INTERPRETING PAUL

THE CANONICAL PAUL
volume 2

Interpreting Paul

Luke Timothy Johnson

WILLIAM B. EERDMANS PUBLISHING COMPANY
GRAND RAPIDS, MICHIGAN

Wm. B. Eerdmans Publishing Co.
4035 Park East Court SE, Grand Rapids, Michigan 49546
www.eerdmans.com

27 26 25 24 23 22 21   1 2 3 4 5 6 7

ISBN 978-0-8028-2466-0

Library of Congress Cataloging-in-Publication Data

A catalog record for this book is available from the Library of Congress.

Unless noted otherwise, Scripture quotations are the author's translation.

CONTENTS

Preface   xiii

Abbreviations   xv

Introduction   1

No "Theology of Paul"   3

The Benefits of Deconstruction   7

1. **Romans 3:21–26 and the Faith of Jesus**   13

Faith as the Confession of Christ   18

Faith as Response to God   20

Faith as Obedience   21

The Obedience of Jesus as the Faith of Jesus   23

Conclusion   26

2. **The Social Dimensions of *Sōtēria* in Luke-Acts and Paul**   27

The Question   27

Comparative Method   29

Criteria for Comparison   31

The Social Character of Salvation in Luke-Acts   32

The Gospel   32

Acts   36

The Social Dimension of Salvation in Paul's Letters   39

Romans   40

Corinthian Correspondence   43

Thessalonian Correspondence   45

Captivity Correspondence   45

Conclusion   47

3. **Transformation of the Mind and Moral Discernment in Romans**   48

A First Look at Romans   49

A Second Look at Romans   52

A Glance at Aristotle   54

The Measure of Faith and the Mind of Christ   58

The Role of the Holy Spirit   62

Evidence from Other Letters   64

Conclusion   67

4. **Life-Giving Spirit**   69

Paul's Argument in 1 Corinthians 15   72

The Functions of the Holy Spirit   80

Conclusion   84

5. **The Body in Question**   86

Thinking Body   87

The Assembly as the *Sōma Christou*   91

Sexual Involvement   96

The Implications of Meals   101

Conclusion   105

6. **Glossolalia and the Embarrassments of Experience**   107

The Nature of the Phenomenon   108

The Pervasiveness of the Phenomenon   115

Evaluations of Glossolalia by New Testament Writers   116

The Ambiguous Character of Glossolalia   120

Glossolalia and Deviance   126

7. **God Was in Christ**   129

    The Mythic Character of 2 Corinthians 5:19   130

    Paul's Language in 2 Corinthians 5:1–21   132

    The Logic of Mythic Language   134

    Conclusion   137

8. **Truth and Reconciliation in 2 Corinthians**   138

    The Reality of Alienation   140

    The Emotional Truth of Hurt and Anger   144

    The Roots of Reconciliation   151

    The Body Language of Reconciliation   156

    Conclusion   158

9. **Ritual Imprinting and the Politics of Perfection**   160

    Reconstructing the Ritual   161

    How Many Initiations?   166

    Initiation into the Mysteries   171

    Mysterious Initiation in Judaism   174

    Ritual Initiation and Status Elevation   177

    Jewish and Christian Practice   179

    The Character of Paul's Response   181

    Conclusion   183

10. **The Truth of Christian Experience**   185

    The Rhetorical Situation   186

    The Story of the Galatians   190

    Paul's Story   193

    The Story of Jesus   200

    The Story of Israel   203

    Conclusion   207

11. **The Expression of Christian Experience**   209

    The Attractions and Perils of Heteronomy   211

CONTENTS

The Paradoxical Character of Christian Freedom 215

Deciphering Galatians 6 220

 Closing Assertions 221

 Mutual Care, Individual Responsibility (Gal 6:1–5) 222

 Sharing All Good Things 225

Conclusion 229

12. **Paul's Vision of the Church** 230

Paul's Ecclesial Focus 231

Israel and the Church 233

Mission of the Church 235

The Church in Metaphor 236

Organization in the Local Church 239

The Church in Colossians and Ephesians 240

The Church in the Pastorals 241

Conclusion 243

13. **The Rise of Church Order** 244

The Church as Historical Phenomenon 246

Eschatology and Church Structure 249

The Rise and Development of Church Order 253

History 258

Theology 260

Conclusion 261

14. **Fellowship of Suffering** 262

The Present Gift: The Power of God and the Power
of the Resurrection 265

The Ambiguities of Weakness 268

Suffering With and For 270

Return to Philippians 272

The Mind of Christ 274

The Mind of the Philippians 278

Living Examples of the Mind of Christ   280

Conclusion   287

15. **Mystery and Metaphor in Colossians**   289

    The Mystery of Christ among the Gentiles   290

      Paul's Usage   290

      Mystērion *in Colossians*   295

      What the Colossians Have Been Given in Christ   298

    The Metaphors of Christian Maturity   301

      Stability   301

      True and False   302

      Life and Growth   303

      Mystery and Metaphor in Baptism   305

    Conclusion   312

16. **Doing the Truth in Love**   313

    The Evidence in Paul on Sex and Gender   314

    Sex and Gender Today   317

    A Necessary Excursus   325

    Doing the Truth in Love   328

    Conclusion   335

17. **Sacrament of the World**   337

    The Church as Place of God's Reconciliation   340

    The Church and Christ, Wife and Husband   346

    A Nonrealized Eschatology   352

    Coda: The Circumstances of Composition   355

18. **Discernment, Edification, and Holiness**   357

    Building the *Ekklēsia* in 1 Thessalonians   361

      Holiness   361

      Edification   364

      Discernment   366

Community Construction in Other Pauline Letters 367

   1 Corinthians 369

   Romans 379

   Ephesians 381

   Conclusion 384

19. **The Apostle as Crisis Manager** 385

   The Crisis in Thessaloniki 386

   Paul's Response to the Crisis 392

     Cognitive Correction 392

     Social Pressure 394

   Social Coercion in Other Canonical Letters 396

     First Corinthians 397

     Second Corinthians 399

     Galatians 401

     The Letters to Paul's Delegates 404

   Conclusion 407

20. *Oikonomia Theou* 409

   Clarifications and Caveats 409

   Composition and Setting 411

   The Theological Perspective of 1 Timothy 415

   Conclusion 423

     Response to an Incisive Critique 423

   The Search for a "Theological Voice" 424

   The Translation and Function of 1 Timothy 1:4 426

21. **The Shape of the Struggle** 428

   Preliminary Observations 435

   The Exegetical Challenge 437

   Further Connections 442

   Conclusion 448

22. Second Timothy and the Polemic against False Teachers   449

   Second Timothy: A Personal Paraenetic Letter   453

     2 Timothy 1:3–2:13   455

     2 Timothy 2:14–4:8   459

   Hellenistic Materials Pertinent to Understanding 2 Timothy   464

     Epictetus   468

     Lucian of Samosata   470

     Dio Chrysostom   473

   Paraenesis and Polemic in 1 Timothy and Titus   476

     First Timothy   477

     Titus   479

   Conclusions   480

23. The Pedagogy of Grace   481

   The Rhetorical Situation   483

   The Rhetorical Response   488

   The Gift That Teaches   490

   The Experience of God's Goodness   492

   Conclusion   496

Conclusion   498

Acknowledgments   501

Bibliography   503

Index of Authors   549

Index of Subjects   559

Index of Scripture and Other Ancient Sources   568

PREFACE

In the seventy-sixth year of my life and at the end of a very long career spent interpreting the New Testament in the service of the church—even when the church did not seem overly excited about my efforts—I am both relieved and filled with a sense of gratitude as I send this second volume of *Canonical Paul* to the publishers, who have waited so patiently for it.

I am relieved because God has granted me the strength and the wit to complete what will almost certainly be my last scholarly book. I am grateful because this late period of writing could finally be devoted completely and thoroughly to Paul, the apostle of the church.

I have always been a "Pauline" Christian, if indeed I can lay claim to the title Christian, because, for me, Paul has always been the most difficult and therefore also most delightful advocate and interpreter of the Lord Jesus Christ and of the human experience of God's transforming power through Christ. In Paul's letters above all I have found the quality of mind and the depth of conviction that could arouse in me both excitement and passion. And it is Paul's letters, above all, that show how important and difficult is life together in the church. But for most of my scholarly life, with some momentary exceptions, and apart from the classes I devoted to the canonical letters, I did not have the chance before these past three years to do Paul straight and without chaser.

Spending the time between late 2016 and now in the study of his canonical letters, while simultaneously going through the process of grief at the loss of my wife, Joy, on December 20, 2017, has reminded me again and again how deeply Paul sees into the human heart and how profoundly his words can speak to the human condition. It may seem strange to speak of so demanding a moralist and so challenging a thinker as a comfort and solace, but so he has been to me. And, I am certain, to countless others as well.

His letters can be both challenge and comfort when they are liberated as much as possible from the elaborate structures of theory and criticism that have been erected around the apostle himself and his correspondence, so that all his canonical letters can be read as cleanly and directly as possible. I hope that this set of essays offers some help in that liberating project.

I have mentioned the great patience exercised by Eerdmans, who should have received these two volumes years before this. But I would be remiss not also to express my deep gratitude to the editors at Eerdmans who have worked so hard to make my prose clearer and my references more accurate. Jarrett Knight and David Carr have been of great personal as well as professional assistance, and I hope they understand, despite my constant teasing, how much I appreciate them and their contributions. As was the first volume, this one also is dedicated to my late wife, Joy, who shared faith's journey with me and, at every moment, her keen intelligence and extraordinary love.

LUKE TIMOTHY JOHNSON
Atlanta, 2019

ABBREVIATIONS

ABD	*Anchor Bible Dictionary*. Edited by David Noel Freedman. 6 vols. New York: Doubleday, 1992
AnBib	Analecta Biblica
ANRW	*Aufstieg und Niedergang der römischen Welt*
AYB	Anchor Yale Bible
BBR	*Bulletin for Biblical Research*
BETL	Bibliotheca Ephemeridum Theologicarum Lovaniensium
Bib	*Biblica*
BZ	*Biblische Zeitschrift*
BZAW	Beihefte zur Zeitschrift für die alttestamentliche Wissenschaft
BZNW	Beihefte zur Zeitschrift für die neutestamentliche Wissenschaft
CBQ	*Catholic Biblical Quarterly*
ER	*The Encyclopedia of Religion*. Edited by Mircea Eliade. New York: Macmillan, 1987.
ExpTim	*Expository Times*
FRLANT	Forschungen zur Religion und Literatur des Alten und Neuen Testaments
Goodspeed	*The New Testament: An American Translation*, by Edgar J. Goodspeed
Hart	*The New Testament: A Translation*, by David Bentley Hart
HBT	*Horizons in Biblical Theology*
IDB	*The Interpreter's Dictionary of the Bible*. Edited by George A. Buttrick. 4 vols. New York: Abingdon, 1962.
Int	*Interpretation*
JAAR	*Journal of the American Academy of Religion*
JB	Jerusalem Bible
JBL	*Journal of Biblical Literature*

JSNT	*Journal for the Study of the New Testament*
JSNTSup	Journal for the Study of the New Testament Supplement Series
JSSR	*Journal for the Scientific Study of Religion*
JTS	*Journal of Theological Studies*
Knox	*The Holy Bible: A Translation From the Latin Vulgate in the Light of the Hebrew and Greek Originals*, by Ronald Knox
KJV	King James Version
LCL	Loeb Classical Library
LXX	Septuagint
Moffatt	*The New Testament: A New Translation*, by James Moffatt
MS(S)	manuscript(s)
NAB	New American Bible
NABRE	New American Bible Revised Edition
NE	*Nicomachean Ethics* (Aristotle)
NEB	New English Bible
NICNT	New International Commentary on the New Testament
NIGTC	New International Greek Testament Commentary
NIV	New International Version
NJB	New Jerusalem Bible
NovT	*Novum Testamentum*
NovTSup	Supplements to Novum Testamentum
NRSV	New Revised Standard Version
NTS	*New Testament Studies*
PIBA	Proceedings of the Irish Biblical Association
PRSt	*Perspectives in Religious Studies*
QD	Quaestiones Disputatae
RB	*Revue Biblique*
RSR	*Recherches de science religieuse*
RSV	Revised Standard Version
SBLDS	Society of Biblical Literature Dissertation Series
SBLMS	Society of Biblical Literature Monograph Series
SBLSBS	Society of Biblical Literature Sources for Biblical Study
SBLSP	Society of Biblical Literature Seminar Papers
SBLTT	Society of Biblical Literature Texts and Translations
SBT	Studies in Biblical Theology
SCJ	Studies in Christianity and Judaism
SNTSMS	Society for New Testament Studies Monograph Series
SNTW	Studies of the New Testament and Its World
SP	Sacra Pagina

SR	*Studies in Religion*
ST	*Studia Theologica*
TD	*Theology Digest*
TDNT	*Theological Dictionary of the New Testament*. Edited by Gerhard Kittel and Gerhard Friedrich. Translated by Geoffrey W. Bromiley. 10 vols. Grand Rapids: Eerdmans, 1964–1976.
TNT	*Theology of the New Testament* (Bultmann)
TS	Texts and Studies
TJ	*Trinity Journal*
TUGAL	Texte und Untersuchungen zur Geschichte der altchristlichen Literatur
WBC	Word Biblical Commentary
WUNT	Wissenschaftliche Untersuchungen zum Neuen Testament
ZNW	*Zeitschrift für die neutestamentliche Wissenschaft und die Kunde der älteren Kirche*

Introduction

This is the second of two volumes dealing with the canonical letters of Paul. The first volume explained why consideration of all thirteen of Paul's letters is justified both by the best canons of critical research—there is truly no valid reason for the common distinction between so-called "authentic" and "disputed" letters—and by the continuous tradition of the church, for whom these canonical letters, rather than a scholarly reduction in their number, have been the source of life and reflection from the time of their first collection until the present. The "canonical Paul" is the church's apostle, and if biblical scholarship is to serve the church, it must learn to engage all the letters ascribed to him in Scripture.

The first volume, *Constructing Paul*, therefore provided a set of studies that form the basis for any construction of Paul based on the canonical letters by present-day readers. A first set of essays examined the available historical sources, a reasonable account of Paul's life and ministry, his place within earliest Christianity, and the shape of his correspondence. A longer collection of essays dealt with the sort of issues necessary for readers to have a historically and literarily responsible engagement with the canonical letters, such as the character of Paul's Jewish identity, the role of Scripture in his letters, the kinds and level of Greco-Roman culture found in them, the important place played by religious and quotidian experience in the shaping of his discourse, and a consideration of Paul's convictions, symbols, myths, and metaphors. A distinguishing feature of all these essays is that they draw their evidence from all of Paul's canonical letters—when, to be sure, the letters make evidence on any of these topics available. To demonstrate the value of reading individual letters in their canonical context, I next considered "Paul's Voice" as it appears in the short letter to Philemon, showing what difference is made in reading Philemon together with rather than apart from Colossians and Ephesians. Finally, in the only essay that moves in the direction of evaluation rather than analysis and explanation, I took up the question of whether Paul is better considered as an oppressive or liberative voice within Scripture and the life of the church, reaching the not unexpected verdict that Paul's letters are emphatically and distinctively liberating when read responsibly and as a whole.

The present volume consists of a set of discrete forays into Paul's canonical letters themselves. They are a deliberately mixed lot. Some have been published before, and others have been composed specifically for this collection. Some are heavily footnoted, and others are not. Some are decidedly exegetical in character—for example, the study of the faith of Jesus in Rom 3:21–26 (chap. 1). Others make an argument concerning literary character and rhetorical context, such as the study "Second Timothy and the Polemic against False Teachers" (chap. 22). Some try to make sense of specific tropes within letters, such as the two studies on 1 Corinthians (chap. 4, "Life-Giving Spirit," and chap. 5, "The Body in Question") or the two essays on narrative and imperative in Galatians (chaps. 10–11).

Other essays try to show how links between letters might usefully be made, such as "*Oikonomia Theou*" (chap. 20, comparing 1 Timothy and 1 Corinthians) or "Ritual Imprinting and the Politics of Perfection" (chap. 9, examining both Galatians and Colossians). Some remain resolutely at the level of "what Paul meant when he wrote," such as "Transformation of the Mind and Moral Discernment in Romans" (chap. 3), and others make suggestions concerning the pertinence of letters for today, such as "Truth and Reconciliation in 2 Corinthians" (chap. 8), "The Pedagogy of Grace" (chap. 23), and "Doing the Truth in Love" (chap. 16). Some take up disputed scholarly issues, such as the meaning of *pistis Christou* (see chap. 1, "Romans 3:21–26 and the Faith of Jesus: The Soteriological Significance of Christ's Obedience") or the character of the church in Paul's letters (see chap. 13, "The Rise of Church Order").

The obviously eclectic nature of the essays is intentional, for the argument spanning the two volumes of *The Canonical Paul* is that the "construction" of Paul (vol. 1) ought to lead, not to a fixed and final edifice or monument called "Paul," but rather to a "deconstruction" consisting of discrete and nonsystematic inquiries into the letters themselves, in relation to each other, and in conversation with contemporary concerns of believers. My goal in the first volume was to prepare readers for such engagement by making them aware of all the issues involved in a responsible reading of the canonical collection. My goal in this volume is to present both a sampler of such readings and a stimulus for further such readings of the canonical letters themselves.

I emphatically do not desire that these volumes in any way deflect from or even replace such direct engagement with the wide range of the canonical letters and the even wider range of questions that might be put to them.

No "Theology of Paul"

I can anticipate the disappointment of the reader who has approached a volume called *Interpreting Paul* expecting a full and magisterial treatment of Paul's thought. Such large books frequently fly under the banner of "Paul's theology." To find instead only a set of discrete essays that do not in the least provide, or even pretend to provide, such a comprehensive construction may seem to the reader a form of dereliction of duty. Is my apparent "failure to launch" a symptom of scholarly fatigue (I am writing at the age of seventy-six), or, worse, of theological ineptitude, or even of cowardice? Such signs of age, or of intellectual and moral decline, may indeed be present in your author, but my refusal to offer something like a theology of Paul, a refusal that has been implicit in all my work from the start, is instead, or so I like to think, based on a principled stand, not only on the impossibility of (anyone) responsibly accomplishing such a task, but also on the positive damage done to the reading of the canonical letters by the very attempt to carry out the task. Allow me to sketch some of the elements of my position.

My first objection to the effort to construct a theology of Paul might be termed philosophical. Since at least the time of Plato, Western thought has tended to privilege the one over the many, the abstract over the particular, the ideal over the real, the synthetic over the analytic. The quest for a singular, comprehensive version of Paul falls squarely within this philosophical bias. Grasping Paul whole in a single vision is thought to be better than struggling with each of his letters in all their quirky specificity; or, to put it another way, we can only understand the individual letters if we have a comprehensive vision of what Paul's over-arching theology was.

It is important to recognize, however, that the preference for the one over the many truly is a philosophical bias rather than a logical neces-sity. It can be argued (and I will argue) that the particular and discrete many is not only the necessary starting point for true science but also the appropriate point of return for authentic inquiry. Engaging the many need not have as its goal the construction of the one. Yet the longing for the one is difficult to eradicate. A reason for this persistent longing may simply be that the singular synthetic is easier for our minds to grasp than the multiple many. Theory is certainly easier to control and manipulate than the messy facts of somatic existence or of literary polyvalence.

To stay on the philosophical point for a moment longer: in surveying the history of philosophy, one cannot but notice how much more excitement is generated by the study of the great theoreticians through the ages than of the masters of aphorism. Aristotle, Kant, and Hegel are appreciated more than Epicurus, Pascal, and Nietzsche. The makers of great systems are granted more importance than the shapers of many sharp observations. There is also this: the history of Western thought has been indelibly stamped by the first historian of thought, Diogenes Laertius. His third-century-CE *Lives and Opinions of Eminent Philosophers* taught all subsequent historians of philosophy to think in terms of individual figures (Parmenides, Plato, Chrysippus) in connection to their ideas on certain well-defined topics (cosmology, epistemology, ethics) and in relation to other thinkers and their ideas. In short, philosophy, rather than being envisaged as a shared quest for wisdom, became a recital of biographically based systems of thought.

The effect of such an approach on philosophy can be found in the example I cited in the first volume and repeat here: college students in a course on the history of philosophy learn something called "Platonism," which they understand to be a set of teachings on knowledge, the cosmos, and human behavior. This set of convictions, so gathered and organized, can then be compared to those held by other philosophers. Students are vaguely aware that this "Platonism" is based on and supposedly stated in a set of literary works called Plato's *Dialogues*. But their knowledge of what they call Platonism turns out not to be based on a reading of those dialogues; it is based on the summary found in their textbook.

If they should happen at some point in their lives actually to read any or all of Plato's dialogues, they would quickly discover two things. First, it is difficult to find in any clear way what was so cogently taught as Platonism in their philosophy class; the dialogues are complex conversations that touch on a world of subjects, and the set of "teachings" that supposedly constitute Platonism appears to be an abstraction drawn from a handful of these dialogues and arranged into a logical order. Second, readers discover that if they forget about finding "Platonism," and instead enter into a close reading of the actual dialogues, they are stimulated to thought in ways they would not have expected.

In the same way we continue to teach Hume and Kant and Hegel and Marx in succession and in terms of their "philosophical ideas" within set categories of cosmology, epistemology, metaphysics, and ethics. The carryover to the teaching of theology is direct and clear. Seminarians study the theology of Thomas Aquinas, Luther, Calvin, Barth, and Tillich as discrete thinkers, with an emphasis on how their "systematic theologies" converge and differ, rather than simply learning to think theologically while engaging these and other authors in all their specificity. The same impulse, I suggest, drives the quest for a theology of Paul: it is abstract and provides an easily grasped handle on the apostle.

My second objection to the quest for a theology of Paul concerns the means that are almost universally employed to construct it. I mentioned all of these in the first volume, so I will be brief here. The process is inevitably selective in one or more ways:

- Certain letters are regarded as authentic, while others are regarded as spurious.
- One or more letters (especially Romans) sets the frame within which everything must fit.
- Since ideas are the stuff of theology (so it is supposed), then "theological concepts" or even "theological terms" are regarded as noteworthy even apart from their literary context; such ideas can be gathered under recognized theological topics, such as soteriology or eschatology, while themes, metaphors, and symbols that are not so recognized may escape notice.
- Similarly, letters that are laden with such theological concepts (Romans, Galatians, 2 Corinthians) are valued more highly than letters in which such concepts appear less frequently (2 Thessalonians, 1 Timothy).

Of all these forms of selectivity, the most egregious is the omission of Colossians and Ephesians from consideration because of their disputed character. If one were to think a "theology of the canonical letters" to be a worthwhile project in the first place, the absence of these letters (above all Ephesians) from the database would be incomprehensible.

My third objection to a theology of Paul is the effect it has on readers. The construction of a synthetic "Paul" consisting of his important theological ideas can serve to distort reading in one of two ways, each of which inhibits direct and vivifying contact with the apostle's letters. One effect is to replace the reading of Paul's letters altogether: Why bother working through all the complexities, ambiguities, and obscurities of Paul's actual discourse when I have available to me a neatly organized version of "Paul" as created by a clever contemporary scholar? Indeed, one may be deluded into thinking that one actually "knew" Paul by means of reading such a theology, without having read the canonical letters at all. A second effect of a systematic theology of Paul is to direct what readers see and value if they should after all have the occasion to read Paul's actual letters. If I have been persuaded that a certain theme (say, righteousness) or concept (say, grace) is the key to understanding Paul, it is natural for me to "find" and "treasure" precisely these elements in the letters, while downplaying, or perhaps not even seeing, other elements that are of equal or even greater importance within a given letter.

The tendencies I have enumerated are abundantly illustrated by the theologies of Paul that presently flourish. Take, for example, the positions represented by the so-called "old" and "new" perspectives on Paul,[1] with the first emphasizing the vertical dimension of individual salvation and the second emphasizing the horizontal erasure of social difference: each uses only a handful of letters; each makes its "perspective" the lens through which everything must be viewed; each leaves entirely out of account the greater part of the canonical correspondence. Of what possible use are such constructions, except to replace the actual reading of Paul's letters? Yet, even as they purportedly make Paul "make sense," they simultaneously block access to his astonishingly rich and difficult discourse as it is found in his actual letters.

A final objection to any effort to secure a theology of Paul is its premise that the canonical letters were produced by a thinker whose letters presented opportunities to express aspects of an internally consistent and coherent body of thought. The premise is faulty on several counts.

First, the "Paul" of the canonical letters is not a philosopher seeking to construct a vision of reality but a pastor and moral teacher. His primary concern is with the formation of character among his readers—in this respect, he is rightly perceived as resembling Epictetus far more than Aristotle.

Second, the production of the canonical letters, as we saw in volume

1. See especially the evenhanded and perspicacious analysis of Westerholm, *Perspectives Old and New on Paul.*

1, was the work of a Pauline school that was present and active through-out Paul's letter-writing career. Paul, I have suggested, authorizes all the canonical compositions in his name, but the actual writing of letters un-doubtedly involved the active participation of the epistolary cosponsors and colleagues who were with him at the time of writing. The Pauline corpus emerges from social more than solitary thinking.

Third, our examination of the canonical writings has revealed that, on any number of "theological" points—our main example was eschatol-ogy—the letters are remarkably inconsistent or, at the very least, various. The disparities and incongruities are more evident, to be sure, when the entire canonical collection is considered; this is one obvious reason why the quest for a theology of Paul always involves the shrinkage of the cor-pus to a more manageable (and supposedly more internally consistent) core. But we have found that even within this hypothetical core, the letters reveal sometimes startling degrees of diversity.

Finally, the letters do not so much show us aspects of Paul's "theol-ogy" as they do moments of Paul's theological "thinking." Paul's thinking, in turn, is not impelled by the need to make a system of thought inter-nally coherent but is stimulated, indeed necessitated, by experience and occasion. We have seen how central both transcendent and quotidian experiences prove to be as generators of reflection in the canonical let-ters; we have seen as well how the occasions of letter-writing affect the content and form of Paul's discourse.

The Benefits of Deconstruction

I do not use the term "deconstruction" as employed by Jacques Derrida and postmodernism.[2] I by no means, for example, regard the text as a tyrannical imposer of meaning. Nor do I resist Paul's authority by tech-niques of what can best be called linguistic nihilism. Quite the contrary: I seek to discover and appreciate the meanings that Paul's discourse dis-closes. Why, then, the term "deconstruction"? I use it because this set of essays *does* resist a single hegemonic reading of Paul's letters, such as is imposed by a theology of Paul that either replaces the close reading of specific texts or dictates what might be seen or not seen in Paul's letters. These essays deconstruct the premise that a single and controlling read-

---

2. See Derrida, *Writing and Difference* and *Aporias*. For postmodernism as the revolt against "grand narratives," see esp. Lyotard, *Postmodern Condition*.

ing of Paul is necessary or even possible. They seek to show how many and various are the meanings revealed by the canonical letters, once we actually set about reading them, rather than imposing on them a priori notions of what they must mean.

For fellow scholars, especially younger ones who seem more and more enmeshed in purely academic debates, my hope for these studies is that—beyond the insight they may offer on this point or others—they will serve as something of a model for a mode of New Testament scholarship that is increasingly rare. I mean a kind of scholarship that seeks to combine breadth of scope with close attention to detail,[3] scholarly integrity with intellectual adventure, a respect for historical realities with present-day concerns. I want to show that the canonical letters can still give rise to new and provocative questions. Such questions can arise, moreover, simply from the careful reading of the Greek text. They need not, in other words, come from some theoretical standpoint.[4]

By far the majority of the essays included in this volume arose not out of an academic *status questionis* but out of puzzles raised by the text itself. Take, for example, the first essay in this collection, on the faith of Jesus. Although it begins with attention to contemporary contributions on the subject, it actually arose completely out of my personal state of

---

3. It is not in the least uncommon today for scholars to identify themselves, not merely in terms of a very narrow body of data (New Testament), not merely in terms of an even narrower subset of compositions (John, or the Synoptics, or Paul), but also in terms of a specific ideological approach (feminist, postcolonial) to that tiny area. Worse, little embarrassment is revealed at the confession—in response to gentle questioning—that such a "New Testament scholar" knows little even of the rest of the New Testament beyond these self-chosen delimitations. Such self-perpetuating ignorance would be inconceivable in, let us say, contemporary STEM disciplines, or even in the the nineteenth-century guild of biblical scholarship, when a grasp of the entire biblical literature was taken for granted and a knowledge of the language and literature of antiquity was assumed.

4. I do not mean to suggest that any reading is totally innocent of bias. In the introduction to the first volume, I gladly acknowledged ways in which my own Catholic and conservative tendencies affect my reading of the canonical collection. And I have both welcomed and enabled the presence of other than Caucasion males at the scholarly table, on the conviction that such diversity enriches and complicates interpretation. My comment has as its target two distressing tendencies. The first is to elevate "diversity in perspective" into a self-evident good in and of itself rather than as a welcome contributor to a search for a shared meaning. The second is to make a specific starting point (or theory) not only the starting point but also the end point, so that the text itself becomes once more a florilegium of potential prooftexts rather than an arena for contestation.

cognitive dissonance when, teaching a Greek exegesis course on Romans at Yale Divinity School, and being justifiably uncertain of my own grasp of Greek, I found myself befuddled by the gap between what seemed the plain sense of the Greek in Rom 3:21–26, which pointed to the faith/faithfulness of Jesus, and the consensus of all contemporary translations of the New Testament, which translated *pistis Christou* as "faith in Christ." The essay was the result of my own direct struggle with Paul's argument. It has enduring value, I think, simply because it engages a genuine and enduring problem posed by the text, rather than an issue generated by an academic theory.

Similarly, I would hope that the studies gathered here would reinforce the perception that each of the canonical letters is *worth* such close examination and can give rise to genuine thought. If engaged with the same seriousness as Romans, for example, the Letter to Titus reveals itself not as a trite, second-generation imitation of Paul that advances no real argument but as a passionate statement of the manner in which God's gift can educate humans in virtue, in the face of a pastoral situation for which the term "dire" is too weak (see chap. 23, "The Pedagogy of Grace"). The real problem with the disputed Pauline letters is that they are no longer treated with the same degree of seriousness that was once brought to them by interpreters before the start of the nineteenth century.[5] They continue to speak powerfully to those willing to engage them with the same scholarly care as is brought to Romans and Galatians. It is my genuine hope that by treating all the canonical letters on the same plane, I may have shown a little more convincingly how artificial is the distinction between disputed and undisputed letters.

Finally, this set of essays seeks to make a strong statement concerning the relationship of biblical scholarship to the life of the church[6] by insisting that the appropriate set of compositions for the interpretation of Paul is precisely the full set of canonical compositions. All thirteen letters ascribed to Paul have fed the life of the church through the centuries. The fact of a New Testament canon is, to be sure, the result of a historical process, but the actualization of canon is an existential faith-decision of

---

5. The state of affairs within New Testament studies is nicely illustrated by the survey of scholarship on Paul by Victor Paul Furnish, "Pauline Studies," in the volume published by Scholars Press to celebrate the centennial of the Society of Biblical Literature: not only are the Pastorals dismissed by a single line; they do not reappear in the entire volume, even though chapters are devoted to New Testament Apocrypha and the Apostolic Fathers. See Furnish, "Pauline Studies," esp. 326.

6. See Johnson, "Scripture for the Life of the Church."

the church in every generation, instantiated first of all through liturgical reading and proclamation.[7] But since the start of the nineteenth century, the church's diet has been restricted to the academically defined "authentic" letters. This is not merely a matter of lectionary selection. It has much more to do with the fact that academically trained pastors are largely ignorant of the possibilities for preaching offered by the "disputed" letters of Paul. Their teachers in seminaries, both university-based and not, have passed on to them, most often uncritically, the dogmas they received from their teachers, who in turn themselves received them, most often uncritically, from their teachers.[8]

The effects of the long academic captivity of the church have been devastating in many ways, but the consequences for the interpretation of Paul within the church are particularly egregious. Not only do pastors assume that the "consensus" of scholars should dictate the usage of the faith community; not only are most preachers sadly deficient in their knowledge of the full canonical collection of letters;[9] such deference and ignorance enables the proliferation of negative perceptions of Paul "the oppressor."[10] And since, within the academy, attempts to argue for the authenticity, or even the authority, of the disputed letters is regarded as wrongheaded,[11]

---

7. See the discussion in Johnson, *Writings of the New Testament*.

8. I make bold to use the term "dogmas" for scholarly positions that are uncritically transmitted, following the sage observation of Bernhard Weiss with regard to the growing "consensus" in the late nineteenth century concerning the late dating of James: "The newer critics also have their unshakeable dogma and their tenacious traditions." *Der Jakobusbrief*, 50.

9. Students for ministry typically take a one-semester survey course in the New Testament, in which the standard views of "the historical-critical method" are purveyed; if they take another course, the exegetical offerings are limited to the compositions with which the faculty are most familiar, and most advanced courses are either thematic or propagate an ideological position (such as postcolonialism).

10. See the final chapter in vol. 1, "Paul, Oppressor or Liberator?"

11. The reviewers of the first edition of my *Writings of the New Testament* (1986), while generally positive toward the evidence it provided of scholarly acumen and clarity, were also uniformly puzzled at the "surprisingly conservative" position that I took on the Pastorals. That such a condescending attitude persists is revealed by the passing comment by N. T. Wright when he suggests that the question of the authenticity of Colossians and Ephesians, at least, ought to be reopened by scholars: "In North America today, you more or less *have* to say that you will regard Ephesians and Colossians as post-Pauline—unless, like Luke Timothy Johnson, you have so massively established your scholarly credibility on other grounds that your acceptance of the letters as fully Pauline can then be regarded, not as a serious scholarly fault, but as an allowable eccentricity." *Paul and the Faithfulness of God*, 1:58-59. Thanks, I think!

and since the career of a young scholar who might try to make that case can actually be scuttled thereby, the situation will not soon get better.

My point concerning Paul and the church therefore spans both volumes and is made in the first place through the simple politics of publishing. Both volumes use the evidence of all the canonical letters, and both volumes assume the worth and authority of all the letters ascribed to Paul in the New Testament. Such inclusiveness of attention and use is a rarity and itself supports the case that the church's Paul is the canonical Paul.

Moreover, although each of the studies in this volume employs scholarly diction and is variously adorned with footnotes, careful observers will note that while the footnotes are often complex (as footnotes tend to be), the prose in the body of each study is for the most part clear and accessible. Even when Greek is used, a translation is usually provided. Even when it is not, the chapter and verse references make it possible to follow along with English translations. In short, the essays are, I hope, useful not only to scholars but also to intellectually curious pastors and congregants.

Chapter 1

Romans 3:21–26 and the Faith of Jesus

The Soteriological Significance of Christ's Obedience

By his recent article on the *pistis Christou* formulations in Paul,[1] Arland J. Hultgren has performed the service of reviewing the scholarship devoted to this issue,[2] and discussing the syntactical points pertinent to the question.[3] He has also shown that the resolution of the

---

1. Hultgren, "*Pistis Christou* Formulations." He discusses, in particular, Rom 3:22, 26; Gal 2:16, 20, 22; Phil 3:9.

2. One can add to the works surveyed by Hultgren ("*Pistis Christou* Formulations," 248–53) Howard, *Paul*, 57–65, in which he argues that the "faith of Christ" means God's fidelity in fulfilling the Abrahamic promises; Hays, "Psalm 143," esp. 114n32, which points in the same direction as the present essay; and S. Williams, "'Righteousness of God,'" who reaches conclusions compatible with those in the present essay, esp. on 272–77.

3. Hultgren's conclusion, that "on the basis of syntax alone—apart from theological considerations—the interpretation of the *Pistis Christou* formulations along the lines of the subjective genitive is excluded" ("*Pistis Christou,*" 258), goes well beyond his own observations. He admits the weakness of the "articular" argument (253) and grants that the argument equating *pistis Christou* with a prepositional phrase can be taken in either direction (254); but in arguing against the subjective, he omits from consideration Col 1:4; 2:5 and misses the importance of 1 Thess 1:8 (254). He constructs a *petitio principil* in his analysis of Gal 2:16 (255), grants that Paul uses both objective and subjective genitives in prepositional phrases using anarthous nouns (255), and too quickly dismisses the strong support given the subjective reading by Rom 4:16b, *tō ek pisteōs Abraam*. Of course, the genitive *Abraam* is "adjectival" (257)—all genitives are. Hultgren refers to Nigel Turner, *A Grammar of New Testament Greek*, vol. 4, *Style* (Edinburgh: T&T Clark, 1976), 83. Turner notwithstanding, however, it is precipitous to classify the use of *hoi ek* simply as a sectarian designation (256). The use in Gal 3:7, 9 as well as in Rom 3:26 argues against that designation. In Rom 4:16, the personal faith-response of Abraham remains central to the understanding of *tō ek pisteōs Abraam*. It is not simply formal. The weakness of the purely linguistic arguments against the subjective genitive is clear from Hultgren's final translation: "One can speak (rather awkwardly) of 'Christic faith' or (more clearly) 'faith which is in and

debate will come about not on the basis of linguistic analysis alone but on the basis of exegesis.[4] Unfortunately, his own exegetical observations, especially those concerning the critical passage, Rom 3:21–26, lack the necessary sharpness. In this short note, I join the growing number of those who are discontented with the abrupt dismissal of the "faith of Jesus" by Ernst Käsemann and other commentators,[5] and who find that, simply on exegetical grounds, a subjective reading of *pistis Christou* is not only sometimes possible but at times (as in Rom 3:21–26) necessary.[6] The basic pieces of my argument have been shaped before, especially by Markus Barth.[7] I will here try to refine his position, taking into account the excellent observations of Sam K. Williams on Rom 3:21–26.[8]

The three phrases employing *pistis* in Rom 3:22, 25, and 26 are awkwardly placed. If Paul was here adding clarification to a traditional formulation, he botched the job rather badly. There are problems with reading the genitives in these phrases subjectively, but they are small compared with those facing the objective rendering found in all the modern translations and purveyed without question by the major commentaries.

First, we must note the literary function of this passage. Paul here restates the thesis of Rom 1:17, after elaborating its antithesis in 1:18–3:20. Two things follow from this simple observation: (1) Paul is here showing how God's way of making humans righteous is being revealed; the emphasis is on the gift rather than on its reception; (2) there is a formal balance between the thesis and its restatement. Perhaps the simple exegetical technique of reading the passage without the phrases in question will help us see this. If we omit *dia pisteōs Iēsou Christou* from 3:22, *dia* [*tēs*] *pisteōs* from 3:25, and *ek pisteōs Iēsou*[9] from 3:26, we see at once that

of Christ,' that is, the faith of the believer which comes forth as Christ is proclaimed in the Gospel (Rom 1:8, 17, Gal 3:2, 5)." This does not advance our understanding.

4. Hultgren, "*Pistis Christou*," 263.

5. Cf. Käsemann, *Commentary on Romans*, 94, 101; cf. Nygren, *Commentary on Romans*, 150–61; Leenhardt, *Epistle to the Romans*, 99–101; Barrett, *Epistle to the Romans*, 74; Schlier, *Der Römerbrief*, 105, 155.

6. Rather than beginning with the notion that these formulations need always be read as subjective genitives, I think it better to ask whether they might *ever* be so read, and if so, what they might mean. Lumping them all together simply makes for poor exegesis. That is why I focus here on what I regard as the most compelling case.

7. M. Barth, "Faith of the Messiah," 363–70. Barth's treatment is especially good for its use of "obedience" as the content of the "faith of Christ."

8. In addition to his "'Righteousness of God,'" see S. Williams, *Jesus' Death as Saving Event*, 34–56.

9. Accepting here the shorter reading in the genitive (of H, A, B, C, K, etc.).

Paul is stating in straightforward fashion what God has accomplished for humans in the death of Christ. The only place where the reception of that gift is mentioned explicitly is in 3:22, *eis pantas tous pisteuantas*.

If, with the RSV and most commentators, we read the three phrases as referring to faith *in* Christ, what happens to the passage? First, in Rom 3:22 we have redundancy. Why should Paul add *eis pantas tous pisteuontas* if he has just said "through faith in Jesus Christ"? The added note of "all" (*pantas*) lends some specificity, it is true, but not enough to make this added phrase necessary. On the other hand, a subjective reading makes the two phrases distinct. Now, with the righteousness of God being revealed *through the faith of Jesus*, the emphasis on God's gift is maintained. Furthermore (and this is, I think, conclusive), we find a formal parallel to 1:17. As Paul there spoke of God's righteousness being *ek pisteōs eis pistin*, so here the *eis pantas tous pisteuontas* corresponds to the second member of that balanced phrase, and *dia pisteōs Christou* corresponds to the *ek pisteōs* of 1:17.

The second phrase, *dia [tēs] pisteōs*, in Rom 3:25 is even worse, if read objectively. The RSV's "to be received by faith" strikes one as a desperation move. The placement of the phrase between *hilastērion* and *en tō autou haimati* is, as Williams has shown, "extremely difficult."[10] The least likely function of the phrase, however, is to refer to the reception of the gift. Precisely the awkward placement of the phrase demands that we regard it as modifying God's action of putting forth Jesus Christ as a redemption, in the expiation effected by the shedding of his blood. The most obvious referent would be God himself. It was "through his faithfulness" that he put forward Jesus. This understanding of God's fidelity is important in Romans.[11] But the close conjunction of the phrase "in his blood" and "expiation" leads me to think that the phrase *dia [tēs] pisteōs* here again (and awkwardly) refers to the disposition of the one who was shedding his blood—namely, Jesus. A decent translation is nearly impossible. I would hazard the following as at least an indication of how I understand the phrase working: "Whom God put forward as an expiation: through faith, in the shedding of his blood." I am reading the last two phrases almost as a hendiadys. The faith of Jesus and the pour-

---

10. S. Williams, *Jesus' Death as Saving Event*, 41–44.

11. Cf. Hultgren, "*Pistis Christou*," 252; Hays, "Psalm 143," 110–11; and Ljungman, *Pistis*, 35–56. Paul's ability to speak at once and in parallelism of God's *pistis* and his *alētheia* in Rom 3:3, 7 (cf. Rom 15:8) alerts us to his willingness to use different words to point to the same reality. The theological weight does not come from *alētheia* itself, however, as the bearer of some "biblical" meaning, but from Paul's usage.

ing out of his blood, together, form the act of expiation. *Dia* and *en* are both to be taken as instrumental. This is convoluted, but it makes more sense than the objective rendering, and there is another place in the New Testament (1 Pet 1:2) where an equally strange construction demands a similar construal.

The final phrase, *ton ek pisteōs Iēsou* (Rom 3:26), is rendered by the RSV "him who has faith in Jesus." This is the least likely of all the objective readings, for it forces the simple meaning of the Greek. One would ordinarily (and free from other considerations) render this "the one who shares the faith of Jesus," meaning "one who has faith as Jesus had faith." The faith of the human being Jesus is here clearly intended. In 4:16 the same phrase occurs in reference to Abraham, *tō ek pisteōs Abraam*. The RSV does not there translate as "those who believe in Abraham" but (quite correctly) as "those who share the faith of Abraham."[12] So should we understand 3:26. This is supported by observing the way Paul uses Jesus's personal name. This is the only time that *pisteōs Iēsou* occurs. Ordinarily, Paul uses the messianic title in such phrases, or in other statements of belief. Indeed, he does not often speak of Jesus simply by name. When he does, his emphasis appears to fall on Jesus's human identity rather than on his messianic role (see esp. Rom 8:11; 1 Thess 1:10; 2 Cor 4:10–14). Paul's meaning in 3:26, then, would seem to be that God, by revealing his saving action in the cross of Jesus, has not only shown himself to be righteous but shown himself to be one who makes righteous those who, on the basis of Jesus's faithful death (I will return to this awkward expression), have faith in God.

By reading Rom 3:21–26 in this fashion, we not only respect its literary function as the restatement of Paul's thesis in 1:17, but allow it to move naturally into the discussion of Abraham's faith in 4:1–25, and (of even greater importance) allow it to be understood in the light of 5:12–21, where Paul again describes the gift of God's grace brought about through Jesus. Indeed, I suggest that the key to understanding Rom 3:21–26 is found in its placement between 1:17 and 5:18–19. But before that can be made clear, a few preliminary points must be made.

It is not always obvious on what grounds resistance to the notion of "the faith of Jesus" is based. There may be fear of a notion of faith as a sort of "work" that might nullify the sovereignty of God's grace, even if this happened to be a work by one whom we confess as God's Son. Therefore, no matter what the plain sense of the Greek seems to

12. Hultgren, *"Pistis Christou,"* 256–57; M. Barth, "Faith of the Messiah," 367.

demand, we conclude that Paul *cannot* mean that Jesus had faith, or, if he did, that this could not be soteriologically significant. Unfortunately, doctrinal presuppositions (from whatever direction) make for poor exegesis. But perhaps there is a more genuine difficulty upon which the resistance is based—a failure of imagination. In what sense could Jesus *be* a believer? If Paul spoke of "the faith of Jesus," what could he mean by it?

It is at this point that the severest criticism has been leveled at those studies that have tried to supply this imaginative picture out of a "biblical theology" perspective. Seeking a "biblical" understanding of *pistis*, some have tried to read *'emun*, "faithfulness," wherever Paul has used *pistis* or *alētheia*.[13] Certainly, the severe criticism of some of these suggestions by James Barr, for example, is correct.[14] On the other hand, this negative reaction seems to have almost paralyzed the imagination of those who read Paul, so that *pistis* and its cognates take only an almost univocal sense, and we find it more and more difficult to imagine how Jesus might have had *pistis*, or how Paul might have spoken of it. For the discussion to proceed, I think it necessary to restate again some fairly simple yet important distinctions. They are: Paul can use *pistis* and its cognates in more than one sense; and Paul can indicate the same reality by more than one word. To be specific, I recall here the distinction made already by Rudolf Bultmann between *pistis* as confession and *pistis* as response to God;[15] and I recall the connection drawn (again by Bultmann, and later by Markus Barth) between faith and obedience in Paul.[16] If the logic of these distinctions and connections is firm, then one can reach a satisfactory understanding of "the faith of Jesus" in Paul and see how Rom 5:18–19 explicates Rom 3:21–26.

---

13. M. Barth does not escape this entirely (see "Faith of the Messiah," 365–66), but it is found particularly in Hebert, "'Faithfulness' and 'Faith,'" and Torrance, "One Aspect."

14. Barr, *Semantics of Biblical Language*. But two remarks should qualify Barr's scathing critique. First, Hebert, in particular, made sharp exegetical observations that remain valid (see "'Faithfulness and 'Faith,'" 376–77). Second, although these writers cast their net too widely and indiscriminately, and without sufficient attention to context, it remains proper to inquire after the broader resonances of terms within the usage of a particular author, when the integrity of the exegetical method is observed (see Hays, "Psalm 143," 110n14).

15. See Rudolf Bultmann, "πιστεύω," *TDNT* 6:217–19.

16. Cf. Bultmann, *Theology of the New Testament*, 1:314; M. Barth, "Faith of the Messiah," 366.

CHAPTER 1

Faith as the Confession of Christ

Pistis as confessional is so important for Paul, and its use so pervasive, that it colors the whole discussion of *pistis Christou*. For purposes of clarity, I here leave aside for the moment the disputed cases. Apart from these, we see in the plainest fashion that Paul makes Christ the object of faith. The clearest examples are when he uses the verb *pisteuō*, as in Gal 2:16, *kai hēmeis eis Christon Iēsoun episteusamen*, and in Phil 1:29, *to eis auton pisteuein*.[17] The noun form is used so unequivocally only in Col 2:5: *stereōma tēs eis Christon pisteōs hymōn*. The fact that Paul speaks so clearly of Christ being the object of belief cautions us against precipitous conclusions regarding the disputed genitive constructions. But in what sense does Paul speak of Christ being the object of faith?

Christ is the object of the Christian's faith in the sense of *specifying confession*.[18] We do not find in these passages that "faith" describes a relationship of trust, fidelity, or obedience to the particular figure designated as Messiah, but rather to God's offer of righteousness (salvation, redemption) through the death and resurrection of Jesus the Messiah. Paradoxically, the fundamental confession is not (for Paul) "Jesus is Christ" but "Jesus is Lord," and this is attached explicitly to "confession" language in Phil 2:11, *kai pasa glōssa exomologēsētai hoti kyrios Iēsous Christos eis doxan theou patros*, and in Rom 10:9, *ean homologēsēs en tō stomati sou kyrion Iēsoun*.[19] The confessional aspect of *pistis* specifies the shape of the Christian response to God. Thus, not only "Christ" but also the gospel can be spoken of as the object of such faith.[20] Likewise, Christians can be referred to by Paul simply as the "believers" (*hoi pisteuontes*),[21] and those outside the community as *apistoi*.[22] Such "faith in Christ" sets Christians apart not only from pagans, "who do not know God" (1 Thess 4:5), but also from Jews, who have faith in the one God (Rom 2:17; 10:2) but who

17. In spite of the ambiguity created by the use of scriptural citations, we should probably add Rom 9:33; 10:11, 14 to this category as referring to belief *in* Christ.

18. Cf. Paul's use of *exomologeō* in the citations of Rom 14:11 and 15:9, as well as the consistently christological shape of the confession (*homologeō*) in 1 John 2:23; 4:2, 3, 15; 2 John 7.

19. Cf. Dahl, "Messiahship of Jesus in Paul," esp. 40–43.

20. Here is found the legitimate nucleus of Hultgren's remark about "Christic faith" coming through the gospel ("*Pistis Christou*," 257). Cf., e.g., 1 Cor 2:4–5; 15:11, 14; and (possibly) Phil 1:27 and 2 Thess 2:12.

21. Cf. 1 Thess 1:7; 2:10, 13; 2 Thess 1:10; 1 Cor 1:21; 14:22.

22. Cf. 1 Cor 6:6; 7:12; 10:27; 14:22, 24; 2 Cor 6:14–15; and esp. 2 Cor 4:4.

do not confess Jesus as Christ and Lord; that is, they do not acknowledge God's way of revealing his justice in the present time.[23]

In those places, then, where Paul is concerned to stress the *particular* shape of the Christian response to God (especially in contrast to non-Christian Jews), there are good reasons beforehand to suspect that a *pistis Christou* formulation would be an objective genitive. Such appears to be the case in Gal 2:16a, combined as it is with the already cited verbal form, "and we have believed in Christ Jesus."[24] Yet, even here, where Paul's contrast between faith and the works of the law is clear, a certain ambiguity is created by the presence of *ek pisteōs Christou* in the same verse, and by the phrase, four verses later, *en pistei zō tē tou huiou tou theou* (Gal 2:20). With *ek pisteōs Christou*, one wonders whether the RSV has adequately captured the sense with "by faith in Christ," for that leaves us with the same sense of redundancy as we had in Rom 3:21.[25] In the case of Gal 2:20, one would like to follow the RSV in reading, "I live by faith in the Son of God," were it not that, again, the sense is that one lives because of the gift and not because of the mode of its reception. It is not "faith in Christ" that gives Paul life. It is "Christ living in me" (Gal 2:20a). The "faith" here, one begins to think, may belong to "the one who loved me and gave himself up for me" (Gal 2:20b).[26] Even where "faith" appears to refer to specifying confession, therefore, we are faced with the possibility that it may be less part of the gift's acceptance than of the gift itself, so that we need to read, "I live now, not I, but Christ lives in me. The life I now live in the flesh I live in virtue of the faith of God's Son, who loved me and gave himself for me."[27] But this returns us to the problem with which we began. In what sense can we speak of Jesus having faith? Clearly, Jesus's faith cannot be confessional. It cannot be faith in the Christ. It must be, therefore, faith in *God*, and this brings us closer to the primary meaning of *pistis* in Paul.

---

23. Cf. the use of *nun* in Rom 3:26; 5:9, 11; 8:1, 22; 11:5, 30; 16:26; 2 Cor 5:16; 6:2; Gal 1:23; Col 1:26.

24. Cf. Hultgren, "*Pistis Christou*," 254–55.

25. The contrast established between *pistis Christou* and *ex ergōn nomou* may appear at first to support the objective reading, but it only makes matters worse for it. We must understand the latter phrase, after all, as a subjective genitive, "the law's works," not as an objective genitive, "works in (?) the law." The only way, therefore, that the two phrases can be functionally equivalent (as they appear to be, given the *ek* and *dia*) is by both being read as subjective.

26. Here, as in Rom 3:21–26, the function of the passage in context is critical.

27. Cf. Hebert, "'Faithfulness' and 'Faith,'" 377.

Faith as Response to God

A more fundamental meaning of *pistis* in Paul is that acknowledgment of God's claim on the world (and on one's life) which is the opposite of idolatry. It refers to that responsive hearing of God's word that allows his way of making humans righteous, rather than human perceptions, to be the measure of reality. It bespeaks that acceptance of God's grace as the source of authentic life which is the opposite of self-aggrandizement. This meaning of *pistis* represents one of the two basic options available to human freedom in the world: openness to God, or a turning from him. It is this understanding of *pistis* that enables Paul to make the otherwise outrageous claim, *pan de ho ouk ek pisteōs hamartia estin* (Rom 14:23). The sin that opposes faith is not an action but a centering of existence in falsehood—that is, idolatry. As idolatry begins with the refusal to acknowledge God's claim to glory as creator (Rom 1:18–23) and leads logically to the attempt to establish one's place in the world (righteousness) on one's own terms (Rom 10:3), so faith begins in the recognition of being God's creature and leads to accepting his way of making humans righteous before him (Rom 3:21–26). So fundamental an orientation of human existence can have as its object only God himself. Thus, Paul speaks of the Thessalonians' *pistis pros theon* precisely in the context of recalling to them *pōs epestrepsate pros ton theon apo tōn eidōlōn douleuein theō zōnti kai alēthinō* (1 Thess 1:8–9).

The *theological* object of this response is found most clearly in Paul's discussion of Abraham. When he cites Gen 15:6 in both Rom 4:3 and Gal 3:6, Paul says of him, *tō theō kai elogisthē autō eis dikaiosynēn*. The thematic connection between this sort of faith and righteousness does not require stressing, but we can note how emphatically Paul repeats that Abraham's faith is directed to God: in Rom 4:5, *pisteuonti de epi ton dikaiounta ton asebē*; in Rom 4:17, *katenanti hou episteusen theou tou zōopoiountos tous nekrous*. It is in this fashion that Paul can present Abraham's faith in God as model for the Christian response to God. So, in Gal 3:5–6, Paul's question to the Galatians places in opposition "the works of the law" and "the hearing which is faith" (*ex akoēs pisteōs*, an epexegetical genitive), as the source of their new life. With the *kathōs* that immediately follows, Paul makes Abraham an example of such faithful hearing. He draws the connection securely in Gal 3:7, *hoi ek pisteōs houtoi huioi eisin Abraam*. As Abraham believed in *God*, so those called his children are regarded as *ek pisteōs* (the resemblance to both Rom 4:16 and Gal 3:26 is striking). Similarly, in Rom 4:22–24 the *dikaiosynē* reckoned to Abraham because of his faith is to be reckoned as well *tois pisteuousin epi ton egeiranta Iēsoun ton kyrion hēmōn ek nekrōn.* The proper object of this fundamental faith, for the Christian as for Abraham, is the one who raises from the dead and calls into existence things that do not exist (Rom 4:17). This is not "faith in Christ" but faith in the one who raised Christ from the dead, God (*patēr theos*). If the confessional aspect of *pistis* is encapsulated by Rom 10:9a, the response aspect of faith is captured by the second part of that same verse, 9b: *kai pisteusēs en tē kardia sou hoti ho theos auton ēgeiren ek nekrōn sōthēsē.* Significantly enough, Paul then proceeds to attach *dikaiosynē*, not to the confession of Jesus as Lord, but to this faith in God: *kardia gar pisteuetai eis dikaiosynēn, stomati de homologeitai eis sōtērian* (Rom 10:10).

Faith as Obedience

It can be objected that Paul rarely uses *pistis* and its cognates in this God-directed sense. But just as he can mean different things by *pistis*, so can he use different expressions for this fundamental response to God. It is here, I think, that the discussions of the faith of Jesus have tended to go astray. The point of advance is less to be found in locating the possible Hebrew resonances of *pistis* (in the direction of "fidelity"), as it is in finding how Paul himself understands the response of *pistis* toward God. For Paul, faith as a fundamental human response is the only option to sin. There is no middle ground. Now, as sin in the fundamental sense is best understood under the category of disobedience (see Rom 5:19), so theological faith is best understood within the framework of obedience toward God.[28] Paul is particularly rich in this terminology, especially in Romans, where the two responses to God are described in what is, for Paul, almost a systematic manner.

The first noteworthy thing about his usage is that faith language and obedience language tend to overlap, functionally. We have seen how, when speaking of faith in a confessional sense, Paul could place Christ and the gospel as objects of this faith. In the same way, he can speak of obedience being directed to Christ, or to the proclamation of Christ in the kerygma. In 2 Cor 10:5 he speaks of taking every thought captive *eis tēn hypakoēn tou Christou* (in contrast to *parakoēn*, 10:6). And in 2 Thess 1:8 he prom-

---

28. In this, Bultmann is surely correct: *"Paul understands faith primarily as obedience;* he understands the act of faith as an act of obedience" (*Theology of the New Testament*, 1:314). The elements of trust and fidelity are certainly to be found in Paul (cf., e.g., Rom 4:18–20; 8:24–25), but at the heart is obedient hearing.

ises retribution to *mē eidosin theon kai tois mē hypakouousin tō euangeliō tou kyriou hēmōn Iēsou* (cf. 2 Thess 3:14). In Rom 6:17 Paul gives thanks because *hypēkousate de ek kardias eis hon paredothēte typon didachēs*, but states of Israel in 10:16, *ou pantes hypēkousan tō euangeliō*. As "faith" could specify the Christian response by being directed to Christ and to the gospel announcing God's work in Christ, so "obedience" can have this specifying role. Functionally, faith and obedience language overlap.

That Paul intends this convergence is indicated by the phrase he uses in Rom 1:5 and 16:26 to summarize the goal of his preaching, *eis hypakoēn pisteōs* (cf. Rom 15:18). Several points should be made concerning this expression. First, whether the genitive is read here in a strictly epexegetical way ("the obedience which is faith") or in a more generally adjectival way ("faithful obedience"), Paul clearly brings the two terms together as mutually interpretative. Paul invites us, in effect, to understand faith as a response of obedience to God, and obedience as a response of faith (cf. Rom 10:16–17; Gal 3:4). Second, the use of this phrase does not seem accidental. Its placement at the very beginning and end of Romans forms something of an interpretative *inclusio* around the letter.[29] Third, the use of this phrase already in 1:5 conditions the way in which *pistis* will be read subsequently in the letter, certainly as early as 1:17, and probably as well in 3:21–26.

Just as the confessional aspect of *pistis* was more prevalent but less fundamental than the "theological" aspect, so also is it with *hypakoē*. This can be seen especially in Rom 6:12–19. Paul is there portraying the human condition under sin and under grace (with, again, but two options). Those under sin are led *eis to hypakouein tais epithymias autou* (6:12), whereas those under grace are freed from this form of "obedience" (which is really disobedience to God; cf. 1:24), and can serve righteousness (6:18), because they have obeyed (*hypakouein*) the teaching given them (6:17). Paul's basic understanding of the matter is stated summarily in 6:16: *ouk oidate hoti hō paristanete heautous doulous eis hypakoēn douloi este hō hypakouete ētoi hamartias eis thanaton ē hypakoēs eis dikaiosynēn*.[30] What is remarkable in this passage is that instead of speaking of *pistis* leading to righteousness, Paul speaks of obedience leading to *dikaiosynēn*. We will meet this again. For now, we note that the functional equivalence of faith and obedience is virtually complete.

29. Cf. the parallelism of Rom 1:8 and 16:19, noted by Bultmann, *Theology of the New Testament*, 1:314.

30. The same pattern (but involving *pronēsis*) is in Rom 8:5–7.

The same connection between obedience and righteousness is found in 6:17–19. Here, obedience is contrasted to sin as a fundamental response to God. Because Christians are not under sin but grace (6:14), they can present themselves to *theō* as people living (as from the dead) and can direct their bodily members as weapons of righteousness to *theō* (6:13). They are to consider themselves as dead to sin but living to *theō* in Christ Jesus (6:11).[31]

The point of these remarks, which have scarcely been novel, is simple and direct. When Paul speaks of obedience, we are justified in seeing at least one important aspect of what he means by faith: faith as the fundamental, responsive "yes" to God. Can we not, therefore, when we read of the *obedience* of Jesus, see there a possible understanding of Jesus's faith? It will be noticed that in speaking of Rom 1–4, we saw the connection between *pistis* and *dikaiosynē*. In speaking of Rom 6, we focused on the connection between *hypakouein* and *dikaiosynē*). We should not be surprised if the connection between the two modes of speaking is to be found in Rom 5.

The Obedience of Jesus as the Faith of Jesus

The question now raised is whether Paul says anything about Jesus's response to God in these terms. It would be surprising if it were entirely lacking. If human beings generally (in Paul's mind) can respond to God only by sin or by faith (by disobedience or obedience), and if Abraham was able to respond to God by faith (which is obedience) and was on that basis justified (Rom 6:16), then Jesus's lack of such response would leave him alone, of all Abraham's children, without faith in God (cf. Rom 4:11–12). No matter how paradoxical Paul's statements concerning the kenotic service of the Son (cf. 2 Cor 5:21), the logic of his thought would seem to demand a similar response of the human being Jesus. This becomes even clearer when we remember that it is by receiving the Spirit of adoption

---

31. This analysis is supported by Paul's use in Romans of *apeitheō* and *apeitheia*. Apart from 2:8, these terms refer to disobedience shown toward God (10:21; 11:30–32), a use reflected as well in Eph 5:6 and the textually disputed reading of Col 3:6. Likewise, Paul speaks of the *apistia* of Israel in the same way as of its disobedience. In Rom 3:3 Israel's *apistia* is contrasted to *pistis tou theou*. In 4:20 Abraham does not allow *apistia* to deflect the movement of his faith from directing glory to God. In 11:20, 23, Paul speaks of the *apistia* of Israel in exactly the same way as of its *apeitheia* (cf. 11:32).

as sons and daughters that Christians are able to call God "Father" and, being children, are heirs together with Christ (Rom 8:15–17). If Christians are to be shaped into the image of this Son by the Spirit of the Lord (2 Cor 3:17–18) and are to present their members as the weapons of righteousness to God in a response of faith-obedience (Rom 1:5; 6:13; 12:1–2), it would be strange indeed if Jesus did not, in Paul's mind, so respond in his earthly life to the mystery of God with that obedience which Paul calls faith.

We need not, of course, rely upon surmise or logic. In fact, Paul speaks clearly of Jesus's obedience to the Father in his human condition. Whether or not the hymn of Phil 2:6–11 is traditional, it obviously corresponds with Paul's own sentiments. And whether or not the initial kenosis from *morphē theou* refers to a descent from a preexistent state,[32] there is no question concerning the significance of 2:7b–8: *kai schēmati heuretheis hōs anthrōpos etapeinōsen heauton genomenos hypēkoos mechri thanatou, thanatou de staurou.* It was as a human being (*hōs anthrōpos*) that Jesus was obedient (*hypēkoos*) to death on the cross. We note here the same connection between the obedience and the sacrificial act that we suggested in Rom 3:25. The obedience, we see, is the attitudinal correlative to the act of sacrifice. That Paul wished to exploit just this aspect of the hymn is shown by Phil 2:12, "*Hōste . . . kathōs pantote hypēkousate.*" The obedience of Jesus is a model for the Philippians' obedience. We might also suggest that Jesus's obedience was the *ground* for their own obedience. He made it possible for them to be obedient. If we transpose this obedience language to that of faith, we can suggest that the "faith" of Jesus in God was the ground of possibility for their "faith" in God. The final expression of that faith in the death on the cross opened up that possibility by revealing the paradoxical power of God to save in weakness; that is, it revealed his way of making humans righteous before him.

But is there reason to connect this response of obedience by Jesus toward the Father to the gift of righteousness that comes to humans from God? There is explicit reason. It is found plainly and emphatically in a passage that has, strangely, drawn little attention in the whole discussion of the faith of Jesus—namely, Rom 5:18–19.[33] This is not the place to

32. Recent exegetical work on the Philippians hymn has tended to support the view advanced already by Cerfaux, *Christ in the Theology of St. Paul*, that the hymn refers above all to the human disposition of the man Jesus as God's Servant. Cf. Talbert, "Problem of Pre-existence"; Murphy-O'Connor, "Christological Anthropology"; Howard, "Phil 2:6–11."

33. Käsemann's view is typically polemical: "Almost grotesque is the attempt, on the basis of the term *anthrōpos*, to emphasize the humanity of the person of Jesus,

discuss the difficult question of the precise function of chapter 5 in the whole argument of Romans.[34] It is clear, however, that in 5:12–21 Paul is again presenting (in somewhat different language) the nature of the gift that has been given humans by God. He does this by the systematic contrast of the two human figures (however representative they may be), Adam and Jesus. The actions or attitudes of these two human beings (and the consequences of them) are the focus of the presentation. Those powers of sin and grace that elsewhere appear in personified form are, in this argument, located in the attitudes and actions of human persons.

Before proceeding, it is important to note the resumptive force of Rom 5:12–21. There is a close correspondence in form and in meaning between 5:15, *hē charis tou theou kai hē dōrea en chariti tē tou henos anthrōpou Iēsou Christou eis tous pollous eperisseusen*, and the statement of 3:24, *dikaioumenoi dōrean tē autou chariti dia tēs apolytrōseōs tēs en Christō Iēsou*. The *eis pantas tous pisteuontas* of 3:22 matches well the *eis tous pollous* of 5:15. The disputed genitives concerning the "faith of" or "faith in" Christ follow this statement in 3:25–26, just as here, in 5:15–19, the language of Christ's *obedience* dominates.

The most important thing to recognize is that here, once more, what is being said of the man Jesus is described as part of God's gift. Paul is describing the objective act of God (through Jesus) by which the gift (*dōrēma*) was given to human beings *eis dikaiōma* (Rom 5:16).[35] The contrast between Adam and Jesus is drawn most sharply in 5:18 and 5:19. In verse 18 we read, "Therefore, just as through the trespass of one man the consequence was condemnation for all, so also the righteous deed [*dikaiōma*] of the one man [Jesus] has led to *dikaiōsin zōēs* for all." Paul is ringing changes on justice language. But the point seems clear enough: the righteous deed of Jesus provided the basis for others reaching righteousness (an "acquittal" for life, or consisting in life). The doing of righteousness here has nothing to do with the response of Christians to Christ, or to the gospel, but everything to do with the response of Jesus to God his Father.

The next verse makes this even clearer. Paul says that many people were established as sinners because of the disobedience (*parakoē*) of the one human being, Adam. In the same way, *dia tēs parakoēs tou henos anthrōpou hamartōloi katestathēsan hoi polloi, hoytōs kai dia tēs hypakoēs*

---

to develop something like an anthropology of Jesus" (*Commentary on Romans*, 143). But see M. Barth, "Faith of the Messiah," 366.

34. Cf. Dahl, "Two Notes on Romans 5," 37–48.

35. Dahl, "Two Notes on Romans 5," 45–46.

tou henos dikaioi katastathēsontai hoi polloi (Rom 5:19). Here, the obedience of Jesus is explicitly said to be the basis for the righteousness of others. The future passive of the verb is important; it is on the basis of his past act that others will be established as righteous before God. The obedience of Jesus is God's way of saving other humans. And by this obedience of Jesus, I suggest, Paul means, simply, Jesus's faith. The human faith of Jesus is certainly not a virtue, nor is it simply a matter of trust and fidelity. For Paul, it is essentially obedience. In Jesus, we see *hypakoē tēs pisteōs* articulated in the death on the cross. The obedience/faith of Jesus is itself the expression of God's gift of grace to humans and, therefore, the way in which (in this present time, apart from the law) God's way of making humans righteous is revealed. The faith of Jesus is soteriologically significant. Rom 5:19 is the plain explication of Rom 3:21–26.

Conclusion

I suggest, therefore, that the faith of Jesus is central to Paul's presentation of the gospel, and that the faith of Jesus, understood as obedience, is soteriologically significant. It provides the basis for the faith response of others. That this understanding does no violence to the principle of righteousness apart from the works of the law is made clear from Rom 3:22 and 3:30. Nor is the point of Jesus's faith that his is just like the faith of Christians. Not at all. The point is (and I believe it is Paul's point) that, by virtue of the gift of the Spirit, the faith of Christians might become like that of Jesus.

The importance of recognizing the proper place of Jesus's faith within the heart of the Pauline gospel may ultimately be that we do not allow a (properly) kenotic Christology to become an (improperly) docetic one. It can happen. If the response to God available to Abraham and to those who have received Jesus's Spirit is systematically removed from the range of possibility of the Son himself, then Jesus has become a cipher. Finally, by reading Rom 3:21–26 in the light of Rom 5:18–19 and as the restatement of Rom 1:17, we might be moved to reflect once more on the precise significance of the citation from Hab 2:4 in Paul's thought and ask whether, for Paul, "the righteous one who will live by faith" might not refer first of all to Jesus.

Chapter 2

The Social Dimensions of *Sōtēria* in Luke-Acts and Paul

Restoration and Belonging

W hat do New Testament writers mean when they speak of salvation? My inability to answer so basic a question has bothered me more in recent years as I worked through two New Testament compositions, Luke-Acts and James, where salvation language figures prominently. It is easier to state the importance of the language than to define its significance.

The Question

Part of my discomfort—perhaps shared by my readers—derives from my increased awareness of the complexity of such a question and the difficulty of carrying out proper inquiry into it. Soteriologies are complex systems of meaning, which often show only a part of themselves publicly. Statements about salvation bear with them an implicit cosmology, anthropology, and eschatology, but it is not always easy to tease these implicit dimensions into visibility. And the accurate delineation of any soteriology is hampered by an assumption that the system as a whole is already understood even as we examine its parts.

The assumption is often wrong. My inherited Catholic Christianity, for example, leads me to assume that the New Testament's language about salvation concerns the future blessedness of the individual human soul in heaven. Using such a code, I can deal easily with passages such as Jas 1:21, which encourages its readers to accept with meekness the implanted word "which is able to save your souls" (RSV). Likewise, I imagine that I understand what Luke means by those who seek to "save their souls" only to end up losing them (Luke 9:24). My assumptive soteriological code makes good (even if erroneous) sense of statements about individual persons in relation to God.

But I have a harder time supplying sense to Paul's statement, "Thus all Israel will be saved" (Rom 11:26 NABRE). Can Israel be saved the way souls are saved? What might that mean? Does this passage demand consideration, as many New Testament theologies suppose, under the rubric of final and universal salvation?[1] The adequacy of my assumed code is challenged. I must scramble for meaning the way Irenaeus was required to when gnostics read Paul's language of "flesh and spirit" cosmologically rather than morally.[2]

Any attempt to deal seriously with New Testament soteriology first must pay close attention to the system implied by explicit statements and, second, must question the assumption that the code for understanding the system is already in possession. The third thing any such analysis must do is resist the impulse to harmonize the divergent witnesses precipitously.

Fresh impetus has recently been given to a reexamination of New Testament soteriology (or soteriologies) by the publication of N. T. Wright's *The New Testament and the People of God*.[3] Wright surveys Jewish apocalyptic literature of the first century and concludes that "the hope of Israel" had nothing to do with a world-ending cataclysm but rather with a this-worldly restoration of God's people.[4] On that basis, he further questions widespread assumptions about the New Testament's "apocalyptic worldview." He suggests that there is little evidence either for a fervent expectation of the end of the world associated with the parousia or for a great crisis created by the "delay of the parousia."[5] Wright suggests that the New Testament writers also may well have viewed salvation as a restoration of God's people here on earth.[6] It is not necessary to deny future or individual

1. See, e.g., Whiteley, *Theology of St. Paul*, 273; Stauffer, *New Testament Theology*, 223; Ladd, *Theology of the New Testament*, 521; Kümmel, *Theology of the New Testament*, 238.

2. Irenaeus, *Adversus haereses* 1.3, 1.8.2–5, 1.20.2.

3. As he explains in his preface (xiii–xix), this is the first of a projected five-volume study on Christian Origins and the Question of God, Wright, *The New Testament and the People of God*.

4. Wright, *New Testament*, 300 and esp. 334–38. On this point as many others in his reconstruction of Judaism (whose main fault is its almost exclusive focus on the Palestinian variety), Wright credits his conversation with Sanders, *Judaism*, 278, 298.

5. Wright, *New Testament*, 459–64.

6. Wright, *New Testament*, 400, 458.

or spiritual dimensions of Christian hope in order to reconsider, as Wright invites us, a this-worldly, socially defined understanding of salvation in early Christianity. It is a good hypothesis.[7] How can it be tested?

Comparative Method

One way to begin to test the hypothesis is through the careful comparison of two New Testament writers for whom salvation is a major theme. Comparison between bodies of literature is difficult to execute properly. But it is of considerable benefit. Comparison sharpens our perception of each writing and enables the generation of more encompassing theories.[8] If the examination of salvation language within two sets of New Testament writings for whom it is most centrally a concern should reveal—despite all the expected dissimilarities—a deep level of fundamental agreement, then a general theory concerning the early Christian conception of salvation is at least one step closer to being demonstrated. Such a comparison, of course, must move beyond the mere lining up of "parallels" to deal with dissimilarities as well as similarities, and the functions of each within the respective compositions.

Luke-Acts and Paul's letters offer themselves as good candidates for comparison on the question of salvation. First, we are dealing with the most substantial bodies of literature in the New Testament attributable to individual authors. Second, the theme of salvation plays a distinctively important role in each author's writings. In support of this last assertion, a few statistics:

- The Gospel of Luke uses *sōzein* seventeen times (cf. Matt, 14×; Mark, 13×; John, 6×), and Acts uses *sōzein* thirteen times; these thirty instances match the twenty-eight uses of the verb by Paul (twenty-one if the Pastorals are excluded). Apart from the Gospel passages already mentioned, *sōzein* is used otherwise in the New Testament eleven times; in sum, Luke and Paul use the verb 58 of its 102 occurrences.
- The noun *sōtēria* is found ten times in Luke-Acts and seventeen times in Paul (fifteen outside the Pastorals).
- The term *sōtērion* is used in the New Testament only in the three

---

7. And this is how Wright identifies his own effort; see *New Testament*, 464.
8. See J. Smith, *Drudgery Divine*, 46.

instances found in Luke-Acts (Luke 2:30; 3:6; Acts 28:28), and the one case of Eph 6:17.

- The title *sōtēr* appears four times in Luke-Acts (Luke 1:47; 2:11; Acts 5:31; 13:23) and twelve times in Paul (but only twice—Phil 3:20 and Eph 5:23—if we exclude the ten instances in the Pastorals).
- Finally, the adjective *sōtērios* is found in the New Testament only in Titus 2:11.

Third, these statistics show not only that these authors, compared to other New Testament writers, are fond of salvation language but also that the various terms are proportionately distributed in each case. We are not in a position of trying to compare a minor theme in one author to a major theme in the other.

Such an evenhanded approach has not always been the rule when comparisons have been made between Luke-Acts and Paul. More often, what has been called comparison has turned out to be a measuring of Luke-Acts against a Pauline standard to Luke-Acts' disadvantage. The approach is classically illustrated by Vielhauer's essay "On the 'Paulinism' of Acts"[9] and is perpetuated by any number of studies that propose to compare the "image of Paul" in the undisputed letters and in Luke-Acts,[10] or that consider some theme thought to be "central" to Paul but regrettably deficient in Luke-Acts.[11]

Because of the assumed connections between "Paul" and "Luke," and because "Paul" appears as a character in both sets of writings, it has proven extraordinarily difficult to disentangle a genuine comparison between the compositions from notions of dependence, derivation, development, and distortion.[12] But precisely such a dispassionate and evenhanded comparison is what is desired if we are to make headway

9. In Keck and Martyn, *Studies in Luke-Acts*.

10. See, e.g., Müller, "Der 'Paulinismus' in der Apostelgeschichte," and Löning, "Der 'Paulinismus' in der Apostelgeschichte."

11. See, e.g., the discussion of "salvation" in Stephen G. Wilson's *Luke and the Pastoral Epistles*, which reads the evidence consistently to show that Luke and the Pastorals not only agree on major aspects of this theme but do so in consistent disagreement with Paul. Unfortunately, the argument is based on faulty method: see my review in *JBL* 101 (1982): 459–60.

12. For a very recent example, see Beker, *Heirs of Paul*. Despite the use of a "comparative method" (chap. 3) and despite protestations of sympathy for the difficulties facing Paul's "adapters," Beker must conclude, "Therefore we can only consider Luke's adaptation of Paul an acute deformation and distortion of the historical Paul" (92).

concerning the role of salvation language in each set of compositions. To make the point emphatically, I turn first to the writings of Luke before considering those of Paul.

Criteria for Comparison

For such a comparison to be adequate, several criteria need meeting. First, all of the relevant data should be included. Ideally, this would include all references to redemption and liberation (among others) as well as terms for "salvation." That ideal will certainly not be met in the present essay, which aims at suggestion rather than demonstration. On the other hand, it is important as well to isolate specific "language games" to see how they work on their own terms (if they do) before invoking language from another "game" to explicate them.[13] Second, the literary character of the respective writings must be taken into account. Although Paul's letters do not lack some narrative character,[14] the implicit story undergirding his argument requires reconstruction. The analysis of salvation in Luke-Acts must take narrative structure much more directly into account.[15] Third, the ways in which each writer appropriates earlier traditions has some significance for the analysis: Paul obviously makes use of creedal formulae and scriptural texts (Rom 9:10; 10:13),[16] but in addition to citing Scripture (Acts 2:21), Luke also takes over and modifies the salvation language already embedded in his Markan gospel source.

Finally, proper comparison demands a consistent set of questions that can appropriately be put to both authors' works. The full range of questions concerning salvation would include the following: who does the saving; what is salvation from; what aids or impedes salvation; how is salvation accomplished; when does salvation take place; what is the telos of salvation; where is salvation accomplished; and, finally, who is saved? Neither Luke nor Paul fills out the survey completely. The questions they most fully and directly respond to are the ones most useful for comparison. Fortunately for the sake of this exercise, the compositions enable us to work toward some answer to our opening question: Do these writers

13. See the helpful discussion in Boring, "Language of Universal Salvation," 274–75; also Beker, *Paul the Apostle*, 256–60, in conversation with Theissen, "Soteriologische Symbolik."

14. See the seminal work by Hays, *Faith of Jesus Christ*.

15. See now Kurz, *Reading Luke-Acts*.

16. For intertextual connections in Rom 9–11, see Hays, *Echoes of Scripture*, 73–83.

conceive of salvation primarily in terms of when or where? Are they thinking mainly about the individual or a social group?

The Social Character of Salvation in Luke-Acts

The most appropriate procedure would be to work through Luke-Acts in its narrative order, since that is clearly the way Luke himself wishes to make his argument.[17] Although constraints of space demand here a more efficient approach, the literary unity of the two volumes and their narrative progression must be kept in mind.[18]

To assess the social dimension of salvation in Luke-Acts, I will deal with the verb *sōzein*, which is primarily embedded in specific stories and pronouncements, and then the use of the substantives *sōtēria* and *sōtērion*, which more frequently occur in programmatic announcements.[19] Narrative sequence is observed only by considering each volume's combined data in turn.

The Gospel

By far the hardest material to evaluate is that involving *sōzein*. One difficulty is presented by the fact that Luke takes over some instances from Mark (Luke 6:9 = Mark 3:4; Luke 8:48–50 = Mark 5:23–24; Luke 9:24 = Mark 8:35; Luke 18:26 = Mark 10:26; Luke 18:42 = Mark 10:52; Luke 23:35–37 = Mark 15:30–31), while also eliminating Mark's use of *sōzein* in other passages (the healing summary of Mark 6:56 and the eschatological declarations in 13:13, 30) and lavishly increasing the use of the verb in still other places

17. See Johnson, *Gospel of Luke*, 1–24.

18. In *Luke: Historian and Theologian*, I. Howard Marshall declared that "the central theme in the writings of Luke is that Jesus offers salvation to men" (116), and he devoted half his book (77–215) to developing that theme. Marshall did not yet have the advantage of the work done on the theme of the people of God in Luke-Acts by Dahl, "Story of Abraham in Luke-Acts," or Jervell, *Luke and the People of God*, and he failed to integrate the theme of salvation into that of the shaping of God's people. In this respect, O'Toole's *Unity of Luke's Theology*, which also takes salvation as a central Lukan theme, is an advance. But far more attention is given to the playing out of the theme in narrative terms by Tannehill in his two-volume *Narrative Unity of Luke-Acts*, esp. 1:15–44 and 1:103–39.

19. For the similar treatment of Lukan strands, see Johnson, *Literary Function*, 127–29.

(Luke 7:50; 8:12, 36; 9:56; 13:23; 17:19; 19:10; 23:39). Luke's practice can usefully be contrasted with that of Matthew, who adds *sōzein* to his Markan source twice (Matt 8:25; 14:30) and otherwise amplifies the language about salvation only by adding the programmatic statement in the infancy account, "for he will save his people from their sins" (Matt 1:21 RSV). Another difficulty is that *sōzein* is found frequently in healing stories, where the verb obviously bears the straightforward meaning of "being rescued/healed" from some specific physical or spiritual ailment, and *individuals* rather than groups are affected (see Luke 7:50; 8:36, 48; 17:19; 18:42). Conclusions about a thematic signifiance of *sōzein* or about any "social dimensions" of salvation must be derived from such passages by inference.

In fact, however, the passages do support some such inferences. We note first that Luke, taking the lead from his Markan source, makes the term of healing not only "salvation" from a physical sickness but a "restoration" to human society (see Luke 4:39; 5:14, 25; 6:9; 7:10; 8:39, 48–56; 14:4; 17:19). Indeed, Luke emphasizes this aspect of *sōzein* by having Jesus return the resuscitated son of Nain to his mother (7:15) and the pacified epileptic to his father (13:10–17). And although the language of salvation is not explicitly used, such also is the obvious point of Jesus's three parables of the "lost and found" in 15:3–32, the last of which (15:11–32) restores a lost son to his father in illustration of Jesus's mission to the outcast of Israel, represented by "tax collectors and sinners" (15:1–2). The coalescence of these ideas is suggested as well by the synonymous character of two declarations by Jesus. In 9:56 he states that "the Son of Man came not to destroy lives but to save [*sōzein*] them," and in 19:10 he says that "the Son of Man came to search out [*zētēsai*] and save [*sōzein*] that which was lost."

That Luke signified something more than physical recovery by his healing stories is also indicated by his expansion of the theme of *faith* beyond trust shown toward Jesus the healer (see 7:50; 8:48–50; 17:19; 18:42) to the message of good news proclaimed by this prophetic Messiah to the poor and outcast of the people (4:16–32; 6:20). Luke combines deeds of healing with the good news proclaimed to the poor (7:22–23) and matches the faith shown toward Jesus the healer with the faith in order to be saved that is directed to the word of God (8:12). As I stated in my recent commentary on Luke, "By combining physical healings with the proclamation of the good news, furthermore, Luke continues to make the point noted earlier, that the ministry of healing involves most of all the 'healing' or the 'restoration' of the people of God."[20]

20. Johnson, *Gospel of Luke*, 125.

CHAPTER 2

The two previous observations are joined by the theoretical question, unique to Luke's Gospel, posed to Jesus as he progresses on his journey to Jerusalem. Luke structures this journey in order to show how, as the prophet Jesus heads toward his death, he is already gathering a people around himself.[21] The question is motivated, therefore, by the events taking place within the narrative itself: "Lord, are those who are being saved few in number [*Kyrie, ei oligoi hoi sōzomenoi*]?" (Luke 13:23). Notice the present progressive sense of the participle. Both the question and Jesus's answer make most sense when "salvation" is understood precisely in terms of inclusion within God's people. Included in the kingdom of God are Abraham and Isaac and Jacob and "all the prophets," as well as those (we note) who will come from the east and west and north and south to recline in the kingdom of God. Excluded are those who do not enter by the narrow gate (Luke 13:24–30). It is surely not by accident that Luke has placed this question so close to the healing of the bent woman who is designated as a "daughter of Abraham" (13:10–17).[22] As the ministry of healing is continuous with the prophetic proclamation of the good news to the poor, so is "saving" of the sick continuous with that "rescuing of the lost" that leads to the restoration of God's people.

The story of Zacchaeus makes the point conclusively. It comes at the climax of Jesus's progression toward Jerusalem. Zacchaeus is the paradigmatic "sinner and tax collector" who, when visited by the prophet, responds to him in faith (as is shown by the disposition of his possessions).[23] Jesus's declaration that "the Son of Man has come to search out and save [*sōzein*] that which was lost" (19:10) is here used to support Jesus's pronouncement that "today salvation [*sōtēria*] has come to this house, because he too is a child of Abraham" (19:9).

As the declaration concerning Zacchaeus shows, Luke's language of *sōtēria/sōtērion* corresponds to that of *sōzein*. The statement that *sōtēria* had "come" (or "happened," *egeneto*) to the house of Zacchaeus (19:9) is the first use of this substantive since the Benedictus, where it occurs three times: Zechariah says that God has "raised up a horn of salvation [*sōtēria*] for us [*hēmin*]" in 1:69 (RSV); that this is understood as a salvation (*sōtēria*) from "our enemies" is stated in 1:71; and that the prophet John would give "knowledge of salvation [*sōtēria*] to his people [*tō laō*

21. See Johnson, *Gospel of Luke*, 163–65, and, with a different emphasis, Moessner, *Lord of the Banquet*.
22. See Hamm, "This Sign of Healing," 64–73.
23. For discussion, see Hamm, "Luke 19:8 Once Again"; Johnson, *Gospel of Luke*, 283–88.

34

autou]" in 1:77. These statements join that in 19:9 concerning Zacchaeus to frame Luke's use of *sōzein*, and move in the same direction. Who saves? God. Through what agency? The visitation of God's prophets. Who is saved? The people Israel. What is the sign of salvation? Negatively, freedom from enemies and freedom from sin (1:75, 77); positively, the freedom to worship God in holiness and righteousness (1:74–75). Salvation "means," then, leading a life before God as a member of God's people.

Mary's designation of God as "my savior [*sōtēr*]" obviously conforms to this understanding, for the entire structure of the Magnificat demonstrates how the "raising up" of this lowly servant is emblematic of the "raising up" of the people Israel (Luke 1:46–55),[24] in fulfillment of the promises to Abraham. The angelic announcement of Jesus as a "savior born for you who is Lord Messiah" (2:11) fits in the same framework, as does Simeon's declaration upon receiving the child Jesus that "my eyes have seen your salvation [*sōtērion*]" (2:30), which he then elaborates as a "glory of your people Israel" as well as a "light of revelation to the Gentiles" (2:32), a proleptic note of universality sounded also by Luke's inclusion of Isa 40:5 in the citation of 3:6, "and all flesh will see the salvation [*sōtērion*] of God."

In the gospel section of his narrative, then, Luke uses salvation language with reference to the restoration of God's people in response to prophetic visitation. This conclusion is supported negatively by the fact that Luke does *not* use salvation language in other contexts where it might have been expected. Luke avoids using salvation for the resting of Lazarus in Abraham's bosom, for example (16:23), or for the reception of the good thief into paradise (23:42–43)—an omission the more striking for failing to match the setup provided by 23:39, "Save yourself and us." Finally, Luke does not use salvation language with reference to the disciples' future experience of the parousia. I have noted already his omission of *sōzein* as found in Mark's eschatological discourse (Mark 13:13, 20). In speaking of the parousia in 17:33, Luke uses the language of "losing and gaining" one's life rather than the language of "losing and saving" (in contrast to 9:24). And in 21:28 those who persevere to the end will find their *apolytrōsis* to be near at hand, rather than their *sōtēria*.

In his efforts to describe the normative story that shapes the worldview of Judaism and early Christianity, Wright makes judicious use of the "actantial model" of narrative analysis associated with A. J. Greimas.[25]

---

24. Johnson, *Gospel of Luke*, 45–54.

25. Wright, *New Testament*, 69–77; it has also been used effectively by Hays, *Faith of Jesus Christ*, 92–125.

Since I have entered into conversation with Wright, it may be helpful to display my findings concerning Luke's salvation language in the Gospel in the form of the model Wright himself has adopted from Greimas. The basic model looks like this:

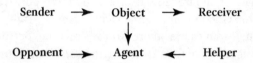

Like Wright, I find the model useful most of all for the way it enables complex data to be organized. My findings with respect to salvation language in the Gospel of Luke fit perfectly into this model:

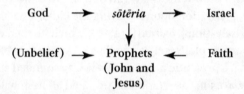

To spell this out: God sent salvation to his people Israel through the agency of his prophets John and Jesus. It could be received by faith and (by implication) impeded by lack of faith. What the model does *not* make clear is that "salvation" has meant precisely to *be* part of this people by faith.

Acts

This discussion of salvation language in Acts will bracket from the start the two cases of *sōzein* in 27:20 and 27:31 as well as the declaration "this will turn out for your salvation [*sōtēria*]" in 27:34. In the context of Paul's sea voyage and shipwreck, these terms bear the obvious meaning of "rescue and survival." It is possible that they might be read for deeper narrative significance, but they need not be.[26]

Otherwise, the salvation language in Acts develops the theme established by Luke's Gospel. Indeed, two of Luke's programmatic statements flesh out the actantial model sketched above. In his recital of Israelite history, Luke has Stephen declare that, in Moses's first visitation of the peo-

---

26. See Johnson, *Acts of the Apostles*, 456–59.

ple, God wanted "to give salvation [*sōtēria*] to them through his hand"
(Acts 7:25). And in Paul's proclamation in the synagogue at Antioch of
Pisidia, he states that from David's seed "according to the promise, he
[God] sent Jesus as a savior [*sōtēr*] to Israel" (13:23) and concludes to his
Jewish audience, "To us the message of this salvation [*logos tēs sōtērias
tautēs*] has been sent [*exapestalē*]" (13:26). This is the point also of Peter's
declaration in 5:31 to the council that "God has raised to his right hand
this one as pioneer and savior [*sōtēr*] in order to give repentance [*meta-
noian*] and forgiveness of sins to Israel [*tō Israēl*]."

On the basis of these texts, the model now looks like this:

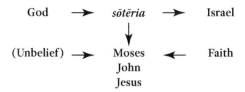

The receiver of salvation, in other words, remains Israel. This social understanding is entirely consistent with Luke's use of *sōzein* in
the first part of Acts. In Peter's Pentecost speech, after announcing on
the basis of Joel 3:5 that "everyone who calls on the name of the Lord
will be saved" (Acts 2:21), Peter says in response to those who ask him,
"What shall we do?" (2:37): "Be saved [or "save yourselves," *sōthēte*]
from this twisted generation" (2:40). Salvation appears here *precisely*
as the formation of a remnant people out of the larger faithless population, which, by being baptized and repenting, receives the gift of the
Holy Spirit (2:38), which Luke has Peter interpret as the "promise to
you and to your children" (2:39).[27] It is not surprising, therefore, to see
those who join this people being referred to as "those being saved [*hoi
sōzomenoi*]." In context, the term means virtually the same thing as "being in community [*epi to auto*]" (2:47) and "those who were believing
[*hoi pisteuontes*]" (2:44).

As the healing of the bent woman in Luke 13:10–17 and the reception
of Zacchaeus in Luke 19:1–10 symbolized the restoration of Israel, so
does the healing of the lame man at the gate in Acts 3:1–10, as has been
shown so well by Dennis Hamm.[28] Peter makes this clear in his speech to

27. For the language of "remnant" for believing Jews in Luke-Acts, see also Moessner, "Paul in Acts."

28. Hamm, "Acts 3:1–10," 305–19.

the council following the healing, when he declares the man to have been "saved" (Acts 4:9) and connects his healing/salvation to the restoration of Israel through the prophet Jesus: "this is the stone that was rejected by you the builders which has become a cornerstone, and there is not in any other the salvation [*sōtēria*], for neither is another name given among humans under heaven in which we must be saved [*dei sōthēnai hēmas*]" (4:11–12). It is, furthermore, undoubtedly this symbolic function of the healing that helps account for the awkward inclusion of "faith" as the other active agent of healing in 3:16.[29]

As the proclamation of the word moves into the gentile world, Luke continues to use salvation language in precisely the same social sense. Cornelius is told by the angel to send for Peter, who will "speak words to you by which you will be saved, you and all your household" (Acts 11:14). In still a third symbolic healing, the lame man of Lystra is perceived by Paul to possess "such faith as to be saved" (14:9). This healing by faith symbolizes the spread of the movement among gentiles through the ministry of Paul, in fulfillment of the programmatic prophecy announced by him at the end of his synagogue speech at Antioch of Pisidia: "I have made you a light to the nations, so that you will be for salvation [*sōtēria*] to the end of the earth" (13:47; see Isa 49:6). The narrative model for Luke's story of salvation can therefore be expanded still further, both with reference to the "receivers" of salvation and with reference to the "agent":

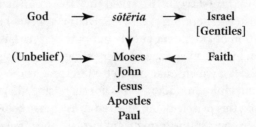

Although the receiver is expanded and the agents multiplied, it remains the same story: God sends salvation to his people through his prophets, and salvation means precisely to be part of that people.

That Luke continues to work with such a fundamentally social understanding of salvation is shown above all by the conflict at Antioch and the Jerusalem Council in Acts 15. Those telling the gentile believers "you cannot be saved unless you are circumcised according to the custom of

---

29. Johnson, *Acts of the Apostles*, 68.

Moses" (15:1) are not stating something about a future life with God but something about status within the restored people of God. For them, to be a part of this people demands the practice of the customary circumcision. The same logic attends the statement of the Pharisaic party that the law of Moses must be kept (15:5). But Peter responds by recounting his experience of God's work among the gentiles, concluding that "through the gift that is the Lord Jesus, we are believing in order to be saved, in the same way that they are" (15:11).[30] He asserts that membership in the people is exactly the same for both Jews and gentiles. Thus also James speaks of the gentile mission in terms of the "raising up of the fallen tent of David" (15:16) by which God "has made visitation to take from the gentiles a people for his name" (15:14).[31]

This decision once made, the message moves even more rapidly into the gentile world through the work of Paul. The Pythian spirit in Philippi announces to the crowd that "these people are announcing to you [*hymin*] a way of salvation [*sōtēria*]" (Acts 16:17). When the frightened jailor in that city asks, "What must I do in order to be saved?" (16:30), Paul's response is in terms of faith and of the group: "Believe in the Lord Jesus and you will be saved, you and your household" (16:31). The upshot is that his entire household is baptized (16:34). The extension of the people of God among gentiles is solemnly enunciated at the end of Acts. Corresponding to Paul's statement in 13:26 that "*to us* was sent [*exapestalē*] the message of this salvation" is his final prophecy in 28:28, "to the gentiles this salvation [*sōtērion*] has been sent [*apestalē*]. And they will listen."

Luke's use of salvation language is utterly consistent. It has to do with God's restoration on earth of a people drawn from the Jews and gentiles alike, a people that responds in faith to the prophetic proclamation of good news. Salvation for Luke involves healing and rescue, but its term is present and social rather than future and individual. Salvation means belonging to a certain community, with faith signifying in behavioral terms the commitment that makes such inclusion actual.

The Social Dimension of Salvation in Paul's Letters

It is a sensible method, therefore, to begin with Romans, where the language is most attested and plays the most central thematic role, and

---

30. For this translation, see Johnson, *Acts of the Apostles*, 263.
31. See Dahl, "'A People for His Name.'"

then compare the other undisputed letters with Romans for consistency, while bracketing the data from the Pastorals for another occasion.[32]

Romans

Read on its own terms, Paul's salvation language in Romans also appears to tell a story of how God was revealing through the good news about Jesus a "power for salvation [*eis sōtērian*] to all who believe, Jews first and gentiles" (1:16). As we all now recognize, that is the "thesis" of Paul's diatribal argument.[33] But it is also the "story line" in whose plot Paul conceives his mission to be playing a critical role. God's plan for salvation, according to Paul's argument, is not directed first of all at scattered individuals but at social groups, at peoples. This becomes clear in the midrashic argument of chapters 9–11, where the bulk of Romans' salvation language is located.

The first suggestion that *sōtēria* is communal is found in Paul's citation of Isa 10:22, which states that "the remnant will be saved [*to hypoleimma sōthēsetai*]" (Rom 9:27). Paul then declares that his prayer is for "them" (*autōn*)—meaning his fellow Jews—"for salvation [*eis sōtērian*]" (10:1). In context, this clearly means that his fellow Jews are not presently part of the remnant people constituted by faith, since their acknowledged zeal for God is not accompanied by "recognition" (10:2).

---

32. Although it must exist somewhere, my limited research has yet to uncover a study that proceeds this way. More often, the subject of salvation is treated without specific attention to the language of *sōtēria*; Beker, for example, pays close attention to the communal concerns of Paul (*Paul the Apostle*, 309), and in particular to the connection of church to Israel (316), but without reference to *sōtēria*; Sanders, *Paul and Palestinian Judaism*, similarly has several of the pieces but treats them separately; likewise, Cerfaux, *The Church in the Theology of St. Paul*. But at least these are aware of the social dimension. More often, salvation in Paul is treated almost entirely in terms of its temporal dimension and in terms of the individual's destiny; the comment by W. Foerster is classic: "In Paul *sōzō* and *sōtēria* are obviously limited quite intentionally to the relation between man and God" ("σῷζω, ktl," *TDNT* 7:992). See also Bonsirven, *Theology of the New Testament*, 271–72; Stauffer, *New Testament Theology*, 223; Kümmel, *Theology of the New Testament*, 145–50, 186, 238. Rudolf Bultmann's *Theology of the New Testament* simply equates salvation with righteousness (1:271) and pays no attention to *sōtēria* as social; not surprisingly, Bultmann has no discussion at all of Rom 9–11! The best treatment of *sōtēria* in social terms that I have yet found is Amiot, *Key Concepts of St. Paul*, esp. 148, 173.

33. Dunn, *Romans 1–8*, 37–49.

The tight cluster of statements in Rom 10:9–13 serves to clarify what "recognition" Paul sees as necessary for "salvation"—that is, inclusion in the remnant people of God. The confessional language of 10:9–10 deserves especially close attention. How does a person become part of the remnant people? First, there is the verbal profession that "Jesus is Lord" (10:9a). This, says Paul, is *eis sōtērian* (10:10b). He means it has the effect of "recognizing" the claim of the messianic community concerning Jesus (see 1 Cor 12:1–3). This recognition signifies membership in the messianic community. But the verbal profession must be accompanied by "believing in your heart that God raised him from the dead" (10:9b). Such faith establishes one as "sharing the faith of Abraham" (4:16–25) *eis dikaiosynēn* (unto righteousness, 10:10a) and therefore as part of that "remnant chosen by grace in the present time" (11:5). Consequently it issues in "you will be saved" (10:9b). The faith from the heart defines the right relationship with God, but the confession with the mouth defines entrance into the "salvation people" (10:10).[34] That Paul is thinking of salvation in terms of membership in the remnant people is shown further by his iteration of the principle of God's impartiality (10:12) and citation from Joel 3:5, "For everyone who should call on the name of the Lord shall be saved" (10:13; cf. Acts 2:21). This reading makes good sense of the next three statements involving salvation. In 11:11 Paul asserts that Israel did not stumble so as utterly to fall. God has not rejected his *laos* (11:1). Rather, their "false step" (*paraptōma*) has meant *sōtēria tois ethnesin* (11:11). This can only make sense in the historical context of the early Christian mission, including that of Paul, which progressed to the gentiles largely because of Jewish rejection. Acceptance by the gentiles of the good news in "the present season" means "salvation for them"—that is, their inclusion in God's *hypoleimma*. Paul also adverts to the deeper game God is playing. The gentiles are included to *parazēlōsai autous*—that is, stimulate his fellow Jews to emulation (11:11). Such, indeed, was the motivation for Paul's own work among the gentiles: he "magnifies his ministry" so that *parazēlōsō mou tēn sarka* ("I may cause my kinspeople to emulate"), which he spells out, saying, "and I might save some from among them [*kai sōsō tinas ex autōn*]" (11:14).

In these passages, salvation cannot mean anything other than inclu-

---

34. It is striking to find a consistent tradition of interpretation that simply equates *dikaiosynē* and *sōtēria* in 10:10, clearly because the social implication of verbal profession have not been thought through: see e.g., Bultmann, *Theology of the New Testament*, 1:271; Conzelmann, *Grundriss der Theologie des Neuen Testaments*, 224; Goppelt, *Theology of the New Testament*, 2:136.

sion of the Jews in the restored Israel according to the promise by faith. That Paul expected his mission to have just that effect is expressed in 11:25–26: "Blindness has come upon a part of Israel until the full number of gentiles come in, and thus all Israel will be saved [*kai houtōs pas Israēl sōthēsetai*]."

Paul's thesis statement in 1:16 and his elaboration of it in chapters 9–11 support the suggestion that *sōtēria* means inclusion in God's restored *laos* (see Rom 9:25, 26; 10:21; 11:1, 2; 15:10–11). It should be emphasized that Paul has *not* used salvation with reference to the individual person's spiritual dilemma or as opposed to life according to the flesh or sold under sin. Nor has it been used for an individual's future life before or with God.

This reading enables us to understand 13:11 in the same context of Paul's ministry. The community is encouraged to pay special attention to the commandment of love, "since you also know the season, that the hour [is here] for you already to rise from sleep, for now [*nun*] our salvation [*sōtēria*] is closer than when we came to believe." In the context of the argument from chapters 9–11, the *sōtēria* Paul has in mind is the inclusion of Jews as well as gentiles in the people rescued from the *orgē tou theou* ("the wrath of God"; see 1:18–32). The gentiles need particularly in "this season" to show that love which is the "fulfillment of the other law" by being its summary (13:8), and by thus demonstrating the "righteous demand of the law" (8:4), cause the Jews to emulate them and turn to Jesus as the *telos gar nomou* (10:4).

The three remaining texts in Romans might be thought to challenge this "horizontal" reading of salvation. In 5:9–10 Paul celebrates the restored relationship between God and humans (5:1) enabled by "this gift in which we stand" (5:2) by declaring: "How much more therefore, now having been put in right relationship by his blood, shall we be saved through him from the wrath. For if when we were enemies we were reconciled to God through the death of his son, how much more, once reconciled, shall we be saved by his life." We notice at once that the contrast in these sentences establishes a rhetorical rather than a real temporal sequence. The contrast posits "salvation" as a condition distinguishable from "righteousness," as in 10:9–10. But no more than there should salvation be read here as an entirely future reality. First, the *orgē* is not only future in Romans (2:5, 8); it is also past and present as well (1:18; 3:5; 4:15; 9:22; 12:19; 13:4–5). Second, there is no question that, for Paul, the gift of Jesus's "life" (*zōē*) is already shared by those who "live by faith" (1:17; see 5:17–18; 6:4; 8:2, 10). In these statements, therefore, *sōtēria* is not only clearly communal (referring to all those who "now have peace with God," 5:1) but is at the very least also incipient in those who, justified and reconciled, now live by the Spirit of Jesus. The same temporal tension is expressed by 8:23–24: "ourselves having the firstfruits of the Spirit, we also groan within ourselves as we await the *apolytrōsin tou sōmatos hēmōn*; for we have been saved [*esōthēmen*] in hope." Here, salvation is grammatically past and the redemption of the body (by resurrection?) is future. But as the plurals suggest, the experience of being in the restored people ("salvation") is proleptic of the future and full realization of redemption/reconciliation by God.

In Romans, therefore, salvation has to do with inclusion within God's remnant people. Negatively, it denotes rescue from the *orgē* that is God's judgment on sinful humanity. Positively, it signifies right relationship and reconciliation with God through recognition of the gift given by the faith of Jesus expressed in his sacrificial death (3:21–26).[35] Apart from 10:9–10, 13, which define the terms of inclusion in this people, salvation language in Romans is entirely social in character. It would not distort the "story line" of Romans, I think, to display it this way:

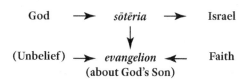

The major difference from the story line of Luke-Acts involves the major role played by the *orgē tou theou* in Romans, and the dialectical character of Jewish/gentile roles in God's plan, only a portion of which appears in Acts.

Corinthian Correspondence

Paul's use of salvation language in 1 Corinthians is almost entirely consistent with that in Romans. The Corinthians are "being saved" (notice the plural present progressive, *sōzesthe*) through the gospel preached by Paul (1 Cor 15:2); the message of the cross is said to be *dynamis tou theou* for those who "are being saved [*tois de sōzomenois*]" (1:18), and through its foolishness God has been pleased to "save those who are believing [*sōsai*

35. On this, see chap. 1 in this volume.

tous pisteuontas]" (1:21). That these statements fit within Romans' understanding of "joining the remnant community" is shown further by the marked resemblance to Rom 11:14 in Paul's declaration that he becomes all things to all people *hina pantōs tinas sōsō* (1 Cor 9:22), as well as his assertion in 10:33 that he seeks the good of the many *hina sōthōsin*.

Such a "social" understanding of salvation gives an edge to Paul's cautionary comment to husbands and wives of unbelievers. He asks each in turn, "How do you know that you will save your husband/wife" (1 Cor 7:16)? In context, this surely does not mean, "How do you know you will influence them for eternal life?" but rather "How do you know whether you can draw them into the community/remnant people?"

Two of the statements in 1 Corinthians seem not to fit this framework. In his discussion of the work of himself and Apollos, Paul says that "the day" will make clear how builders of the house have done their work, "for it is revealed in fire" (3:13). The one whose house is burnt up will "suffer loss but himself be saved [*sōthēsetai*], but thus, as though through fire" (3:15). Here the future judgment of the individual seems to be the clear focus for salvation language. And with reference to the sexually deviant member of the church in 1 Cor 5:1–5, Paul expresses the desire that the *olethron tēs sarkos* (destruction of "his" flesh, or destruction of his "fleshly lusts"?) will have an effect: "*hina to pneuma* [his spirit? the spirit operative in the community?] *sōthē* on the day of the Lord." Once more, future judgment is in view for the individual person. But even in these two texts, we notice, the fate of the individual is very much related to that social reality that is the community (the "house"/ the "gathering").

Turning to 2 Corinthians, the use of *tois sōzomenois* in 2:15 has exactly the same valence as in 1 Cor 1:18. In 2 Cor 6:2 the citation of Isa 49:2, "In an acceptable season I heard you, on a day of salvation I have helped you," is applied by Paul to the community's present circumstances: "Behold, now is the acceptable season; behold, now is the day of salvation," and used as part of the presentation of his ministry as one that "avoids giving offense" (6:3); the combination reminds us of Rom 13:11–14. The precise meaning of 2 Cor 1:6 is harder to pin down: "If we are afflicted, it is for your encouragement and *sōtēria*"; as is that of 7:10: "sorrow according to God works repentance without regret *eis sōtērian*, but the sorrow of the world works death." There is no doubt, however, that the context in both cases is social rather than individual, present rather than future.

Thessalonian Correspondence

If 1 Thess 2:16 is not an interpolation—as I believe it is not—then the statement concerning the Jews who "are preventing us from speaking to the gentiles *hina sōthōsin*" corresponds exactly with the missionary language employed by Paul in Rom 11:11–14. Likewise, the two statements in 1 Thess 5:8–9 make sense precisely when understood in application to life in the present time within the messianic remnant community: "But let us who are of the day be alert, having put on the breastplate of faith and love and the hope of salvation as a helmet. Because [*hoti*] God has not destined us for wrath [*orgē*] but for the possession of salvation [*sōtēria*] through our Lord Jesus Christ."

When 2 Thess 2:10 characterizes those who "are being destroyed [*tois apollymenois*]" (cf. 1 Cor 1:18; 2 Cor 2:15) as those who by deception "do not accept the truth *eis to sōthēnai autous*," the salvation language functions straightforwardly to designate those who belong to the community and those who do not.[36] This can be seen even more clearly when placed next to the sequel in 2:13: they are to thank God, "because God chose you to be the firstfruits unto salvation [*aparchēn eis sōtērian*] in holiness of Spirit and fidelity to truth." Note in passing that "first-fruits unto salvation" echoes the language of Rom 11:16 concerning the remnant people.

Captivity Correspondence

The usage in Philippians is more mixed. In 1:27–28 the language of salvation suggests just the sort of insider/outsider distinction found in the Corinthian and Thessalonian correspondence. The Philippians' living according to the good news and not being intimidated by "those who are opposing" is "proof of your salvation [*sōtēria*]" as it is also for those opposing "proof of their destruction [*endeixis apōleias*]" (cf. 1 Cor 1:18; 2 Cor 2:15; 2 Thess 2:10). Likewise, Paul's instruction in 2:12 to "work out your own salvation [*tēn heautōn sōtērian*] in fear and trembling," when addressed to all "my beloved," suggests that they live out their community identity according to the "mind of Christ" in mutual service

---

36. For salvation language used in defining insiders and outsiders, see Boring, "Language of Universal Salvation," 276–77.

(Phil 2:1–12a). In contrast, the expectation from heaven of the Lord Jesus Christ as *sōtēr*, while communal, is certainly oriented to the future. And in 1:19 Paul's assertion that Christ's being preached in whatever circumstances "will turn out to me *eis sōtērian*" has his individual future as its obvious point of reference, especially since this is what is developed by the verses following in 1:20–26.

The salvation language in Ephesians is virtually identical to Romans, no surprise in light of the overall resemblance between these letters.[37] In 2:5 and 2:8 the statements *chariti este sesōsmenoi* and *tē gar chariti este sesōsmenoi dia pisteōs* refer precisely to the inclusion of the gentiles with the Jews in the one people being shaped by God. Likewise in the opening blessing, the *euangelion tēs sōtērias* (1:13) is mentioned with reference to the gentiles (*kai hymeis*) who by faith have become heirs of the promise. In contrast to Philippians, Ephesians' designation of Jesus as *sōtēr* fits within this present and social context: he is "head of the church, himself *sōtēr* of the body" (5:23). Finally, the exhortation to "accept the helmet of salvation and the sword of the Spirit, which is the word of God" (6:17) is addressed to the community and has the same sense of 1 Thess 5:8— namely, to live out their identity as God's remnant people even in the face of spiritual opposition.

Such is the evidence in Paul's letters, absent the complicating data from the Pastorals.[38] We have found that Paul's most deliberate use of salvation language is in Romans, and that with a few exceptions his usage elsewhere fits comfortably within its framework. Salvation language is used more consistently of present circumstances rather than of the future. It almost entirely has a social rather than an individual application. It seems to mean primarily belonging to a remnant people chosen in the present time by God (by grace and through faith), a people that itself escapes the wrath that is God's judgment turned even now toward the world of sinful humanity, and yet also lives in hope of a future in which the remnant will be filled out (Rom 11:12) by Paul's fellow Jews, whose joining of the remnant people, Paul thinks, will mean "all Israel will be saved" (11:26) and all will experience "the resurrection of the dead" (11:15).

37. See Roon, *Authenticity of Ephesians*.
38. This chapter began as a paper for the Society of Biblical Literature in 1993. The constraints of time and setting led me to exclude the evidence of the Pastorals, which I would not do today.

Conclusion

This essay began as an effort to test Wright's hypothesis concerning the conception of salvation in early Christianity by carrying out a careful comparison of salvation language in two New Testament writers. The sketchy comparison of Luke-Acts and Paul's letters suggest the following conclusions:

- The use of *sōtēria/sōzein* language in both writers serves to identify present social realities more than the future destiny of individuals.
- Both writers share the same basic story and worldview: salvation means belonging to the remnant people God is creating out of Jews and gentiles in the present season. For Luke and Paul, *extra ecclesiam nulla salus* would not only be true but tautologous.
- Comparison on the basis of this deliberately limited set of data tends to support the view that at least these two important New Testament writers shared the overall story and worldview that Wright has described as that of Jewish apocalyptic. Yet by defining the remnant people in terms of grace and faith and spiritual transformation, that story was given a decisive turn and that worldview a definitive new shaping.[39]
- If doing comparisons adequately is so arduous, it is no wonder that it is also done so rarely.

---

39. In this respect, Wright's consideration of the ways in which the messianists reshaped Jewish symbols in light of the experience of Jesus (*New Testament*, 365–70), and redefined hope in light of the continuing presence of Jesus (459–64), is a more adequate account than Bultmann's flat "what for the Jews is a *matter of hope* is for Paul a *present reality*—or, better, is also a present reality" (*Theology of the New Testament*, 1:279).

Chapter 3

Transformation of the Mind
and Moral Discernment in Romans

Paul's Spirit-Filled Ethics

In this chapter I examine the possible connection between two kinds of language in Paul's letters about the way human behavior is directed. The first kind of language is explicitly and obviously religious in character. It aligns human agency with a transcendental spiritual power. The second kind is moral or paraenetic in character.[1] It advocates the practice of virtue and the avoidance of vice. Is there an intrinsic link between these two modes of discourse? Does Paul himself indicate such a link? Is a connection to be inferred from language that Paul himself does not explicate?

To put the question another way: Does Paul allow his readers (whether ancient or contemporary) to appreciate any role for the human *psychē* between the power of the *pneuma* that comes from God and the disposition of the *sōma* by human persons?[2] The question concerns consistency in Paul's thought, the way in which he did or did not think through his convictions concerning human relatedness to God (expressed in the symbols of Torah) and his directives concerning human moral behavior. The question is also critical to the appropriateness of speaking of "character ethics" in Paul.[3]

---

1. No one in our generation has done more to make us aware of this dimension of Paul's letters than Abraham Johannes Malherbe, among whose students I am proud to be included; see esp. *Paul and the Popular Philosophers*.

2. For the use of these terms in Paul's anthropology, see Bultmann, *Theology of the New Testament*, 1:191–220, and Dunn, *Theology of Paul the Apostle*, 70–78.

3. An earlier draft of this essay was delivered to the "Character Ethics in the Bible" consultation of the Society of Biblical Literature's annual meeting, New Orleans, Louisiana, November 1996.

As always when asking such questions of Paul, the shape of the Pauline corpus makes methodology an issue impossible to avoid. The occasional character of Paul's correspondence means that we have in each composition only so much of his thinking on any subject as has been raised by the circumstances he considered himself to be addressing. The fact that many of the letters traditionally ascribed to Paul are also regarded by the majority of contemporary scholars as pseudonymous means that discussions of "Paul's thought" are bound to be either conventional or contentious.[4] The best way to overcome the problem of fragmentation is to embrace it. In this essay I take a single letter and try to figure out its logic. Such a procedure allows other Pauline letters and, as in the present case, other ancient compositions to serve as intertexture that might inform both ancient and present-day readers as they try to fill those gaps that might have "gone without saying" for Paul but may not have to his first readers and certainly do not to us.[5]

I argue a threefold thesis in this essay. First, Paul's letter to the Romans both presents the problem in the sharpest form and provides clues to its solving. Second, placing Paul's clues against the backdrop of Aristotle's discussion of *phronēsis* in the *Nicomachean Ethics* provides a framework that makes them more coherent. Third, the hypothesis thus derived from Romans is supported by evidence drawn from other Pauline letters and is disconfirmed by none of them.

A First Look at Romans

How can we account for the fact that the language about the Holy Spirit, which dominates the theological argument in Rom 5–8, is virtually absent from the moral instruction in chapters 12–14? To appreciate the difficulty, it is helpful to review the language in some detail. The "spirit of holiness" (*pneuma hagiosynēs*) is introduced in 1:4 in connection with that power (*dynamis*) designating Jesus as Son of God because of his resurrection from the dead. In 5:5 this Holy Spirit is given to those who have been made righteous, pouring out the love of God into their hearts.

4. My own position on these matters, that all letters ascribed to Paul could well have been written during his lifetime in a complex process of composition that already involved his "school," is sketched in *Writings of the New Testament*, 271–73, 393–95, 407–12, 423–31.

5. For the notion of intertexture, see V. Robbins, *Tapestry of Early Christian Discourse*.

In chapter 6, Paul shows the irreconcilability of "walking in newness of life" and continuing in sin (6:1–23). He does not speak there of the Holy Spirit, but as we see in 7:6, the power of the Spirit in this newness of life has been assumed, for Paul states there that they are now able to serve God "in the newness of the Spirit and not the oldness of the letter."

The power of the Holy Spirit to direct human behavior is most extensively elaborated in Rom 8. The "law of the Spirit of life" has freed them (8:2) and enables them to "walk according to the Spirit" (8:4–5). As in 5:5, the presence of this Spirit is expressed by terms of astonishing intimacy: they are "in" the Spirit, the Spirit of God "dwells in" them, and they "have" the Spirit of Christ (8:9). The Spirit who raised Jesus from the dead—note the echo of 1:4—"dwells in them" (8:11). As a result, they have received a "spirit of adoption" making them children of God (8:15). As children of God, furthermore, they are "led about" by the Spirit (8:14), who testifies with their own spirits concerning their identity as God's children (8:16), comes to their assistance when they are weak (8:26), and prays for them when they are unable (8:26), so that God, who knows the "intention of the Spirit" (8:27 NABRE), heeds their prayer. Finally, as Paul begins his long exposition concerning Jews and gentiles in God's plan, he begins by invoking the "shared witness" of his own conscience and the Holy Spirit to the truth concerning his loyalty to his own people (9:1).

Reading Romans to this point could easily conclude that God's Holy Spirit was most actively and intimately involved in the moral life of believers. Everything in Paul's argument leads the reader to this expectation. Yet when Paul turns in 12:1 to the moral consequences of his argument (note the *oun*), such language about the Holy Spirit virtually disappears.[6] Especially intriguing is 12:1–2, the statement by which Paul makes a transition from the indicative to the imperative mood often in the participial form frequently used in paraenesis (see esp. 12:10–13).[7] Paul says his readers should present their bodies to God as a living sacrifice, their "reasonable worship" (*logikēn latreian*). He spells out this general imperative in three discrete stages. Negatively, they are not to "conform themselves" (*syschēmatizesthe*) to this world. Instead, they are to be "transformed by the renewal of mind" (*metamorphousthe tē anakainōsei*

---

6. For taking the *oun* at its full weight, see Moo, *Epistle to the Romans*, 748.

7. For discussion of the use of the participle as imperative, see W. Wilson, *Love without Pretense*, 156–65.

tou noos). The purpose of this renewal is to enable the "testing [*dokima-zein*] of what is God's will, the good, the pleasing, and the perfect."

I note at once that each stage is assumed to be under their control. It is done, the readers might assume, by their own capacities, not under the control of another, such as God's Holy Spirit. Observe further that there is an emphasis on the readers' cognitive capacities rather than affective dispositions: they are to offer reasonable worship (or the worship of their minds), they are to avoid one way of measuring, they are to change their "mind," and they are to test. These are all mental activities. And here, where we most might have expected it, we find no role at all assigned to the Holy Spirit.

Indeed, in the next part of the letter (Rom 12:3–13:14), which is usu-ally considered to be a classic example of paraenesis in the proper sense of the term—that is, a set of exhortations or maxims of a traditional char-acter joined together without any obvious line of argumentation[8]—the only mention of spirit is in a threefold exhortation, "do not be lacking in zeal, be fervent in spirit, serve the Lord" (12:11). This may or may not refer to the Holy Spirit; it may equally likely refer to simple spiritual fer-vor. Likewise in Paul's subsequent discussion of differences in worship and diet (14:1–15:12), he makes only one reference to the Holy Spirit, when he declares, "For the kingdom of God is not food and drink, but rather righteousness and peace and joy in the Holy Spirit" (14:17). Only at the very end of this discussion does Paul revert to language about the Holy Spirit, when he prays: "May the God of hope fill you with all joy and peace in your believing, so that you may overflow in hope in the power of the Holy Spirit" (15:13). Finally, turning to his own work as an apostle, Paul mentions the "power of signs and wonders, in the power of the Holy Spirit" that has accompanied his preaching among the gentiles (15:16–19).

It seems, therefore, that Paul's language in Romans about the work of the Holy Spirit is restricted to what might be called *religious* rela-tionships. It does not appear to affect, except in the most formal and tangential fashion, his language about *moral* behavior among believers. Between pneumatology and ethics there is no obvious connection. Un-less we are missing something.

---

8. For discussion and literary parallels, see W. Wilson, *Love without Pretense*, 71–81, 91–125.

A Second Look at Romans

What we may be missing are subtle connections Paul establishes at the level of the Greek text that have largely escaped translators into English but which may have been recognized by ancient readers.

The use of the noun *noos* in Rom 12:2 deserves attention. What does Paul mean by "mind" or "intelligence" here? The question is made more pertinent by the omission, in the best manuscripts and the twenty-seventh edition of Nestle-Aland, of the personal possessive pronoun, "your" (*hymōn*).[9] The absence of the pronoun leaves some ambiguity about whose mind Paul means. We remember that *noos* also appeared in 7:23–25, with Paul declaring in 7:23 that his inner self agrees with God's law, but that he also sees another law in his members warring against "the law of my mind [*tō nomō tou noos mou*]." And in 7:25 he states, "Therefore with my mind [*tō noi*] I serve the law of God, but with my flesh [*tē sarki*] the law of sin." As a Jew, Paul has the proper understanding of the relationship with God (2:18–20) but, under the influence of the flesh, lacks the capacity to live it out.

Even more pertinent is the way Rom 12:2, addressed to gentile believers (see 11:13), reverses the situation of the gentiles that Paul had developed in 1:18–32. There he had argued that idolatry had rendered gentiles foolish in their ways, and he mocked their self-proclaimed wisdom; each stage of alienation from God, in fact, leads them to a further corruption of understanding: "Having not decided [*ouk edokimasan*] to hold God in recognition [*en epignōsei*], God handed them over to an undiscerning mind [or "untested mind," *adokimon noun*], doing what they should not [*ta mē kathēkonta*], filled with every sort of wickedness" (1:28–29). Paul concludes in Rom 1:29–32 with the list of gentile vices that flow from such perverted understanding.

Note further that the *renewal* of the mind in Rom 12:2 has as its purpose that Paul's gentile readers will be able to discern or test the will of God (cf. 2:17) in practical circumstances. The phrase *eis to dokimazein hymas ti to thelēma tou theou* is surely an intentional echo and response to the *adokimon noun* ascribed to the gentiles who did *not* "present [their] bodies as a living sacrifice that is pleasing to God, a rational worship," but whose preference for the creature over the Creator led to the darkening

9. The pronoun is read by Sinaiticus, the first corrector of Bezae, ℵ, 33, the Koine tradition, some old Latin MSS, and the Syriac. It is absent from P46, Alexandrinus, Vaticanus, the original hand of Bezae, F, G, and many other witnesses.

of their own minds and hearts. Paul shares the logic of ancient moralists, who assume that moral behavior follows upon right perception, enabling ancient polemic to argue that just as good perceptions led to proper behavior, so did wicked deeds suffice to demonstrate a derangement in thinking.[10] Thus, just as the "untested mind" of idolaters led inevitably to vice, so the "renewed mind" of the gentile believer is to lead to virtue. The link between this understanding and specific attitudes and actions is a process of mental testing (*dokimazein*).

The connection between *noos* and *dokimazein*, in turn, allows us to take with full seriousness the remarkable incidence of *phron-* cognates in this section of Romans: *phronimos* occurs in 11:25 and 12:16; *phronēma* in 8:6, 7, 27; *hyperphronein* in 12:3; and *phronein* in 8:5; 11:20; 12:3, 16 (twice); 14:6 (twice); 15:5. The threefold usage in 12:3 is especially striking, since it picks up directly from *dokimazein* in 12:2: *Legō gar dia tēs charitos tēs dotheisēs moi panti tō onti en hymin mē hyperphronein par' ho dei phronein alla phronein eis to sōphronein hekastō hōs ho theos emerisen metron pisteōs.*

The statement is difficult to translate. Standard translations miss the important play on words represented by *phronein eis to sōphronein*. The Douay version has "Let him rate himself according to moderation"; the Jerusalem Bible, "Let him judge himself soberly"; the New American Bible, "estimate himself soberly;" the Revised Standard Version and the New Revised Standard Version, "think with sober judgment"; the New International Version, "think of yourself with sober judgment."[11]

The problem with the translations is twofold. First, they miss the link to Greco-Roman moral philosophy established by *sōphronein*.[12] Second, by translating *eis to sōphronein* adverbially, they miss the parallelism to *eis to dokimazein* in 12:2. Both constructions are final clauses expressing purpose and/or result.[13] Just as *eis to dokimazein* is correctly rendered "in order to test/discern," or "so that you can test/discern," so should

---

10. See chap. 22 in this volume and Johnson, "New Testament's Anti-Jewish Slander."

11. A glance at several standard commentaries shows a similar consistency: Käsemann's *Commentary on Romans* has "think with soberness"; Fitzmyer, *Romans*, "think of yourself with sober judgment"; Dunn, *Romans 9–16*, "observe proper moderation"; Moo, *Epistle to the Romans*, "think with sober thinking."

12. The commentaries recognize the allusion but give it scant attention. They invariably refer in passing to the article by U. Luck, "σώφρων, ktl," *TDNT* 7:1097–102.

13. Moo, *Epistle to the Romans*, 760, recognizes that the construction could indicate purpose but prefers to see it functioning adverbially.

eis to sōphronein be translated as "so that you can think rightly/moderately." Among recent scholars, Stanley Stowers has correctly suggested the importance of this statement within Paul's argument as a whole.[14] Paul's language points us to discussions of practical reason, and the role of prudence (*phronēsis*), in moral discernment. The solemn warning not to overestimate oneself but to *phronein eis to sōphronein* is programmatic for Paul's entire moral argument concerning life in the community.

A Glance at Aristotle

No extended justification is required for a turn to Aristotle in any discussion of "character ethics," nor for the use of his *Nicomachean Ethics* (*NE*) as the main point of reference.[15] It may be helpful, however, to recall the key role played by prudence in Aristotle's discussion of moral virtue. For example, Aristotle concludes in *NE* 2.5.6 that "if virtues are neither emotions [*pathē*] nor capacities [*dynamis*], it remains that they are dispositions [*hexeis*]," and he states briefly concerning prudence (*phronēsis*): "Virtue then is a settled disposition [*hexeis*] determining the choice of actions and emotions, consisting essentially in the observance of the mean relative to us, this being determined by principle [*logō*], that is, as the prudent man would determine it [*hō an ho phronimos horiseien*]" (2.6.15).[16]

Aristotle delays a direct discussion of prudence until *NE* 6.5.6. Here he characterizes *ho phronimos* as *ho bouleutikos* (6.5.2), so it may be useful to note how he speaks of "deliberation" in 3.3.10–11: "Deliberation [*to bouleuesthai*] then is employed in matters which, though subject to the rules that generally hold good, are uncertain in their issue; or where the issue is indeterminate . . . and we deliberate not about ends [*peri tōn telōn*] but about means [*peri tōn pros ta telē*]." This statement is particularly important for its distinction between means and ends, and for its recognition of the element of "indeterminacy" that calls for deliberation

14. See Stowers, *Rereading of Romans*, 42–82. Given the weight he has assigned to the entire theme of *sōphrosynē*, however, Stowers gives little specific attention to the actual verses where Paul's argument becomes explicit on the point. Likewise, W. Wilson, *Love without Pretense*, 141, provides some comparative passages but does not develop the theme.

15. Käsemann certainly saw the connection: "Thereby he [Paul] falls back surprisingly on Greek ethics. For Aristotle, *sōphrosynē* is in the *Nicomachean Ethics* 1117b.13 one of the four cardinal virtues." Käsemann, *Commentary on Romans*, 320.

16. Throughout this discussion, I use the translation of Rackham, LCL.

or prudence: between the general rules and the specific applications, some mediation is required.

Aristotle's explicit discussion of *phronēsis* begins in *NE* 6.5.1. He observes that the definition of prudence is best learned by observing "the persons whom we call prudent [*tinas legomen tous phronimous*]." Distinguishing prudence from science and art, he considers it "a truth-attaining rational quality, concerned with action in relation to things that are good and bad for human beings" (6.5.4; see also 6.5.6). It is therefore preeminently a form of *practical* reasoning, the ability to discern what is good and bad for oneself (and, in the case of statesmen like Pericles, for others as well) amid the complexity of changing circumstances (6.5.6).

Aristotle can speak of deliberative excellence as "correctness in deliberation" (*orthotēs boules euboulia*) in the sense of "arriving at something good" (*hē agathou teutikē*) (*NE* 6.9.4). At the start of his treatise, Aristotle places prudence among the intellectual rather than the moral virtues (1.13.20), but by the end of his discussion, he recognizes that "prudence is intimately connected with moral virtue, and this [viz., moral virtue] with prudence, inasmuch as the first principles [*archē*] which prudence employs are determined by the moral virtues, and the right standard [*orthon*] for the moral virtues is determined by prudence" (10.8.3).

Four aspects of Aristotle's rich discussion of *phronēsis* are of particular pertinence for the reading of Romans:

1. Like Paul in Rom 12:3, Aristotle connects *phronēsis* to *sōphrosynē*. Having declared that prudence is the faculty for discerning what things are good for the self (and for statesmen like Pericles, for humankind), he says, "This accounts for the word temperance [*sōphrosynē*] which signifies 'preserving prudence' [*sōzoun tēn phronēsin*]" (*NE* 6.5.6). We may question the etymology and wince at the pun, but his point is serious: temperance does in fact keep intact the apprehension (*hypolēpsin*) that is critical for moral discernment. Vice will not destroy one's capacity to perceive mathematical truths, says Aristotle, but love of pleasure or fear of pain can disable the ability to perceive clearly the moral *archē* (first principle), and therefore the person thus corrupted "cannot see that he ought to choose and do everything as a means to this end and for its sake; for vice tends to destroy the sense of principle" (6.5.6). This, I submit, sounds a great deal like Paul's view of how the gentiles' corruption of mind disabled them from seeing clearly and led them ever deeper into darkness and vice (Rom 1:18–32).

2. The resemblance is not accidental, for Aristotle also establishes an explicit if complex link between the *noos* and *phronēsis*, just as Paul does in

Rom 12:2–3. In *NE* 6.6.2, Aristotle says that the *noos* is that which apprehends first principles (*archē*) by which prudence is guided in its decision-making. "Intelligence [*noos*] apprehends definitions, which cannot be proven by reasoning, while prudence deals with the ultimate particular thing, which cannot be apprehended by scientific knowledge" (6.8.9; see also 6.11.4). Since prudence depends on experience, it cannot be asked of the young: "Prudence includes a knowledge of particular facts, and this is derived from experience, which a young man does not possess, for experience is the fruit of years" (6.8.5). On the other hand, "intelligence [*noos*] is both a beginning and an end [*archē kai telos*], for these things are both the starting point and the subject matter of demonstration" (6.11.6).

Aristotle distinguishes cleverness and prudence by making one a natural facility and the other a virtue: "True virtue cannot exist without prudence. Hence some people maintain that all the virtues are forms of prudence" (*NE* 6.8.3). This is because "it is a disposition [*hexis*] determined by the right principle; and the right principle is the principle determined by prudence" (6.13.4). Does this sound convoluted? It must have to Aristotle as well, for he tries once more: "Virtue is not merely a disposition conforming to right principle but one cooperating with right principle, and prudence is right principle in matters of conduct" (6.13.5).

If I understand this rather tangled exposition correctly, Aristotle is struggling to express the dialectical relationship between that "mind" (*noos*) that can understand "first principles"—which is the realm of properly human action having to do with moral virtue, and which here stands as the "end" toward which specific actions ought to tend—and that form of practical intelligence (*phronēsis*) that is able in specific complex circumstances to rightly determine those "means" that tend toward the desired "ends," namely the ways of acting that "cooperate" with or conform to those first principles of morality apprehended by the mind (*hē men gar to telos hē de' ta pros to telos poiē prattein*, *NE* 6.13.7). Understanding makes judgments, and prudence issues commands, "since its end is a statement of what we ought to do or not to do" (6.10.2).

3. Aristotle recognizes that prudence "is commonly understood to mean especially that kind of wisdom which is concerned with oneself, the individual," leading people to use the term "to mean those who are wise in their own interest" (*NE* 6.8.3). At the same time, he notes that the term has wider application, as in the case of statesmen like Pericles, who have the capacity to discern "what things are good for themselves and for mankind" (6.5.5), and notes that "prudence is indeed the same quality of mind as political science, though their essence is different"

(6.8.1). Indeed, the two realms cannot entirely be separated: "Probably as a matter of fact a man cannot pursue his own welfare without domestic economy and even politics," although "even the proper conduct of one's own affairs is a difficult problem and requires consideration" (6.8.4). For the present analysis, it is sufficient to note that Aristotle's understanding of moral (or prudential) reasoning includes consideration for others, under the category of "what is equitable," for "equitable actions are common to all good men in their behavior toward each other" (6.11.2–3). We see the same tension between the individual and the community concern in Paul's discussion.

4. Finally, for Aristotle, the role of prudence in moral discernment is to hit the "mean" between two extremes wherein Aristotle thinks virtue is to be found, and doing it well: "Hence, while in respect of its substance and the definition that states what it really is in essence, virtue is the observance of the mean, in point of excellence and rightness it is an extreme" (*NE* 2.6.17). And finding this mean "is determined by principle [*logō*], that is, as the prudent man [*phronimos*] would determine it" (2.6.15). The point I make here is that the determination of virtue is with reference to a measure or framework. Prudence itself is guided by those moral "first principles" (*archē*) perceived by the *noos* and seeks to express them in action. In this light, Paul's otherwise obscure references to a "measure of faith" (*metron pisteōs*) in Rom 12:3 and "proportion of faith" (*analogian tēs pisteōs*) in 12:6 might appear more intelligible. We note that in each case it is a question of standard: *phronein eis to sōphronein hekastō hōs ho theos emerisen metron pisteōs*, and *eite prophēteian kata tēn analogian tēs pisteōs*. It will be remembered how critical the concept of "proportionality" (*analogia*) is to Aristotle's notion of that "mean between two extremes" that is justice (*dikaiosynē*) (see *NE* 5.3.1–12).

I do not suggest that Paul was writing with a copy of the *Nicomachean Ethics* in hand, or that Aristotle was a direct influence.[17] I am suggesting that Paul's language about moral discernment follows a strikingly similar kind of logic. In Paul as in Aristotle, the capacity to "test" or "estimate" morally derives from the *noos*, not simply intelligence as a capacity, but perhaps something closer to what we would call a "mindset"—that is, a moral intelligence that grasps certain fundamental principles or values. In Paul and in Aristotle, the corruption of the *noos* makes moral dis-

---

17. See Stowers, *Rereading Romans* 58–65, for a good discussion of the widespread theme of self-mastery in Hellenistic Jewish literature; see also Wilson, *Love without Pretense*, 137.

cernment impossible rather than simply difficult. In Paul and Aristotle, prudence or discernment involves what is good for the individual but inevitably involves as well what is good for other humans. And in both writers, moral deliberation takes place within a framework that enables it to be measured.

To this point, my exposition of Rom 12:1–6, especially in its emphasis on the relationship between *noos* in 12:2 and the language of *phronēsis*, has shown an impressive resemblance to Aristotle not least in the way both authors lack any transcendental referent when speaking of moral decision-making, which appears in both to be entirely rational in character. I seem to have failed in my effort to link Paul's religious and moral discourse, his language about the Holy Spirit, and his language about virtue. Unless still something else has been missed.

The Measure of Faith and the Mind of Christ

What I have missed is that although Paul shares with Aristotle the terms and understandings of *noos* and *metron* and *analogia*, he gives each of them a distinctive turn. Here is the first way in which Paul's religious and philosophical language can be seen as merging.

Paul could not be clearer in Rom 12:3 that the framework for prudence/discernment is not a theory of virtue—a matter of hitting the mean between two extremes, for example—but "the measure of faith" (*metron pisteōs*), and that this measure comes not from human calculation but from God: *phronein eis to sōphronein hekastō hōs ho theos emerisen metron pisteōs*. Each phrase has its own difficulty. Does *hekastō* refer back to the act of discerning, so that Paul's readers are to exercise moral discernment appropriately *toward each one* according to the measure of faith? In that case, the dative *hekastō* refers to other members of the community. Or does it anticipate the second clause: "as God has given to each one [*hekastō*] a measure of faith." The word order suggests the first option, and I consider it the more likely reading. Commentators, however, tend to take *hekastō* as referring to the recipient of the measure of faith.[18] In either case, however, the norm for measuring moral deliberation is that of faith.[19]

18. See Fitzmyer, *Romans*, 645–46; Dunn, *Romans 9–16*, 721; Moo, *Romans*, 760; Käsemann, *Romans*, 331.

19. For the different possible understandings of "measure of faith," see Moo,

Similarly in Rom 12:6, the phrase *kata tēn analogian tēs pisteōs* should be taken as referring not simply to the exercise of prophecy but to the measurement of all the *charismata diaphora* according to the gift given to them,[20] the gift-giver understood once more as God; although we can note once more in passing that Paul does not use the explicit language of the Holy Spirit here either.

If *metron* can be understood as a measure, then what are we to understand by Paul's use here of the term "faith"? Rather than repeat the several opinions offered by the commentators ranging from charismatic gift to community creed,[21] we should proceed exegetically by observing the way Paul speaks of faith in this part of the letter. If we take as a hypothesis that *pistis* serves as a measure for moral discernment, we can make good sense of Paul's otherwise odd usage in Rom 14:1. Discussing diversity of practice in the community, Paul instructs his readers to "receive those who are weak in faith." Since the context concerns believers who eat everything and the weak who eat only vegetables (14:2), the clear implication is that "weakness" here means an inability to live according to the measure given by faith. This becomes even clearer in 14:22-23: "The faith you hold, hold according to yourself before God. Happy is the one who does not condemn himself in his discerning. But the one who is doubting yet eats has already condemned himself, for it was not out of faith. And everything that is not out of faith [*ek pisteōs*] is sin [*hamartia*]."[22]

The obvious question raised by making faith the measure for moral discernment is "Whose faith?" In one sense Paul clearly refers to the faith and the mind of the individual believer: "the faith that you hold" (Rom 14:22). So he says also in 14:5-6, "One person judges a day over a day; another judges all days [alike]. Let each one be fully assured in his or her own mind [*en tō idiō noi*]. The one who chooses [*phronōn*] the day chooses [*phronei*] the Lord." But can Paul also mean more than the

---

The Epistle to the Romans, 760–61; Käsemann, *Commentary on Romans,* 335; Fitzmyer, *Romans,* 645–46. Since my own reading resembles Fitzmyer most, but moves in another direction, I will not try to adjudicate between the opinions. But I vigorously take exception to Dunn's view that "it is very unlikely here that *metron* has the sense of 'standard by which to measure, means of measurement'" (*Romans,* 721). That is precisely what it means.

20. See esp. Käsemann, *Commentary on Romans,* 333–34.

21. E.g., Käsemann, *Commentary on Romans,* 335; Moo, *Epistle to the Romans,* 761; Dunn, *Romans 9–16,* 722; Fitzmyer, *Romans,* 647.

22. Among commentators, Käsemann in particular notes the pertinence of 12:3 for the understanding of *pistis* in this statement (*Commentary on Romans,* 379).

individual's personal faith? Can there be another Mind involved here and functioning as a measure beyond that of the individual believer?

It is at this point that Paul's way of speaking of Jesus with reference to the moral behavior of believers in this part of Romans becomes pertinent. Immediately after the statement in 12:3 warning against self-overestimation and calling for *phronein eis to sōphronein* according to the measure of faith, Paul draws the comparison between a body with many parts and many functions, and the community: "in the same way we are one body in Christ, individually members related to each other" (12:4–5). Depending on how strongly we take this metaphor of "the Messiah's body," we might ask whose *noos* is directing it.[23] The link between the dead and raised Messiah Jesus and this specific human community is for Paul very real (see also 1 Cor 6:15–20; 10:16–17; 12:12–31; Col 3:15; Eph 4:4, 15). The one who lives by the rule of God in righteousness and peace and joy in the Holy Spirit is "one who serves Christ in this way" and is pleasing to God as well as approved by humans (Rom 14:18, cf. the language of 12:1). Even more emphatically, Paul states in 14:7–9: "None of us lives for oneself, and no one dies for oneself. For if we live, we live for the Lord, and if we die, we die for the Lord. Whether we should live or die, we are the Lord's. Because it was for this reason that Christ died and came back to life, that he might be Lord over the dead and the living."

Two aspects of this intense and intimate relationship between the risen Christ as Lord and the believer as obedient servant deserve special attention.

1. In a statement that connects moral activity and the bond between believers and Jesus in the most explicit fashion, Paul reminds his readers that they should no longer "walk" as in the night but "decently" (*euschēmonōs*) as in the day with no more revelry, drunkenness, debauchery and licentiousness, contention and jealousy (Rom 13:13). The vice list reminds us of the one in Rom 1:29–32 that condemned gentile behavior as directed by an *adokimos noos*. Instead, they are to "put on the Lord Jesus Christ, and make not provision [*pronoian mē poieisthe*] for the flesh" (13:14). The metaphor of "putting on" a quality as one puts on clothing is not uncommon in Paul; just before this, Paul says that they must "put on" the weapons of light (14:12; cf. 1 Thess 5:8; Col 3:10, 12; Eph 6:11, 14; 2 Cor 5:3; 1 Cor 15:53–54). But what does it mean to "put on" a person? At the very least, it suggests that the qualities found in

23. The use of *sōma* in 12:5 is particularly intriguing only four verses after Paul tells his readers to present *ta sōmata hymōn* to God as living sacrifices.

that person are to be the qualities adopted by them. So Paul speaks in Eph 4:24 of "putting on the new person," and in Gal 3:27 he says that those who have been baptized into Christ have "put on Christ." Certainly, such language allows the inference that the same "mind" that was in Christ should also be in the believers. Paul's statement in Rom 14:14 would seem to support this suggestion: "I know and have become fully convinced [*oida kai pepeismai*] in the Lord Jesus that nothing is common [*koinon*] by itself, but for the person reckoning it as common, for that person it is common." The grammatical relationship between Paul's mental conviction and the phrase "in the Lord Jesus" can be construed in such fashion as to point at just such an adoption of the "mind of the Messiah" as I am suggesting.

2. Paul invokes the example of Jesus himself as a guide to the moral behavior of his readers. Thus he warns those who consider themselves free to eat any food: "Do not by your eating destroy that one for whom Christ died" (Rom 14:15b; cf. 1 Cor 8:11). Explicit in the statement is the mutual relatedness of all in the community to the one Lord Jesus (see Rom 14:7-9). But the exhortation also implies that just as Jesus died for another, so should their behavior follow a similar pattern: they should walk according to love and not grieve a brother or sister by their behavior (14:15a).

The exemplary role of the human Jesus is manifest in Rom 15:1-3. Paul says that those who are strong should bear with the weaknesses of those who are not strong, *and not please themselves*; rather "each one should please the neighbor unto the good thing for the sake of building up the community." "For Christ also did not please himself, but as it is written, 'the reproaches of those who reproach you have fallen upon me.' . . . May the God of patience and comfort give to you so that you might think the same way [*to auto phronein*] toward each other, according to Christ Jesus. . . . Therefore accept one another, just as Christ accepted you unto the glory of God" (15:3-7).[24]

If we place these pieces against the backdrop of Aristotle's discussion in the *Nicomachean Ethics*, we can at least entertain the possibility that Paul understands the process of moral discernment within the community to be exercised not only within the measure of faith but specifically within the "faith of Christ" (see Rom 3:21-26, 5:12-21) that was demonstrated by Jesus's obedience to God and loving self-disposition toward others.[25] The transformation of believers "in the renewal of mind" means

24. See Hays, "Christ Prays the Psalm."
25. In the ever-growing literature devoted to the question of the faith of Jesus,

therefore their "putting on" the mind of Christ, so that the process of *phronēsis* is aligned with the *archē* apprehended by their *noos* thus renewed and informed.

The Role of the Holy Spirit

We have seen that Paul's religious and moral language does coincide in Rom 12–14, but the role of the Holy Spirit remains elusive. If we read only Rom 8, we might conclude that the Spirit completely took over the direction of human freedom, yet Rom 12–14 has shown that moral discernment is very much an exercise of the human *noos*. I have suggested that Paul implies that this human *noos* is itself shaped by the *noos Christou*. But Paul does not draw an explicit connection between the Spirit given to humans and this process of moral testing and decision-making. Closer examination, however, reveals a number of important implicit connections.

1. The Holy Spirit empowers moral choice in accord with God's will (Rom 8:1–3), so that human *phronēma* can be "according to the Spirit" and not simply "according to the flesh" (8:5–8). This power of the Spirit comes to the assistance of human "weakness" (*astheneia*), so that when "we" don't know how to pray, the Spirit prays and God who knows the hearts (of humans!) knows the *phronēma tou pneumatos*! Here Paul brings this spirit of God into the closest possible connection with the disposition of human freedom. Note also that Paul concludes the moral instruction of 12:1–15:12, so otherwise devoid of language about the Spirit, with a prayer that concludes, "in the power of the Holy Spirit" (*en dynamei pneumatos hagiou*).

2. The Holy Spirit "leads" humans who are "children of God" (Rom 8:14), and Paul's readers have "received not a spirit of slavery leading you again into fear, but a spirit of sonship by which we cry 'Abba, Father'" (8:15). Shortly after declaring how the Spirit assists them in their weakness (8:27), Paul asserts that God has set aside those whom God has chosen "to be conformed [*symmorphous*] to the image of his son, so that he can be the firstborn of many brothers" (8:29). Here, the close identification of believers and Christ is mediated by the Spirit. The Spirit itself testifies "to our spirit" (or "with our spirit") that "we are children

---

see Hays, "*Pistis* and Paul's Christology"; Stowers, "ἐκ πίστεως"; and chap. 1 in this volume.

of God" (8:16). Those who call out to God as "sons" can be said to have "the mind of Christ."

3. Indeed, the Spirit "dwelling" in them is at work to replicate the same pattern of dying and rising as in Jesus: "If the Spirit of the one who raised Jesus from the dead dwells in you, the one who raised Christ from the dead will also give life to your mortal bodies through his spirit which dwells in you" (Rom 8:11). We remember the first appearance of the "spirit of holiness" in Rom 1:4, in connection with the resurrection of Jesus and his demarcation of "Son of God in power."

4. Paul uses "newness" language only three times in Romans. The first instance speaks of the "newness of life" (*kainotēti zōēs*) in which those baptized were supposed to "walk" (i.e., conduct their moral lives): "We were buried therefore with him by baptism into death, so that as Christ was raised from the dead by the glory of the father, we too might walk in newness of life" (Rom 6:4 RSV).[26] The second speaks of the "newness of the Spirit" (or "that comes from the Spirit") that enables service of God: "Now we are discharged from the law, dead to that which held us captive, so that we may serve not under the old written code but in the new life of the Spirit [*kainotēti pneumatos*]" (7:6 RSV). Finally, in 12:2 Paul tells his readers to be transformed "in the newness of mind" (*tē anakainōsei tou noos*).

5. Paul declares that the one thing owed to each other is love (Rom 13:8), since love fulfills the other law by doing no harm to a neighbor (13:9-10).[27] Paul follows this with the command to "put on the Lord Jesus Christ" (13:14). We remember that the "love of God" was said to be poured into the hearts of believers "through the Holy Spirit which has been given to us." Once more, the connections between the work of the Spirit, the model of Christ, and moral discernment are intricate.

In Romans as in Aristotle, then, moral discernment (*phronēsis/ dokimazein*) is a fully rational exercise of the human intelligence (*noos*) that operates within a certain framework and according to certain first

26. In his response to the original form of this paper, Professor Stephen Fowl helpfully pointed out that Paul also anticipates chapter 12 by his heavy use of cognitive language in Romans 6; see *hē agnoeite hoti* (6:3), *touto ginōskontes* (6:6), *pisteuomen* (6:8), *eidotes* (6:9) and *houtōs kai logizesthe* (6:11).

27. I follow the minority view by translating *ho gar agapōn ton heteron nomon peplērōken* in this fashion. For the more common translation of *heteros* as referring to the neighbor ("the one who loves the other has fulfilled the law"), see Dunn, *Romans 9-16*, 776-77, and Fitzmyer, *Romans*, 678.

principles. But in Romans the measure is faith rather than virtue, and the human *noos* is in process of renewal by the mind of Christ, so that the expression of *phronēsis* within the community that is the body of the Messiah is to act according to the pattern of life demonstrated above all in the obedient faith and self-disposing love of Jesus. In a shorthand that is anachronistic but also useful, the Holy Spirit may be seen as the effective cause of this transformation, and the messianic pattern as the formal cause.

Evidence from Other Letters

The *Nicomachean Ethics* proved helpful in filling what appeared at first to be some logical gaps in Paul's moral exhortation in Rom 12–14. Even more support is offered by three of Paul's letters: 1 Corinthians, Philippians, and Galatians bring together in the same combination the elements we have identified in Romans.

1. Paul's attempt in 1 Cor 1:18–2:16 to rectify his readers' perceptions concerning their call and identity is of particular interest, not least because of his flat affirmation in 2:16, "we have the mind of Christ" (*noos Christou*), which makes implicit what I suggested was implicit in Rom 12:2. The *noos Christou* in this case is explicitly connected to the revelatory work of the Holy Spirit (1 Cor 2:10–11). In a contrast not unlike that in Rom 12:2, Paul opposes the "spirit of the world" to the "spirit of God" (*pneuma tou theou*), which the believers have been given (1 Cor 2:12a), and the function of this Spirit is to enable them to know the things given to them by God (2:12b)—in other words, to exercise discernment. Paul insists that such discrimination is not available to the "natural person" (*psychikos*), because they are "spiritually discerned" (*pneumatikōs anakrinetai*, 2:14).

Paul's presentation of Jesus in 1 Cor 1:18–30 is directly pertinent to his discussion of spiritual discernment, for the cross is the supreme example of that which was "given by God" but could not be "spiritually discerned" by those lacking God's Spirit (1:18; 2:8), whereas for believers the crucified Messiah is "Christ the power of God and the wisdom of God" (1:24). The "hidden wisdom" in Christ that the rulers of this world could not see is the way in which God chooses to exercise power through weakness; but this is both the message Paul proclaims and the manner of his proclamation (2:2–4), in order that their faith be based not in human wisdom but in the power of God (2:5). And as the rest of 1 Corinthians as well as 2 Corinthians makes abundantly clear, this same pattern of exchange based on the obedient death and self-disposing love of Jesus (foolishness for wisdom, weakness for strength, sin for righteousness, poverty for wealth, death for life) is to be the pattern that structures their moral thinking within the community (see, e.g., 1 Cor 6:7; 8:11–13; 9:19–22; 10:31–11:1; 11:23–29; 13:1–7; 14:1–5; 2 Cor 4:7–12; 5:16–21; 8:9; 13:3–10).

2. In Phil 2:2 Paul appeals to his readers to "think in the same way" or "think one thought" (*to auto phronēte, to hen phronountes*). He uses the same language for moral discernment that we found in Aristotle and Romans (see also the use of *phronein* in Phil 1:7; 3:15, 19; 4:2, 10). He joins this manner of moral reasoning to the comfort that is "in Christ" (*en Christō*) and the fellowship that is "of the Spirit" (*koinōnia pneumatos*, 2:1). This link is unsurprising, since in Phil 1:19 Paul speaks of the *pneuma Iēsou Christou* that is at work among them.

In Rom 12:16 Paul warned his readers against thinking too highly of themselves and recommended associating with the lowly (*tapeinois*). Here in Phil 2:3 their *phronēsis* is likewise to avoid overestimation of the self: "in lowliness [*tapeinophrosynē*] reckon others as having it over yourselves." The use of "reckon" (*hēgoumenoi*) is important both because it will run through Paul's argument in chapters 2 and 3 and because it suggests once more the genuinely *rational* character of moral discernment.[28] We note further that as "putting on the Lord Jesus Christ" in Rom 13:14 was opposed to "contention and jealousy" (Rom 13:13), so here the attitude of considering others more than oneself is contrasted to the measurement of strife and vainglory (Phil 2:3).

Aristotle recognized that prudence inevitably involved looking to the common good as well as that of the individual, but he agreed with the common recognition that *phronēsis* had as its main task seeking what was good for the individual. As in Rom 12:4–5, Paul reverses the priority: they can look to their own interest but must *prefer* that of others: *mē ta heautōn hekastos skopountes, alla kai ta heterōn hekastoi* (Phil 2:4).

Finally, as we know, Paul presents to them the pattern of the obedient servant who did not "reckon" his own interest in being equal to God but emptied himself out in an obedient death (Phil 2:6–11), introducing the example with the exhortation: *touto phroneite en hymin ho kai en*

28. See Kurz, "Kenotic Imitation."

Christō Iēsou (2:5), a phrase almost impossible adequately to translate. The RSV does not do badly when it supplies "Have this mind among yourselves, which is yours in Christ Jesus," but the substantive "mind," however appropriate and accurate an echo of 1 Cor 2:16 and Rom 12:2, misses the dynamism of the present imperative ("keep on discerning"), and, more important, the phrase *ho kai en Christō Iēsou* should be rendered "which is also in Christ Jesus." The *touto* and *ho* connect: the "way of thinking" that they should pursue is the "way of thinking" that is found in Jesus.

That Paul intends the Christ-hymn to be understood as exemplary[29] is demonstrated by the way he proceeds to offer three other examples to the Philippians of a "moral reckoning" that gives up an individual's interest for the sake of the greater good: Timothy (2:19–24), Epaphroditus (2:25–30), and Paul himself (3:1–16). Having given these moral examples, he says in 3:15–16, "Therefore let us think this way [*touto phronōmen*] whosoever are perfect [*teleioi*]. And if you are thinking in another way [*ti heterōs phroneite*], God will show you this way [*touto*]. But we should stay in line with what we have reached." And he concludes, "Brethren, become imitators together and pay attention to those who walk thus, just as you have us for a model" (3:17).

3. In Gal 5:13–6:5 we find the same elements as in the other letters. Most striking here is the way Paul's moral instruction is folded almost entirely into his religious language. The struggle to act according to one's perception of what is right is now described as a battle between the flesh and the spirit (5:17). The vice list of 5:19–21 are the "works of the flesh" that exclude people from inheriting the "kingdom of God" (5:21). In contrast, the virtue list of 5:22–23 is described as the "fruit of the Spirit" (5:22). And the moral life is defined directly in terms of the Spirit's guidance: "If you are led by the Spirit, you are not under the law" (5:18), and "If we live by the Spirit, let us also walk by the Spirit [or: align ourselves with the Spirit]" (5:25 RSV).

Yet there is also the very clear sense that the Galatians have the freedom to dispose of themselves in a manner not in accord with the Spirit: they can "provide opportunity for the flesh" (5:13).[30] It is striking that, as in the other letters we have examined, Paul does not define such fleshly

29. See Hooker, "Philippians 2:6–11."

30. Note the similarity between Gal 5:13, *mē tēn eleutherian eis aphormēn tē sarki*, and Rom 13:14, *kai tēs sarkos pronoian mē poieisthe eis epithymias*.

behavior primarily in terms of bodily excess but in terms of antisocial and solipsistic behavior: the rivalry that leads to snapping and biting at each other to their mutual destruction (5:15); the vices of enmity, rivalry, jealousy, rage, party spirit, divisiveness, sect-forming, envy (5:20–21); the attitude of vainglory; the practice of mutual provocation; the presence of mutual envy (5:26).

Paul tells his readers that those elevating themselves are self-deluded (Gal 6:3). Rather, each person is to "test" one's own deeds (6:4) and each person is to carry one's own burden (6:5). Against solipsistic tendencies, Paul proposes "serving one another through love, for the entire law is fulfilled in this one saying, you shall love your neighbor as yourself" (5:13–14). This means in practice that those who are "spiritual" (*hoi pneumatikoi*) will look after a fellow member in trouble; they will not use the failure as a basis to build themselves up, but (looking to themselves and knowing that they too can be tested) they tend to such a one in the spirit of meekness (6:1).

They are in fact to "bear one another's burdens and thus fulfill the law of Christ [*nomos tou Christou*]" (Gal 6:2). Paul's constant punning makes such language hard to render. Surely here he means much the same as he meant by the *noos Christou* in 1 Cor 2:16, or the "way of thinking that was in Christ Jesus" in Phil 2:5—namely, that pattern of life revealed in the Messiah Jesus, obedient faith toward God and loving service to others. That Paul intends his readers to reach just this conclusion is supported by Gal 5:24: "Those who belong to Christ Jesus have crucified the flesh with its passions and desires" (RSV).

Conclusion

This investigation into the connection between Paul's religious and moral language, between his pneumatology and ethics, has shown that while Paul's moral logic is remarkably similar to the character ethics of Aristotle, so much so that some of the assumptions that Paul leaves unexpressed can helpfully be supplemented by reference to the *Nicomachean Ethics*, the framework for that logic is pervasively colored by his religious convictions. Human prudential reasoning and testing is demanded, but it is informed not only by one's own mind but also by the mind of Christ. The capacity to see truly and to act appropriately is enabled by the Holy Spirit. The point of prudence is not only one's own interest but above all the good of the community that is the body of Christ. The measure of sound moral reasoning is not hitting the mean that is virtue but corresponding to the faith of Christ that is spelled out in lowly service to others.

In short, the habits Paul seeks to shape in his readers are the habits of Jesus, and the character he seeks to mold in his communities is the character of Jesus Christ.[31]

31. It is perhaps worth noting that in the character ethics of Thomas Aquinas, which depends so heavily on Aristotle, we find in at least two places the effect of reading Paul. In *Summa Theologica* II-II, 47, 10, Thomas explicitly departs from Aristotle with respect to the private nature of prudence, using Paul, specifically 1 Cor 13:5 and 10:33, to argue that prudence must include concern for the neighbor as well as the self. And in II-II, 52, 1–2, Thomas argues that the human virtue of prudence is helped by the divine gift of the Holy Spirit, specifically the gift of counsel.

Chapter 4

Life-Giving Spirit

The Ontological Implications of Resurrection in 1 Corinthians

The resurrection is undoubtedly the foundation for all Christian confession and practice. The statement "Jesus is Lord" (1 Cor 12:3) definitively distinguished the first believers from other Jews and continues to demarcate Christians from all other religions. The confession has three essential parts. First, it states something about Jesus, a historical Jewish man of the first century who was executed under Roman authority. Second, the implied verb "is" makes a declaration about a present situation rather than a past event: the confession concerns the status of Jesus now. Third, it declares that the one who was crucified (a historical fact) is now Lord. That is, he fully participates in divine life and rule, since the term *kyrios* bears with it the full weight of the divine name, following the Septuagint's use of *kyrios* to render the tetragrammaton.[1]

Two further preliminary observations on this simple but all-important confession. Linguists term this a performative statement; that is, it does not merely state a fact potentially observable to all but it declares a personal commitment to a reality that perhaps others cannot perceive.[2] As Paul says in 1 Cor 8:6, although there are many so-called gods and lords in the world, "for us" there is but one Lord Jesus Christ. Indeed, Paul insists that no one can make the performative utterance "Jesus is Lord" except in or through the Holy Spirit (*en pneumati hagiō*, 1 Cor 12:3).

The significance of the title *kyrios*, moreover, is clarified by the New Testament's frequent use of Psalm 110:1 (LXX 109:1) with reference to Jesus's resurrection: "The Lord [*kyrios*] said to my Lord [*kyrios mou*], Sit at my right hand until I place your enemies beneath your feet."[3] The

---

1. As in Gen 2:4; Exod 3:15–16; 34:6; Ps 24:1; Isa 53:1.
2. See Austin, *How to Do Things with Words*.
3. Hay, *Glory at the Right Hand*.

lordship of Jesus—that is to say, the resurrection of Jesus—is understood as royal exaltation: Jesus enters fully into the life and rule of God. The confession "Jesus is Lord" is the resurrection confession, involving or implicating both Jesus and the one who confesses.[4]

Jesus's resurrection is the starting point, the good news from God. Such good news, however, is both amazing and confusing in that a singular human being, to say nothing of an executed criminal,[5] should after his death enter into the life and power of God. Small wonder, then, that almost from the start, even Christians have struggled to grasp the truth of the gospel (Gal 2:14) in its fullness and have tended, in a variety of ways, to slip away from the full paradox of the resurrection faith.

Some have diminished the confession's power by making it exclusively about the believer: Jesus "lives on" in some spiritual fashion in the lives of his followers through the memory of his teaching or the imitation of his acts or the continuation of his prophetic program or even through a form of self-knowledge that constitutes an elevation of the individual psyche. But, while the earliest Christian writings do attest to these postmortem presences of Jesus, they are never identified with the resurrection presence.

Others, concerned that the subjective interpretation seems *too* subjective, seek to secure the objective character of the resurrection by insisting that it was, on some level, a historical event. Jesus was not killed; someone else was. Jesus got really sick but then got better. Or, more often, Jesus died but was resuscitated, proof of which was found in the empty tomb and Easter appearances. Making the resurrection historical—that is, making it an event in time and space that can be empirically verified—also falls short of the confession that Jesus is Lord. In resuscitation, mortality is not transcended but deferred; it means simply continuing on the same plane of empirical human existence rather than sharing in God's rule of the universe.[6]

Christians today likewise are unsteady in their grasp of the central truth of their existence, the reality that alone makes real everything they say and do in the name of Jesus. Rather than being the ground and power of every act of preaching, the resurrection becomes a past event proclaimed once a year as part of the liturgical cycle.[7] Rather than being a

---

4. For a discussion of the resurrection as the fundamental experience that generates the Christian movement, see Johnson, *Writings of the New Testament*, 95–107.

5. See Hengel, *Crucifixion in the Ancient World*.

6. For these options, see Johnson, *Living Jesus*.

7. See Johnson, "Preaching the Resurrection."

celebration of the greatest display of God's power to "bring into being that which is not" (Rom 4:17; cf. 1 Cor 1:28), enabling us to gladly use the language of myth and mystery (1 Cor 2:1–5), the resurrection is an embarrassment that must be defended or explained away, using the very Enlightenment-based epistemological instruments that make its serious interpretation impossible.[8]

A key element in the present diminished appreciation for the resurrection among Christians—to the extent that some seriously consider a reconstruction of a "historical Jesus" to be an adequate norm for Christian identity[9]—is the lack of an appropriate language. It is difficult to speak of "Holy Spirit" with no phenomenology.[10] In a world that rejects the notion of soul and in which intellectuals eschew talk even about "mind" for "brain chemistry," how can "spirit" be discussed in any meaningful way? How can "spiritual body" be addressed without first considering the meaning of any form of embodied existence apart from the default Western image of the body that is derived from Descartes?[11] The same conceptual/linguistic flattening affects our very reading of the New Testament witness concerning the resurrection so that even when the text is plainly speaking of something more than resuscitation, Christians insist on thinking it is speaking of something historical.

This essay engages some very difficult texts in Paul's first letter to the Corinthians, the first extended and explicit discussion of the resurrection, dating from about twenty-five years after Jesus's crucifixion,[12] in order to show how Paul's language demands of us an ability to think and speak in ontological rather than exclusively historical terms.[13] This

8. So, despite every effort to the contrary, Wright, *Resurrection of the Son of God.*

9. See esp. Johnson, *Real Jesus.*

10. The work of Karl Rahner has had a great influence on me; for an orientation, see the short entries by L. B. Puntel, "Spirit," and K. Lehmann, "Transcendence," in K. Rahner, *Encyclopedia of Theology,* 1619–21 and 1734–42.

11. See esp. the important monograph by Placher, *Domestication of Transcendence.*

12. For my position concerning the date, occasion, and argument of 1 Corinthians, see Johnson, *Writings of the New Testament,* 261–77. The date of this discussion is all the more important when it is remembered that Paul here speaks of events within his and the community's experience some fifteen years before the most plausible date for a narrative gospel.

13. I speak of "ontological" in the looser philosophical sense as roughly equivalent to "metaphysical"—that is, thought engaged with questions of existence/being (*esse*) as such, rather than with the study of individual existents or events; see Albert Keller, "Ontology," in K. Rahner, *Encyclopedia of Theology,* 1106–10.

essay begins with 1 Corinthians 15. Although Paul's statements concerning the resurrection come at the end of the composition, they provide, like the truth of the confession itself, the ground for everything he has said previously.[14]

Paul's Argument in 1 Corinthians 15

The first eleven verses of Paul's discussion[15] are a robust reminder to the Corinthians of both dimensions of the resurrection confession as it concerns them and as it concerns Jesus. First, as it concerns them, the good news of Christ's death, burial, and resurrection is *en prōtois*, among the "first things" (or "things of first importance"), that Paul proclaimed to them (1 Cor 15:3). They accepted this good news (15:1); they stand in it and are now being saved by it, if they indeed remain in it (15:2). Second, as concerns Jesus, the Scriptures attest to his death and his resurrection on the third day (15:3–4). He was seen as resurrected by many witnesses, some of whom are still alive (15:5–6), and he was seen by Paul himself (15:8; see also 1 Cor 9:1), who has expended all his efforts on the basis of this gift (15:10). Paul draws the two dimensions together when he declares in 15:11, "whether then it was I or they [the other witnesses], so we preach and so you believe." The death (and burial) and resurrection of Jesus are the bedrock of the shared apostolic proclamation and of shared Christian identity, what Paul calls earlier in the letter, "fellowship with [God's] son, Jesus Christ our Lord" (1:9).

Paul next reasserts the centrality of the resurrection against the claim, apparently made by some among his readers, that "there is no resurrection of the dead" (1 Cor 15:12–19). It is not clear who made this declaration or what precisely they meant by it.[16] Following Paul's logic in the subsequent argument, however, it seems safe to conclude it involved these people's perception of their own present and future. They saw no need for a resurrection of the body because they were so impressed by the "already" of God's rule active among them. Paul begins his letter, in fact, with an acknowledgment of being enriched with every kind of

14. See, e.g., Thiselton, *First Epistle to the Corinthians*, 1169.

15. I offer my own reading of 1 Cor 15 in the following paragraphs. For analysis of specific issues, see esp. R. Collins, *First Corinthians*, 525–84; Fee, *First Epistle to the Corinthians*, 713–809; Conzelmann, *1 Corinthians*, 248–93; and Thiselton, *First Epistle to the Corinthians*, 1169–314.

16. For a survey of theories, see Fee, *First Epistle to the Corinthians*, 7–15.

knowledge and speech (1:4), and his discussion of *ta pneumatika* ("spiritual powers") in chapters 12–14 recognizes the existence of such impressive displays of speech and knowledge among them. If Paul's mockery of them in 4:8 is read in this connection, then they saw themselves, in their present bodily condition, as "already ruling"—that is, already fully entered into God's kingdom and exercising authority within it.[17]

Paul's response in 1 Cor 15:13–19 has a powerful rhetorical structure, built on three conditional sentences (15:13, 15:16, and 15:19). The first two are identical, "If the dead are not raised, then neither is Christ raised," and are followed by, "but if Christ is not raised." In each case, the protasis is followed by three distinct apodoses that deal not with Christ but with the state of believers.

In 1 Cor 15:14 the set is the emptiness of the proclamation, the emptiness of their faith, and the preachers as false witnesses against God. In 15:17 it is the foolishness of their faith, the continuation of the condition of sin, and the loss of those who have already died in Christ.

The point of stressing the resurrection of Christ as the test case for the truth of the resurrection is that, without Jesus's resurrection, "the good news they received, in which they stand, and by which they are being saved" (1 Cor 15:1–2) is total fantasy. The resurrection is not simply about Jesus but about them, their present way-of-being in the world. Thus the force of Paul's final conditional sentence in 15:19, "If we have hoped in Christ in this life only, then we are the most pitiable of humans." For Paul and all those who preach as he does, the resurrection of Jesus is not about Jesus alone; it is not simply an event of the past; it is an existential reality that at once determines their present existence and shapes their future hope.[18]

Having secured the link between Christ's resurrection and their present condition, Paul turns to the "future hope" intimated by 1 Cor 15:19:

---

17. "You are already satisfied [*kekoresmenoi*]; you have already grown rich [*eploutē-sate*]; you have become kings [*ebasileusate*] without us! Indeed, I wish that you had become kings, so that we also might become kings with you" (1 Cor 4:8 NABRE). Paul's argument of chap. 15 is here contained *in nuce:* the presence of resurrection power does not yet mean the full realization of God's *basileia*. They are like pretend monarchs sitting on imaginary thrones.

18. Using a term like "reality" illustrates both the necessity and the difficulty of using ontological language. Christ's resurrection as his exaltation to God's presence is, for Paul, "real" in a way that transcends empirical categories, and at the same time, it creates a new "state of existence" among humans still very much within empirical constraints. Yet neither aspect of this conviction can adequately be expressed in historical terms.

their future is to go where Christ has already gone. He is the firstfruits of those who have fallen asleep.[19] Christ is as paradigmatic for humanity's elevation in life as the first human was paradigmatic for humanity's standing under death (15:21–22): in Christ all will be brought to life (*pantes zōopoiēthēsontai*).[20] But by saying that "each one will be brought to life in his own rank" (15:23), Paul reminds those who think they already have the fullness of resurrection that they are wrong. Indeed, not even the exalted Lord has yet reached the *telos* of God's plan (15:24). Christ's dominion has yet to conquer all inimical powers and authorities or even the ultimate enemy of death; when all that has been accomplished, then Christ will hand over rule to God, who will be, at the last, (*ta*) *panta en pasin* (15:24–28).[21]

During the course of his argument, Paul's language has shifted from the historical (what was preached to them / Jesus's death and resurrection) and the experiential (those who witnessed him / the present faith and salvation of the believers) to the mythological (the parousia of Christ / his enthronement / his triumph over all enemies / his handing over the kingdom to God). How could it not?[22] The matters of which Paul now speaks are not on the present empirical plane of Paul and the Corinthians but on a future, cosmic plane, where the exalted Christ, spiritual powers, and God are the contenders. When Paul concludes with the statement "so that God might be all things in all things," however, his language becomes unavoidably metaphysical/ontological/existential. He makes a declaration concerning the invisible but real cause of all that exists with respect to all things (visible and invisible) that exist, in a relation (*en*)

19. Paul's use of *aparchē* here and in 15:23 echo the LXX's translation of *reshit* in passages such as Exod 23:19; Lev 2:12; 23:10; Num 15:20–21; 18:12; Deut 18:4; 26:2; 33:21. Whereas the offering of the sacrificial "firstfruits" represents the "part for the whole," Paul's use here and in Rom 8:23; 11:16; 16:5; and 1 Cor 16:15 indicates that *aparchē* means "first of the whole," as is made clear in 15:23: "Christ the firstfruits, then, at his coming, those who belong to Christ [*hoi tou Christou*]."

20. The same verb *zōopoioun* recurs decisively in 15:45.

21. The MS evidence for the inclusion or exclusion of the definite article is well split, making the precise rendering of the phrase even more problematic. The avoidance of ontological language among scholars is illustrated by Fee's agreement with C. K. Barrett that the words "are to be understood soteriologically, not metaphysically" (Fee, *First Epistle to the Corinthians*, 760).

22. Paul's language in 15:24–28 is mythic in the proper sense: it has a narrative form (this will happen, then that will happen). God and God's agent are actors; death and sin are personified as cosmic enemies; and none of the statements is even potentially verifiable.

suggesting immediate power and presence, or even identity: God being all that is with, or within all that is. The resurrection/exaltation of Jesus as Lord, it appears, has consequences for the very structure of reality.

After a series of statements in 1 Cor 15:29–34 that rhetorically connect to the earlier objection to the reality of the resurrection (15:12), and point forward to the argument's final moral exhortation (15:58),[23] Paul returns to the mystery of Christ's (and their) future exaltation. He responds to a question posed by an imagined interlocutor, "How will the dead be raised? With what sort of body do they come?" (15:35). His first response is a dismissive "You fool!"

Given Paul's assumptions, the question appears foolish on two counts. First, it seems to assume that the dead who are raised will have empirical bodies like those of the presently alive Corinthians. Perhaps this is for some of them, as it is for many present-day skeptics, a major stumbling block to a wholehearted acceptance of future resurrection. Besides sounding a bit like the classic horror movie *The Night of the Living Dead*, the misconception of a steady increase of material bodies simply leaves no room. A simple coming back to empirical life is not good news for the earth or for the ones awakened. Second, the question is also foolish because, no more than any other human on this side of mortality, Paul was scarcely in a position to describe "what sort of body" the resurrected might possess or be possessed by.

But Paul does have a way of getting at the question that will also address the arrogant assumptions of the readers who consider themselves "already ruling." Paul can argue about the future resurrection of all by drawing an analogy between it and the resurrection of Jesus, since he has already intrinsically linked the two. What does not work analogously is the status of Christ as Lord, or his exaltation to God's right hand. But on the question of the "kind of body"—again, an inescapably ontological query—Paul can draw some analogies.

He prepares his readers for his central analogy by drawing them into observations of the natural world (as they understand it). Seeds that are sown must die before they come back to life, and when they do, God gives the bare seed that was sown a "proper body" (*idion sōma*, or

---

23. Paul poses two "why" questions based on practice: Why does the community practice baptism for the dead if the dead are not raised (15:29)? Why does Paul endure dangers, rather than simply pursue pleasure, if mortal life is all there is (15:30–32)? He concludes by exhorting them to virtue rather than to be influenced by the bad morals of those who "are ignorant of God" (15:33–34).

"body of its own") as God wills (1 Cor 15:36–38).[24] He reminds them of the different kinds of "flesh" (*sarx*) to be observed in humans as distinct from birds and beasts and fish (15:39), and of the qualitative differences between the "bodies" (*sōmata*, 15:40) on earth and those in the heavens. Here, Paul introduces the term "glory" or "radiance" (*doxa*) to distinguish the heavenly bodies—the sun, moon, stars—from the earthly; indeed, he says, stars differ from stars in their radiance/glory (15:41).[25]

The effect of these comparisons is to emphasize two points. The first is that while there is some continuity between what is sown and what is raised, there is even greater discontinuity. The second is that God can surprise with new bodies, and God's range of inventiveness with respect to bodies is displayed not only on the earthly level, the diverse meanings of "flesh" when applied to animals and humans, but on the heavenly level, where radiance/glory defines the meaning of "body."

With the transition "Thus also it is with the resurrection of the dead" in 1 Cor 15:42, Paul turns to his main analogy between the resurrection of Christ and the future state of the resurrected dead. The adverb "thus" (*houtōs*) suggests that the same two points made by his earlier analogies (continuity/discontinuity; God's range of creativity with respect to bodies) carry over as well to this prime example. He begins with three dramatic contrasts that not only echo his earlier comparisons but also reflect language that he used earlier in the letter when speaking of God's surprising creation of the Corinthian community.[26] The body is sown in corruption but is raised in incorruptibility, sown in dishonor but raised in glory/radiance, sown in weakness but raised in strength. These three sets anticipate the fourth, for Paul's language clearly points to the contrast between the merely material, which is always corruptible, weak, and liable to shame, and the more-than-merely material, a body that shares in incorruption, glory, and strength.

The fourth contrast is between the *psychikos* and the *pneumatikos*.

24. This is not really an "argument from nature" in the scientific sense, because Paul inserts God's will directly into the choice of the plant's body (*theos didosin . . . kathōs ēthelēsen*, 15:38).

25. Elsewhere, Paul uses *doxa* primarily with respect to God (see Rom 1:23; 2:7; 3:7; 4:20; 5:2; 6:4; 1 Cor 11:7; 2 Cor 3:8–10, 18; Phil 2:11; 1 Tim 1:11; 3:16) and the human future with God (Rom 8:18–21; 9:23; Phil 3:21; Col 1:27).

26. In 1 Cor 1:20–28 Paul opposes foolishness and wisdom, strength and weakness, glory and shame, and uses for God's election language that echoes creation itself: God chose *ta mē onta, hina ta onta kataischynē* ("the things that have no existence in order to shame the things that have existence").

Both terms are more obscure than the ones preceding them, but if Paul is consistent in his contrast, then *psychikos* must align with the "merely material" or empirical—that is, always corruptible, subject to dishonor, and weak. By the same logic, *pneumatikos* must align with the strength, incorruptibility, and radiance of the more-than-merely material, or the super-empirical.

Paul insists on the seriousness of this last, most important contrast by adding, "if there is a *psychikos sōma* there is also a *pneumatikos sōma*" (1 Cor 15:44).[27] All these disjunctions contrast the kinds of flesh or bodies with which we and the Corinthians are familiar—bodies that are fleshly, corruptible, liable to dishonor and weakness—with bodies with which they are unfamiliar, unless they think of those far-off bodies of the sun, moon, and stars and think of them as radiant, incorruptible, and strong, because they partake of *pneuma*. By using the term *sōma pneumatikos*, however, Paul pushes the Corinthians—and modern Christians—beyond the range of the empirical and verifiable to the realm of the ontological and nonverifiable. A "spiritual body" is at the very least oxymoronic. Within contemporary cosmology, the two terms do not seem to go together.

But Paul's next statements make clear that his speaking of a spiritual body is not language he has stumbled into. Rather, it is where his entire argument has been heading, as he shows immediately by supporting it by a scriptural citation from LXX Gen 2:7, which he reads retrospectively from the perspective of the resurrection. The text of Genesis has, "The Lord God formed man out of the clay of the ground and blew into his nostrils the breath of life, and so man became a living being." Paul quotes only the last line, *eis psychēn zōsan* (1 Cor 15:45). As earlier, the term "psychic" refers here to ordinary human existence. Paul has this term characterize *ho prōtos . . . Adam* in order to set up the typology (employed also in Rom 5:12–21) between the first and new creations.[28]

---

27. This disjunction also appears earlier in Paul's distinction between persons in the Corinthian community: the *psychikos anthrōpos* does not receive "the things of the spirit of God" (*ta tou pneumatos tou theou*, 1 Cor 2:14). For discussion, see Pearson, *Pneumatikos-Psychikos Terminology*. Notice that this distinction corresponds to that between *sarkinois* ("fleshly") and *pneumatikois* ("spiritual") in 1 Cor 3:1: "I was not able to speak to you as spiritual people but as fleshly." The Corinthians engaging in rivalry are "fleshly"—that is, "all too human." Paul again contrasts fleshly and spiritual with respect to the collection in Rom 15:27.

28. I have already pointed to Paul's use of creation language concerning the election of the Corinthians in 1:28. The reality brought into being through the resurrec-

The first Adam became a living being because God's breath animated the clay from which he was formed. But Paul contrasts the first human (a paradigm for all humans) with the one he calls *ho eschatos Adam* ("the last Adam"), who became *eis pneuma zōopoioun* (1 Cor 15:45). The phrase is important not simply because it opposes *psychikos* and *pneuma* but because the adjective *zōopoioun*, "life-giving," can be applied properly only to God.[29] The contrast between Adam and Christ, then, is between natural life and resurrection life. But in the case of Christ, resurrection means exaltation into the presence and power of God, since God alone is giver of life.

Paul drives home his point in 15:46–48: the *pneuma* was not first (with respect to humans) but the *psychē*; the first human was drawn from clay, while the second human (Christ) was from heaven. And as before, he makes the connection between the paradigmatic human and those "in his image":[30] as with the earthly one, so with those who are earthly; as with the heavenly one, so with those who are heavenly. If humans have borne the "image" of the one made from clay, so do they now also bear the image of the one from heaven. Once more: although followers of Christ have not reached the state of being "life-giving" like the exalted Jesus, they do participate somehow in his image—and Paul suggests that the medium of this participation, both for the future and the present, has to do specifically with *pneuma*.

Paul closes his argument in chapter 15 not with exposition but with exhortation. He turns to the behavioral correlates of "standing in the good news" of Christ's resurrection. The message is simple: they must

---

tion of Jesus is understood by Paul as a "new creation." See above all 2 Cor 5:17: "If anyone is in Christ, there is a new creation; the old things have passed away; behold, they have become new [*kaina*]." See also Gal 6:15 and the startling statements in Rom 4:17–25: Abraham "believed in the God who gives life to the dead and calls into being what does not exist" (*episteusen theou tou zōopoiountos tous nekrous kai kalountos ta mē onta hōs onta*, 4:17); God brought life to the womb of Sarah, although Abraham was "as good as dead" and Sarah's womb was "dead" (4:19); God "raised Jesus our Lord from the dead" (4:24).

29. See LXX 2 Kgs 5:7; Neh 9:6; Job 36:6; Ps 70:20. As pointed out in the previous note, Paul uses the verb for God's creating power in Rom 4:17 and specifically with reference to the future resurrection in Rom 8:11, "he who raised Christ Jesus from the dead will give life [*zōopoiēsei*] also to our mortal bodies." In Gal 3:21 he denies this life-giving ability to the law, and in 2 Cor 3:6 he declares, "For the letter kills, but the spirit gives life [*to de pneuma zōopoiei*]."

30. For Paul's use of *eikon*, see Rom 1:23; 8:29; 1 Cor 11:7; 2 Cor 3:18, 4:4; Col 1:15; 3:10.

change. Full participation in God's rule is not available to "flesh and blood"—that is, ordinary human existence—much less such an existence defined precisely by "flesh." The corruptible—that is, the mortal—cannot without change inherit immortality (1 Cor 15:50). Whether believers die before the coming of Christ or not, all will necessarily be changed (15:51). The dead will rise *aphthartoi* (incorruptible) and "we will be changed" (15:52): "this corruptible being will be clothed with incorruptibility and this mortal being will be clothed with immortality" (15:53).

The process of this ontological transformation through the *pneuma*, however, begins already in this mortal, empirical existence that humans share. They simultaneously bear both the image of Adam and the image of Christ. It is entirely legitimate to read in this connection a passage from Paul's second letter to the Corinthians, which serves as a virtual commentary on the argument Paul makes in 1 Cor 15: "Now the Lord is the Spirit [*ho de kyrios to pneuma estin*], and where the Spirit of the Lord is, there is freedom. All of us, gazing with unveiled face on the glory of the Lord, are being transformed into the same image [*tēn autēn eikona metamorphoumetha*], from glory to glory, as from the Lord, who is Spirit [*apo kyriou pneumatos*]" (2 Cor 3:17–18 NABRE, adapted). Reading the passages from the two Corinthian letters side by side, it seems evident that Paul sees the process of ontological transformation as already at work through the resurrection spirit that defines the resurrected Jesus as "life-giving Spirit."

For Paul in 1 Corinthians, however, such ontological change demands also a moral change. He speaks of death as the last enemy conquered by resurrection in the end time but insists that the sting of death is sin (15:56). He declares that if the resurrection is not real, then they are still in their sins (15:17), and he says of those who live as though there were no future resurrection ("Let us eat, and drink, for tomorrow we shall die") that they are self-deceived, and their influence is dangerous: "bad company corrupts [*phtheirousin*] good morals" (15:33 NABRE).[31] He tells them, "Become sober righteously and stop sinning. For some of you do not know God" (15:34). Such insistence on moral change extends throughout the letter (see esp. 14:20). But 1 Cor 15 provides the eschatological-ontological assumptions underlying Paul's moral exhortations and makes of them something much more than mere moralism.

This essay has shown how Paul refers to the exalted Lord Jesus as "life-

---

31. The choice of "corrupt" (*phtheirousin*) in the present context cannot be accidental (see 15:42, 50).

giving spirit" (*to pneuma zōopoioun*) and of the future bodies of the resurrected believers as "spiritual bodies" (*sōmata pneumatika*). It is appropriate,
then, to pursue the question of the ontological implications of the resurrection by inquiring into the role of the *pneuma* throughout 1 Corinthians.

The Functions of the Holy Spirit

Since Paul nowhere defines *pneuma*, we are required to learn how he
understands it from the terms he uses in association with it and by the
functions he assigns to it. The eschatological discourse of chapter 15 has
linked *pneuma* to the incorruptible rather than the corruptible, to the
immortal rather than the mortal, to strength rather than weakness, to
glory rather than shame; it has been described as "life-giving." That discussion, in short, connects *pneuma* to the divine rather than to ordinary
human existence.

As we turn to the earlier parts of Paul's composition, however, we
see at once that he confuses the issue slightly by speaking with some
frequency of *pneuma* not as an eschatological, divine reality but as a
present-time dimension of ordinary human psychology. Thus, Paul can
speak of being holy both in body and spirit (1 Cor 7:34) or of having his
spirit refreshed (16:18) or of someone's spirit praying when speaking in
tongues (14:14) or of an excommunicated man having his flesh destroyed
so that his *pneuma* might be saved (5:5). When he says he will come to
the community in a "spirit of mildness," he refers to his own human
disposition (4:21).

Even some of these statements, though, suggest that Paul understands
the human spirit to have characteristics that might apply as well to the way
he thinks about God's Spirit. Thus, in 1 Cor 2:11 he speaks of the human spirit
in terms of a power of introspection: "among human beings, who knows
what pertains to a person except the spirit of the person that is within (*ei mē
to pneuma tou anthrōpou to en autō*)?" (NABRE). And in 5:3 Paul tells his
readers that although he is absent in body, he is "present in spirit" (*parōn
de tō pneumati*), suggesting that even at the level of human psychology,
pneuma is not confined by space or the individual body. The same passage,
indeed, describes a gathering of the community in which, Paul says, "I am
with you in spirit with the power of the Lord Jesus" (5:4 NABRE).[32]

32. The passage reads, *en tō onomati tou kyriou [hēmōn] Iēsou synachthentōn
hymōn kai tou emou pneumatos syn tē dynamei tou kyriou hēmōn Iēsou.*

Most of the time in 1 Corinthians, however, Paul's language about *pneuma* refers to "the Holy Spirit" (6:19; 12:3) or the "Spirit from God" (2:11–12, 14; 3:16; 6:11; 7:40; 12:3), even in cases where he omits such specific qualification. At least three aspects of such usage requires attention as we inquire into the ontological implications of resurrection.

First, Paul closely associates *pneuma* with Jesus—not the Jesus of human history but the Jesus who is *kyrios*. Most dramatically, Paul makes the Spirit the basis for the confession of Jesus as Lord: "Nobody speaking by the spirit of God [*en pneumati theou*] says, 'Cursed be Jesus'"—that is, sees Jesus simply as a false messiah cursed by God—"and nobody is able to say, 'Jesus is Lord,' except by the Holy Spirit [*en pneumati hagiō*]" (1 Cor 12:3). Similarly, when speaking of the Corinthians' transition from their former vice to a state of being cleansed, made holy, and made righteous (6:11), Paul combines the instrumentality of "the name of the Lord Jesus Christ" and "the Spirit of our God." This Spirit of God is thus closely linked to the risen Jesus as Lord.

Second, the spirit also mediates the presence of Jesus as risen Lord to believers. After declaring the intimate unity that results from sexual relations—"the one who clings/adheres to a prostitute becomes one body, for it says, 'The two become one flesh'"—Paul makes this remarkable statement about another form of intense intimacy: "And the one who cleaves/adheres to the Lord is one *pneuma* [we must supply "with him"]" (1 Cor 6:16–17). Note how this pneumatic unity has somatic implications for believers, a theme pursued in the next chapter. Note, for now, another text pointing to the spirit as mediator of presence: "For by means of one spirit we have all been baptized into one body, whether Jews or Hellenes, whether slaves or free, and we have all been made to drink the one spirit" (12:13).

Third, Paul sees the Spirit's relation to humans as a form of intimacy or even interiority. The Corinthians have received the spirit that comes from God (1 Cor 2:12), the spirit that penetrates the deep things of God in the way that a person's own spirit examines the self (2:10), so that they can know the gifts given them by God. The Corinthians are to discern "spiritual things" (*ta pneumatika*) "spiritually" (*pneumatikos*) because they are "spiritual people" (*pneumatikoi*) who have been "taught by the spirit" (*didaktois pneumatos*, 2:12–13). Or at least that is the ideal if they are mature (*teleiois*).

In fact, Paul regards them as immature, as babes, as fleshly and as psychic, because their competitive behavior shows they don't get what the spirit is about (1 Cor 3:1–4; see 2:14). He needs to remind them repeatedly about the ontological implications of resurrection. "Do you not know that you [plural] are God's sanctuary and that the Spirit of God dwells in/among you [*oikei en hymin*]?" (3:16). This is something they should know but they act as though they did not, so he warns them, "If anyone destroys/corrupts [*phtherei*] God's sanctuary, God will destroy this one" (3:17). He tells them again in his discussion of sexual immorality, "Or do you not know that your [plural] body is the sanctuary of the Holy Spirit within/among you, which you have from God, and you are not your own?" (6:19).

These three aspects are in truth closely interconnected. If Paul uses spirit language for the designation of Jesus as Lord, and for the intimate presence of Jesus to believers, this has implications for other places in this letter where Paul speaks of Christians' being "in Christ" (eleven times) and "in the Lord" (nine times). Just as he can speak of "drinking the one Spirit" and of the Spirit "dwelling in them," so he can speak of them being "in Christ" and "in the Lord." The manner suggests a sharing or communication at the level of being rather than at the level of shared physical space or a sphere of moral influence. The conclusion that seems to be demanded by the way in which Paul uses language in 1 Corinthians is that the mutual indwelling of the risen Lord Jesus, the Spirit, and the Corinthians is, at the very least, a mutual influence at the level of energy, power, and presence.

Such an impression is not diminished when we turn to the functions that Paul ascribes to the Spirit. Thus, in 1 Cor 1:5–6 he thanks God for the enrichment of the Corinthians in speech and knowledge, "just as the witness of Christ was confirmed among you." But in 2:4 he speaks of his kerygma as accompanied not by convincing words of wisdom but "by the demonstration of the Spirit and of power," so that their faith might be based "not in the wisdom of humans but in the power that comes from God" (2:5). The powerful demonstration of the Spirit is precisely the way the witness of Christ "was confirmed/established" among them.

Similarly, in 2:10 Paul speaks of the Spirit as the one who has revealed the mysteries otherwise unknowable to humans. Paul and his associates speak with words taught by the Spirit rather than in words taught by human wisdom (1 Cor 2:13). The contrast here is between mere human capacity and the empowerment given by the Spirit. Paul is taught the words to say by the Spirit; the Spirit's power confirms his proclamation. He works in an energy field that comes from the risen Lord in whose name he speaks (see 1:2, 10; 5:4; 6:11), and the energy field is the Spirit.

Not only does the Holy Spirit empower the words of the apostle, so that he can declare, "I think that I too have the Spirit of God" (1 Cor 7:40 NABRE), but the Spirit also lifts and transforms the words of the community as it engages in worship. The Spirit bestows and energizes all the gifts within the community. Paul's explicit elaboration of this truth in 1 Cor 12:4–11 falls between two statements concerning the spirit described above. The first, in 12:3, declares that only in the Holy Spirit is it possible to declare that Jesus is Lord. The second, in 12:13, states that Paul and his readers have all drunk the one spirit and have all been baptized in one spirit into one body. Between these statements, which intimately link the power of the spirit both to Jesus and to the community, falls Paul's declarations concerning the spiritual gifts (*ta charismata* / *ta pneumatika*) given to the community.

This well-known passage offers three points that are particularly pertinent. First, and most obvious, all the "manifestations of the Spirit" (*phanerōsis tou pneumatos*, 1 Cor 12:7) and "gifts" (*charismata*, 12:4) of which Paul speaks serve to elevate human existence through the exercise of powers not ordinarily available to them. Some are notably exceptional to normal human experience, such as the gifts of healing and the performance of wonders, prophecy, tongues, the discernment of spirits, and the interpretation of tongues (12:9–10). Others appear as a heightened expression of more ordinary human capacities: words of wisdom, words of knowledge, even faith (12:8–9). But all are elevations of human ability through the Spirit's power.

Second, Paul here speaks of the Spirit in distinctly personal terms. In 12:11 he declares that the Spirit gifts each one "as he wills." The Spirit is not simply an impersonal energy but freely chooses in the manner of God (1 Cor 1:28). The rhythmic assertions of 12:4–6 also affirm the personal character of the Spirit: "There are a variety of gifts, but the same Spirit; and there are a variety of ministries, but the same Lord; and there are a variety of activities, but it is the same God who activates them all in every way [*ta panta en pasin*]."[33] Scattered references are concentrated in a single affirmation: God, the Lord Jesus, and the Spirit join in providing the elevation of human capacities.

Third, Paul insists in 12:7 that the manifestation of the Spirit to each individual is *pros to sympheron* ("for the common good"), a theme that

---

33. The use of the same phrase for the distribution of gifts in the community and for the final eschatological victory of God in 1 Cor 15:28 cannot be accidental.

he will develop explicitly in his discussion of tongues and prophecy in chapter 14 and that is stated as a fundamental principle in 1 Cor 6:12, 7:35, and 10:23, 33.

Conclusion

Observations concerning Paul's discussion of the resurrection in 1 Cor 15, and his use of spirit language throughout that composition, lead to five conclusions and two questions.

- The resurrection is for Paul (and those who preach as he did) more than a historical event of the past concerning Jesus. It is an eschatological reality that affects believers in the present and anticipates the character of their future existence in which God will be "all things in all things."
- The exalted Lord Jesus is life-giving Spirit and the source of the power that touches and transforms the Corinthians. The confession of Jesus as Lord and the possession of the Holy Spirit are correlative and mutually defining realities.
- The Holy Spirit that examines the deep things of God and is the medium of the risen Lord's presence to the Corinthians is also the medium of an intense and mutual indwelling among God and humans: the Corinthians have drunk the one Spirit, and the Spirit dwells in them—they are in the Spirit, and in Christ and in the Lord. The consistent use of such locative prepositions connotes a deep and intersubjective relationship.
- The presence of the Holy Spirit among and within the Corinthians is the basis for the process of their personal and social transformation. Once sinners, they are now made clean, made holy, made righteous (1 Cor 6:11); the "Spirit from the Lord" has empowered them to know, speak, and perform in ways not available to, and not grasped by, the "merely natural man."
- The resurrection, therefore, initiates what Paul elsewhere calls a "new creation" (2 Cor 5:17; Gal 6:15), and indeed a "new humanity" (Col 3:9–10; Eph 4:24), based on the "last Adam" who became "life-giving spirit." Not a forgiveness of sins from the outside is here meant, but an ontological change in the structures of human existence.

Such conclusions, in turn, raise important questions, two of which form a transition to a study of the next chapter:

- If the end point (*telos*) of the new creation is a "spiritual body" (*sōma pneumatikon*), what are the implications here and now, in the perdurance of the empirical body, for the understanding and use of the body? How does the ontology of resurrection require a reconsideration of body? How seriously should we take Paul's calling the Corinthian assembly "Christ's body" (*sōma Christou*)?
- If, as Paul states, "we must all be changed," how does the process of moral growth work for the transformation of the individual and social self? Or, to put it another way, how can living according to the "mind of Christ" (1 Cor 2:16) direct Christ's body to its proper goal (*telos*)?

Chapter 5

The Body in Question

The Social Complexities of Resurrection in 1 Corinthians

In the previous essay, I argued on the basis of a close examination of
1 Cor 15, as well as of Paul's language about *pneuma* throughout the
composition, that Paul sees the resurrection as more than an event of the
past that involved Jesus alone. Instead, he understands resurrection as a
reality of the present that involves, indeed defines, the present existence
of believers. The crucified messiah Jesus has been exalted. As Lord he
shares God's rule over all things. He has become not simply a living being (through resuscitation) but life-giving spirit—that is, a source of the
spirit who gives life (1 Cor 15:45). An analysis of Paul's language about
the Holy Spirit, in turn, shows that it is precisely the presence of that
Holy Spirit among and in believers that enables them to confess Jesus as
Lord, that gifts them with extraordinary capacities, and that makes them
holy. Paul's language about the Holy Spirit is a way of speaking about the
resurrection/exaltation of Jesus as a new creation that fundamentally
affects human existence. I suggested, further, that this state of affairs
demands of us, in turn, a mode of thinking and speaking that engages
the conditions of human existence (i.e., ontology) and not merely the
actions of human agents (i.e., history).

Paul's way of thinking and speaking about spirit (*pneuma*), in turn,
demands as well a fresh consideration of body (*sōma*).[1] Three statements
in 1 Corinthians impel such reconsideration. First, when Paul responds

---

1. My claim to "freshness" here is relative rather than absolute. Certainly, Paul's
language about *sōma* has received massive attention, especially by scholars interested
in Paul's theological anthropology; see, e.g., Robinson, *The Body*; Bultmann, *Theology
of the New Testament*, 1:190–210; Gundry, *Sōma in Biblical Theology*; Jewett, *Paul's
Anthropological Terms*; Dunn, *Theology of Paul the Apostle*, 55–78. Such analyses, however, have tended to be both synthetic (drawing from all the "great letters") and lexi-
cal (focusing, for example, on the semantic nuances of *pneuma*, *sōma*, and *sarx*). My

to the question of an imagined interlocutor concerning the future resurrection, "With what sort of body do they come?" (15:35), he ultimately
replies that the body "is raised a spiritual body" (*sōma pneumatikon*,
15:44). Second, in his discussion of sexual immorality, Paul rebukes the
Corinthians for forgetting that "your bodies are members of Christ"
(6:15). Third, he states flatly in 12:27, "You [plural, *hymeis*] are the body of
Christ." The three statements point to three aspects of Paul's perception
of the body among those who have been baptized in the Holy Spirit and
profess Jesus as exalted Lord: (a) the future condition of body as totally
suffused with Spirit; (b) the persistence of the empirical body (*sōma
psychikon*) that remains at the disposal of the individual as the medium
of worldly (and spiritual) expression; (c) the communal or collective
sōma of the community, which is at once the sanctuary of the Holy Spirit
(3:16–17) and the *sōma* of the Messiah. Given these three aspects, the
meaning of *sōma* in any specific instance will not necessarily be perfectly
clear. The presence of the resurrection *pneuma* complicates the language
of the body.

Thinking Body

A good preparation for examining Paul's language about *pneuma* and
sōma is to recollect how our default mode of thinking about the body—
inherited from Descartes and extended by science and technology—
prevents us from truly engaging what Paul is saying.[2] Our tendency is to
think in terms first of the individual human body. Pervasive individualism—evident above all in contemporary American culture—makes talk
about a "social body" seem secondary and derivative, at best a metaphor.[3]
The individual body, moreover, tends to be considered in isolation from
the world and from other bodies. The sense of separate somatic existence
is expressed and reinforced by the development of distinctive posture,
clothing, housing, and variable zones of personal safety.[4] In pathological

---

essay more modestly seeks only to examine the complexities of *sōma* in view of the
resurrection *pneuma*, and stays almost completely within the frame of 1 Corinthians.

2. Placher, *Domestication of Transcendence*.

3. The premise of the American experiment—derived from John Locke (*Second
Treatise on Government*, 1690) and other Enlightenment thinkers—is that society is
formed by contract among independent individuals, who must "consent" to being
governed by common rules or authority; more recently, see Rawls, *Theory of Justice*.

4. A direct symbolic line runs from the "body language" of individualism to the

cases, the bodies of others—whether the "others" are animals, people, microbes, or even food—are viewed essentially in terms of threat to the integrity of the individual organism, which must maintain itself against dangerous entanglement.[5]

The individual body, furthermore, is considered in purely physical terms. Indeed, the progression in contemporary thought has been from the ghost in the machine to simply the machine or, perhaps better, the workings of brain chemistry within the machine.[6] Finally, the body is thought of in terms of problem-solving: the dramatic exchanges of blood and vital organs in medical technology is matched by the routines of exercise and diet and, more drastically, in the kind of body engineering expressed by fetal harvesting, gender changing, plastic surgery, and cloning.[7] In this construal, the body is considered a form of property. It is something I have. I own it and can dispose of it as I choose. I can sell my body for profit. I have rights over my body just as I have rights over my other property.[8]

The development of cultural criticism has slightly modified such a mechanistic view of the body by alerting us to the ideological interests that can be at work in the social construction of the body in diverse cultures.[9] Such analysis reminds us that different cultures have different notions of what is beautiful or admirable in human bodies—bald is not always bad and bowed legs can suggest qualities of leadership[10]—and that body-typing can and has played a role in a variety of racist and sexist political programs.[11] But the modification offered is slight, for the body

---

acquisitive use of possessions: corresponding to the *noli me tangere* of political individualism is the keep-off-the-grass of gated "communities." For a brilliant fictional rendering, see Boyle, *Tortilla Curtain*.

5. See, e.g., Baker, *The Body Toxic*.

6. For accessible discussions of the complex issues in the philosophy of mind, see Heil, *Philosophy of Mind*, and Jaworski, *Philosophy of Mind*.

7. One must wonder whether any sense of irony went into the efforts of James Villepigue and Hugo Rivera as they wrote *The Body Sculpting Bible for Women* and the companion volume for men.

8. The premise is foundational especially for early feminist discourse; see, for example, the Boston Women's Health Course Collective, *Our Bodies, Our Selves*.

9. The work of Michel Foucault in this regard is of fundamental importance; see, e.g., *Discipline and Punish*.

10. See the instructive essay on ancient body assumptions in Malherbe, "Physical Description of Paul."

11. Obvious examples are the propaganda posters produced in Nazi Germany depicting Jews with subhuman features, and the stereotypical representations of African

is still regarded as a problem to be solved, or as an object to be manipulated, or as a property to be negotiated. And it is still the individual rather than the social body that is of primary interest.

A more fruitful way of thinking of body is through reflection on our own bodily experience. When I reflect bodily—that is, tap my foot, wrinkle my brow, sigh deeply, ponder the itch in my left ankle, and, above all, perform the amazing mental trick of remembering the former me—I realize that every sense of my self is of my bodily self. As long as I remember me, I remember my body. I cannot conceive of me absent from my body. Although my cells have sloughed off and been replaced endlessly, somehow what I call me has been borne through the years—and through entropy to ever greater corpulence—by the body. I realize, then, that whereas there is some truth to the claim that I "have" my body—I can indeed dispose of it in a variety of ways—there is an equal truth to the claim that I "am" my body. I cannot dispose of body completely without also disposing of me. In the strict empirical sense, when my body disappears, so do I. Likewise, when I commit my body, I commit me. This is the basis of all covenant and all witness.[12]

If this is so, and all our experience confirms that it is, then the body does not lie outside myself as a problem to be solved, as a sculpture to be carved, as a project to be engineered. If I so objectify my body, I alienate myself from my true somatic condition. As the philosopher Gabriel Marcel has instructed us, the body-self does not lie in the realm of the problematic but properly in the realm of the mysterious.[13] I cannot detach myself from my body as though it were not me. That way lies the most profound alienation. The mysterious, Marcel tells us, is that in which we are inescapably involved as persons.[14] A budget is a problem, but marriage is a mystery. A broken timepiece is a problem, but a dying friend is a mystery. Making budget decisions mysterious is simply silly, but treating a marriage like a problem is tragic. Weeping over a stolen automobile shows confusion; failure to weep for a dying friend reveals alienation.

My body, furthermore, is not isolated from its physical environment.[15]

Americans in the USA during the era of segregation; similar are the pictorial representations of "the Hun" and the "Yellow Peril" by World War II Allied propaganda.

12. For the connection between body and possessions, see Johnson, *Sharing Possessions*, 1–10, 29–34; for the body as the basis of witness and covenant, see Johnson, "Revelatory Body."

13. See esp. Marcel, "Outline of a Phenomenology of Having."

14. See Marcel, *Mystery of Being*, 1:242–70.

15. The intersection of theology and ecology is currently a busy one; see, among

The world is as much within me as outside me. The microbes, thank goodness, are not simply out there; they are in here, doing their quiet good work. I suck in and expel the world's atmosphere, in the process feeding the green things around me that in turn feed me. I have, in fact, eaten quite a considerable part of my environment over the past sixty-five years and, while retaining some of it in storage, have also returned an astounding mountain of body-stuff for the world's cycle of regeneration. As I take, so do I gift; as I eat, so am I eaten, while alive and assuredly when I die.[16] My body is not the exception to the world, it is the rule; it is not separate from the world, it is the world in concentrated form.

Finally, my reflection on my own experience of being and having a body suggests to me that thinking first if not always in terms of my individual body rather than in terms of the social body is also, in its way, a form of alienation. It is obvious that we are born out of the bodies of others, and in fact bear their bodies within us, just as when we give birth, our bodies are carried forth by our children and their children. Just as we derive from the bodies of others, so also are we dependent on other bodies. Not only at birth but also at burial, not only in first but also in second infancy, we are utterly dependent on other bodies, other selves, in all essentials.[17] These moments of entry and departure, however, only accentuate the fundamental dependence of any individual body on the bodies of others throughout human life; indeed, a life cut off from other bodies becomes less and less human. When John Donne declared that "no man is an island, entire of itself," he spoke the soberest truth.[18]

Such reflection on the lived experience of somatic existence does not bring us all the way to Paul's perceptions, but it serves to call into question the default sense of the body peddled by radical individualism and late capitalist commodification. When we recognize how, even when thinking of the empirical body, we can speak of being as well as having body, and can perceive that the membrane distinguishing the human body from the world is permeable with traffic moving both ways, and can acknowledge the ways in which the body of every individual person is willy-nilly implicated in the bodies of others, we are better able to consider the statements that Paul makes as he seeks to sort out the

many offerings, Van Houtan and Northcott, *Diversity and Dominion*; Oord, *Divine Grace and Emerging Creation*; and my own small contribution, Johnson, "Caring for the Earth."

16. A point made brilliantly by Crace, *Being Dead*.
17. See esp. Jackson, "House Divided Again."
18. Donne, "Meditation 17."

complexities of somatic existence in light of the resurrection and the empowerment of the Corinthian community through the Holy Spirit.

It is precisely in the turn to language about *pneuma* and *sōma* that we encounter the greatest difference between Paul's assumptions and our own. Whereas the two terms seldom touch for us,[19] for Paul they are always mutually implicated. Paul would have agreed with his contemporary James that "the body without a spirit is dead" (Jas 2:26), but he also shared the conviction of the entire prophetic tradition that spirit without a body is powerless and inarticulate. Spirit, even God's Holy Spirit, requires a body for its self-expression. We do not find in 1 Corinthians any trace of a dualism that privileges the spirit and seeks its release from the body; instead, we find spirit and body in mutual dependence. What makes the language in 1 Corinthians so complex, however, is that Paul does not have in mind only the animate (natural) body that he calls *psychikos* but the consequences for human bodies of being animated by God's *pneuma*. Thus, Paul refers to God's breathing into the clay so that the first Adam became a living being, *psychēn zōsan*, but his concern throughout the letter is the social implications of Christ becoming "life-giving spirit" (*pneuma zōopoioun*, 15:45).

The Assembly as the *Sōma Christou*

Unlike our contemporary focus, Paul's attention is given primarily to the social rather than the individual body. As with his language of the *pneuma*, he can speak of the individual's *sōma* in terms of self-disposition. Thus, husband and wife each have *exousia* over the body of the other in their sexual relationship (1 Cor 7:4), and the unmarried woman whose concern is for the things of the Lord is holy in "body and spirit" (7:34). Paul pummels and enslaves his own body to keep himself worthy of proclaiming to others (9:27). He proposes the possibility of "handing over" his own body (13:3). But in the majority of instances, *sōma* has a collective sense.

The body is one of three metaphors that Paul uses for the Corinthian assembly as such: in 3:6–9 he tells them that they are God's field (*geōrgion*), which Paul has planted and which Apollos has watered, but to which God gives growth. They are also God's building (*oikodomē*),

---

19. Our usage retains a vestigial element of the ancient strong conviction when we refer only to a living ("animate") human's "body" and to a dead human's "corpse."

whose foundation of Jesus Christ Paul, as a wise builder, has established, and on that foundation others can build (3:9–15). And because the Holy Spirit dwells in/among them (*to pneuma tou theou oikei en hymin*), they are in fact God's temple (*naos*, 3:16–17). Paul's favorite metaphor for the assembly, however, is that it is the Messiah's body, which he develops fully in chapter 12 and exploits also in chapters 6 and 10. That this is Paul's favorite community metaphor is indicated by his use of it throughout 1 Corinthians, and with some frequency elsewhere in his letters (see Rom 12:4–5; Eph 4:4–16; 5:30; Col 1:18, 24; 3:15). The metaphor is not a passing figure that Paul seizes on to make a single point but rather represents a fixed conviction concerning the character of the assembly. The fact that Paul uses it so widely and in such differing contexts, plus the fact that he develops it so extensively in 1 Corinthians, raises the question of whether *sōma Christou* is only a metaphor, or is it, for Paul, perhaps something more?

We are able to ask this question more responsibly in 1 Cor 12 because, as most commentators observe, the use of "body" as a metaphor for the city-state was common among ancient rhetoricians.[20] Especially when the topic was one of political harmony addressed to city-states in conditions of discord and strife, the metaphor was frequently and usefully deployed. Members of a society should think of themselves as analogous to a human body, all of whose parts work together peacefully for the common good. It would be foolish to deny that Paul's language about the body in 1 Cor 12 bears precisely the same sort of force and points in the same direction. This is a community, after all, whose fleshly, all-too-human condition is described in terms of rivalry and competition and strife and schism (3:1–4), and it is incontestable that Paul seeks among them harmony and cooperation rather than division (1:10). Paul's emphasis in 12:14–26 on unity within diversity, and on the mutually useful functions of the parts of the body, makes the political point in a fairly conventional fashion.

Several aspects of Paul's discussion, however, suggest that something more than a political metaphor is at work.[21] We note at once that as he discusses the mutual functions of the members, he twice states that it is

20. See M. Mitchell, *Paul and the Rhetoric of Reconciliation*, 157–64; Martin, *Corinthian Body*, 38–46.

21. While impressed by the wealth of comparative material and etic analysis brought to bear on the question of the body in 1 Corinthians by, respectively, Martin, *Corinthian Body*, 87–103, and Neyrey, *Paul, in Other Words*, 102–46, I find their approach less satisfactory than a more traditional emic appreciation. It is noteworthy

God who has placed the members as they are and has arranged the social body the way it is (1 Cor 12:18, 24). While an appeal to divine order would not in the least be out of place in a Greco-Roman discourse on harmony,[22] there is a directness and concreteness to Paul's statements that is exceptional. When we look at how Paul sets up this discussion, moreover, we see that he has prepared his hearers for God's direct involvement in the social body.

Paul says in 12:3 that no one can declare "Jesus is Lord, except in the Holy Spirit." This statement is followed by a series of affirmations concerning the Spirit. In 12:4–7 Paul attributes the diversity of gifts, the diversity of ministries, and the diversity of powerful deeds, respectively, to the same Spirit, the same Lord, the same God, concluding that "it is the same God who works *ta panta en pasin*" ("all things in every one," 12:6), a phrase that provocatively anticipates Paul's later description of the eschatological *telos* as *ho theos (ta) panta en pasin* ("God will be all things in all things," 15:28). The specific presence of the Spirit within all the community's activities is repeated several times in the verses that follow: gifts are given "through the Spirit" and "according to the Spirit" (12:8), "in the same Spirit," and "in the one Spirit" (12:9). Paul concludes, "All these the same Spirit energizes, distributing specific [gifts] as it chooses" (12:10). To summarize: the Holy Spirit not only enables the confession of Jesus as Lord, but the Spirit is the power (*energeia*) at work in every activity of the assembly.

When Paul subsequently states in 12:12 that just as bodies have many members but are nevertheless one body, "so also [is] the Christ," he requires us to think in terms other than of simple comparison. The "Christ" in this context cannot be the empirical Jesus who ministered in Palestine some twenty years earlier and then was crucified. It can refer only to the present social body that is the assembly, which Paul daringly terms "the Christ." Paul means, I think, that the Corinthian assembly *is*, in a very real—that is, in an ontological and not merely moral—sense, a bodily expression of the risen Jesus who has become life-giving spirit (1 Cor 15:45). Certainly, it is not yet the *sōma pneumatikon* of the eschatological resurrection. But it is definitely an anticipation of that spiritual body. If Paul were asked, "Where is the body of the resurrected Jesus now?" he has given his response in 1 Cor 12: "the body of the resurrected Christ"

---

that neither study pays sufficient attention to the ways in which *pneuma* and *sōma* interpenetrate in 1 Corinthians.

22. See, e.g., Dio Chrysostom, *Orations* 38.9, 11, 18, 20, 51; 39.8; 40.5, 15, 35; 41.10.

is this assembly—"together with all those who call on the name of the Lord in every place, theirs and ours" (1:2).

Such, I think, is the conclusion to be drawn from Paul's statement in 12:13, "For in one Spirit we have all been baptized [*ebaptisthēmen*] into one body—whether Jew or Hellene, whether slave or free—and we have all been given to drink [*epotisthēmen*] one Spirit."[23] The Spirit stands instrumentally at the beginning and end of this statement. The ritual of baptism into the community is also, by means of the Spirit, a baptism "into the body" that is Christ; such baptism is, says Paul, also a matter of this body "drinking the one Spirit." In light of Paul's later declaration in 15:45 that the eschatological Adam became "life-giving spirit," as well as Paul's alignment of Spirit-Lord-God in 12:4–7, there cannot be any doubt, I think, that Paul regards the Corinthian community as the bodily expression of the resurrected one, living through the Spirit that comes from him. Thus, he concludes in 12:27, "You [plural] are Christ's body, and individually members [of it]." This is more than metaphor for Paul. Perhaps a better term would be *symbol*, in the strong sense of a sign that participates in that which it signifies.[24]

Taking Paul's language so seriously makes more intelligible two further features of his language concerning the community. In his discussion of eating foods offered to idols in 1 Cor 8:1–13, Paul makes a distinction between a knowledge that puffs up the individual and a love that builds up the other (8:1). When Corinthians convinced of the rightness of their position concerning idols act without consideration for the effect their actions might have on others, they are puffed up but do not build up: "the weak person is destroyed by your knowledge, the brother for whom Christ died" (8:11). Paul here uses a fragment of the Jesus story to provide a norm for behavior that "builds up"—namely, living (and dying) for the sake of others as Christ did for them.[25] In contrast, the one acting obliviously of the effect on others does not build up but tears down. But this is not a mere matter of imitation (acting toward others as Christ

---

23. The balanced passive verbs perhaps suggest the ritual actions of initiation into the community: being plunged into water (by others) and being given to drink (by others). Compare the similar constructions in Gal 3:27, "you were baptized into Christ, you were clothed [*enedysasthe*] with Christ."

24. See J. Splett, "Symbol," in K. Rahner, *Encyclopedia of Theology*, 1654–57.

25. Here, the reference to the Jesus story is an allusion; in 11:24 ("this is my body for you") it takes the form of a direct citation of the words of Jesus. The implication in both instances is the same: the pattern of Jesus's self-donation is to be the pattern of their own. For Paul's subtle use of the Jesus story, see esp. Hays, *Faith of Jesus Christ*.

acted for them); it is more a matter of identification. Paul adds, "Thus, by sinning against the brothers and by pummeling their conscience while it is weak,[26] you are sinning against Christ (*eis Christon hamartanete,* 8:12). The phrase "sinning against Christ" assumes the strongest sort of connection between each member of the community (or the community as a whole) and the resurrected Lord.[27]

The second aspect of Paul's language that gains greater intelligibility in light of his understanding of the church as the body of Christ is his striking use of the phrase "mind of Christ" (*nous Christou*) in 1 Cor 2:16. The phrase occurs at the conclusion of Paul's discussion of the wisdom that has been given to the Corinthians through the Holy Spirit. They have received, he says, not the Spirit from the world but the Spirit that is from God, so that "we might know the gifts that have been given to us by God" (2:12). Rather than the Spirit as the power of extraordinary performance (as in tongues, healing, and prophecy), Paul here stresses the Spirit as means of elevating and shaping human thinking. The context of this passage makes it clear that the most important spirit-guided perception is the recognition that the crucifixion of Jesus has reversed ordinary human status markers. The cross that appears to the world as weak and foolish is God's strength and God's wisdom (1:18–31). Paul wants them to measure themselves by this paradoxical, cruciform, norm. Thus, they also were among the weak and foolish, among the things that are not, which God has brought into being (1:26–29).

But having "the mind of Christ" pushes the perception given by the Spirit even more. As Paul's use of the Jesus story in 8:11 ("the brother for whom Christ died") makes clear, the Spirit is to lead the community to perceive and act in imitation of Jesus. Having "the mind of Christ" enables the members of the body to act in harmony, to seek the good of the whole rather than the good of the individual alone, to build up the body of Christ through love. If the Corinthian community is for Paul the body of Christ, then the mind that guides this body's behavior should be Christ's own mind.[28] Growing progressively into such maturity through

26. For the translation of *typontes*, see Thiselton, *First Epistle to the Corinthians*, 654–55.

27. It is clearly impossible for a member of the Corinthian assembly to "sin against" the human Jesus; commentators are correct to see in this passage an assumption concerning the identification of Christ and the church implied by Acts 9:5, "I am Jesus, whom you are persecuting." Something more than a moral "identifying with the weak" is meant here. See Wikenhauser, *Pauline Mysticism*.

28. On this, see chap. 3 in this volume.

mutual love and service is the sort of moral activity that transforms Christians according to the image of Christ in anticipation of full participation in God's life that is future resurrection.

Sexual Involvement

The two behavioral issues most preoccupying Paul's readers in Corinth involve sex and food. Paul's perception of the community as the body of the Messiah, enlivened and empowered by the Holy Spirit, profoundly affects his treatment of each subject. Almost all of 1 Corinthians 5–7 deals in one way or another with sexuality.[29] I will comment briefly on Paul's discussion of marriage in 7:1–40 and on his instruction for excommunication in 5:1–12, before concentrating on his puzzling statements in 6:12–20.

Readers familiar only with the stereotype of Paul as misogynistic and against sex are surprised to discover not only the most liberated ancient discussion of sexuality (Paul addresses both genders equally in terms of power and refuses to define females in terms of marriage and progeny)[30] but also one of the most robust and positive treatments of sexual activity anywhere.[31] Let us grant that Paul prefers celibacy in the present circumstances as a way of dedicating oneself to the Lord without anxiety (1 Cor 7:1, 7, 32–34); let us grant as well that Paul regards marriage as a means of avoiding sexual immorality (*porneia*) and disordered passion (7:2, 9). But when Paul speaks of sexual activity within the covenant relationship of marriage, he is entirely positive, and his discussion reveals, indirectly, some of his basic assumptions about spirit and body.

29. Helpful guidance is found in Deming, *Paul on Marriage and Celibacy*; Yarbrough, *Not Like the Gentiles*; and, most recently, Thaden, "Wisdom of Fleeing Porneia."

30. In sharp contrast to a standard treatment of *oikonomia* (such as Xenophon's), Paul does not address men as householders with young wives whom they must instruct but begins his discussion in 7:2–3 by addressing both female (*gynē*) and male (*anēr*) with regard to their reciprocal sexual rights and responsibilities, and continues with the same reciprocity through 7:10–16. Similarly, Paul's discussion of the unmarried in 7:32–40 makes it clear that the value of women is not totally defined by their role in the household. In this respect, Paul is more "liberated" than the closest parallel in Greco-Roman philosophy; see Ward, "Musonius and Paul."

31. A failure to seriously engage Paul is a notable deficiency in Foucault's *History of Sexuality*; for a creative effort at engaging Paul and Foucault, see Nicolet-Anderson, *Constructing the Self*.

Husbands and wives have authority (*exousia*) over each other's bodies—that is, each can expect the other to engage sexually. They are to "give what is owed" (*tēn opheilēn apodidotō*, 1 Cor 7:3) to each other. Indeed, so seriously does Paul take this that he forbids withdrawing from sexual activity except by mutual consent, and then only for a time, and then only in order to pray. After a short time, they are to "come together again" (*palin epi to auto*, 7:5). More prolonged sexual abstinence in marriage allows Satan to test the couple through their lack of self-control (*akrasia*, 7:5). Even more striking is Paul's statement concerning the spiritual effect of married sex. He considers that, although such is not always the case (7:16), it is possible that an unbelieving man in a mixed marriage is "made holy" (*hēgiastai*) through the (believing) woman and the unbelieving woman is "made holy" through the (believing) man. He is convinced of this, it seems, from the conviction that the children of such a relationship are also made holy (*hagia*, 7:14). His language almost suggests that holiness is a kind of infection that can be sexually transmitted.[32] I pause over this point because it shows us how Paul thinks of body not in mechanical but in relational terms, so that the body sexually engaged with another has spiritual implications.[33]

This same potentially "infecting" power of sexual activity—now opposite the "holiness" that is communicated through sex within marriage—lies behind Paul's command to the Corinthians in 5:1–12 that they excommunicate a member whose *porneia* (sexual immorality) is grotesquely incompatible with a holy community. Paul shows himself concerned more with the integrity of the body of the church than the body of the man living in (at least legal) incest (1 Cor 5:1).[34] He draws the comparison to yeast that infects a whole lump of dough—so can such immoral sexual activity infect the common body of the church (5:6). Paul expects the members to gather together and "expel from your midst the one who has acted this way" (5:2). They are not to "mingle" (*synanamignysthai*) or to "eat with" (*synesthiein*) such a one (5:11).[35]

32. Both Neyrey, *Paul, in Other Words*, and Martin, *Corinthian Body*, are helpful in providing anthropological perspectives on such language.

33. Note in 7:34 that Paul states "being holy both in body and spirit" (*kai tō sōmati kai tō pneumati*) as the goal.

34. See the discussion with ancient references in Thistleton, *First Epistle to the Corinthians*, 382–88; also Fee, *First Epistle to the Corinthians*, 194–228.

35. The command here is directly contrary to the advice in 7:5, where temporary separation is to be followed by being *epi to auto*; in both cases, however, the premise is the same: somatic contact bears pneumatic implications.

Two aspects of this intriguing passage are of special interest to our topic. The first is the way Paul speaks of the man being handed over to Satan "for the destruction of the flesh, so that the spirit might be saved in the day of the lord" (1 Cor 5:5). The image of Satan as an inimical power on the fringes of the community is found elsewhere in Paul (see 2 Cor 2:11; 11:14; 12:7; 1 Thess 2:18; 2 Thess 2:9; 1 Tim 1:20; 5:15) and anticipates the statement we have just seen in Paul's discussion of marriage (1 Cor 7:5). That the individual man's fleshly (i.e., merely human) body is affected by such excommunication is clear.[36] But whose *pneuma* is being saved? Is it his, or is it the Holy Spirit of the community? If we avoid harmonizing this passage with the more clearly pedagogical intention expressed by the parallel in 1 Tim 1:20, excommunication in the 1 Corinthians passage seems entirely for the purpose of protecting the holiness of the corporate body of the church.[37]

The second aspect is the way Paul describes the communal act of expulsion. Paul is absent in body, he says, but is present in spirit and has already made his judgment on the case (1 Cor 5:3). Now, the entire assembly is to come together in the name of the Lord (*en tō onomati tou kyriou hēmōn Iēsou*), with Paul's and their spirit gathered together (*synachthentōn hymōn kai tou emou pneumatos*) with the power of the Lord Jesus (*syn tē dynamei tou kyriou hēmōn Iēsou*, 5:4). The assembly is not merely a gathering of individuals that vote on membership. It is the body of Christ that acts in the power of the Holy Spirit. In the way Paul expresses the corporate action of the community in the act of excommunication, we detect the premises for his later explicit designation of the church as the *sōma Christou*.

The final passage concerning sexual activity is both the most important for appreciating Paul's extraordinarily strong view of the body as redefined by the resurrection of Christ and, alas, also the most difficult. It is difficult above all because Paul's language about the body shifts between the singular and the plural. In 6:12–14 he speaks of the individual bodies of the Corinthians. He begins by citing (or crafting) the slogan "food for the belly, the belly for food," whose implication is that sex is a closed

---

36. But not without ambiguity: the noun *olethros* ("destruction") is clear enough (see 1 Thess 5:3; 2 Thess 1:9; 1 Tim 6:9), but given the semantic range of *sarx* in Paul's correspondence, the destruction could be to the "fleshly body" itself or to the "fleshly dispositions" leading to immorality (cf. Gal 5:13, 16–17, 19); see Thiselton, "Meaning of *ΣΑΡΧ*."

37. On this, see now M. K. W. Suh, *Power and Peril: Paul's Use of Temple Discourse in 1 Corinthians*, BZNW 239 (Berlin: De Gruyter, 2020).

physical transaction with no further meaning.[38] Paul clearly rejects this position not only for sex but, as we shall see in a moment, for food as well. He redirects the Corinthian's perception by insisting that the *sōma* is not for sexual immorality but "for the Lord," and, reciprocally, "the Lord is for the body" (6:13). The singular term "body" (*sōma*) here still seems to mean the individual; but stated without qualification, it points the way toward the collective meaning.

What does Paul mean by stating that the body is for the Lord and the Lord is for the body? He asserts the impact of the resurrection on the understanding of the human body: "God both raised the Lord and will raise us by his power" (1 Cor 6:14). At the very least, Paul here establishes the connection between the (past) raising of Jesus and the (future) resurrection of believers. The implications Paul draws from his statement, however, indicate that for him the reality of the resurrection is not merely either past or future; it is above all a present reality. The power of the Lord is already present and active in the somatic existence of the all-too-empirical Corinthians to whom Paul writes. Paul therefore reminds them of this reality of which they should have been aware: "Do you not know that your bodies [both terms plural, *ta sōmata hymōn*] are members (*melē*) of Christ?" (6:15).[39] The moral inconsistency of having sex with a prostitute—Paul uses the expression *mē genoito*[40]—derives from the fact that believers' individual bodies also form the body of the resurrected one: "Shall I take the members of Christ and make them members of a prostitute?" (6:15).[41]

As in chapter 7, Paul's understanding of sexual intimacy bears ontological implications; Paul implicitly rebukes the Corinthians (*ouk oidate*, "do you not know") for their failure to recognize the meaning of Gen

38. It is difficult to determine whether Paul is citing slogans of the Corinthian assembly (perhaps deriving ultimately from his own preaching) or is setting up straw-positions of fictive interlocutors. Among responsible discussions, see Hurd, *Origin of I Corinthians*, and M. Mitchell, *Paul and the Rhetoric of Reconciliation*, 65–99.

39. Paul concentrates his use of the implied rebuke, *ouk oidate* ("do you not know"), in this discussion of sexual behavior (5:6; 6:2, 3, 9, 15, 16, 19). The statement that they are members of Christ's body clearly anticipates 12:27.

40. See Malherbe, "*Mē Genoito.*"

41. "The members" (*ta melē*) respectively "of Christ" (*tou Christou*) and "of a prostitute" (*pornēs*) might refer to the bodily parts of the individual Christian engaged in sex with a prostitute—the body parts that belong to Christ should not be made the property of a prostitute—as in Rom 6:13, 19; 7:5, 23), or might refer to the community members who are *melē tou Christou* who are entangled sexually with the body parts of prostitutes.

2:24, which he quotes, "the two shall become one flesh,"[42] when he affirms that "the one who clings to a prostitute becomes one body [with her]" (1 Cor 6:16). Using the same participle (*kollōmenos*), he adds, "but the one who clings to the Lord is one spirit [*pneuma*] with him" (6:17). Everything we have seen in the discussion of the body of Christ in 1 Cor 12 we find also in this discussion of sexuality: the individual members are, because of the resurrection of Jesus, intimately joined to his Spirit and, by that means also, become the bodily expression of the life-giving spirit in the world. Their actions involve not simply their own private bodies and spirits; they implicate the body of Christ and the Holy Spirit.

Once more in 1 Cor 6:19 Paul reminds them of what they already should know: their (plural) body (singular) is the sanctuary of the Holy Spirit, which they (plural) have from God that is "among/within them" (plural).[43] And they do not, therefore, belong to themselves. They have been bought for a price and should therefore glorify God in their (plural) body (singular) (6:20).[44] By "glorifying God" Paul means that they must recognize and live by the recognition that God is indeed present among them, both individually and corporately.[45] Only such a strong ontological sense of the unity between the spirit of the resurrected one and the community can make intelligible Paul's command and explanation in 6:18. Flee sexual immorality, he tells them. This is the straightforward moral implication of what he has been telling them. But his explanation appears extremely odd.

Paul declares that every sin a person commits is outside the body (*ektos tou sōmatos*), but the one who commits sexual immorality sins against his own body (*eis to idion sōma hamartanei*). But surely this is wrong if

---

42. "The members" (*ta melē*) respectively "of Christ" (*tou Christou*) and "of a prostitute" (*pornēs*) might refer to the bodily parts of the individual Christian engaged in sex with a prostitute (the body parts that belong to Christ should not be made the property of a prostitute, as in Rom 6:13, 19; 7:5, 23), or might refer to the community members who are *melē tou Christou* who are entangled sexually with the body parts of prostitutes.

43. In 1 Cor 15:45 Paul also cites the second chapter of Genesis when he refers to the first Adam becoming "a living being" (*eis psychēn zōsan*, Gen 2:7), in contrast to the eschatological Adam who is *sōma pneumatikon*. The use of Gen 2 in the present passage testifies to the in-between state of the Corinthian bodies: they are possessed by the Spirit but are still empirically involved and not yet at the stage of being "spiritual bodies."

44. Greek: *ēgorasthēte gar timēs· doxasate dē ton theon en tō sōmati hymōn.*

45. The meaning of *doxazein* here is that found in Rom 1:21: to "glorify God" is to recognize and respond to the claims of God; see Johnson, *Reading Romans*, 32–36.

we understand things in a common-sense fashion. Many sins are "inside the body" and affect one's "own body" with at least the same severity as does fornication. Drunkenness has obvious physical consequences; so do rage, gluttony, and sloth. If we think of body simply in terms of the individual, Paul is certainly mistaken. But perhaps by "his own body" (*to idion sōma*) Paul does not mean the individual but the corporate body, the body, that is, of Christ. We remember his statement concerning making another stumble: "by sinning against your brother for whom Christ died, you have sinned against Christ" (8:12). By implicating body and spirit sexually with the body and spirit of a prostitute, Paul thinks, harm is done to the body of Christ and the Holy Spirit in a distinctive fashion. We might still debate the proposition's truth or falsity. But it makes sense at least if Paul's intended meaning for "one's own—proper—body" is, in fact, the body of Christ.

The Implications of Meals

When we turn to the way Paul connects the Corinthian meals with the resurrection—and thereby further complicates the social meanings of body—we must acknowledge from the start that some of Paul's language is strange to us not because of his distinctive theological perspective but because he shares ancient cultural convictions concerning meals that are no longer our own. In no other context is the default Enlightenment understanding of the body—especially in First World countries—more clearly revealed than with respect to eating food. Americans mostly eat apart rather than together; food is fast and take-out and devoured in the car or, if at home, before the television.[46] We obsess about food, but mostly in terms of the technology of the body: its safety in processing, its fat and sodium content, its nutrients, how it will make us slimmer or fatter. Food is certainly not a mystery; it is a problem. As Robert Farrar Capon has astutely observed, contemporary Americans neither fast nor feast (both profoundly religious responses to reality); we diet.[47] Dieting is the supreme expression of body technology, and the triumphal expression of somatic individualism.

In contrast, ancient Greco-Roman and Jewish culture agreed with most cultures in most times and places in regarding meals as the most

46. For a snapshot, see Lambert, "The Way We Eat Now."
47. See Capon, *Supper of the Lamb.*

profound expression of human communion. Meals were magical because they both made and expressed the one social body that consisted in many individual members.[48] Meals, indeed, enabled those not joined by biological or ethnic ties to establish *koinōnia*. The ancient conviction that "friendship is fellowship" (*philia koinōnia*) meant the most profound sort of sharing at both the physical and the mental level: physical through the sharing of possessions (*tois philois panta koina*), and mental through the sharing of ideas and ideals (friends are *mia psychē*).[49] It is not an exaggeration, I think, to state that, for Paul's world, meals were a far more important means of expressing such unity and intimacy than was sexual activity. To eat together signified spiritual agreement, just as spiritual estrangement was expressed by inhospitality or, as we have seen in 1 Cor 5:1–12, excommunication.[50] Eating together was serious business, all agreed, because eating expressed and established spiritual bonds. Cultic meals both in Judaism and in Greco-Roman religion extended this understanding by regarding meals partaken in honor of the god—and in which the god partakes through sacrificial offering—as establishing and celebrating a specific unity (vertically) between the god and worshipers and (horizontally) among the worshipers of the god.[51] Our interest, then, is how Paul's convictions concerning the presence of the resurrected Christ in the church affects such shared cultural norms.

After delicately examining the issues of conscience and community concern in his discussion of food offered to idols—he agrees with the strong that idols are not real, since "for us" there is one God and one Lord, but he rebukes the strong for their willingness to exercise their freedom without concern for those less strong in their convictions (1 Cor 8:1–13)—and after presenting himself as an apostolic example of relativizing individual rights for the sake of others (9:1–27), Paul warns his readers in 10:14–22 against participation in meals at idol shrines. Idols may not be real, but idolatry is real, and the act of eating in the presence of idols, just like sexual activity with a prostitute, affects the social body that is the church. Paul considers things offered to idols as sacrifices to demons, and eating at the table of idols as a fellowship (*koinōnia*) with demons (10:20–21). He relies here on the common view of Jews, found already in the Septuagint's translation of Ps 95:5, that "all the gods of the

48. See Johnson, "Meals Are Where the Magic Is."
49. For the topos on friendship, see Gustav Staehlin, "φίλος, φίλη, φιλία," *TDNT* 9:146–57; Bohnenblust, *Beiträge zum Topos Peri Philias.*
50. Johnson, *Religious Experience*, 163–79.
51. See J. Smith, *Drudgery Divine*, 116–43.

nations are demons." Participation in a common meal signifies for Paul participation in the powers present at the meal. He reminds his readers that this is the premise of Jewish sacrifice as well: "Those who eat the sacrifices are sharers [*koinōnoi*] in the altar" (10:18).

The most powerful backing for Paul's warning, however, comes from his readers' experience of their own common meals, which include the blessing of a cup and the breaking of a loaf of bread. Paul asks them rhetorically, "The cup of blessing that we bless, is it not a *koinōnia* ["participation"] in the blood of the Messiah? The bread that we break, is it not a *koinōnia* in the body of the Messiah?" (1 Cor 10:16). He wants them to answer resoundingly, "Of course they are!" The physical sharing of the cultic meal establishes and expresses the fullest sort of fellowship between worshipers and the one worshiped, and Paul assumes that his readers understand the matter in precisely the way he does. I need not point out, I hope, that such "fellowship" supposes the presence and power of the resurrected one among them—a presupposition running all through this letter. Paul then adds a statement that fills out the ancient understanding of fellowship: those who share in the meal are also "one body"; "all those of us who partake of the same loaf are one bread, one body" (10:17). Just as Paul will speak in chapter 12 of the ritual of baptism as a drinking of the one spirit that makes them the body of the Messiah, so does he here understand the cultic meal in the same highly realistic terms, as an eating of a loaf that makes them partakers of the body of Christ and one body.

In 11:17–34 Paul returns to the common meals of the Corinthians by way of rebuke, for their "coming together" is not for the better but for the worse (11:17). There are parties formed among them when they "gather together" (11:18–19); in fact, when they "gather together" they do not really celebrate "the Lord's banquet" (*kyriakon deipnon*)—that is, a meal of fellowship with the resurrected Lord as the body of Christ (11:20). Instead, they falsify the act of gathering into a body, because their party spirit is revealed by each one eating "his own meal," with the result that some become drunken with excess, while others go hungry (11:21). They bring into the cultic meal the individualism and competition that belongs in the world, not in the body of Christ. As a result, they show contempt for God's assembly and they shame the poor (11:22). We cannot be certain precisely what the Corinthians are doing—it is reasonable to suppose, as some studies have suggested, that the practices common to patronage may be at play.[52] More important is Paul's

---

52. See Theissen, "Social Integration."

perception that the cultivation of the individual interest to the shaming of the poor and weak offends in a fundamental way the meaning of living according to the mind of Christ and building the Messiah's body. The Corinthians may gather at a meal as a body, but their behavior fragments and weakens that body.

Paul understands the effect of this weakening quite literally. Because some eat and drink "without discerning the body," they eat and drink judgment (*krima*) to themselves (1 Cor 11:29, 34),[53] and their condemnation is expressed by some of them "being weak, and without health, and not a few dying" (11:30). In the case of the excommunicated man, the immoral person was turned over to the zone of danger and destruction that Paul designates as Satan, for the destruction of the flesh and for the saving of the spirit (5:5). When the Lord's banquet is corrupted by selfishness and competition, the damage to the body of Christ is expressed internally by the mortal weakness and even death of the members of that body. Paul connects such judgment with "not discerning the body" (*mē diakrinōn to sōma*, 11:29), and with "eating the bread and drinking the cup unworthily [*anaxiōs*]" (11:27).

These statements follow immediately upon, and logically refer to, Paul's citation of the words that the Lord Jesus spoke "on the night he was handed over," words that Paul received from the Lord—we know not how—and handed on to the Corinthians as the inner meaning of the meal they called the Lord's banquet (1 Cor 11:23–25). Many things can be said about these words, which represent one of the clearest cases of Paul handing on specific Jesus traditions. Given the interest of the present essay, I focus on three. First, the "body which is for you" and the "covenant in my blood" clearly interpret the bread and wine of Jesus's final meal with his disciples in terms of Jesus's death for others. Second, this is the part of the Jesus story that is most intimately associated with their celebration of the *kyriakon deipnon*—in his remembrance (*anamnēsis*), that is, in the form of ritual memory that makes actual in the present the effect of what was done in the past.[54] The words spoken at the ritual meal communicate and remind the Corinthians *in nuce* of "the mind of Christ" (2:16) that is to guide their mutual behavior. Third, it is striking that Paul quotes Jesus as telling them not to "say this" but rather to "do this" (*touto poieite*, 11:24). The eating and drinking in the assembly in remembrance of Jesus is to enact the meaning of his death for others. The point is made

---

53. For *krima* in the sense of condemnation, see Rom 2:2–3; 3:8; 5:16; 13:2; 1 Tim 3:6; 5:12.

54. See Dahl, "Anamnesis."

clear when Paul adds that whenever they eat this bread and drink this cup, they proclaim the Lord's death until he comes (11:26).

Paul means not the fact of Jesus's death, as in a historical report, but the meaning of that death, as an expression of the mind of Christ. Thus, the "body given for you" must remind us, and it should have the Corinthians, of "the brother for whom Christ died" (1 Cor 8:11), just as their shaming the poor should have reminded them that "when you sin against your brother, you sin against Christ" (8:12). So it is that when they eat and drink unworthily—by not discerning the body of Christ that is the church—they are "liable for the body and blood of the Lord" (11:27).

Here is the perfect example of how Paul perceives the ontological transformation of the Corinthian body through the power of the Holy Spirit as demanding moral transformation as well. The mind of Christ (1 Cor 2:16) requires of them that they dispose of their individual bodies in service to each other for the common good (*pros to sympheron*, 12:7), for the building up of the common body through love (8:1; 13:1–13). Rather than threaten the health of Christ's body through a competitive eating that mirrors the "spirit of the world," the "spirit they have received from God" (2:12) should lead them, "when [they] come together to eat," to "wait upon one another" (11:33) as Christ has shown them how to do through the gift of his body for them (11:24).

Conclusion

I offer a series of short conclusions in summary of what 1 Corinthians says about *pneuma* and *sōma*.

- Paul's understanding of the human body is complex: it is both the self and what the self can dispose in relationships with others. Meals and sexual activities establish and express powerful spiritual realities.
- Paul's default understanding of the body is not the individual but the community. Specifically, because of the gift of the Holy Spirit given by the exalted Lord Jesus, he perceives the community to be the body of the resurrected Christ in the world.
- When Paul, speaking of baptism, says that believers have been given to drink of the one spirit, and when, speaking of the Lord's banquet, he declares that those who have eaten the one loaf are one body, his language pushes beyond metaphor to symbolism in the proper sense.

- Because of the resurrection of Jesus and his exaltation as Lord, the primary *pneuma* both of the individual and the community is the Lord's, and the primary loyalty must be to the Lord.
- Paul understands both sin and holiness to have an infectious character because of the psychosomatic complex that is the individual and social body. Sexual immorality threatens the holiness of the church; covenantal sexual love makes partners and children holy. Eating with demons weakens and sickens the church; eating at the table of the Lord saves and makes holy.
- In contrast to the forms of individualism and competition that characterize the spirit of the world, Paul demands that the Spirit from God find expression in Christ's body through a pattern of moral behavior that is directed by and conforms to "the mind of Christ": the Spirit works for the common good; the members serve each other and build each other up according to the pattern of the one who gave [his] body for them.

Chapter 6

Glossolalia and the Embarrassments of Experience

The Corinthians and the Hellenistic World

Even at Pentecost, speaking in tongues divided the crowd.[1] Since then, glossolalia has been singled out as either the supreme criterion for the direct action of the Holy Spirit in Christian lives[2] or the supreme example of how enthusiasm is a bad thing for Christian piety.[3] Opinions vary concerning the authenticity of tongues as a religious experience or as the expression of religious experience.[4] But no one denies that for some Christians it is the experience most highly prized, the palpable sign that their life has been taken over by the power of God.[5] What is more, such Christians claim that this experience is precisely the same as that reported in the New Testament of the first believers.[6] If present-day

1. Even those positively impressed "were astonished and confused, asking each other what this meant" (Acts 2:12). The negative reaction resembles that repeated through the ages: "But others mockingly declared that they were filled with new wine" (Acts 2:13). For translation and discussion, see Johnson, *Acts of the Apostles*, 41–47.

2. E.g., see Bruner, *Theology of the Holy Spirit*, 19–149; Lawless, *Handmaidens of the Lord*, esp. 7, 23, 59–65, 99–101; Obaje, *Miracle of Speaking in Tongues*, 26–37; Garrett, *Spirit Possession and Popular Religion*.

3. In his classic study, Ronald A. Knox shows how glossolalia figures in some but not all manifestations of that religious impulse he calls "enthusiasm"; see *Enthusiasm*, 360–66, 380, 549–59, 564. Despite his basically positive appreciation, Kelsey, *Speaking with Tongues*, begins by noting the way tongues create controversy in churches (5–8).

4. See Heyd, *"Be Sober and Reasonable,"* 31–38, 51–64, 80–98, 239, for the way in which glossolalia was reduced either to a medical cause (*melancholia*) or the influence of demons. The general idea can be gained from the title of the work by Casaubon, *A Treatise Concerning Enthusiasme as It Is an Effect of Nature*; similarly, Foster, *Natural History of Enthusiasm*.

5. See Kelsey, *Speaking with Tongues*, 17, 78; Hinson, "Significance of Glossolalia"; Laurentin, *Catholic Pentecostalism*; Jones, "Black Pentecostal."

6. See on this point W. MacDonald, "Place of Glossolalia."

Christians have exactly the same experience of God, it is patent that their Christianity above all must be regarded as authentically continuous with that of earliest Christianity.[7] The present-day prevalence of this practice and the claims that continue to be made for it make the study of glossolalia of particular pertinence for any examination of religious experience in earliest Christianity.[8]

The Nature of the Phenomenon

Determining the character of glossolalia is not easy.[9] The New Testament evidence is sparse and inconsistent.[10] In Acts, tongues are treated as real languages—Galileans speak "other tongues" (2:6-8)—and as a form of prophecy (2:16-18). In contrast, Paul emphasizes the unintelligibility of tongues (1 Cor 14:6-11) and explicitly contrasts this activity with that of prophecy (1 Cor 11:3-5).

The conflicts in our sources raise a number of questions. Should we assume that tongues takes a single consistent form? Then we might want to value one source more than another. Paul's report, for example, might be taken as that of a firsthand observer—indeed participant (see 1 Cor 14:18)—and therefore as more reliable. Acts correspondingly might be viewed as a narrative interpretation that camouflages the "real" phenomenon. Or should we begin with the assumption that even in the New Testament period glossolalia took several forms?[11] Then Paul and Acts might witness to a diversity of practice as well as of interpretation.

Another decision has to do with what evidence counts in determining the nature of glossolalia in earliest Christianity. What weight should be

7. See C. Williams, *Tongues of the Spirit*, 73.

8. The literature on glossolalia grew enormously under the impetus of the "charismatic movement" or "Pentecostal movement" within both Protestantism and Catholicism in the 1960s and 1970s. For a helpful collection of articles, see Mills, *Speaking in Tongues*, esp. his full bibliography on 493-528.

9. The term "glossolalia" derives from *glōssais lalein* (to speak in tongues) (see 1 Cor 14:6). The Greek word *glōssa*, which otherwise in the New Testament refers to the physical tongue (Luke 16:24), ordinary speech (1 John 3:18), or human language (Rev 5:9), is used in some passages for ecstatic utterance associated with possession by the Holy Spirit (see Mark 16:17; Acts 2:3, 4, 11; 10:46; 19:6; 1 Cor 12-14). See Johannes Behm, "γλῶσσα," *TDNT* 1:719-27; Harrisville, "Speaking in Tongues."

10. For surveys of the pertinent texts, see Beare, "Speaking with Tongues"; W. MacDonald, "Glossolalia in the New Testament."

11. See, e.g., D. Brown, "Acts of the Apostles."

assigned to similar phenomena in early Hebrew prophecy or Hellenistic mantic prophecy? Or how seriously should the experiences of contemporary glossolalists be taken, together with the claim that their experience represents the same "gift of the Holy Spirit" as that mentioned by Paul (1 Cor 12:10)?[12] Can the extensive studies of contemporary practice carried out by linguists, ethnographers, and psychologists validly be employed to explicate the New Testament phenomenon?

Unfortunately, research into contemporary glossolalia is divided on such critical issues as whether tongues is a uniform or pluriform phenomenon,[13] whether it is invariably accompanied by or even to be identified with states of psychological dissociation,[14] and whether such parallel speech patterns as those found in shamanism can be considered glossolalic.[15] Concerning antiquity, debate continues on the ecstatic character of the Hebrew prophets and the manifestations of mantic prophecy.[16]

Given this range of uncertainty, any definition of glossolalia in the New Testament must remain tentative, avoiding such easy characterizations as that expressed by the *Interpreter's Dictionary of the Bible* a generation ago: "The psychological aspects are patent."[17] Patience and discipline are particularly required in a phenomenological analysis of tongues. Neither a reductionistic assumption that tongues is attributable to charlatanism or self-delusion, nor an apologetic assumption that

12. Note J. Massingberd Ford's dismissal of the hypothesis that tongues is ecstatic utterance: "It must be noted that no one who has ever heard the exquisitely beautiful choral singing in tongues at a quiet prayer meeting could ever declare this to be 'bedlam.'" And later: "All these articles appear to speak from the standpoint of persons who have no empirical experience of the phenomenon which they wish to evaluate." "Toward a Theology of 'Speaking in Tongues,'" reprinted in Mills, *Speaking in Tongues*, 268, 270. Likewise Kelsey, *Speaking with Tongues*, 144, dismisses the work of a scholar on the grounds of unfamiliarity with the contemporary phenomenon. It is fascinating that some of the same writers who insist that tongues is absolutely unique to Christianity in antiquity and cannot be compared with Greco-Roman phenomena (e.g., Kelsey, *Speaking with Tongues*, 141) also assume that the contemporary phenomenon can, without more ado, be taken as equivalent to that addressed by Paul.

13. See Samarin, *Tongues of Men and Angels*, 129–49.

14. Goodman, *Speaking in Tongues*, 124; Kelsey, *Speaking with Tongues*, 142; Maloney and Lovekin, *Glossolalia*, 112. Maloney and Lovekin provide a valuable survey and include a rich bibliography (263–79); see also Kildahl, "Psychological Observations," 124–42; Hine, "Pentecostal Glossolalia."

15. See Eliade, *Le Chamanisme*, 98–102; May, "Survey of Glossolalia."

16. C. Williams, "Ecstaticism," 328–38; Aune, *Prophecy in Early Christianity*, 36–48; Bunn, "Glossolalia in Historical Perspective."

17. E. Andrews, "The Gift of Tongues," *IDB* 4:671–72.

tongues is a direct result of divine inspiration, helps us understand the experience of glossolalia. Like any religious activity, glossolalia can be either sincere or phoney (or a complex mixture of both). Like other religious experiences, it can involve human and transcendental causes simultaneously.[18]

Scholars have generally worked with the hypothesis that glossolalia is a single phenomenon, and they have offered two standard definitions.[19] The first has it that tongues is the divinely inspired ability to speak actual but untaught human languages, a skill technically known as *xenoglossia*.[20] In this understanding, the report in Acts 2:4–11 is determinative. The disciples receiving the Holy Spirit speak "other languages" that are understood by pilgrims from the diaspora who also happen to speak those languages. Appeal is also made to Mark 16:17, which refers to "new tongues" (or "languages") as a sign that will accompany disciples. Some aspects of Paul's discussion in 1 Cor 14 are also isolated to support this hypothesis—for example, his comparison of tongues to known human languages of the earth (14:10–11).[21] Most of all, Paul lists with "tongues" another spiritual gift called "interpretation of tongues" (*hermēneia glōssōn*, 1 Cor 12:10). In light of 1 Cor 14:13, and especially 14:27–28, such interpretation is taken to mean "translating from a real but unknown language into another real but known language."[22] Modern glossalalists chime in with the evidence that their ecstatic speech is in fact a language unknown to them. A substantial oral tradition has it that such languages

18. See Maloney and Lovekin, *Glossolalia*, 249–51.

19. A third, rather odd hypothesis is that tongues are, literally, a heavenly language. The basis of this position, which is folkloric rather than scientific, is Paul's phrase "If I speak with the tongues of angels" in 1 Cor 13:1, his references to revealing mysteries (1 Cor 14:2) and speaking with God (1 Cor 14:28), and his cryptic allusion in 2 Cor 12:4 to heavenly visions that he is incapable of expressing in human speech. Paul's characterization has something in common with the ecstatic speech in the Testament of Job 48:1–50:3. The obvious problem with the hypothesis is that it is unhelpful for determining the linguistic or psychological dimensions of speech as it was practiced by early Christians. For a discussion of the texts, see Currie, "'Speaking in Tongues.'"

20. May, "Survey of Glossolalia," 75–96. See the reports given by Stevenson in *Xenoglossy* and *Unlearned Language*.

21. See Harpur, "Gift of Tongues"; Gundry, "'Ecstatic Utterance' (N. E. B.)?," esp. 306. This is the position advocated as well by Ford, "Theology of 'Speaking in Tongues,'" and Forbes, "Early Christian Inspired Speech."

22. J. Davies, "Pentecost and Glossolalia," esp. 231.

are spontaneously recognized by visitors from foreign climes who recognize in these utterances languages they themselves speak.[23]

The weight of textual evidence, however, does not support this understanding of tongues as real human languages. The Pentecost story does emphasize the intelligibility of the tongues spoken, but a careful reading indicates that the miracles occurred in the *hearing* rather than in the *mode of speaking.* The bystanders do not ask, "How can they all be speaking our native languages?" but rather, "Since all who are speaking are Galileans, how is it that *we hear them* in our own native languages?" (Acts 2:8).[24] The other references to tongues in Acts stress their source rather than their intelligibility. The isolation of Pentecost in this respect suggests that the element of communication was emphasized by Luke to suit his narrative purposes at that point in his story.[25]

The mention of "new tongues" in Mark 16:17 is too obscure to provide help in defining the nature of the phenomenon. The "longer ending of Mark" in which it occurs is certainly a later addition to the Gospel and indebted to other traditions, such as those found in Acts and Paul.[26] At best, the phrase provides another witness to the practice of tongues among early Christians. As for Paul, he could hardly emphasize more strongly that, in his view—and he *was* a speaker in tongues himself (1 Cor 14:18)—glossolalia is an intrinsically noncommunicative form of utterance (1 Cor 13:1; 14:2, 4, 7–9, 16–17, 23). What, then, does he mean by "interpretation of tongues"? A study of the verb *diermēneuein* by Paul's Jewish contemporaries Josephus and Philo suggests that it often means simply "to put into words," or "bring to articulate expression."[27] When Paul tells the tongue-speaker to pray that he or she might "interpret,"

23. Samarin, "Linguisticality of Glossolalia." For examples of such reports, see Sherrill, *They Speak with Other Tongues*, 98–107; Kelsey, *Speaking with Tongues*, 160–63.

24. For the contrary view, see Taylor, "Tongues of Pentecost"; Beel, "Donum Linguarum." But the divided response of the crowd is decisive: not all there heard in the same manner; some concluded from the apparently incoherent character of their raving that the speakers were in fact drunk (Acts 2:13); Peter's "interpretation," furthermore, was not of their discourse but of their ecstatic condition; see Johnson, *Acts of the Apostles*, 53–54.

25. See Johnson, *Acts of the Apostles*, 45–47.

26. The manuscript support for "new" (*kainais*) in the phrase "they will speak with [new] tongues" (*glōssais lalēsousin kainais*) in Mark 16:17, furthermore, is even weaker than for the passage as a whole. For a discussion of the longer endings of Mark and variants, see Metzger, *Textual Commentary*, 122–28.

27. See Thiselton, "'Interpretation' of Tongues."

therefore (1 Cor 14:13), he does not mean "provide a translation" but "change to a mode of speech intelligible to the assembly."

The purported evidence offered by contemporary glossolalists that their utterance is real language, finally, is spurious. Careful linguistic study has demonstrated that glossolalia is not a "real but unknown language" but rather a "language-like patterning" of sound.[28] Observation of the "interpretation of tongues" in actual Pentecostal practice, furthermore, shows that it is not the translation of a language, which would require some coincidence of sound-segment, but a separate utterance altogether, often lengthier by far than the glossolalic segment.[29] The stereotypical character of the reports of real languages being heard by native speakers, along with the impossibility of verifying such reports, suggests that they are essentially folkloric and legitimizing in character.[30]

The second major hypothesis concerning tongues is that it is not a real language but an ecstatic utterance that takes the form of an ordered babbling.[31] Paul clearly regards tongues as unintelligible, contrasting speech that is "in the Spirit" (*en tō pneumati*) but does not use the mind (*nous*) with speech that does use the mind and therefore builds up the community (1 Cor 14:14–15, 19). Because glossolalia is private and noncommunicative, God may be praised by it and the person praying may be edified, but neither the mind nor the community gains any benefit from the performance (1 Cor 14:2–3, 14, 17, 28).

This definition of glossolalia also better corresponds with most of ancient and contemporary parallel phenomena. In at least the older forms of Israelite prophecy, there is evidence of inspiration by God's Spirit, trancelike states with the physical indications of dissociation and the uttering of inarticulate cries (see, e.g., 1 Sam 10:5–13; 19:18–24). Whether classical Hebrew prophecy was also accompanied by ecstatic states remains a matter of debate.[32] An important parallel to early Christian glossolalia is the Hellenistic religious phenomenon known as mantic prophecy. In contrast to nonecstatic, "technical" prophecy, such as discerning the auspices or practicing divination,[33] such prophecy involved so complete a

---

28. Samarin, *Tongues of Men and Angels*, 74–128; Maloney and Lovekin, *Glossolalia*, 38; Kildahl, "Psychological Observations," 362.

29. See the example that is provided by Maloney and Lovekin, *Glossolalia*, 32.

30. See Christie-Murray, *Voice from the Gods*, 248–52; Stevenson, *Xenoglossy*, 1–14; May, "Survey of Glossolalia."

31. See, e.g., C. Williams, "Glossolalia in the New Testament."

32. See Robert R. Wilson, *Prophecy and Society*, 21–35.

33. See Cicero, *De divinatione* 18, 34.

possession (*enthousiasmos*) by the divine spirit (*pneuma*) that the mind of the prophet (*mantis*) was inoperative and the oracles were literally spoken by the god.[34] The prophetic oracles delivered at Delphi played a key role through much of the religious and political life of ancient Greece.[35] Our evidence suggests that such oracles were linguistically intelligible, if obscure in meaning. Even so, they often required "interpretation" by qualified cultic personnel who were called "prophets" (*prophētai*).[36]

Such prophecy was highly esteemed, even by the philosophically sophisticated, as a sign of direct divine involvement with humans.[37] It is not certain, however, how inevitable was the state of trance or ecstasy (*furor*, *mania*) in such prophecy, although it is frequently mentioned.[38] Still less certain is the presence of glossolalic utterance.[39] Some references are made to the occurrence of strange sounds and garbled or foreign words,[40] but these tend to be associated with wandering prophets—especially the priests of the goddess Cybele—and soothsayers,[41] or with those attacked as charlatans,[42] than with the oracles of the fixed pro-

---

34. For an orientation, see Dodds, *The Greeks and the Irrational*, 64–101. The classic monograph is Fascher, *Prophētēs*; citations to comparative material can be found also in Helmut Kramer, "προφήτης," *TDNT* 6:784–96; Bacht, "Wahres und Falsches Prophetentum."

35. For a sense of the cultural importance of Delphi, see Herodotus, *Persian Wars* 1.51, 61, 67; 5.42–43, 62–63, 91; 6.52, 57, 66, 76, 86; 7.220, 239; 8.114, 141; Thucydides, *Peloponnesian War* 2.7.55, 3.11.92, 4.13.118, 5.15.17.

36. See Plato, *Timaeus* 72B; Herodotus, *Persian Wars* 8.135. The picture of ancient prophecy is made even more complex by the traditions concerning the Sibyls, who produced their prophecies in *mania* but did so in clear (and written) prose; see Parke, *Sibyls and Sibylline Prophecy*.

37. See Plato, *Ion* 534A–D; *Phaedrus* 244A; *Timaeus* 71E–72B; Plutarch, *The E at Delphi* 387B, 391E; *The Obsolescence of Oracles* 432A–D; *Oracles at Delphi* 399A, 397C. Once more, Philo's language and perceptions concerning prophecy are those of the Greek world: the divine *pneuma* "seizes" humans (*Questions on Genesis* 4.196), "falls on" them (*Life of Moses* 2.291), "possesses" them (*Life of Moses* 1.175), and "fills" their mind (*Questions on Genesis* 4:140). He consistently speaks of the *pneuma* replacing the human mind in prophecy (see *On the Special Laws* 4.49; *Who Is the Heir?* 264–65; *Questions on Genesis* 3.9; *Life of Moses* 2.188–92). This is how God "speaks through" the prophets (*On the Special Laws* 1.65). See Weaver, "Pneuma in Philo of Alexandria," 115–41; note in particular the comparison Weaver draws between this language and that used of the Pythian Oracle (131–34).

38. See, e.g., Plutarch, *The Obsolescence of Oracles* 417C; Cicero, *De divinatione* 32.70; Virgil, *Aeneid* 6.42ff.

39. See Aune, *Prophecy in Early Christianity*, 30–35.

40. See Herodotus, *Persian Wars* 8.135; Plutarch, *The Obsolescence of Oracles* 42A.

41. See Apuleius, *Metamorphoses* 8.27; Dio Chrysostom, *Orations* 10.23–24.

42. See Lucian, *Alexander the False Prophet* 13, 22, 27–28, 49, 51, 53.

phetic shrines like Delphi or Dodonna. That Paul himself considered tongues as equivalent—at least in manifestation—to such mantic prophecy seems certain from his word choice in 1 Cor 14:23, when he suggests that "ignorant and unbelieving" people (i.e., outsiders) who came across a whole congregation speaking in tongues would conclude, "you are raving" (*hoti mainesthe*), which, in context, should be understood as "you are prophesying in the way all cults do, in a frenzy."[43]

The understanding of glossolalia as a structured babbling, furthermore, corresponds with the best evidence provided by the linguistic analysis of modern tongue-speaking,[44] although the degree of ecstasy involved in the contemporary phenomenon is a matter of debate. Problems of definition are here obvious. Some observers virtually define glossolalia in terms of psychological dissociation, considering it to be the oral expression of a trance state.[45] Others point out that the *initial* experience of tongues is often accompanied by dissociation but that subsequent performances frequently lack any signs of an altered consciousness.[46]

First-person accounts of the experience of glossolalia emphasize, especially with regard to the first occurrence, positive feelings of release, freedom, and joy.[47] Although some modern glossolalia occurs in private,[48] it is ordinarily a public and cultic activity. It is connected above all with the experience of conversion, being "born again" or "baptized in the Holy Spirit" (in explicit continuity with Acts 10:46 and 19:6), and with the practice of prayer (as in 1 Cor 14:2, 28).[49] The understanding of tongues as a form of prophecy (as in Acts 2:4–11) is rarer, as is the actual practice of "the interpretation of tongues."[50]

In summary, the convergence of evidence suggests that glossolalia is a verbal expression of a powerful emotional state. It is not a real language but a kind of structured or ordered babbling. Especially in its first mani-

---

43. Cf. Homer, *Iliad* 6.131; Euripides, *Bacchae* 299; Pausanias, *Description of Greece* 2.7.5; Herodotus, *Persian War* 4.79; Plato, *Phaedrus* 244C. Paul's usage here must be taken, together with his emphasis that tongues does not use the *nous*, as decisive in pointing the phenomenon of glossolalia toward the manifestations of Greco-Roman prophecy. See Fascher, *Prophētēs*, 168: "Wenn Paulus I Kor 14:23 *mainesthe* von den Glossolalen gebraucht, dann heisst es 'rasen oder in Verzuchung reden.'"

44. Samarin, "Linguisticality of Tongues," 55–73.

45. Goodman, *Speaking in Tongues*, 58–86.

46. Samarin, *Tongues of Men and Angels*, 26–34; Kelsey, *Speaking with Tongues*, 142.

47. Goodman, *Speaking in Tongues*, 24–57; Kildahl, "Psychological Observations," 359, 364; Kelsey, *Speaking with Tongues*, 221; Maloney and Lovekin, *Glossolalia*, 185.

48. See Hutch, "Personal Ritual of Glossolalia."

49. See Maloney and Lovekin, *Glossolalia*, 126–46.

50. See, however Maloney and Lovekin, *Glossolalia*, 23–26.

festation, it is experienced by the speaker as an expression of a powerful spiritual presence. It is human utterance whose entire significance lies in its directly expressing a certain kind of religious experience.

The Pervasiveness of the Phenomenon

It is impossible to determine how widespread glossolalia was in earliest Christianity. The evidence supports only that tongues were spoken by Paul and some members of the Corinthian congregation in the mid-fifties of the first century[51] and was thought by Luke to have been a feature of some early conversion experiences.[52]

Although Paul lists "tongues" and the "interpretation of tongues" among the spiritual gifts (*charismata*) in 1 Cor 12:10, it is noteworthy that neither appears in the two other Pauline lists of spiritual gifts (Rom 12:3–8; Eph 4:11). He makes no mention of the experience of tongues in connection with his own call (Gal 1:15–17) nor in connection with the conversion of others. The case of Gal 3:1–5 is particularly striking because of Paul's emphasis there on the work of the Spirit and its "powerful deeds." Indeed, we shall see that Paul is deeply ambivalent in his attitude toward tongues. But, for that matter, not even Luke connects tongues to Paul's conversion experience (Acts 9:3–8). Nor is tongues linked to the laying on of hands, except in Acts 19:6. Finally, there is no hint of the

---

51. Clement makes no reference to the phenomenon when writing to them some forty years later.

52. Other evidence sometimes adduced in favor of larger claims is difficult to assess. Apart from the problematic longer ending of Mark (16:17), the gospel tradition has nothing about glossolalia. Indeed, Jesus's condemnation of the "babbling" of gentiles in prayer (Matt 6:7) could well have been taken by Christians as an implied criticism of glossolalia. Among passages that *could* be used with reference to glossolalia but need not be are Paul's mention of "spiritual hymns" by which Christians could praise God "in their hearts" (Col 3:16; Eph 4:19), his command to the Thessalonians not to "quench the Spirit" (1 Thess 4:19), and his claim that the Holy Spirit helps Christians when they do not know how to pray "with unutterable groanings [*stenagmois alalētois*]" (Rom 8:26). Still more difficult to assess are the traces of early Christian bilingualism. Certainly "amen" as a response to prayer could scarcely be thought of as an ecstatic utterance (see 1 Cor 14:16). But what about the Aramaic cry *maranatha* uttered in worship (1 Cor 16:22), and the Aramaic diminutive *abba*, the proclamation of which is directly connected by Paul to the experience of the Holy Spirit (Gal 4:6; see Rom 8:15)? Both words are wonderful candidates for the sort of "ordered babbling" that makes up glossolalia. Unfortunately, we have no way of positively linking these expressions to the practice of tongues.

practice of glossolalia in any other Christian writing before the middle of the second century.

Even for the earliest period of the Christian movement, therefore, glossolalia appears as at best a sporadic and ambiguous phenomenon. Two inferences about that first period are therefore emphatically *not* supported by the evidence: that tongues was a normal and expected accompaniment of the Holy Spirit (and therefore, by implication, a necessary indicator of the authentic presence of the Spirit); and that tongues demonstrates how the first Christians lived in a charismatic fog of trance or dissociation.

Evaluations of Glossolalia by New Testament Writers

The discussion of glossolalia is further complicated by the disparate evaluations of the phenomenon in the two New Testament sources that report it. Luke gives a completely positive valuation to glossolalia. As the tongues of fire at Pentecost are the *visual* sign of the Spirit's presence, which transforms followers into ministers of the word (see Luke 1:4), so the speaking in tongues is the *auditory* sign. It is the Holy Spirit who "gives them utterance" (Acts 2:4). In the Pentecost account, the first experience of tongues is an expression of praise: the disciples tell "of the great things of God" (Acts 2:11).

Peter's speech following this event provides Luke's own interpretation, not of the tongues, but of the experience of ecstatic utterance itself. He begins by citing Joel 3:1–5 (LXX), indicating thereby that this gift of the Spirit is in fulfillment of prophecy. Luke's emendations to the Joel citation, furthermore, have the effect of making this outpouring of the Spirit an eschatological event ("in the last days"), signaled by the spirit of prophecy (see Acts 2:17–18), and by the "signs and wonders" worked by God (2:19).[53] These touches serve to make Pentecost a programmatic statement for the rest of Acts, in which the apostles are depicted as the prophetic successors to Jesus, filled with the same Holy Spirit he was and working as he did signs and wonders among the people.[54] By making the diverse tongues intelligible to Jewish pilgrims from all over the diaspora,

---

53. Johnson, *Acts of the Apostles*, 48–55.

54. For the notion of "programmatic prophecy" as a literary technique in Luke-Acts, see Johnson, *Gospel of Luke*, 16; and for the depiction of the apostles as prophets in succession to Moses and Jesus, see ibid., 17–20.

furthermore, Luke indicates that the prophetic Spirit is the fulfillment of the promises to Abraham, extended first to Abraham's descendants and only then to the nations of the earth (2:38–39).[55]

Glossolalia functions as a sign of the Spirit in the two other Acts passages, where it also marks a new stage in the mission. When the Spirit falls on the household of the gentile Cornelius, the Jewish Christians present at the scene can hear the tongues and conclude that the gentiles had received the same Holy Spirit that they had at Pentecost (10:45). Likewise, when Paul lays hands on the former followers of John the Baptist in Ephesus and they begin "to speak in tongues and prophesy" (19:6), it shows that people of Asia have also received the Holy Spirit and that this baptism in Jesus is greater than that of John's (19:2–3; see Luke 3:16; Acts 1:5; 11:16). In short, Acts treats glossolalia as a nonambiguous symbol of the Spirit's presence and a sign of the mission's success.[56]

In contrast, Paul's attitude toward glossolalia is more complex and ambivalent, at least in part because of the problems he thinks it is causing in the Corinthian community.[57] The elitist tendencies in that assembly led some of them to regard all spiritual powers (*ta pneumatika*, 1 Cor 12:1) as a means of self-aggrandizement.[58] Just as some of them used "liberty" and "knowledge" in ways careless of community edification (8:1–2; 10:23), so the spectacular gift of tongues seems to have been claimed by some as a superior "sign of the Spirit." Indeed, some may well have been claiming that only tongues truly certifies a spiritual person: "tongues is a sign for believers" (see 14:22).[59]

55. Johnson, *Acts of the Apostles*, 47.

56. While rejecting the historicity of the Cornelius episode in Acts 10:44–48, Philip F. Esler argues that, together with the evidence in 1 Cor 12–14, it provides genuine historical evidence that speaking in tongues among gentiles functioned as a sign for their admission into the church; see his "Glossolalia and the Admission of Gentiles."

57. For discussions of Paul's treatment of glossolalia and prophecy in 1 Cor 12–14, see Johnson, "Norms"; Callan, "Prophecy and Ecstasy"; Hunt, *Inspired Body*, 18–30; Gillespie, *First Theologians*, 97–164; Bruner, *Theology of the Holy Spirit*, 283–319; Grudem, *Gift of Prophecy*.

58. Martin, "Tongues of Angels"; and Martin, *Corinthian Body*, 87–103, is certainly on target concerning the ways in which the Corinthians themselves were using tongues, although the evidence he adduces for ecstatic speech as a broad cultural status enhancer, while provocative, is not probative. Neyrey, in *Paul, in Other Words*, 128–35, reads both 1 Cor 11:2–16 and 14:1–34 in light of Mary Douglas's analysis of societal freedom and control; he also touches briefly on the question of honor/shame on 67–68.

59. Hurd, *Origin of I Corinthians*, contains this line of questioning—"Concerning

Paul acknowledged from the start of this letter that his readers had been "enriched with all speech and knowledge" (1 Cor 1:5). But when he takes up the issue of tongues explicitly in 1 Cor 12–14, it is to relativize the claims being made for it. He begins by reminding them that there is a difference between *ta pneumatika*, which can refer to any sort of "spiritual phenomenon," and *ta charismata*, the term Paul uses for the gifts given by the Holy Spirit (see 1:7; 12:4, 9, 28, 30, 31).[60] He does not deny the reality of *ta pneumatika* but stresses their ambiguity. When the Corinthians were still pagans, such impulses led them away into idolatry (12:1–2).[61] Ecstasy is not self-validating but must be tested by its results. Thus the gift of the Holy Spirit leads to the confession "Jesus is Lord" (12:3),[62] and every *charism* given by that Spirit must be shaped according to the "mind of Christ" (2:16)—that is, in service to the upbuilding of the messianic community (8:12; 10:31–33).[63] Each part of the messianic body should work for the common good rather than for the benefit of individual members (12:7).[64] Although Paul acknowledges "tongues" and "the interpretation of tongues" as gifts of the Holy Spirit, therefore, he already relativizes their importance by placing them last, after the "foundational" gifts that build up community identity (12:8–10), and by emphasizing that private experience is secondary to the good of the whole body (12:12–31).

In chapter 13, Paul continues to diminish the importance of tongues—as indeed of all the gifts of speech—by asserting *agapē* as the most funda-

---

spiritual gifts: how is it possible to test for the Spirit? How can we (or anyone else) distinguish between spiritual men? When you were with us and spoke with tongues you gave us no instructions on this point" (195)—but recognizes that behind the question lay the vested interests of the glossolalists (192). See also Johanson, "Tongues," esp. 186–90.

60. Käsemann notes that it is with his choice of terms that Paul begins his theological critique; see "Ministry and Community," esp. 66.

61. The text is very difficult, but its basic sense is clear enough: "Il est fort naturel que l'Apôtre rappelle ici les phénomènes extatiques d'un passe païen; c'est pour rappeler aux Corinthiens qu'ils sont pas en soi une manifestation du Saint-Esprit" ("It is entirely natural that the apostle here recalls the ecstatic phenomena of a pagan past; it is to recall to the Corinthians that they are not in themselves a manifestation of the Holy Spirit"). Héring, *La Premiere Epître*, 108. See also Maly, "I Kor 12:1–3," esp. 86.

62. On the issue of the opposing formula, "cursed be Jesus," see Brox, "*ANATHEMA IĒSOUS*"; Pearson, "Did the Gnostics Curse Jesus?"; Maly, "I Kor 12:1–3," 93–95.

63. Hunt, *Inspired Body*, 125–27; Gillespie, *First Theologians*, 142–55.

64. For Paul's appropriation of a common rhetorical topos, see M. Mitchell, *Paul and the Rhetoric of Reconciliation*, 157–64; Martin, *Corinthian Body*, 92–96.

mental expression of God's Holy Spirit (cf. Rom 5:5). *Agapē* is defined in terms of service to the other in preference to personal gain. Using himself as an example, Paul declares that "the tongues of humans and of angels" are meaningless without *agapē* (1 Cor 13:1).[65] Tongues is a gift that will pass away (13:8), and Paul clearly intimates that it is among the "childish" things that must be put aside if real maturity is to be reached (13:11).[66]

When he turns to the discussion of the "higher gifts" that the community should pursue (1 Cor 12:31), Paul makes glossolalia the foil for prophecy, which he considers superior in every respect (14:5). Prophecy uses the mind, whereas ecstatic babbling does not (14:14–15). It builds up the identity of the community, whereas tongues improves only the speaker (14:3–4). It is intelligible, whereas tongues is not (14:6–10). Glossolalia also escapes the discernment of the entire community, which Paul considers essential for the healthy expression of the spiritual gifts. He regards glossolalia as an optional form of prayer, one that can be abandoned with no great loss. He speaks in tongues himself but would gladly give them up for the sake of building up the community (14:18–19). He can leave the impulses of the prophets to the prophets themselves since they are under rational control (14:31–32), but he must impose rules for glossolalia: tongues are restricted to their function of private prayer (14:13–16). The only time they can be spoken in public is when they can be followed by "interpretation" (14:27–28).[67]

Paul's evaluation of glossolalia is best summarized by 1 Cor 14:20–25. He reverses the glossolalists' claim by suggesting that tongues are far from an unambiguous sign of belief: they can mean anything, can come from anywhere.[68] If the assembly has glossolalia as its dominant mode of speech, outsiders can legitimately conclude that this assembly is simply a cult like every other one (14:23).[69] Only if prophecy is active can they be brought to recognize that God is at work in this community (14:25).

65. That chap. 13 functions rhetorically as an *exemplum* in the same fashion as chap. 9 is shown decisively by Holladay, "I Corinthians 13," 80–98.

66. It is difficult to imagine that Paul did not intend to connect the rebuke to the Corinthians' "childishness" in 3:1–3, this declaration that "when I became a man, I put away childish things" (13:11), and his command with reference to tongues in 14:20: "Brethren, do not be children in your thinking; be babes in evil, but in thinking be mature." See also Hunt, *Inspired Body*, 102–5, 129–32.

67. See W. Richardson, "Liturgical Order"; Schweizer, "Service of Worship," 405.

68. See Johanson, "Tongues," 186–90.

69. "Paul has the unbeliever mistake the Christian prayer meeting as just one more enthusiastic Hellenistic cult. The scandal here, in the strict sense, is that the distinctive word of the Gospel is not heard." Johnson, "Norms," 41.

To make tongues more than an interesting variety of private prayer is to think like a child and not like an adult (14:20; cf. 13:11).

The Ambiguous Character of Glossolalia

Paul's delicately nuanced treatment of glossolalia suggests that it was, at least in his eyes, a deeply ambiguous phenomenon. To elicit dimensions of this religious experience that lie just below the surface of the text, some controlled use of the imagination is required.

There is every reason to suppose that for the Corinthians who spoke in tongues, the gift was unequivocally positive. Such ecstatic babbling must have seemed to them—as it does to us—all the more dramatic a "religious experience" because of its exotic character. Here is not a concept about God or the will to please God. It is instead a somatic invasion by God's own power, lifting not only their feelings to states of joy and liberation but even their tongues to lalic freedom. For the speakers themselves, the gift (see 1 Cor 12:10, 28) must indeed have seemed a pure expression of *ta pneumatika* (12:1; 14:1), in which one "drank the Spirit" (12:13) and was activated and directed by the Spirit (12:11). Since it was the Holy Spirit itself that activated their speech (12:6, 11), furthermore, it must have appeared to them that the overwhelming of their *nous* was all the more impressive a sign of God's immediate presence, literally inside them and speaking through them! In their speech, God spoke as through angels, God clashed the cymbals, God made music on the harp, God blew the trumpet (13:1; 14:7–8). What could be a more unmistakable sign of God's empowering and transformative presence than to have their speech directed not by their own puny minds but by the direct breath of God![70] For that matter, how could the truth of the resurrection—that Jesus is Lord—be more emphatically expressed than by them speaking ecstatically "in the Spirit" (see 12:3)?

For those seeing and hearing the tongue-speakers, the phenomenon was undoubtedly impressive as well. Surely in such Spirit-driven speech could be found the "powerful deeds" energized by the Spirit as a sign of faith (Gal 3:1–5), the palpable demonstration that the kingdom of God does not consist in speech but in power (1 Cor 4:20). For the observers as much as for the speakers themselves, the phenomenon of glossolalia among those gathered in the name of Jesus must have served as proof

70. Cf. Gunkel, *Influence of the Holy Spirit*, 77–86.

that he was alive and powerfully present among them (see Matt 18:20). Especially if tongues was regarded (as it was by Luke and by the wider gentile world) as a form of prophecy, then glossolalia served as well to demonstrate that the age of prophecy had now been reborn in this messianic sect of Judaism. As a result, this sect had a legitimate if not compelling claim to be considered as the authentic people of God, the rightful heir of the biblical tradition. In short, by enlivening their hearts and by liberating their tongues, this gift of the Holy Spirit made clear to all that prophecy was alive and that Jesus was alive as well.

If Paul was a glossolalist as he claimed to be (1 Cor 14:18), then his appreciation for this gift must have been real. Indeed, he does call it a *charisma* of the Holy Spirit (12:10, 30), and he does "thank God" that he can speak in tongues more than any them (14:18). But his appreciation, as we have seen, is muted by equally real apprehensions. What sort of concerns led him to emphasize what he considered prophecy—namely, rational discourse—in preference to glossolalia?

Two of Paul's concerns are explicit. The first is his worry that the form of glossolalia might be mistaken for the mantic prophecy prevalent in Greco-Roman culture. His caution in 1 Cor 12:1 that *ta pneumatika* drew them away to idolatry when they were pagans, and his conclusion in 14:23 that outsiders would assume that an assembly of glossalalists "are raving as mantic prophets rave," both point in this direction. In a sense, Paul wants to protect the "one Spirit" here just as he did the "one baptism" in Galatia, as a means of affirming the "one God."[71] His concern here is a variation of the command in 1 John 4:1 to "test the spirits to see if they are from God."

Paul's second manifest concern is the way in which tongue-speaking can lead to disorder in the assembly. He suggests that an ecstatic cannot exercise self-control in the way that "the spirits of prophets are subject to prophets" (1 Cor 14:32 RSV). Out of the conviction that God is a God of peace and not of confusion, therefore (14:32), Paul himself sets limits on glossolalia. At most, two or three should speak in tongues; but if there is no one to "interpret," a glossolalist should "keep silence in church and speak to himself and to God" (14:28 RSV). Paul's stringency here stands in contrast to his leniency with prophets: "You can all prophesy one by one so that all may learn and be encouraged" (14:31).

Thus far we have examined the surface of the text and the surface reasons for limiting glossolalia's expression. But are there unexpressed issues

---

71. See my discussion in chap. 3 on pp. 48–68 in this volume.

as well? It may be that glossolalia was not only messy but also a challenge to established, and especially male, authority. We can take our first cue from social-scientific work on contemporary glossolalia. More recent psychological studies reject the older view that glossolalia is intrinsically connected to psychopathology.[72] On the other hand, glossolalia appears to be mimetic behavior; that is, new speakers in tongues follow the patterns of sounds uttered by the lead glossolalist.[73] Not surprisingly, extroversion, the ability to be hypnotized, and a willingness to submit to authority are positively correlated with the experience.[74] For the most part, while the experience of tongues has an integrating effect on the individual, it also fosters among those who practice glossolalia a sense of elitism that proves disruptive in communities.[75] These findings throw possible light on the divided allegiances in the Corinthian community (1 Cor 1:10–12). Certainly Cephas was a glossolalist by reputation (Acts 2:4–11) and Paul by self-acknowledgment (1 Cor 14:18). It is certainly conceivable that the party spirit of those who cried out "I am for Paul" or "I am for Cephas" (1 Cor 1:12) could be correlated with the sociopsychological tendencies of submission to authority figures, elitism, and divisiveness attributed to contemporary glossolalists.[76]

Such speculation is given some support by I. M. Lewis's classic study of spirit possession and shamanism, *Ecstatic Religion*.[77] Lewis makes no mention of glossolalia. But he does demonstrate how, in cultures that have a generalized belief in transcendental spiritual powers, claims to the possession of such powers have specific sociological implications. In particular, spirit possession serves to empower groups otherwise marginal within a society. "In its primary social function, peripheral posses-

---

72. J. Richardson, "Psychological Interpretations of Glossolalia"; Maloney and Lovekin, *Glossolalia*, 93; Coulson and Johnson, "Glossolalia"; see also the survey of studies in C. Williams, *Tongues of the Spirit*, 125–91.

73. For tongues as learned behavior, see Kildahl, "Psychological Observations," 355; Mayers, "Behavior of Tongues."

74. Kildahl, *Psychology of Speaking in Tongues*, 50–53; Kildahl, "Psychological Observations," 353, 365; Maloney and Lovekin, *Glossolalia*, 77; Gonzalez, "Theology and Psychology," 107; Kelsey, *Speaking with Tongues*, 220.

75. Kildahl, *Psychology of Speaking in Tongues*, 66–75; Kildahl, "Psychological Observations," 365–66; despite his overall positive evaluation of tongues, Kelsey emphasizes their tendency to breed arrogance and elitism in the individual, and consequently divisiveness within groups (*Speaking with Tongues*, 223, 231).

76. Esler suggests that the Corinthians may well have imitated Paul's glossolalic practice; see "Glossolalia," 48.

77. Page references appear in the text.

sion thus emerges as an oblique aggressive strategy" (32). The claim to spirit possession does not rupture relationships but helps vent frustrations among those who do not enjoy overt power within the group (121). Such claims would understandably have more appeal among the lesser orders (101, 104–6, 110), enabling them functionally to destabilize a given authority structure[78] while also grasping a share of power by providing what is, in such contexts, an obvious status enhancement (109–10).

Lewis's analysis is most pertinent, and provocative, for our present topic, however, because of the role that spirit-possession plays in gender battles. Lewis shows how certain ritualized forms of sickness, which are interpreted by males as a form of demonic possession, are evaluated quite differently by the women involved: "What men consider demoniacal sickness, women convert into a clandestine ecstasy" (30; see also 77). Specifically with regard to women's possession cults, Lewis notes that they are "thinly disguised protest movements directed against the dominant sex" (31).

If Lewis's analysis has any pertinence to ancient glossolalia as an expression of spirit-possession, then we are led to still another aspect of Paul's treatment of tongues—namely, his general difficulties with the speech of *women* in the Corinthian church. We note that the discussion of glossolalia is framed at either side by Paul's efforts to control women's speech in the assembly. In 1 Cor 11:3–16 the topic is the veiling of women who "pray or prophesy";[79] in 14:33b–36 Paul issues a blanket directive for women to "keep silent in the assembly."[80] The apparent contradiction in the two passages is notorious and has led to various resolutions.[81] In the first instance, some sort of ecstatic speech is clearly at issue, for "prayer and prophecy" are included among the *charismata*.[82] The second case

---

78. "Enthusiasm thrives on instability." Lewis, *Ecstatic Religion*, 175.

79. For a analysis of the passage as a whole in the light of recent literature, see M. Black, "I Cor 11:2–16."

80. The critical issues attaching to this passage are discussed, with recent literature, by Osburn, "Interpretation of 1 Cor 14:34–35."

81. Including considering one or both passages interpolations. For 11:2–16, see Walker, "1 Cor 11:2–16"; Cope, "1 Cor 11:2–16"; Jerome Murphy-O'Connor, "Non-Pauline Character." For 4:33b–36, see Murphy-O'Connor, "Interpolations in 1 Corinthians"; Conzelmann, *First Corinthians*, 246; Fee, *First Epistle to the Corinthians*, 699–702.

82. In the present passage, we have "every man praying or prophesying" (*proseuchomenos ē propheteuōn*, 11:4), to which corresponds "every woman who prays or prophesies" (11:5) and "it is fitting that every woman be covered while praying" (11:13). In 1 Cor 14 we find prayer in 14:13, 14, 15, and prophesying in 14:1, 3, 4, 5, 24,

appears to involve teaching, for Paul instructs the women to learn from their husbands at home rather than speak in the assembly.[83] Nevertheless, both instances involve women's speech.

We observe furthermore that in both discussions Paul appeals to the custom of the other churches concerning the roles of women.[84] More strikingly still, in both places Paul invokes the concept of shame (*aischros*).[85] Finally, we note the element of specifically sexual embarrassment that appears to be connected with the uncovering of women's heads in Paul's appeal to what "nature [*physis*] itself teaches you" (1 Cor 11:14) or what is "proper" (*prepei*) in women's public behavior (11:13). Even if his alternatives of wearing short hair or having the head shaved (11:5-7) do not necessarily refer, as sometimes thought, to prostitution,[86] the probable allusion to the lust of the angels (11:10; cf. Gen 6:1-4)[87] sexualizes women's unveiled ecstatic speech.

Elisabeth Schüssler Fiorenza and Antoinette Clark Wire have placed Paul's delimitation of women's speech in the context of the activity of

---

31, 39. We cannot be certain that Paul uses the terms with absolute consistency, but if chap. 11 is to be fitted to the distinctions Paul draws in chap. 14, then the "praying" may be discourse in tongues (and therefore ecstatic), and "prophesying" rational discourse (using the *nous*).

83. The passage obviously resembles 1 Tim 2:11-15, which is one reason some want to find it an interpolation (see Scroggs, "Paul and the Eschatological Woman"); for a discussion of similarities, see Johnson, *Letters to Paul's Delegates*, 132-41.

84. In 1 Cor 11:2, "I commend you because you remember me in everything and maintain the traditions even as I have delivered them to you," and in 11:16, "If anyone is disposed to be contentious, we recognize no other practice, nor do the churches of God." In 14:33c, "As in all the churches of the saints, women should keep silent," and in 14:36, "What! Did the word of God originate with you, or are you the only ones it reached?"

85. He declares that it is shameful—*aischron estin*—for a woman to pray with unveiled head or to speak in public (1 Cor 11:6; 14:35). The expression is all the more stunning for occurring only here and in closely connected passages (Eph 5:12 and Titus 1:11) in all of Paul's letters. Note also in 11:14-15 the contrast between "dishonor" (*atimia*) and "honor" (*doxa*).

86. M. Black cites a text from Dio Chrysostom to the effect that a woman caught in adultery should have her head shaved and be a harlot, but also gives evidence that a shaven head can be associated with mourning; see "1 Cor 11:2-16," 206.

87. See the argument in Martin, *Corinthian Body*, 242-46, and Corrington, "'Headless Woman.'" The passage in Joseph and Aseneth 15:2 is also pertinent: in the presence of the "man from heaven," Aseneth is told to remove her veil, so that her head is "like that of a young man."

"women prophets" in the Corinthian community.[88] Paul's concern with veiling can thus be connected to the practices of ecstatic speech among women prophets in shrines such as that of Apollo at Delphi: the tossing of the unveiled and unbound hair by the enthused maiden was a notable feature of such prophecy.[89] Just as Paul was concerned that ecstasy could "lead them off to dumb idols" (1 Cor 12:2) and that an assembly of glossalalists could be mistaken for a seance of mantic prophets (14:23), so he feared that women speaking ecstatically with unveiled or loose hair could be regarded as a manifestation of the Pythian spirit. And if Lewis is correct, Paul might also, at some level, have intuited that such speech among women might prove threatening to the orderly patriarchal world constructed by "the law" (14:34).

We can, however, go one step further. Why does Paul's discussion sexualize such ecstatic speech and speak of it in terms of shame? Here the recent research by Dale Martin and Mary Foskett concerning the ways in which the body was construed in Greco-Roman medical and moral discourse offers significant insight.[90] If serious medical opinion considered male sperm as bearing the *pneuma* of life into a woman's womb;[91]

88. See Wire, *Corinthian Women Prophets*, 116–58; Schüssler Fiorenza, *In Memory of Her*, 226–36. Schüssler Fiorenza in particular argues that the inconsistency in Paul's argument and the cultural probabilities suggest that the issue is not one of veiling but rather one of wearing the hair loose or bound. While I agree with Martin, *Corinthian Body*, 233, that veiling is at the heart of the passage, I think it a false dilemma: not wearing a veil when prophesying in a *furor* would in all likelihood lead to its loosening and thus to the sexual and cultic associations suggested by both Schüssler Fiorenza and Martin.

89. In his account of the restrictions placed on the cult of Dionysius in Rome (ca. 186 BCE), Livy lists among the troubling aspects of the cult that it involved sexual misbehavior, men prophesying with contorted bodies, and women with disheveled hair (*Annals of Rome* 39.13). He adds that in the Roman decree concerning the matter, it was noted that "a great part of them are women, and they are the source of this mischief" (39.15). See the references in Schüssler Fiorenza, *In Memory of Her*, 227, and Kroeger and Kroeger, "Evidence of Maenadism."

90. Martin's discussion of this passage is provocatively and appropriately titled "Prophylactic Veils" (*Corinthian Body*, 229–49), and he adduces convincing evidence from the medical literature. One is only surprised that he, unlike Schüssler Fiorenza, does not explicitly connect this discussion to the one on glossolalia. Foskett advances this research by connecting it explicitly to the cultural construction of virginity in the Greco-Roman world and the frequent link between virginity and prophecy; see "A Virgin Conceived."

91. See Aristotle, *Generation of Animals* 1.20; the entire discussion of *sperma* is in 1.17–21.

if some ancient physiology pictured the woman's body as a receptive vessel, open both at the mouth and vagina;[92] if the ravings of the Delphic Oracle sitting over the smoking tripod came from her being suffused from below by the *pneuma* of Apollo, so that the god spoke out above through her mouth;[93] and if these ravings could be heard, by clients as well as by critics, as a sort of orgasmic frenzy,[94] then the sexual connotations of female prophecy in this culture are obvious. If any of these associations were in Paul's mind (and the allusions to sex and shame are his, after all), it is small wonder that he was worried not only about the disorder that glossolalia could create but also about the deep confusion over the sort of *pneuma* by which Christians were being possessed. In this light, his restrictions are less surprising than his willingness to credit this ecstatic gift and give it some degree of expression. He does conclude, after all, "Do not forbid speaking in tongues, but let all things be done decently and in order" (1 Cor 14:39–40).

Glossolalia and Deviance

In the second and third centuries, glossolalia appears only infrequently. The most noteworthy outburst is associated with the figure of Montanus (ca. 160) and the two women prophets who accompanied him.[95] Montanus apparently regarded himself as a passive instrument of the Holy Spirit, "like a lyre struck with a plecton."[96] He understood his "strange speech" (*xenophonein*) as a form of prophecy, and his speech was accompanied by the frenzy associated with mantic prophecy.[97] Even in Montanism, however, such inspired utterance did not seem long to survive the founders,[98] although the Montanist Tertullian does evoke the

92. Aristotle, *History of Animals* 10.5; Hippocrates, *Aphorisms* 5.51; see Martin, *Corinthian Body*, 237–39.

93. See the vivid story of Apollo closing the throat of the Oracle in prophecy in Lucan, *Pharsalia* 5.160–97; Plutarch, *The Obsolescence of Oracles* (*Moralia* 432D–E, 404E, 405C); Martin, *Corinthian Body*, 239–40.

94. Virgil, *Aeneas* 6.77–101; Martin, *Corinthian Body*, 240–42.

95. See Eusebius, *Ecclesiastical History* 5.15–18; Hippolytus, *Refutation of All Heresies* 8.12.

96. Epiphanius, *Refutation of All Heresies* 48.4.1.

97. Eusebius, *Ecclesiastical History* 5.16.7–10.

98. Eusebius, *Ecclesiastical History* 5.17.4; but see Epiphanius, *Refutation of All Heresies* 49.1–3.

presence of ecstatic speech in his community as a proof against Marcion of its authenticity.[99]

Irenaeus of Lyons (ca. 200) also claims acquaintance with tongues, although his report is succinct and influenced by Pauline language: "We have heard many brethren in the church having prophetic gifts and speaking through the spirit in all tongues and bringing to light men's secrets for the common good and explaining the mysteries of God. Such persons the Apostle calls spiritual."[100] Irenaeus apparently understands tongues to mean "other languages." But he also reports on the activities of a Valentinian gnostic called Marcus, whom Irenaeus regards as a charlatan and magician, but whose repertoire includes prophecy. According to Irenaeus, Marcus seduces women and coaxes them to prophesy, and the manner of their speech once more suggests glossolalia or mantic prophecy.[101] It is worth noting that in the case of Montanism and Gnosticism, glossolalia is associated with women.

Apart from these notices, there are only the occasional patches in gnostic compositions of strung-together syllables that resemble transcribed glossolalia,[102] and the numerous concatenations of sounds in the magical papyri that are used in spells. Phenomenologically, it is difficult to distinguish these from "praying in tongues."[103] In such cases, however, it is impossible to determine what sort of oral activity generated or was generated by the literary text. Some preachers apparently even used babbling speech in public, at least according to the anti-Christian polemicist Celsus, who calls their utterances "without form or meaning."[104]

Arguments from silence are deservedly suspect, but the paucity of evidence for glossolalia in the second two hundred years of Christianity suggests that it became an increasingly marginal activity. Most of the occurrences appear in groups rejected by the orthodox tradition. This is no surprise. As Lewis notes, "The more entrenched the religious au-

---

99. Tertullian, *Against Marcion* 5.8.

100. Irenaeus, *Against Heresies* 5.6.1, in *The Ante-Nicene Fathers*, ed. Alexander Roberts and James Donaldson (1885–1887, 10 vols.; repr., Peabody, MA: Hendrickson, 1994); see also Eusebius, *Ecclesiastical History* 5.7.6.

101. Irenaeus, *Against Heresies* 1.14–16.

102. See Pistis Sophia 4.142; Gospel of the Egyptians 44 and 66; Zostrianos 127.

103. *PGM* III. 560–85; IV. 945, 960, 1120–25; XII. 345–50. Aune thinks that the differences are more important than the similarities; see "Magic in Early Christianity."

104. Origen, *Against Celsus* 7.9. Note also Origen's sexualized portrayal of pagan prophecy in *Against Celsus* 7.3.

thority, the more hostile toward haphazard inspiration."[105] The silence itself, however, can variously be weighed. It may indicate that tongues was practiced rarely and by dissident groups. Or it may suggest that orthodox writers, suspicious of charismatic activity generally, ignored manifestations of popular religion that did not meet their increasingly high standards of rationality.[106]

In either case, our information comes mainly from the orthodox side, and at our present distance we can only observe that by the late fourth century John Chrysostom confesses himself at a loss interpreting the passage about tongues in 1 Corinthians. He can only guess that Paul was referring to foreign languages.[107] And in the fifth century, Augustine of Hippo dismisses the significance of tongues as a special dispensation of the primitive church, no longer of pertinence to the church in his day.[108] An experience of the Holy Spirit that in the end seemed as embarrassing as it was impressive, glossolalia began its long subterranean life, surfacing only now and then as a form of enthusiasm that inspired some and repelled as many others.[109]

---

105. Lewis, *Ecstatic Religion*, 34.

106. See Eusebius, *Ecclesiastical History* 5.17.2–4; Lewis, *Ecstatic Religion*, 132.

107. "This whole place is very obscure; but the obscurity is produced by our ignorance of the facts referred to and by their cessation, being such as used to occur but now no longer take place." John Chrysostom, *Homilies on First Corinthians* 29.32.35.

108. Augustine, *Homilies on First John* 6.10; see also *Baptism* 3.18.

109. It is a fascinating aspect of this history that the gender dimension analyzed by I. M. Lewis remains an important element; see the role of women in enthusiastic movements, described by Knox, *Enthusiasm*, 30, 55, 68, 162, 319.

Chapter 7

God Was in Christ

Second Corinthians 5:19 and Mythic Language

W ithout question, 2 Corinthians is the hardest of Paul's letters to read and understand. This is partly due to the complex character of its composition: even if we do not accept its segmentation into several fragments,[1] the *logos* rhetoric, especially in its arrangement, remains opaque.[2] Paul's extraordinarily dense language intertwines the specific circumstances of Paul and his readers with the work of God in Christ. Readers have always found it difficult to discern precisely where Paul speaks to the very human situation of alienation existing between him and the Corinthian church and the very concrete project of his collection for the saints in Jerusalem, on the one hand, and where he speaks of God's reconciliation of the world through Christ, on the other.

Two recent Emory dissertations (now published) have revealed just how intricate are those connections. In *The Character of Jesus: The Linchpin to Paul's Argument in 2 Corinthians*, Thomas Stegman analyzes the letter from the perspective of *ethos* argumentation and finds that Paul challenges his readers to display the same character as that shown by Jesus and, Paul is confident, found in himself as well. As Jesus showed obedient faith toward God in his human condition, so are Christians, filled with the power of the Spirit, to demonstrate the same disposition of obedient faith. Similarly, in *Snatched into Paradise (2 Cor 12:1–10): Paul's Heavenly Journey in the Context of Early Christian Experience*, James Buchanan Wallace shows how Paul's account of his ascent to heaven is continuous with the way he speaks elsewhere about both his own religious experi-

---

1. For representative positions, see H. Betz, *2 Corinthians 8 and 9*; Bates, "Integrity of II Corinthians 1"; DeSilva, "Measuring Penultimate against Ultimate Reality"; Furnish, *II Corinthians*, 30–48.
2. See, e.g., Witherington, *Conflict and Community in Corinth*.

ence and the experiences of God's power shared by his readers. These recent studies confirm the observation that in this letter Paul stretches the
capacity of language by the way in which he confidently merges rather
than distinguishes the realms of the human and the divine.

Indeed, the greatest difficulty in reading the Greek of 2 Corinthians is
due precisely to such interconnections of divine and human persons and
power; in this letter it is impossible to avoid the conclusion that Paul's
language about himself and his readers, God and Christ, is mythic. For the
purpose of this essay, I define *myth* as first-order statements, often but not
necessarily in the form of narrative, that place human and divine persons
in situations of mutual agency.[3] Because human agency is involved, such
statements can appear to be talking about the empirical world that we all
recognize. But because divine agency is also, perhaps primarily, involved,
such statements are also impervious to empirical verification.

I begin by affirming the thoroughly mythic character of the statement in
2 Cor 5:19. I then place this statement within its immediate literary context
of 2 Corinthians, with the specific interest in teasing out the connections
among experience, perception, and claim in Paul's argument. Next, I offer
by way of analogy some contemporary experience-based claims that both
resemble and differ from Paul's mythic language. In the process, I suggest
that the truth claims of mythic statements can in fact be tested—at least
in part—through assessment of the experience and of the symbolic world
within which they make sense. In all this, I write as someone who celebrates rather than deprecates mythic language, who is in fact convinced
that without such mythic language Christians—indeed all religious people—could not express what they consider most true about their lives.[4]

The Mythic Character of 2 Corinthians 5:19

My essay cannot give adequate attention to all the exegetical problems
that—characteristic for 2 Corinthians—this verse poses. But I can at least
indicate what they are.

3. The definition of myth is a classic battleground where several scholarly fields—
including classics, history, religion, philosophy, and anthropology—stake out positions. For a sample of discussions, see Sebeok, *Myth*; Murray, *Myth and Mythmaking*;
Kirk, *Myth*; Schremp and Hansen, *Myth*. Given the variety of definitions abroad, the
best bet is to make one's own definition and apply it consistently.

4. I have made this argument in a variety of places, including *The Real Jesus*, *Living
Jesus*, and *Writings of the New Testament*, 2nd ed.

The verse appears to repeat and expand the verse immediately preceding it: 5:18, *ta de panta ek tou theou tou katallaxantos hēmas heautō dia Christou kai dontos hēmin tēn diakonian tēs katallagēs* ("all things are from God who has reconciled us to himself through Christ and has given us the ministry of reconciliation"); in turn, 5:19, *hōs hoti theos ēn en Christō kosmon katallassōn heautō, mē logizomenos autois ta paraptōmata autōn kai themenos en hēmin ton logon tēs katallagēs*, which I translate as: "that is, God was in Christ reconciling a world to himself, by not reckoning against them their sins, and by placing among us the message of reconciliation." Despite their resemblance and interconnectedness, the clauses are not identical. In 5:18 God reconciled "us" and in 5:19 "a world"; in 5:18 such reconciliation is clearly through the instrumentality of Christ (*dia Christou*), whereas in 5:19 the *en Christō* is more ambiguous. The statement concerning the entrusting of reconciliation "to us" is in the first case a *diakonia* and in the second a *logos*. And the clause "by not reckoning against them their sins" in 5:19 expands (and presumably explicates) the process of reconciling "world" or "us."

The precise meaning and function of the connective *hōs hoti* in 5:19 is unclear. Most commentators agree that it does not, as in 2 Cor 11:21 or 2 Thess 2:2, suggest something not the case ("as though"),[5] but some think that it may bear some of the sense of those passages by referring to something written or at least traditional, so that Paul in the second clause appeals to what his readers have already been taught (Furnish paraphrases, "as it is said").[6]

Most difficult are the participles and prepositional phrases. Should *theos ēn en Christō katallassōn* be read as an imperfect, and the preposition as locative ("God was in Christ"), or should the prepositional phrase be read as instrumental, with the imperfect as part of a periphrastic participle, "was reconciling"? In the first instance, God appears to be "in Christ" at least analogously to the way someone is "in Christ" in 5:17;[7] in the second, "in Christ" simply provides a stylistic variation on *dia Christou* in 5:18. Also unclear is the precise syntactical function of the other participles that I have translated instrumentally: "by" not counting trespasses and "by" entrusting the message of reconciliation.[8]

5. 2 Cor 11:21 reads, *kata atimian legō, hōs hoti hēmeis ēsthenēkamen*; 2 Thess 2:2 has: *hōs hoti enestēken hē hēmera tou kyriou*.
6. See the discussion in Furnish, *II Corinthians*, 317–18.
7. "If anyone is in Christ, a new creation" (*ei tis en Christō, kainē ktisis*).
8. Furnish, *II Corinthians*, 306, for example, translates "not charging their trespasses to them" in flat apposition to "reconciling the world to himself," and makes

The main point I want to make about these interpretive difficulties, however, is that their resolution one way or another does not fundamentally alter the mythic character of both statements. Whether *theos* is "in Christ" in a locative (ontological) sense or achieves reconciliation "through Christ," God is still the subject of a narrative fragment concerning the past, and *kosmos* is an object of such generality as to be intrinsically nonverifiable. The same can be said of the designation "Christ": Paul's statement is set in the past tense (aorist and imperfect) and logically must refer to the historical figure Jesus of Nazareth, but the term *Christos*, like the instrumentality ascribed to him as the agent of God's action, lacks any historical specificity; it is unattached to any specific action, or even any specific character disposition. As for the verbs "reconciling" and "reckoning" and "giving/entrusting," they also are too broad and nonspecific to be placed within the realm of empirically verifiable history.

The most specific elements in the statements are the "we" and "they," who presumably stand for "world" and have been reconciled through the nonreckoning of their transgressions, and to whom the ministry or word concerning reconciliation has been entrusted. The statement "God through Christ was reconciling the world to himself" is just as mythic as "God was in Christ as he reconciled the world to himself"; it is a narrative fragment that speaks of God's agency within the realm of human activity.

Paul's Language in 2 Corinthians 5:1–21

The character of Paul's statements in the immediate context of 2 Cor 5:19 might help us begin to discern the distinctive combination of elements that constitute Paul's mythic language.

Some fourteen statements have humans as their subject and refer entirely to human actions and dispositions at the empirical plane, most of them in the first-person plural: "we are groaning" (5:2), "longing" (5:2), "burdened and groaning" (5:4), "bold" (5:6); "we walk by faith" (5:7); "we are ambitious to be pleasing" (5:9), "persuade" (5:11), "not commending ourselves" (5:12); "we are ecstatic" and "we are sober" (5:13); "we are ambassadors" (5:20); "we make appeal" (5:20); "we beg" (5:20). In addition

---

the second participle into a discrete statement, "and he has established among us the word of reconciliation."

to these "we" statements there is one in the first person, "I hope that" (5:12), and one in the third person, "those who boast in appearance" (5:12). In such statements, agency belongs to Paul, his associates, and his rivals, although Paul asserts that this activity is carried out "before God" (5:13).

Five other statements have quite a different character. In these, Paul's "we" is the recipient of action or disposition, and God or Christ is the agent. These statements place the empirical "we" in realms that are beyond the empirical. Thus we "have a building from God, a dwelling not made with hands, eternal in heaven" (5:1), "have been given the Spirit as a first installment" (5:5), "must all appear before the judgment seat of Christ" (5:10 RSV), are "in Christ a new creation" (5:17), are "reconciled to [God]" (5:18). Unlike the first set of statements, none of the referents here can be located in the arena of ordinary human exchange. They suppose an understanding of reality that includes more than what can be tested by the senses: a dwelling in heaven, a future judgment, a gift of the Spirit.

Perhaps most striking in this context is the presence of a set of statements that are explicitly cognitive in character. Again, the "we" that includes Paul and his associates is the subject. Thus, while Paul states in 5:7 that we walk by faith, not by knowledge, his other cognitive statements affirm the importance of a certain form of knowledge: we know that we have been given a heavenly dwelling (5:1); we know that when we are clothed with the body, we are away from the Lord (5:6); we know the fear of the Lord (5:11); and we have made the judgment (*krinantas*) that "one died for all; therefore all have died" (5:14). Most elaborate is 5:16: "Consequently, from now on we regard [know] no one according to the flesh; even if we once knew Christ according to the flesh, yet now we know him so no longer." By such statements Paul places human agency within a distinctive understanding of reality that belongs to those included in his "we."

The immediate context of 5:19 contains a large number of statements concerning nonempirical persons. The judgment seat before which we will stand is Christ's (5:10); Christ's love constrains us (5:14); in Christ is a new creation (5:17); reconciliation is through Christ (5:18); God is in Christ (5:19); for the sake of Christ we make appeal and beg (5:20); in him (*en autō*) we are made God's righteousness (5:21). In these statements, Christ is less an active agent and more a means or instrument or identifier. The partial exception is one statement in which Christ is the implied subject: "and he died in behalf of all, so that those who are living might no longer live for themselves but for the one who died and was raised for them" (5:15). In this declaration, which serves to explain the judgment made by Paul and his associates that "one died for all; therefore all have died" (5:14), Christ is the agent of dying, and God is the (implied) agency by which Christ was "raised up."

Finally, there are the statements in which agency is ascribed directly to *ho theos*. The heavenly dwelling is from God (*ek theou*, 5:1); God gave us the pledge that is the Holy Spirit (5:5); human actions and dispositions are "before God" (5:11, 13), and humans can be reconciled to God (5:20) and be God's righteousness (5:21); all things are from God (*ek tou theou*, 5:18); God was in Christ (5:19); God made Christ to be sin (5:21).

The Logic of Mythic Language

I think we can all agree that although Paul's language in 2 Cor 5 is mythical in the way I have defined, it is also unlike the sort of mythic narrative we associate with, say, Enuma Elish or Gen 6:1–4. Paul does not speak about figures of the distant past with heroic dimensions, but of his contemporaries and a man who died violently within the lifetime of Paul and his readers. Paul uses mythic language in order to express convictions concerning what is happening in the empirical realm that he shares with his readers.

The question arises, then, as to the logic of such language. On what is it based, and how does it make sense (we assume) to Paul and his readers?

We can approach these questions by means of analogy. There is a class of statements that take the form of an abbreviated narrative escaping any real empirical verification. Such statements are grounded in a historical reality but are not completely defined by it. Take, for example, a widow of one of the men who rushed the pilot's compartment of Flight 93 on 9/11 when the airplane had been taken over by terrorists, and who was killed with all aboard that flight when the plane crashed in a Pennsylvania field. She tells her son who never knew his father, "Your daddy was a great patriot. He died for his country."

There is, we observe, some historical basis for her declaration: her husband actually died in an effort to save lives—those who rushed the cockpit had learned of the terrorists' mission to use the plane as a weapon of destruction. To be sure, it is impossible to verify anything about her spouse's precise motivation or emotions at the critical moment. Perhaps he lingered reluctantly in the back of the group that rushed the cockpit. Perhaps he vomited in fear when the rush began. His widow's statement to her son does not rely, however, on the determination of such things.

It is instead based on her experience of and knowledge of her deceased husband: the kind of man she knew him to be.

Her judgment is based on something real beyond the brute fact of the historical event. She does not, however, simply aver that her husband was a good man. Her statement places his action within the symbolic framework of national identity, in which "patriotism" (from the time of Horace on) is most fully expressed by "dying for one's country."[9] This language elevates the sacrificial act of her husband by placing it in a more public and value-laden framework.

Take another example. An Irish-Catholic father reassures his children when his harried wife lashes out in frustration at them while cooking dinner, "Your mother is a saint. You know that she would do anything for you children." In this case, the wife's behavior is negative rather than positive: she shows irritation toward her family. Is the father's interpretation therefore false? Not necessarily. First, he invokes a frame of reference that both he and the children share: saints are those who show heroic love toward others. In the case of their mother, the husband reminds the children, her cooking supper is one among a multitude of ways that her love is in service to them; indeed, he suggests, there is no real limit to that love in practical terms—she would do anything for them. The issue of her momentary anger is subsumed by an appeal to the overall character of the mother demonstrated in repeated actions. The father also bases his statement on his privileged understanding of his wife's true character that he has learned through his constant experience of her.

Such homely examples are, to be sure, only analogies. These statements are not "mythic" in the sense of the definition I have given. There is a great distance between stating that a father dies for his country and stating that the Messiah died for all humans, so that all have died. Similarly, there is a great distance between claiming one's wife is a saint (of sorts) and claiming that God was in Christ. Nevertheless, the examples provide us a sense of how mythic language concerning the present has a definite logic.

It is based, first, on a speaker's personal experience of the one to whom larger-than-life status is ascribed on the ground of knowing of actions of that person that define his or her character. Second, it involves a judgment concerning that person's character as revealed by such action. Third, it involves a frame of reference, or symbolic structure, within which such ascription makes sense. In the case of Paul's statement in

---

9. "Dulce et decorum est pro patria mori" (Horace, *Odes* 3.2.13).

2 Cor 5:19, then, an experience commensurate with the judgment that "God was in Christ" would be required, a judgment concerning an action of Christ that reveals his character, and an understanding of the world within which such predication makes sense. The context for this statement in 2 Corinthians contains evidence for all three.

First, the experience: when Paul states in 2 Cor 5:5 that the one who works in him and his associates to prepare them for a heavenly habitation is the God who has given them the pledge that is the Holy Spirit, he echoes a statement that he made earlier in the letter: "God is the one who has secured us together with you into Christ [*eis Christon*] and has anointed [*chrisas*] us. And he has sealed us, and has given us the pledge that is the Holy Spirit in our hearts" (1:21–22). For Paul, the experience of the power of the Holy Spirit is the personal experience of God ("in our hearts") in and through Christ, the experience that "anoints" Paul and others, giving them a participation (pledge) in Christ's work (see other passages on the Spirit in 2 Cor 3:3–18; 4:13; 6:6; 11:4; 12:18). They have a "fellowship in the Holy Spirit" (13:13).

This experience of God's powerful Spirit through Christ, in turn, grounds the judgment that Paul shares with his readers concerning Jesus's apparently shameful death by execution—a negative historical fact. Paul and his associates have "reached the judgment" (*krinantas*) concerning Jesus's death, that it was a sacrifice in behalf of all, indeed an expression of love "for us" (5:14): "He died in behalf of all, so that those who are living might no longer live for themselves but for the sake of the one who died and was raised in their behalf" (5:15). We observe in this statement that not only Jesus's death but also his resurrection was for the sake of Paul and his readers. It is by Jesus's exaltation, Paul tells his readers in 1 Cor 15:45, that the *eschatos Adam* became "life-giving Spirit" (*to pneuma to zōopoioun*). Thus Paul says earlier in 2 Cor 4:14 that "we know that the one raising the Lord Jesus will raise us also together with him and place us with you in his presence."

We note also that Christ's death is interpreted in terms of an exchange: his life for all, so that all might live for him. Participation in the Spirit coming from Christ therefore means participation in the pattern of his existence, as Paul declares in 2 Cor 6:9, "We are as people dying, and behold, we live!" Even when they receive the sentence of death, they put their "trust in the God who raises the dead" (*tō theō tō egeironti tous nekrous*, 1:9). If Christ's death on the cross is experienced by others as life, and if his weakness is experienced by others as power, then the power of God is at work in such a fundamental way that the judgment "If anyone is in Christ, there is a new creation" (5:17) follows, and with it a cognitive reevaluation of everything that appears as empirically real: our real home is in heaven, not on earth (5:1–2); when we are in the body, we are away from our home (5:6); when we suffer and groan, it is because we long for heaven (5:2); and when God made Christ to be sin (through a death that was cursed by Torah), it was so that we might become "God's righteousness in him" (5:21).

The experience of the resurrection Spirit out of an empirical death demands the use of mythic language as the only possible means of expressing the truth, enables a restructuring of the symbolic world shared by all Jews, and impels a proclamation to the world of a new paradigm of power-in-weakness that is God's message of reconciliation.

Conclusion

My analysis has not made Paul's language any easier to understand. I hope that it has at least pointed to the importance of the resurrection experience—the conviction that the crucified Jesus has become exalted Lord and life-giving Spirit—in generating and making sense of Paul's mythic language. It may be worth asking whether readers who understand the resurrection of Jesus (even when they claim to believe in it) simply as a form of resuscitation, rather than Christ's exaltation to a participation in God's power, can ever adequately grasp Paul's language concerning the implications of that Spirit of life being given to others as a pledge.

For that matter, it is also worth asking whether those of us fundamentally shaped by Enlightenment epistemology can ever really appreciate the truth-telling capacity of myth. Without a phenomenology of Spirit that enables us to understand the capacity of bodies to transcend themselves and inhabit other bodies, we are not able to make sense of Paul's language about our being "in Christ" or God's being "in Christ" without reducing it to a weak form of moral allegiance or, worse, to pious nonsense. But to demythologize Paul's language in 2 Corinthians is to eliminate more than its poetry and power; it is to deny its claim to truth. The passage I have considered challenges contemporary readers to ask whether it is really myth speaking of unseen realities that deceives, or whether it is thought that remains only at the level of appearances that deceives.

Chapter 8

Truth and Reconciliation in 2 Corinthians

The Complexity of the Process

In the twenty-first century, the term "truth and reconciliation" is regularly associated with the word "commission" and refers to the political process set up in response to what is, or is perceived to be, the grievances of a population that has suffered under an oppressive regime.[1] The process involves those guilty of such oppression to confess to their wrongdoing before those they have oppressed (thus "the truth") as the necessary precondition for their continued participation—often enough after paying a penalty or "reparations"—in a newly constituted society. The process transposes to the secular realm of politics the ancient premises of the sacrament of penance: the honest acknowledgment of sins (even of the most grievous sort) to a priest, a genuine profession of contrition, the doing of a penance, and full reconciliation with the church.[2]

It is legitimate to debate whether the contemporary political process actually accomplishes the revelation of much truth, or whether it effects any lasting reconciliation. As with the sacrament of penance on a much smaller scale, it is possible to wonder whether the process can even serve as a cover for another sort of falsity. One set of oppressors may be replaced by another, with the "commission" functioning as one of the levers of their new power. Likewise, "going to confession" can, in a bizarre fashion, serve as a pious cover for continuing sin.

---

1. The paradigmatic case was South Africa's Truth and Reconciliation Commission, established in 1996 to address the abuses of human rights under apartheid. Canada likewise began a Truth and Reconciliation Commission in 2008 to heal the wounds inflicted on indigenous peoples. More than forty other nations (including Chile, Guatemala, Ecuador, Kenya, and Liberia) have established similar commissions. Their efforts at "restorative justice" in place of "retributive justice" have received both praise and criticism, and their success has been, at best, mixed.

2. See Tutu, *No Future without Forgiveness*; for a sober assessment, see Nussbaum, *Anger and Forgiveness*, esp. 211–46.

Still, the terms "truth" and "reconciliation" retain their capacity to compel our attention, even when their practical realizations have often enough proven to be disappointing. We persist in thinking that authentic reconciliation must have something to do with truth, and that truth must be a component in authentic reconciliation. Perhaps unconsciously, this has something to do with the lingering (and unconscious) influence of Paul's second letter to the Corinthians, wherein, as I hope to show, the truth is an essential element in reconciliation between persons. But in 2 Corinthians, both truth and reconciliation are more complex realities than seem to be assumed by contemporary political processes.[3]

Second Corinthians is rightly recognized as one of the most, if not the most, difficult of Paul's letters, not alone because of its diction and ideas, but because it does not seem to hold together as a single, logically developed composition, leading scholars to develop a variety of source theories that break one letter into several.[4] While fully recognizing the difficulties posed by the letter, I here assume that it is a single composition[5] and argue that its disparate parts serve as elements in a rhetoric that seeks reconciliation on the basis of truth.[6] Truth in relations human and divine, it turns out, is a complex and multifaceted thing, by no means reducible to the recital of facts.

I begin by sketching the rhetorical situation (as viewed by Paul) in terms of alienation between Paul and at least some members of the Corinthian church. I then discuss three aspects of truth in service of reconciliation: the truth of hurt and anger (2 Cor 10–12), the truth of God's call to reconciliation (2 Cor 1–7), and the truth of embodying reconciliation (2 Cor 8–9). I conclude with some reflections on how Paul's way of think-

3. The only example I have seen of a scholar making a similar contemporary connection to the one I am making is Brink, "From Wrongdoer to New Creation." One can add the recent efforts of Khobnya, "Reconciliation Must Prevail," and (on the collection) Andemicael, "Grace, Equity, Participation."

4. For arguments and theories, see, e.g., Furnish, *II Corinthians*; H. Betz, "2 Cor 6:14–7:1" and *2 Corinthians 8 and 9*; Bates, "Integrity of II Corinthians"; DeSilva, "Measuring Penultimate against Ultimate Reality"; Fitzgerald, "Paul, the Ancient Epistolary Theorists."

5. For examples of works that treat 2 Corinthians as a literary whole and make sense of its complex rhetoric, see Stegman, *Character of Jesus*; Vegge, *2 Corinthians*.

6. Among the many studies on 2 Corinthians under the general rubric of reconciliation, see Martin, *Reconciliation*, 90–110; Kim, "2 Cor. 5:11–21"; and several of the articles in Bieringer et al., *Theologizing in the Corinthian Conflict*; Bieringer, "Reconciliation with God." For an appendix that lists some thirty-five articles and monographs on the topic, see Fitzgerald, "Paul and Paradigm Shifts."

ing about truth and reconciliation may or may not have significance for thinking about contemporary political situations.

The Reality of Alienation

When Paul sets out to write 2 Corinthians, his position with regard to his beloved but restive community in Corinth is far from ideal.[7] Already in his first letter to them, he clearly regarded them as arrogant in their assumption that they could pick and choose among teachers, with their rivalrous party spirit threatening the unity and stability of the church.[8] Paul considered such dispositions signs of immaturity rather than maturity (1 Cor 3:3-4) and showed them how he and Apollos were collaborators rather than rivals (3:4-4:6). At the same time, he sought to assert his special authority to teach them as the "father" who had founded the community (4:15-16), and he sent his delegate Timothy to represent his teaching among them, while simultaneously threatening to visit them "with a stick" (NRSV) if necessary (4:17-21).[9]

The first order of practical business he takes up in that first letter is the distasteful and difficult excommunication of the member practicing (at least legal) incest while remaining within the community (1 Cor 5:1-13). The second order of business is rebuking them for settling disagreements about everyday matters in pagan courts rather than having them adjudicated by their own assembly (6:1-9). The third order of business is shaming those engaging in sexual immorality (6:10-20). The tone of these opening exercises in authority is preemptory. Paul seeks less to persuade than to command obedience. Given what the letter suggests about the temperament of the Corinthians, Paul's commands, despite his appeal to *koinōnia* (1:9), may well have stirred up as much resentment as respect.

Paul then turns to answer questions, which came to him by way of letter,[10] concerning marriage and virginity (1 Cor 7:1-40), eating meat

7. For works that deal with the character of the Corinthian community (in sociological and ideological terms) that are pertinent to 2 Corinthians, see Horrell, *Social Ethos*, esp. 199-235, where he posits 2 Cor 10 as preceding 2 Cor 1-9; Kloppenborg, "Greco-Roman *Thiasoi*"; Barrett, "Sectarian Diversity at Corinth."

8. See the classic study of Dahl, "Paul and the Church at Corinth," and esp. M. Mitchell, *Paul and the Rhetoric of Reconciliation.*

9. Unless otherwise indicated, Scripture quotations in this chapter are from the NABRE.

10. The letter undoubtably comes from those in the divided community who

offered to idols (8:1–13), participation in pagan worship (10:1–32), their inappropriate conduct in the exercise of women's prophetic gifts (11:3–16), the unworthy conduct in the celebration of the Lord's Supper (11:17–34), and their preference for spiritual gifts that establish their own position rather than build the church (12:1–14:40). After a lengthy exposition concerning the resurrection (15:1–58), whose moral as well as metaphysical point is that "we all must change" (15:51, author's translation),[11] Paul concludes with his own projects and plans (16:1–18), which very much involve them.

- He expects them to join the Galatian churches in incrementally contributing to the collection he is taking up "for the saints" (16:1–3);[12] when he comes to them from Ephesus, where he is now working (16:8), it will be by way of Macedonia (16:5), and he will write letters of recommendation for those they will send to Jerusalem with the gift, and possibly even join them (16:4).
- Although he professes that he wants to even "spend the winter" with them, he persists in staying in Ephesus until Pentecost. The situation in Ephesus is that Paul has had a "door of opportunity opened" (presumably for preaching); at the same time, "there are many opponents" (16:9).
- In the meantime, he is sending Timothy to them as his delegate and asks that they not disdain him (16:10). Rather oddly, Paul seems to expect them to send Timothy back to him "with the brothers." Who are "the brothers," anyway? We do not know, except that they are called "messengers of the churches" in 2 Cor 8:23 and play a role in the collection (9:3–5).
- Even more mysteriously, Paul states that Apollos—one of their favorite teachers (see 1 Cor 1–4)—has chosen not to visit them, despite Paul's declaration that "I urged him strongly to go to you with the brothers" (16:12).
- He exhorts them to respect and even be subordinate to those local householders/leaders who have financially supported the church (16:15–18).

---

regard Paul as a teacher from whom they wish to hear, and the sending of questions to him may have hardened the divisions; see Hurd, *Origin of I Corinthians*.

11. See Gillman, "Transformation in 1 Cor 15:50–53."

12. See Georgi, *Remembering the Poor*; Nickle, *The Collection*; and Downs, *Offering of the Gentiles*.

In brief, 1 Corinthians can be read (especially in hindsight) as a missive that was almost bound to create problems for Paul. In it, he combined the assertion of his authority,[13] severe rebukes of the Corinthians' behavior, and expectations for their participation in his personal projects, none of which are spelled out with any real clarity. Especially for readers who may have been as self-regarding and arrogant as Paul suggests, the combination could easily fail in its rhetorical goal of securing *koinōnia*. Paul clearly sought to unite the Corinthians, but he may have succeeded mainly in joining together at least some of them against himself.

Much of what transpired between the composition of 1 and 2 Corinthians, unfortunately, remains obscure to readers, like ourselves, who are left with only the two letters as evidence. As Paul writes 2 Corinthians, the delegate beside him is Timothy (see 2 Cor 1:1), whom the previous letter portrayed as having been sent to Corinth, and whom Paul had expected back, perhaps with other "brothers" (1 Cor 16:10–11). Timothy co-sponsors (and possibly aids in writing) the letter, and he may well be represented in the "we" used so frequently in this second letter (2 Cor 3:1–18; 4:1–18; 5:1–6:12; 7:2–3, 13; 8:1–2, 4–7). In terms of place, Paul now appears to be writing not from Ephesus but from Macedonia (2:13; 7:5).

The earlier travel plans stated in 1 Cor 16:1–5 have evidently been disrupted. Paul had stated there that he expected to come to the Corinthians through Macedonia, but now he declares that he had intended to go to Macedonia through Corinth, and then come back from Macedonia to them—a change in plans he must defend lest he be charged with deceit (2 Cor 1:15–21). His failure to come directly to Corinth, he now says, was to "spare" them (1:23). Yet Paul's movements remain opaque. He moved on to Macedonia from Troas, he says, because he could not find his delegate Titus in Troas (2:12–13); so, despite a "door being opened" for him in Troas, he moved on to Macedonia. At the time of this writing, however, Titus had arrived in Macedonia, bringing relief to Paul both by his presence and by the news he brought from Corinth (7:5–16).

Also unclear are the kinds of experiences Paul has had during his stay in Ephesus and travel to Macedonia. He speaks of affliction in Asia that made him despair of life itself but from which God had rescued him (2 Cor 1:8–10), and he speaks as well of his flesh having no rest when he came to Macedonia: "we were afflicted in every way—external conflicts,

13. For how this might be taken negatively, see the reading by Castelli, *Imitating Paul*.

internal fears" (7:5). Whatever the causes, the effects of such affliction deeply mark this letter.

Above all, Paul's contacts with the Corinthian community are hazy: how many (if any) visits did Paul make to Corinth after the writing of his first letter (see 2 Cor 1:23–2:1; 10:11–14)? He says in 2 Cor 13:1, "This third time I am coming to you," and speaks of "my second visit" in 13:2. It appears that whenever Paul came to them prior to this letter, the outcome was not positive: he appeared (by his own admission) as less powerful when among them than he did in his letters; he quotes them as saying, "His letters are severe and forceful, but his bodily presence is weak, and his speech contemptible" (10:10). But what letters did he write? He speaks of writing to them "out of much affliction and anguish of heart . . . with many tears" in a manner that caused pain (2:1–9). Later, he says, "Even if I saddened you by my letter, I do not regret it; and even if I did regret it, I see that it saddened you . . . unto repentance" (7:8–9), and he suggests that the letter was written "on account of the one who did wrong or was done wrong" (7:12, author's translations). To which letter does he refer? To 1 Corinthians? To the letter referred to in 1 Cor 5:9? To a part of the present 2 Corinthians (say, chaps. 10–12), if in fact 2 Corinthians is a composite of letters? Or to a letter that is lost completely?

In all this confusion, however, two things are starkly clear. The first is that Paul is continuing his project of gathering funds from gentile communities to be brought to the church in Jerusalem, a collection that for him is not simply in relief of the impoverished but also symbolizes the *koinōnia* between Jews and gentiles in Christ (see Gal 2:10 and esp. Rom 15:25–29). The collection is so important to him that he has spent considerable time and effort in bringing it to conclusion. In 2 Cor 8–9 Paul urges the Corinthians to meet their commitment to this cause, and his embarrassment at the fact that they are resisting is palpable: how can his most impressively gifted gentile church turn its back on this effort, especially when he has used their pledge as leverage to convince other churches to contribute (8:10–12; 9:2–6)? The Corinthians are on the verge of bringing public shame on Paul because, at the very moment he seeks to accomplish a cosmic act of fellowship, they seem not to be interested in fellowship with him. And this is the second aspect of 2 Corinthians that stands out—namely, the state of alienation between Paul and at least some members of the apostle's signature community.

The precise causes of the estrangement are complex and seem incapable of complete disentanglement, but three elements appear to be involved and interconnected. The first is the resentment of some in the

Corinthian church at Paul's behavior toward them: when he speaks of a painful visit and of a letter that caused hurt to a church member, and when he quotes the Corinthians to the effect that he is strong in his letters and weak when among them, we get the sense that Paul's efforts to lead the church at a distance, or correct it at close hand, have not been appreciated, resulting in a loss of respect for his apostolic authority.

The second cause is the Corinthians' suspicion concerning Paul's financial dealings. In his first letter to them, he made the bold claim that the preached among them for free, even though he could have demanded pay from them (1 Cor 9:1–27). Indeed, even in this letter, he contrasts himself to "peddlers of the word," who presumably take their money for preaching up front (2 Cor 2:17). They are transparent. But it turns out that when Paul was among them, he did not in fact need their money, since he was being supported by the Macedonian church at Philippi (see Phil 4:10–20; 2 Cor 11:8–10). Now he has asked them to contribute much larger sums of money (week by week) for a collection that he is purportedly taking up for people in a land far away (1 Cor 16:1–4). Can he be trusted? Their suspicion is deepened, apparently, by Paul's sending his delegate Titus to pick up the money when he had told them he would come himself (2 Cor 12:16–18).

The third cause is the Corinthians' growing fascination with and allegiance to other teachers, those whom Paul calls "super-apostles," who are, evidently, more impressive in their self-presentation than Paul and, at least in the eyes of the Corinthians, more honest and straightforward in their financial dealings (2 Cor 10:12–11:6).

Whether we read 2 Corinthians as a single literary composition (as I do), or as an edited series of notes, the fact of alienation and Paul's desire to effect reconciliation with the Corinthian community draws us to the heart of his effort. It is therefore worthwhile to focus on the aspects of truth that can be discovered within Paul's rhetoric of reconciliation.

The Emotional Truth of Hurt and Anger

People truly grow apart from each other and even reach a state of enmity because of perceived hurt and the consequent anger stimulated by that perceived hurt. The hurt is magnified and the anger turns to a chronic resentment when the fault remains unacknowledged or, worse, when subsequent behavior continues along the lines of what gave offense in the first place. In human relationships, to be sure, perceptions of injury and responses of anger generally go both ways: faults can easily be ascribed to either party, and the cataloging of the respective faults is a favorite tactic in family quarrels that have too long been delayed and therefore have grown far huger than their original causes. If hurt and anger so regularly occur between those of (presumed) equal status as siblings, how much more can they break out between those in authority and those whom they command?

The difficulty facing Paul when he composes 2 Corinthians is suggested by the convoluted character of the letter. Here, Paul does not lay out in orderly fashion a *logos* argument concerning God's righteousness, as he can do for a Roman church whose members he has not yet met and cannot possibly have offended. Nor does he celebrate the constant ties of affection and fellowship he has enjoyed with the Philippians, who from the start have supported his ministry even in other cities. Paul struggles in this letter at once to win back the support of his signature community and to gain their continued cooperation in completing the project of the collection. Second Corinthians is dominated by *ethos* arguments (appeals to character) and *pathos* arguments (involving feelings).

The first element of truth-telling in Paul's search for reconciliation is therefore the recognition of the emotional hurt that has been done and the emotional anger it has aroused. This is not simply truth at the cognitive level. It is above all an *emotional* dimension of truth. One of the most striking aspects of 2 Corinthians, even among the Pauline letters—matched only partially in this respect by Galatians—is the degree and intensity of such emotional recognition. Paul acknowledges the ways he has hurt and angered his readers—at least as far as he understands them—and, while also defensive, is unusually transparent concerning the hurt that he has experienced from them, and he expresses appropriate anger in response.

The catalog of the injuries Paul has done against members of the community is long and appears, sometimes indirectly, throughout the letter. By "indirectly" I mean that we must infer the charge that lies behind Paul's defensive responses, as well as the real hurt that lies behind apparently trivial matters. When Paul asks in 2 Cor 1:17 whether his change in travel plans makes him an unreliable person (someone who is both "yes" and "no"), for example, it is clear that his *character* and not merely his actions are at issue. Thus, the question of Paul's reliability, sincerity, or deceit repeatedly appears (2:17; 4:2; 6:8), with the implication that he (and his delegate Titus) have wronged the Corinthians, or ruined them, or taken advantage of them (7:2) especially in the handling of the collection (8:20). He and Titus got the better of them by deceit (12:17–18). By not telling them the whole truth about his support from the beginning, he has, in effect, sailed under false colors and deceived them from the start. Why should they trust him with their money now?

But Paul is more than inconsistent or unreliable. He has actually given pain by his behavior when visiting them (2 Cor 2:2, 4), and by his letters, which have saddened them (7:8–10, 12) and frightened them (10:9). He has caused some to stumble (6:3). More subtly, and perhaps contradictorily, they perceive Paul as ineffectual: he appears to be commending himself (3:1; 5:12; 6:4), thereby "acting according to the flesh" (10:2) in his boasting (10:8, 13); he seeks to "lord it over" their faith (1:24). Yet, when he shows up, he is not strong as he pretends to be in his letters; he shows himself to be physically weak and rhetorically insignificant (10:10; 11:6). Perhaps he is even crazy (5:13).

Such is the list of the Corinthians' complaints against the apostle, as they have been reported to him by Titus or others. Perhaps more precisely, this is the list as Paul understands it. And if Paul were a politician of the present day dealing with his constituents, "reconciliation" would necessarily begin with a ritualized "recognition" and "apology" (meaning, in the contemporary sense, a statement of regret).

But things are not so simple as the media-driven and media-defined social interactions of today would make them appear. Even if the Corinthians' charges are accurate at the level of fact, they may not be true at the level of intention or motivation. Paul may indeed have unexpectedly changed his plans, but the conclusion that he has an unreliable character is not a necessary inference from that fact. His motivations may have been positive, or they may have had nothing to do with his disposition toward the Corinthians, much less been a deliberate slight of them. The same might apply to the collection: Paul's "misspeaking" on the matter of his personal support in 1 Cor 9 (as we would put it in our present jargon)—that is, his stressing one side of the truth (his not burdening the Corinthians for his support) while leaving out the other side (the Philippians were sending him money)—does not amount to a full-scale scheme to defraud the Corinthians by means of the collection. Even if Paul were abjectly to acknowledge his every failing toward them, in short, the really hurtful thing is the way in which his character itself has been called into question.

Paul therefore also has a catalog of injury. It is essential to note here that, from Paul's perspective, there is a fundamental and unavoidable asymmetry in the *koinōnia* that the Corinthians and he have in Christ

(1 Cor 1:8). They exist as an *ekklēsia theou* (1 Cor 1:1) only because of Paul. He is the apostle who came to them in the first place "in weakness and fear and much trembling" with the message concerning a crucified messiah, not with "persuasive words of wisdom" but with a "demonstration of spirit and power" (1 Cor 2:3–5).

Through his work and that of Apollos, "everything belongs to you. Paul or Apollos or Cephas, or the world or life or death, or the present or the future: all belong to you, and you to Christ, and Christ to God" (1 Cor 3:21–23). But Paul begins that remarkable assurance in his first letter to them by admonishing them, "Let no one boast about human beings" (3:21). Already there, he reminds them not to make comparisons between leaders on the basis of their own sense of self-importance: "Who confers distinction upon you? What do you possess that you have not received? But if you have received it, why are you boasting as if you did not receive it?" (4:7).

Because he is the founder of the community, however, the one who laid the foundation of Christ among them and who planted them as God's field (1 Cor 3:6–17), they should regard Paul as having a special paternal role over them: he is the father, whose particular role is to protect, support, nurture, and correct them (4:6–17). In plain fact, Paul and the Corinthians are not on the same plane. He has *exousia* (authority) as an apostle who has seen the Lord Jesus (9:1), and they owe their very existence as church to him.

Paul therefore has his own list of hurts, shorter in length but equal in emotional weight. He is clearly offended first by the Corinthians' misunderstanding of him: they mistake his lack of rhetoric for a lack of knowledge, his physical weakness as a deficiency in authority, his care not to burden them (2 Cor 11:9) as fraudulent deceit. Second, Paul thinks that they have abandoned him by failing to participate in the collection as they had promised they would (8:6–7, 11; 9:3–4), thereby exposing him to shame before his other communities (9:4; 10:8). Third, they have allowed themselves to be deceived by "super-apostles" whose credentials appear superior to Paul's (with letters of commendation, rhetorical skill, wonder-working power, and a record of suffering for Christ), thereby putting Paul into a shameful position of having to compete for their allegiance (3:1–5; 5:12; 10:12), a practice he detests and has warned them against demanding in his first letter to them (1 Cor 3:1–12).

These are scarcely minor matters, for by abandoning Paul in favor of other teachers, they are turning their backs on their own experience of God's power. It is through Paul, after all, that "the signs of an apostle were performed among you with all endurance, signs and wonders, and mighty deeds" (2 Cor 12:12; see 1 Cor 2:4: "with a demonstration of spirit and power"). Paul ought to need no other recommendation than themselves: "You are our letter, written on our hearts, known and read by all, shown to be a letter of Christ administered by us, written not in ink but by the Spirit of the living God, not on tablets of stone but on tablets that are hearts of flesh" (2 Cor 3:2–3).

This, indeed, is the final and greatest hurt: rather than criticize and disparage Paul, they ought above all to be his loyal defenders: "I ought to have been commended by you" (2 Cor 12:11). By forcing Paul into a passionate (and angry) defense of himself and his apostleship—by forcing him to boast of himself in such an extravagant fashion as we see in 10:1–12:21—they have only increased his sense of shame by making him appear as a foolish suitor (11:1–3, 16; 12:6, 11).

That Paul's response to the Corinthians in this letter contains expressions of anger cannot be doubted. Anger, indeed, is another essential element in the "truth" of alienation. Anger is generated by perceived hurt; perception of a great hurt can stimulate great anger. As a biological/ psychological response to challenge or threat, anger is both natural and necessary to survival. The expression of anger, however, can vary greatly in appropriateness. The attempt to deny or suppress anger, for example, can lead to surreptitious, indirect, and toxic modes of hostility that are all the more lethal because they remain covert. We think of passive aggression, defensiveness, slighting, teasing, taunting, and—on a much higher scale—the setting of psychic and physical traps; these are all forms of "lashing back."[14] Healthy expressions of anger, in contrast, are proportionate to the perceived injury or challenge, are expressed verbally rather than physically, are direct rather than indirect, and seek to clear the air rather than annihilate the other. And the healthy expression of anger in response to hurt can be of great service in the task of reconciliation.

It is possible to see some of Paul's statements as defensive expressions of anger, such as when he complains that they prefer outward appearances (2 Cor 5:12), or insists that he and his colleagues "caused no one to stumble, and no fault can be found in our ministry" (6:3), or declares that "you are not constrained by us but by your own affections" (6:12), and insists that he and his team have "wronged no one, ruined no one, taken advantage of no one" (7:2, author's translations). Other statements indirectly reveal anger by the way in which Paul denies the Corinthian complaints by reframing or reinterpreting their charges. He did not come

14. For a helpful analysis of such pathologies, see Rubin, *Angry Book*.

to Corinth as planned so as to "spare [them]" (1:23); his team are "not like many who are peddlers of the word of God" (2:17, author's translation). Rather, "we have renounced shameful, hidden things; not acting deceitfully or falsifying the word of God" (4:2); they work openly before God's gaze (5:11), and they have always spoken the truth (7:14). The painful letter he wrote them was not intended to cause pain but was so that they "might know the abundant love" he has for them (2:4); it was intended in fact to "test [them]" (2:9). Everything Paul does is for them (4:15). Even though the letter saddened them, it was a sadness unto repentance, and stimulated their concern for Paul (7:12). In the matter of the collection, he did not burden them out of love for them (11:9–11). They may think that they have been testing Paul and his character, but in fact he has been testing them and the character of their obedient faith (12:19–13:9).

Paul's overt expression of anger—which makes him appear weak and vulnerable, or, as he says, "foolish"—appears most vividly in 2 Cor 10–11. Here, Paul does not explain or reinterpret his own actions. Instead, he countercharges. He is not weak and powerless; rather, he is one who does battle against cosmic forces, destroying arguments (10:1–5) and punishing the disobedient (10:6). If such is their wish, he will be powerful in their presence (10:11). Paul declares himself to be as jealous of them as a husband whose wife is being deceived, as Eve was by Satan (11:3). The Corinthians put up with falsity (11:4) and mistake humility for weakness. They are impressed by those who camouflage themselves as apostles of Christ the same way Satan masquerades as an angel of light (11:13–15). The Corinthians "put up with" a charlatan who proclaims a different Jesus, Spirit, and gospel than those taught them by Paul (11:4), and who thereby "enslaves you, or devours you, or gets the better of you, or puts on airs, or slaps you in the face" (11:20)! Paul says, ironically, "To my shame I say that we were too weak" to commit such outrages against the Corinthian community (11:21).

One can almost feel Paul's anger as he enters, to his chagrin, a point-by-point comparison with the false apostles, on their chosen ground (2 Cor 11:23–32):[15] his Jewish pedigree is, if anything, superior to theirs, and, as his catalog of sufferings demonstrates, he has shown himself many times over a servant of Christ.[16] It is noteworthy that Paul adds to the

15. For efforts to identify Paul's actual rivals, see Georgi, *Opponents of Paul*; Kolenkow, "Paul and His Opponents"; Barrett, "Paul's Opponents in Corinth"; Sampley, "Paul and His Opponents"; Sumney, *Identifying Paul's Opponents*. For the question of Paul's "opponents" generally, see vol. 1, chap. 4.

16. See esp. Fitzgerald, *Cracks in an Earthen Vessel*; O'Collins, "Power Made Perfect in Weakness."

list of afflictions "the daily pressure upon me of my anxiety *for all the churches*," a reminder to the Corinthians of the trouble they cause Paul, of the reality that they are only a small part of Paul's pastoral responsibility, and of the higher vision to which he wants to elevate them. In all of this boasting,[17] which Paul regards as foolishness and therefore as a form of weakness, Paul's anger at the Corinthians as well as at the false apostles is manifest: "I have been foolish. You compelled me, for I ought to have been commended by you" (12:11).

Paul's climactic boast concerns his experience of being snatched into the third heaven and hearing things of which no one may speak (2 Cor 12:1–5), but he follows this allusive account with the report that to keep him from being too elated, he was penetrated by a stake in the flesh and, when he begged for relief, was told by the Lord, "My gift is sufficient for you, for power is made perfect in weakness" (12:7–9, author's translation). By this point, Paul's overt anger is spent, and he concludes, "I will rather boast most gladly in my weaknesses, in order that the power of Christ may dwell with me. Therefore, I am content with weaknesses, insults, hardships, persecutions, and constraints, for the sake of Christ; for when I am weak, then I am strong" (12:9–10).[18]

By this final statement, Paul pushes us back into the earlier part of the letter, in which weakness and strength, death and life, are central to his argument concerning human reconciliation with God.[19] But he also reminds us that the self-revelation of emotional hurt and anger is a "weakness" that plays a real and important role in human reconciliation. It is a foolishness that is actually wise when we seek to restore relations, for even as such naked exposure makes us vulnerable to others, it also invites them to greater intimacy with us. Human alienation can be overcome only if someone moves. In most cases, those who are truly weak are in fact unable to move—that is, to reach across the divide of hostility. In most cases, the ones who are genuinely strong are obliged to move, precisely because they have the strength to do so, and as in the case of Paul, by making themselves, for the sake of the other, "weak." As Paul declares toward the end of the letter, "We rejoice when we are weak but you are strong. What

---

17. See Pawlak, "Consistency Isn't Everything."

18. See Wallace, *Snatched into Paradise*. For a fascinating *Auseinandersetzung* on this section of the letter, see Andrews, "Too Weak Not to Lead," and the devastating reply by Lambrecht, "Strength in Weakness."

19. Especially helpful is Kraftchick, "Death in Us, Life in You."

we pray for is your improvement" (2 Cor 13:9). This pattern of strength becoming weakness for the sake of making others strong, as we shall see, is at the theological heart of Paul's understanding of reconciliation.

The Roots of Reconciliation

As important as emotional truth is, the mutual expression of anger and the mutual recognition of hurt will not by themselves achieve authentic reconciliation. By themselves, such "truths" might actually exacerbate a state of alienation. Reconciliation requires a positive appeal to a prior and profound commonality that is sufficiently strong to have survived the strains of separation.

In the case of estranged families, this may mean the affirmation of ancestors or the good memories of past sharing. In the case of divided nations, it may mean the invocation of earlier covenants and constitutional loyalties. In the case of Paul and the Corinthians, it requires an awareness that the bond of fellowship among them involves more than mutual affection. From the first, their *koinōnia* has been rooted in the presence and power of God at work among them (1 Cor 1:8).

Thus, in 2 Corinthians, Paul mentions in short asides how he and the Corinthians remain bound by positive dispositions: prayer (1:11), joy (7:13), love (2:8), grace (4:15; 6:1), concern (7:12); through all of these, Paul and the Corinthians receive and give encouragement (2:7; 7:7, 11, 13). More importantly, however, Paul and the Corinthian believers are bonded by a shared commitment to, and relationship with, the God revealed through Jesus Christ. Paul regards reconciliation in vertical more than horizontal terms. Paul and the Corinthians must be rightly aligned not only with each other—as though they were simply friends—but above all with the living God, who, through Christ, brought into being and enabled both Paul's apostleship and their very existence as a community. This realization helps us understand the rhetorical function of two passages whose purpose might otherwise seem obscure.

The first is the seemingly intrusive passage in 2 Cor 6:14–7:1, which appears to be inserted between exhortations from Paul to receive him as openly as he receives them, and seems to introduce a minatory note within an otherwise encouraging appeal.[20] But if we understand it as Paul

20. For efforts to make sense of the passage as authentically Pauline, see Dahl,

seeking to turn them from their fascination with teachers they regard as "super-apostles," but whom Paul regards as agents of Satan camouflaging as angels of light (see 11:3–15), the passage functions as a summons to renew their commitment to the one true God: they need to make, and keep, a choice for the God who has chosen them:

> Do not be yoked with those who are different, with unbelievers.[21] For what partnership [*metochē*] do righteousness and lawlessness have? Or what fellowship [*koinōnia*] does light have with darkness? What accord [*symphōnēsis*] has Christ with Beliar? Or what has a believer in common [*meris*] with an unbeliever? What agreement [*synkatathesis*] has the temple of God with idols?[22] For we are the temple of the living God,[23] as God said, "I will dwell and move among them, and I will be their God and they shall be my people. Therefore, come out from them and be separate, says the Lord, and touch nothing unclean; then I will receive you and be a father to you, and you shall be sons and daughters to me, says the Lord almighty."[24] Since we have these promises, beloved, let us cleanse ourselves from every defilement of flesh and spirit, making holiness perfect in the fear of God. (Adapted)

Reconciliation with Paul's apostolic team, in other words, demands of the Corinthians that they emphatically distance themselves from those who proclaim another good news, another Jesus, another Holy Spirit (11:4). Fellowship with the followers of the living God means separating from the allure of idolatry, even in its most subtly camouflaged forms.

The second significant passage in this connection is the thanksgiving (2 Cor 1:3–7)—or, better, blessing formula—with which Paul opens his letter immediately after the greeting:

"A Fragment and Its Context"; Beale, "Old Testament Background"; Rabens, "Paul's Rhetoric of Demarcation"; Nathan, "Fragmented Theology in 2 Corinthians."

21. The Greek is literally "do not be 'other-yoked' with unbelievers" (*me ginesthe heterozygountes apistois*).

22. Paul has lined up all the synonyms for "fellowship" and "agreement" that come readily to mind.

23. When Paul says, *hemeis gar naos theou esmen zōntos*, he clearly echoes the ecclesial definition he used in 1 Cor 3:16: *ouk oidate hoti naos theou este?*

24. A thoroughly mixed citation from Scripture that has elements from Lev 26:11–12; Ezek 37:27; Isa 52:11; Ezek 20:34; 2 Sam 7:14; and Isa 43:6.

Blessed be the God and Father of our Lord Jesus Christ, the Father of compassion [*oiktirmōn*] and God of all encouragement [*paraklēseōs*], who encourages us [*parakalōn hēmas*] in our every affliction [*thlipsei*], so that we may be able to encourage [*parakalein*] those who are in any affliction [*thlipsei*] with the encouragement [*dia tēs paraklēseōs*] with which we ourselves are encouraged by God [*parakaloumetha autoi hypo tou theou*]. For as Christ's sufferings overflow to us [*ta pathēmata tou Christou*], so through Christ does our encouragement [*hē paraklēsis hemōn*] also overflow. If we are afflicted [*thlibometha*], it is for your encouragement and salvation [*paraklēseōs kai sōterias*]; if we are encouraged [*parakaloumetha*], it is for your encouragement [*hymōn paraklēseōs*], which enables you to endure the same sufferings [*pathēmatōn*] that we suffer [*paschomen*]. Our hope for you is firm, for we know that as you share in the sufferings [*pathēmatōn*], you also share in the encouragement [*paraklēseōs*].

By this opening statement, Paul establishes three fundamental points, all the more rhetorically effective because made in the form of prayer.[25] The first is the extraordinarily positive note that he strikes with his readers; in the midst of affliction and suffering, he emphasizes not division or hostility but fellowship and comfort. Second, the blessing reminds his readers that he and the Corinthians are related to each other above all by their shared relationship to God, which is enabled by Jesus Christ; we remember 1 Cor 1:9 ("you were called to fellowship [*koinōnia*] with his Son, Jesus Christ our Lord"). Thus, the vertical dimension of reconciliation. The third point is that their fellowship is one of reciprocal suffering and comfort—their lives are not simply about themselves but about each other.[26]

Paul here introduces the central theological conviction of this letter: that the pattern of self-emptying for the sake of others revealed by the ministry of Christ (above all in his death on the cross) not only reveals how God's weakness serves to empower humans but also sets the manner

25. For the rhetorical function of Paul's opening prayers, see above all Schubert, *Form and Function*, and O'Brien, *Introductory Thanksgivings*.

26. Note the two uses of "empower": God encourages Paul and his associates in their affliction *so that they can empower* them to encourage those in every affliction (2 Cor 1:4), and the encouragement of Paul and his associates is for the sake of their encouragement *that is empowered* in the endurance of the same sufferings. Their life before God is not only linked; it is mutually influential.

of the ministry of reconciliation practiced by Paul's company.[27] In 2 Corinthians, Paul elaborates and extends his understanding of the cruciform pattern of Christian existence found already in 1 Corinthians (1:17–2:5; 3:18–23; 4:9–12; 8:11–12).[28]

The paradigm of the cross and resurrection, which is, as Paul understands it, the paradigm of death for others leading to the empowerment of others, is stated most directly at the end of 2 Corinthians, but it forms the premise for his argument throughout: "[Christ] is not weak toward you but powerful in you. For indeed he was crucified out of weakness, but he lives by the power of God. So also we are weak in him, but toward you we shall live with him by the power of God" (13:3–4). In this remarkable statement, Paul links death and life, weakness and strength, and maps these exchanges on the relationship between God-in-Christ, Paul, and the Corinthians.

Similar is the statement of exchange in 2 Cor 5:21, which uses forensic language: "For our sake he made him to be sin [*hamartia*] who did not know sin, so that we might become the righteousness of God [*dikaiosynē theou*] in him."[29] To heal the rift between God and humans caused by human sin (and weakness), God put Jesus in the position of sin and weakness (through his cursed death; see Deut 21:23; Gal 3:13), so that through his exaltation in power humans might be put in right relationship (*dikaiosynē*) with God.

The stronger one had to move, since the weaker party could not. The living God had to occupy the place of the weak in order to make the weak stronger. It is possible to read 2 Cor 1:17–20 as a variation of the same pattern, this time with an emphasis on the character of Jesus's human faith: because Jesus was not "yes and no" but all the promises of God found their "yes" in him, humans are able to also say "yes" to God in faith (see 4:12–13): "therefore, the Amen from us also goes through him to God for glory."[30]

Paul's perception of the Corinthians and his ministry to them is therefore marked by deep paradox. In fact, he sees them as full of the power given by the Holy Spirit that comes through Jesus's resurrection and exaltation. They are a letter written by the Holy Spirit on the hearts. They

27. See, e.g., Wedderburn, "2 Corinthians 5:14."

28. See Ibita, "Mending a Broken Relationship." See also A. Harvey, *Renewal through Suffering.*

29. Among many others, see Porter, "Reconciliation"; Moore, "2 Cor 5:21"; Wright, "On Becoming."

30. Stegman, *Character of Jesus.*

should be Paul's letter of recommendation as an apostle (2 Cor 3:1–6); among them were worked "signs and wonders, and mighty deeds" (12:12). As he noted in his first letter, they were richly endowed with every sort of gift (1 Cor 1:5). Yet this power has led them to a kind of arrogance, a false sense of strength and wisdom, an inflated sense of themselves that presumes to pick favorites among God's emissaries.[31] They see themselves as strong and Paul as weak, themselves as wise and Paul as foolish (1 Cor 1:10–2:16; 4:6–13). They have forgotten that all that they have has come as gift (1 Cor 4:7) from the despised, weak, and foolish apostleship of Paul. More important, they forget that the source of the Spirit that empowers them is the crucified one who gave himself that they might live.

Reminding them of this "truth" as the real root of reconciliation is the goal of Paul's rhetoric especially in chapters 1–7 of 2 Corinthians. First is the fact that they live in God's power and are rightly related to God because of God's Son saying yes to all God's promises, undergoing the shame of the cross, and becoming sin, all for their sake. Out of God making himself weak, humans are given strength: "God was reconciling the world to himself in Christ, not counting their trespasses against them" (2 Cor 5:19).[32] But Paul continues, "So we are ambassadors for Christ, as if God were appealing through us. We implore you on behalf of Christ, be reconciled to God" (5:20). Second, then, is that Paul and his colleagues continue the reconciling ministry of Christ through—and this is most important—continuing the same pattern of "life for others." As he declares in 5:14, "For the love of Christ impels us, once we have come to the conviction that one died for all . . . so that those who live might no longer live for themselves but for him who *for their sake* died and was raised."

What Paul needs to work hardest at convincing his readers, however, is that the pattern of human reconciliation—indeed all of Christian life—ought to follow the pattern displayed by God in the weakness, sin, and foolishness of the cross of Christ. "Life for others" demands not overt displays of power but the willingness to be exposed and vulnerable, "foolish" and "sinful" and "weak" in the eyes of others, especially those more impressed by human reputation than by divine commendation. In some sense, all of the rhetoric Paul has deployed has worked toward this goal. He has been willing to reveal his sense of hurt, has expressed his anger, has worked to remind the Corinthians of the bonds of fellowship in Christ.

31. Note the strategic use of *physioun* in 1 Cor 4:6, 18, 19; 5:2; and 6:1, a disposition to which Paul explicitly contrasts *agapē* in 1 Cor 13:4.
32. See chap. 7 in this volume.

But the most impressive statement of how he perceives the ministry that he carries forward with his colleagues is found in 2 Cor 4:5–11, which deserves quoting in full. After declaring that the good news concerns "the glory of Christ, who is the image of God" (4:4), he continues:

> For we do not preach ourselves but Jesus Christ as Lord, and ourselves as your slaves for the sake of Jesus. For God who said, "Let light shine out of darkness," has shone in our hearts to bring to light the knowledge of the glory of God on the face of Christ. But we hold this treasure in earthen vessels, that the surpassing power may be of God and not from us. We are afflicted in every way, but not constrained; perplexed, but not driven to despair; persecuted, but not abandoned; struck down, but not destroyed; always carrying about in the body the dying of Jesus, so that the life of Jesus may also be manifested in our body. For we who live are constantly being given up to death for the sake of Jesus, so that the life of Jesus may be manifested in our mortal flesh.[33]

The body that was crucified, with all its attendant foolishness and shame, was the medium through which God brought about reconciliation with humans. The bodies of Paul and his associates likewise carry out the ministry of reconciliation through a weakness that empowers the Corinthians.

Reconciliation demands more than positive dispositions or verbal formulas; it must ultimately be expressed through the body. Paul wants the Corinthians to show their fellowship with Paul and the Lord by fulfilling their pledge concerning the collection of money for the saints, which will ultimately be to their benefit: "Everything indeed is for you, so that the grace [or "gift"] bestowed in abundance on more and more people may cause the thanksgiving to overflow for the glory of God" (2 Cor 4:15).

The Body Language of Reconciliation

Paul's language concerning the *koinōnia* between himself and the Corinthians, and their shared *koinōnia* with the Lord, has specific connotations within the symbolic world of ancient Greco-Roman culture. From at least the time of Aristotle, *koinōnia* was regarded as equivalent to *philia* (friendship). The saying had it, "friends hold all things in common" (*tois philois*

---

33. See esp. Fitzgerald, *Cracks in an Earthen Vessel.*

panta koina).[34] Certainly, friends shared values and dispositions: they were "one soul" (*mia psychē*). But they also shared all their material possessions: "what is mine is thine and what is thine is mine" in the manner of brothers who share freely in each other's goods.[35] When Luke describes the "one mind and heart" among the first believers in Jerusalem, he uses the trope concerning friendship: "no one claimed that any of his possessions was his own, but they had everything in common" (Acts 4:32).[36] And we have seen in 1 Cor 9 that Paul assumed the same logic of material reciprocity for the spiritual goods he shared with the Corinthians, even though he eschewed making use of his right in that regard (9:1–3). Aristotle used the term "equality" (*isotēs*) for the sort of sharing that had elements of dispro-portion:[37] a teacher may contribute spiritual goods, whereas the student shows fellowship by giving the teacher material support (see Gal 6:6).

We have seen how the Corinthians' suspicions concerning the way Paul and his delegates were managing the collection was a major factor in their alienation from him. For this very reason, their rejoining the effort can also signify their full reconciliation. Once more, we observe how "truth and reconciliation" involves more than a balancing of the books, or even a recognition of the deep bonds of the past that still endure. It means being pulled upward together by some higher purpose in the present.[38]

Paul's appeal to the Corinthians in 2 Cor 8–9—whether they are sep-arate notes or not—offers his readers just such an opportunity. They can seal their reconciliation with the Pauline mission by joining wholeheart-edly in his larger effort at reconciling the gentile mission with the Jewish mother church in Jerusalem. Paul and the Corinthians can make their *koinōnia* more actual and powerful by their shared labor to secure the *koinōnia* among all the churches everywhere that "call upon the name of our Lord Jesus Christ, their Lord and ours" (1 Cor 1:2). Paul is now experiencing shame because they have lagged in their cooperation with his great project, even while he has boasted of them to others (2 Cor 9:3–4). But it is not too late. They can fully heal the rift between Paul and themselves by joining him in helping those in need in Jerusalem.

The importance of this collection for Paul is evident from the canon-ical letters. His providing assistance for the poor in Jerusalem was a fun-

---

34. For guides to the ancient topos, see Bohnenblust, *Beiträge zum Topos Peri Philias*, and Dugas, *L'amitié Antique*.

35. Plutarch, *On Brotherly Love* 484B–C.

36. Johnson, *Literary Function*, 1–28.

37. Aristotle, *Nicomachean Ethics* 1130b–32b.

38. For the cultic dimensions of Paul's language, see Downs, *Offering of the Gen-tiles*, 131–45, and J. Wilson, "Old Testament Sacrificial Context."

damental part of the agreement with the Jerusalem leaders concerning the division of labor between Cephas's ministry to the circumcised and Paul's ministry to the gentiles (Gal 2:10). The efforts he was making even at a distance to raise and deliver money from the Galatian and Achaian communities is made clear in 1 Cor 16:1–4. In Rom 15:27 Paul makes the ancient logic of friendship explicit for the relationship between Jerusalem and his gentile communities: "they are indebted to them, for if the Gentiles have come to share in their spiritual blessings, they ought also to serve them in material blessings." In 2 Corinthians also, Paul uses the language associated with friendship for the collection: "It is acceptable according to what one has, not according to what one does not have; not that others should have relief while you are burdened, but that as a matter of equality [*isotēs*] your surplus at the present time should supply their needs . . . that there may be equality [*isotēs*]" (8:12–14).

That the Corinthians' generosity in this matter is regarded by Paul as a participation in the reconciling work of God in Christ is made clear by another of his exchange statements in 2 Cor 8:9: "For you know the gracious act of our Lord Jesus Christ, that for your sake he became poor although he was rich, so that by his poverty you might become rich."[39] Jesus reconciled the world to God through his weakness given for their strength, by his sin given for their righteousness, by his poverty given for their richness. The Corinthians can join this work by the body language of material donation for the poor in Jerusalem and, by so doing, help effect reconciliation among all the churches, whether Jewish or gentile.

Did Paul's efforts with the Corinthians succeed? We have two clues that they did. The first is Paul's statement in Rom 15:25–26: "Now, however, I am going to Jerusalem to minister to the holy ones, for Macedonia *and Achaia* have decided to make some contribution for the poor among the holy ones in Jerusalem." By Achaia, he means those to whom he wrote in this letter (see 2 Cor 1:1). So, they joined in the collection after all. The second clue is that they saved his letters.

Conclusion

We have been able to consider "truth and reconciliation" in 2 Corinthians only from Paul's perspective, but given that limitation, the composition is remarkable, especially for an ancient writing, above all for a religious

---

39. As in other key instances, the noun *charis* is surely best understood as "gift"; see J. Barclay, *Paul and the Gift*.

writing, for its transparency and candor. The letter allows us to glimpse the emotions of hurt and anger caused by Paul's alienation from his churches in Achaia, hurt and anger that move in both directions. We see thereby that the honest recognition of emotional truth is an essential element of genuine reconciliation. We have seen as well how Paul appeals to the bonds of *koinōnia* that they share, and have shared, despite their present distance and misunderstanding. Such an appeal to a common history and identity is also familiar to us in contemporary contexts. The declaration that "we are, after all, everyone of us South Africans," or "we are, despite our divisions, all Americans," remains a powerful motivation for overcoming alienation.

Two elements in the rhetoric of 2 Corinthians, however, are especially instructive. The first is that Paul reminds his readers that it is not merely their relationship with each other that matters but that it is their reconciliation with and from God that defines their *koinōnia*. The roots of reconciliation lie not in their mutual good will but in God's infinite grace. God's self-giving in Christ, furthermore, is more than simply the cause of reconciliation between God and humans; it is also the pattern for reconciliation between humans: the strong must be willing to become weak so that the other can be empowered; the wise must become foolish so that those who act foolishly might become wise; those without sin must be willing to be regarded as sinful for the sake of right-relatedness in God. Because the weak cannot move because they are weak, the strong must move toward them, for reconciliation to take place.

Finally, although Paul summons the Corinthians to express reconciliation through the body language of sharing possessions—and in that regard it resembles superficially the notion of paying "reparations"—there is an important difference. Yes, reconciliation is expressed by sharing possessions, with Christ's becoming poor so that others might become rich serving once more as the model. But the sharing of possessions is not among the formerly estranged parties. Instead, the reconciliation between the Corinthians and Paul is solidified bodily by their joining together in helping communities other than their own. Here reconciliation means turning from the plusses and minuses of the past and joining together as a single body in assistance of others, moving forward rather than looking backward.

Chapter 9

Ritual Imprinting and the Politics of Perfection

Galatians and Colossians

If religious experience issues in the organization of life around a perception of power,[1] first of all in the demarcation of sacred time and sacred space,[2] then the study of ritual provides an obvious point of access to the religious experience of the earliest Christians.[3] For ritual—broadly defined as repetitive communal patterns of behavior[4]—we need not rely entirely on reports about personal experience, for ritual is embodied and visible, and often, though not always, public.[5] It therefore enables us to move from ritual gestures, with their symbolic valences, in two

1. For the organization of life around the perception of power, see Leeuw, *Religion*, 1:27–28, 191–205; 2:339–42; Wach, *Sociology of Religion*, 17–34.

2. See Durkheim, *Elementary Forms*, 52–55; Eliade, *The Sacred and the Profane*, 20–113.

3. For the connection between ritual and the demarcation of sacred time and space from very different perspectives, see Eliade, *Cosmos and History*, 3–92; J. Smith, *To Take Place*, 102–8; Bell, *Ritual Theory, Ritual Practice*, 124–30.

4. Cf. Bell, *Ritual Theory, Ritual Practice*, 91–92. Note that my definition includes rituals that are not necessarily or specifically "religious," although—like some college sporting events—they may indeed *function* religiously. Compare the definition of ritual by E. M. Zuesse: "conscious and voluntary, repetitious and stylized symbolic bodily actions that are centered on cosmic structure and/or sacred presences" ("Ritual," *ER* 11/12:405). Jonathan Z. Smith offers a number of partial characterizations in *To Take Place*: "Ritual is, first and foremost, a mode of paying attention" (103); it "is, above all, an assertion of difference" (109). "Ritual represents the creation of a controlled environment where the variables (the accidents) of ordinary life may be displaced precisely because they are felt to be so overwhelmingly present and powerful. Ritual is a means of performing the way things ought to be in conscious tension to the way things are" (109). "Ritual, concerned primarily with difference, is, necessarily, an affair of the relative" (110).

5. See Bell, *Ritual Theory, Ritual Practice*, 94–117, on recent attention in scholarship to the "ritual body."

directions. We can move laterally to compare ritual patterns, and we can move inward—tentatively to be sure—from public gesture to the personal experience.

In the case of nascent Christianity, the ritual of baptism offers the best possibility for such analysis. It is the most pervasively attested ritual activity in the New Testament. The evidence is insufficient to reconstruct completely either the ritual or its significance, but it is adequate to support some reasonable hypotheses. As a ritual of initiation into an intentional community, furthermore, baptism can be compared with similar ritual activities in religious communities contemporaneous with nascent Christianity. Finally, cross-cultural anthropological studies of rituals of initiation provide us with a fuller sense of what the experiential and social dimensions of baptism might have been. In sum, baptism allows the sort of convergence of perceptions that enriches a phenomenological analysis.[6]

Reconstructing the Ritual

Although the author of Ephesians speaks of "one baptism" as an identifying mark of unity among believers,[7] we cannot assume that the ritual took the same form or had the same significance everywhere it was practiced.[8] Some things, however, can be stated with a degree of probability, especially if we suppose—as it seems we should—some degree of continuity between the baptism practiced by John and received by Jesus,[9] and that practiced by Christians in the name of Jesus.[10] Our re-

6. Cf. Walter Burkert's attempt at a "comparative phenomenology of ancient mysteries" in *Ancient Mystery Cults*, 4.

7. "There is one body and one Spirit, just as you were called in the one hope that belongs to your call, one Lord, one faith, one baptism, one God and Father of us all, who is above all and through all and in all" (Eph 4:4–6). We will see the connection between "one baptism" and "one God" again later. Unless otherwise indicated, Scripture quotations in this chapter are from the RSV.

8. My language here is deliberately cautious, for there are even cases in which we cannot be sure baptism was practiced at all. See Hickling, "Baptism."

9. See Matt 3:1–16; 11:11; 14:2; 16:14; 17:13; 21:25; Mark 1:4–9; 6:25; 8:28; 11:30; Luke 3:7–21; 7:19–20, 33; 9:19; 20:8; John 1:25–33; 3:22–26; 4:1–2; Acts 1:5, 22; 10:37; 13:24; 18:25; 19:34.

10. See Matt 28:19; Mark 16:16; Acts 2:38–41; 3:12–28; 9:18; 10:47–48; 11:16; 16:15, 33; 18:8; 19:3–5; 22:16; Rom 6:3; 1 Cor 1:13–17; 12:13; 15:29; Gal 3:27; Eph 4:5; Col 2:12; 1 Pet 3:21. For the premise of continuity, see Lampe, *Seal of the Spirit*, 19–20.

constructive effort must take into account all the possible allusions to baptism in the epistolary literature,[11] as well as schematic descriptions in New Testament narratives.[12]

As the word itself suggests and as the language associated with it supports, baptism is first of all a washing, probably through immersion, in water.[13] In contrast to most other ancient lustrations, baptism is an initiation into an intentional community,[14] a *rite de passage* that marks a transition from outsider to insider status.[15] The circumstances of the ritual are not altogether clear. It seems to have been performed in public rather than in private.[16] It was passive rather than active: one did not bathe oneself but was "baptized," apparently by one other person,[17] when possible in the presence of others.[18]

Concerning the specific actions involved in the ritual, we can only make informed guesses based on the symbolism associated with baptism in the New Testament writings. We cannot assume that they were part of every, or even any, baptismal ritual. The metaphor of taking off and putting on qualities, for example, which is used in the context of baptism,

11. In addition to the passages involving *baptizein* and *baptisma* given above, this means considering as well the references to "bath" (*loutron*) in Eph 5:26 and Titus 3:5, "bathing" (*louein/apolouein*) in 1 Cor 6:11 and (possibly) Rev 1:5, and "sprinkling" (*rantizein*) in Heb 10:22.

12. The fullest description is that of the baptism of Jesus by John (Matt 3:16–17; Mark 1:9–11; Luke 3:21–22; John 1:32–34). Given the connections that will be shown below, it is highly likely that the depiction of this event in the Gospels has been at least in some degree affected by community practice and conviction. Other brief narrative accounts are in Acts 8:26–40; 9:17–19; 10:44–48; 16:15, 33; 19:1–7. For an attempt to flesh out the ritual in Pauline communities, see esp. Meeks, *First Urban Christians*, 150–57.

13. See Albrecht Oepke, "βάπτω, βαπτίζω," *TDNT* 1:529–46.

14. The question of proselyte baptism in Judaism will be discussed below. For the variety of washings in ancient traditions, see Oepke, *TDNT* 1:530–35; Delorme, "Practice of Baptism"; Wagner, *Pauline Baptism*, 127–35; Burkert, *Ancient Mystery Cults*, 101–2.

15. See Gennep, *Rites of Passage*, 1–13. See also Eliade, *Rites and Symbols*, x: "The term initiation in the most general sense denotes a body of rites and oral teachings whose purpose is to produce a decisive alteration in the religious and social status of the person to be initiated." For further bibliography, see Barbara G. Meyerhoff, Linda A. Camino, and Edith Turner, "Rites of Passage," *ER* 11/12:380–87.

16. See Matt 3:1–17; Mark 1:5; Luke 3:7, 21; Acts 2:41; 8:12; 10:47–48; 16:15, 33.

17. See Matt 3:11; Mark 1:8–9; John 1:26, 33; Acts 16:33; 19:5; 1 Cor 1:12–17. That Thecla "gave herself the bath" is clearly regarded as exceptional (see Acts of Paul and Thecla 34, 40).

18. See Acts 2:41; 10:47–48; 16:15, 33; 19:5; 1 Cor 1:15.

can with some likelihood be connected to ritual divestment and reclothing before and after immersion.[19] Similarly, language about illumination and enlightenment might be connected to the ritual use of lights such as candles, perhaps in a nighttime ceremony.[20] It is conceivable that some form of ecstatic utterance accompanied the baptized person's emergence from the water.[21] Finally, it is likely that the ritual initiation of baptism also involved a longer or shorter period of instruction, the imparting of a body of lore concerning the significance of the ritual itself and of the larger mystery of which it was a part,[22] and some sort of profession of faith.[23]

In a 1907 essay, Sigmund Freud perceptively noted the similarity between obsessive behavior and religious ritual.[24] Both involve the repetition of patterned actions. But whereas obsessive acts like hand-wringing are pathological because they inhabit only a private world of meaning, religious rituals take their significance from a larger and more public symbolic world.[25] To those who do not share it, this symbolic world may appear as no less strange than that of the obsessive-compulsive. For its adherents, however, ritual both mirrors and models fundamental truths

19. See Gal 3:27; Col 3:9–10; Eph 4:22. See Meeks, *First Urban Christians*, 151, 157; Wainwright, *Christian Initiation*, 14–15.

20. See Wainwright, *Christian Initiation*, 15. Hebrews speaks of "having been enlightened" (*phōtisthentes*), with clear reference to the readers' initiation (6:4; 10:32). The statement cited by Eph. 5:14, "Awake, O sleeper, and arise from the dead, and Christ shall give you light," is plausibly connected to a baptismal ritual, given that composition's extensive use of darkness/light symbolism (cf. Eph 1:18; 3:9; 5:8–9, 13). For other light symbolism possibly connected to baptism, see Rom 13:12; 2 Cor 4:6; Col 1:12; 1 Pet 2:9).

21. Note the reports of ecstatic speech in Acts 2:1–4; 10:46–47; 19:6. Meeks, *First Urban Christians*, 151–52, makes the very plausible suggestion that the bilingual cry of *abba* (Gal 4:6; see Rom 8:15–17) may well have been one form of such utterance.

22. The imparting of knowledge is such a standard feature of all initiations (see La Fontaine, *Initiation*, 15; Eliade, *Rites and Symbols*, 3), and of ancient initiations in particular (see Burkert, *Ancient Mystery Cults*, 69, 153n14), that we should take seriously such oblique indications as Acts 18:26; Heb 6:2; Luke 1:4, the explicit allusions to shared traditions (see esp. Rom 6:1–11), and possible samples of such instruction (1 Pet 3:18–4:6).

23. Note in particular the statement of faith in Acts 8:37 (variant reading); 16:15, 31; and the element of "calling on the name" in Acts 2:38; 4:12; 8:16; 9:14, 21; 10:43; 22:16; 1 Cor 1:2; 6:11; as well as such creedal statements as Rom 10:9. See Meeks, *First Urban Christians*, 152; Crehan, *Early Christian Baptism*, 8–22.

24. Freud, "Obsessive Acts and Religious Practices"; cited in J. Smith, *To Take Place*, 110–11.

25. Freud, "Obsessive Acts," 9:118–19.

about the world.[26] To get closer to the experiential dimension of early Christian baptism, therefore, we must move beyond physical actions to a consideration of the symbols attached to these actions.

The most obvious religious symbolism for a ritual of washing is purification.[27] Some New Testament passages speak of baptism as cleansing the initiate.[28] Ritual purifications frequently have the effect of providing access to the sacred.[29] Thus in Judaism the cleansing of physical objects either results from contact with what is holy or enables access to such contact.[30] In Hebrew prophetic literature, in turn, the language of ritual purification was given an ethical dimension, so that purification could signal a conversion from patterns of idolatry and sin.[31] The same moral connotation is given to baptism in the New Testament by the frequent connection to forgiveness of sins and admission to a sanctified people.[32]

A second symbolic dimension of Christian baptism is new life. Such symbolism is common in rituals of initiation, for behaviorally the initiate enters a community with distinctive observances and new obligations.[33] Thus we are not surprised to find baptism called the "bath of regeneration" (Titus 3:5, author's translation), for *palingenesia* is widely attested in ancient literature for a variety of rebirths and new beginnings, whether cosmological, ethical, or mystical.[34] The language of birth or rebirth is closely connected to that of regeneration.[35] The most distinctive Christian symbolism for baptism, however, is that of death and resurrection,

26. See Geertz, "Religion as a Cultural System," esp. 113–18.

27. See, e.g., Wagner, *Pauline Baptism*, 127–35; Burkert, *Ancient Mystery Cults*, 101–2.

28. Eph 5:26; Titus 2:14; Heb 10:22; for possible allusions, see Acts 15:9; Heb 1:3; 9:14; 1 John 1:7.

29. This is obviously the case in the initiatory washing at Eleusis; see Kerényi, *Eleusis*, 45–61; Nock, "Hellenistic Mysteries," 2:792–93.

30. See LXX Exod 19:10; Num 8:21; 19:12; 31:23; Lev 16:19–20, 30; m. Yadayim 1:1–4:8; Matt 15:2; Mark 7:2–5.

31. See LXX Ps 50:1–12; Isa 57:14; 66:17; Jer 40:8; Ezek 36:25; 37:23.

32. Matt 4:11; Mark 1:4; Luke 3:3; Acts 2:38; 3:19; 15:9; 22:16; 1 Cor 6:11; Eph 5:26–27; Titus 2:14; 1 Pet 3:21; Heb 10:22. See also A. Collins, "Origins of Christian Baptism," esp. 40.

33. See Eliade, *Rites and Symbols*, xii–xv; La Fontaine, *Initiation*, 15.

34. For discussion and references to primary sources, see Dibelius and Conzelmann, *Pastoral Epistles*, 148–50.

35. See John 1:13; 3:3–8; 1 John 3:9; 1 Pet 1:3, 23. Paul's speaking of "giving birth" to individuals (Phlm 10) or communities (1 Cor 4:15; Gal 4:19) may well be connected to the practice of baptism. Notice also how the language of "those born of the flesh / into slavery" in Gal 4:23–29 has as its explicit contrary "those born of the gospel," but by implication also "those born of the Spirit / into freedom," as in baptism (Gal 3:27–4:7). See F. Bueschsel, "γεννάω" and "γίνομαι," *TDNT* 1:665–75 and 1:681–89.

most clearly attested in Paul's letters but found elsewhere as well.[36] This symbolism most obviously connects the Christian ritual to the foundational narrative of Jesus's passion, death, and resurrection.[37]

A final aspect of baptismal symbolism is particularly complex. It can perhaps best be characterized as relational. Baptism establishes a bond between the initiate and two spiritual powers, themselves in some fashion interconnected. First, baptism brings the initiate into connection with a power designated as Holy Spirit.[38] The degree to which this power is perceived as personal is not clear, especially since *to pneuma to hagion* is itself brought into close association with the person of Jesus.[39] In the accounts of Jesus's baptism, we see that the descent of the Holy Spirit and the declaration of Jesus's divine sonship go together.[40] Paul's allusion to the "spirit of adoption" received by the baptized certainly seems to support the conclusion that the Holy Spirit was regarded as the medium through which the unique relationship between Jesus and God was transferred to others, so that at baptism this same filial relationship was established, as expressed by the initiate's shouting out the Aramaic caritative designation for God, *Abba*.[41]

Such a mystical identification is clearly understood as a form of status enhancement. It also points to the conviction that the Jesus who was cru-

36. Rom 6:1–11 is the most obvious Pauline example. On this, see Tannehill, *Dying and Rising*; Schnackenburg, *Baptism*, 105–70. 1 Cor 15:29 must certainly also be placed within this understanding, as also Col 2:12–15; 2:20–3:7. See also 1 Pet 3:18–4:2, and the implication of "the baptism with which I am to be baptized" in Mark 10:38–40. For the whole theme, see Cullmann, *Baptism in the New Testament*, 9–22.

37. By "foundational" I mean that the basic story of Jesus's passion and death was formed very early—probably the first part of the Jesus tradition to reach narrative expression—before the time of Paul and widely disseminated in non-Pauline as well as Pauline churches; see the argument in Johnson, *Real Jesus*, 141–68. I thereby take a position directly contrary to Mack, *Myth of Innocence* and *Who Wrote the New Testament?*, for whom the passion narrative is a late narrative elaboration of the "Christ Myth."

38. Acts 1:3, 8; 2:1–4, 38; 8:16–17; 9:17–19; 10:45–48; 11:16; 19:5–6; Rom 5:5; 1 Cor 12:13; Gal 3:27–4:6; Eph 4:4–6; Titus 3:5–6; Heb 6:4.

39. John 14:25; 20:21–23; Acts 2:33; 4:30–31; 10:36–45; Rom 1:4; 8:2–4, 9–11; 1 Cor 6:11, 15–19; 12:3, 12–13; 15:45; 2 Cor 3:18; 13:14; Gal 5:5–6; Eph 1:13; 2:21–22; Phil 2:1–5; 2 Tim 1:13–14; 1 Pet 3:18–20; 1 John 4:13–14; 5:6–8; Jude 20–21; Rev 1:9–10; 19:10.

40. Matt 3:16–17; Mark 1:9–11; Luke 3:21–22; John 1:32–34.

41. "In Christ Jesus you are all sons of God, through faith. For as many of you were baptized into Christ have put on Christ.... And if you are Christ's, then you are Abraham's offspring, heirs according to the promise.... And because you are sons, God has sent the Spirit of his Son into our hearts, crying, 'Abba! Father!' So through God you are no longer a slave but a son, and if a son then an heir" (Gal 3:26, 29; 4:6–7).

cified was now more powerfully alive as "Lord" and capable of contacting humans across time and space, touching them with this life through the Spirit, so that they could live a "new life" and a "resurrection life" according to the pattern of his own.[42] In short, Christian baptism not only signaled passage from one population to another but generated a new form of identity.[43] No wonder baptism is the ritual constantly mentioned and most frequently recalled in the New Testament writings, for in this ritual Christians were both empowered and imprinted[44]—or, to use the language soon to become technical, they were "sealed."[45]

How Many Initiations?

A description like the one I have attempted can leave an impression of uniformity of practice, understanding, and experience that may not have

---

42. Rom 6:1–11; 8:2–11; 12:1–2; 15:1–7; 1 Cor 2:16; 11:1; Gal 5:25–6:2; Eph 4:20–24; Phil 2:1–11; Col 3:10–17; 2 Tim 2:1–13; 1 John 4:17–19; 1 Pet 2:21–25; 4:1–6; Heb 13:12–13.

43. What is shocking, of course, is that this man, whose *nous* they now have (1 Cor 2:16), was executed as a criminal under Roman authority. The resemblance between this conviction and necromancy is obvious. In necromancy it is thought that those who have died, especially those who have died violently or criminally, have spirits that can operate powerfully when controlled by the appropriate mechanisms. Usually the dead are summoned for purposes of divination, but "the calling up of the dead may occur for purposes other than information seeking" (Erika Bourguignon, "Necromancy," *ER* 10:345). Such a belief seems to lie behind the response of Herod to the wonders worked by Jesus: Was it possible that the beheaded John the Baptist was more powerfully at work in this man whom he had baptized? Grasping how small a distance separates the phenomena of necromancy and baptism can, once we overcome resistance to what appears an intolerable reduction, help us understand more vividly the realism, indeed the sheer physicalism, of some of the New Testament's language: the Holy Spirit was poured over them (Acts 2:33; Titus 3:6), it was poured into them (Rom 5:5), it was drunk by all of them (1 Cor 12:13), they were "filled with the Holy Spirit" (Acts 4:31) and could therefore speak "in" the spirit (1 Cor 14:12) and live "by" the Spirit (Gal 5:25); and all of this is pretty much equivalent to speaking and acting "in the name of Jesus" (1 Cor 5:4) and "in the Lord" (1 Cor 7:39).

44. My use of "imprinting" here is metaphorical, borrowing partly from the ancient imagery of the seal, which shows identity, and partly from the psychological theory that certain human life experiences have a particularly important role in determining other sorts of responses. See, e.g., Hess, *Imprinting*, 1–61; Sluckin, *Imprinting and Early Learning*, 1–15, 116–26.

45. See esp. the use of *sphragizein* in 2 Cor 1:22; Eph 1:13, 4:30; Rev 7:3–8. For this aspect of baptism, see Wainwright, *Christian Initiation*, 14, and Lampe, *Seal of the Spirit*, 3–18.

existed. Precisely the notion of ritual imprinting, however, can lead us to a closer consideration of what the actual experience of baptism may have involved for some early Christians. Suppose it be granted that baptism imparts a certain of identity or "sealing": what is the corollary? Does it necessarily follow that baptism is the single and final initiation to be undergone, for example, or is it possible that Christians are to move through a series of rituals leading them progressively toward full perfection or maturity? This question lies at the heart of two letters attributed to Paul addressed to Christians in the territory of ancient Phrygia— namely, Galatians[46] and Colossians.[47]

The differences between the letters are obvious. In Galatians, Paul appears as a founder of the churches to whom he writes,[48] and the linked issues of his own apostolic authority and the observance of Torah figure prominently in his argument.[49] His language in Galatians is defensive and passionate,[50] even as his argument is rhetorically shaped[51] and midrashically sophisticated.[52]

In contrast, Paul writes to believers in the city of Colossae,[53] not as the

46. I am using the expression "Phrygia" loosely, since the precise boundaries of what Luke in Acts 16:6 calls "the Phrygian and Galatian region" did not seem terribly clear to him, or for that matter to Pliny (*Natural History* 5.95) or Strabo (*Geography* 12.7.1–5). For the problems of ethnic, geographical, and political designations, see F. F. Bruce, "Phrygia," *ABD* 5:365–68. The debate over a "North Galatia" or "South Galatia" destination for the letter has at least something to do with reconciling Paul's founding of these churches with the accounts in Acts; see, e.g., Lightfoot, *St. Paul's Epistle to the Galatians*, 1–35; Bruce, "Galatian Problems 2."

47. The main critical issue pertaining to Colossians is its authenticity, which is not of particular importance in the present discussion. For arguments against authenticity from the perspective of literary connections, see Sanders, "Literary Dependence in Colossians"; and from the perspective of theological consistency, see Lohse, "Pauline Theology." An extensive argument in favor of authenticity is mounted by Cannon, *Traditional Material*. The case for Colossians' authenticity, and indeed for its having been written from Ephesus *before* 1 Corinthians, has recently been made by Murphy-O'Connor, *Paul*, 237–39.

48. Gal 1:11; 4:13–20.

49. His apostolic authority: Gal 1:12; 1:17–2:10; 4:12–20; 5:2–3, 10–11; 6:17; the observance of Torah: Gal 2:3, 14–19; 3:2, 10–22; 4:21–5:4; 5:11, 18; 6:12–13.

50. See Gal 1:1, 6, 8, 9; 3:1; 4:11; 5:7, 12; 6:17.

51. For the use of rhetoric in Galatians, see H. Betz, *Galatians*; Brinsmead, *Galatians*; Hall, "Rhetorical Outline for Galatians"; Smit, "Letter of Paul to the Galatians."

52. See, e.g., Dahl, "Contradictions in Scripture"; Wilcox, "'Upon the Tree'"; Callan, "Pauline Midrash."

53. On the little that is known about the Phrygian city in the Lycus valley that disappeared from history after a devastating earthquake in 60 or 64 CE, see C. E. Arnold, "Colossae," *ABD* 1:1089–90.

founder of their community,[54] but as the senior colleague of Epaphras, from whom they learned Christ[55] and who is at the time of writing Paul's fellow prisoner.[56] As we might expect in such circumstances, neither the issue of Paul's apostolic authority[57] nor his particular investment in Torah emerges with the same vividness.[58] Instead, using language far less dialectical than that in Galatians, Paul works out the implications of what he considers shared traditions and understandings,[59] particularly concerning baptism and the identity of Christ.[60]

Despite these differences, the situations addressed have some striking similarities:

- The ethnic and cultural background is gentile rather than Jewish: believers have turned to Christ directly from paganism.[61]
- Whether under the influence of outside proselytizers or inside agitators,[62] some members in each community are seeking a further

54. Paul has only "heard of" their faith (Col 1:4, 9); they have not "seen his face" (2:1), and Tychichus will report to them on Paul's affairs (4:7–8). It is possible that Colossians is part of a three-letter packet carried by Tychichus as he accompanied the slave Onesimus back to his owner, Philemon (see Col 4:9): the note to Philemon is a letter of recommendation for Onesimus, Colossians is a cover letter to the local church (similar to the one for the Laodiceans; see Col 4:16), and Ephesians is a circular letter to Paul's gentile congregations. See Johnson, *Writings of the New Testament*, 353–55.

55. Paul refers to Epaphras as "one of yourselves" (Col 4:12) and makes clear that they learned the grace of God in truth from Epaphras (1:6–7).

56. Paul calls himself a prisoner (Col 4:3). And although in Colossians he does not call Epaphras a "fellow-prisoner" as he does Aristarchus (4:10), it is a fair inference, given the fact that Epaphras is with Paul, sends greetings, but is not returning to the church with Tychichus. The reference to Epaphras in Phlm 23 as "fellow prisoner" is decisive.

57. Paul's authority is not under threat but assumed (Col 1:1, 23, 25; 2:5; 4:2–4, 8–9, 18).

58. Not only is Torah not cited in this letter, but the diction employed in Col 2:11–15 and 2:22 is, apart from the term *peritomē*, extremely general: *cheirographon tois dogmasin* and *entalmata kai didaskalias tōn anthrōpōn*.

59. See Col 1:5–7; 2:6–7; the conditional constructions in 2:20 and 3:1 also assume shared knowledge.

60. The argument in Colossians proceeds by intertwining the two: Christ (1:15–20, 27–29; 2:2–3, 6, 9; 2:14–3:1; 4:2); baptism (1:12–13, 21–23; 2:11–15; 2:20–3:4; 3:9, 12).

61. For Galatians, see 2:8, 15–16; 3:2; 4:8–9, 21; 5:2, 4; 6:12–13; for Colossians, see 1:21, 27; 2:13; 3:11; 4:11.

62. In both letters, Paul is either uncertain of the identity or remarkably circumspect. For Galatians, see 1:7, 9; 3:1; 4:17; 5:7, 10, 12; 6:12–13; for Colossians, see 2:8, 16, 18.

initiation beyond baptism. In the case of Galatians, it is clear that
some believers are having themselves circumcised.[63] In Colossae,
there is also apparently the desire for circumcision,[64] as well as
some additional visionary experience.[65]

- In each group, such ambitions are connected to a desire for "perfection" or "maturity."[66]
- In each case, there is the suggestion that those having additional initiations are in a superior position to those who have received only baptism into Christ.[67]

The most pressing *religious* question is why some Phrygian Christians
were seeking an additional initiation beyond baptism. The question gains
even more point when we remember that circumcision is, after all, a
mutilation of the body which, when carried out on an adult male—as it
would be in such cases—is also extraordinarily painful.[68] What impulse

---

63. There is a note of coercion sounded in Gal 2:3 and 6:12, but more of a voluntary desire in 4:21 and 5:2–4. Note Paul's apparent necessity to deny that he himself is a preacher of circumcision in 5:11.

64. See the need to designate baptism as a "circumcision made without hands" and the "circumcision of Christ" in Col 2:11; the regulations against handling, tasting, and touching in 2:22; and the denial of distinction between Jew and gentile in 3:11.

65. The key phrase is Col 2:18, which the RSV renders "insisting on self-abasement and the worship of angels, taking his stand on visions." The term *embateuein* has definite associations with ritual initiations; see Eitrem, "Embateuō"; Francis, "Background of *Embateuein*." Martin Dibelius argued that the visionary experience involved an initiation into an Isis-style mystery after baptism; see "Isis Initiation in Apuleius." Fred O. Francis argues for a form of Merkabah mysticism; see "Humility and Angelic Worship." Lucien Cerfaux thinks that a form of syncretistic Jewish mystery like that expressed by Philo is involved; see "L'influence des 'Mystères.'"

66. Of particular importance in Galatians is the use of *epitelein* in 3:3. The RSV translates, "Having begun in the Spirit, are you now ending with the flesh?" But the term has definite connections with the "perfection" that comes from the completion of initiation ritual; see Ascough, "Completion of a Religious Duty," esp. the inscriptional evidence collected in 590–94. See also *plērōma* in Gal 4:4, *plēroun* in 5:14, *telein* in 5:16, and *anaplēroun* in 6:2. In Colossians, see *teleios* in 1:28 and 4:12; *teleiotēs* in 3:14; *plēroun* in 1:9, 25; 2:10; 4:17; *plērōma* in 1:19; 2:9; *plērophoria* in 2:2; and *plērophorein* in 4:12.

67. See Gal 4:17; 5:5; 6:12–13; Col 2:8, 16, 18, 23.

68. The debilitating effects of the procedure are graphically depicted in the story of Dinah and Shechem in Gen 34:25. For an instance when gentiles were compelled to be circumcised "as a condition of life among them [the Jews]," see Josephus, *The Life* 113; or for when they themselves sought the procedure, see Josephus, *Jewish Antiquities* 13.258; LXX Esth 8:17.

drove such an ambition? The letters to the Galatians and Colossians have rarely been read together, and even less frequently, if ever, with this question in mind. The reason is that our question is less historical than it is religious: we are asking a phenomenological question of ancient texts in order to apprehend better the human experience of ritual.

Because Colossians is often relegated to the ranks of pseudonymous Pauline letters, the two compositions are rarely even brought together as evidence for religious practice in a specific region of the Mediterranean world, although, even if not both from Paul, they address remarkably similar situations in communities in the same region and within a relatively short timespan.[69] The letters are ordinarily studied to yield information about "Pauline opponents"[70] and the theological response made by the author.[71] In the eyes of most observers, the important action is that taking place between Paul and his rivals for his churches' allegiance. Little effort is spent trying to figure out what Paul's readers were themselves experiencing and thinking, or what the religious logic of their position might be. But precisely that should be of most interest to the study of religion. So we pose the question: What was the character of the experience of baptism for these Phrygian Christians such that they would seek further ritual initiations?

The clue is to be found, I think, in the fact that, on the evidence of

69. On the Phrygian/Galatian region, see note 46 above. Galatians could have been written any time "fourteen years later" than Paul's conversion (see Gal 2:1; 2 Cor 12:2) during his active ministry, therefore between 49 and 57. If Colossians is authentic, as I think, then it would be written during an imprisonment, therefore possibly between 57 and 64. Remember the presumed impact of the earthquake of 60/64 (see note 53 above). The convolutions required by the premise of pseudonymity are illustrated by Meeks, *First Urban Christians*. He notes that we are dependent for locating the destination of Philemon (a universally recognized authentic letter) on Colossians (a disputed letter) (210n219). He even holds open the possibility that the letter could have been authorized by Paul (see his signature in Col 4:18) and written by Timothy under Paul's authorization (125). It is difficult to see how this does not constitute "Pauline authorship" in the broad sense of the term (see Johnson, *Writings of the New Testament*, 255–57).

70. For Galatians, see, e.g., Schmithals, *Paul and the Gnostics*, 13–64; Tyson, "Paul's Opponents in Galatia"; Jewett, "Agitators"; Munck, "Judaizing Gentile Christians"; for Colossians, see Bornkamm, "Heresy of Colossians"; Bandstra, "Colossian Errorists"; Evans, "Colossian Mystics."

71. For Galatians, see, e.g., M. Barth, "Kerygma of Galatians"; Cerfaux, "Christ Our Justice"; Hays, *Faith of Jesus Christ*; for Colossians, see, e.g., Dahl, "Christ, Creation, and the Church"; Francis, "Christological Argument of Colossians"; Hanson, "Conquest of the Powers."

both letters, these Christians were converted gentiles. In the context of their symbolic world, it was natural for them to regard their baptism into Christ as initiation into a mystery.[72] Their cultural expectation (or imprinting, if you allow) was that one initiation would lead to another. The reasons for seeking circumcision, in other words, may have had much less to do with theology than with the logic of ritual practice in antiquity and the tendency of religious people to seek perfection—that is, to finish the course on which they have set themselves.

Initiation into the Mysteries

Information about the ancient mysteries is notoriously and understandably difficult to assess.[73] The *disciplinum arcanum* functioned with sufficient rigor to make even our most explicit witness to ritual practice within the mysteries models of indirection and circumspection.[74] What is abundantly

---

72. Although the term *mystērion* occurs in Colossians (1:26; 2:2; 4:3), my suggestion is not based on terminology alone; nor am I debating the origins of Christian baptism. For the fruitless debates on these points, see J. Smith, *Drudgery Divine*; there is no need to rehearse all the literature that he dissects so skillfully. There appear to be four basic approaches to the study of earliest Christianity in the context of the mysteries. The first is to ignore them completely and pay attention only to Jewish antecedents (and Palestinian Jewish ones at that); see, e.g., Cullmann, *Baptism in the New Testament*, 14n2; Beasley-Murray, *Baptism in the New Testament*. The second is to recognize the pervasiveness of mystery practice and language but refuse to grant it any influence for nascent Christianity, reserving that for later "Catholic" development; see, e.g., Wagner, *Pauline Baptism*, 259–75; Metzger, "Considerations of Methodology"; Nock, "Hellenistic Mysteries," esp. 809–10. The third is to subsume early Christianity into the mysteries more or less completely; see, e.g., Reitzenstein, *Hellenistic Mystery-Religions*; Loisy, *Les Mystères Païens*; Angus, *Mystery Religions and Christianity*. The fourth is to be fundamentally open to the ways in which the symbolic worlds of the mysteries and Christianity may have intersected, without demanding causal connections in the strict sense and respecting the distinctiveness of the diverse cults; see H. Rahner, "Christian Mystery"; Casel, *Mystery of Christian Worship*; Cerfaux, "L'influence des 'Mystères.'" My argument makes clear that I find the fourth position most congenial and, in fact, demanded by the sort of phenomenological analysis that I am attempting.

73. The literature on the mysteries is obviously enormous. In addition to the works cited in note 72, see Metzger, "Classified Bibliography"; Aldernick, "Eleusinian Mysteries"; Beck, "Mithraism since Franz Cumont." For basic orientation, see Burkert, *Greek Religion*, 276–304; Burkert, *Ancient Mystery Cults*; Meyer, *Ancient Mysteries*.

74. See Motte, "Silence et Sécret"; Alderink, "Eleusinian Mysteries," 1477; Burkert, *Ancient Mystery Cults*, 90.

clear, however, is that initiation into one mystery by no means excluded initiation into another.[75] In the polytheistic system that dominated ancient Mediterranean cultures, even the most ardent devotion to a specific god allowed recognition of the dignity and importance of the other gods. Someone who boasted of initiation into a multitude of mysteries was revealing not religious unreliability but most profound and catholic piety.[76]

More pertinent to our present discussion, the most ancient and pervasively influential Eleusinian mysteries had multiple well-defined initiations, beginning with a purification bath and moving through the "lesser mysteries."[77] A first initiation into the cult of a specific god or goddess, then, could ordinarily be regarded as preliminary to still further initiations.[78] Our clearest direct evidence for this comes form Apuleius's *Metamorphoses* (*Golden Ass*), deservedly esteemed not only as a picaresque novel[79] but also as an account of religious conversion and transformation.[80]

After his careless dabbling in magic potions had turned him into an ass, and vengeful Fortune had led him through a series of progressively more alienating experiences, Lucius encounters the goddess Isis on the moonlit beach at Cenchrae.[81] Isis saves him by restoring him to his humanity,[82] and Lucius becomes a devotee of the goddess.[83] Apuleius's

75. See Nock, *Conversion*, 107–21, 155; Angus, *Mystery Religions*, 187–204.

76. Apuleius of Madura boasts of having undergone multiple initiations into mysteries (see *Apology* 55). Libanius reports of the emperor Julian that he "consorted with *daimones* in countless rites (*teletai*)" (cited in Nock, *Conversion*, 115). The extreme case is presented in Theophrastus's "Portrait of the Superstitious Person," who goes to the priest of Orpheus monthly (cited in Luck, *Arcana Mundi*, 65–66).

77. Clement of Alexandria, *Stromateis* 5.71–72, speaks of three stages, but there were actually four stages in the complete Eleusinian initiation: the purification, initiation into the lesser mysteries (at Agrae), then initiation into the greater mysteries (at Eleusis), and a year later the *epopteia*, also at Eleusis. See Nock, "Hellenistic Mysteries," 792–93; Wagner, *Pauline Baptism*, 71–88; Kerényi, *Eleusis*, 45–102; Alderinck, "Eleusinian Mysteries," 1478–82.

78. For seven degrees of initiation in the Mithras cult, see Cumont, *Mysteries of Mithra*, 152–58; Merkelbach, *Mithras*, 86–145; Burkert, *Ancient Mystery Cults*, 42, 98–99.

79. See Conte, *Latin Literature*, 166–90.

80. Nock, *Conversion*, 138, calls Apuleius's account "the high-water mark of the piety which grew out of the Mystery religions."

81. *Metamorphoses* 10.38; for text, translation, and full commentary, see Griffiths, *Isis-Book*.

82. *Metamorphoses* 11.3–15.

83. *Metamorphoses* 11.26.

veiled description of Lucius's initiation into the cult of Isis is one of our most important sources of knowledge of the mysteries.[84] We note that it involves a purificatory bath[85] and the putting on of new clothing.[86]

However dramatic and decisive, though, Lucius's initiation is by no means final. It is really only a first step. He discovers that a still more advanced form of initiation into the cult of Osiris, the consort of Isis, is desirable,[87] and after some delay and considerable expense he undergoes that second initiation.[88] Nor is this the end. Soon he is informed that still a third initiation is available. Lucius begins to have questions about the good faith of those who had initiated him in the first place, but he undergoes a third initiation,[89] with the same result as with the first two: his expense is well repaid by the even greater prosperity he enjoys as a lawyer, and he gains an exalted status as a member of the priesthood of the Osiris cult.[90] While Lucius was hesitating before his third initiation, wondering if something had gone wrong in the first two times, he is re-assured by a prophecy, which tells him: "There is no reason to be afraid of this long series of ritual, as if something had been omitted before. Rejoice and be happy instead, because the deities continually deem you worthy. Exalt, rather, in the fact that you will experience three times what is scarcely permitted others even once, and from that number you should rightly consider yourself forever blessed."[91]

From Apuleius's story, then, we learn that multiple initiations within the same cult were not only possible but to be expected as progressive movement toward perfection; that the passage from Isis to Osiris was considered not an apostasy but an enhancement; and that each state of initiation led to greater knowledge, dignity, and status within the cult. Ritual imprinting was toward the politics of perfection.

84. "It is the only first-person account of a mystery experience that we have." Burkert, *Ancient Mystery Cults*, 97.

85. *Metamorphoses* 11.23.

86. *Metamorphoses* 11.24.

87. *Metamorphoses* 11.27; for the entire myth, see Plutarch, *Isis and Osiris* (*Moralia* 351D–384C).

88. *Metamorphoses* 11.29.

89. *Metamorphoses* 11.29; Nock notes, "The second and third initiations have been regarded as invented by the Roman priesthood for their personal gain . . . but it is possible that these additional ceremonies were genuine and due to a tendency else-where observed to multiple rites" (*Conversion*, 150).

90. *Metamorphoses* 11.30.

91. *Metamorphoses* 11.29.

Mysterious Initiation in Judaism

The question of how much the language and sensibility of the mysteries had entered into the Judaism of the Hellenistic period remains disputed. At one extreme is Erwin Goodenough, who argued that Hellenistic Judaism was, in effect, a form of Mystery, and who interpreted a variety of archaeological data and literary texts in support of that strong position.[92] For Goodenough, the discovery of the synagogue at Dura-Europos with its murals depicting Moses in the garb of a mystagogue was the key to unlocking the specific religiosity of Hellenistic Judaism as found above all in the writings of Philo, who for Goodenough is not an idiosyncratic but a representative figure.[93] At the other extreme is Arthur Darby Nock, who, while recognizing the validity of many of Goodenough's discrete observations, resists the transmutation of Judaism in the diaspora into a single coherent religious system fundamentally different from that of a halakically based Palestinian Judaism.[94]

What neither position can deny is the pervasive use by Philo of language that takes its origin in the mysteries yet is employed with direct reference to the practice and self-understanding of Judaism.[95] There is no question here of syncretism in the crude sense. As a passionate defender of Judaism, Philo engages in the same sort of rejection of the pagan mysteries that we find in the Wisdom of Solomon (14:22–31).[96] He

92. Goodenough, *By Light, Light*; Goodenough, *Introduction to Philo Judæus*.

93. Goodenough, *Jewish Symbols*. Before Goodenough, Lucien Cerfaux argued for widespread influence of the mysteries on Alexandrian Judaism, focusing esp. on Pseudo-Orpheus; see "Influence des Mystères"; for a full examination of the pertinent non-Philonic texts, see Holladay, *Fragments from Hellenistic Jewish Authors*, esp. vol. 2, *Poets* (1989), vol. 3, *Aristobulus* (1995), and vol. 4, *Orphica* (1996). Certainly the vision of the heavenly man in Joseph and Aseneth 14–17 shares the same sensibility.

94. See in particular Nock's three reviews of Goodenough's *Jewish Symbols*, under the titles "Religious Symbols and Symbolism I," "Religious Symbols and Symbolism II," and "Religious Symbols and Symbolism III." In his "Hellenistic Mysteries," 802, Nock insists that Philo's language is no more than a "philosophic metaphor" and that his interests are the same as those of Palestinian Judaism. A critical yet appreciative review of Goodenough's contribution is found in M. Smith, "Goodenough's *Jewish Symbols*."

95. Nock grants, "Undeniably, Philo used Mystery terms for hidden theological truths," in "Religious Symbols and Symbolism II," 899. Nock's reference to this usage as a "philosophical metaphor" ("Hellenistic Mysteries," 802) derives from the fact that Plato had already employed the Eleusinian "lesser and greater mysteries" language with respect to spiritual transformation through knowledge (see *Symposium* 209E; *Phaedrus* 150B–C; Burkert, *Ancient Mystery Cults*, 91–93).

96. For Philo's rejection of an accommodation that would mean abandonment of ancestral customs, see *On the Migration of Abraham* 89–92; *Against Flaccus* 50.

speaks of "the lore of the occult rites and mysteries and all such imposture and buffoonery," scorns their "mummeries" and "mythic fables," and declares, "Let none, therefore, of the followers and disciples of Moses either confer or receive initiation to such rites."[97] In other places, he associates the mysteries, especially that of Demeter, with the exhibitions of licentiousness and effeminacy.[98]

What we find in Philo, then, is not a mingling of Judaism and the mysteries but rather a conceptualization of Judaism as Mystery: Philo's loyalty to the literal prescriptions of the law, including the obligation of circumcision, cannot be doubted.[99] But he regards such observance, based on a literal reading of the text of Scripture, as only the first stage of initiation. More is required if "perfection" is to be reached—namely, an initiation into a manner of reading that is allegorical and a transformation of the self that is spiritual in nature. It is the cultivation and perfection of the human soul through contemplation of the divine realities that is the real goal of Scripture.

Philo employs the symbolism of the mysteries at three levels. First, he contrasts the stage of perfection available to the patriarchs to the higher level of knowledge and transformation available to Moses, who entered into the presence of God. The movement from the stories of Genesis (which provide protreptic in the virtues) to the revelation of the law by Moses is the movement from the lesser to the greater mysteries. The moral virtues demonstrated by those *nomoi empsychoi* are available to all humans, but the divine secrets of the law are available only by revelation. In this understanding, Moses is a mystagogue. Second, Moses is also the one who initiates into the higher, allegorical reading of the law, so that the reader understands God's concern not to be simply with the cleansing of utensils and the separation of foods but always with the purification of the human mind and the separation of the spirit from earthly entanglements. Third, by displaying these two levels and by portraying them in terms of a mystery cult into which one can enter progressively through successive initiations, Philo has constructed himself as a hierophant, drawing his reader into deeper levels of knowledge and perfection.

If we scan Philo's language of perfection (*teleiōsis*), we find that it focuses on the human soul (*psyche*) or mind (*nous*),[100] which, schooled

97. Philo, *On the Special Laws* 1.319 (Colson, LCL).
98. Philo, *On the Special Laws* 3.37–42.
99. See Philo, *On the Migration of Abraham* 118.
100. Philo, *On Agriculture* 133, 146, 165; *On the Migration of Abraham* 73; *On the Cherubim* 69.

in the virtues exemplified by the patriarchs[101] and guided by God,[102] reaches its perfection in divine knowledge[103] acquired by the vision of God.[104] His language concerning the mysteries, in turn, coincides exactly with that concerning perfection. The mind that still knows sensibly has not yet attained "the highest mysteries,"[105] and it is the mind that is the "initiate of the divine mysteries"[106] received by God's revelation.[107] The mind is purified by such initiation into the "great mysteries."[108] It can soar aloft and be initiated into the "mysteries of the Lord."[109] Those who have such knowledge deserve to be called "initiates."[110] The movement from sensible knowledge and the practice of the virtues to this higher apprehension of God is characterized as initiation respectively into the "lesser mysteries" and "greater mysteries."[111]

For Philo, it is Moses who has uniquely entered into God's presence,[112] the "darkness of God" where he learned the "essence of unseen things,"[113] the "patterns and originals of the things of the sense."[114] It is Moses's mind that has been initiated into God's mystery.[115] Moses is therefore the one who can lead others into this greater mystery.[116] He is, indeed, a hierophant and teacher of the divine rites.[117] Moses is such through the oracles of the law, which themselves bear clues, when properly detected, of how they are to be read at a deeper than literal level.[118] Even the Septuagint is to be received as the oracles of a mystery.[119] Logically, then,

101. Philo, *On the Life of Abraham* 26; *On Agriculture* 157; *On Giants* 26.
102. Philo, *On the Change of Names* 23–24.
103. Philo, *On the Sacrifices of Abel and Cain* 7.
104. Philo, *On Rewards and Punishments* 36; *Who Is the Heir?* 121; *On Drunkenness* 82; *On the Change of Names* 12; *On the Posterity of Cain* 132.
105. Philo, *On the Life of Abraham* 122 (Colson, LCL).
106. Philo, *On Rewards and Punishments* 121 (Colson, LCL).
107. Philo, *On the Cherubim* 42.
108. Philo, *Allegorical Interpretation* 3.100 (Colson and Whitaker, LCL).
109. Philo, *Allegorical Interpretation* 3.71.
110. Philo, *On the Cherubim* 48; *On Flight and Finding* 85 (Colson and Whitaker, LCL).
111. Philo, *On the Sacrifices of Abel and Cain* 62 (Colson and Whitaker, LCL).
112. Philo, *On the Giants* 53–54; *On the Sacrifices of Abel and Cain* 53–54.
113. Philo, *On the Life of Moses* 1.158 (Colson, LCL).
114. Philo, *On the Creation of the World* 71 (Colson and Whitaker, LCL).
115. Philo, *Allegorical Interpretation* 3.101–3.
116. Philo, *On the Virtues* 178.
117. Philo, *On the Posterity of Cain* 173; *On the Giants* 54.
118. Philo, *On Dreams* 1.164.
119. Philo, *On the Life of Moses* 2.40.

those who hear the oracles of the law and learn to read them allegorically are themselves "initiated into the mysteries of the sanctified life."[120]

My point in this exposition is to demonstrate that, in at least one writer roughly contemporaneous with Paul, Judaism was not only consistently portrayed in terms of a mystery but was one with multiple initiations. Philo states clearly, furthermore, that "initiation into the lesser mysteries must precede initiations into the great,"[121] with Moses being the hierophant of the higher rites. The pertinence of this sequence to our present discussion should be obvious, especially in the case of Galatians, where an initial purificatory baptism into the Messiah is considered as prelude to a higher "perfection" accomplished by initiation into Moses. Note how Paul addresses those seeking circumcision: "Tell me, you who *want to be* under the law, do you not hear the law?" (Gal 4:21, author's translation). Philo intimates in one passage, in fact, that even more initiations might be possible: "I myself was initiated under Moses the God-beloved into the greater mysteries, yet when I saw the prophet Jeremiah and knew him to be not only himself enlightened but a Hierophant of the holy secrets, I was not slow to become his disciple."[122]

Ritual Initiation and Status Elevation

A third line of evidence is provided by cross-cultural anthropological studies of ritual.[123] Analysis of initiation rituals from a variety of cultures indicates that the multiple initiations found among the ancient Greco-Roman mysteries are by no means exceptional.[124] The Hopi, for example, have a two-stage initiation, with the second occurring some years after the first.[125] The Navaho practice a four-stage initiation.[126] The Gisu and Samburu also practice multiple initiations.[127] Initiations into secret so-

---

120. Philo, *On the Contemplative Life* 25, 28 (Colson, LCL); see *On the Life of Abraham* 122; *That God Is Unchangeable* 61.

121. Philo, *On the Life of Moses* 1:62; see *On the Sacrifices of Abel and Cain* 61–62.

122. Philo, *On the Cherubim* 49 (Colson and Whitaker, LCL).

123. Richard Ascough's application of ritual theory to the ritual of baptism in the Didache ("Analysis of the Baptismal Ritual") reveals the tripartite movement described by Van Gennep and Turner but no evidence for a stage of liminality (see below).

124. See La Fontaine, *Initiation*, 145, 152–53.

125. La Fontaine, *Initiation*, 90.

126. See Gennep, *Rites of Passage*, 79.

127. La Fontaine, *Initiation*, 145.

cieties, which are almost always hierarchical, especially involve a series of stages.[128] Jean S. La Fontaine analyzes the intricate stages of initiation into the Chinese Triad societies[129] and refers to as many as ninety-nine levels of membership in the Poro associations of West Africa, each with its own initiation.[130] Arnold van Gennep mentions the seven grades of initiation found among the Arioi in Tahiti and other parts of Polynesia, as well as the eighteen degrees of initiation into the Melanesian *suge*.[131] Such initiations involve an increase in both knowledge and power by the initiates,[132] especially in what Victor Turner calls "rituals of status elevation."[133] Indeed, rituals of initiation consistently invest initiates with greater status within a specified group. In La Fontaine's precise formulation, "maturity is a social status."[134]

Other anthropological aspects of initiation that might shed light on the present discussion are the frequent use of oaths and professions in such rituals,[135] the widespread symbolism of death and rebirth in connection with initiation,[136] the way that circumcision—especially in some African tribes—functions as an ordeal whose successful endurance proves maturity,[137] and the manner in which the suffering of an ordeal at initiation involves a pattern of submission to the authority of the initiator.[138] But of the greatest pertinence is Turner's analysis of the dialectic of structure and structurelessness in the ritual process.

Turner used his fieldwork among the Ndembu of northwestern Zambia in central Africa as a means of providing greater nuance to Van Gennep's classic analysis of *rites de passage*.[139] Van Gennep's work was a classic for two reasons. First, across a bewildering variety of specific ritual forms he was able to detect a basic pattern: in rituals negotiating a passage from one condition to another, he consistently saw the moment of separation, the moment of liminality, and the moment of reintegration.[140] Second,

128. La Fontaine, *Initiation*, 39; see also Turner, *Ritual Process*, 190–94.

129. La Fontaine, *Initiation*, 42–18.

130. La Fontaine, *Initiation*, 94.

131. Gennep, *Rites of Passage*, 84.

132. La Fontaine, *Initiation*, 15–17.

133. Turner, *Ritual Process*, 167.

134. La Fontaine, *Initiation*, 104; see also Milner, "Status and Sacredness."

135. La Fontaine, *Initiation*, 15.

136. La Fontaine, *Initiation*, 15 and 102; see Eliade, *Rites and Symbols*, 73–76, 89–93.

137. La Fontaine, *Initiation*, 112–14, 146–47.

138. La Fontaine, *Initiation*, 147–85.

139. Turner, *Ritual Process*, 4; see also Turner, *Process, Performance, and Pilgrimage*, 15–16.

140. Gennep, *Rites of Passage*, 7–25.

he saw that such rituals involved a social construction: puberty rituals, for example, did not mark a biological event but created a social event; what they effected was a transition from one social status to another.[141]

Turner gave his attention above all to the middle stage of liminality. Two of his observations are of special interest. The first is that the condition of liminality, experienced after the preliminary rites of separation and before the rites of reintegration, involves what Turner calls *communitas*[142]—namely, a sense of structureless cohesion and harmony that is frequently expressed by an absolute egalitarianism: "the passage from lower to higher status is through a limbo of statuslessness."[143] The second is that the condition of liminality is normally a temporary and preparatory condition. It prepares the way for the reintegration of the initiate at a higher status in society: "There is a dialectic here, for the immediacy of the *communitas* gives way to the mediacy of structure."[144]

Particularly those going through rituals of status elevation expect to pass through a stage of status reduction before reaching that higher state: "Such liminality may also, when it appears in *rites de passage*, humble the neophyte precisely because he is to be structurally exalted at the end of the rites."[145] If we were to apply Turner's analysis to the situation in Paul's Phrygian churches, we would say that those who had undergone an initial ritual of separation (such as baptism) could well agree with Paul that they were thereby neither male nor female, neither Jew nor Greek, neither slave nor free (Gal 3:28). But they would also have a great deal of anthropological evidence on their side if they were to add, "'For the time being,' that is, until we are initiated into the higher status of initiation into Moses offered through the ordeal of circumcision."

Jewish and Christian Practice

Finally, we can consider the evidence concerning the multiple relations of baptism to other initiations within Judaism and nascent Christianity itself. Most obvious is the practice of proselyte baptism for gentiles

141. Gennep, *Rites of Passage*, 65–70.
142. Turner, *Ritual Process*, 102–28; Turner, *Process, Performance, and Pilgrimage*, 40–44.
143. Turner, *Ritual Process*, 97; Turner, *Process, Performance, and Pilgrimage*, 98–101.
144. Turner, *Ritual Process*, 129; Turner, *Process, Performance, and Pilgrimage*, 44–45.
145. Turner, *Ritual Process*, 201.

converting to Judaism. Our knowledge of the ritual is inadequate, but it seems to have been considered a preliminary initiation, to be followed later by circumcision.[146] The pertinence of this precedent to gentile converts to the Messiah in Galatia should be obvious. There is also the baptism of John, which was extended to Jews who had already been circumcised, including Jesus.[147] John's Gospel provides slight evidence for a baptizing ministry of Jesus concurrent with that of John (3:22; 4:2). Thus we would have at least the theoretical possibility that a single individual could undergo, in sequence, Jewish proselyte baptism, circumcision, the baptism of John, and the baptism of Jesus.

The Acts of the Apostles shows those who heed Peter's proclamation at Pentecost being baptized "in the name of Jesus" (2:38). This group could well have included some who had also been baptized by John (see 1:21–22). After his encounter with the risen Lord, Paul, a circumcised Jew, receives the Holy Spirit (9:17) and is then baptized (9:18). Finally, we see Paul baptizing "in the name of Jesus" those disciples who had been baptized by John (19:1–5), and then placing hands on them so that they receive the Holy Spirit (19:6).[148] In light of these combinations, we should not wonder overmuch at a reference to "instruction about ablutions [baptisms]" in the plural, as part of the "elementary doctrine of Christ" (Heb 6:1–2), nor should we be too much surprised if new gentile converts in Phrygia, recently baptized into Jesus, should think that perhaps still more initiations were in store for them.

By means of these separate lines of evidence, I have tried to move from the clues in the text of Galatians and Colossians to some sense of the *kind* of "religious experience" baptism was for them. Since in this case we have no direct emic evidence, we are obliged to move from the external pattern of behavior toward some sense of the meaning of the

---

146. The basic texts are b. Yevamot 46a; Pesahim 8.8; 91b–92; Epictetus, *Discourses* 2.9.9–21; Sibylline Oracles 4.62–78; Josephus, *Jewish Antiquities* 20.38–48. For discussions, see Beasley-Murray, *Baptism in the New Testament*, 18–31; Crehan, *Early Christian Baptism*, 24; Lampe, *Seal of the Spirit*, 24; Cullmann, *Baptism in the New Testament*, 9; Delorme, "Practice of Baptism."

147. See Josephus, *Jewish Antiquities* 18.5.2; Matt 3:1–17; Mark 1:1–33; Luke 3:2–19; John 1:31–34; 3:22–24; 4:1–2; Acts 1:5; 18:25; 19:3–4; for discussion, see Beasley-Murray, *Baptism in the New Testament*, 31–44.

148. On the fruitless effort to derive some theological consistency on the question of the Holy Spirit in Luke's narrative by asking other than narrative questions, see Shepherd, *Narrative Function*, 11–26.

ritual as suggested by ancient texts and modern studies. Yet the yield is not insignificant. We have put ourselves in the position of understanding why these Phrygian Christians would have wanted to receive circumcision and undergo additional initiations beyond baptism; the reason is simply that such was the symbolic imprinting of initiation, certainly in their world, and in most other worlds we have been able to survey as well. To be initiated once was to be separated from "the world" and enter the community of the "sanctified." It meant dwelling in a state of liminal *communitas*, where social differentiations between gender, race, and status were dissolved. But this was only to be a temporary and preliminary state of affairs. If one was to "mature" or "grow perfect" in this religion, then surely other initiations would follow, and with them greater status. At the very least, we can appreciate that this desire was far from perverse and was, in fact, the natural impulse of human religiosity within the symbolic world of the ancient mysteries.

The Character of Paul's Response

Paul's response to his churches becomes more intelligible when placed in this context. In Gal 3:3 Paul's rhetorical question should be given its full ritual connotation. Rather than the RSV's neutral "Having begun in the Spirit, are you now ending with the flesh?" we should read something like, "Having begun in the Spirit, are you being perfected [*epiteleisthe*] now in the flesh?"[149] Paul perceives the logic of their endeavor.

Likewise, Paul's strange question in Gal 4:8-9 becomes a little clearer: "Formerly, when you did not know God, you were in bondage to beings that by nature are no gods; but now that you have come to know God, or rather to be known by God, how can you turn back again to the weak and beggarly elemental spirits, whose slaves you want to be once more?" Quite apart from the difficulty of identifying the "elemental spirits,"[150] how could Paul equate a desire for circumcision and the observance of Torah with a return to idolatry? The implied equation makes more sense against the backdrop I have sketched. To treat initiation into Christ as preliminary to initiation into Moses is, for Paul, to deny the ultimacy of Christ and, finally, the oneness of God (see Gal 3:30). It is to continue to

---

149. See Ascough, "Completion of a Religious Duty."

150. For the literature on *stoicheia tou kosmou* in Gal 4:3 and 8, see H. Betz, *Galatians*, 204-5.

act within the framework of polytheism, where initiation into a second deity in no way suggests rejection of the first. Paul's (to us) outrageous identification of Torah with idolatry makes sense if he is in fact opposing the logic of ritual imprinting in the mysteries.[151]

Above all, we can better understand why Paul hinges his entire argument on the reality of the gift of the Spirit the Galatians received when they accepted the proclamation of the crucified Messiah (Gal 3:2) and had "put on Christ" by baptism (3:27).[152] That Paul can appeal to their experience suggests that he knew they had experienced the working of powerful things among them (3:5). But he needs to convince them that this gift of the Spirit is indeed the fulfillment of God's promise (3:14), bringing them into full maturity before the one God: "Because you are sons, God has sent the Spirit of his Son into our hearts, crying, 'Abba! Father!' So through God you are no longer a slave but a son, and if a son then an heir" (4:6–7).

Paul therefore sets up a fundamental opposition between initiation in the Spirit and initiation "in the flesh" (i.e., circumcision). So the desire to be circumcised cannot be something more added on by way of perfection but can only be a fundamental betrayal of the first gift. "If you receive circumcision, Christ will be of no advantage to you. . . . You are severed from Christ" (Gal 5:2, 4). He extends the opposition also to the moral sphere. Paul declares, "If we live by the Spirit, let us also walk by the Spirit" (5:25), which means living according to the principles of *communitas* established by the gift of the Spirit: egalitarianism, mutual upbuilding, the positive "fruits of the Spirit" (5:22). In a word, Paul advocates living in what Turner would call a state of permanent liminality. For Paul, the desire to be initiated "in the flesh" is itself an expression of a "fleshly morality," which he spells out in terms of attitudes of rivalry, envy, self-seeking (5:19–21). In short, Paul argues for the sufficiency of baptism as a ritual of initiation because through it Christians enter into full inheritance of God's promise (3:27–4:7).

In Colossians, Paul's argument is based even more emphatically on the adequacy of the experience of God in Christ through baptism. Those seeking to disqualify others (2:18) or judge others (2:16) on the basis of

151. It may also be possible that Paul's polemical statement, "they desire to have you circumcised that they may glory in your flesh" (Gal 6:13), also fits within this framework, for success in recruiting devotees to higher stages of initiation also has implications for the authority of the mystagogue.

152. For the importance of the *experience* of the Holy Spirit in Paul's argument, see Lull, *Spirit in Galatia*, 53–152.

circumcision (2:11) and ascetical regulations (2:21) and mystical initiation (2:18) are both deceiving and self-deceived. They are like people who chase after shadows but do not see the solid body that casts the shadow. Festivals and new moons and sabbaths are "only a shadow of what is to come; but the body is Christ's" (2:17, author's translation). Their practices only puff them up (2:18) with the appearance of religious rigor (2:23) but do not really transform the person spiritually (2:23). Indeed the very fact that the promotion of further initiations leads to rivalry and judgment demonstrates that "they are of no value in checking the indulgence of the flesh" (2:23). Paul seeks to remind his readers that the power at work in Christ is the very power of God: "in him all the fulness of God was pleased to dwell" (1:19). Therefore, by their initiation into Christ through baptism (1:21; 2:11–12), they have entered into "the inheritance of the saints in light," for God has "qualified" them (1:12).

Once more, then, Paul exhorts his readers to follow through the ritual imprinting of baptism into the death and resurrection of Jesus. They are to live in a community where there is no "Greek and Jew, circumcised and uncircumcised, barbarian, Scythian, slave, free man, but Christ is all, and in all" (Col 3:11). They are to "put on" the qualities of meekness and compassion and harmony that reflect the state of *communitas*. The letter is filled with the language of mystery and maturity (see 1:6; 3:28; 4:12). But for Paul the *mystērion* is above all the way in which God has reached out to the gentiles through Christ, "in whom are hid all the treasures of wisdom and knowledge" (2:3). And perfection (see 1:28; 3:14; 4:12) consists above all in a deeper knowledge of this gift that has been given (1:6–7, 9–10; 2:2), a knowledge spelled out in a consistent manner of life that enacts the ritual imprinting of death and resurrection (1:10; 3:1–17).

Conclusion

Paul's arguments are powerful, even compelling. And they tell us a great deal about *his* understanding of the experience of baptism.[153] But Paul's theological rhetoric had an uphill fight against the deep impulses of religious imprinting. We have no idea how successful he was in his ancient

---

153. Note, however, that his arguments also depend on his readers' agreement that they had, in fact, experienced powerful things through baptism and the reception of the Holy Spirit.

Phrygian battles.[154] We do know that he secured for baptism its unique status as a ritual of initiation for Christians and established the *nomos tou christou* (law of the Christ), the pattern of the dying and rising Christ, as the ritual imprinting through which Christians would grow in perfection. But it is equally clear that the religious impulses of the Phrygian Christians were not confined to them. After not too many years, Christians everywhere followed the sacrament of baptism with the second initiation rite of confirmation and, for those more dedicated still, a third initiation into the priesthood.[155] As with Apuleius in the cult of Isis, so with Augustine in the cult of the Christ. In this particular game, religion trumps theology.

154. We may wonder, however, what his Galatian and Colossian readers might have thought had they heard him assure his Corinthian congregations that "we do speak a wisdom among the perfect [*teleiois*], but not a wisdom of this age nor of the rulers of this age who are being destroyed. But we speak a wisdom of God that has been revealed in a *mystērion*" (1 Cor 2:6–7, author's translation).

155. Concerning confirmation, Gregory Dix notes that it performed the same function of excluding the less-than-fully-initiated from sacred meals in Christianity as circumcision did in Judaism: by the time of Hippolytus, "The old jewish [*sic*] rules against table-fellowship 'with men uncircumcised' have been transferred by the church to any form of table-fellowship 'with men unconfirmed'" (*Shape of the Liturgy*, 83).

Chapter 10

The Truth of Christian Experience

The Fourfold Narrative in Galatians 1–4

Some of the canonical letters of Paul suffer from neglect; they are scarcely read and seldom regarded as having more than historical significance—they may reveal something of their circumstances, it is thought, but have little to say to later generations. Such is the case, surely, with the so-called Pastoral Letters (above all Titus) and with the Second Letter to the Thessalonians.

Other letters, by contrast, have been made to bear a theological weight that threatens to obliterate the homely circumstances of their composition. This has certainly been the fate of Romans and Galatians.[1] As I tried to demonstrate in the first volume, these "great" letters of Paul have represented, for good and ill, the "theological Paul," who is regarded by champions as the heart of authentic Christianity and by detractors as the chief destroyer of the Jesus movement.[2]

Despite its impressive sweep and magisterial argument, however, Romans was written by Paul as a fundraising letter seeking to persuade the Roman church to support his new mission to Spain. Recognizing such homely origins does not diminish Romans, but it serves to place his longest and most logically worked out composition in the same general class of missionary and pastoral concerns that dominate the canonical collection as a whole.[3] While Paul speaks in Romans with great theological energy and weight, his argument serves not to develop a systematic

1. See, e.g., Froehlich, *Biblical Interpretation*; Allen and Linebaugh, *Reformation Readings of Paul.*
2. The commotion has not quieted; among many others, see Elliott, *Galatians in Christian Theology*; Hacker, *Colonizers' Idols*; Nanos, *Galatian Debate*; Lozada, *Toward a Latino/a Biblical Interpretation*; Kahl, *Galatians Re-imagined*; Lee and Yoo, *Mapping and Engaging.*
3. See Johnson, *Reading Romans.*

soteriology but to be an effective instrument for acquiring financial support for his mission to the gentiles.

In this and the subsequent chapter, I pursue the question of whether Galatians is best read as a theological treatise adjudicating the respective claims of Judaism and Christianity—as it has so often been read—or is better understood as an expression of Paul's pastoral concern for a set of regional churches who are in danger of division and perhaps even dissolution. Is it possible that his readers' confusion is based not in conflicting theological positions but in basic human competitiveness and the quest for status? Is it possible that Paul's language about the works of the law and faith looms large in this letter not because those topics were the most important either for Paul or his hypothetical opponents but because the competitive conflicts within the churches arose out of envy for Paul's own privilege as a Jew?

Is it perhaps the case that Paul's concern in Galatians is not first of all soteriological (how humans are saved) but ecclesial (how believers should live out together the implications of their experience). Can Galatians be read, that is, as concerned less with the (fairly abstract) issue of how humans are put in right relationship with God and more with the practical (even material) issue of living in right relationship with each other? Perhaps most provocatively, should we read Galatians less as a logical argument developed on the basis of theological premises—"truth" in the sense of correct principles—and more as an invitation to enter into and continue a complex set of narratives to which the "truth" of their experience has already initiated them?

The Rhetorical Situation

In the previous chapter, I offered a quick sketch of the crisis Paul considered himself to be facing among "the churches throughout Galatia" that required a response from him "and all those with me" (Gal 1:2). The team character of Paul's ministry is indicated by this cosponsorship, and the phrase "throughout Galatia" suggests that the tendency Paul counters is found not in a single community but in an entire region. Apart from these broad references, however, the letter has an intensely personal (even individual) tone. There is no mention in this letter, for example, of Paul's sending or receiving delegates, back and forth. Rather, the personal experience of Paul and that of the Galatians—separately and in tandem—dominates the letter. Even more than the Corinthian correspondence, this letter points to direct interactions between the apostle and his readers.

The readers were among Paul's gentile converts, who came to faith in Christ straight from the worship of beings that were not really gods and who, in all likelihood, learned what little they knew of Judaism from Paul himself. It may well have been Paul the Pharisee who inadvertently stimulated the rivalry among some Galatian believers who considered baptism only a starting point and craved the further ritual "perfection" they could have through being circumcised and observing the law of Moses, and who, not incidentally, could both look down on others still lacking their exalted status and seek to pressure them to follow their path toward full (ritual) perfection.

Although a great deal of scholarly effort has been dedicated to locating the "agitators" or "opponents" of Paul in Galatia,[4] the simplest and most elegant hypothesis is that the "certain ones" who are stirring discontent and envy among the churches are from inside the circle of Pauline churches rather than from the outside, and are themselves gentiles who—under whatever influence—have come to regard full inclusion in Judaism as having higher status than mere membership in Christ. Why, they may well have asked, can't they have the same status enjoyed by Paul by undergoing the initiation that Paul had and following the law of Moses as Paul had? For those with such an ambition, the cost of disturbing or even disrupting the community might seem a small one.

Paul's language in response, as has often been noted, combines emotional and polemical outbursts with tightly argued logic. Thus, on the first point, he replaces his customary thanksgiving with a statement of astonishment (Gal 1:6) and calls his readers stupid (3:1, 3) and bewitched (3:1). As for those imposing circumcision, he wishes they would castrate themselves (5:12), and themselves be cursed (1:8–9) and cast out of the community (4:30); they are cowards who seek to avoid the persecution that comes with the cross (6:12); they only seek to impose circumcision on others only so that they can boast (6:13). On the second point, Paul engages in the reading of scriptural texts with sophisticated techniques (3:10–13, 16–22; 4:21–31) that seem deliberately intended to expose the ignorance of those who "think they know the law" (4:21).[5]

What has been less noticed until very recently is the way in which Paul's response depends on the convergence of four narratives, all of them touch-

4. Among such efforts, see Schmithals, *Paul and the Gnostics*, 13–64; Tyson, "Paul's Opponents in Galatia"; Jewett, "Agitators"; A. Harvey, "Opposition of Paul"; Robert McL. Wilson, "Gnostics—in Galatia?" By far the most levelheaded and sober assessment is offered by Munck, "Judaizing Gentile Christians."

5. See, e.g., Lindars, *New Testament Apologetic*, 232–37; Dahl, "Contradictions in Scripture"; Wilcox, "'Upon the Tree'"; Callan, "Pauline Midrash."

ing on the lives of his readers. By recalling these stories to their minds, Paul seeks to redirect their energy from an ambition for status that threatens to exclude, to an ambition for service that seeks to embrace. I am suggesting that when Paul speaks of "the truth of the gospel" (Gal 2:5, 14) and accuses the Galatians of turning to "another gospel" (1:6–9), he is speaking not in theoretical terms of turning from a true theology to a false one but of turning their back on God's work in the world and in their lives.

There is no need, I think, to construct an elaborate exposition of or defense for the term "narrative" (or its virtual synonym, "story") as frequently used in epistolary literature. I am building on the excellent work especially of Richard Hays, who has shown how elements of a narrative about Jesus form the substructure of Paul's theology in Galatians, an approach that has successfully been extended to Romans by Katherine Grieb and Valérie Nicolet-Anderson.[6] But I am especially assuming the thorough analysis of narrativity in ancient rhetoric and its applicability to Galatians by Richard Manley Adams.[7] Three definitional points of my own may, however, prove helpful.

First, I think of narrative as an ordered sequence of events or experiences (a plot) enacted by human or divine characters. Events may be visible to others; experiences may or may not be. Thus, "I bought a dozen eggs for your breakfast this morning" is a short but clear narrative segment, whereas "Eggs are good for your health" is not a narrative but a proposition. The event of egg-purchasing can be verified by the presence of actual eggs where there had been none, whereas the experience of egg-phobia is less available to testing. We cannot assume, however, that even so brief an account will be without some ambiguity. Does the phrase "this morning," for example, refer to the time when the eggs were purchased, or to the time when breakfast was prepared, or perhaps even both? If the phrase was placed at the start of the sentence, then it would clearly refer to the time of purchase; but where it stands now, it could have either of the two points of reference I have identified.

Second, narratives or stories can be in varying degrees either explicit or implicit within other genres, such as speeches, dramas, and letters. Im-

6. See Hays, *Faith of Jesus Christ*; Grieb, *Story of Romans*; Nicolet-Anderson, *Constructing the Self*.

7. Adams, "'The Israel of God.'" Three essays taking up aspects of narrative in Galatians are found in B. Longenecker, *Narrative Dynamics in Paul*—namely, B. Longenecker, "Sharing in Their Spiritual Blessings," and D. Campbell, "Story of Jesus" and "Stories of Predecessors." A dissenting voice is offered by Das, *Paul and the Stories of Israel*.

plicit elements of story require some explicit signposts for the full form of the story to be filled in. From "I bought a dozen eggs for your breakfast this morning," for example, we can properly infer at the level of plot the discovery of a need for eggs, an excursion to a place that provides eggs, a purchase of eggs, and the (planned or actual) cooking of breakfast. At the level of character, we can infer as well a probable relationship (spousal, parental, servile) between at least two persons, as well as a motivation ("for your breakfast") that is rich in possible significance.

Third, explicit and implicit parts of a narrative, although always possessing a temporal or causal sequence or both, may not appear within nonnarrative genres in that "natural" sequence. Elements may be, and often are, referred to out of sequence. The "natural" chronological or causal sequence may require reconstruction by the reader or listener when a writer or speaker states or alludes to parts of the story out of sequence. But an important truth lies within this difficulty. The more allusive and fragmented the story fragments appear within a rhetorical argument, the more we can conclude that the intended readers (or hearers) of the rhetoric have a prior or "assumed" knowledge of those elements in the story. These are the simple premises I bring to the reading of Galatians.

The present chapter focuses on the first four chapters of the letter in order to identify the four narratives that Paul uses to enable his Galatian readers to understand and affirm the truth of the Christian experience. The stories are, as one might expect, intertwined in Paul's polemical and argumentative rhetoric. The distinctions between them that I draw are made only to make clear the several strands that Paul wants to be heard as coexisting and codependent. In the next chapter, I show how Paul argues that this fourfold story should be carried forward in the lives of the Galatian believers.

The four stories I consider here are those concerning Paul himself, concerning Jesus, concerning God (and God's people Israel), and concerning the Galatians. It is noteworthy that elements of all four narratives are already intertwined in the epistolary greeting (1:1–5):

- We learn more than we have suspected we might about God: that he is the Father who sends gift (grace/*charis*) and peace (*eirēnē*) to the churches throughout Galatia, that he raised Jesus from the dead, that with Christ he appointed Paul as his representative (apostle). It was by his will, moreover, that these things happened, so that he should receive eternal glory—that is, the recognition of his presence and power.

- About Jesus we learn that God raised him as Messiah, that as Lord he also sends grace and peace to the Galatian churches, that he appointed Paul as an apostle, and that he gave himself for the sake of their sins in order to rescue them. Thus, we have both the past event of Jesus's self-giving for the sake of the Galatians and the present existential reality of Jesus (as risen Lord) commissioning Paul and now greeting the Galatians.
- About Paul we learn that he was appointed as an apostle not by human authority but by God the Father and Jesus the Lord, and that he writes to the Galatian churches together with those who are with him.
- About the Galatians we learn that the risen Lord Jesus gave himself for their sins and rescued them from the present evil age, and that both God the Father and the Lord Jesus Christ send grace and peace, together with Paul and his entourage, to the assemblies throughout their region.

In sum, the greeting of the letter introduces the major characters and makes clear (above all by the use of the first-person plural pronoun "us") that the four stories go together to form one story that has unfolded among them, and still is (or ought to be) unfolding, "according to the will of God." Paul's opening rhetoric so weaves together God with Christ, and God and Christ with himself, and himself with the Galatian churches (and God and Christ), that his readers—then and now—assume that all these characters belong together. The twofold plot mechanism linking them is the self-giving of Jesus for their rescue and the appointment of Paul as their apostle. We are now able to pick up the discrete strands in this story to see how they ought (in Paul's view) to be so joined together.

The Story of the Galatians

In the case of Paul's readers in the churches of Galatia, it is again necessary to reconstruct a narrative that within the letter appears mostly in allusive fragments, yet when these are arranged chronologically, a coherent story appears. Like Paul, the Galatians have experienced a dramatic turn in their lives. But their starting point was dramatically different from Paul's. He began "in Judaism" as a strict and competitive observer of the law of Moses. They began as gentiles who "did not know

God" and served "beings that were not gods" (4:8).[8] Paul came among them while they were in this condition, and they gladly welcomed him. Despite his physical affliction, they received him as a "messenger from God," indeed "as Christ Jesus," and would have plucked out their eyes for Paul (4:13–16). There is no indication that they had ever even heard of Judaism or the law before Paul's arrival; what they knew of it, we can assume, they knew because they became acquainted with Paul's "former life in Judaism" (1:13)—in all likelihood, from Paul himself.

It was appropriate that they received Paul as a messenger from God, and even as Christ Jesus, because Paul proclaimed to them "the good news from/concerning Christ" (*to euangelion tou Christou*, Gal 1:7). He preached Christ as "publicly displayed as crucified," and on the basis of their hearing this message with "the hearing of faith," they received the Holy Spirit (3:1–2). Paul stresses the point that this experience (*pathein*, 3:4), which manifested itself in "mighty deeds" (*dynameis*) was worked through the Holy Spirit (3:5) and had nothing to do with "works of the law" (3:2, 5).[9] Not only that: in addition to such extraordinary manifestations, in baptism the Galatians received an even more intimate and transforming experience of the Spirit:

> Through faith you are all children of God in Christ Jesus. For all of you who were baptized into Christ have clothed yourselves with Christ. There is neither Jew nor Greek, there is neither slave nor free person, there is not male and female; for you are all one in Christ Jesus. And if you belong to Christ, then you are Abraham's descendent, heirs according to the promise. . . . As proof that you are children, God sent the spirit of his Son into our hearts, crying, "Abba! Father!" So you are no longer a slave but a child, and if a child then also an heir, through God. (3:26–29; 4:6–7 NABRE)

The experience of God's Holy Spirit in baptism, in short, has at once made the gentile Galatians children of God and children of Abraham. In Christ, furthermore, the three kinds of differentiation that in the ancient world (and, for that matter, every world) define status—namely,

8. There is no compelling reason to make the Galatians' enslavement to *stoicheia tou kosmou* in 4:3 equivalent to "beings that were not gods" in 4:8. The more cosmologically modest translation of "worldly regulations" suits both the immediate and broader contexts nicely.

9. For the importance of this point in Paul's argument, see Lull, *Spirit in Galatia*.

ethnicity, social class, and gender—have been relativized: they are "all one in Christ Jesus" (3:28). Paul acknowledges that the Galatians at first made appropriate progress within this "new creation" of liminality, where neither circumcision nor uncircumcision matter (6:15): "you were running well" (*etrechete kalōs*).[10] He then expresses puzzlement over the present commotion: "who hindered you from following the truth?" (5:7 NABRE).[11]

We share Paul's puzzlement, uncertain whether those advancing the cause of circumcision with its attendant obligation to perform the works of the law come from the outside or (as I think more likely) from within the Galatian congregations. Whoever they are, Paul regards them as "preaching a different good news" than the one he proclaimed and the one which transformed the Galatians (Gal 1:6–9). They have "bewitched" (*ebaskanen*) their hearers,[12] whom Paul twice castigates as "senseless" (*anoētoi*) for being persuaded by them (3:1–3). The reason they are senseless is that they have failed to connect the experience of life through the Spirit with the faith of the crucified Messiah and instead have chased after the status that might come to them by further ritual perfection.[13] They are getting their own story wrong.

Those who seek to be circumcised are desiring more, but in so doing, they are cutting themselves off from the gift they have been given. In contrast to Paul, who "did not nullify" the grace that came to him in Christ (*ouk athetō tēn charin tou theou*, Gal 2:20), those who seek circumcision are separated from Christ (*kathērgēthēte apo Christou*) and have fallen away from the gift they had been given (*tēs charitos exepesate*), because by seeking circumcision they are obligated to the whole law (5:3–4), and placing oneself under the whole law means regarding Christ as a curse rather than as the source of life (see 3:13). The Galatians who regard circumcision simply as the means to a higher social position in the church have therefore turned their backs on the profound transformation Christ's Holy Spirit has made in their lives. By "observing days, months, seasons, and years" under the aegis of the Jewish law, they have,

10. The use of the imperfect denotes continuous action in the past; their progress was more than momentary.

11. At the risk of excessive repetition, I note that the "truth" here is the reality of what they had experienced through the Holy Spirit.

12. See the discussion of witchcraft and the evil eye in Neyrey, *Paul, in Other Words*.

13. For the ritual connotations of *epitelein* in 3:3, see the preceding chapter, "Ritual Imprinting and the Politics of Perfection."

ironically, once more placed themselves in slavery to "weak and destitute guidelines [*stoicheia*]"[14] just as they had when they did not know God or, more important, when they were not known by God (4:8–10). No wonder that Paul feels he has labored among them in vain (4:11); no wonder he is in labor until Christ be formed among them again (4:19). No wonder he is "perplexed" because of them (4:20).

Paul's Story

Paul, to be sure, is the narrator of all four stories. The account of his own life experience demands extended consideration not only because it occurs first in the letter and is told at such length and in such detail but also because it plays such an important exemplary role: Paul clearly wants his own narrative to provide a model to his readers.[15] Despite all the circumstantial detail he provides, Paul's story is basically a simple one in three stages: his life before encountering the risen Lord Jesus, the transformation of his life with and in Christ, and his extended fidelity to that experience of transformation despite human opposition.

Paul saw himself as "set apart" (*aphorisas*) by God from his mother's womb (Gal 1:15) for a special destiny; this language, as I showed in volume 1, echoes the prophetic call of Jeremiah and Isaiah.[16] In the first stage of his life, however, he understood this destiny in terms of a deep commitment to the observance of Torah and the persecution of those who, in his eyes, threatened the status of the law. He quickly summarizes this

14. The most obvious way to translate *stoicheion* in Galatians is as "elementary principles" or "basic observances" (see Xenophon, *Memorabilia* 2.1.1; Plutarch, *On the Education of Children* 16). See especially this sense in Heb 5:12. The cosmological translation in Galatians, in turn, has affected the cosmic translation in Col 2:8, 20. In my view, the use of the verb *stoichein* in the obvious sense of "observe" or "line up with" is dispositive (see Acts 21:24; Rom 4:12; Phil 3:16; and above all Gal 5:25 and 6:16).

15. Hans Dieter Betz deserves full recognition for helping bring rhetorical analysis back to the study of Paul—it had already been a feature of interpreters like Calvin—and in particular Galatians; see Betz, "Literary Composition" and *Galatians*. Because he mistakenly identified Galatians as a form of forensic rhetoric, however, he saw Paul's *narratio* as serving a defensive function. The work of Adams ("'The Israel of God'") and others has shown how wide are the functions of narration within Greco-Roman rhetoric, and how the story of Paul in Galatians should be seen above all as exemplary.

16. See vol. 1, chap. 5 ("What Kind of Jew Is Paul?").

part of his story in 1:13–14, noting that the Galatians had already "heard of" (*ēkousate*) his former "manner of life" (*anastrophē*).[17] Although this segment of the story is brief, both its arrangement and diction deserve attention. We note how Paul characterizes his life "within Judaism" (*en tō ioudaismō*)[18] in what might be thought of as an inverted order, undoubtedly in order to make a point. He begins with his persecution of the church ("beyond measure"[19]): he had persistently "sought out" (*ediōkon*) and "tried to destroy" (*eporthoun*) those whose allegiance was to Christ. The use of the imperfect tense indicates repeated or continuous behavior (it is an *anastrophē*) rather than an isolated act: destroying the church was Paul's program.

By placing his agenda of opposing the church first, Paul enables his hearers to understand his characterization of his "Judaism" as the basis of his destructive disposition toward the church. As one set apart by God from birth, Paul understood in this former stage that his opposition to believers in Christ was in accord with, an expression of, God's will: he was acting to defend the manner of life that was in accord with Torah. Paul brings together in Gal 1:14 (NABRE) two striking statements concerning his life "in Judaism," how he "progressed . . . beyond many of my contemporaries among my race" and how he was "even more a zealot for my ancestral traditions." Taken together, the statements show first how Paul's dedication to "my ancestral traditions"[20] was the basis for his persecution of the church: he was a "zealot," someone whose fervor had an aggressive and oppositional edge to it,[21] and he was intensely competi-

17. *Anastrophē* means, broadly, the conduct of life or manner of living. See Epictetus, *Discourses* 1.9.24, 1.22.13; 2 Macc 6:23; Letter of Aristeas 130. Paul uses the noun form also in Eph 4:22 and 1 Tim 4:12, and the verb form *anastrephein* in 2 Cor 1:12; Eph 2:3; and 1 Tim 3:15, all with this same sense of the character of life.

18. Paul's double use of *Ioudaismos* is unparalleled in the New Testament but clearly corresponds to *anastrophē* to mean "the Jewish way of life," as in 2 Macc 2:21; 8:1; 14:38; and 4 Macc 4:26. It corresponds to Paul's other *hapax legomenon* in Gal 2:14, *Ioudaikōs*—that is, "live in a Jewish manner"—by observing laws distinctive to Jews and not found among gentiles. Paul's usage makes clear why an insistence on making the term *Ioudaios* simply a geographical designation ("Judean") is anachronistic nonsense; see for example, how Hart, *New Testament*, insists on the consistent translation "Judean" even here.

19. The adverbial phrase *kath' hyperbolēn* when used with persecution suggests a rabid fanaticism (see Sophocles, *Oedipus Rex* 1195; 4 Macc 3:18). The phrase is used positively by Paul in Rom 7:13; 1 Cor 12:31; 2 Cor 1:8; 4:7, 1; 12:7.

20. The double use of the personal pronoun *mou* (my) is particularly revealing of Paul's proprietary stance toward Israel's traditions.

21. In Greek, the cognates of *zēloun* can be used positively for an ardent allegiance

tive, measuring himself and his "progress in Judaism"[22] against that of his contemporaries. The rhetorical point of this characterization, given the crisis in Galatia, should have been obvious: the competitive marking of progress and status can lead to destroying the people of God.

Paul's way of framing this first part of his story has extraordinary rhetorical importance, for the stage *from which* he has been moved through the experience of God in Christ is precisely the stage *toward which* the agitators in the Galatian community want to go. The kind of fierce competitiveness Paul displayed *en tō Ioudaismō*, he wants them to see, is exactly the same as the "politics of perfection" they are practicing.

The second stage of Paul's own story is the transformation that God worked in him through Christ.[23] He speaks of God being pleased to "reveal his Son to me [or "in me," *en emoi*]" (Gal 1:16). So cryptically does he speak of this experience of Jesus as God's Son that it is best understood as an encounter with the resurrected one, since it happened well after Jesus's death and after Paul's period of persecuting the church. No detailed account of this "revelation" is given, but it results in a complete reversal of Paul's story. The one who persecuted the followers of Jesus in defense of Torah is now commissioned by God to proclaim "him" (i.e., Jesus) as good news to the gentiles, and he at once obeys, without consulting any human authority ("flesh and blood"), or going to Jerusalem to those who were apostles before him; rather, he preached in Arabia before turning back to Damascus (1:17). God, then, "reveals" Jesus as his Son to Paul and commissions Paul as an apostle to the gentiles, a commission he obeys unequivocally and without human authorization. As he identifies himself in the greeting of the letter, Paul is an "apostle, not through humans, but through Jesus Christ and God the Father who raised him from the dead" (1:1).

Was Paul's turning point only an epistemic episode, by which he came

---

to or pursuit of something good (see, e.g., Rom 10:2; 1 Cor 12:31; 14:1, 12, 39; 2 Cor 7:7, 11; 11:2; Titus 2:14), or negatively as a form of jealousy (e.g., Rom 13:13; 1 Cor 3:3; 13:4; 2 Cor 12:20; Gal 4:17). It must be confessed that the usage here and in 2 Cor 11:2 have aspects of both senses. Paul also speaks of his persecution of the church as *kata zēlos* in Phil 3:6.

22. In moral literature, the verb used by Paul, *prokoptein*, is used for "making progress" either in a good or bad direction, toward virtue or vice (see, e.g., Philo, *On the Sacrifices of Abel and Cain* 7; Epictetus, *Discourses* 2.17.4; Testament of Judah 21:8). In Paul, see the negative use of the verb in 2 Tim 2:16; 3:9, 13, and the positive use of the noun (*prokopē*) in Phil 1:12, 25; 1 Tim 4:15.

23. For transformation language in Galatians, see now Carr, "Subject of the New Creation," 48–96.

to new insight into Christ, or was there more involved? Paul's language in Gal 2:19–21 suggests something much more—a transformation that involved his total self, a form of dying with Christ and being raised to a new life in Christ:

> For through the law I died to the law, that I might live for God [*hina theō zēsō*]. I have been crucified with Christ [*Christō synestaurōmai*];[24] yet I live, no longer I, but Christ lives in me [*zē de en emoi Christos*]; insofar as I now live in the flesh [*ho de nyn zō en sarki*], I live by the faith of the Son of God [*en pistei zō tē tou huiou tou theou*],[25] who has loved me and given himself up for me [*tou agapēsantos me kai paradontos heauton hyper emou*]. I do not nullify the grace of God [*ouk athetō tēn charin tou theou*];[26] for if justification comes through the law, then Christ died in vain [*dōrean*]. (NABRE, adapted)

Paul here states a mystical or existential identification with the one whom God revealed in him. Paul was "co-crucified" with Christ, and his present life is "Christ living in me." We cannot say where or how this change in Paul occurred; did it, for example, come about through his own baptism? The language here finds its most explicit parallel in Rom 6:1–11, where Paul speaks of the baptism experienced by believers as a form of dying with Christ and rising to newness of life. More important here is the fourfold repetition of "life" and "living." For Paul, the issue is truly a matter of life and death. The experience of God in Christ gave what the law, even when obeyed, could not give, which is life with and from God (see Gal 3:21).[27]

This remarkable symbiosis (to use an inadequate term) between Christ and Paul, we note, is not simply a punctiliar event of the past; it

24. Paul elsewhere uses this utterly strange construction, "to be crucified together with" (*synstauroun*), only with reference to the baptismal experience of the believers in Rome (see Rom 6:6).

25. For the modification of the NABRE translation of "faith in the Son of God" to "the faith of the Son of God," see Hays, *Faith of Jesus Christ*, and chap. 1 in this volume. The syntax of the sentence resembles that in Phil 3:9, with the phrase "in faith, the one that is of the Son of God" appearing in the secondary attributive position, making the subjective sense of the genitive far more likely.

26. Cf. the similar declaration in 1 Cor 15:10: "by the gift of God [*chariti tou theou*] I am who I am, and his gift to me has not become empty [*kenē*]."

27. In a contrary-to-fact conditional construction, Paul says in Gal 3:21, "If a law was given that could give life (*zōopoiesai*), then righteousness really would be from the law."

is, rather, a continuous condition, the life Paul now lives in the flesh. At the end of this letter, Paul states the change he experienced—and was still experiencing—in dramatic fashion: "But may I never boast except in the cross of our Lord Jesus Christ, through which the world has been crucified to me, and I to the world" (Gal 6:14 NABRE). Such a new form of existence cannot be measured by the human status markers of circumcision or uncircumcision; it is, indeed, a "new creation" (*kainē ktisis*, 6:15). So profoundly and permanently has his transformation in Christ "marked" him that Paul can even identify his physical disability (see 4:13–14) with the experience of being co-crucified with Christ: "From now on, let no one make trouble for me; for I bear the marks of Jesus [*ta stigmata tou Iēsou*] on my body [or "in my body," *en tō sōmati mou*]" (6:17 NABRE, adapted).

This life, moreover, follows the pattern of Jesus himself. Paul lives "by the faith that is the Son of God's," which in Jesus is articulated by his self-donation to others; "he loved me and gave himself for me" (Gal 2:20). Paul's words here echo the greeting: "the Lord Jesus Christ, who gave himself for our sins to rescue us from the present age" (1:3–4). The self-donation was not for Paul alone; it was for the Galatians as well. Here the stories of Jesus, Paul, and the Galatians intersect.

The third stage of Paul's story is spelled out most fully in the text and therefore must here be summarized most crisply. Nothing of what Paul recounts is accidental or incidental to his rhetorical purposes, but a detailed reading is unnecessary for my present purpose, which is to give a sense of how in Galatians he weaves together four stories. Two aspects of Paul's recital, however, are of special significance. The first is his obedience to God's call of him as an apostle to the gentiles. Paul did not "nullify" (*athetein*) the gift that God had given him in the experience of transformation (Gal 2:21) but spent his life in the faithful fulfillment of his prophetic/apostolic sending. Without human consultation, he immediately went to preach in Arabia (1:16–17), and then, after spending fifteen days with Cephas in Jerusalem, he proclaimed the good news also in Syria and Cilicia (1:20–24).

With curious yet revealing diction, Paul notes that the churches in Judea heard that "the one who once was persecuting us is now proclaiming [*euangelizetai*, "announcing good news"] the faith [*tēn pistin*] he once sought to destroy" (Gal 1:23).[28] His bringing of the good news to the

---

28. Paul here brings under the awning of "the faith" both the good news and the churches he once persecuted.

Galatians in the first place was an expression of that fidelity. Even as he came to them in weakness (4:13), he preached to them Christ as crucified (3:1).[29] They welcomed him as a messenger (*angelos*) from God, indeed as Christ Jesus himself (4:14), hearing the good news with faith (3:2). Even though Paul asks whether he has now become their enemy by speaking truth to them (4:16), he continues to "give himself for them" as Jesus did (as evidenced by this letter). Paul is like a mother in labor pains until "Christ be formed among you" (*mechris hou morphōthē Christos en hymin*, 4:19 RSV).

Paul has, in short, remained faithful to God's call and gift.[30] Of even greater rhetorical significance, however, is the way Paul recounts his defense of the "truth of the gospel" when challenged by those seeking to impose circumcision on new gentile believers. When Paul went in response to a revelation of God to Jerusalem to consult with the leaders there "so that I might not be running . . . in vain" (Gal 2:1–2 NABRE), his gentile delegate Titus was not required to be circumcised (2:3). When "false brothers" infiltrated to "spy on our freedom that we have in Christ Jesus," Paul did not submit to them, "so that the truth of the gospel might remain intact for you" (2:4–5 NABRE).[31] Paul's struggle to preserve the freedom of the gentiles was a struggle "for them"—that is, the Galatians themselves. The Jerusalem leadership, Paul relates, sided with him and recognized that Paul had been "entrusted" (*pepisteumai*)[32]—that is, by God—with the good news for the uncircumcised, that the same one who worked through the other apostles was at work in him, and that he had been given this gift by God. Recognizing all this, the leadership extended the right hand of fellowship (*koinōnia*): Cephas, James, and John would work among the Jews, while Barnabas and Paul would work among the gentiles (2:7–9).

---

29. This characterization cannot but remind us of 1 Cor 2:1–5, where Paul also links his personal weakness to the proclamation of the crucified Jesus.

30. Paul's interjection in Gal 1:20 (NABRE), "As to what I am writing to you, behold, before God, I am not lying," reveals the fragility of such personal testimony. Compare Paul's statement concerning his experience of the resurrection in 1 Cor 15:15.

31. Note how elements of Paul's argument are embedded in the narration. The false brothers sought to impose a slavery (*katadoulōsousin*) to take away the freedom (*eleutheria*) that they had "in Christ Jesus." Paul here uses the economic metaphor rather than the language of death and life, anticipating 5:1 (NABRE): "For freedom Christ set us free; so stand firm and do not submit again to the yoke of slavery." As he does elsewhere, Paul subverts the Pharisaic understanding of Torah as the "yoke of freedom." See, e.g., m. Avot 6:2.

32. See the similar use of the perfect tense of *pisteuō* in 1 Tim 1:11; 2 Tim 1:13; Titus 1:3.

The stipulation that the gentile mission would "remember the poor" of the Jerusalem church, Paul had already intended (2:10).

Paul's defense of the freedom of the right of gentile believers to be recognized as full-fledged members of the church, not on the basis of birth or circumcision, but on the basis of the experience of the promise of the Holy Spirit (see Gal 3:1–5), continued in the dramatic confrontation between Cephas and himself in Antioch (2:11–14). The agreed-upon *koinōnia* between Jewish and gentile believers in Christ would be expressed most forcefully in the sharing of meals—a material sharing with gentiles forbidden to Pharisaic Jews. Although at Antioch Cephas had joined Paul and Barnabas in such fellowship meals, under the influence of some "people from James,"[33] Cephas gave way and withdrew from such fellowship, with other Jewish Christians following him; even Barnabas was drawn into their hypocrisy (2:12–13). Paul regarded Cephas as "clearly wrong" (*kategnōsmenos*, 2:11) and "not walking rightly according to the truth of the gospel" (*ouk orthopodousin pros tēn alētheian tou euangeliou*, 2:14) and challenged him openly before everyone, with the statement that sets up the argument to follow: "If you, though a Jew, are living like a Gentile and not like a Jew [*ethnikōs kai ouchi Ioudaikōs zēs*], how can you compel the Gentiles to live like Jews [*Ioudaizein*]?" (2:14).

Paul's story has a paradigmatic character. Through the narrative of his own experience, he shows the gentile Galatian readers at least three things.

- His former life in Judaism was one of competitive law-observance that led to the attempt to destroy the church: being as he was in his former life does not represent the future for them that God desires.
- His life was transformed by God through Christ; indeed, he underwent a death with Christ and now lives with Christ in him: such a new life given by God through Christ should also be theirs.
- Paul has remained faithful to this transforming experience and has steadfastly defended the "truth of the gospel" against all efforts to displace the freedom given by Christ with a slavery to law-observance. So should they stand firm against those trying to impose circumcision within their communities.

33. For an effort to provide an even-handed historical analysis of James and Paul, see Johnson, "James' Significance for Early Christian History," 1–23.

The Story of Jesus

In contrast to Paul's story, which is mostly recounted in sequence and with considerable detail, the story of Jesus in Galatians is allusive and elliptical. Readers must construct a story of Jesus from a set of short narrative fragments that Paul deploys with rhetorical intent. Like Paul's own story in which human and divine agents interact, the story of Jesus contains mythic discourse as well as historical fact. Thus in 4:4–5, while Jesus is embedded in human particularity—he is born of a woman and born under the law—he is also "sent by God" in order to ransom those under the law, so that they might receive the inheritance. Thus also, while Christ is rooted in the history of Israel—he is the singular "seed" (*sperma*) to receive the promise to Abraham and is therefore supremely the son and heir of Abraham (3:16; 4:22–28)—he is also "the Son of God" (1:16; 2:20; 4:4) sent to save all humans, gentiles as well as Jews (3:28), so that they become at once "sons of Abraham" (3:29) and "sons of God" (3:26).

In Galatians, the story of Jesus therefore represents the continuation (and true telos) of the story of Israel, and the revelation of God's presence and power among humans. The singular story of "Jesus" is, in effect, part of a "meta-story" involving God and humanity.

With regard to that short segment of Jesus's mortal existence, Paul stresses two things in particular. The first is his death by crucifixion. Galatians contains by far the greatest proportion of Paul's language concerning crucifixion and the cross.[34] Paul's initial preaching to the Galatians "publicly displayed Jesus Christ as crucified" (3:1).[35] Since Torah placed under God's curse anyone hanging on a tree (Deut 21:23), Jesus's death was cursed by Torah (Gal 3:13). His death by crucifixion was therefore a stumbling block to anyone (like Paul himself in his prior life) who defined righteousness solely in terms of conformity to the law; it was, in brief, "the scandal of the

34. *Stauros* ("the cross") appears three times in Galatians (5:11; 6:12, 14), and seven times in the remaining twelve canonical letters; *stauroun* ("to crucify") three times in Galatians (3:1; 5:24; 6:14) and only three times in the other twelve canonical letters; *synstauroun* ("co-crucify") appears only in Gal 2:19 and Rom 6:6. Nine of the twenty instances of the cognates are in Galatians.

35. Paul's use of *prographein* ("set forth as a public notice," Plutarch, *Life of Camillus* 11) in Gal 3:1 may refer to the ancient rhetorical practice of *ekphrasis*—that is, using words (oral or written) to "bring to life" a scene (see Lucian, *How to Write History* 20), in this case the death of Jesus on the cross. For the ancient practice, see Koopman, *Ancient Greek Ekphrasis*. For a famous example, see Fitzgerald and White, *Tabula of Cebes*. For a Christian example, see Henning, *Educating Early Christians*.

cross" (*scandalon tou staurou*, 5:11; cf. 1 Cor 1:23). We have already seen Paul's own identification with the cross of Jesus: he has been "co-crucified with Christ" (Gal 2:19); he "glories in the cross . . . , through which the world has been crucified to me and I to the world" (6:14); he bears in his body the "marks of Jesus" (*stigmata tou Iēsou*, 6:17). Paul's singular emphasis on the cross of Jesus in this letter, I think, has to do both with his own experience of transformation (see above) and with the fact that the mode of Jesus's death is the sticking point of the choice between Christ and Torah as the ultimate expressions (and therefore norms) of God's righteousness.

Paul's second emphasis is on Jesus's human dispositions, specifically his faith toward God and his self-donation to others. I am firmly convinced that, in the scholarly argument concerning *pistis Christou*, the stronger position is that held by those who see the phrase (and its equivalents) as subjective, denoting the human response of trust and obedience of Jesus toward God,[36] rather that that held by those who regard the phrase (and its equivalents) as objective, denoting the response of Christians toward Christ.

It is certainly the case that Paul can and does speak of "faith in Christ" in a confessional sense, as in Gal 2:16, when Paul declares, "and we have come to have faith in Christ." But that confessional declaration is bracketed on one side by this: "we know that a human being is not made righteous on the basis of [*ex*] the works of the law[37] unless [*ean mē*] through [*dia*] the faith of Jesus Christ";[38] and on the other side by this: "so that we might be made righteous on the basis of Christ's faith [*ek pisteōs Christou*] and not on the basis of the works of the law [*ex ergōn nomou*], for no one in the human condition [*pasa sarx*] is made righteous on the basis of the works of the law" (2:16). Even more compelling is Paul's statement in 2:20 that the life he now leads in the flesh, he lives *en pistei tē tou huiou tou theou*, both because of the grammatical construction[39] and because

---

36. For this understanding of faith, see chap. 1 and Johnson, *Reading Romans.*

37. Note that the genitive is subjective here: "the works that belong to the law" or "the deeds prescribed by the law."

38. The use of *ean mē* is consistently exceptive in New Testament grammar, and certainly in Paul (cf. Rom 10:15; 11:23; 1 Cor 9:16; 14:6, 9, 11, 14; 2 Thess 2:3; 2 Tim 2:5). This is important both because the usual translation "and not" is grammatically incorrect in itself and because it constructs an either/or that could (and did) lead to the inference that law-observant Jews were excluded from sharing in the faith of Jesus. The preposition *dia* is instrumental: the faith of Jesus is the efficient cause (in Aristotelian usage) of human righteousness.

39. The secondary attributive position of the phrase points strongly to the sub-

it is followed at once by another attributive clause ascribing to this same subject the loving of Paul and the giving of himself for Paul.

So closely, indeed, does Paul associate faith (*pistis*) with Christ that in chapter 3 he can make them virtually synonymous. Thus in Gal 3:11 his citation from Hab 2:4, "The righteous one shall live on the basis of faith [*ek pisteōs*]," in all likelihood has here, as in Rom 1:17, the human Jesus as the proper referent for "the righteous one" (*ho dikaios*).[40] Likewise we see in 3:14 that Paul draws a virtual equivalence between the gentiles receiving the blessing of Abraham *en Christo* and the reception of the promise that is the Holy Spirit *dia tēs pisteōs*.[41] Similarly in 3:22 he speaks of "the promise on the basis of the faith of Jesus Christ" being given "to those who have faith," and in the next line equates the coming of Jesus with *pistis*: "before faith [*pistis*] came . . ."

Jesus's faith toward God is expressed, in turn, by his self-giving to other humans. Paul speaks of the Son of God as one who "loved me and handed himself over for my sake" (Gal 2:20), and as one who "gave himself in order to rescue us from the present age" (1:4). Of his crucifixion, Paul declares, "Christ ransomed us from the curse of the law by becoming a curse for our sake" (3:13). Christ was sent by God "to ransom those under the law, so that we might receive adoption" (4:5 NABRE). Paul defines the human Jesus, in short, in terms of what has come to be called "alterity";[42] thus Paul can tell the Galatians, "Bear one another's burdens, and so you will fulfill the law of Christ [*nomon Christou*]" (6:2 NABRE).

The story of Jesus, however, does not end with his mortal existence. God raised him from the dead (Gal 1:1), so that his existence continues among other humans in a more powerful fashion as Lord (*kyrios*, 1:3). His presence is mediated by the Holy Spirit, which is his own Spirit: "God sent the spirit of his Son into our hearts" (4:6 NABRE; see 3:2) in such fashion that believers are "clothed" with Christ (3:27) and are "in Christ" (3:26–28), having become through him both children of God and heirs (4:7). As we have seen, Paul speaks of his own life as one in which "Christ

---

jective character of *huiou tou theou*: it is the faith that belongs to the Son of God by which Paul lives; see note 21 above.

40. Johnson, *Reading Romans*; see also Heliso, *Pistis and the Righteous One*.

41. In the phrase *ten epangelian tou pneumatos*, the genitive is epexegetical: Paul identifies the Holy Spirit with the promise.

42. For discussion of Emmanuel Levinas, who drew heavily on the Jewish tradition in his phenomenology, see Critchley and Bernasconi, *Cambridge Companion to Levinas*.

lives in me" (2:20 NABRE), and Paul's work among the Galatians has as its goal that "Christ be formed in you" (*morphōthē Christos en hymin,* 4:19 NABRE).[43] The story of Jesus continues, through the Holy Spirit, in the story of his followers.

The Story of Israel

This fourth narrative is intended to instruct those gentile Galatians who are tempted to turn aside from the good news as it touched their lives—changing them into sons of God and sons of Abraham—in order to seek circumcision as the true sign of "being rightly related" to God (the basic sense of "righteousness"). Paul asks rhetorically in 4:21 (NABRE), "Tell me, you who want to be under the law, do you not listen to [or hear] the law?" Here Paul constructs the story of Israel, and therefore the narrative precedents to the other three stories, through a reinterpretation of Scripture.

Paul actually provides two versions of the story, the first in Gal 3:15–22 and the second in 4:21–31. The first appears to be a straightforward, chronologically ordered account, whereas the second Paul acknowledges to be a form of allegory (4:24). But both accounts center on Abraham, and both accounts work with the premise that the meaning of the promise to Abraham is the Holy Spirit. This simple premise is the basis for the boldest and most radical reinterpretation of Torah undertaken by Paul, for if the promise equals the Holy Spirit and if the gentiles have received the Holy Spirit, then the gentiles have become receivers of the promise and the gentiles are equal to the children of Abraham. Necessarily, the distinctions between "Jew and gentile," between "circumcision and uncircumcision," become nugatory, for both Jews and gentiles share in a "new creation" (6:15).[44]

---

43. The extraordinary character of this expression should not be slighted. At the very least, Paul desires the formation of a "Christlike" character among the Galatian believers; at the most, he hopes for the same sort of coexistence of Christ with them that he himself experiences. In either case (or both), "Christ" is a recognizable identity transferable to others.

44. That Paul without any argument simply equates "the promise" made to Abraham with "the Holy Spirit" is his most transgressive rereading of Scripture—far more radical than the creative adjustments made in 2 Cor 3 or Rom 9–11. In the Septuagint, first of all, the term *epangelia* scarcely even appears (see LXX Ps 55:8; Amos 9:6), so Paul's making it the hinge point for the narrative is itself bold. But in the Old Tes-

Or, to put it in different terms, "Scripture saw beforehand that God would make the gentiles righteous by faith" and announced the good news ahead of time when God told Abraham, "Through you all nations [all gentiles] will be blessed" (Gal 3:8). "Consequently," Paul declares, "those who have faith [or, better, who are "out of faith," *ek pisteōs*] are blessed along with Abraham who had faith [*tō pistō Abraham*]" (3:9 NABRE).

It is critical to note that Paul launches his reinterpretation of Torah from the experiential basis he has established with the three narratives that have intermeshed Jesus, Paul, and the Galatians; the faith of Jesus, the faith of Paul, and the faith of the Galatians; and the transforming power from Christ experienced by Paul and, most important for his rhetorical purposes, the Galatians. It is not by accident that his first reading of Scripture follows immediately after his reminder to the "senseless" Galatians of the basis of their receiving the Holy Spirit—namely, the proclamation of a crucified Messiah which they received with faith (3:1–5).

Paul prefaces his chronological summary in 3:15–23 with a nonnarrative section of midrashic interpretation of statements from Scripture that oppose, on one side, faith and life and righteousness and, on the other side, the law. First, Abraham had faith in God and it was reckoned to him as righteousness (Gen 15:6), and Abraham was "pre-evangelized" (*proeuēngelisato*) regarding the blessing of all the nations (gentiles) in him (Gen 12:3; Gal 3:6–9). This is the narrative starting point. But the law intervenes to say that everyone who does not remain within the things written in this book to perform them is under a curse (Deut 27:26; Gal 3:10). This text from Moses plainly refers to keeping the law; if you don't do it, you are cursed—excluded from the people and possibly God. And this statement has an absolute and inclusive application. It presents the Deuteronomic principle under which Paul had lived his earlier life and on the basis of which he had persecuted believers in Christ in defense of Torah. On the same side of the ledger, Paul adduces another text from Deuteronomy, that everyone who hangs on a tree is under a curse (Deut 21:23; Gal 3:13). Here appears the specific textual basis of Paul's attack on believers. They did not do all that the law required, and their crucified

---

tament, the *idea* of the promise (or blessing) to Abraham is consistently connected to many descendants, possessions of the land, safety from enemies, etc., all material realities. That the content of the promise to Abraham should be the Holy Spirit may to some degree be an extrapolation from passages in the prophets (Isaiah, Jeremiah, Ezekiel, Zechariah) but most certainly is grounded in the experience of the Holy Spirit by Paul and his readers.

Messiah was cursed by God. But the law claimed not only to impose a curse but also to bestow a blessing. Leviticus claimed that everyone who performed the works of the law "would live [*zēsetai*] in them" (Lev 18:5; Gal 3:12).

Against this array of texts promising blessing and woe on the basis of the Law, Paul adduces two texts, the first being the declaration of righteousness and blessing to Abraham on the basis of his faith (Gen 15:6; 12:3; see Gal 3:6, 9), and the second being the statement by the prophet Habakkuk (Hab 2:4, which Paul quotes also in Rom 1:17): "The righteous one shall live on the basis of faith" (*ho dikaios ek pisteōs zēsetai*, Gal 3:11). The contradiction between these texts is resolved or transcended not by another text from Scripture but by the narrative of experience: Christ rescued them from the curse of the law by taking it on himself (3:13), and Christ is, preeminently, the righteous one who lives on the basis of faith. His death on the cross, therefore, does not signify his being cursed by God but instead signifies the means by which the promise to Abraham might be realized among all nations, all those who receive the promise that is the Holy Spirit with faith (3:14).

Having so dealt with the main issue, which is the basis for "life" and "right-relatedness" with God, Paul can reduce his first narrative to three moments: (1) the promise of a blessing to Abraham and his seed on the basis of faith (Gal 3:15–16); (2) the intrusion of the law and its claims that never had anything to do with faith (3:17–22); (3) the coming of faith with the coming of the faith of Jesus Christ, Abraham's seed and the blessing to the gentiles (3:23–29). In this brief recital—and radical reinterpretation—the real problem is not the claim to live by faith but the existence and claims of the law.

Against the exalted claims for Torah made by law-observant Jews, especially Pharisees trained in law, as he formerly was, Paul seeks to diminish the status of the law: it is not eternal but came into being hundreds of years after Abraham (Gal 3:17) and was a stopgap until the coming of the Messiah (3:19); it was revealed not directly by Moses but through intermediaries (3:20); it was not so much the guide to wisdom as a lowly pedagogue that gave elementary rules and kept the heirs of the household as little children out of trouble (3:19, 22).

The one thing the law could not do is the one thing that really matters, which is to give life. Life came on the basis of faith, and until faith (Christ) came, those under the law were no better than the gentiles enslaved by idolatry; they too were like children kept from their inheritance (the blessing) by supervisors and nannies. The children were freed and entered their inheritance through "the faith of Jesus Christ" (Gal 3:22). Paul finishes the story by reminding the Galatians of their experience of the blessing through their faith in the crucified Messiah, their baptism into Christ, and their reception of his spirit of adoption (3:23–4:7).

The effect of this first iteration of the story of Israel is to make it also the prior part of the Galatian story: because they belong to Christ, because they have the promise of the Spirit, they too are children of Israel and rightful heirs of the promise made to Abraham. They too live on the basis of faith and not on the basis of law.

Paul's second iteration of Israel's story (Gal 4:24–31) is told to "those who want to be under the law" and has a much sharper edge than the first version. By means of allegory, it actually collapses the biblical account concerning the birth of Abraham's sons into the present situation of the Galatians.[45] Here chronological sequence is replaced by the oppositional identification of characters (4:24). The gentile believers to whom Paul writes are the children of the promise through Abraham's wife, Sarah, a free woman; they represent Isaac and allegorically have "the Jerusalem above" as their mother. They fulfill the words of Isaiah concerning such a surprising birth: "Rejoice, you barren one who bore no children; break forth and shout, you who were not in labor; for more numerous are the children of the deserted one than of her who has a husband" (Gal 4:27 NABRE, citing Isa 54:1).

In contrast are those whose allegiance is to the present Jerusalem. Allegorically, this earthly Jerusalem represents Mount Sinai (where the law was revealed), which is another earthbound point in Arabia.[46] In the story of Abraham, they represent Ishmael, the son of the slave woman Hagar (Gal 4:23–24), who "bears children for slavery." Paul used the metaphor of the household and kinship as the vehicle for his first account; the second account uses the economic metaphor of slavery and freedom, making the Jewish observance of law derived from Sinai a kind of slavery, which might be compared to the religious practices the Galatians practiced before they were rescued by Christ (see 4:8–10).

45. For a discussion of the textual variants, see Barrett, "Allegory of Abraham," esp. 163–64.

46. The geographical placement of Sinai and Jerusalem enables them to equal "the flesh," whereas the "Jerusalem above" of the promise equals "the spirit." The children of slavery are the children according to the flesh and are observers of earthbound laws. The children of freedom are the children according to the promise (spirit) and walk according to faith. For lively discussion, see Boyarin, *Radical Jew*, 13–38; Gignac, "Lorsque Paul 'Raconte' Abraham."

Paul also locates the present situation of the Christ-believers in Scripture: "Just as then the child of the flesh persecuted the child of the spirit, it is the same now" (Gal 4:29 NABRE). It is not entirely clear what Paul means here. The letter indicates elsewhere that Paul persecuted the church (1:13), that he displeased people by proclaiming Christ (1:10), that he was still being persecuted (5:11), and that the agitators within the Galatian community seek to avoid persecution for the cross of Christ by seeking circumcision (5:12) and try to coerce others to be circumcised so they can "boast of your flesh" (5:13) even if they do not themselves observe the law! The best clue may be provided by 4:17 (NABRE): "They show interest in you, but not in a good way; they want to isolate you, so that you may show interest in them." But Paul's own recollection of his "zeal" concerning the law in his earlier life (1:14) throws light on their "zeal" toward them and their "isolation" or "shutting off" (*ekkleisai*) of the faithful—they want to thus force an "emulation" (*zēloun*) of them as circumcised.

In any case, Paul reads the Genesis account as legitimation for cutting off (placing under the ban; see Gal 1:9) the members of the community who have already cut themselves off from Christ by seeking to be under the yoke of Torah through circumcision (5:4), or who have tried to persuade others to do the same: "But what does the scripture say? 'Drive out the slave woman and her son! For the son of the slave woman shall not share the inheritance with the son'" (4:30 NABRE; see Gen 21:10). Paul concludes the account, saying, "On this account, brothers, we are children not of the slave woman but of the free woman" (Gal 4:31).

Conclusion

The first four chapters of Galatians make an argument by means of the weaving together of three stories that have as their common element a fourth, the story of Jesus, which intersects and transforms the story of Paul, of the Galatians, and of Israel. The powerful point made by the conjoining of narratives is, first, that right relationship with God (and therefore authentic life) is accomplished not by the performance of the commandments revealed on Sinai but through the obedient faith revealed through the crucified Messiah Jesus. Those who share this faith, both gentiles and Jews, share in the promised inheritance, which is the Holy Spirit, the source of true life. The premise underlying each of these narratives, we have seen, is real-life experience. The experience of God

in Christ is at once so powerful and so paradoxical as to force the reinterpretation, not only of Paul's own biography and the history of the
Galatians, but even of the God-given Scriptures themselves.

The rhetorical point of Paul's interweaving of these stories is that the
Galatians should understand the basis of their standing in right relationship with God, should resist those in their communities who insist that
Christ is not enough and that more initiations would lead to perfection,
and should, if necessary, excommunicate those who disrupt the fellowship of the free with "another gospel" that would lead them back to slavery. But the question still requiring answer is how those thus freed are to
live their lives before God, if Christ rather than Torah is to be the norm
for their continuing stories. To that question we must devote attention
in the next chapter.

The Expression of Christian Experience

The Imperatives of Galatians 5–6

In the first four sections of Galatians, I have shown, Paul sought to persuade the gentile believers in the Galatian churches by weaving together four narratives. By showing them how their story intersected those of Jesus, Israel, and Paul himself, he affirmed their identity as at once children of God and the true heirs of the promise made to Abraham through the gift of the Holy Spirit that came to them through the crucified and raised Messiah Jesus. Paul constructed these intermingled narratives in order that the Galatians would realize their unity as church "in Christ," a unity that made nugatory the differences between Jew and Greek, male and female, slave and free.

Paul wanted his gentile readers to resist agitators (from without or from within) who advanced the desirability of circumcision, observance of the law, and differences of status within the church. By insisting that for both Jews and gentiles "the faith of Jesus Christ" was the basis of a right relationship with God, and that sharing in such faith enabled both Jews and gentiles to be children of the promise and children of God, Paul hoped to enable the Galatians to move forward together as unified communities.

Narratives of the past, however, even when they extend themselves into the present, do not by themselves determine how a story ought to continue. Paul has insisted that the upshot of the narratives is that his readers are "children not of the slave woman but of the freeborn woman" (Gal 4:31).[1] Yes, but what does that freedom look like? How is it expressed? If the law of Moses is not the norm of right-relatedness to God, but rather the faith of Jesus is, what does that mean in actual life?

---

1. Unless otherwise indicated, Scripture quotations in this chapter are from the NABRE.

If law does not give life, but rather life comes by gift through the Holy
Spirit, then how is that life to be expressed in everyday matters? How
can "freedom," of all things, not devolve into another form of individualism and competition, leaving the community even more fragmented and
making the orderliness of law seem even more attractive?

Such are the questions that the Galatians—and present-day readers—
are left with after following Paul through four chapters of fundamentally
narrative argument. These are the questions that Paul seeks to answer
in chapters 5-6, now not through stories but through imperatives. The
shift in rhetoric is evident. Less apparent is how Paul's imperatives adequately meet the queries concerning the practical carrying out of life
that his confident narratives stimulate in thoughtful readers. Take, for
example, the first of these imperatives in Gal 5:1: "For freedom Christ set
us free; so stand firm and do not submit again to the yoke of slavery."[2] In
the context of the letter, the exhortation is both clear and confusing. If
they are children of the free woman (4:31), they should remain free and
should not submit to slavery. That is not difficult to grasp.[3]

But two aspects of the command are puzzling. First, how can the
Pharisee Paul, for whom Torah had been the yoke of freedom, speak of
observance of the law as a form of slavery? Second, how could gentile
believers submit *again* (*palin*) to slavery, unless Paul (even more daringly) implicitly identifies submission to the ritual observances of the law
of Moses with the gentile observance of days, months, and years when
they did not know God and were enslaved to beings who were not God
(Gal 4:8-10)? We can make some headway if we consider more carefully
Paul's disjunction between law-observance, or moral heteronomy, on
one side and faith-freedom, or moral autonomy, on the other side.[4]

2. The Greek is *tē eleutheria hēmas Christos ēleutherōsen; stēkete oun kai mē palin
zygō douleias enechesthe.*

3. The point is made by all commentaries and such books as Barrett, *Freedom
and Obligation*; Harmon, *She Must and Shall Go Free*; Loubser, *Paul Cries Freedom
in Galatia!*; F. Watson, *Paul, Judaism and the Gentiles.*

4. The term "heteronomy" adequately describes the dominant mode of religiosity
among both Jews and gentiles in the ancient world, that of "participation in benefits" through the observance of ritual and moral commands (see Johnson, *Among the
Gentiles*, 32-63). In the context of this letter, the term "theonomous" may seem more
appropriate than "autonomous" to describe the alternative. But for the ancients, law
was also "God-given," and "autonomous" as I use it by no means is the sort of Kantian
ethic associated with the Enlightenment. By it I mean, rather, the religious and moral
dispositions found among the second class of ancient religious people—namely,
"moral transformation" (see *Among the Gentiles*, 64-78, 158-71). The distinction

The Attractions and Perils of Heteronomy

There is much to be said for a religiosity based on the observance of externally imposed *stoicheia*,[5] such as those governing the rituals of gentile religion and the law of Moses. For the individual, the carrying out of the prescriptions provides the security of knowing that what God wishes, one is doing. Thus, one is "righteous," or "rightly related," to God and the world created by God. Most commandments, moreover, are clear and able to be observed. This is the case especially with negative commands such as "Do not kill" or "Do not steal" or "Do not commit adultery" (see Exod 20:13–15). Such prescriptions cut off one narrow band of human activity but also provide the freedom to act in ways that do not kill or steal or commit adultery. Security, predictability, and controllability are all benefits of law-observance. An added bonus is the sense of accomplishment that accompanies observance, and the social status of being a "righteous person" when all such prohibited activities are in fact avoided.

Positive commandments such as "Keep holy the Sabbath day" (see Exod 20:8–11) or "Preserve a corner of the field for the poor and sojourners" (see Lev 19:9–10) are, to be sure, more difficult to fulfill perfectly, precisely because of their open-endedness: thus the vast interpretive effort put into the midrash that determines the kinds of "work" that would profane the Sabbath, or the casuistry demanded by deciding what in fact constitutes a "corner" in a manner that is fair both to a property owner and to the needy.[6] More difficult still are the commandments that prohibit internal dispositions, such as those forbidding the "coveting" of a neighbor's wife or property. Avoiding the physical act of adultery with the neighbor's wife is doable if difficult, but the internal disposition is trickier. Likewise, avoiding stealing the neighbor's donkey is doable and easy, but what about desiring it so profoundly that if the opportunity arose, one might filch it? That also is trickier. These are the sort of conundra posed by law that fuel, for the zealous keeper of the law, the need

---

points mainly to whether behavior is dominantly conformed (*stoichein*) to externally derived guidelines or to internal dispositions that discern appropriate responses.

5. See chap. 10, p. 194, note 14 for my everyday translation of *stoicheion*: in Galatians, the cognates must mean "basic guidelines" if both uses of the noun in 4:3 and 4:9, as well as the verb form in 5:25 and 6:16, are to make sense.

6. See, e.g., the list of "works" forbidden on the Sabbath in m. Shabb 7:2, and the regulations governing the corner of field or orchard in m. Pe'ah.

to do midrash, to measure both the self and others, and to defend Torah against those playing fast and loose with the rules.[7]

A set of *stoicheia* like the law of Moses works best, however, at the social level. Common observance establishes and solidifies social cohesion. Law enables community. We recognize each other as Jews because we are all circumcised, and all keep the Sabbath, and all offer sacrifice to God in the Jerusalem temple. Precisely the visibility of such observances "in the flesh" gives them their social value; we are given a greater sense of being "God's People" when we join together to do the same things in the same way at the same time.

Finally, according to the canons of ancient religiosity, religious observance provides access to the divine *dynamis* (power) to the community and to the individual. The "works of the law" are not empty performance; they are rather powerful performative gestures. The presence of God and the power of God are secured through the right-relatedness of adherents through the performance of divinely ordained rules and regulations.

Given all these precedents and advantages, it is not difficult to understand the "politics of perfection" advocated by the circumcisers in the Galatian churches,[8] or its appeal to gentiles who had left behind their own *stoicheia* when they heard the good news of Christ and had received the Holy Spirit. They now needed some sort of guide to live out their experience of the power and presence of God. Getting circumcised and taking on the law of Moses might have seemed to them not only logical but highly desirable. After all, wasn't this Paul's own set of *stoicheia* by which he lived? Why should they be deprived of the ancient law that he himself had formerly showed such zeal in defending? Why not gain "in the flesh" such signs of advancement and the status derived from the adoption of the law? Why not encourage or even coerce others to follow the law, and shun them if they refuse?

But there are also perils to defining religion in terms of law-observance. Precisely the performability of law can, at the individual level, encourage a certain moral immaturity (choices are predetermined and discernment is not required) or even arrogance ("see how well I observe what is required"). At the social level, law-observance can threaten community cohesion through competition and even contempt toward the less ob-

---

7. For a brilliant tracing of a single command through the entire history of Talmudic discussion and debate, see Wimpfheimer, *Talmud*.

8. See chap. 9, "Ritual Imprinting and the Politics of Perfection."

servant.[9] For both individual and community, the performance of law can be religiously deceptive, not because the commandments are wrong (like the commandments in the law of Moses, they can be spiritual and good and holy), but because they may promise what they cannot deliver. The law of Moses promises, for example, that the observance of all the commandments will give life (Gal 3:12). But, in fact, life is always a gift from the life-giving God, and no human performance can secure such life. Likewise, the promise of righteousness through obedience to law is deceptive, for right-relatedness between persons cannot adequately be expressed by obeying commands.

The analogy of children being rightly related to parents can be illuminating. We all recognize that it is possible (as in Jesus's parable of the two sons in Luke 15:11–31) to do all that a parent asks, yet at the same time be filled with resentment and envy. Conversely, parental orders can be neglected or even disobeyed without the bonds of trust and affection between parents and child being threatened. Obsessive law-observance can even distract from or inhibit true right-relatedness. We would not consider a child to be rightly related to parents if she should say, "Look, I am doing all that you ask of me perfectly, even though I despise you in my heart." Or if he should say, "Reward me with affection because I keep even the smallest of your directions, even though I am doing it to secure my own place more than out of affection for you."

Strict adherence to the letter of the law can, indeed, block perceptions essential to being rightly related to another: it is not helpful if a child tells his parent, "Look, I am doing what you told me to do yesterday," when in fact the parent needs this other thing done today. It is not adequate to make a set of parental commands serve as the full expression of the parent-child relationship. The child of whatever age who says, "My eyes are on these practices you require; do not distract me with anything new or surprising," is by that declaration stating a focus on self-performance rather than on a responsive relationship. Such a stance is strikingly different from the one that says, "I trust in the new direction you are leading me, and I will say yes to this new thing you show me." Such trust and obedience, I think, is at the heart of what Paul calls faith, articulated above all by the obedient faith of Jesus Christ (Rom 3:21–26; Phil 2:5–11).

These simple reflections can point us to a better understanding of the

9. See Paul's acute observations on just these tendencies in Rom 14:1–23.

tension between law, which is a set of prescriptions, and faith, which is a relational disposition. The law, to be sure, as Paul notes in Gal 2:16, can be compatible with the human disposition of faith. But it cannot be taken as either a replacement for faith or the adequate measure of faith. In some circumstances, Paul suggests, the desire for circumcision and law-observance can amount to a choice for slavery rather than freedom and for death rather than life.

The Galatians, for example, were without the "works of the law" when Paul proclaimed the good news of a crucified and raised Messiah to them; they responded with faith, and they received the Holy Spirit (Gal 3:1–5). They were, in other words, already alive with the very life-breath of God (3:5). They were not children needing nannies and wards. They were free children by the spirit of adoption (4:1–7). For them to now place themselves under the law as the comprehensive measure for righteousness signifies, for Paul, that they are repudiating the gift they have been given and the manner of its giving (5:2–4). Paul is clear that they cannot have both a crucified Messiah and an absolute adherence to Torah, for by the terms of Torah, Christ cannot be "the righteous one" (3:13).

But since the gift of the Spirit *is* the gift of life, that these gentiles are choosing circumcision means they are implicitly making a choice for death. Since the gift of the Spirit is the gift of freedom, they are also making a choice for slavery.

Again, an analogy may clarify. We can think of someone who is fully healthy and breathing well. Someone else proposes that an artificial respirator "gives life" to those attached to it. This is a perfectly valid claim, so long as one understands that it applies to those who cannot breathe well on their own, who are unhealthy. But if someone already breathing well thinks that the respirator is a necessary instrument for healthy breathing, and uses it around the clock, under the apprehension that without it his life is in peril, such a person is massively self-deluded. Healthy people do not need a respirator in order to breathe. Worse than that: using a respirator around the clock is a form of captivity or slavery: I can only go where the respirator allows me. Worse, my dependence on a breathing machine may ruin my capacity to breathe on my own through the weakening of my muscles and organs; thus, what was intended to support life becomes the occasion of ill-health and even death. The Galatians are breathing just fine through the gift of the Spirit. Making law-observance a necessary mark of perfection or advancement means slavery and death.

Rather than having them revert to Paul's own starting point, which he abandoned when co-crucified with Christ ("I died to the law, that

I might live to God," Gal 2:19), Paul urges the Galatians to continue their story in continuity with the gift of life they have been given through the Spirit. They are to live out the story that is now theirs together with Paul: "I implore you, brothers, be as I am, because I have also become as you are" (4:12). Paul does not "[build] up again those things that [he] tore down" (2:18). He does not nullify (*athetō*) the gift of God, because he knows that "if righteousness comes through the law, then Christ died in vain" (2:21, author's translation).

No, the new creation he shares with the Galatians (6:15) is one that comes on the basis of the "faith of the Son of God who loved me and gave himself for me" (2:20, author's translation). Therefore, the way forward for them is not on the basis of either circumcision or uncircumcision but through "faith working through love" (5:6).[10] The shape of the gift should in turn shape their continuing story: the moral dispositions of Jesus himself (faith expressed through love) are also to be the dispositions they express.

The Paradoxical Character of Christian Freedom

After a short interlude (Gal 5:7–12) in which Paul expresses his confidence that the Galatians—or at least those listening to him—are thinking along the same lines as him, that they know he is not the one responsible for causing this commotion (if he were, why was he still being persecuted for the cross?), and that the ones causing the trouble will be punished (perhaps even by self-castration!), Paul returns to the imperative mood and the consideration of what he meant by "faith expressing itself through love" (5:6, author's translation) by taking up again the subject of freedom: "For you were called for freedom, brothers, but do not use this freedom as an opportunity for the flesh; rather, serve one another through love." It is an extraordinarily powerful and paradoxical exhortation, drawing Paul's ancient readers, and us, to a consideration of the difference and connection between "freedom from" and "freedom for."[11]

---

10. The Greek is: *en gar Christō Iēsou oute peritomē ti ischuei oute akrobystia alla pistis di'agapēs energoumenē.* Both the verbs *ischuein* and *energein* denote power; here the fleshly markings either of circumcision or uncircumcision "have no power/do not signify." But faith "works itself out" through love, precisely as we have seen the *pistis* of the Son of God expressed through "his loving me and giving himself for me" (Gal 2:20).

11. Nobody has provided a more succinct or brilliant summary than Martin Luther, "A Christian is a perfectly free lord of all, subject to none. A Christian is a per-

The Galatians have been "called to freedom." Paul here turns the affirmation of the gift they have been given in 5:1, "for freedom Christ set us free," into a mandate: they are "called" to live out that freedom in a certain way.[12] Freedom here clearly does not signify a complete lack of conditions. It is not the "freedom of choice" celebrated by liberal individualism, although such ability to choose is assumed as a baseline by the very binary structure of Paul's argument. If they did not have "freedom of choice," then his entire argument concerning the direction of their lives would be nonsensical. But beyond that, *eleutheria* (or *libertas*) in the deeper sense points to the appropriate expression of human choice.[13] True freedom is not living in any which way we please, but is, rather, living in accord with the truth of our existence. For Paul, we know, this means living in accord with the gift of God in the Spirit, in accord with the pattern of the story of Jesus Christ into which they have been incorporated.

In negative terms, Paul commands, "Do not use this freedom as an opportunity for the flesh" (*mē tēn eleutherian eis aphormēn tē sarki*, 5:13). Two terms demand attention. The first is *aphormē*, which is used elsewhere by Paul, as here, in the sense of an "opening" or "advantage point" (see Rom 7:8, 11; 2 Cor 5:12; 1 Tim 5:14), and once in the sense of "pretext" (2 Cor 11:12). Paul does not want the Galatians' gift of freedom to provide the basis, or excuse, for something contrary to freedom in the fullest sense, here designated as "flesh" (*sarx*), a term that, even within the short compass of this letter, can rightly be called polyvalent. Thus, *sarx* can connote the human condition as somatic (Gal 1:16; 2:16, 20), or biological descent as opposed to descent according to the promise (4:13, 14, 23, 29). It can mean the physical in contrast to spiritual (6:8). It can be used as shorthand for the ritual of circumcision, a visible marking "in the flesh" that can be the source of boasting (6:12–13), which Paul opposes to "the Spirit" as an empowerment from God that transforms humans. This is clearly the sense in 3:3, where Paul asks rhetorically, "Are you so stupid? After beginning with the Spirit, are you now ending in the flesh?"[14]

---

fectly dutiful servant of all, subject to all," in the short treatise "The Freedom of a Christian" (1520), in Luther, *Three Treatises*, 277. The disjunction "freedom from" and "freedom for" is popularly associated with Fromm, *Escape from Freedom*.

12. Helpful for this section of Galatians is Furnish, *Theology and Ethics in Paul*, 59–65; J. Barclay, *Obeying the Truth*; and Westerholm, "'Letter' and 'Spirit.'"

13. The Augustinian distinction (as in *Enchiridion* 28.105; *City of God* 22.30) is carried forward in medieval theology, as in Thomas Aquinas, *Summa Theologica* II-II, 183–84, ad 1.

14. As I note in chap. 9, the use of *epitelein* here has unmistakable resonance with

This last sense bleeds into the meaning of *sarx* as a moral disposition that is distinct from, and indeed opposed to, the Spirit in the following exhortation (Gal 5:13, 16, 17, 19, 24). In the present context, therefore, "an opportunity for the flesh" means choosing to live by a simply human measure (rather than God's), with base human dispositions and with hostile human actions. "According to the flesh," then, is shorthand for the attitudes that disrupt rather than build true human community. Here it gets at the basic motivations driving the circumcision agenda.

Paul spells out the positive "call" of freedom, which paradoxically is a new form of slavery: "Rather, serve [*doulouete*] one another [*allēlois*] through love [*dia tēs agapēs*]" (Gal 5:13). Such self-donation is, however, not like the slavery they had experienced with "worldly *stoicheia*" (4:9) when they did not know God, or the "yoke of slavery" imposed by law-observance. It is, rather, an expression of the freedom they have in the Spirit, which enables them to dispose themselves—as Jesus had—for other humans. It is, moreover, reciprocal: they are to serve "one another," which is the antithesis of a social arrangement in which some command and others serve. This is a service "through love," which means that it is an expression of the story of Jesus they now share (2:20); it is "faith working itself out through love" (5:6, author's translation). Such mutual service, Paul declares, is in fact the true telos of the law: "For the whole law is fulfilled in one statement [*en heni logō*], namely, 'You shall love your neighbor as yourself'" (5:14; see Lev 18:19).[15] The opposite of such mutual regard and service is the dispositions and behaviors that manifest "an opportunity for the flesh." Paul declares, "But if you go one biting and devouring one another, beware that you are not consumed by one another" (5:15).[16] The meaning of flesh in this section of Galatians, therefore, shifts to signify the underlying moral attitudes and actions opposed to the way of the Spirit revealed in the story of Jesus and in their own experience. Jesus's story was one of self-giving for the sake of others. The continuation of his story in their own means living in mutual service to each other.

Paul's subsequent statement concerning the opposition of flesh and spirit, then, is not a distinction between the physical and the mental, and a control of the body by the mind; it is, rather, a distinction between two

---

ancient ritual initiations: "Are you seeking ritual advancement/perfection through circumcision?" is a fair paraphrase.

15. Cf. Rom 13:9; see also Westerholm, "On Fulfilling the Whole Law."

16. The metaphorical body language of "biting" (*daknete*) and "devouring" (*katesthiete*) is extraordinarily vivid; note also that the "dissolving" or "destruction" (*analuein*) of the community occurs *hyp' allēlōn*, from such selfish, aggressive, and destructive behavior turned against each other.

moral tendencies (or desires, *epithymia*) that struggle for dominance: "I say, then: live by the Spirit [*pneumati peripateite*][17] and you will certainly not gratify [*telesēte*] the desire [*epithymia*] of the flesh. For the flesh has desires against the Spirit, and the Spirit against the flesh; these are opposed to each other, so that you may not do what you want.[18] But if you are guided [*agesthe*] by the Spirit, you are not under the law" (Gal 5:16–18).

Paul then proceeds to enumerate the "works of the flesh" (Gal 5:19). The phrase points to the kinds of behaviors/works resulting from "the desire of the flesh," and the choice of "works" (*erga*) must deliberately echo the earlier expression "works of the law" (*erga tou nomou*, 2:16; 3:2). While the use of such vice lists was standard among ancient moralists,[19] the content of the lists is not necessarily standard in every respect; the specific items included in a list often have particular pertinence to the rhetorical situation, and such is the case here: "Immorality, impurity, licentiousness, idolatry, sorcery,[20] hatreds, rivalry, jealousy, outbursts of fury, acts of selfishness, dissensions, factions, occasions of envy,[21] drinking bouts, orgies, and the like. I warn you, as I warned you before, that

17. Here the NABRE's "live" is more precisely "walk," in the sense of moral behavior (see Rom 6:4; 8:4; 13:13; 14:15; 1 Cor 7:17; 2 Cor 5:7). Compare the use of *ouk orthopodousin* for Peter's behavior in Antioch (Gal 2:14).

18. Paul here slips in a thought that is developed more fully in Rom 7:15–23: the flesh is a power within humans that—unaided by God's Spirit—blocks them from doing the good that they desire. The thought is not really germane to the present argument, which concerns not so much the incapacity to perform (e.g., the commandments) as the aggressive advocacy of the law as a means of "biting and consuming" others.

19. See John T. Fitzgerald, "Virtue/Vice Lists," *ABD* 6:858–59.

20. The vices of sexual immorality (*porneia*), impurity (*akatharsia*), and licentiousness (*aselgeia*) are all part of the standard items associated with "idolatry" (*eidōlolatreia*) as practiced by gentiles, and by the Galatians in their former life. Although it might be found on such lists, the inclusion of "sorcery" (*pharmakeia*) may here echo the charge of "bewitching" in Gal 3:1: *tis hymas ebaskanen?* The inclusion of "drinking bouts and orgies" (*methai, kōmoi*) at the end of the list would also be standard indicators of "the desires of the flesh" in the most obvious sense.

21. At the heart of this list, Paul includes eight dispositions that are of a profoundly antisocial and hostile character and point to precisely the attitudes and actions of those who "bite and consume" others in the community: hatreds (*echthrai*), rivalry (*eris*), jealousy (*zēlos*)—see Paul in 1:14 and the agitators in 4:16!—outbursts of fury (*thymoi*), acts of selfishness (*eritheiai*), dissensions (*dichostasiai*), factions (*haireseis*), and forms of envy (*phthonoi*). For the way in which *phthonos* is regarded by both Greco-Roman and Jewish moralists as the cause of all social unrest, upheaval, and violence, see Johnson, "*Topos Peri Phthonou.*"

those who do such things will not inherit the kingdom of God" (5:19–21; cf. 1 Cor 6:9–11).

To this set of misanthropic vices that epitomize the "works of the flesh," Paul opposes the "fruit of the Spirit" (*karpos tou pneumatos*, Gal 5:22).[22] In contrast to the vice list, which mixed dispositions, like envy, with actions, like witchcraft and orgies, Paul's list of virtues consists entirely of moral dispositions and attitudes. And in contrast to the vices, which are mostly selfish, antisocial, and divisive, the virtues are peaceable and serve community cohesion: "Love [*agapē*], joy [*chara*], peace [*eirēnē*], patience [*makrothymia*],[23] kindness [*chrēstotēs*], generosity [*agathōsynē*], faithfulness [*pistis*], gentleness [*prautēs*], self-control [*enkrateia*]. Against such there is no law [*kata tōn toioutōn ouk estin nomos*]" (5:22–23).[24] This classic list of virtues is overwhelmingly made up of qualities that are positively related to others, in sharp contrast to the misanthropic qualities making up the "works of the flesh." These are the virtues not of the Greco-Roman warrior-hero but of person who seeks what is good for others in the community. There can be "no law against them" for two reasons: they conform admirably to the deeper dispositions required by the full observance of the law (dispositions of peace, gentleness, and long-suffering), they are necessary for those who love the neighbor as the self (5:14), and they are internal dispositions of humans that are given to them through the gift of the Holy Spirit, whom God sent "into our hearts" (4:6). As the free expression of gentle qualities toward the other, they owe their existence neither to law nor the flesh but to the Spirit. They are the "fruit of the Spirit."

In a striking allusion to the account of his own transformation in Christ (see Gal 2:19–20), Paul declares, "Those who belong to Christ [*hoi de tou Christou*] have crucified their flesh with its passions and desires [*tēn sarka estaurōsan syn tois pathēmasin kai tais epitymiais*]" (5:24). Paul

22. The singular *karpos* is striking, suggesting that all these dispositions together make up a singular outcome in human behavior of the Spirit's life among them. For the unity of virtue in Greco-Roman moral teaching, see Maximus of Tyre, *Discourse* 36.2, and Dio Chrysostom, *Oration* 4.83–96. Similarly, the use of "fruit" rather than "works" intimates the organic unfolding of a life force rather than the result of human effort.

23. For the linguistic evidence supporting the reading of *makrothymia* as a form of "patience" or "forbearance" toward another, rather than a passive "endurance," see Johnson, *Letter of James*, 312–13.

24. Paul's statement is strikingly similar to the one in 1 Tim 1:9, "with the understanding that law is meant not for a righteous person but for the lawless and unruly."

had been co-crucified with Christ that he might live to God, by dying to the law. Because they are now "in Christ" (3:28), the gentile Galatians have died to all the vicious and misanthropic dispositions of the flesh that led to community rivalry and destruction. They are not any longer to be conceited, provoking one another, envious of one another (5:26). Rather, their existence from now on is to be measured and guided by the gift they have been given—namely, the Holy Spirit: "If we live in the Spirit, let us also follow the Spirit" (5:25).[25]

Paul has clearly shown the imperatives that follow from the new experience of freedom enjoyed by the Galatian believers. They have not needed the law to be the recipients of the Holy Spirit, which is the fulfillment of God's promise to Abraham. They have been given the power to become adopted children of God, able to greet God in the manner Jesus did, as "Abba."[26] They have undergone a fundamental change or transformation. They are not to continue as they were (in vice) or seek for the easy guidance of heteronomous norms. The question of how to use their freedom is answered clearly in two simple directives. First, they are not to submit again to any sort of slavery to externally applied norms, all of which are "worldly *stoicheia*," even when revealed by God. Second, they are not to enslave their freedom to the sorts of vice that lead humans to destroy each other. Instead, they are to be led by the Spirit that empowers them, displaying the positive virtues that cultivate human harmony. They have "crucified" that old self; now they must live according to the measure of the power of new life given to them by God in Christ.

Deciphering Galatians 6

The final section of Galatians presents distinctive problems of interpretation. As difficult conceptually as 5:1–26 is, Paul's imperatives, as we have seen, follow logically from the questions posed by his fourfold narrative argument of chapters 1–4. Gal 5:26, indeed, would seem to form an intel-

---

25. Although the preposition *en* can be taken locatively, Paul's thought pushes us toward regarding it also as instrumental: "since we live *by* (the power of) the Spirit." Similarly, we should not miss the presence of *stoichein* in the exhortative subjunctive *stoichōmen*: they are to be measured by, follow along the lines of, the Spirit. See also 6:16: *hosoi tō kanoni toutō stoichēsousin.*

26. Despite its overconfidence, and despite above all its blithe overuse by some theologians, the work of Joachim Jeremias on the remarkable use of *Abba* in Mark 14:36, Rom 8:15, and Gal 4:6 is still worth considering; see *The Central Message of the New Testament.*

lectually satisfying conclusion to the missive. Paul could have appended his actual ending at that point—"the grace of our Lord Jesus Christ be with your Spirit, brothers. Amen." But he does not. He continues with what appear to be disjointed and even confusing exhortations. The character of these exhortations is actually distinguished by the interjection of 6:11, "See with what large letters I am writing to you in my own hand." The remarks following the interjection are intensely personal and polemical, continuing and concluding the arguments made earlier (5:12–16). In contrast, the exhortations preceding them in 6:1–10 appear to be so general as to be obscure. In order to seek some clarity of this more difficult section, I begin by quickly summarizing the points that Paul had already made earlier in the letter but that he repeats here in 6:12–16.

Closing Assertions

Paul makes four passionate declarations in the final section of the letter. The first concerns those who are seeking to advance the circumcision agenda; the second concerns his own stance; the third wishes a blessing on all those following the path of the Spirit; the fourth angrily asserts the special status he holds with regard to Christ.

Paul first identifies the scurrilous designs of the agitators.[27] The ones seeking to coerce circumcision on the Galatians are "seeking a good appearance in the flesh"[28] (Gal 6:12, author's translation). They do not themselves keep the law, Paul insists (6:13), but they wish to "boast in your flesh" (6:13). They seek the security and safety that comes from persuading others to adopt their position. But at a deeper level, Paul says, they do this "only so that they will not be persecuted for the cross of Christ" (6:12, author's translation). Here he sharply delineates the stakes underlying all his earlier arguments: human acceptability measured by ritual conventions, or the work of God measured by the scandal of the cross.

Second, in contrast to the agitators, Paul makes his boast only in the cross of the Lord Jesus Christ, through which the world is crucified to him and he to the world. His experience of Christ has alienated him not just from making the law the frame for righteousness but from the entire

---

27. On the importance and import of this passage, see Prokhorov, "Taking the Jews Out of the Equation."

28. The verb *euprosōpein* is a hapax, but its meaning is clear from its etymology: to put on a good face, or mask—in this case *en sarki*, which, given the polyvalence Paul uses elsewhere, can mean "through the marks of circumcision" or "through self-aggrandizing behavior" or both.

"world" that measures status in terms of external markings rather than internal transformation: "For neither does circumcision mean anything, nor does uncircumcision, but only a new creation [*kainē ktisis*]" (Gal 6:15).

Third, Paul declares "peace and mercy" on all those who are measured by this rule (*tō kanoni toutō stoichēsousin*, Gal 6:16)—the rule he has just stated—and for the "Israel of God," that is, the Israel according to the promise that is gifted by and lives by the Holy Spirit enjoyed by the gentile Galatians. This blessing represents at the same time the implicit banishment from the community of those who want to advance another measure: these proclaimers of "another gospel" are to be put under the ban (1:8–9) and cast out (4:30).

Finally, Paul exclaims, "From now on, let no one make trouble for me [*kopous moi mēdeis parechetō*]; for I bear the marks of Jesus on my body [*egō gar ta stigmata tou Iēsou en tō sōmati mou bastazō*]" (Gal 6:17, adapted). Although the words are clear enough, their import is not. Having just denied that the presence or absence of fleshly marks are significant, why does he return to the marks he bears on his body as somehow dispositive? His intention must be not to establish a fundamental chasm between the "physical" and the "spiritual" but to remind his readers that, in his case, the spiritual (meaning the gift of the Holy Spirit) came to him precisely through, not his being a circumcised Jew, but his being "co-crucified with Christ" (2:19, author's translation). The marks he bears on his body, then—the *stigmata Iēsou*—are the marks of the new creation embracing both Jew and gentile without distinction. These marks of the cross of Jesus that are visible on his body stand as the best evidence that he does not seek to avoid persecution for the cross of Christ as do the circumcisers. Those wounds are already his.

Like the greeting to the letter in Gal 1:1–4, these four final points intertwine the stories of Paul, Jesus, the Galatians, and Israel. They provide a fine summary of the chapters 1–4. That they may well have been written in Paul's own hand is suggested by 6:11 and is supported by the intensely personal tone of the statements. But precisely the clarity of the closing words of Galatians increases the puzzlement posed by 6:1–10.

Mutual Care, Individual Responsibility (Gal 6:1–5)

Paul concluded his consideration of living according to the Spirit rather than the flesh in Gal 5:26 by exhorting his readers, "Let us not be conceited, provoking one another, envious of one another." And in the sentences following, he enunciates two cases of community interaction that appear to flow from his desire that the believers not be in hostile competition with each other.[29] Each is posed in the form of a conditional, as cases often are.

First, then, is Gal 6:1–2 (adapted): "Brothers, even if a person [*ean kai . . . anthrōpos*] is caught out [*prolēmphthē*] in some transgression [*paraptōmati*],[30] you who are spiritual [*hymeis hoi pneumatikoi*] should correct that one with a gentle spirit [*katartizete ton toiouton en pneumati prautētos*], looking to yourself, so that you also may not be tempted [*skopōn seauton mē kai ou peirasthēs*]. Bear one anothers' burdens, and so you will fulfill the law of Christ [*allēlōn ta barē bastazete kai houtōs anaplērōsete ton nomon tou Christou*]." This first exhortation seems completely other-directed, fitting comfortably within the ancient philosophical tradition of mutual correction.[31] Given what Paul has said about gentleness as a fruit of the Spirit, it is no surprise that such correction of an erring brother or sister by "those who are spiritual"[32] be carried out gently rather than harshly—as was sometimes part of the same tradition.[33] Also consistent with this philosophical tradition is that the one correcting be self-mindful—the corrector may be liable to fall into the same transgression or, even more subtly, use such correction of the other as an occasion for subtle envy and competition (see again 5:26).

This statement concerning mutual correction concludes, however, with a legitimation that far exceeds even the love of neighbor that "fulfills the whole law" (Gal 5:14). In a dramatic appropriation of the symbolism of Torah, Paul makes the bearing of one another's burdens (again, note the reciprocity) the fulfillment of the "law of Christ." The reader cannot

29. For a thoughtful thinking-through of this difficult passage, see Lambrecht, "Paul's Coherent Admonition."

30. Given the heavy use of *paraptōma* elsewhere in the canonical letters as a rough equivalent for "sin" (against God)—see Rom 4:25; 5:15, 16, 17, 18, 20; 11:11, 12; 2 Cor 5:19; Eph 1:7; 2:1, 5; Col 2:13—this singular appearance in Galatians seems entirely removed from the realm of law-keeping and seems to refer to ordinary "transgressions" people commit against each other.

31. See, e.g., Hierocles, *On Duties* 4.25.53; Dio Chrysostom, *Oration* 77/78.37–45; Plutarch, *How to Tell a Flatterer from a Friend* 30–37 (*Moralia* 70D–74E); Philodemus, *On Frankness* 37. From the side of Judaism, see Ezek 3:21; Pirqe Aboth 5:18; 1QS 5:24–25.

32. Although the expression *hoi pneumatikoi* ("the spiritual ones") follows naturally enough from "those led by the Spirit" (5:25), it only appears in this sense elsewhere in Paul's letters in 1 Cor 2:13–15; 3:1; 14:37 (?).

33. For this, see Malherbe, "'Gentle as a Nurse.'"

but think of the way Paul's telling of the story of Jesus emphasized his "giving of himself" for the sake of others (1:4; 2:20; 4:4–5). The "law of Christ," then, means the same as Paul's use of "the mind of Christ" in 1 Cor 2:16: it is a way of living according to the Spirit, to the point of perceiving and acting on reality according to the pattern revealed by the Messiah himself. Paul's statement here corresponds perfectly to Phil 2:1–11.[34]

The second case, however, seems to move away from other-directedness and toward a concern for individual integrity:[35] "For if anyone thinks he is something when he is nothing,[36] he is deluding himself. Each one must examine [*dokimazetō*] his own work, and then he will have reason to boast with regard to himself alone [*eis heauton monon to kauchēma hexei*], and not with regard to someone else [*kai ouk eis ton heteron*]. For each will carry his own load [*hekastos gar to idion phortion bastasei*]" (Gal 6:3–5, adapted). This set of statements is at home even more obviously within the world of Greco-Roman moral philosophy, calling for accurate self-assessment as the premise for any assertion of self ("boast," *kauchēma*) over others. The language of boasting is not exceptional among the moralists, nor is it always regarded negatively.[37] The issue with regard to boasting is its basis and accuracy. A great rhetorician like Aelius Aristides has a legitimate basis for advertising his rhetorical skills.[38] Paul will shortly accuse those advocating circumcision as seeking to "make a boast" (*kauchēsōntai*) in the flesh of the Galatians (6:13). They do this even though they themselves do not observe the law. The Galatians' subservience to law makes such advocates appear to "be something," which they are not of themselves but only on the basis of others. Read contextually, therefore, this aphoristic declaration could have application to the circumcisers who think they are something but are not, and who are therefore self-deceived.

The principle, however, also clearly has more general applicability within the social life of a community of faith. It points to the necessary

---

34. See Hays, "Christology"; Schäfer, "Die Torah der messianischen Zeit"; Strelan, "Burden-Bearing"; Murphy-O'Connor, "Unwritten Law of Christ"; Konradt, "Die Christonomie der Freiheit."

35. See Martyn, "Apocalyptic Antinomies."

36. The phrase *dokei tis einai* ("thinking one is something") inevitably recalls to mind the characterization of the Jewish leadership in 2:6.

37. See Plutarch, *On Inoffensive Self-Praise* (*Moralia* 539B–547F).

38. Aelius Aristides's *Orations* 28, 33, 34 amply display the great orator's *philotimia*; see also Philostratus's *Lives of the Sophists* 582.

corollary of mutual correction, which is honest self-discernment. No one can do this for us. Each one "carries his or her own load." Each one is called to "test [*dokimazetō*] one's own practice" before venturing to address or offer counsel concerning the failure of others. This admonition, therefore, picks up from the qualifying phrase of the previous case, "looking to yourself that you may not also be tempted [or "tested," *peirazein*]" (Gal 6:1).

Although Paul's language in 6:1–5 is recognizable within the Greco-Roman moral tradition, it also shows the complex internal tensions that are found within any community of those who are led by the Spirit and are called to freedom. The appropriate expression of authentic freedom is found, as the previous chapter has shown, not in the carrying out of specific instructions, but in the cultivation of internal moral dispositions. Such dispositions are those that reflect the "fruit of the Spirit" and eschew the "works of the flesh" that are selfish and self-aggrandizing. The disposition and practices of believers are to build rather than destroy the church. Edification, however, requires a delicate balance between mutual assistance and self-discernment, between individual and corporate responsibility, between the apparently contrary ideals of "each one carrying one's own load" and "bearing one another's burdens."

The key element in discernment would seem to be the actual need of the other, in contrast to one's own agenda to change another. The project of the circumcisers, by this measure, is "fleshly" precisely because they seek to impose an obligation (that they themselves do not meet) in order to secure their own safety and to have a reason to boast. Their "thinking they are something" is empty self-deceit.

In contrast, authentic "bearing of one another's burdens" begins not with one's personal agenda but with the failing and need of the other, and proceeds with the cautious care appropriate to one who knows one's own susceptibility to the same faults. These short instructions by Paul illustrate that for a community gifted with freedom by the Spirit (Gal 5:1) and "called to freedom" (5:13), living "according to the Spirit" (5:25, author's translation) is not easier than keeping the law but more difficult.

Sharing All Good Things

After the complexities of Gal 6:1–5, the straightforward imperative in 6:6 seems refreshingly clear: "One who is being instructed [*katechoumenos*] in the word [*ton logon*] should share all good things [*koinōneitō*

... *en pasin agathois*] with his instructor [*tō katēchounti*]." Considered in itself, the instruction is a commonplace of ancient pedagogy: the teacher who shares wisdom should receive material support. The "fellowship" (*koinōnia*) through nonequivalent goods is a classic example of how the ideal of friendship establishes reciprocity between persons of unequal social status.[39]

The principle is one that Paul applies to himself and the Corinthian church, although he refuses to take advantage of it and preaches to them for free: "If we have sown spiritual seed [*ta pneumatika*] for you, is it a great thing that we reap a material [*sarkika*] harvest from you?" (1 Cor 9:11). More strikingly, in Romans, Paul applies the same principle to the collection that he has taken up among gentiles for the relief of the Jerusalem church: "they are indebted to them, for if the gentiles have come to share in their spiritual blessings [*ta pneumatika*], they ought also to serve them in material blessings [*ta sarkika*]" (15:27; see also *isotēs* concerning the collection in 2 Cor 8:13).

In light of this tradition, and of Paul's usage, Gal 6:6 can be read as expressing the way material and spiritual *koinōnia* can combine "everyone must bear one's own load" with "bear one another's burdens."

Does it, then, offer a conclusion to 6:1–5, making reciprocal sharing "in all good things" the resolution of the tension we observed between individual and communal responsibility? But in that case, the restriction to the teacher and the one taught seems arbitrary, in addition to introducing the sole instance of leadership functions into the letter. Or does 6:6 stand isolated, without any particular reference to what precedes or follows it? In a composition that is otherwise so logically put together, the position that 6:6 is simply an isolated dictum seems least likely.

Before trying to resolve the problem posed by 6:6, the language of the immediately following verses demands close attention. Paul begins with a solemn warning: "make no mistake; God is not mocked" (*mē planasthe, theos ou myktērizetai*, 6:7).[40] Such a negative command in the aorist, followed by a present indicative, would ordinarily be premonitory in character: "Don't fall into self-deception; God is not mocked." But what actual or possible behavior should elicit this somber reminder? Can it possibly refer only to the payment or nonpayment of catechists? How

---

39. See above all Aristotle, *Nicomachean Ethics* 8–9.

40. The verb *myktērizein* (derived from *myktēr*, "nostril") means "to sneer at or make mock of"; it is found mostly in the LXX, not as directed to God but to human enemies; see Prov 1:30; Jer 20:7; Ps 43:13; 79:6.

would God be "mocked" or "shamed" by that sort of negligence? In all likelihood, the warning points forward. Unfortunately, Paul's diction in the next lines has polyvalent possibilities.

One possibility is that Paul's language intensifies his earlier distinction between moral behavior according to the flesh and the Spirit in Gal 5:16–26.[41] Thus, "a person will reap only what he sows, because the one who sows for the flesh [or "into the flesh," *eis tēn sarka*] will reap corruption from the flesh [*ek tēs sarkos*], but the one who sows for the spirit [*eis to pneuma*] will reap eternal life from the spirit [*ek tou pneumatos*]" (6:7–8, adapted). Such a moral referent seems perfectly logical, if perhaps a bit redundant. It is supported by the seriousness of the declaration that God is not mocked, and by the mention of corruption on one side and "eternal life" on the other.

But why use the language of sowing and reaping in this connection? Paul earlier had spoken of the "fruit of the Spirit" (*karpos tou pneumatos*) in 5:22, but in that place it meant a set of moral dispositions rather than eternal life. And Paul did not speak of "the works of the flesh" in connection with any agricultural metaphor. Finally, thinking of the disjunction in moral terms does not help clarify the odd prepositional phrases *eis tēn sarka* and *eis to pneuma*. Are they roughly locative, so that one plants "into" flesh or spirit as the place of sowing? Or are they roughly expressing purpose, so that one sows "for the purpose of the flesh" or "for the purpose of the Spirit"?

The lines that follow, in turn, tend to open another possibility for understanding the entire sequence of passages. Paul says in Gal 6:9, "Let us not grow tired of doing good, for in due time [*kairō idiō*] we shall reap our harvest [or, better, "we shall reap"], if we do not give up." Here Paul's point is not making a choice between good and evil, but not giving up in the doing of good; not reaping different sorts of harvests, but the patient waiting for an expected harvest. Finally, Paul says in 6:10 (adapted), "So then, while we have the opportunity [*koiros*], let us do good to all, especially to those who belong to the family [*oikeious*, "household members"] of the faith." Here the "doing good to all" echoes the "sharing in all good things" of 6:6. Is it possible that this whole section makes sense best when it serves as a cryptic reminder to the gentile Galatian church that they are to participate in the collection for the poor in the Jerusalem church, which Paul mentions as an essential condition of the Jerusalem leadership's recognition of the validity of Paul's gentile mission (2:10)?

41. See, e.g., Matera, *Galatians*, 222–23; Bruce, *Epistle to the Galatians*, 263–66; Cousar, *Galatians*, 146–47.

The points in favor of that reading can briefly be noted:

1. The strange interjection of the *koinōnia* through "all good things" between the instructed and the instructor makes sense if the reference is not simply to teachers and those taught within the Galatian assembly but also between gentile communities and Jerusalem. What could be a better example of "bearing the burdens of others" than sharing possessions in this context?

2. Although Paul uses "fruit" in a moral/religious sense in Rom 6:21–22 and 7:4–5 in a way that is similar to the suggested use in Gal 5:22, he also uses "fruit" as a euphemism for financial support in Rom 1:13 and 1 Cor 9:7, just as he uses the language of "refreshment" (*anapauein*) in 1 Cor 16:18; 2 Cor 7:13; and Phlm 7 and 20, and the language of "harvesting" (*therizein*) in 1 Cor 9:11 and 2 Cor 9:6.

3. The language of "doing good to all" without growing weary, especially for "members of the household of God," could easily apply to the collection, especially in light of Paul's use of kinship language in Gal 4:1–4 (see also Paul's invoking of the relational gift of "peace" [*eirēnē*] upon the Israel of God)—the gentiles can now see themselves as part of Israel according to the promise; an expression of thanksgiving for this gift would be a "sharing in all good things" with those who are Jews according to the Spirit as well as the flesh.

4. Paul's warnings that God is not mocked, that they should not grow weary, and that they should "take the opportunity" (*kairos*) suggest the filling of a solemn obligation that has not yet been filled.

5. Finally, the circumcision agenda takes on added significance: if the Galatians—whom Paul says elsewhere he has recruited for the collection (1 Cor 16:1)—become circumcised and another "Jewish" community, then the symbolic significance of Paul's collection, and even the significance of his own ministry to the gentiles, is threatened. Thus, the warning: God is not mocked![42]

---

42. I am not the first to make this connection. Although Keith F. Nickle notes the strong resemblance between the language here and in 2 Cor 8–9 in *The Collection*, 59n55, it is Larry W. Hurtado who makes a strong case for the collection here being in view; see "Jerusalem Collection," esp. 53; even earlier, see Bligh, *Galatians*, 484. Basil S. Davis sees the verses as referring to the collection, and adds (with the help of a fifth-century interpreter) the nuance that Paul further does not want the Galatians to be supporting the wrong teachers—namely, the Judaizers; see "Severianus of Gabala."

It may be simply that we must be content with recognizing an irresolvable polyvalence in these verses, since the question of referentiality cannot be settled completely. But it can be added that if the Galatians were involved in the collection, had pledged to contribute as *gentile* believers to their Jewish brethren, and had then shirked that commitment because of their concern to become Jewish themselves through circumcision, then it would make sense that Paul would regard such behavior as "sowing for the flesh" that would yield only corruption.

Conclusion

The study of Gal 5–6 demonstrates that the chapters are far from an afterthought or add-on. The rhetorical shift from intertwined narratives to community imperatives reveals where Paul was heading all along and makes clear that his interest from the first was less soteriology than ecclesiology.

Paul wants the Galatian church, which began in idolatry, was transformed by the experience of God's power by the Holy Spirit, and is now divided by those seeking to impose circumcision, to understand how to continue their story as God's children through the Spirit and as God's promised people through the Spirit. He wants them to live out the truth of the Christian experience, which means never swerving from the gift that had been given them—the power of freedom through the Spirit—to fall back again into the slavery of obedience to worldly *stoicheia* represented by any form of heteronomy, even that of the law.

Instead, they are to learn to express the experience of freedom through moral dispositions that nurture rather than fracture community. And since such dispositions cannot adequately be captured by any set of laws, the Galatians must learn the difficult art of discernment: how to live within the tension of individual responsibility and mutual care, between carrying their own load and bearing one another's burdens. But they must above all, if they are to live according to the Spirit and the story of Jesus, stop manipulating others in order to serve their own ends.

Chapter 12

Paul's Vision of the Church

The Community of the Risen Lord

Addressing Paul's understanding of the church (*ekklēsia*) means raising other difficult questions that a brief essay cannot adequately answer. The most critical question concerns which of the letters ascribed to Paul should be considered. Ephesians and 1 Timothy, for example, provide fuller information on aspects of the church than do some undisputed letters. But they are commonly regarded as pseudonymous. Should they be excluded altogether, read as a faithful continuation of themes in the authentic letters, or adjudged betrayals of the authentic Paul's spirit? In order to maintain conversation with the dominant scholarly position, this essay will discuss the evidence of the undisputed letters before that in Colossians, Ephesians, and the Pastoral Letters, even though there are strong reasons for accepting all thirteen letters attributed to Paul as authored by him through a complex process of composition. The present analysis does, however, emphasize thematic links between the disputed and undisputed letters in order to respect the genuine lines of continuity among them and the marked diversity within even the collection of undisputed letters.

Another procedural question concerns consistency and variation among the expressions of Paul's thought. Which images and understandings are of fundamental character, and which are brought to the surface only by the peculiar circumstances that Paul faces in a specific community? Is it accurate, for example, to call Paul's basic outlook "charismatic" if he deals with the spiritual gifts extensively—and cautiously—in only one letter (1 Cor 12–14) and briefly in two others (Rom 12:6–8; 1 Thess 5:19–21)? Is Paul's commitment to an egalitarian membership (Gal 3:28) absolute, or a function of his concern about competitiveness? These questions remind us of the occasional character of the Pauline correspondence. By no means are his letters simply spontaneous outpourings of the moment; recent analysis has confirmed how pervasively Paul used the conventions of ancient rhetoric in his letters. They are, however, genuine letters that respond to situations—sometimes critical—in Paul's own ministry or in the life of his communities. We never find Paul's thought on any subject laid out systematically, therefore, but only as directed to a specific occasion.

Finally, it is difficult to assess the impact of social realities on Paul's statements concerning the *ekklēsia*. The basic structure of the Greco-Roman club or society, already substantially appropriated by the Hellenistic Jewish synagogue, was immediately available for Paul's congregations as he worked in the diaspora. And the fact that his churches met in the *oikos* (home) of leading members (e.g., Rom 16:5; 1 Cor 16:19; Col 4:15; Phlm 2) had a number of implications, supplying a range of metaphors, a model of leadership functions, and a source of leaders, as well as creating a source of tension in deciding the appropriate social roles for women and men in the assembly. This short essay cannot take up these disputed questions but can remind the careful reader to assess the following summation, which is necessarily general, in light of the complex and diverse witness of the letters themselves.

Paul's Ecclesial Focus

The main point on the topic of Paul's ecclesiology can nevertheless be stated clearly and emphatically: the central concern in Paul's letters is the stability and integrity of his churches. He was the founder of communities (1 Cor 4:15; Gal 4:13; 1 Thess 1:5) and expended his energies on their behalf. He lists his daily care for the churches in climactic position in his list of tribulations (2 Cor 11:28). When absent from his churches, Paul sought to visit them (e.g., 1 Cor 4:18; 1 Thess 2:17–18). When he was not able to visit, he stayed in contact through the sending of his delegates (e.g., Phil 2:19; 1 Thess 3:2) and the writing of letters. It is significant that all but one of Paul's letters are to be read in churches. The only truly private letter is 2 Timothy. Although addressed to an individual, Philemon includes members of the local church in its greetings (Phlm 3); 1 Timothy and Titus, as *mandata principis* ("commandments of the ruler") letters, have a semipublic character. Paul's primary concern in his letters, furthermore, is not the individual but the community as such. He appeals to all the members of the church as his readers, and in the letters to his delegates, his focus is on their administration of a local community in

Paul's absence. Paul characteristically addresses his readers as "brothers" in the plural (e.g., Rom 1:13; 1 Cor 2:1), and his instruction is directed to their life together rather than to the good of any individual. As a moral teacher, Paul seeks to shape communities of character. The intrinsic legitimacy of certain practices—such as circumcision, visions, or spiritual gifts—is less his concern than the possible divisiveness such practices might generate within communities through rivalry and competition. Ecclesiology is as central to Paul as soteriology. Indeed, it can be argued that for him soteriology *is* ecclesiology: all of his language about salvation (*sōtēria*) has a communal rather than an individual referent (e.g., Rom 1:16; 8:24; 11:11, 14).

The Pauline church resembled other *ekklēsiai*, such as the many clubs and philosophical schools of the Hellenistic world, in its basic structure, its location in the household rather than the cult shrine, and its patterns of mutual assistance. Paul is also capable of presenting himself in terms used by Greco-Roman philosophers (1 Thess 2:4–12; Gal 4:14). The inherently fragile nature of the *ekklēsia* as an intentional community—that is, one dependent on the commitment of its members rather than natural kinship—helps account for Paul's constant concern for "building up" the church by mutual exhortation and example (1 Thess 5:11; 1 Cor 8:1; 14; Eph 4:12, 16). Paul shows himself willing to exclude or even dismiss those in the church whose behavior threatens the stability or integrity of the church (e.g., 1 Cor 5:1–5; 2 Thess 3:14–15; Gal 4:30).

Paul's understanding of his own work and that of the church owes more, however, to the symbolic world of Torah and the heritage of Judaism. He speaks of his own role as an apostle in terms reminiscent of the call and work of God's prophets (Gal 1:15), who were sent out to speak God's word. He refers to the church in terms of God's "call" (*kalein, klēsis*; Rom 11:29; 1 Cor 1:26; 1 Thess 2:12), giving the noun *ekklēsia* some of the resonance of God's *qahal* ("assembly") in Scripture (Deut 23:1–2; Josh 9:2; Ps 21:22). Thus, members of the community have not simply chosen to belong to the church as another club; rather, God has called them out of the world. Even with his gentile communities, Paul can employ the narratives of Torah concerning the people of Israel as exemplary for the church (1 Cor 10:1–13; 2 Cor 3:7–18; Gal 4:21–31). Similarly, the church is to be characterized, as was ancient Israel, by holiness: "This is the will of God, your sanctification" (1 Thess 4:3 RSV). The boundary between those in the church and outside it is marked by a ritual act (baptism) but is defined by moral behavior rather than ritual observance (Rom 6:1–11). Formerly, members lived in the vice typical of those who are without

God in the world and given to idolatry (1 Thess 1:9; Rom 1:18–32). But by the ritual washing of baptism (Eph 5:26), they have been cleansed morally and now are called to holiness of life. This basic distinction is expressed by Paul as the contrast between "the world" and "the saints" (*hoi hagioi*, the holy ones; 1 Cor 6:2).

Israel and the Church

In some real sense, therefore, Paul sees his churches as continuous with Israel, considered not simply as an ethnic group but as God's elect people. But three elements in Paul's experience introduced an element of discontinuity with the Jewish heritage as well. The first (in chronological order rather than order of importance) was his own life experience as one who had persecuted the church precisely out of zeal for Torah (Gal 1:13–14; Phil 3:6). The appeal to Deut 21:23 in Gal 3:13 ("cursed be everyone who hangs upon a tree," NABRE), as a rebuttal to those who would claim Jesus as the righteous one, may well have been Paul's own before his encounter with the risen Jesus. His statement that "no one in the Holy Spirit can say, 'Cursed be Jesus'" (1 Cor 12:3) may well have an autobiographical basis. For Paul the Pharisee, if one held to the Torah as absolute norm, then one could not claim Jesus as Lord. It was the experience of Jesus as the powerfully risen Lord that put Paul in a state of cognitive dissonance. If Jesus is the righteous one, then Torah cannot be an absolute norm: God is capable of acting outside God's own scriptural precedents.

The second element follows the first: Paul perceives the resurrection of Jesus as something more than the validation of a Jewish messiah in the traditional sense of a restorer of the people. The resurrection of Jesus is more than a historical event like the exodus. It is an eschatological event that begins a new age of humanity. Indeed, the resurrection is best understood as new creation: "If anyone is in Christ, there is a new creation. The old things have passed away. Behold, everything is new" (2 Cor 5:17).

The third element is Paul's sense of his own mission and its consequences. If Paul was sent to the gentiles with the good news of what God had done in Jesus (Gal 1:16), and if gentiles were to be included in the church without the requirement of circumcision (Gal 5:1–6), then the perception that the resurrection is a new creation and Jesus is a new Adam is confirmed (1 Cor 15:45; Rom 5:12–21). If, as he had done, Paul's fellow Jews reject that proclamation despite their zeal for Torah (Rom

9:30–10:3), and if, as he had done, Paul's fellow Jews even resist and persecute the proclaimers of the good news (2 Thess 2:13–16), then there is some real rupture within God's people that must be reconciled. For Paul, then, the relationship between the church and Israel is not simply a matter of continuity or of discontinuity; it must rather be seen in terms of a dialectic within history.

In Paul's undisputed letters, the various sides of this dialectic are expressed in several ways. An obvious example is the way Paul appeals to the principle that in Christ there is neither Jew nor Greek, male nor female, slave nor free (Gal 3:28), thereby rendering the three great status markers dividing people (ethnicity, gender, class) nugatory for those in the church ("in Christ"). Paul makes this appeal most emphatically in the context of resisting those within a gentile community who seek to be circumcised, and who would thereby make the church a community in which Jews and males have higher status than gentiles and women. Note that at the end of Galatians he puts two statements in tension, saying first, "Neither circumcision counts nor uncircumcision, but a new creation" (6:15), but then also, "Peace upon the Israel of God" (6:16). In Galatians, Paul's polemic would lead one to conclude that the "Israel of God" was made up only of gentile believers, so severe are his characterizations of the law (3:19–22) and of "the present Jerusalem" (4:25). Indeed, in his more negative moments, reacting against the resistance or harassment of fellow Jews, Paul even designates them as "false brethren" (Gal 2:4 RSV), unbelievers who are perishing, blinded by "the god of this world" (2 Cor 4:3–4 RSV), unable to understand even their own Scripture, and subject to the wrath of God (1 Thess 2:16).

On the other side of the dialectic, Paul confirms the truth of Torah's narratives (Rom 4:1–25) and the words of the prophets (11:8–27; 15:4), recognizing moreover that, unlike gentile idolaters, the Jews had not only the "words of God" (3:2) but also the knowledge of God's will (2:18). Thus, although he insists that Jew and gentile stand in fundamentally the same relationship before God both in their sin and in their capacity for faith (3:9, 22), he also acknowledges that the Jew has a considerable advantage because of the knowledge of God's revelation (3:1–4).

The full dialectic is worked out in Romans 9–11, the climax of Paul's most extended reflection on his mission to the gentiles. Beginning with three unshakable convictions—his solidarity with his fellow Jews (9:1–3), God's election and blessing of the Jews (9:4–5), and the infallibility of God's word (9:6)—Paul engages in a midrashic reflection on Scripture impelled by the implications and consequences of the gentile mission. He interprets the present situation (9:30–10:4) in terms of a longer history of election and rejection (9:6–29), and understands himself with other believing Jews as a faithful remnant (11:1–6). Jews who now stumble over the crucified Messiah will perhaps, out of jealousy for the favor that God is now showing to those who formerly were "no people," also in the end be joined to the increasingly gentile church, and "thus all Israel will be saved" (11:13–32). While passionately committed to the cause of the mission to the gentiles, Paul remains as unswervingly devoted to his own people and to the fidelity of the God who had elected them.

Mission of the Church

Paul describes the church's mission never in terms of a specific task that it is to perform but in terms of a character of life that it is to exhibit. It is to "walk worthily of its call" (Eph 4:1). At the most obvious level, this involves a life of righteousness before God (Rom 6:13, 18). Just as it is not physical circumcision but the circumcision of the heart expressed in obedience to the commandments that identifies the genuine Jew (Rom 2:25–29), so within the church it is not a matter of circumcision or not but of "keeping the commandments of God" (1 Cor 7:19 RSV). Like Jesus and James, Paul identifies the love of neighbor as the perfect summation of God's commandments, because "love does no harm to the neighbor" (Rom 13:8–10). Paul thus emphasizes a communal understanding of righteousness; it is not only a matter of being right with God but also a matter of being in right relationship with others (1 Cor 8:1–3; Rom 14:17). Here it is impossible not to detect the influence of the story of Jesus on Paul's understanding of the church. In 1 Cor 1:18–2:5 Paul challenges the arrogance and rivalry of his Corinthian readers by appealing to the message of the cross, which demonstrates how God's power works through weakness and God's wisdom through foolishness. The cross that reverses human valuations is the paradigm for those in the church who "have the mind of Christ" (2:16): they are to live together not in competition but in cooperation, not in rivalry but in mutual edification.

Paul shows little or no concern for the perfection (*teleiōsis*) of individuals but is constantly concerned that his churches mature as communities of reciprocal gift-giving and fellowship. And the norm is the human Jesus: "Little children, how I am in labor until Christ be formed among you" (Gal 4:19). Paul understands Jesus as the one "who loved us and gave himself for our sins" (Gal 1:4). Jesus's kenotic (self-emptying) and faithful obedience toward God, which implied the rejection of any competitive claim toward God (Phil 2:5–11), and which established the possibility for all to be righteous through sharing his faithful obedience (Rom 5:18–21), is also the perfect expression of Jesus's love for humans, and therefore the model for relations within the church. Those who "put on the Lord Jesus Christ" (Rom 13:14) are able to "welcome one another as Christ has welcomed [them]" (15:7). Those who "bear one another's burdens" also "fulfill the law of Christ" (Gal 6:2). Those who are guided by love are willing to give up their rights for the sake of "the brother for whom Christ died" (Rom 14:15; 1 Cor 8:11). Paul considers attitudes of envy and rivalry to threaten such relationships (Gal 5:16–21). Envy and rivalry foster a spirit of competition that seeks the good of the individual at the expense of the community (Gal 5:13). Paul therefore advocates another spirit, that of fellowship or reconciliation (Gal 5:22–24; Phil 2:1–4). In his view, the paradigm of God's saving action as revealed in the faith and love of Jesus demands of the strong in the community not to dominate or assert their will but to place themselves in service and humility at the disposal of the weak (1 Cor 8:7–13). As Paul measures the integrity of his own mission by this norm of reconciliation (2 Cor 5:12–21), so does he measure the integrity and maturity of his churches (2 Cor 13:1–11). The task of collecting money from gentile churches for the impoverished church in Jerusalem, a task to which Paul committed himself in agreement with the Jerusalem leaders (Gal 2:10) and to which he devoted—with varying degrees of success—his best energies (1 Cor 16:1–4; 2 Cor 8–9), and for which he was willing to risk even his life (Rom 15:24–32), becomes the body language of the church's identity as a place of reconciliation.

The Church in Metaphor

Paul's understanding of the church is expressed as much by a series of metaphors as by propositions. Metaphors, especially root metaphors, are much more than rhetorical ornaments; they structure a perception of reality. The metaphors that Paul employs for the church combine elements of a living organism and structure. The simplest metaphors of this kind are agricultural and used only once, perhaps because of Paul's limited ability to handle horticultural terms. The church is a field that Paul has planted and Apollos has watered, but God gives the growth (1 Cor 3:6–9). Similarly, God's people is a domestic olive tree (the Jewish people) that, although pruned, is "holy in root and branches" (Rom 11:16). God has grafted the branch of a wild olive (gentile believers) onto it and is capable of grafting the domestic olive on again (Rom 11:16–24)—a clumsy metaphor indeed. These agricultural metaphors were probably derived from the imagery of the prophets.

A much more complex metaphor drawn from Paul's Jewish heritage is that the church is a family. The note of continuity with Judaism is found in the designation of Abraham as "our father" (Rom 4:1) and the affirmation that the gentiles are the "children of Abraham" through faith and thus part of Israel, indeed more so than those Jews who are not believers (Gal 3:4). Also in continuity with Judaism, Paul calls the creator God "Father" (Gal 1:1; Rom 1:7). But Paul connects God's fatherhood directly to "our Lord Jesus Christ," whom he recognizes as "Son of God" (e.g., Rom 1:4; 2 Cor 1:19). Jesus, however, was intended by God to be "the firstborn of many children" (Rom 8:29). Believers become children of God through "the spirit of adoption" that they receive at baptism (Rom 8:15; Gal 4:6). The church is therefore a fictive family in that it is not made up of biologically related people, but because of Paul's realistic sense of the Holy Spirit as "indwelling" humans (Rom 8:11), the bonds connecting members of the community are not, for him, simply imaginary. When Paul addresses his readers as "brothers" (*adelphoi*) or refers to coworkers as "brother" (*adelphos*) or "sister" (*adelphē*) (Rom 15:14; 16:1; 1 Cor 1:11), this kinship language works powerfully to strengthen community identity and unity. And since in antiquity the relationship between brothers is the supreme paradigm for fellowship (*koinōnia*), kinship language also encourages the patterns of equality and reciprocity that are Paul's moral concern.

A third metaphor is found in only two of the undisputed letters (1 Cor 12:22; Rom 12:4–5) but is attested also in two of the disputed letters (Col 1:18; Eph 4:12). Although it derives from Greco-Roman politics rather than Torah, Paul's use of it is distinctive. In this metaphor, the church is the body of the Messiah. The metaphor of the body combines the sense of a living organism and an articulate, many-membered structure. Paul's use emphasizes the legitimacy of many gifts in the community (1 Cor 12) and the need for those gifts to be used for the "building up" (*oikodomē*) of the community as a whole (1 Cor 14:26). Once more, however, Paul's perception of the community's life as one that is literally given by God through the Holy Spirit (Rom 5:5) and shaped by transformation into the image of Christ (2 Cor 3:17–18) gives the metaphor both depth and complexity. Since Paul can speak of the resurrected Jesus as "life-giving Spirit" (1 Cor 15:45) and can declare, "We have all drunk of the one Spirit" (12:13), it appears that the metaphor of the body may better be called a symbol in the strict sense—that is, a sign that participates in that which it signifies. Such participation seems demanded by Paul's language concerning the implications of eating the body of the Lord (10:16–22) and the ambiguity of reference present in his statement concerning "disregarding the body" at the Lord's Supper (11:27–30). When, in the same letter, Paul says of the community (using the plural), "And we have the mind of Christ" (2:16), it is legitimate to ask whether Paul might truly understand the church as the bodily presence of the resurrected Jesus. Such a mystical understanding— supported by a variety of other expressions (e.g., Gal 2:20; 1 Cor 6:17)—may also in turn undergird his statements concerning the disposition of the physical body (as in sexual relations) by members of the church (1 Cor 6:15–18; 7:14).

The previous two metaphors reveal the important roles Paul assigns to the Holy Spirit in his ecclesiology as the source of its (divine) life and as mediator of its (christic) identity. The Spirit "dwells in" the community (Rom 8:9, 11); as a result, Paul also speaks of the community as being "in Christ" (Rom 6:11; 1 Cor 1:2) and "in the Lord" (1 Cor 7:22; Gal 5:10), as shorthand for the sphere of influence (or energy field) that is the community. As with the contrast between the saints and the world, these designations serve to remind members powerfully of their special identity: they are "in Christ" as "the body of Christ," and they are "in the Lord" because they belong to the Lord (1 Cor 6:13). It is impossible to avoid the conclusion that Paul's understanding of the church involves a deep and mystical identity between this community and the risen Jesus mediated by the Holy Spirit.

Another metaphor is the church as a building (*oikodomē*, 1 Cor 3:9). Once more, the image combines unity and multiplicity and has roots in Torah, in Greco-Roman political philosophy, and in the social situation of early Christians whose *ekklēsia*, in fact, met in the houses of wealthier members. The house is a root metaphor that generates a number of other images: Paul and his associates are household managers (*oikonomoi*, 1 Cor 4:1–2) who dispense the mysteries of God; members of the community whose speech and actions serve to strengthen the community are said to "edify" the church (*oikodomein*, "to build a house"; 1 Cor 8:1; 1 Thess 5:11). Paul's distinctive version of the metaphor once more comes from his sense that the community derives from and is ordered by God.

The church is therefore "God's house." Given Paul's sense of the community as enlivened and guided by the indwelling Holy Spirit, furthermore, it is but a short step to a refinement of the house metaphor: the church is God's temple (1 Cor 3:16-17). This image combines the elements of unity and multiplicity together with a profound sense of the divine presence within the community, and supports as well the mandate to holiness of life within the church.

Organization in the Local Church

The notion that Paul's churches either were directed exclusively by the apostolic authority of Paul himself or were charismatic organisms guided exclusively by the Spirit without any human organization is contradicted both by sociological logic and by evidence in the undisputed letters. Paul's frequently expressed frustration reveals how his own visits, the sending of his delegates, and even his letters failed to enable him to resolve even the larger crises of his churches, much less the everyday affairs (*ta biōtika*, 1 Cor 6:3-4) that require attention in every community. Intentional communities do not survive without mechanisms that enable them to carry out common tasks and make decisions. On one side, they need to settle disputes; on the other side, they need to provide hospitality, organize fellowship, care for the sick, even receive and read letters from the apostle. They can take communal action in such matters as the collection (1 Cor 16:1-4) or providing supplies requested by Paul's agent for a future mission (Rom 15:24; 16:1-2). Pauline churches had available to them from the start, moreover, the simple and flexible structure of the Greco-Roman *ekklēsia* and the Jewish synagogue. The diaspora synagogue had a board—often made up of wealthy benefactors of the community—that administered finances and settled disputes and oversaw the study and teaching of Torah, as well as the system of organized charity to the needy within the community.

The undisputed letters provide sparse but significant evidence that some such simple structure was present also in Pauline churches from the beginning. Paul can speak of those in the Thessalonian church—presumably in existence for a very short time—who preside over others and exhort them (1 Thess 5:12). Paul is angry at the Corinthians for picking inadequate members to settle disputes over *ta biōtika* in that church (1 Cor 6:18). In 1 Cor 12:28 he lists "governing" as one of the gifts of the Spirit (see also Rom 12:8) and instructs the Corinthian church to "be submissive" to such benefactors (and householders) as Stephanas and Achaicus (1 Cor 16:15–18). Galatians recognizes that there are those who instruct others in the word who should receive financial support in return (6:6). The Letter to Philemon assumes that the addressee has some authority over the *ekklēsia* that meets in his house (1–3, 21–22). Finally, Paul addresses *episkopoi* (supervisors) and *diakonoi* (helpers) in the Philippian church (Phil 1:1). These brief notices support the conclusion that Paul's churches had local leadership.

The Church in Colossians and Ephesians

The letters to the Colossians and Ephesians form a set within the Pauline corpus much like Galatians and Romans. In addition to sharing substantially in diction and style, the two letters work at similar themes from slightly different perspectives. As the position worked out polemically in Galatians is shaped by Romans into a magisterial argument, so also is the position worked out polemically in Colossians shaped by Ephesians into a magisterial reflection. Neither Colossians nor Ephesians adds significantly to our knowledge of structure in the Pauline church, although Ephesians does include a list of ministries (4:11). But both letters share Paul's focus on the *ekklēsia* as a community of mutual upbuilding and reconciliation. Their distinctive contribution is to heighten the sense of mystical identification between Christ and the church found also in the undisputed letters. Paul treats such leadership in purely functional terms, without providing any theological legitimation in its support.

In Colossians, Paul opposes those who seek to measure maturity by the addition of circumcision (2:11), ascetical observances (2:21–22), and even mystical experiences (2:18) by appealing to the adequacy of the gentiles' experience of God through baptism into Christ (2:9–15). Against the individualism inherent in the competition for higher status within the community (2:16, 23), Paul calls for a new sense of humanity that unites rather than divides persons on the basis of their status (3:11), and for a maturity based on an ever deeper insight into the mystery of Christ, spelled out in attitudes of mutuality and cooperation (3:5–17). To support the "fullness of God" that is made accessible through baptism into Christ (2:9–12), Colossians emphasizes the primacy of Christ over both creation and the church (1:15–20). In this letter, the church is the body, but Christ is the head (1:18, 24; 2:19).

Ephesians, which may well have been a circular letter, lifts the local concerns found in Colossians into a reflection on the nature and mission of the church that is the fullest and most mature in the Pauline collection. Virtually every ecclesial theme of Paul's other letters is brought together in Ephesians in a manner so metaphorically complex as to deflect easy summation. In brief, Paul portrays God's will in terms of an *oikonomia* (household administration, 1:10; 3:2) that has cosmic range: God seeks the reconciliation of all humans (1:9–14). The need for reconciliation between God and humans because of sin is expressed socially in alienation among humans. The prime example is the enmity between Jews and gentiles (2:11–12). Jesus's death and resurrection had the goal of reconciling humans to God and humans to each other in a new humanity that is created in his image in the Holy Spirit (2:13–18). Eph 2:1–11 elaborates these points through extraordinarily complex metaphors of body, house, and temple that make it clear that as the Jewish temple symbolized lack of access to God for all humanity and with it the enmity between Jew and gentile (2:14–15), so the church is to be the new house of God in the Spirit where all have equal access to God (2:19–22). The church is the place in the world where this mysterious plan of God is being revealed (3:9–11). The nature and mission of the church is therefore the same: to be the symbol of the world's possibility by being the place in the world where human differences do not separate but provide the basis for a deeper unity in the Spirit (4:11–16). The measure of the community's life is therefore "the unity of the Spirit in the bond of peace" (4:3 NRSV), and every behavior that falls short of "doing the truth in love" (4:15) must be rejected. If the church fails to be a community of reconciliation, it has no reason to exist. Positively, the love between female and male in marriage (5:22–31) points to the reconciliation possible between Jew and gentile: "This is a great mystery, by which I mean Christ and the church" (5:32).

The Church in the Pastorals

The letters to Paul's delegates Timothy and Titus are regarded by the majority of scholars as inauthentic and as representing a development of Pauline ecclesiology in the direction of institutional complexity. Whether the judgment concerning authenticity is correct or not, it is not substantially supported by differences in ecclesiology. Indeed, it is a mistake in method to combine these three letters as though they were uniform. Second Timothy focuses completely on the character and behavior of Paul's delegate in contrast to the practices of false teachers (2:14–4:5). The church enters the discussion only implicitly when the author develops the metaphor of the great house in which some vessels are destined for honorable use and others for shameful (2:20–23), as an encouragement to become a "proven workman" for God within the community of faith (2:15). In Titus, the only explicit mention of ecclesial organization comes in the instruction to establish elders/supervisors in every church, with a short list of qualities desirable in the supervisor (1:5–9). Otherwise, Titus concentrates on the threat that is implicitly posed to the church by the disruption of households by those challenging the adequacy of grace and advocating observance of the law (1:10–16).

It is 1 Timothy that provides a fuller view of the church, most obviously in its description of the moral and intellectual qualities desired in those who hold the positions of supervisor (*episkopos*, 3:1–7), helper (*diakonos*, 3:8–10, 12–13), and female helper (3:11). Although these descriptions are not found in the undisputed Pauline letters, we have seen that the titles themselves occur in Philippians. Since there is no description of the duties attached to these offices, furthermore, it is only by inference that we conclude that they involved oversight of the community's finances, teaching, settlement of disputes, and administration of charity—the same functions that we infer fell to those designated as "standing over" others in the undisputed letters. Most strikingly, there is also no theological legitimation of these positions. As in the other Pauline letters, the positions are assumed to be in existence and are regarded in purely functional terms.

First Timothy shows Paul excommunicating those upsetting the community (1:20) and refusing women permission to speak in the assembly (2:11–15), but these reflexes are also found in the undisputed letters (1 Cor 5:1–5; 14:33–36). Of the major Pauline metaphors for the church, 1 Timothy develops only that of the household (*oikos*). Management ability in one's household is a good indicator of leadership ability in the *ekklēsia* (1 Tim 3:4; cf. 1 Cor 16:15–18). False teaching draws attention away from "God's ordering of things" (*oikonomia theou*), to which faith responds (1 Tim 1:4). And in an explicit development of the metaphor, good behavior in the *ekklēsia* enables one to be a "pillar and support of the truth" within the "household of God, which is the church of the living God" (3:15).

Conclusion

There is great diversity within the Pauline collection concerning the images used for the church or the precise aspect of the church under discussion. But the letters are remarkably consistent in their basic understanding of the church as a community defined by its relationship with God through the risen Lord Jesus Christ and called to be a community of moral character, recognizable for its patterns of mutual support and fellowship.

The Rise of Church Order

An Examination of Bultmann's Theology of the New Testament

Ifirst read Bultmann's amazing book in my late twenties. I was then
a Benedictine monk and a student of theology. At that time, *Theology of the New Testament* stood as a colossus, demanding to be taken
into account. It would have been inconceivable to me—as it would to
other young scholars in the 1960s—that Bultmann would ever come
to resemble Shelley's "Ozymandias," needing excavation to be fully
appreciated.

The same copy I read then lies before me now as I write. Every page
is scarred and scratched with notes, queries, and objections. Many of
my questions arose because Bultmann was saying things much different
from the views of scholars who were then more familiar to me (Brown,
Dupont, Cerfaux, Wikenhauser, Cullmann). Like another book I read
and fought with in that same period of my life, Peter Berger's *Sacred Canopy*, I found Bultmann's *Theology* to be challenging, even threatening, to
my (supposedly) stable monastic existence. As so often happens when
books stimulate such a fearful and angry response, Bultmann and Berger
ended up shaping my perceptions far more profoundly than the Browns
and Fitzmyers and Cullmanns who up to then had been my heroes.

My notes, queries, and objections to the *Theology*, however, came not
only from an emotional reaction to the intellectual—shall I say existential—challenge Bultmann posed to my monastic certitudes, but above all
in response to his stunning exposition of Paul. They arose as well from
genuine difficulties I had even then with the construction of the book
itself. And whenever I reread the *Theology*, as I often do in my doctoral
seminars on the New Testament and Theology at Emory, I find two convictions confirmed. The first is that Bultmann's is the only version of the
odd enterprise in intellectual history called "New Testament theology"
that is truly grown-up; other entries in the field pale in comparison,

lacking either the sharp appreciation of the hermeneutical problem presented by the New Testament, or the energy to enucleate a genuinely "pure" biblical theology.[1]

The second conviction is that I remain deeply unconvinced by a number of aspects of his presentation. It is, I think, precisely the lack of *argument* within Bultmann's work that makes his book most frustrating. By "lack of argument" I do not mean that the *Theology* lacks a strong thesis or the coherent development of that thesis, much less that it is deficient in learning; the book bristles with the citation of specific texts from Scripture and other ancient writings and consistently locates itself within scholarly discourse. Any reader wanting to challenge Bultmann must be willing to be master of the same wide range of learning, and that remains a daunting task. I mean rather that the book proceeds by way of assertion more than by way of genuine analysis—seldom is a New Testament text presented as problematic and effort given to deciphering it. Much in the manner of his teacher Adolf Schlatter, rather, Bultmann tends to array textual evidence in support of meanings he has already determined; the reader is less often offered options to consider than conclusions presented as self-evident,[2] while the premises underlying the overall demonstration are seldom if ever exposed for critical assessment. His amassing of data is so apparently exhaustive, and his overall vision so apparently comprehensive, that a reader finds it difficult to find a vantage point from which to ask how things might have been read differently or what might have been left out.

In fact, his work is so constructed that the examination of any of its individual parts must be considered within the whole, and the treatment of any specific topic can adequately be assessed only by taking into account what Bultmann has said on the topic in other parts of his work. The chapter I consider in this essay, "The Rise of Church Order and Its Earliest Development" (vol. 2, chap. 5), for example, must be placed in the context of Bultmann's treatment of the church in *The History of the Synoptic Tradition* and elsewhere in *Theology*.[3]

1. The distinction between a "true" biblical theology and a "pure" biblical theology derives from Johann Philipp Gabler's inaugural lecture in 1787; for full discussion see Boers, *What Is New Testament Theology?*

2. That this style is not peculiar to Bultmann among German scholars is shown by the recent study of the theology of Hans Urs von Balthasar by Kilby, *Balthasar*.

3. Before this chapter, see the dicussions in vol. 1, chap 2, sec. 6; vol. 1, chap 2, sec. 8; vol. 1, chap. 3, sec. 10; vol. 1, chap. 3, sec. 11; and vol. 1, chap. 5, sec. 34; as well as as his concluding comments in vol. 2, chap. 8, sec. 61.

The Church as Historical Phenomenon

As the subject of historical inquiry, the church remains a consistent focus for Bultmann, especially since he is far more confident in a scholar's ability to reconstruct the history of the earliest church than he is in the ability to reconstruct the historical Jesus. In *The History of the Synoptic Tradition*, for example, he acknowledges that his formal analysis of Jesus traditions is as much in service of constructing a history of the church as was Dibelius's study of the community and its needs. He declares that all historical work must move in a circle: "The forms of the literary tradition must be used to establish the influences operating in the life of the community and the life of the community must be used to render the forms themselves intelligible."[4] Thus, by distinguishing between those elements in the Jesus tradition that are apocalyptic or eschatological in character and those that are sapiential, he considers that a theory concerning ecclesial development is demonstrated: "An essential part of my inquiry concerns the one chief problem of primitive Christianity, the relationship of the primitive Palestinian and Hellenistic Christianity."[5] Bultmann pays minimal attention to the Synoptic Gospels as compositions: he sees them primarily in terms of how they organize and edit tradition; only Luke does he recognize as having a "literary" quality.[6] Much as the church itself, the Gospels appear primarily as the medium for the transmission of tradition.

The same presuppositions and procedures concerning the historical study of the church are found in *Theology*. Here is the same disinterest in the overall literary or rhetorical shape of the New Testament compositions in favor of a concentration on them as sources for historical reconstruction. Here also is the conviction that (in circular fashion) levels of tradition within compositions can be assigned to various stages of historical development of the church, so that the placement of the tradition and the securing of the development are mutually reinforcing. Here, finally, is the history of religions scheme (borrowed from Heitmüller and Bousset)[7] of geographical/cultural development in the church from Palestinian to Hellenistic to Paul, a development that continues after Paul—the subject of the chapter I am engaging—in the direction of institutionalization.

---

4. Bultmann, *Synoptic Tradition*, 5.
5. Bultmann, *Synoptic Tradition*, 5.
6. Bultmann, *Synoptic Tradition*, 337–67.
7. See Heitmüller, "Zum Problem Paulus und Jesus"; Bousset, *Kyrios Christos*.

Before taking up the specific subject of institutional development, however, it may be helpful to add a few further comments on Bultmann's practice as a historian, specifically with respect to his historical knowledge, method, and perspective. I have already noted his impressive command of earliest Christian literature, even though he gives scant actual attention to some canonical compositions (James, Revelation) and makes much heavier use of some second-century evidence (Clement, Hermas, Ignatius) than others (the apocryphal acts and gospels). In contrast, the real but limited knowledge of the *Umwelt* displayed in the *Theology* shows how much information concerning that world has been discovered since Bultmann wrote. He alludes to "associations," for example, but does not have the benefit of the analyses that have shown how the structure of such associations parallels that of the diaspora synagogue and the early church.[8] As is well known, Bultmann vastly overestimates the coherence and pervasiveness of Gnosticism as a pre-Christian phenomenon. He could not have used "Gnostic" so casually or so often had he known the cautions issued by later scholarship.[9] Similarly, his use of "the mysteries" would have benefited from the vast new knowledge concerning them made available since Bultmann's time.[10]

As for Second Temple Judaism, Bultmann does not appear aware of the complexities of "eschatological/apocalyptic" exhibited in the extant literature; instead, like his predecessors (Schweitzer, Weiss), he uses "eschatological" as an abstract category that can be put to many uses. Similarly, he does not know how mysticism and mystery occupied a place even at the heart of the rabbinic tradition.[11] In this and in other respects, such as the pervasiveness of what Sanders calls "covenantal nomism,"[12] the fact that the discoveries at the Dead Sea were not yet available to him at the time of his writing meant a major lacuna in his knowledge of Palestinian Judaism. He was not aware, for example, that a community

8. See Harland, *Associations*; it would be more accurate to say that Bultmann is *aware* of these parallels but does not systematically work out their implications (see *Theology*, 2:101–2).

9. See the challenges to the history of religions understanding, ranging from Yamauchi, *Pre-Christian Gnosticism*, to M. Williams, *Rethinking "Gnosticism."*

10. See, e.g., Metzger, "Considerations of Methodology"; Burkert, *Ancient Mystery Cults*.

11. Following the pioneering work of Gershom G. Scholem, *Jewish Gnosticism, Merkabah Myticism and Talmudic Tradition*, research in this area has proliferated; see, e.g., Himmelfarb, *Ascent to Heaven*.

12. Sanders, *Paul and Palestinian Judaism.*

could be at once eschatological, law observant, and mystical and have a highly elaborate hierarchical structure.[13] Finally, research in Judaism since the time of Bultmann has simply obliterated the easy linguistic and cultural distinctions between Palestine and the diaspora that fueled the history of religions school's tripartite theory of development.[14] In short, the historical evidence for many of his assertions concerning the *Umwelt* is inadequate or wrong.

Bultmann can scarcely be blamed for such lack of knowledge. He worked with what was available to him, as do we all. It is simply unfortunate that his masterful synthesis appeared just as research into the world of the New Testament was about to change the perception of that world dramatically. More questionable—again in hindsight—is his historical method. He is utterly confident in form criticism as the key to historical reconstruction. Not only does this method demand treating compositions as repositories of tradition rather than as rhetorical arguments (more on this later), its actual handling of those traditions is sometimes maddeningly inconsistent: Why, for example, is the Letter of James, with its strong eschatological expectation and vision of a community of solidarity, not considered as evidence for the early Palestinian church, or why is the collection for Jerusalem discussed as an aspect of the Hellenistic church rather than as an effort in which Paul was intimately involved? The method is almost always circular as well: the determination of what tradition is "early" or "late" depends on a prior conception of development, and that conception of development is also supported by traditions being assigned as "early" and "late." Finally on this point, Bultmann's fondness for notions of "self-understanding" is at best only loosely connected to the texts and structures he is describing: it is difficult to avoid concluding, for example, that his construction of the self-understanding of the primitive church as the "eschatological congregation" is anything more than a form of reification.

Most problematic in Bultmann's practice as a historian, however, is the way in which theological judgments intrude into his historical analysis. This may seem a strange complaint for a book that seeks to be a theology of the New Testament, but it is a complaint that cuts to the heart of his endeavor. Like his predecessors and peers, and in fact like many of his successors, Bultmann simply did not make an adequate distinction between the discrete epistemologies demanded for doing history and

13. See Flint and VanderKam, *Dead Sea Scrolls*.
14. See Johnson, *Among the Gentiles*, 26–31.

theology. The result is something of a muddle, in which theological pre-suppositions affect historical description, and historical developments are the subject of theological judgments. And as Nils Dahl observed in his classic review of Bultmann's masterwork, those theological presup-positions and judgments are entirely those of the Reformation.[15]

Eschatology and Church Structure

The topic of church structure is not entirely lacking in Bultmann's early historical analysis. His discussion in "The Earliest Church as the Escha-tological Congregation" (vol. 1, chap. 2, sec. 6) is heavily dependent on the Gospels and the first chapters of Acts: the Twelve are "eschatologi-cal regents" whose leader possesses the keys of the kingdom of heaven (*Theology of the New Testament* [*TNT*] 1:37).[16] But Bultmann says nothing more about any specific leadership activities, a surprising omission in light of Acts' portrayal of the apostles as administering the community of goods (4:32–5:11) and overseeing the mission (8:1–9).[17]

The subject recurs in "Beginnings toward Development of Ecclesiasti-cal Forms" (vol. 1, chap. 2, sec. 8): since the eschatological congregation does not conceive of itself as a new religion—"a new historical phenom-enon" (*TNT* 1:53)[18]—its main preoccupation is negotiating its boundary with Judaism, specifically with respect to observance of the law and the inclusion of the gentiles (*TNT* 1:53–56). With regard to the decision to include gentiles by the apostolic council, Bultmann relies solely on Gal 2:1–10, dismissing the account in Acts 15 because "the source on which it rests told about another meeting and decision" (*TNT* 1:56). He discusses the first congregation's ties to synagogue and temple with respect to its place of meeting, its practice of baptism, and the meal (*TNT* 1:57–58), and then turns to the subject of the "direction of the church." Although Jerusalem plays a symbolic role as the center for the entire church, the

---

15. Dahl, "Rudolf Bultmann's *Theology of the New Testament*."

16. It is striking that Bultmann omits the name of Peter from his quick allusion to Matt 16:18–19 or any consideration of what the entailments might be for "building the church" on Peter.

17. Bultmann's reliance on Acts 2:42–47 for his description is clear from his dis-cussion of baptism and common meals (*TNT* 1:39–41). This makes the omission of the leadership role of the apostles more glaring.

18. This is an important phrase, for the endgame of the "eschatological congrega-tion" will be when Christianity concieves of itself as a new religion (*TNT* 2:116–18).

portrayal in Acts of "the legal right of supervision" over the church by Jerusalem "is certainly legendary" (*TNT* 1:61). The Twelve do not really hold an office: their task is the proclamation of the word (*TNT* 1:58–59). The elders, in contrast, serve as a real center of authority in the congregation, as they did in the synagogue (*TNT* 1:59). Bultmann stresses the necessity of tradition from the beginning but insists that this "need not be mediated by institution or sacraments" and declares that the idea of an "apostolic succession" based on the imposition of the hands appears only later with the Pastoral Letters (*TNT* 1:60). Nevertheless, even in the eschatological congregation there was need for a "certain regulation" with regard to the common life (*TNT* 1:61–62).

In the Palestinian church, then, Bultmann sees "tendencies and beginnings in the direction of institutional forms" that pose "questions which arise for the future" (*TNT* 1:62). I think it important to observe at once the decidedly nonhistorical considerations that Bultmann introduces from the start, since these considerations influence his later discussions. When speaking of the office of elders, for example, Bultmann asserts that the congregation is not constituted—as if it were a club or association—by its members "but is conscious of having been founded by God's deed," so that the question that really matters is "*what office can appropriately be instituted* for the direction of the eschatological Congregation? Undoubtedly, it can only be one *founded upon the proclamation of the word*" (*TNT* 1:59, emphasis original here and elsewhere).[19] Even in these early descriptions, then, we see the ecclesial values that Bultmann espouses: institution must be measured by the community's eschatological calling—how it remains somehow "other" from the world—and specifically by the primacy of the proclaimed word over any form of human-based authority.[20]

Bultmann's discussion in "The Kerygma of the Hellenistic Church Aside from Paul," in turn, pays almost no attention to questions of ecclesial institution or authority. In "Church Consciousness and the Christian's Relation to the World" (vol. 1, chap. 3, sec. 10), his focus is entirely on the concept of church and the way in which the eschatological consciousness of the primitive community was translated into the Hellenistic context. The Hellenistic church grew out of the

19. He supports this assertion by reference to 2 Cor 5:18–19.
20. Thus, Bultmann works hard in his depiction of the "eschatological congregation" to minimize any actual administrative acts or structures, as when he insists that tradition "need not be mediated by an institution or sacraments" (*TNT* 1:60).

synagogue and carried forward the awareness of being the people of God (*TNT* 1:95–98); indeed, the concept of church applied first to the movement as a whole more than to particular assemblies (*TNT* 1:93–95).[21] In its emphasis on the community rather than the individual, the Hellenistic church showed itself superior to the mysteries (*TNT* 1:93). As the people of God, the church separated itself from "non-Christian cults of every sort" (*TNT* 1:99) and cultivated a dualistic view of outsiders (borrowing elements of Stoicism and Gnosticism) that expressed itself in forms of asceticism, eschatological expectation, and moral transformation (*TNT* 1:100–107). Everything in Bultmann's treatment of this "church concept" suggests that the Hellenistic church successfully maintained, *mutatis mutandis*, its identity as an eschatological community.

His subsequent discussion in "The Church's Relation to Judaism and the Problem of the Old Testament" (vol. 1, chap. 3, sec. 11) likewise pays exclusive attention to the spectrum of early Christian responses to the Old Testament (*TNT* 1:108–15) and raises a question concerning ecclesial structure only with reference to the nullifying of ritual commands while retaining the symbolic language of sacrifice. He asks whether cult and cult leadership would also be abolished and whether the office of priest would appear (*TNT* 1:116).

Bultmann's treatment of "The Word, the Church, the Sacraments" in the section of *Theology* devoted to Paul (vol. 1, chap. 5, sec. 34), as might be expected, focuses entirely on the church as eschatological community and is therefore also entirely positive. Paul's eschatology combines elements of Gnosticism and apocalypticism (*TNT* 1:306–7), but central to it is the proclamation of the word: "In the 'word,' then, the salvation-occurrence is present. . . . The 'day of salvation' . . . is present reality in the Now in which the word encounters the hearer. . . . The apostle," therefore, "belongs intrinsically to the eschatological occurrence" (*TNT* 1:307). It is the word that calls the church into being as an eschatological congregation, and as a result the church belongs to the salvation occurrence. Bultmann here speaks of the "peculiar double character of the eschatological Congregation. On the one hand, it is no phenomenon of the world but belongs to the new aeon; on the other hand, this eschato-

---

21. Not only does this assertion fly in the face of the evidence—the usage in Paul, apart from Ephesians, moves in the opposite direction—but the example of the collection cited by Bultmann (*TNT* 1:94–95) seems to support the position that the sense of a larger "church" actually arose through such efforts.

logical Congregation, which as such is invisible, takes visible form in the individual congregations within the world" (*TNT* 1:308).

What kind of actual historical shape might such a "visible yet not visible" church take? It takes its "purest form" in the cultic gathering, "from time to time" (*TNT* 1:308). Bultmann emphasizes again that the church is "not a club in which like-minded individuals have banded together . . . [nor] a conglomeration of the Spirit-endowed, each of whom has and enjoys his private relationship to Christ." From the side of Judaism, the notion of the people of God stresses this communal character; from the side of Gnosticism, the image of the body of Christ does the same (*TNT* 1:310). The structure of the church is determined by its eschatological holiness, defined by its rejection of worldly distinctions (Gal 3:28), but, Bultmann asserts, such rejection "does not mean a sociological program within this world; rather, it is an eschatological occurrence which takes place only within the eschatological Congregation" (*TNT* 1:309). From the center of this cultic gathering, to be sure, "there develops a secular faith-determined community of living" in which there are various reciprocal ministries and services, but Bultmann emphasizes that "official representatives" of the community (*episkopoi* and *diakonoi*) appear "for the first time" only in Phil 1:1 (*TNT* 1:309–10).

After this remarkably brief characterization of structure in the Pauline church, Bultmann turns to an extensive examination of Paul's language about baptism and the Lord's Supper, paying particular attention to the way in which Paul modifies the tradition regarding each so as to distance it from the practice of the mysteries—they are to be understood not mystically but eschatologically, and nothing of *ex opere operato* should be associated with them. He asserts, indeed, that "the sacrament of the Lord's Supper like that of baptism is also coordinate with the word-proclamation and ultimately only a special mode of it" (*TNT* 1:313; cf. 1:311–14). From Bultmann's historical analysis of the church to this point, it is clear that the church as eschatological congregation—the ideal—is corrupted when it is overly determined by outside influences (such as the law or the mysteries) rather than the proclaimed word, or when its structures (of worship or leadership) are not subordinate to the proclaimed word. It might almost be said, paradoxically, that the church begins to lose its identity as soon as it becomes "historical," for to that extent it can no longer be fully eschatological. From this perspective, "development" must almost necessarily mean "decline." Such would be the logical conclusion to draw from Bultmann's analysis to this point, and such is the paradox within which he begins my target chapter.

The Rise and Development of Church Order

Bultmann begins his discussion with the commonsense observation that no human society can survive without regulations; it was therefore natural for Christianity to develop in structure, a process that eventually became the Catholic Church. But he then raises the question of whether "the Ecclesia in the New Testament sense" is a historical entity, a "thing of history at all." "Is it not, rather, the eschatological Congregation of those who are divorced from the world . . . ?" If that is true (and everything in Bultmann's presentation has sought to convince the reader that it is true), then if the Ecclesia should constitute itself as an entity within the world, having a history within which it works out its regulations, it would mean "a falling away from its own nature." It would fall even further if its regulations were a matter of coercion and were attached to specific offices. Such a development would "directly contradict the nature of the Ecclesia" (*TNT* 2:95). This set of statements perfectly summarizes the prior analysis and anticipates the rest of the chapter: one can have the authentic eschatological Ecclesia, or one can have a historical institution, but one cannot have both.

Bultmann locates his discussion within the debate between two influential predecessors, the great church historian Adolf von Harnack and the legal scholar Rudolf Sohm.[22] Sohm regards the development of ecclesiastical regulation as "the sinful fall of the church," a denial of its nature; Harnack, in contrast, argues that structure was there from the beginning and its development does not contradict the nature of the Ecclesia (*TNT* 2:95–96). Bultmann declares that in terms of history Harnack is correct, but that in terms of what he calls "the decisive factor"—namely, the church's "self-understanding" as an eschatological congregation defined by separation from the world—Sohm must be considered correct (*TNT* 2:96). What this opening discussion reveals above all, I think, is Bultmann's deep ambivalence about the church as something other than a pure ideal. The more it moves from the invisible to the visible, the more problematic it is.

As his presentation proceeds, Bultmann considers from a slightly different angle some of the aspects of the starting point—the incipient reg-

22. In the bibliography for this chapter, available in the 1951 Scribner Original English Edition (2:255), Bultmann refers to Rudolf Sohm, *Kirchenrecht*, 2 vols. (Leipzig: Verlag von Duncker & Humblot, 1892) and *Wesen und Ursprung des Katholizismus*, 2nd ed. (Teubner, 1909), as well as to Adolf Harnack, *Entstehung und Entwickelung der Kirchenverfassung und des Kirchenrechts in den zwei ersten Jahrhunderten* (1910).

ulations of the local church as they were "determined by the congregation's understanding of itself as an eschatological community ruled by the Spirit." The starting point must be the Pauline church, where the Spirit-endowed are the chief persons of authority and the Spirit-endowed are primarily the proclaimers of the word (*TNT* 2:97). Bultmann disagrees with Sohm that any and all regulation is a betrayal of the Spirit; Paul's churches show the proper alignment: the Spirit guides the proclamation of the word, and that proclamation guides everything else (*TNT* 2:98). What Bultmann sees as an ideal state of affairs, however, depends on a misreading of the evidence. He states that compared to the Spirit-endowed authorities, "those who act for the external order and welfare of the congregation's life play at first a subordinate role" (*TNT* 2:97).

But this is simply not what our earliest datable evidence (Paul's letters) supports. Four things should be noted. First, as Paul's own experience indicates, the claim to possess the Holy Spirit (1 Cor 7:40) or to be an apostle called by God (1 Cor 9:1) by no means assured acceptance of the authority thus claimed. Second, those exercising leadership in the local assembly (1 Thess 5:12–13)—to whom the congregation should submit—are not identified as the Spirit-endowed. The congregation in Corinth is told to be "subordinate" to the heads of household enumerated in 1 Cor 16:15–18, without any reference to their possession of the Holy Spirit. Third, in Rom 12:8 and 1 Cor 12:28 the gifts of the Spirit include the homely exercise of local leadership. Fourth, some of the Spirit-endowed, in turn, even those speaking a "word" in the assembly (such as glossolalists and prophets), require regulation and the discernment of the community (1 Thess 5:21; 1 Cor 14:29–32). By the selective and slightly tendentious use of the evidence, Bultmann has created an ideal starting point that does not actually appear in Paul's letters.

Bultmann sees the starting point as an ideal as well because the Spirit was at work in congregations as well as in Spirit-endowed leaders. This is a critical point: the real question, he says, is "In what form will the rule of the Spirit, or of Christ, realize itself in history?" (*TNT* 2:99). For the earliest church, he speaks of a "congregational democracy" or "pneumatocracy" to describe the participatory role of congregants and explicitly contrasts this to the development of a monarchical episcopate and a distinction between priests and laymen. Bultmann dedicates a lengthy paragraph to the data supporting such democratic activity in the earliest church. What bewilders the reader is that, apart from the Pauline passages dealing with discernment (see above), the bulk of the evidence for such activity comes from Acts, Clement, Ignatius, and the Pastorals, writings that Bultmann otherwise assigns to the later stage of development (*TNT* 2:99)!

As Bultmann traces the development (or decline) toward ecclesiastical offices, then, the reader must keep in mind this primordial, Spirit-filled ideal and the criterion for the authentic authority to make regulations in the church it establishes: when leadership and regulations are Spirit-led, they are appropriate to the nature of the church as eschatological congregation, but to the degree that "authority behind the regulations is represented by individuals, then the ecclesiastical office arises." And for Bultmann, that is what becomes what Sohm called the "sinful fall of the church" (*TNT* 2:100).

Bultmann finds no fault with the organization of the elders in the Palestinian church or the equivalent structure in the Hellenistic churches, where the use of *episkopos* (taken from associations) probably is roughly equivalent to *presbyteros*; a real distinction comes only with the monarchical episcopate in Ignatius (*TNT* 2:101–2). But his nonchalance here is at first puzzling: are not such boards of elders precisely offices based on persons rather than Spirit? The reason Bultmann does not object to them is that they are simply local authority structures; the "church" as a whole—remember his insistence that this was the initial "conception" of church from the start—continues to be directed by the Spirit-endowed leadership of the apostles, and such charismatic leadership, he insists, is *not* an office. It is, rather, their proclamation of the word that constitutes the church (*TNT* 2:103). The charismatic leader is not one appointed by a local church but "is the inspired man endowed with miraculous power" (*TNT* 2:104).

Things begin to go awry when the double stream of authority (charismatic/general and institutional/local) become merged and appointment to office comes to be seen as the transmission of charism. Now the proclamation of the word becomes "an affair of congregational officers," and local bishops come to be seen as successors of the apostles: "The decisive step has then been taken: henceforth the office is regarded as *constitutive of the Church*. The whole Church rests upon the office-bearers, whose office is held to go back in uninterrupted succession to the apostles (= the twelve)" (*TNT* 2:107). The final stage is when bishops become leaders of the sacramental cultus (*TNT* 2:108–9) and an absolute distinction is drawn between clergy and laity. The church has now become an institution of salvation: "*the regulations of the Church all together become ordinances of divine law* and make the Church into an institution of salvation" (*TNT* 2:110). The only remaining step in the church's decline is the development of a system of discipline (see *TNT* 2:221–26).

There is much that can be challenged in this section of Bultmann's historical/theological reconstruction. One is his focus on the presence/absence of office or institution as the most important criterion for the church's authentic identity. Even if one allows that "eschatology" is the enemy of history—a concession not all find easy to make—that "eschatological consciousness" is the mark of authentic Christianity, an intense eschatological consciousness is perfectly compatible with hierarchical and even legalistic structures, as Qumran and many subsequent communities have shown. It is by no means obvious, furthermore, that the elaboration of ecclesial structure in Christianity completely routinized the work of the Spirit. Second-century literature above all is replete with examples of Spirit-filled leadership: evidence is provided by the apocryphal Acts, by the Acts of the Martyrs, by Montanists, and by gnostics. The struggle between charism and order was real in these instances, but it is a historical falsification to reduce Christian existence in the second and third century to a caricature of institutional cult and hierarchical order.

Bultmann's use of sources also requires attention. He recognizes that the last stages of development take place after the New Testament, and the earliest explicit evidence for them is Clement and Ignatius. But he sees a key role also played by the New Testament compositions called the Pastoral Letters. Here, he says, we find the laying on of hands as charism; here we have the offices of bishop, elder, and deacon; here we have the command to appoint others to office (*TNT* 2:106–8). Because Bultmann—like the great majority of scholars of his generation—regarded the inauthenticity of the Pastorals as self-evident, he was confident that they served as witnesses to the critical stage of development he called "decisive": the collapse of charismatic authority into institution. Indeed, from F. C. Baur to Walter Bauer, the so-called church order in the three letters to Paul's delegates was regarded as the clinching evidence for their inauthenticity.[23] Some present-day scholars, however, continuing a long tradition of resistance to the "assured result" of critical consensus in the nineteenth century, consider it possible that the Pastorals were written within the frame of Paul's ministry.[24]

But even those who think they are inauthentic must agree on several points with respect to their so-called church order. First, the elements

23. For the history of scholarship, see Johnson, *First and Second Letters to Timothy*, 20–54.

24. E.g., Johnson, *First and Second Letters to Timothy*, and Towner, *Letters to Timothy and Titus*.

dealing with ecclesial structure amount to two chapters in 1 Timothy and at best one line each in 2 Timothy and Titus; there is much more to these letters than church order. Second, the depiction of community organization in 1 Tim 3 and 5 is utterly simple and finds parallels in contemporary associations and diaspora synagogues. Third, what is said about leadership and its functions, moreover, agrees substantially with the fragmentary evidence in Paul's undisputed letters (see 1 Thess 5:12; Gal 6:6; 1 Cor 6:1–8; 12:28; 16:15–18; Phil 1:1; Rom 12:7–8; 16:1–3). Fourth, in sharp contrast to both Qumran and Ignatius, these letters totally lack any theological legitimation for the exercise of leadership; it is entirely straightforward and functional. Finally, more than that, because the letters portray the delegates as under the direction of the apostle, they agree completely—in terms of literary presentation—with Bultmann's portrayal of the ideal relationship between apostolic/charismatic authority and local leadership.

Just as Bultmann began with the self-understanding of the church as an eschatological congregation, so does he bring the tale of development to a conclusion with a discussion of what he considers the transformation in the church's understanding of itself (*TNT* 2:111). The portrait he draws is essentially that which has become familiar in scholarship under the rubric "early Catholicism" (*Frühkatholizismus*).[25] Rather than an eschatological community shaped by the transcendent proclamation of the word, the church as institution claims possession of salvation. Eschatology is transmuted from a stance of opposition to the world in response to the proclaimed word, to an expectation of a future return in the far distance, so that the church stands now as the ready and available instrument of grace through its sacraments and is ever more comfortable facing a prolonged existence within secular history: "the Christian faith, losing its eschatological tension, is becoming a Christian-bourgeois piety" (*TNT* 2:114; cf. 2:112–16).

And just as Bultmann began his treatment of the primitive church by insisting that it did not conceive of itself as a "new religion—i.e., a new historical phenomenon" (*TNT* 1:53), he concludes his discussion of the development of church order by asserting that the church now conceived of itself precisely as a new historical phenomenon, and indeed "*as a new religion* existing side by side with the Jewish and the heathen religion (the latter regarded as a unity)" (*TNT* 2:116). The fullest literary expression of this new consciousness is the Acts of the Apostles. The author of Luke

---

25. Cf. Campenhausen, *Ecclesiastical Authority*.

and Acts, Bultmann asserts, "is guided in his presentation by *a conception of Christianity as an entity of world history*" (*TNT* 2:116). The very composition of a historical account, which in Bultmann's view would have been incomprehensible to those seeing the church as the eschatological congregation, reveals Luke's own understanding: "the history of salvation continues" in "the history of Christianity" (*TNT* 2:117). The story of the early church's development, according to Bultmann, is a tragic one: the Spirit is imprisoned by institution, and eschatology is stifled by history. By becoming more humanly visible and real within the ancient world, Christianity inevitably lost its true identity, becoming not a challenge to the world through the word but a part of the world through the machinery of salvation.

Moving "beyond Bultmann" demands more, I think, than correcting what one regards in his account as incidentally inadequate or in error. It demands asking in a more fundamental way how to provide a responsible account of two separate things that Bultmann treated as one. One task is to attempt a historical description of the Christian movement from its diverse first-century beginnings to the time of its first real consolidation in the middle to late second century. Another task altogether is to engage theologically the understanding of church as it is found in the discrete compositions of the first and second centuries. Although these two tasks intersect in many ways, they nevertheless require distinct modes of knowing and different methods of engagement.

History

The task of historical description has its own importance, but it is not fundamentally a theological enterprise. In this regard, Harnack's position (with which Bultmann partially agreed) is better than Sohm's (with which Bultmann more fundamentally agreed). To carry out the task more adequately, I think, the following principles need to be operative.

First, the accurate dating and the appropriate use of sources is imperative. Although the practice of tradition criticism need not be abandoned altogether, greater skepticism concerning it is required; by no means is the "prehistory" of Rom 3:21–26 or Phil 2:5–11 certain. Paul's letters give us our earliest evidence, together, perhaps, with James and Hebrews. Colossians, Ephesians, 2 Thessalonians, and the Pastoral Letters may also need to be considered within the Pauline framework. The Synoptic Gospels and Acts must be treated with the greatest caution as providing information concerning Christianity before Paul. In any case, dates and location of traditions need to be argued for rather than assumed. Even for the Pauline letters, furthermore, it cannot be assumed that the same structures, practices, and images were at work in every one of his churches.

Second, the historical account must be inclusive. This means that more than the presence or absence of structure should be analyzed. Rather, the entire range of practices and images concerning the assembly found in the respective compositions needs to be considered, without reference to how they do or do not meet or fall away from a supposed ideal. Inclusivity means as well the willingness to acknowledge the multiple ways in which believers interacted with the symbolic worlds within which they lived and from which they entered the assembly. In this regard, Bultmann is relentlessly either/or in his perspective: the eschatological congregation must be distinguished from the mysteries or from Judaism. But history is usually much more a matter of both/and: just as there were a variety of ways of being Jewish, so there were a variety of ways of being religiously gentile, and Christians from the beginning brought aspects of those worlds into the believing assembly.[26]

Third, the diverse geographical location of early communities is also important, for development happens in different places in different ways and at different speeds. Bultmann's Palestinian/Hellenistic distinction is too simple and serves more as a way to organize data than as description of datable and locatable communities. Rather than start with a single place (Palestine) with a universal conception of church that precedes local assemblies, which then undergoes a transformation, proper historical method would begin with all the diverse communities (and their conceptions) and recognize that through a variety of exchanges (leaders, goods, letters, convictions) a broader fellowship and a more inclusive sense of Ecclesia developed.[27]

Finally, from a historical perspective, institutional development is simply natural to communities as they grow in size and complexity. From a historical perspective, there can be no asking of what structures are "appropriate" to the proclamation of the word or "endowed" by the Spirit or consistent with an eschatological self-understanding. From a historical perspective, institutional development may be measured by effectiveness or by sustainability, but it cannot be measured by theological criteria.

---

26. See Johnson, *Among the Gentiles*, 130–71.
27. See Johnson, *"Koinonia,"* and Johnson, "Making Connections."

The development of the early church in the direction of Catholicism cannot in historical terms be regarded as a "fall from grace," or a "corruption," or a "decline." It is, in historical terms, simply what happened.

Theology

The large problem of how best to read the New Testament theologically can clearly not be addressed fully in this essay.[28] But I think the way forward is in a different direction than that taken by Bultmann (and all other "New Testament theologies")—namely, seeking to locate historically some principle of unity that can give usable coherence to the diverse New Testament compositions within a single book. I think the right direction rather lies in affirming two complex realities and working to put them in an ongoing dialectical conversation. The first complexity is the world of readers, who approach these texts for a variety of reasons and from a variety of perspectives. The second complexity is the irreducible diversity of the New Testament compositions themselves, which resist reduction to a single historical or thematic unification. The best possibility for an authentic theological engagement with the New Testament is not to be found in a book, however learned, but in a living conversation among believers who take the otherness of the canonical texts with full seriousness.

It is as a collection of diverse literary compositions with distinct literary and rhetorical shaping, moreover, that the New Testament must be engaged by contemporary readers. The "otherness" of the texts is secured not simply by their historical distance from readers but also by the resistance posed by their specific rhetoric. Consequently, whatever any of the New Testament compositions has to say on any specific topic—such as the church—must be assessed within its rhetorical shaping and purposes. The true inadequacy of Bultmann's historical method is that it does not enable him to get at much of what the New Testament writings have to say theologically about the church.

Because Bultmann does not read Romans rhetorically, he does not see how Paul's discussion of Jew and gentile in God's plan (Rom 9–11) has everything to do with Paul's vision of how his readers are to live within community with mutual acceptance of differences (Rom 14). Because he does not read Hebrews rhetorically, he fails adequately to appreciate its

28. A sketch of my own position is found in Johnson, *Scripture and Discernment*.

powerful vision of the church as a people on pilgrimage to God. Because he does not read James rhetorically, he does not grasp that it challenges readers to the most radically countercultural stance in the New Testament. Because he considers Ephesians only from the point of view of its (presumably) late date and does not read it rhetorically, he misses the New Testament's most powerful evocation of the church as the place of reconciliation in the world and the sign of the world's possibility. Finally, because Bultmann does not read Luke-Acts as a literary whole but considers Acts separately as a historical source alone, he considers it the supreme expression of the church's transformation of consciousness from eschatological congregation to historical church. He fails to see that Luke continues in his second volume the same prophetic challenge that he began with the portrayal of Jesus in his Gospel: the church in Acts embodies and enacts the same radical challenge to the world as a Spirit-guided institution that Jesus did as God's Spirit-anointed prophet.[29]

Conclusion

I suggest that quite different perspectives on the church past and present are offered in turn by Bultmann's historical reading and the literary engagement I have proposed. From Bultmann's tale of development as decline, the church appears as most authentic when least visible, and the Christian reality as the sad loss of an eschatological dream. From the ongoing engagement with the New Testament's diverse compositions in all their literary and rhetorical complexity, in contrast, emerges a set of visions that are various indeed and, precisely in their variety, offer diverse possibilities for authentic expressions of the church and a diverse set of challenges to corruptions of the church.

29. See Johnson, *Prophetic Jesus, Prophetic Church.*

Chapter 14

Fellowship of Suffering

The Paradox at the Heart of Paul

P aul's letters challenge present-day readers not only because they
emerge from an ancient world no longer our own and only with
great difficulty understood by us, not only because they are addressed
to situations only partially recoverable by us, but above all because they
speak of religious realities as though they were perfectly intelligible to
their first readers but which remain opaque to us. A prime example is
Paul's language about power and weakness, and about power and suffering. In this chapter, I probe some of the connections among these
realities that appear to be assumed by Paul the correspondent, connections that require some considerable work to grasp. By so doing, I hope
to cut close to the heart of the paradox that pervades the writings of the
apostle for whom the experience of God in Christ is, as we have seen,
the starting point of the new creation in which he now participates, but
also the beginning of the mystery he seeks to penetrate.

A text that can begin and (I hope) also conclude this reflection is
Paul's remarkable declaration in Phil 3:7–11. Having laid out all the rea-
sons why he might have confidence in his impeccable Jewish heritage,
Paul says:

> But whatever gains I had, I have come to consider as a loss, because of
> Christ. More than that, I even consider everything to be a loss because
> of the supreme good of knowing Christ Jesus my Lord. For his sake
> I have accepted the loss of all things and I consider them so much
> rubbish, that I might gain Christ and be found in him, not having
> any righteousness of my own based on the law but that which comes
> through the faith of Christ, the righteousness from God, depending on
> faith, to know him and the power of his resurrection and fellowship of
> his sufferings [*tou gnōnai auton kai tēn dynamin tēs anastaseōs autou*

kai koinōnian pathēmatōn autou] by being conformed to his death
[*symmorphizomenos tō thanatō autou*] if somehow I may attain the
resurrection from the dead [*ei pōs katantēsō eis tēn exanastasin tēn ek
nekrōn*]. (NABRE, adapted)

The language of *koinōnia* is not in itself surprising, since it is commonly used in Greco-Roman discussions of friendship[1] and in the New
Testament generally.[2] Philippians uses such language so fluently and pervasively that it can quite properly be regarded as a kind of "friendship
letter,"[3] appropriate to the correspondence between the apostle and his
dearest community, with whom he shared bonds of affection,[4] and from

1. For the topos of fellowship and friendship in Hellenistic literature, see F. Hauck,
"κοινός, ktl," *TDNT* 3:789–809; Eglinger, "Der Begriff der Freundschaft"; Bohnenblust, *Beiträge zum Topos Peri Philias*; Dugas, *L'amitié antique*; Konstan, *Friendship
in the Classical World*; Fitzgerald, *Greco-Roman Perspectives on Friendship*. There
was broad agreement in antiquity that friendship (*philia*) was roughly equivalent
to "fellowship" (*koinōnia*), involving elements of identity ("friends are 'one soul'"
[*mia psychē*] and a friend is "another self"; "friendship is equality" [*philia isotēs*])
and elements of indiscriminate sharing ("friends hold all things in common" [*tois
philois panta koina*]), both spiritual and material; friendship is "life together" (*syn-
bios*); friends "think the same way" (*to auto phronein*). For all these, see esp. Aristotle,
Nicomachean Ethics 9.9.

2. See, e.g., John Campbell, "KOINΩNIA"; McDermott, "Biblical Doctrine of
KOINŌNIA"; Panikulam, *Koinōnia in the New Testament*; Seesemann, *Der Begriff
KOINONIA im Neuen Testament*.

3. Although the term *philia* or its cognates do not appear in the letter, Philippians is extraordinarily rich in language associated with friendship in Greco-Roman
literature. Paul uses *koinōnia* in 1:5; 2:1; 3:10; and 4:15. Especially notable is the frequent use of the *syn-* prefix, which might consistently (if awkwardly) be translated
as "fellow": thus, Paul connects it to the verbs "to struggle" (1:27; 4:3), "to rejoice"
(2:17), "to be formed" (3:10), "to receive" (4:3), and "to share" (*synkoinōnein*, 4:14).
He connects it to nouns such as "sharer" (*koinōnia*, 1:6), "soul" (2:2), "worker" (2:25;
4:3), "soldier" (2:25), "imitator" (3:17), "form" (3:21), and "yoke" (4:3). He speaks of
being "one soul" (*mia psychē*, 1:27) and "one spirit" (*hen pneuma*, 1:27) and of thinking
the same thing (2:2). He utilizes variants on "the same thing" (*to auto*, 1:6, 30; 2:2,
18). Finally, he uses *isos* ("equal") twice, once with reference to Jesus (2:6) and once
with reference to Timothy (2:30). See O'Brien, "Fellowship Theme in Philippians."
For Philippians as a "friendship letter" in the generic sense, see Alexander, "Hellenistic Letter Forms." See also White, "Morality between Two Worlds"; Witherington,
Friendship and Finances in Philippi. Another approach to partnership language is
taken by Sampley, *Pauline Partnership in Christ*.

4. In contrast to Galatians, affectionate language pervades this letter: Paul "hold[s]
[them] in [his] heart" (Phil 1:7); "yearn[s] for [them] with all the affection of Jesus
Christ" (1:8); he says that "I am glad and rejoice with you all; likewise you should

whom he received material benefits in support of his ministry (4:10–15).[5]
The language of friendship is all the more appropriate when the issue that
Paul seems to address most fully in this letter is the vice of envy (*phthonos*), which leads to community disharmony (*eritheia, eris*), displayed in
grumbling and disputes (1:5; 2:14; 2:2–3); in ancient moral philosophy,
such competitive rivalry was regarded as the opposite of friendship.[6]

That Paul can speak of his own sufferings to the Philippian church is
also clear. He is in prison (Phil 1:12) and can refer to himself and his co-
worker Timothy as "slaves of/for Christ" (1:1). He experiences separation
from and longing for (4:1) his beloved community; he is like a sacrifice
poured out on the altar for them (2:17). In his absence, as stated above,
some in the community have displayed a spirit of rivalry and envy (1:15;
2:14; 4:2–3). Suffering need not consist in flogging and mockery; frustration and anxiety can serve nicely.

More puzzling is the use of *koinōnia* in this precise connection:
Are we to understand it as a sharing or participation in the suffering
of Christ? But the suffering of the mortal human being Jesus was in the
past, revealed most starkly in his slave-death on the cross (Phil 2:7–8).
How can Paul "participate" or "have a share" in the sufferings of Jesus
now? How fungible is suffering—any kind of suffering—anyhow? Also
puzzling is the way that Paul begins with his "knowing" the "power of
the resurrection" but ends with the hope of attaining "resurrection from
the dead." What is the distinction between what Paul has already experienced (known) and what he hopes for? Finally, how does this passage
correspond, clarify, or stand in tension with 3:20–21: "For our citizenship
is in the heavens, from which we also expect our Lord Jesus Christ as savior, who will change the form of the body of our lowliness [*metaschēmatisei to soma tēs tapeinōseōs hēmōn*] into conformity [*symmorphon*] to his
body of glory [*tō sōmati tēs doxēs autou*] according to the effective energy
that empowers him to submit all things to him [*kata tēn energeian tou
dynasthai auton kai hypotaxai autō ta panta*]." Once more in this passage
we find the language of power presently in the hands of Christ, together
with a contrast not between resurrection and suffering (as in 3:10) but
between lowly bodies and glorious bodies.

---

be glad and rejoice with me" (2:18), and "My brethren whom I love and long for, my
joy and my crown" (4:1). He thinks it "kind of [them] to share [his] troubles" (4:14).
Above all, Philippians evinces a quality of quiet joy (1:4, 19; 2:2, 17–18, 19, 28, 29; 3:1;
4:1, 10) that derives from their distinctive fellowship (1:5; 2:1; 3:10; 4:15).

  5. See Johnson, "Making Connections."
  6. On this, see esp. Johnson, "James 3:13–4:10."

I hope to circle back to these passages in Philippians, after a fairly lengthy detour through all the canonical letters, in an effort to sort out Paul's language about power, on one side, and weakness, lowliness, and suffering, on the other side. By so doing, I think we can approach the paradox that lies at the heart of Paul's effort to interpret what has happened to him and his readers. [7]

The Present Gift: The Power of God and the Power of the Resurrection

Paul uses the language of power with great frequency and fluency, employing a number of terms. Take first the cognates of *dynamai* ("to be able, to have a capacity"). This verb is used often with respect to human *incapacity* apart from God: they are not able to see God (1 Tim 6:2), keep God's law (Rom 8:7) or please God (Rom 8:8), be taught spiritually when fleshly (1 Cor 2:14; 3:1-2), or inherit the kingdom of God as flesh and blood (1 Cor 15:50). Israel could not see through the veil (2 Cor 3:7). The law could not give life (Gal 3:21). Sins cannot be kept secret (1 Tim 5:25). Humans cannot take anything with them when they die (1 Tim 6:2). Women in households constantly seek knowledge from false teachers but cannot attain recognition of the truth (2 Tim 3:7). Similarly, the adjective *adynatos* is used for human incapacity apart from God (Rom 8:3; 15:1). On the human side, Paul's emphasis is on weakness rather than strength. More on that later.

In sharp contrast, Paul employs *dynamai* to characterize God (Rom 1:20; 9:17; 16:25; 1 Cor 2:5; 6:14 [who will raise us as he raised Jesus]; 2 Cor 1:8; Eph 3:20); Jesus (Rom 1:4; 1 Cor 1:24; 5:4; 15:24; 15:43 [his resurrection]; Phil 3:21); the Holy Spirit (Rom 15:13, 19; 1 Cor 2:4; 12:3 [who enables humans to proclaim Jesus as Lord]); the good news (Rom 1:16; 1 Cor 1:18); faith (1 Cor 2:5); the kingdom of God (1 Cor 4:19-20); and the giving of comfort to humans (2 Cor 1:4). God's power communicated to humans enables them to confess Jesus as Lord (1 Cor 12:3) and to be raised as Jesus was (1 Cor 6:14), but also to recognize God's work (Eph 3:4), to stand fast and resist evil (Eph 6:11-16), and to bear troubles (1 Thess 2:6). Paul's use of the verb *dynamai*, then, can be summed up in this fashion: human incapacity is transformed by the communication to them of power that belongs properly to God.

---

7. See the helpful essay by Fitzmyer, "'To Know Him and the Power of His Resurrection.'"

The same basic pattern applies to Paul's use of the noun *dynamis*. He does not use it for the power of the empire, of the military, of riches, or of physical prowess of any sort. The noun is, instead, regularly attached to God (Rom 1:20; 8:3; 9:17; 1 Cor 2:5; 4:19–20; 6:14; 2 Cor 1:8; 4:7; 6:7; 8:3; Eph 1:19, 21; 3:7, 20; Col 1:11, 29; 2 Thess 1:7, 11; 2 Tim 1:8); to Jesus (Rom 1:4; 1 Cor 1:24; 5:4; 15:24, 43; 2 Cor 12:9; 13:4; Phil 3:10); to the Holy Spirit (Rom 1:4; 15:13, 19; 1 Cor 2:4; Gal 3:5; Eph 3:16; 2 Tim 1:7); and to the good news (Rom 1:16; 1 Cor 1:18; 1 Thess 1:1).[8] As with the verb form, the noun *dynamis* is used also for the mighty acts performed by humans through God (Rom 15:19; 1 Cor 12:10, 28, 29; 2 Cor 12:12). The communication of power from God to humans is clearly found as well in the use of the cognates *dynamoun* ("to enable"; see Eph 6:10 and Col 1:11), *dynatein* ("to be able"; see Rom 14:4; 2 Cor 9:8; 13:3), and the adjective *dynatos* ("capable/powerful"; see Rom 4:1; 9:22; 11:23; 2 Cor 10:4; 12:10; 13:9; 2 Tim 1:12; Titus 1:9), as well as in the passive use of the compound verb *endynamoun* ("to empower"; see Rom 4:20; Eph 6:10; Phil 4:13; 1 Tim 1:12; 2 Tim 2:1; 4:17).

Paul uses still another set of cognates describing power, this time with an emphasis on the "energy" or "effectiveness" of power (see the adjective *energes* in 1 Cor 16:9).[9] The same pattern observed with respect to the *dynamis* word group is, if anything, even more obvious in the cognates of *energeia*. Thus, the noun itself is used exclusively for God in Eph 1:19; 3:7; Col 1:29; 2:12. In Phil 3:21, as we have seen, Paul speaks of the *energeia* that empowers the resurrected Lord Jesus; and in Col 2:12 Paul speaks of believers having been raised with Christ, "through the faith of the *energeia* of God."

As for the verb *energein* ("to be effective, to energize"), Paul speaks in 1 Cor 12:6 of God himself who "energizes" everything in all things (*panta en pasin*; cf. Eph 1:11), and of the gifts as all being "energized" by the Holy Spirit (1 Cor 12:11). Paul declares that the one "energizing" Cephas to preach to the circumcised also "energized" Paul to preach to the uncircumcised (Gal 2:8). So here we have the concept of God's power not simply being communicated to humans but also effectively working within and among them: the Corinthians' consolation is "energized" in endurance (2 Cor 1:6); God "energizes" the working of powerful deeds

8. The term is applied to sin in 1 Cor 15:56 and to the deeds done by the antichrist in 2 Thess 2:9.
9. See Clark, "Meaning of *energeō*."

among the Galatians (Gal 3:5); and faith is "energized" or "working effectively" through love (Gal 5:6; cf. Phlm 6). God's power is "energized" among Paul's readers in Ephesus (Eph 3:20) and Philippi (Phil 2:13) and Thessalonica (1 Thess 2:13). It can be perceived in the "operations/effective displays of power" (*energēmata*) among the Corinthians (1 Cor 12:6, 10). God's power is most "energized" in the resurrection of Christ (Eph 1:20).[10]

Paul's other terms for power likewise center in a characteristic of God that is communicated and made effective in humans through Christ. Thus, *kratos* in Eph 1:19; 6:10; Col 1:11; 1 Tim 1:16; *krataomai* in 1 Cor 16:13 and Eph 3:16; *ischyein* in Phil 4:13; and *ischyros* in 1 Cor 1:25, 27; 4:10; 10:22.[11]

It is a fair summation of Paul's usage to say that God's power is communicated to humans, specifically through the resurrection and exaltation of Jesus, and empowers them with real and effective power. There is nothing immediately startling in Paul's statement in Philippians that, "being found in Christ," he might "know him and the power of his resurrection [*tēn dynamin tēs anastaseōs autou*]" (Phil 3:9–10). It is entirely consistent with his language throughout the canonical letters concerning power.

The question, to be sure, is the point of the power that is thus communicated to humans. Paul makes clear that the human existential condition is fundamentally altered by God's act of power in the resurrection and exaltation of Jesus. Humans have been placed in a "new creation" (2 Cor 5:17; Gal 6:15). But how has their actual experience of life been changed? Paul speaks, as we have seen, of the powerful deeds and gifts that God does among them as the expression of his rule. He speaks as well of their being transformed "from one degree of glory to another" as they gaze on the image of Christ, a transformation that comes from "the Lord [who] is Spirit" (2 Cor 3:17).

Is such "glory" (*doxa*), then, a matter of manifest and effective control over the circumstances of human existence—is it to occupy a privileged position within God's rule? Does it mean that humans have transcended their own mortality and vulnerability, that they need no longer to suffer

---

10. Paul can also speak of the mystery of lawlessness being "energized" in 2 Thess 2:7, and of "death being energized among us" in 2 Cor 4:12; this last usage will point us to the paradoxical character of Paul's language about power.

11. Paul also speaks (ironically?) of his letters being "weighty and strong [*ischyros*]" in contrast to his unimpressive physical presence (2 Cor 10:10).

(*pathein*)? Does the communication of God's power to humans result in their having a "fellowship in his glory" here and now? Is the "power of the resurrection" that Paul seeks to "know" (i.e., experience) to be identified with the glory of the exalted Jesus? We can approach an answer to this query by examining Paul's language concerning the opposite of power and strength—namely, weakness and suffering.

The Ambiguities of Weakness

Paul can use the cognates of "weakness" (*astheneia, asthenein, asthenēma, asthenēs*) with reference to the frail and mortal condition even of believers, as when he advises Timothy to drink a little wine because of the weakness of his stomach (1 Tim 5:23), or when he speaks of Epaphroditus as being "weak to the point of death" (Phil 2:26–27), or when he refers to the social condition of the Corinthians as "the weak of the world" (1 Cor 1:27 NABRE), or when he speaks of the "parts of the body we consider weaker" (1 Cor 12:22).[12]

But he also uses weakness to designate the human condition apart from God, the "weakness of the flesh" (Rom 6:19; 8:3): thus, Christ died for us when we were "weak" (Rom 5:6). What is most remarkable here, however, is that Paul envisages the "weakness" of God as the very medium of saving weak humans, which is possible because "the weakness of God is stronger than humans" (1 Cor 1:25). Thus, Jesus was "crucified out of weakness, but lives out of the power of God" (2 Cor 13:4). The power-transfer between God and humans is accomplished by God's "sharing" or "having fellowship" with human weakness. The human Jesus who died for others was therefore "sown in weakness" before being "raised in glory [*doxa*]" (1 Cor 15:43). The Holy Spirit that is given to humans through Christ's death (Rom 5:5–6) therefore "comes to our assistance in our weakness" (Rom 8:26). The Christ who speaks through Paul is now not weak but is powerful among them (2 Cor 13:3).

The way in which God communicated power through the weakness of the crucified Jesus becomes the basis for Paul's own understanding of his ministry as one of weakness. Paul "boasts" in his weakness before the Corinthians (1 Cor 2:3; 2 Cor 11:21, 29–30; 12:5, 9, 10; 13:9) and the Galatians (Gal 4:13). He is convinced that "whenever I am weak, I am powerful" (2 Cor 12:10), and that "strength is made perfect in weakness"

---

12. For full discussion of the data, see D. Black, *Paul, Apostle of Weakness.*

(2 Cor 12:9). He shares in the weakness of others in order that they might become stronger (2 Cor 11:29). The language of power and weakness here correspond to Paul's language concerning death and resurrection earlier in 2 Corinthians; after listing the afflictions experienced by his ministry team, he says that they are "always carrying about in the body the dying of Jesus, so that they life of Jesus may also be manifested in our body. For we who live are constantly being given up to death for the sake of Jesus, so that the life of Jesus may be manifest in our mortal flesh. So death is at work ["is energized," *energeitai*] in us, but life in you" (2 Cor 4:10–12 NABRE).

Paul's mode of ministry, in turn, is paradigmatic for the life of discipleship within the Christian community, in the same way that the cross of Christ is paradigmatic for Paul's mode of ministry. Paul cautions the Roman believers who are strong in faith to "bear with the weaknesses [*asthenemata*]" of those who are "weak in faith" (Rom 14:1–2, 21; 15:1). He tells the church in Thessalonica to "bear with the weak" (*antecheste tōn asthenōn*, 1 Thess 5:14). Similarly, he warns the stronger ones in Corinth to be attentive to those who are weaker in conscience among them and not allow their strength and freedom in the matter of eating certain foods to "assault the conscience of the weak one" (1 Cor 8:12) so that "through [their] knowledge, the weak person is brought to destruction, the brother for whom Christ died" (8:11 NABRE). To act in this way is to "sin against Christ" (8:12). They ought to imitate Paul, who "to the weak . . . became weak, so that [he] might win the weak" (9:22 NRSV).

In sum, just as Paul sees God's power communicated to humans through the exaltation of Christ, so he connects the exercise of that power by believers with the crucifixion of Jesus. Power is made manifest and perfected in weakness, just as Christ was crucified in weakness but is powerful among them. And just as God's "weakness" in Christ was for their sake, so that they might be given a share in the power of God, so is the weakness of believers for the sake of others, so that out of the "death at work in their mortal bodies" life might be at work among others. From the side of God, power is given to humans through the weakness of the crucified Messiah; among believers, the power of God is exercised through weakness for the sake of others, so that they might be strong. What is communicated both vertically and horizontally is the power that comes from God. The paradox, both vertically and horizontally, is that the gift of power for others comes through the weakness of the giver.

Suffering With and For

Having made a circuit through the canonical letters to discern Paul's paradoxical language concerning power and weakness (and death and life), I now briefly note how he speaks of "suffering" outside Phil 3:10. As in the case of the other word groups, Paul can use the verb *paschein* and the noun *pathēma* either in the straightforward sense of "experience" (Gal 3:4) or in the moral sense of "passions" (more or less equivalent to *epithymia*), as in Rom 7:5 and Gal 5:14.

Mostly, though, Paul uses "suffering" to refer to the Christian experience of distress and pain inflicted by others, especially through persecution—thus "the sufferings of the present age" in Rom 8:18. Similarly, Paul reminds Timothy of how he had "followed" Paul's "persecutions" and "suffering" (2 Tim 3:10–11). In this sense, Paul stresses the sharing of such experience and (as in the case of weakness and power) its altruistic character. Thus, in the body of Christ, "if one member suffers, all members suffer with it" (1 Cor 12:26).

In the same way, Paul says that the Thessalonians are "suffering the same things" as the churches in Judea (1 Thess 2:14). The churches in Judea were persecuted; so are the believers in Thessalonica. The Corinthians, he states, are undergoing "the same sufferings" as Paul's team (2 Cor 1:6) and are, indeed, "fellows of [their] sufferings" (*koinōnoi este tōn pathēmatōn*, 2 Cor 1:7); they undergo "the same suffering that we are suffering" (2 Cor 1:6 NABRE). The language here is remarkably close to that in Phil 3:10.

Paul also speaks of suffering "for" something or someone, as in 2 Thess 1:5 when he refers to "the kingdom of God for which you are suffering," or in 2 Tim 1:12 when Paul speaks of "suffering these things" for the cause (*di' hēn aitian*) of preaching the good news. In 2 Cor 1:5 Paul connects the shared suffering of the Corinthians and Paul to the suffering of Jesus: "as Christ's sufferings overflow to us" (NABRE). And in Phil 1:29 Paul speaks of the Philippian believers in this extraordinary fashion: "For to you has been granted for the sake of Christ [*to hyper Christou*] not only to have faith in him [*ou monon to eis auton pisteuein*] but also to suffer for the sake of him [*alla kai to hyper autou paschein*]." The most powerful of all Pauline statements along this line is, to be sure, Col 1:24 (NABRE): "Now I rejoice in my sufferings for your sake [*en tois pathēmasin hyper hymōn*], and in my flesh I am filling up what is lacking in the afflictions of Christ [*kai antanaplērō ta hysterēmata tōn thlipseōn tou Christou en tē sarki mou*] on behalf of his body, which is the church [*hyper tou sōmatos autou ho estin hē ekklēsia*]."

Paul's language about weakness, power, and suffering is consistent in meaning—although not consistently dense in its presence—across the canonical letters. It invites us to consider some of the implications of his linguistic usage concerning God, humans, and the world, implications that appear to be at odds with the premises that govern much of our own understanding of reality.

- Humans are not private and isolated individuals but are constituted by sets of relationships.[13] Their bodies, indeed, are interconnected by spirit (specifically the Holy Spirit) in such fashion that they can be thought of as a "body."[14]
- Humans are intrinsically related to spiritual realities, some of them on their own plane, some of them at a higher plane; above all, they are all caught up in a cosmic drama involving God and the world; they are players within a drama whose preceding (and even present) plot they have some notion of, but whose denouement is available only through hope.
- The conditions and experiences of which Paul speaks have a transitive character, so that the weakness of one can work to empower another, the death of one can work to give life to another. Suffering is not, as we tend to think of it, individual and incommunicable.[15] Suffering can both be "shared" and "in behalf of" others, to their benefit. Even if we grant that this makes some sense, although extremely paradoxical sense, in the case of God and humans, it is much harder to grasp in the case of human vis-à-vis each other (absent the unseen power of the Spirit).
- The power that God has gifted humans through the resurrection of Jesus to begin a "new creation" has as its goal the establishment of those so empowered not in positions of privilege but rather in roles as servants. "Strength perfected in weakness" applies not only to the cross of Jesus but to the resurrection life.[16]
- The way God empowered humans through Christ's shameful crucifixion as a slave is the paradigm of the apostolic ministry (life through death, power through weakness) and of Christian behav-

13. See Eastman, *Paul and the Person*; Carr, "Subject of the New Creation."
14. See chap. 5 in this volume.
15. See the reflection in Johnson, "The Body in Pain."
16. It is of first importance to stress that my emphasis on the power of the resurrection does *not* imply, in the present condition of humans, the sort of "theology of glory" that is the bugaboo of some Protestant systematic theology; just the opposite.

ior within the community (bearing one another's burdens, putting up with the weak, "becoming weak to win the weak"). The suffering of Christ is not a past event but a continuing experience within and for his resurrection body that is the church.

Return to Philippians

After this long linguistic excursus, we can return to the text of Philippians in the expectation that Paul's language about power and weakness, death and resurrection, suffering with and for others, may help us grasp some of the things he says in this letter and why he says them.[17] I begin with the (I hope forgivable) lengthy citation of a passage in chapter 1 that has received attention because of its portrayal of Paul as undecided between the preferability of his life and death, and whether he was contemplating suicide,[18] but whose real significance lies in what it reveals about the principles Paul assumes concerning his life before God and with his beloved community:[19]

My eager expectation and hope is that I shall not be put to shame in any way, but that with all boldness, now as always, Christ will be magnified in my body [*megalynthēsetai Christos en tō sōmati mou*], whether by life or by death [*eite dia zōēs eite dia thanatou*]. For to me life is Christ [*to zēn Christos*], and death is gain [*kerdos*]. If I go on living in the flesh, that means fruitful labor for me. And I do not know which I shall choose. I am caught between the two [*synechomai de ek tōn duo*]. I long to depart this life and be with Christ [*syn Christō*], for that is far better. Yet that I remain in the flesh is more necessary for your benefit [*di' hymas*]. And this I know with confidence, that I shall remain and continue in the service of all of you [*menō kai paramenō pasin hymin*] for your progress and joy in the faith, so that your boasting in me may abound in Christ Jesus [*to kauchēma hymōn perisseuē en Christō Iēsou en emoi*] when I come to you again. (Phil 1:20–26, NABRE, with last line adapted)[20]

17. For other approaches to the theme of suffering in Philippians, see Ahern, "Fellowship of His Sufferings"; Bloomquist, *Function of Suffering*; Proudfoot, "Imitation or Realistic Participation?"
18. See esp. Droge, "*Mori Lucrum*"; also Droge, *Noble Death*.
19. See, e.g., Vogel, "Réflexions on Philipp. 1:23–24"; Dailey, "To Live or to Die"; Hawthorne, "Interpretation and Translation"; Reeves, "To Be or Not to Be?"
20. The NABRE translation, "that your boasting in Christ Jesus may abound

The significance of this passage in the first chapter of Philippians deserves attention above all because of its intensely personal character and the fact that it does not present a well-thought-out set piece of moral instruction. We catch Paul, as it were, in midthought. He is not making an argument but is trying to think through his own situation in the face of death and life as he is in prison—that is, as he is experiencing the suffering of shame and isolation and immobility imposed by others on him. He thereby reveals the values by which he defines himself, not values he uses to describe others.[21]

He confesses himself "caught between" (*synechomai*) his own desire (*epithymia*) and what will be to the benefit of the Philippians. His own desire? To "be released" (*analysai*),[22] and thereby be "with Christ" (*syn Christō*).[23] This represents for Paul both what he wishes and a clear "gain" (*kerdos*). And he is unequivocal: this would be a "much, much better thing" (*pollō gar mallon kreisson*) for himself. But he is constrained by his consideration for them (*di' hymas*): remaining in the flesh means the ability to "remain and be of service to all of you" (*menō kai paramenō pasin hymin*) and thus to do "fruitful work" among them. At one level, then, we see Paul weighing the options of seeking his own desire and what might serve others.

At another level, however, this set of options, which might be presented to any of us—should we leave or should we stay, what's to my good and what's good for you?—is completely relativized by another conviction—namely, that in either Paul's death or Paul's life, *megalynthēsetai Christos en tō sōmati mou*: Paul's "body" is the arena of God's glorification/manifestation and is so through the entire process of life ("for me to live is Christ") and death ("which is gain to me . . . I will be with Christ"). His decision to remain among them and serve them, therefore, does not represent his own fear of death or his own desire to prolong his mortal existence but is to enable them to perceive in his body the manifestation of Christ: their boast will be "in Christ Jesus in me" (*en Christō Iēsou en emoi*). Although for Paul himself life is defined utterly by his being "in Christ," his choosing to remain among them to serve them is a way of "displaying Christ in his body." Rather than follow his desire to share

---

on account of me," misses, I think, the odd and tellingly asyndetic *en Christō Iēsou en emoi*.

21. I am not suggesting that the passage lacks rhetorical shaping or intention, only that, in contrast to 3:2–16, Paul presents his discernment "in the moment" rather than as part of a narrative of his past.

22. Although in context *analysai* clearly means "death," the verb can also suggest "liberation"; see Acts 16:26.

23. See esp. Dupont, *Syn Christōi*.

in the "body of glory" that is the exalted Christ's (Phil 2:11; 3:21)—for him the far better thing—Paul chooses to remain in service in his "lowly body" (3:21), precisely to enact what it means for Christ to be displayed "whether in life or in death" (1:20).

The Christic pattern of life for others, and suffering for others, is also to be the way the Philippians are to "carry out [their] lives worthily of the good news of Christ" (Phil 1:27). Indeed, insofar as they also experience opposition and persecution (or the suffering of internal dissension), they can, with Paul, also suffer in behalf of Christ: "To you has been granted, for the sake of Christ [*to hyper Christou*], not only to believe in him [*ou monon to eis auton pisteuein*] but also to suffer for him [*to hyper autou paschein*]." And how is this possible? "Yours is the same struggle such as you saw in me and now are hearing about [in] me [*ton auton agōna echontes, hoion eidete en emoi kai nyn akouete en emoi*]" (1:29–30). Here we see in very concrete circumstances—the imprisonment and indecision of Paul, the opposition and conflict within the Philippian community—the sense of how the suffering of believers also continues the suffering of Christ in the world: as his existence was defined by *hyper pasin* ("in behalf of all"), so is the existence of Paul and the Philippians defined by being at once suffering for and with each other (*hyper pasin hymon*) and in his behalf (*hyper autou*).

The Mind of Christ

In Phil 1:20–26 we find Paul in the process of making the critical moral discernment between death and life, between what is gain for him and what is needed by the Philippians. We are privy to what we might call the mind of Paul in midstride. In Greco-Roman moral philosophy, such practical moral reasoning was called *phronēsis* in Greek and *prudentia* in Latin. The term pointed to the application of higher principles (*sophia*) to the changeable circumstances of everyday life.[24] *Phronēsis* lies between premise and act. It can be translated into English as "disposition" or even "inclination," for it is the habitual mode of practical thinking that gives virtue embodiment. As it happens, the verb form *phronein* appears proportionately more often in Philippians than any other Pauline letter and is outdone in terms of cognates only by Romans.[25] It occurs the first time in Phil 1:7, where after his thanksgiving and statement of confidence in his

24. For the evidence in Aristotle, see chap. 3 in this volume.
25. See Phil 1:7; 2:2 (2×); 2:5; 3:15, 19; 4:2, 10. These eight instances are matched

congregation, Paul declares, "It is right that I should think this way about all of you [*touto phronein hyper pantōn hymōn*], because I hold you in my heart, you who are all partners with me in grace, both in my imprisonment and in the defense and confirmation of the gospel" (NABRE). This instance shows how "be disposed" could serve as well as "think this way"; each points to a characteristic attitude and mode of discernment.

The reason I give so much attention to this term is that it holds such an important place within the Pauline paradox I am seeking to unravel in this chapter. It occurs five times, we notice, in chapters 2 and 3, and three times in 2:1–5. Here is where Paul seeks to shape the "way of thinking" of his readers in terms of the paradox of weakness leading to power, death leading to life, shameful lowliness leading to glory (see Phil 3:20). The paradigmatic instance of God's way of working in such paradoxical fashion, we have already learned, is the death and resurrection of Jesus, and it is this full pattern that Paul presents to his readers in Philippi with the so-called Christ-hymn in 2:6–11.

For my investigation, it matters not at all whether this passage is actually a "hymn,"[26] or is "pre-Pauline,"[27] or even whether it begins with Christ's preexistence or deals entirely with the dispositions of his mortal existence.[28] What matters is the use to which Paul puts his recital concerning Jesus,[29] and this is plainly, as Phil 2:5 indicates, to shape the disposition or way of thinking of his readers, by presenting Christ's "way of thinking" as an example for how they are to think.[30]

---

by the use of the verb form six times, the adjective *phronimos* twice, and the noun *phronēma* three times in the much longer letter to the Romans.

26. Most recently, Gordley, *New Testament Christological Hymns*; Gloer, "Homologies and Hymns"; Hengel, "Hymns and Christology"; Martin, "Some Reflections"; Stanley, "Carmenque Christo."

27. D. Black, "Authorship of Philippians 2:6–11"; Fee, "Philippians 2:5–11"; Furness, "Authorship of Philippians ii. 6–11"; Gamber, "Der Christus-Hymnus"; Georgi, "Der vorpaulinishe Hymnus Phil ii. 6–11."

28. For discussions, see Howard, "Phil 2:6–11"; Hurst, "Re-enter the Pre-existent Christ"; Hurtado, "Jesus as Lordly Example"; Murphy-O'Connor, "Christological Anthropology"; Talbert, "Problem of Pre-existence"; Wanamaker, "Philippians 2.6–11."

29. My approach is closer to those who see the hymn as having a rhetorical role within the letter as a whole; see, e.g., Basevi and Chapo, "Philippians 2.6–11"; Fowl, *Story of Christ in the Ethics of Paul*; Hooker, "Philippians 2:6–11"; and esp. Kurz, "Kenotic Imitation."

30. For a representative sample of other studies on the hymn, see Bornhäuser, "Zum Verständnis von Philipper 2,5–11"; Cerfaux, "L'hymne au Christ-Serviteur de Dieu"; Feinberg, "Kenosis and Christology"; Feuillet, "L'hymne Christologique"; J. Harvey, "New Look"; Hofius, *Der Christushymnus*; Käsemann, "Critical Anal-

Unfortunately, the RSV and NRSV mistranslate slightly—although they capture the idea—by rendering Paul's Greek in 2:5, *touto phroneite en hymin ho kai en Christō Iēsou*, with variations of "have this mind in you which was also in Christ Jesus," making Paul's verb into a noun (which, to be fair, nicely echoes the "mind of Christ" in 1 Cor 2:16), suggesting that this "mind" is "within" each reader. The NABRE does much better, I think, when it offers, "Have among yourselves the same attitude that is also yours in Christ Jesus." I like the "among you," because it picks up the emphasis of Phil 2:1–4: this is a community mode of discernment Paul seeks, not simply an individual one. And "attitude" is better than "mind." But it still replaces the verb with a noun, and the phrase "is also yours" misleadingly supplements the Greek. Here is the most straightforward rendering I can manage: "Have this disposition among you that was also in Christ Jesus." Paul is exhorting them to the same sort of discernment in their circumstances that characterized Jesus in his:

> Who, though he was in the form of God,
>> did not regard [*ouk ... hēgēsato*] equality [*isa*] with God
>> something to be grasped [*harpagmon*].
>> Rather, he emptied himself [*ekenōsen*],
>> taking the form of a slave,
>> coming in human likeness;
>> and found human in appearance,
>> he humbled himself,
>>> becoming obedient to death,
>>> even death on the cross.
>
> (Phil 2:6–8 NABRE)

Although this mythic segment (it represents a divine agent—"in the form of God"—acting in the empirical realm) opens itself to endless reflection, I want to focus on only two aspects. The first is the successive self-diminishment from the highest privilege to the lowest and most shameful condition: the self-emptying from the form of God to taking on the form of slave; and, as human, the lowering of the self through obedience even to death on a cross—a slave's death.[31] It is the movement

---

ysis"; Kraftchick, "Necessary Detour"; Michel, "Zur Exegese von Phil. 2, 5–11"; Moule, "Further Reflexions"; C. Robbins, "Rhetorical Structure"; Stagg, "Mind in Christ Jesus."

31. See Hengel, *Crucifixion in the Ancient World*.

downward from glory to shame. The second aspect is the cognitive and volitional character of the movement. This is self-diminishment. Christ "did not reckon" (*hēgēsato*) equality with God as a "possession for the grasping" (*harpagmon*); he chose to humble himself (*etapeinōsen heauton*) through his life of obedience that led to his shameful death on the cross. Paul here presents Jesus not only as the means of human salvation but as the model for his understanding of what the obedience of faith actually entails. Thus, as Christ "reckoned" in a manner that led to his humbling in place of his "equality with God," Paul wants the Philippians to have this same manner of "reckoning" among themselves (Phil 2:5).

The hymn continues, as we know, with the most dramatic possible reversal, in which God exalts the one who emptied and humbled himself:

> Because of this [*dio kai*], God greatly exalted him
> and bestowed on him [*echarisato autō*] the name
> that is above every name,
> that at the name of Jesus
> every knee should bend,
> of those in heaven and on earth and under the earth,
> and every tongue confess that
> Jesus Christ is Lord [*kyrios Iēsous Christos*],
> to the glory [*doxa*] of God the father.
>
> (Phil 2:9–11 NABRE)

The exaltation of Christ, Paul declares, is not something that Jesus could grasp but came from God as gift, and that divine gift that was stimulated by Jesus's self-emptying obedience (*dio kai* = "and for that very reason"). In a slightly different form, we recognize the pattern of "strength becoming weakness so that others might become strong" found in 2 Corinthians: Christ dying in weakness so that he can be powerful among them (2 Cor 13:4); Christ, though not knowing sin, becoming sin so that they can be God's righteousness (2 Cor 5:21); Christ, though rich, becoming poor so that by his poverty they might become rich (2 Cor 8:9). In the present case, the element of "for them" is missing, for the story of Jesus here serves to demonstrate the paradox of divine power working through human weakness, and the sequence of suffering now and glory later (see Phil 3:10, 20).

The implication is clear enough: if the Philippians have "fellowship" with Christ in the way they presently conduct their lives, they can expect to share as well in the glory that is gifted Christ in his exaltation.

We note how the ending of Phil 3:20–21 (NABRE) echoes the ending of the Christ-hymn: "He will change our lowly body to conform with his glorified body by the power that enables him also to bring all things into subjection with himself."[32]

The Mind of the Philippians

The point of Paul's telling them to think in the way (*touto phroneite*) that characterized Christ Jesus is made clear by his instructions to the Philippian believers in 2:1–4, a passage that reveals how "fellowship of suffering" does not mean a literal imitation of Christ's suffering on the cross, nor even a participation in the imprisonment and persecutions of Paul. It does not mean becoming a slave (*doulos*) in the literal sense. It does mean, rather, sharing in a way of living (see 1:27) that combines wise perception and prudential discernment such as is found in the suffering *doulos* Jesus and, we shall see, in other living examples. As an *anastrophē* ("manner of life"), suffering shifts from an incidental aspect of obedience to God to the essential ingredient of such obedience. "Fellowship of suffering" means living out, in completely different (and constantly changing) circumstances, the same disposition of self-relativization and service of others that was Christ's, not once for all, not only by some members, but chronically and constantly by all members of the community:

> If there is any encouragement in Christ, any solace in love, any particip-
> ipation in the Spirit [*koinōnia pneumatos*], any compassion and mercy,
> complete my joy by being of the same mind [*to auto phronēte*], with
> the same love, united in heart, thinking one thing [*to hen phronoun-
> tes*].[33] Do nothing out of selfishness or out of vainglory; rather, hum-

32. We cannot miss in Paul's language here of "the body of his glory" (*sōma tēs doxēs autou*) the echo of his diction concerning the body of the resurrected in 1 Cor 15:42–44: "So also is the resurrection of the dead. It is sown corruptible, it is raised incorruptible. It is sown dishonorable, it is raised glorious. It is sown weak; it is raised powerful. It is sown a natural body; it is raised a spiritual body" (*houtōs kai hē anastasis tōn nekrōn. speiretai en phthora, egeiretai en aphtharsia; speiretai en atimia, egeiretai en doxē; speiretai en astheneia, egeiretai en dynamei; speiretai sōma psychikon, egeiretai sōma pneumatikon*).

33. Both *to auto phronēte* and *to hen phronountes* obviously correspond to the *touto phroneite* that follows in Phil 2:5. They are to have the same disposition/attitude/way of thinking that Paul describes as defining Jesus. For this reason, the "same thing" that they are to think cannot possibly mean uniformity at the level of content ("we

bly [*tē tapeinophrosynē*][34] regard others as more important that yourselves [*allēlous hēgoumenoi hyperechontas heautōn*],[35] each looking
out not for his own interests, but [also] everyone for those of others
[*mē ta heautōn ekastos skopountes alla [kai] ta heterōn ekastoi*]. (Phil
2:1–4 NABRE)[36]

As my notes suggest, the linguistic links between 2:1–4 and 2:6–11
make the exemplary intent of 2:5 clear: the Philippians are to display
in their attitudes toward each other precisely the willingness to empty
themselves of their own glory—the selfishness and vainglory inherent
in looking only to "one's own interests"—and humbly take on the reckoning of the slave: the "interests of the other" are at least as important
as theirs. Here the suffering of Christ in which they participate is not a
matter of afflictions imposed from the outside, such as imprisonments,
persecutions, and enslavement; it is a matter of the self-emptying and
humility demanded by life together in the faith of Jesus Christ. Just as
Christ was "obedient to death," Paul exhorts them to be "obedient as
you have always been, not only when I am present but all the more now
when I am absent"; they thus "work out [their] salvation with fear and
trembling" (2:12 NABRE). They are able to have such dispositions because of the "support from the Spirit" (1:19) and the "participation in the
Spirit" that they share (2:1). As Paul declares in 1:6 (NABRE), "I am confident of this, that the one who began a good work in you will continue
to complete it until the day of Christ Jesus." The process that might be
called "fellowship of the sufferings of Christ"—that is, the very process

---

all agree that red is the best color") but rather a common attitude/disposition/way
of thinking precisely in the midst of diversity of opinion ("we each like a different
color, but we will not make such diversity divide us"). The following line in verse 3
is therefore critical.

34. The "lowliness" (*tapeinophrosynē*) here deliberately anticipates the "lowered
himself" (*etapeinōsen*) ascribed to Christ in the hymn (Phil 2:8).

35. Three things need noting. First, the use of *hēgeomai* once more deliberately
anticipates the "reckoning" of Christ (Phil 2:6). Second, their "reckoning" is functional rather than essential; that is, it is not the judgment that another is better than
oneself always and in all respects (false humility), but it is viewing the other as a more
significant element in making a moral choice: it is a reckoning. Third, such humble
calculation is to be carried out reciprocally: "each other" (*allēlous*).

36. The plural neuter pronoun *ta* in both clauses is of particular importance, for it
points, as the NABRE translation correctly sees, to all "the things/interests/issues/points
of view" in any community. Total uniformity of opinion is the death of thought. Diversity
of perspective/opinion/interest enables both thought and mutual consideration.

by which the obedient faith of the *douloi theou* (see 1:1) is lived out in mutual service—is begun and brought to completion by God.

Living Examples of the Mind of Christ

Paul follows this section of the letter devoted to the instruction of the Philippians concerning an *anastrophē* that follows the pattern of the slave-Messiah Jesus (2:1–11) through mutual self-emptying with what appears to be at first sight a recital of banal news concerning his fellow workers. The NABRE, for example, titles the section "Travel Plans of Paul and His Assistants." What Paul tells his readers about Timothy (2:19–24), Epaphroditus (2:25–30), and finally himself (3:2–14) does communicate information about all three, but his goal is less information than transformation. Paul shapes his recital to present his readers with three living examples of living according to the mind of Christ.[37] Such personal examples show that the pattern of selflessness and service that Paul had shown them in Christ and enjoined them to practice among themselves was not an impossible ideal but was being lived out in people whom they knew, including himself.

As the cosponsor of this letter, Timothy has already been designated together with Paul as a slave (*doulos*) belonging to Jesus Christ (Phil 1:1). Now Paul hopes to send him to the Philippians in order to receive news of them. And here is how Paul characterizes his delegate: "I have no one comparable to him for genuine interest in whatever concerns you. For they all seek their own interests, not those of Jesus Christ" (2:20–21 NABRE). Even in the NABRE translation, Paul's commendation manifestly echoes his earlier exhortation, but the Greek makes the connection even clearer. Timothy is *isopsychos* with Paul: he is, by the classical measure, a "friend" who views the world exactly as Paul does, and as a *doulos* of Jesus Christ would. His disposition is revealed by genuine or authentic (*gnēsiōs*) concern for their interests (*ta peri hymōn*). To ensure that we do not miss the point, Paul adds, "For they all seek their own interests [*ta heautōn zētousin*] rather than the interests of Jesus Christ [*ou ta Iēsou Christou*]. But you know his worth [*dokimēn autou*], how as a child with his father [*hōs patri teknon*] he served along with me [*syn emoi edouleusen*] in the cause of the gospel" (2:21–22). Timothy worked

---

37. I am especially indebted to Kurz, "Kenotic Imitation," for insight into the paradigmatic roles played by the characters mentioned in Phil 2–3.

"as a slave" at the side of Paul for the sake of the Christ who was a slave, seeking the interests of others rather than his own.

Paul gives similar shape to the pedestrian news that he was sending back Epaphroditus, a member of their congregation ("your brother," Phil 2:25) who has served with Paul—not least by supporting him materially in behalf of the Philippians (2:25, 30; see 4:18).[38] Paul begins with the same term "I reckoned" (*hēgēsamēn*) that he used for Christ (2:25; see 2:6); although in every respect Epaphroditus was equal to Paul ("my . . . fellow worker and my fellow soldier") and in every way a "benefit" to Paul ("your delegate to me and the supplier of my needs"), Paul chooses to send him back because of Epaphroditus's longing (*epipothōn*) to see his home congregation and because of their sorrow at the news of the delegate's sickness/weakness (*ēsthenēsen*, 2:26). Paul chooses in favor of their benefit rather than his own, all the more eagerly since this will lead to their joy (at seeing him) and to Paul's being without the sort of "sorrow upon sorrow" that he would have if God had not, in his mercy, spared his delegate's life (2:27–28). The last lines concerning Epaphroditus reveal how Paul imprints the pattern of the suffering and exalted Christ even on the quotidian experience of a return home. Paul declares that it was "on account of the work of Christ" that he came close to death, risking his very life so that he might make up to Paul whatever was lacking in their service to him [*anaplērōsē to hymōn hesterēma tēs pros me leitourgias*] (2:30).[39] Thus the self-emptying even unto death in imitation of—and for the cause of—Christ. For this reason (*hoti*), Paul tells the Philippians, they should "welcome him then in the Lord with all joy and hold such people in esteem" (2:29 NABRE). The present share in suffering leads to joy and honor (*entimos*).

The final example Paul provides his readers is himself (Phil 3:2–16), which he again recounts according to the pattern of the Christ-hymn.[40] Before turning to that autobiographical sketch, however, it may be helpful to note the import of 3:1, a transition verse that has seemed to many critics to serve mainly as a break that helps support theories of letter fragmentation.[41] It is better, though, to take 3:1a, "as for the rest, my

---

38. See J. Harris, "Epaphroditus, Scribe and Courier."

39. It is impossible to miss here the similarity to Col 1:24, *chairō en tois pathēmasin hyper hymōn kai antanaplērō ta hysterēmata tōn thlipseōn tou Christou.*

40. See esp. Kurz, "Kenotic Imitation." See also DeSilva, "No Confidence in the Flesh."

41. It is obvious from my argument that I regard Philippians as having literary unity and rhetorical coherence. For the debate on integrity, see Koperski, "Early His-

brothers, keep on rejoicing in the Lord [*chairete en kyriō*]," as continuing the thought of the previous passage (see 2:28–29). The next sentence represents an authorial comment on Paul's argument-by-example as a whole: "Writing the same things [*ta auta*] to you is no burden for me but is a safeguard [*asphales*] for you" (NABRE).

If we read what follows this as some sort of warning in the time of crisis, then *asphales* might legitimately be translated as "safeguard," but in that case, what are the "same things" that Paul is writing? Taking 3:2–16 as polemic against opponents truly does make the statement nonsensical, for nowhere else in Philippians do we find "the same." But if we take 3:2–26 as presenting still another example reinforcing the "mind of Christ" that Paul has been trying to communicate since 2:1, then "writing the same things" makes perfect sense as an introduction to his final, personal, example of "thinking as Jesus thought."

It is too bad that Paul's recital of his Jewish credentials in 2 Cor 11, which truly is comparative and defensive over against claims made for or by real rivals, has so shaped scholarly perspective on the other such autobiographical moments, such as those in Galatians and 1 Timothy. The point in both those instances is not to defend Paul's authority against challenge but to provide his readers with a lesson drawn from his own experience. In Galatians and 1 Timothy, Paul wants to contrast his life under the law with his life under grace. In both accounts, Paul's persecution of the church is intimately tied to his allegiance to the law. His persecution of the church appears in Phil 3:6 as well, but it is not the central point. Paul's point in this passage, rather, is his giving up of all his privileges as a Jew in order to "be found in" Christ. Paul tells his story as fitted to the paradigm of the self-emptying Messiah who is now Lord by the gift of God (2:6–11).

If another than polemical understanding of Phil 3:2–16 is to make sense, then we must properly assess the use of the verbs *blepete* in 3:2 and *skopeite* in 3:17.[42] In each case, the command to see/observe means "to pay attention to"; *blepete*, in particular, should not be read as meaning "beware," in the sense of "watch out for," as though those described were

---

tory"; Rahtjen, "Three Letters"; Koester, "Purpose of a Polemic"; Dalton, "Integrity of Philippians"; Garland, "Composition and Unity"; Rolland, "La structure litteraire et l'unite de l'epitre aux Philippiens," 213–16; Pollard, "The Integrity of Philippians," 57–66; Watson, "A Rhetorical Analysis of Philippians and its Implications for the Unity Question," 57–88.

42. For the imperative *blepete* with the neutral sense of "observe," see 1 Cor 1:26; 10:18; Col 4:17; see Kilpatrick, "*BLEPETE*: Philippians 3:2," 146–48.

active opponents or proselytizers who represent an active threat to the Philippians. There is not the slightest hint of such an issue elsewhere in the letter.[43] We do better to translate 3:2–3 along these lines: "Look at the dogs. Look at the evildoers. Look at the chop.[44] For we are the circumcision, we who worship God in the Spirit and make our boast in Christ Jesus and not in any confidence in the flesh." Paul sets up a comparison between his congregation of believers and those who place their confidence in circumcision, and he wants his readers to observe closely not only where they are but where he now is. No actual Jews or Judaizers are in sight.

If there are actual people (possibly within the community) whom Paul wants his readers to "beware of," they are found after his call for them to imitate himself, Epaphroditus, Timothy, and Christ: "For many, as I have often told you and now tell you even in tears, conduct themselves as enemies of the cross of Christ [*tous echthrous tou staurou tou Christou*]. Their end is destruction. Their God is their stomach; their glory is in their 'shame.' Their minds are occupied with earthly things [*hoi ta epigeia phronountes*]" (Phil 3:18–19 NABRE). In what sense are these people "enemies of the cross"? Not, as in Galatians, because they advocate circumcision. Paul, I submit, could not characterize anyone following Judaism as having their stomach as their god. No, the people he describes here are the sort of people who do not "have the mind of Christ," do not "look to the interests of others as well as their own," as the use of *phronountes* makes clear. They are, in short, the counterexample to Paul, Epaphroditus, Timothy, and Paul himself. They are as much a "representation" for contemplation as are the other examples provided by Paul in this section.

43. The isolation of the topic of circumcision to this one chapter, to be sure, is one of the specious arguments made for seeing it as an interpolation; see Koester, "The Purpose of the Polemic of a Pauline Fragment (Philippians III)." There have been many attempts at identifying the purported "opponents" in Philippians; see, e.g., Baumbach, "Die von Paulus im Philipperbrief bekaempften Irrlehrer," 293–310; Ellis, "Paul and his Opponents," 1:268–98; Grayston, "The Opponents in Philippians 3," 170–72; Gnilka, "Die Antipaulinische Mission in Philippi," 258–76; Holladay, "Paul's Opponents in Philippians 3," 77–90; Jewett, "Conflicting Movements in the Early Church as Reflected in Philippians," 362–90; Klijn, "Paul's Opponents in Philippians III," 278–84; Mearns, "The Identity of Paul's Opponents at Philippi," 194–204; Tyson, "Paul's Opponents at Philippi," 82–95.

44. *Katatomē* is a hapax in the New Testament, though it is widely attested in the sense of "cutting a notch" in Greek literature. Paul clearly intends a negative contrast to his usual term for circumcision (*peritomē*) which he applies to the Christians. Compare Colossians 2:11.

Paul begins, then, by reciting the grounds he had for "confidence in the flesh"—that is, for a sense of privilege measured in human terms. He was "circumcised on the eighth day, of the race of Israel, of the tribe of Benjamin, a Hebrew of Hebrew parentage, in observance of the law a Pharisee, in zeal I persecuted the church, in righteousness based on the law I was perfect" (Phil 3:5–6 NABRE, adapted). The résumé can be compared to the ones Paul recites in Gal 1:13–14 and 2 Cor 11:22–23, but to gain a sense of the exalted place among humans Paul considers his heritage to be, we should be reminded of his description of "one calling himself a Jew" in Rom 2:17–20 (NABRE): "You . . . rely on the law and boast of God and know his will and are able to discern what is important since you are instructed from the law . . . confident that you are a guide for the blind and a light for those in darkness, that you are a trainer of the foolish and teacher of the simple, because in the law you have the formulation of knowledge and truth." With such an exalted sense of himself, in short, Paul was in a position of privilege analogous to Christ being "in the form of God" (Phil 2:6).

But Paul abandons all this privilege to associate himself with the shameful slave—Messiah Jesus, whom he now calls Lord (Phil 3:7–9). That he deliberately shapes this "self-emptying" along the pattern of Christ's is indicated by his threefold use of "reckoning" (*hēgeomai*). As Christ did not "reckon" equality with God as something to be grasped, so Paul reckons (*hēgeomai*) everything that was gain for him as loss (*zēmia*), and he has reckoned (*hēgeomai*) all this loss as so much rubbish (*skybalon*). He "reckoned" (*hēgeomai*) all that once was important to his standing in the world as rubbish to be discarded (*panta zēmian einai*). Why such a dramatic revaluation? "On account of Christ" (*dia ton Christon*, 3:7); "because of the supreme good of knowing Christ Jesus my Lord" (*dia to hyperechon tēs gnōseōs Christou Iēsou tou kyriou mou*, 3:8); it came about "on account of him" (*di' hon*, 3:8). It is Paul's "knowing Christ" that is both the cause and the compensation for his loss of privilege. He counts everything else as loss so that he might "gain Christ" (*hina Christon kerdēsō*, 3:8).

But there remains still a deeper cut. If the great gain for Paul is to be "found in" Christ, the greatest loss is his exchange of a righteousness that he could call his own because it was based on performance of the law (*emēn dikaiosynēn tēn ek nomou*) with a righteousness that is based entirely on the obedience of the slave-Messiah Jesus (*tēn dia pisteōs Christou, tēn ek theou dikaiosynēn epi tē pistei*, Phil 3:9).[45] Paul's recital of

45. Again here, both logic and syntax argue for taking *pistis Christou* as subjective—it is Christ's faith in God, not Paul's in Christ, that constitutes the gift. Once

his own loss of prestige and gain of being found in Christ brings us full circle to the statement with which I began this inquiry: "to know him and the power of his resurrection and the sharing of his sufferings by being conformed to his death, if somehow I may attain the resurrection from the dead" (3:10–11 NABRE). We now understand that the "power of the resurrection" is the power of the Holy Spirit (1:19; 2:1) at work in Paul and his readers because of the exaltation of Christ as Lord (2:11).

And we also are in a position to understand that a "sharing in sufferings, being conformed to his death" includes for Paul all the ways in which humans are led to act in ways analogous to the suffering servant Jesus, who was obedient unto death. Obedient faith is itself, in its very nature, a form of suffering. This is because faithful obedience always demands letting go of an absolute hold on one's own desire/place/privilege/interest in order to respond to the needs of others. And such letting go hurts in small matters as well as large.

Paul's share in the sufferings of Christ, his participation in Jesus's obedience unto death does not consist only in Paul's experience of persecution and the shame of imprisonment. It began with his self-emptying of his Jewish privilege to "be found in" and to proclaim one who died the death of a slave. It includes his decision to go on living in service to the Philippians even though his "gain" is to be "with Christ" in death. For Timothy, it means constantly looking not to his own interests but to the interests of the Philippians. For Epaphroditus, it means carrying out his service to Paul and the Philippians even when he is weak to the point of death. And for each of the Philippians themselves, it means regarding others as having a greater claim on themselves, so that in lowliness they look not only to their own interests but also to the interests of others. All of these represent "fellowship in the sufferings of Christ" because they all express a manner of life expressive of the mind of Christ (Phil 2:1–5).

The full pattern of the Christ-hymn, however, is not yet realized either in Paul or in his readers. He concludes in 3:11 with "if somehow I might attain to the resurrection of the dead" (*ei pōs katantēsō eis ten exanastasin tēn ek nekrōn*). Paul can and does share in the sufferings of Christ, but although the experience of the power of the resurrection enables him to "be found in Christ," he is not yet "with Christ" (*syn Christō*) in triumph.

Paul continues to stress this eschatological reservation in the verses that follow. He has been seized by Christ, but he has not yet seized the

---

again, as 2:6–8 makes clear, *pistis Christou* is understood by Paul as equivalent to Christ's obedience to God (compare Rom 3:21–26 and 5:12–21); see the argument in chap. 1, "Romans 3:21–26 and the Faith of Christ," in this volume.

final victory that is Christ's—like a good athlete, he forgets the past and pushes toward the future, "the prize of God's upward calling, in Christ Jesus" (*eis to brabeion tēs anō klēseōs tou theou en Christō Iesou*, Phil 3:14 NABRE).[46] All the Philippians who are mature (*teleioi*) should think in this fashion (*touto phronōmen*); if they have another sort of attitude (*ei tis heterōs phroneite*), God will show them the way (3:15).[47] In any case (*plēn*), Paul says, "that which we have attained, let us continue along the same lines" (*eis ho ephthasen, tō autō stoichein*, 3:16).

The fact that Paul has presented Jesus, Epaphroditus, Timothy, and himself as models of an *anastrophē* that is shaped by having the same attitude as the human Jesus—that is, living by an obedient faith that seeks not what is to the benefit of the self but what is to the benefit of others—is made clear by Phil 3:17: "Join together as imitators of me [*symmimētai mou ginesthe*], brothers, and pay attention [*skopeite*][48] to those who conduct themselves in this manner [*houtō peripatountas*] just as you have an example in us [*kathōs echete typon hēmas*]." Not only Paul but all those he has presented as "walking in this way" serve as examples for the Philippians to imitate.

As is the custom in such paraenesis, Paul presents the counterexample of living according to the mind of Christ. He reminds them even in tears of what he has told them before, that some "conduct themselves" (*peripatousin*)[49] as "enemies of the cross of Christ" (*echthrous tou staurou tou Christou*, Phil 3:18). It is of great importance that we do not read Gal 5:12 into this context. A Judaizing agenda is not, and has not been, present in this letter. Here, being an "enemy of the cross of Christ" means living in a manner that is selfish rather than self-giving, in a fashion that caters to the self rather than serves one's brothers and sisters. Thus, Paul continues, "Their end is destruction, their god is their stomach, their glory is in their shame. Their minds are occupied with earthly things [*hoi ta epigeia phronountes*]" (Phil 3:19 NABRE, adapted). Paul's diction in this last phrase provides a perfect contrast to "having this attitude among you [*touto phroneite en hymin*] that was in Christ Jesus" (2:5).

---

46. Cf. the athletic language in 1 Cor 9:24–27 and see Pfitzner, *Paul and the Agon Motif*.

47. Note the double use of *phronein* here, which decisively ties together this entire section of 2:1–3:16 as an exhortation to live according to the mind of Christ.

48. The "watching" here corresponds to the *blepete* in 3:2. See McMichael, "Be Ye Followers"; Brant, "Place of *Mimēsis*."

49. The repetition of "conducting themselves" clearly links this warning with the positive model presented by those who live according to the pattern of the crucified Messiah in 3:17.

Conclusion

By seeking better to understand Paul's phrase "fellowship of his sufferings" in Phil 3:10, we have been drawn into the paradoxical heart of Paul's
thinking, or perhaps better, of Paul's imaginative world.[50] It is a world
with both mythic and moral elements. At the mythic level, the divine
power unleashed by the exaltation of Jesus at his resurrection is enabled
by the weakness and shame of the crucified Messiah in his human existence. That same divine power is made effective in the realm of human
existence through the mortal weakness of Christ's agents: "strength is
made perfect through weakness" (*hē gar dynamis en astheneia teleitai,*
2 Cor 12:9). What I term as mythic—divine power working in the empirical realm of human agency—can also be called "ontological." As Paul
makes clear everywhere, but above all in Phil 2:6–8, God has entered
into and embraced the human condition in such fashion that the human
condition is fundamentally altered.

Enter the moral dimension. Paul invites the Philippians—as he does
the Romans, Corinthians, and Galatians—to "this attitude among you
that was also in Christ Jesus" (Phil 2:5). As sharing in the human condition, Christ exercised a certain moral *phronēsis,* and this moral disposition—emptying the self for the sake of others, taking other's interests
into account as well as one's own—has an ontological (mythic) effect. It
was "for this very reason" (*dio*) of Christ's *tapeinōsis* (lowliness) within
his human body, expressed by his obedience even to the death of the
cross, that God exalted him and gave him the name that is above every
other name, commanding from all the acknowledgment of him as Lord
(2:9–11). Likewise, because the *dynamis theou* that comes from the exalted Christ is at work in believers whose *phronēsis* corresponds to that
of Christ, who "share in his suffering" in ways small and great in all the
discernments and choices of life, they also will, in the eschaton, share
in the ontological condition of the risen Lord, in the most profound
and paradoxical of transformations. Thus, Paul follows his long exhortation in 2:1–3:19, concluding in a call to those whose manner of life
makes them "enemies of the cross" to imitate those who follow the moral
path of Christ, with this declaration: "Our citizenship is in heaven,[51] and
from it we also await a savior, the Lord Jesus Christ. He will change
our lowly body [*hos metaschēmatisei to sōma tēs tapeinōseōs hēmōn*] to

50. For "imaginative world" and "symbolic world," see Johnson, "Imagining the
World Scripture Imagines," 165–80, and *Writings of the New Testament* (3rd ed.), 9–18.
51. See Brewer, "Meaning of *Politeuesthe* in Phil 1:27."

conform to his glorified body [*symmorphon tō sōmati tēs doxēs autou*] by the power that enables him also to bring all things into subjection to himself" (3:20–21).

But that amazing transformation is future.[52] For now, Paul and his readers seek to think and act—through the power of the Spirit—in a way that their manner of life (*anastrophē*) and moral decision-making (*phronēsis*) begin the ontological/mythic alteration of their very selves that will make their eschatological metamorphosis the completion of their fellowship in the sufferings of Christ.

52. See Carr, "Subject of the New Creation," 97–121.

Mystery and Metaphor in Colossians

The Treasure That Is Christ

In *Constructing Paul*, and in chapter 9 of this volume, I have dealt at some length with the occasion of and rhetorical response of Paul in his letter to Colossae and do not need to repeat everything here. You will remember that Paul had never met these inhabitants of the Lycus Valley but has heard from his fellow prisoner Epaphras, who founded the church, that believers were being agitated by the claims by some that more initiations beyond baptism were needed for full Christian maturity, or perfection (*teleios*): such add-ons included circumcision and the observance of the law, physical asceticism, and visions. Those claiming the high status given by such advancement in religion were apparently "disqualifying" those who did not. As I have argued earlier, such "politics of perfection" not only resembles that found among the Galatian churches (in the same broad geographical area) but quite likely arises from the same gentile "imprinting" concerning initiations into mysteries: one is never enough; more is always better.[1]

The differences between the rhetoric in Galatians and Colossians can be ascribed, I think, to interconnected factors. First, Paul knew the Galatians firsthand as their founder, whereas he knew the Colossians only by the reports of Epaphras. Second, Paul's argument in Galatians relied heavily on Torah, which the Galatian agitators may well have learned about (and craved) from Paul himself. In contrast, the argument in Colossians is carried completely by the shared traditions concerning faith and baptism—with no explicit citation of Torah at all.

More significant than the differences between the two letters is the fact that they share the same rhetorical goal of convincing readers (or

---

1. See chap. 9 in this volume. See also my treatment of the argument in Colossians in *Writings of the New Testament*, 393–404.

hearers) to stand firm within the experience they had been granted, and to "mature," not by adding on further ritual initiations or practices but by gaining a deeper insight into their experience and, on the basis of that experience, developing a keener moral awareness.

With all this stipulated, I should like in this chapter to look more closely at the sort of language Paul uses to shape the imagination of his readers. Specifically, I want to get a clearer picture of what Paul means when he speaks of *mystērion* ("mystery") and to appreciate the impressive range of metaphors that Paul uses to express, or suggest, aspects of the *mystērion*.

The Mystery of Christ among the Gentiles

Paul's use of *mystērion* in Col 1:26, 2:2–3, and 4:3 was appropriate to the rhetorical situation, for in gentile religion initiations were above all associated with the mysteries and the perfection (*teleios*, see Col 1:28; 3:14) they progressively accomplished for those who underwent them.[2] But Paul's use of the term elsewhere in the canonical letters seems to bear more of the sense found in the Septuagint, where *mystērion* refers not to a ritual process but to the revelation by God of a previously hidden truth (secret), translating *raz* in the few instances where it translates a Hebrew or Aramaic *Vorlage* (see Dan 2:18, 19, 27, 28, 29, 30, 47; 4:6; Sir 2:18; 22:22; 27:16, 17, 21) and maintaining that sense in scriptural texts originally composed in Greek (see Tob 12:7, 11; Jud 2:2; Wis 2:22; 6:21; 14:15, 23; 2 Macc 13:21).[3]

Paul's Usage

Paul is generally consistent concerning the character of *mystērion* as a truth or reality that is otherwise unavailable to humans and is disclosed

2. See, e.g., Herodotus, *Histories* 2.51; Thucydides, *History* 6.28; Xenophon, *Hellenica* 1.4.27; Euripides, *Suppliants* 173, 470; Plato, *Gorgias* 497C; *Menon* 76E. For further linguistic evidence, especially drawn from epigraphy, see Gunther Bornkamm, "μυστήριον," *TDNT* 4:802–11; Caragounis, *Ephesian Mysterion*. For archaeological, artistic, and other dimensions of the scant body of knowledge (relative to the cultural importance) concerning the ancient religious rites, see in addition to the references in chap. 9, Bianchi, *Greek Mysteries*; Cosmopoulos, *Greek Mysteries*; Joseph Campbell, *Mysteries*; Clinton, *Myth and Cult*; Bremmer, *Initiation*.

3. See R. E. Brown, *Semitic Background*; Gladd, *Revealing the Mysterion*.

or revealed to them by God. Thus, three times in 1 Corinthians, he uses the plural form *mystēria* as the communications to humans through apostolic preaching (1 Cor 4:1), through prophecy in the assembly (13:2), or through glossolalia (14:2). Using the singular *mystērion*, Paul declares in 1 Cor 2:1 that he proclaimed the "mystery of/from God" without sublimity of words or wisdom. In this case, the *mystērion* seems to point to "Jesus Christ, and him crucified" (2:2).[4] Four verses later, Paul states:

> Yet we do speak a wisdom to those who are mature [*en tois teleiois*], but not a wisdom of this age, nor of the rulers of this age, who are passing away. Rather, we speak God's hidden wisdom in a mystery [*theou sophian en mystēriō tēn apokekrymmenēn*], which God predetermined before the ages for our glory, and which none of the rulers of this age knew, for if they had known it, they would not have crucified the Lord of glory. (2:6–8, adapted)

In this passage as well, it appears that it is how God has revealed God's power through the weakness of the cross of Jesus that forms the content of what "God has revealed to us through the Spirit" (1 Cor 2:10).[5] Paul's final use of the term in 1 Corinthians is once more in the singular and shifts our attention from the source or means of revelation to its content; in his discussion of the resurrection and the end time, Paul says, "Behold, I tell you a mystery [*mystērion*]. We shall not all fall asleep, but we will all be changed" (15:51). In sum, 1 Corinthians shows how Paul thinks of *mystērion* (as process) in terms of something revealed by God to humans that, even when disclosed, might remain not fully intelligible, and (as content) as having several possible referents, including the power released through the cross of Christ and the transformation of all believers at the end time.

In Romans we see that the content of the mystery revealed can be a portion of God's plan for the world, a plan that, as a whole, is by its very nature inaccessible to humans (see Rom 9:14–23; 11:33–36). Paul tells his gentile readers, "I do not want you to be unaware of this mystery [*mystērion touto*], brothers, so that you will not become wise in your own estimation: a hardening has come upon Israel in part, until the full

4. Unless otherwise indicated, Scripture quotations in this chapter are from the NABRE.

5. I am passing over the intervening words, which have a long and complex interpretive history of their own, but not one, I think, germane to the argument I am making here: "What eye has not seen, and ear has not heard, and what has not entered the human heart, what God has prepared for those who love him."

number of the gentiles has come in, and thus all Israel will be saved" (11:25–26, adapted). An even fuller, doxological expression of the mystery that is God's work through Paul among the gentiles concludes the letter to the Roman congregation from whom he expects support in his new missionary endeavors in Spain: "Now to him who can strengthen you, according to my gospel and the proclamation of Jesus Christ, according to the revelation of the mystery [*kata apokalypsin mystēriou*] kept secret for long ages but now manifested through the prophetic writings and, according to the command of the eternal God, made known to all nations [gentiles, *ethnē*] to bring about the obedience of faith [*eis hypakoēn pisteōs*, see 1:5], to the only wise God, through Jesus Christ be glory forever and ever. Amen" (16:25–27).[6]

By far the strongest resemblance to Paul's use of *mystērion* in Colossians is to be found in Ephesians. This should be no surprise since, as I showed in my discussion of Philemon in volume 1 of this work, the three letters (Ephesians, Colossians, Philemon) are connected both in the historical circumstances of their composition and canonically. To summarize quickly: Paul takes the occasion of returning the slave Onesimus to his owner Philemon, accompanied by Tychichus and a letter of commendation (the Letter to Philemon), to write letters to the local churches in Colossae (founded by his fellow prisoner Epaphras) and Laodicaea and the circular letter we know as Ephesians. Tychichus is the mailman and the delegate who delivers both the letters and the news about Paul to the circle of assemblies. In my discussion of these letters, I have already noted the strong stylistic and thematic resemblances between Colossians and Ephesians. Surveying Paul's use of *mystērion* in

---

6. This same sense of *mystērion* as part of God's overall plan for the world underlies the most obvious outlier in Paul's usage in 2 Thess 2:7: "For the mystery of lawlessness [*to mystērion . . . tēs anomias*] is already at work." Although negatively stated, the 2 Thessalonians passage fits within the framework of *mystērion* as an insight into God's activity in the world. By contrast, the two uses of *mysterion* in 1 Timothy are much less dramatic, referring in fact to the content of the Christian message and life. In 1 Tim 3:9 the ideal supervisor is one who should "have the mystery of the faith [*mystērion tēs pisteōs*] with a pure conscience" (author's translation), and in 3:16 Paul's delegate representing him until Paul's return is to know "the manner of life" (*anastrophē*) in the church that is the household of God, for "great indeed is the mystery of piety [*to tēs eusebeias mystērion*]" (author's translation). Paul then provides the content of that mystery: "Who was manifested in the flesh, vindicated in the spirit, seen by angels, proclaimed to the Gentiles, believed in throughout the world, taken up in glory." Despite its abbreviated and hymnic structure, this summary can be seen to contain the same elements identified as the contents of *mystērion* in 1 Corinthians and Romans.

Ephesians therefore contributes to an appreciation of its precise significance in Colossians, by way of both comparison and contrast.

The first Ephesian use of the term *mystērion* occurs in the opening
blessing. Having noted that in the beloved Son "we have redemption
through his blood [*apolytrōsin dia tou haimatos autou*], the forgiveness
of trespasses according to the richness of his grace [*kata to ploutos tēs
charitos autou*]" (1:7, author's translation), Paul says that "he lavished
upon us all wisdom and insight." Into what? "He has made known to us
the mystery of his will [*mystērion tou thelēmatos autou*] in accord with the
favor he has set forth in him as a plan for the fullness of times, to sum up
all things in Christ [*anakephalaiōsasthai ta panta en tō Christō*], things in
heaven and things on earth" (1:9–10, author's translation). Continuous
with Paul's other uses of the term is the notion of *mystērion* as God's plan
for the world to which believers have been given privileged access "now"
or in the "fullness of times," in contrast to its being hidden from earlier
generations. Distinctive here is the singular and cosmic concentration
on "the Christ"; the notion of "recapitulation of all things" has a cosmological and eschatological nuance only implicit in passages such as Rom
11:25, 16:25, and 1 Cor 15:51.

The term recurs three more times in a passage that is the more helpful
to cite at length because it involves Paul's sense of both his own mission
and that of the church:

> Because of this, I, Paul, a prisoner of Christ Jesus for you Gentiles—if,
> as I suppose, you have heard of the stewardship of God's grace that
> was given to me for your benefit, that the mystery was made known
> to me through revelation [*hoti kata apokalypsin egnōristhē moi to
> mystērion*], as I have already written briefly. As you read this, you are
> able to approach perceiving my understanding in the mystery that is
> Christ [*pros ho dynasthe anaginōskontes noēsai tēn synesin mou en tō
> mystēriō tou Christou*]. It was not made known to human beings in
> other generations as it has now been revealed [*hos nyn apekalyphthē*]
> to his holy apostles and prophets by the Spirit, that the gentiles are
> are coheirs, members of the same body, copartners in the promise in
> Jesus Christ through the gospel. Of this I became a minister by the
> gift of God's grace that was granted me in accord with the exercise
> of his power. To me, the very least of all the holy ones, the grace was
> given, to preach to the gentiles the inscrutable riches of Christ [*to
> anexichniaston ploutos tou Christou*] and to bring to light for all what
> is the plan of the mystery hidden from ages past in God who created

all things [*hē oikonomia tou mystēriou tou apokekrymmenou apo tōn aiōnōn en tō theō tō ta panta ktisanti*], so that the manifest wisdom of God might now be made known through the church [*dia tēs ekklēsias*] to the principalities and authorities in the heavens. This was according to the eternal purpose that he accomplished in Christ Jesus our Lord, in whom we have boldness of speech and confidence of access through faith in him. (Eph 3:1–12, author's translation)

As in the other passages, Paul's use of *mystērion* here clearly contrasts what was formerly hidden but is now made known. And Christ is once more central to the content of the mystery that was formerly "hidden in God" but has now been made known. The mystery here also is an expression of God's eternal plan. What is distinctive in this passage is the emphasis on the full share of the gentiles in the promise, and that the preaching of this truth is the heart of Paul's call to be an apostle, as well as the cosmic, revelatory function of the church itself. In both passages, I have provided the Greek for "the richness of his grace" and "the inscrutable riches of Christ" because of the way in which financial metaphors will help Paul express the reality of this mystery in Colossians.

The last appearance of *mystērion* in Ephesians similarly makes the good news the content of Paul's special mission from God. His last words to the readers of this encyclical before signing off are that they should pray for him, "that speech may be given to me to open my mouth, to make known with boldness the mystery that is the gospel [*to mystērion tou euangeliou*], for which I am an ambassador in chains, so that I will have the courage to speak as I must" (Eph 6:19–20, adapted). But by far the most singular use in Ephesians is in 5:32. At the conclusion of the passage 5:21–32—in which Paul enjoins mutual submission of all believers, exhorts wives to be submissive to their husbands ("as the church is subordinate to Christ," 5:24) and husbands to love their wives ("as Christ loved the church and handed himself over for her," 5:25), and cites the passage from Genesis that has a man leaving his father and mother to be joined to his wife as one flesh[7]—Paul adds, "This is a great mystery [*to mystērion touto mega estin*], but I speak in reference to Christ and the church [*egō de legō eis Christon kai eis tēn ekklēsian*]." What Paul's readers would take from this startling statement, I think, is that just as the church is the place where the reconciliation of Jew and gentile reveals the

---

7. Gen 2:24; for full discussion, see Sampley, *"And the Two Shall Become One Flesh."*

mystery of God's plans for the world (to recapitulate all things in Christ), so does the reciprocal relationship of male and female in the household express the reconciliatory character of the church itself. Marriage, then, is not so much a separate "mystery" as it is an expression (or symbol) of the "great mystery" that is Christ and the church, which has been Paul's subject all along.

Mystērion *in Colossians*

The focus on Christ is clear in the final mention of *mystērion* in Col 4:3, where Paul asks the Colossian community to support him in its prayers, "so that God may open a door to us for the word, to speak of the mystery of Christ [or "the mystery that is Christ," *mystērion Christou*], for which I am in prison, that I may make it clear, as I must speak."[8] The resemblance to Eph 6:19–20 is patent, with this exception, that in the Ephesian passage it is the *mystērion tou euangeliou* ("mystery of the good news") rather than, as here, the "mystery that is Christ" (*mystērion tou Christou*). We are pointed to the distinctive quality of Paul's other uses in Colossians, all of which appear in a single passage, and in which we see Paul's presentation of his mission to a gentile church that he had not met in person.

The lengthy passage is now separated by chapter numbers, but Col 1:24–29 actually flows naturally into 2:1–3. The artificial division effected by critical editions and translations does, however, provide a handy break for considering Paul's three uses of *mystērion* within the passage as a whole. To begin, then, Paul says:

> Now I rejoice in my sufferings for your sake, and in my flesh I am filling up what is lacking in the afflictions of Christ on behalf of his body, which is the church,[9] of which I am a minister in accordance with God's stewardship given to me to bring to completion for you the word of God, the mystery hidden from ages and from generations past [*to mystērion to apokekrymmenon apo tōn aiōnōn kai apo tōn geneōn*].

---

8. The genitive *Christou* modifies the noun *mystērion* and is objective. It is not "Christ's mystery" but is a mystery concerning Christ. The genitive may even be epexegetical, in which the noun in that case serves to identify the content of the noun it modifies—thus the alternative, "mystery that is Christ."

9. In chap. 14, I pointed to the extraordinary character of Paul's claim; see p. 270.

But now it has been manifested [*nyn de ephanerōthē*] to his holy ones, to whom God chose to make known the riches of his glory of this mystery [*to ploutos tēs doxēs tou mystēriou toutou*] among the Gentiles [*en tois ethnesin*]; it is Christ in you, the hope of glory [*ho estin Christos en hymin, hē elpis tēs doxēs*]. It is he whom we proclaim, admonishing everyone and teaching everyone with all wisdom, that we may present everyone perfect in Christ [*parastēsōmen panta anthrōpon teleion en Christo*]. For the sake of this [mystery][10] I labor and struggle, in accord with the exercise of his power working within me [*kata tēn energeian autou tēn energoumenēn en emoi en dynamei*]. (1:24–29, adapted)

Our interest in this dense passage is Paul's understanding of mystery, which has several fascinating dimensions. First, the pattern of "once hidden but now made known" is clearly stated. Second, the proclamation of this mystery is the "fulfillment" of the word of God Paul has been commissioned to proclaim. Third, once more "richness" (*ploutos*) is associated with this mystery that is the "hope of glory" (*elpis tēs doxēs*)—if it is now a "hope," then we understand the "glory" to be a future (eschatological) realization of the richness now present. Fourth, the content of the mystery is the figure of Christ "among" or "within" the gentiles. The phrase *en hymin* would naturally be read in external terms as "the extension of the message about the Christ among the gentiles" and thus resemble the statements on *mystērion* in Romans and Ephesians. But the next statement and the remainder of the letter make it possible that Paul might mean as well (or even in the first place) the presence of Christ "within" the Colossian believers in a mystical union—we remember the use of *mystērion* as referring to "Christ and the church" in Eph 5:32. Fifth, the possibility that Paul means by "Christ within you" such a mystical presence and power is enhanced by his final words: he admonishes and teaches everyone so that he might "present everyone perfect [*teleios*] in Christ." The term *teleios*, as I have observed before, is naturally associated with the mysteries in Greek religion. But there, such perfection is a matter of adding on further ritual initiations. Here, Paul sees maturity or perfection as a process of growing awareness (*sophia*) resulting from instruction into the one in whom they are found, or who is found in them (*en Christō*).

10. Apart from this phrase, I have followed the NABRE, which simply has "for this." But the neuter relative pronoun in *eis ho* clearly points back to the only available neuter antecedent, *mystērion*. Thus my clarification.

Col 2:1–3 continues the previous words seamlessly and should be read continuously with them. Paul declares:

> For I want you to know how great a struggle I am having for you and for those in Laodicea and all who have not seen me face to face, that their hearts may be encouraged as they are brought together in love [*symbibasthentes en agapē*], to have all the richness of fully assured understanding [*pan ploutos tēs plērophorias tēs syneseōs*], for the knowledge of the mystery of God, Christ [*tou mystēriou tou theou Christou*], in whom are hidden all the treasures of wisdom and knowledge [*en hō eisin pantes hoi thēsauroi tēs sophias kai gnōseōs apokryphoi*].

As in the first part of this extended passage, running from 1:24–29, the mystery Paul discloses to the Colossians is Christ, and his effort is to increase their recognition and knowledge of "the richness" of this mystery. That is clear enough. What remains obscure is the precise sense of the phrase "the mystery of God, Christ." The critical Greek text of the twenty-eighth edition of Nestle-Aland has *mystērion tou theou, Christou*, which could be translated as "God's mystery, namely Christ" or "mystery of God, who is Christ."[11] The external support for this longer reading is impressive, while the shorter (and usually preferable) readings of "mystery of Christ / mystery that is Christ" (*mystērion christou*) and "mystery of God" (*mystērion theou*) have support only from later and lesser witnesses.[12] Other manuscripts appear either to provide an explanation of the odd construction, as in *mystērion tou theou ho estin Christos* ("the mystery of God which is Christ"),[13] or wander off into theologically motivated expansions, such as "of God the one who is in Christ" (*tou theou tou en Christō*),[14] "of God the father and of Christ" (*tou theou patros kai tou christou*), and "of the God who is also father and of Christ" (*tou theou kai patros kai Christos*).[15] The combination of external support, brevity, and difficulty makes the case for accepting the judgment of the twenty-

---

11. This reading is supported by P46, Vaticanus, a MS of the Vulgate, and a citation in Hilary of Poitiers.

12. *Mystērion Christou* is found in 81, 1241, and Fulgentius; *mystērion theou* is supported by D1, H, P, and the Sahidic.

13. In the original hand of D, several manuscripts of the Vulgate, and Augustine.

14. In Clement and Ambrose.

15. These last two expanded, theologically motivated versions are represented in the vast number of extant witnesses.

eighth edition of Nestle-Aland.[16] The upshot of the text and translation here is that the mystery revealed by God in the present is "Christ among them," and in this mystery the Colossians have been given infinite riches and treasure.

The overall effect of Paul's usage of *mystērion* in Colossians, written to believers who are being urged by agitators to seek further degrees of ritual initiation beyond baptism, is to assert that perfection is to be found, not in the addition of further status markers granted by circumcision, asceticism, or mysticism, but through deeper insight into, and a further living out of, what has been given to them through their initiation into this mystery that is Christ.

What the Colossians Have Been Given in Christ

It is helpful, then, to examine what Paul means by "Christ among/within you" as the content of the *mystērion* that he proclaims, and as the reality into which he exhorts to greater insight and growth. The gist of his argument is stated in Col 2:9–10, where, having warned his readers against being deceived by human teachings that are not according to Christ, he declares, "For in him dwells the whole fullness of the deity bodily [*hoti en autō katoikei pan to plērōma tēs theotētos sōmatikōs*], and you share in this fullness in him [*kai este en autō peplērōmenoi*]" through their baptism into him (2:12). Christ is the fullness of the divine reality, and they are already fully incorporated into this fullness. The way forward, then, is not through addition but through deepening.

Paul gives this argument its full expression in 1:12–22, where he gives thanks to God for the gift that he has given the Colossians. The passage links together two distinct truths: what God has done for them, which forms a bracket in 1:12–14 and 1:21–22, and, within that bracket, the affirmation of how and by whom God's gift was given. Paul begins by "giving thanks to the Father, who has made you fit to share in the inheritance of the holy ones in light. He delivered us from the power of darkness and transferred us to the kingdom of his beloved Son, in which we have redemption, the forgiveness of sins" (1:12–14, adapted); and after the Christ-hymn, he continues, "And you who once were alienated and hos-

---

16. Paul uses *mystērion theou* in 1 Cor 2:1 and 4:1, and *mystērion Christou* in Eph 3:9, but the immediate context that speaks of the mystery as "Christ among/within you" makes the difficult and provocative reading the most likely.

tile in mind because of evil deeds he [Christ] has now reconciled in his fleshly body through his death, to present you holy, without blemish, and irreproachable before him [God]" (1:21–22). On either side of the Christ-hymn, then, is the short narrative of what God has accomplished for them in Christ.[17] God, Paul says, has saved them—that is, brought them from darkness to light, from alienation to reconciliation, from a state of enmity to a share in the inheritance of the holy ones, from the power of darkness into the kingdom of his Son.

The Christ-hymn—if such it is properly called[18]—serves to make the point that it truly was God who accomplished all this, that by being incorporated into mystery of Christ through baptism, they were truly in touch with the ultimate religious reality, and that there was no need to search for something further and supposedly better. The hymn therefore

17. The use of metaphorical language in these statements is both abundant and mixed. Before the hymn, Paul uses the language of law/athletics in speaking of God as "qualifying" or "making fit" (*hikanōsanti*, 1:12), the diction of law and kinship in speaking of "a share in inheritance with the holy ones in light" (*tēn merida tou klērou tōn hagiōn en tō phōti*, 1:12), the metaphor of politics in stating that "he delivered us [*errysato hēmas*] from the power of darkness and transferred us to the kingdom [*kai metestēsen eis tēn basileian*]" (1:13), and the metaphorical field of economics in speaking of "redemption" (*apolytrōsis*, 1:14) and "forgiveness/release of sins" (*aphesis tōn hamartiōn*, 1:14). After the hymn, his language is a combination of the diplomatic—alienated/enemies (*apēllotriōmenous/echthrous*, 1:21), reconciled (*apokatēllaxen*, 1:22), and "presenting" (as at court, *parastēsai*, 1:22)—and cultic ("presenting" [as a sacrifice], "holy, without blemish, irreproachable" [*hagious kai amōmous kai anenklētous*, 1:22). As we saw in vol. 1, chap. 9 ("Convictions, Myths, Symbols, and Metaphors"), when Paul speaks of salvation, no single metaphor suffices.

18. I have no real difficulty with the form-critical conclusion that passages such as this one and Phil 2:6–11 were "hymns," although the determination of what that designation really signifies is difficult. It is striking, for example, that the language of the hymns in Colossians and Philippians are so dissimilar from each other and at the same time so closely conform to the language of the letter in which they are embedded. Has Paul shaped the language of the letter around the hymn to match that of a piece of tradition he has taken over, or has he himself constructed the "hymn" in a heightened version of the specific letter's distinctive diction? Scholars need to be wary of the seductive effect of textual formatting. The highly rhythmic and balanced period in 1 Cor 15:12–19, if properly indented, could plausibly be called "hymnic." No great harm is done by the designation, but the stylistic conformity I have noted ought to lead us to place mental quotation marks around the phrase when we use it. For a recent treatment—leaving out the "hymn" in 1 Tim 3:16 but including the prologue to John's Gospel—see Gordley, *New Testament Christological Hymns*. On the Colossian passage specifically, see Vawter, "Colossian Hymn"; Wink, "Hymn of the Cosmic Christ"; Wright, "Poetry and Theology."

asserts the primacy of "the Son of his love" (Col 1:13, author's translation) through five affirmations that go to show that he is "preeminent in all things" (*en pasin autos prōteuōn*, 1:18):

- In his divine status: he is the image of the unseen God, the first-born of all creatures (1:15); in him "all the fullness was pleased to dwell" (1:19). The implication? Where the Son is present, God is present.
- In his creative activity: in him all things in heaven and earth were created, including all spiritual powers, and all hold together in him; his power over and within all reality, in short, is absolute (1:15–17).
- In his resurrection/exaltation: he is the *archē* (the first/the beginning), the firstborn from the dead (*prōtotokos ek tōn nekrōn*), so that he might be "first/preeminent" in all things (*en pasin autos prōteuōn*) (1:18).
- In his saving activity: through him all things were reconciled (*apokatallaxai*) to God (*eis auton*), both on earth and in heaven, since he brought about peace through the blood of his cross (*eirēnopoiēsas dia tou haimatos tou staurou autou*) (1:20).[19]
- In his life-giving presence in the church: he himself is the head of the body that is the church (*kai autos estin hē kephalē tou sōmatos tēs ekklēsias*, 1:18). The implication? When baptized into the *ekklēsia*, one is organically connected to the *kephalē*, in whom all the "fullness of divinity dwells" (2:9, author's translation).

The mystery that is "Christ among them," then, is not a trivial statement concerning the extent of the Pauline missionary outreach among gentile populations. It states in the shortest possible way that the gentile Colossians have, by their baptism into the Christian community, been given the gift of the full divine presence and power. There is no need to seek further. There is no need to add on other initiations and further status markers. If they think so, they have missed the point. What they need to do is to stay within this mystery as they have learned it, to dig deeper, to understand it more fully, and above all, not to be deceived and deluded by those who do not grasp that they have already been grasped by the only power that counts.

19. The explicit use of diplomatic language is picked up immediately by its application to the Colossians in 1:21: they were alienated but are now reconciled.

The Metaphors of Christian Maturity

Paul's explication of the *mystērion* makes clear that it does not consist, as do the cults familiar to the Phrygian gentiles, in a ritual that bears with it an arcane lore and a set of ritual demands. The *mystērion*, rather, is the revelation of God's utterly changing their existence through the death and resurrection of Jesus. Baptism is a ritual initiation, to be sure, but it is much more; baptism incorporates an individual into this inconceivable reality of the fullness of God "dwelling bodily" in the one who shed his blood on the cross to reconcile humans, and into the body of believers, which is, in truth, the body whose head is Christ, the very image of the unseen God (Col 1:15). There is no "going further" than such a "qualification" (*hikanōsis*, 1:12) gifted them (1:6) by God.

Paul's rhetorical task in this letter, as I have already suggested, is to persuade his readers not to allow agitators to "judge" (*krinein*, 2:16) or "disqualify" (*katabrabeuein*, 2:18) them[20] because they do not follow them in the pursuit of circumcision and the law, or asceticism, or mystical visions, but to stay firm in the "word of truth" (*logos tēs alētheias*) just as they have learned it from their founder, Epaphras (1:5, 7). Paul's persuasion is strengthened by the varied and pointed metaphors he uses in making it. At least six metaphorical fields are employed—not to express the act of salvation but to shape the imagination of the Colossians concerning what they have been given and concerning the way in which their gift from God should be directed.

Stability

Immediately after telling the Colossians of what God has done to reconcile them to himself, Paul adds a condition, "provided that you persevere [*epimenete*] in the faith, firmly grounded [*tethemeliōmenoi*], stable [*hedraioi*], and not shifting [*metakinoumenoi*][21] from the hope of the gospel

---

20. The verbs of *hikanoun* (see 2 Cor 3:6), *krinein*, and *katabrabeuein* in combination evoke an athletic context, in which one is qualified, judged, or disqualified (the *brabeus* was the judge at the games; see Plato, *Laws* 949A).

21. They are not to be "moved" because they have already definitively been "moved" (*metestēsen*) by God from the power of darkness to the kingdom of God's Son (Col 1:13). "To be grounded" is to have a foundation laid; the metaphor is architectural (see Xenophon, *Cyropaedia* 7.5.11); similarly, *hedraios* is used for "sitting" or

which you heard" (Col 1:23).²² Paul states in 2:5 that he rejoices in the "good order [*taxin*] and firmness [*stereōma*]" of their faith in Christ.²³ The images of agricultural and architectural stability are expanded as Paul continues: "As you received Christ Jesus the Lord, walk in him, rooted in him [*errizomenoi*] and built upon [*epoikodomoumenoi*] him and established [*bebaioumenoi*] in the faith as you were taught" (2:6-7).²⁴ The metaphors are, to be sure, mixed, but they effectively make their point: the Colossians are to hold fast and dig deep.

True and False

The reason for the Colossians' standing firm is not mere stubbornness. Paul says they have received "the word of truth" that is the good news (Col 1:5) and "the gift of God in truth" (1:6, author's translation) from Epaphras, their founder. The "advancements" offered by the agitators are based on a philosophy of empty error (*kenēs apatēs*, 2:8); they are not from God but are human traditions (*paradosin tōn anthrōpōn*) based on worldly practices (*stoicheia tou kosmou*). They are not based on Christ (*ou kata Christon*) in whom the fullness of the divine dwells bodily (*en autō katoikei pan to plērōma tēs theotētos sōmatikōs*, 2:9). They are the products if people with "puffed up" minds of flesh (2:18 RSV).

Paul uses two significant metaphors that point to this contrast between true and false. The first is the metaphor of wealth. I have noted earlier how Paul speaks of "the richness [*ploutos*] of glory of this mystery" in Col 1:27 (author's translation) and "the richness [*ploutos*] of the fully assured understanding, for the knowledge of the mystery of God, Christ, in whom are hidden [*apokryphoi*] all the treasures [*thēsauroi*] of

---

"being stationary" in contrast to moving (see Plato, *Republic* 407B; Plutarch, *Roman Questions* 102 [*Moralia* 288E).

22. We recall that Paul speaks of the *mystērion* in Col 1:27 as "Christ among/within you, the hope of glory."

23. Once more, the image of a solid building is evoked, with its straight lines (*taxis*) being "in good order" and its overall solidity; Aristotle, *Parts of Animals* 655a, uses the term *stereōma* for the skeleton that holds together the body.

24. The use of *epoikodomein* ("to build upon") clearly continues the architectural motif, but the term "established" (*bebaiomai*) draws more from the legal realm (see Epictetus, *Discourses* 2.18.32) where something needs "confirming" by evidence (cf. Rom 15:8; 1 Cor 1:6, 8; 2 Cor 1:21). And the notion of being "rooted in" (from *rhizoō*, meaning "to plant"; see Xenophon, *Oeconomicus* 19.1; Theophrastus, *Characters* 1.21), connects to Paul's agricultural metaphors in Col 1:6 and 1:10.

wisdom and knowledge" in 2:2. In contrast, the agitators are seeking to "defraud" them (*paralogizētai*, 2:4)—that is, take away their riches given by God—through their "plausible argments" (*pithanalogia*).[25] Even more impressive is Paul's plea that they should watch out so that there is no one who "captivates" them through empty error (2:8); the verb *sylagōgōn* is a hapax but is clearly derived from *sylan* ("to rob/deprive of money"; see 2 Cor 11:8). The translation of "carry you off as booty" would get at some of the financial metaphor here, but even better would be the contemporary idiom "don't get ripped off." The agitators want the Colossians to trade the pure gold of God's gift for the false coinage of religious status-seeking.

A second metaphor contrasting the true and false, or the real and the illusory, occurs in Col 2:17. Paul tells his reader not to allow anyone to pass judgment on them in matters of diet or the keeping of festivals: "these are shadows of things to come [*ha estin skia tōn mellontōn*]; the reality belongs to Christ [*to de sōma tou Christou*]." Although the NABRE rendering of *sōma* certainly captures the meaning Paul intends, it misses the metaphorical play between "shadow" and "body" in the Greek.[26] As the church, they are, in fact, the body that belongs to Christ (see 1:18, 24). Why should they be looking back at their own shadow, when they are "the things to come" that earlier religious practices intimated?

Life and Growth

The real inadequacy of the agitator's program lies in the fact that the add-ons they advocate do not fundamentally change persons; they simply represent religious variations on the theme of human striving, adding new status markers without fundamental alteration of the impulses of the flesh. Paul declares that "they have a semblance of wisdom in rigor of devotion and self-abasement and severity to the body," but "they are of no value against gratification of the flesh" (Col 2:23). By elevating some over others, by judging and disqualifying some on the basis of individ-

25. The financial associations of *paralogizein* cannot be missed; see Aristotle, *Rhetoric* 1374b; Demosthenes, *Orations* 27.29, 41.30; LXX Gen 31:41. While *pithanalogia* can be used in a neutral sense (see Plato, *Theaetetus* 162C), the combination with *paralogizein* demands understanding it negatively: the agitators are deceiving through the arguments they offer.

26. The present-day reader may be reminded of Plato's allegory of the cave (*Republic* 514A–520A), but it is doubtful Paul consciously made such an allusion.

ual effort, they reveal the true nature of the "flesh" as competition and rivalry. They dance to the *skia* (shadow) rather than cling to the *sōma* (body) that is Christ (2:17).

Continuing to develop the metaphor of Christ and the church as the head and the body, Paul declares that the agitators "do not grasp" or "hold on to" (*ou kratōn*) the source of life for the entire body—not just one individual but the entire community—who is Christ, the head (*kephalē*, Col 2:19; see 1:18). Paul therefore emphasizes that "the entire body" (*pan to sōma*) that is the church "grows the growth" (*auxei tēn auxēsin*) that is "of or from God" (*tou theou*)—my translation throughout here—precisely because "it is supplied and held together through its ligaments and joints"[27] from the head (*ex hou = ek kephalēs = ek Christou = ek tou theou*).[28] Although the idea of "head" and "body" as applied to the cosmos is found in Philo and some few other ancient writings, the application in those cases seems to be to the mental direction provided by the reason that orders or organizes the world.[29] In the case of Paul, however, the notion of the head as the supplier of life itself seems unavoidable, given the conclusion of the sentence, "grows with the growth that comes from God."[30]

Paul also twice uses an agricultural metaphor for the way to the Colossian church's maturity. In the thanksgiving period of 1:3–8, he speaks of the Colossians' having already heard "the word of truth, the gospel,

27. Paul's imagery and diction strongly resemble that used in Eph 4:16, but the passages are by no means identical. The verb *epichorēgein* means to fund or provide for another at one's own expense (see Dionysius of Halicarnassus, *Roman Antiquities* 1.42, 10.54; Diogenes Laertius, *Lives of Eminent Philosophers* 5.67; see also God supplying "seed" in 2 Cor 9:10 and "spirit" in Gal 3:5). For *haphē* as ligament or, more precisely, the touching points of the body, see Aristotle, *On Generation and Corruption* 326b and 327a; for *syndesmoi* as joints, see Aristotle, *Parts of Animals* 642a, and Euripides, *Hippolytus* 199.

28. This implied *sorites* is entirely my own; it has the intention of showing the logical connections Paul is drawing.

29. See Philo, *On Dreams* 1.128; *Questions on Exodus* 2.68, 2.117; *On the Special Laws* 3.184; *Life of Moses* 2.117–35. For other ancient sources, see Lohse, *Colossians and Philemon*.

30. Given the position I have taken throughout this work concerning the authorship of the canonical collection, I do not find it helpful to stress the distinction between the use of *sōma* in Rom 12:4–5 and 1 Cor 12:12–27 and the use here and in Eph 1:23 and 4:16. Metaphors are not theological propositions, even though, as I have argued vigorously elsewhere, this particular metaphor is much more than a verbal ornamentation or rhetorical trope. It comes closer, indeed, to being a symbol in the proper sense.

that has come to you. Just as in the whole world [*en panti tō kosmō*] it is bearing fruit and growing [*karpophoroumenon kai auxonomenon*], so also among you [*kathōs kai en hymin*]." The term "growing" is the same that Paul uses when speaking of the body joined to the head in 2:19, but he adds here "bearing fruit," which connects more closely to the image of "being rooted" in 2:7. Then, very shortly after this statement, he repeats that he prays that they "live in a manner worthy of the Lord [*peripatē-sai axiōs tou kyriou*], so as to be fully pleasing [*eis pasan areskeian*], in every good work bearing fruit and growing [*karpophorountes kai aux-anomenoi*] in the knowledge of God [*tē epignōsei tou theou*]" (1:10).[31] As with the metaphor of the head and the body, Paul sees the Colossians as reaching his desired condition of maturity (*teleios* in 1:28 and 4:12) not through the addition of further religious practices but through a deepening insight "in all wisdom and spiritual understanding" (*en pasē sophia kai synesei pneumatikē*, 1:9) into the *mystērion* that has been given them in Christ. Such insight, we are at once reminded, is not simply intellectual but involves the doing of "every good work" (1:10), as we shall see more clearly as Paul develops the existential and moral implications of baptism, their initiation into that mystery.

Mystery and Metaphor in Baptism

The topic of baptism is at once the key experience on which Paul builds his argument to the Colossians concerning the *mystērion* that is Christ "within/among" them and the topic that is most challenging for the analysis of Paul's language. In other places, I have been able to make a fairly firm distinction between Paul's use of "mystery," which has as its content, on one side, the work that God's Son Jesus—the very image of the unseen God—has done to reconcile them to God through his death on the cross and, on the other side, a set of metaphors that Paul employs in his effort to persuade the Colossian believers to stay firm to the "word of truth" that is the good news concerning Christ's work and to resist the

---

31. Note that Paul spoke of their *epignōsis* of God's will in 1:9 and will speak again of their *epignōsis* of the mystery of God in 2:2, and, climactically in 3:10, of the new person who is made new for the purpose of *epignōsis* according to the image of the one creating him/her. The NABRE translation of "knowledge," therefore, is, I think, too general; Paul means by *epignōsis* here something closer to the "recognition" or "insight" of which he speaks in Rom 1:28; 3:20; 10:2; Eph 1:17; 4:13; Phil 1:9; 1 Tim 2:4; 2 Tim 2:25; 3:7; Titus 1:1.

false enticements of the agitators. But already, in the analysis of Paul's language about the head and the body with reference to Christ and the church, I suggested that the designation of metaphor was perhaps too weak, and that Paul may have thought of the church as "Christ's body" in stronger, symbolic, terms: the "body" of believers actually participated in Christ, or had Christ "within" it, in a manner than went beyond any verbal expression.

The problem of categorization becomes worse when we approach the extensive section of Colossians, stretching from 2:11 to 3:17, that speaks of baptism directly or indirectly. Without question, this is one of the most important pieces of evidence for the practice and understanding of baptism within the canonical Pauline letters.[32] It is certainly one of the most difficult to disentangle. Some have found in the supposed discrepancies between the discussion of baptism in Rom 6:1–11 and Col 2:11–3:17—especially in Col 3:1–3—a reason to challenge the Pauline authorship of this letter. But a quick comparison of the two passages makes it clear that they have much more in common than not:

- Both letters address readers whom Paul has not converted or even met. He must rely, therefore, on shared traditions within the Christian movement.
- In both passages, Paul speaks of a ritual immersion (baptism) that initiates not only into the community but "into Christ" in such fashion that the one baptized is connected existentially to the death and resurrection of Christ.
- In both passages, the effect of the ritual is a real change in the believer: they have "died" to their past sin and are "alive" or "raised to" a new form of existence.
- In both passages, baptism contains a moral imperative to think and act in a new manner, consistent with the transformation they have undergone. "Newness of life" (Rom 6:4) demands a new manner of living in the world.

With that ground cleared, we can look more closely at the specific language of Colossians. Paul begins speaking of baptism in 2:12 immediately after warning against the agitators and assuring his readers that "the fullness of the divinity" dwells in Christ (2:9) and that they themselves

32. See also Rom 6:1–11; 1 Cor 1:13–17; 10:2; 12:13; 15:29; Gal 3:27; Eph 4:5; Titus 3:5–7.

are "filled up in him" (*en autō peplērōmenoi*, 2:10, author's translations). He begins by speaking of baptism as a circumcision that they have undergone, a circumcision not done by hand, a "circumcision of Christ" (*peritomē tou Christou*, 2:11). The choice of this phrasing is unparalleled in Paul,[33] and in all probability it is due to the offer of circumcision by the agitators as an advance in perfection beyond baptism.

Paul uses this language to assert that what they offer, his readers already have in a preeminent degree through their experience of baptism. Not only is this "circumcision of Christ" one that is "not done with hands"—that is, not a literal excision of a male foreskin—but it accomplishes a profound change in being, which had never been claimed for the ritual of initiation into Judaism: they have "stripped off the body of the flesh" (Col 2:11, author's translation).[34] This change in them has come about because by baptism they have somehow been incorporated (I use the term advisedly) into the death and resurrection of Jesus: "You were buried with him in baptism, in which you were also raised with him through faith in the power of God who raised him from the dead.[35] And even when you were dead in transgressions and the uncircumcision of your flesh [*akrobystia tēs sarkos hymōn*],[36] he brought you to life along with him, having forgiven us all our transgressions" (2:12–13).

This passage reveals the complexity of Paul's figural language and the difficulty of its definition. I am convinced that whereas "circumcision" here is properly a metaphor, for example, the language of death and rising with Christ—while clearly not literal or, better, material in the strict sense—corresponds, for Paul, to a reality that is more than linguistic: the believers have truly been changed through the mystery of Christ "within/among them."

In a dramatic turn, Paul now connects the experience of baptism to the event of Christ's saving act, into which baptism has inserted believ-

33. The closest is Phil 3:3, where Paul declares, "We are the circumcision, we who worship through the Spirit of God," but this is not a direct reference to baptism.

34. We shall see the language of "taking off" and "putting on" again in 3:8–12. The metaphor of clothing and unclothing for gaining and rejecting of a certain character, or identity, is in all probability linked to the ritual of baptism itself; see Lohse, *Colossians*, 141.

35. Cf. 1 Cor 6:14, "God raised the Lord and will also raise us by his power," and 1 Thess 4:14; 5:10.

36. With this allusion to "uncircumcision" Paul refers not only to their gentile status but to their alienation from God prior to the saving work of Christ (see Col 1:22–23); as elsewhere in Paul, "flesh" is not only a foreskin but a moral disposition (see esp. Gal 5:16–26).

ers. He picks up from the metaphor of "circumcision" the entailments of initiation into the law of Moses: "obliterating the bond [*cheirographon*] against us, with its legal claims [*tois dogmasin*], which was opposed to us, he also removed it from our midst, nailing it to the cross [*prosēlōsas auto tō staurō*]; despoiling [*apekdysamenos*] the principalities and powers [see Col 1:16], he made a public spectacle of them, leading them away in triumph by it" (Col 2:14–15).[37] Baptism has displaced circumcision because Christ's death and exaltation have displaced the absolute claims of all forms of heteronomous, written norms, including those of the law of Moses.

Thus, when Paul encourages the Colossians in 2:16 not to let others disqualify them on the basis of "food and drink or with a regard to a festival or a new moon or sabbath" it is because these things are but a "shadow of things to come," whereas Christ is the "reality" ("body," *sōma*, 2:17); similarly, he asks them in 2:20 (adapted), "If you have died with Christ to the elemental principles of the world [*stoicheia tou kosmou*], why do you submit to regulations [*dogmatizesthe*] as if you were still living in the world?" Instructions of any sort, including those of the Mosaic law, do not pertain to those who have, with Christ, "died" to all heteronomous norms.[38] Paul insists that instructions concerning what to handle or what to touch or what to taste (2:21) are, even if derived from Torah, only human precepts and teachings that will perish (2:22); they appear to be holy and humble, but they do nothing to curb the "gratification of the flesh" (2:23). In contrast, the baptism that the Colossians have already experienced "stripped off the body of flesh [*sōma tēs sarkos*]" that had been their "uncircumcision" because of sin (2:11–13). As in Paul's argument to the Galatian churches, he regards the desire for more as a failure to grasp the gift that has already been given.[39]

Paul now turns to the positive exhortation of the Colossian believers. Corresponding to the "if you died with Christ" in 2:20 is the "if then you

---

37. For the language of a political triumphal march in which captives are displayed in procession, cf. 1 Cor 4:9; 2 Cor 2:14. The Greek at the end of the sentence is difficult: *thriambeusas autous en autō* can be translated, as in the NABRE above, as "leading them away in triumph by it," with *en autō* referring to the cross. But I think the antecedent is probably "Christ" in 2:11, in which case the phrase *en autō* would be read "in/through him."

38. As in Gal 4:9, I think the *stoicheia* do not refer to cosmic powers but to codes of conduct, a meaning much closer to the dominant usage in Greek. The verb *dogmatizein* echoes the *dogmasin* in Col 2:14.

39. See esp. Gal 5:1–6 and my treatment in chap. 11, pp. 209–29.

were raised with Christ" in 3:3: their new identity requires of them that they "seek what is above [*ta anō*], where Christ is seated at the right hand of God" (3:1).[40] Their lives are no longer to be measured by human standards, even, or especially, those claiming religious credentials. Their existence is rather one that is to follow the pattern of God's work in the death and exaltation of Christ. If their very existence has been transformed, so must also be their moral dispositions, as Paul's next sentence makes plain: "Think [*phroneite*] of what is above [*ta anō*], not of what is on earth [*mē ta epi tēs gēs*]" (3:2). As we have seen through examination of Paul's language employing *phronein* elsewhere, what he calls for is an epistemic transformation; the measure for the Colossians' present and future moral practice must not be the competitive urge of the flesh that leads to religious competitiveness but instead the pattern of death and exaltation revealed through the *mystērion* that is Christ within/among them.

This by no means implies that the Colossians already enjoy the condition "above" that belongs to Christ. He is their "hope of glory" (*elpis tēs doxēs*, 1:27), but although they are, through baptism, "in Christ" (*en Christō*, see 2:11), they are not yet in the eschatological condition of being "with Christ" (*syn Christō*), even though their dispositions and actions in the present prepare for that reality. Paul says, "For you have died, and your life is hidden with Christ in God. When Christ your life appears, then you too will appear with him in glory" (3:3-4). Paul here performs a brilliant reversal on the theme of the hidden and manifest. The *mystērion* that is Christ was formerly hidden but has now been made known (1:26-27); yet the mystery is not totally transparent: "in [him] are hidden all the treasures of wisdom and knowledge" (2:3). Those who belong to Christ, in turn, are now hidden but will be revealed "in glory" when Christ himself fully appears. It is in this time of present hiddenness that the ongoing transformation of the Colossians is to occur.

Paul begins his moral instructions with a continuation of the death/life pattern: they are to "put to death, then [*nekrōsate oun*], the parts of you that are earthly [*ta melē ta epi tēs gēs*]:[41] immorality, impurity, passion, evil desire, and the greed that is idolatry" (Col 3:5), such as

---

40. For "being at the right hand of God" (from Ps 110:1) as shorthand for Christ's exaltation elsewhere in the New Testament, see Matt 26:24; Mark 12:36; 14:62; Luke 20:42; 22:69; Acts 2:33-34; 5:31; 7:55-56; Heb 1:3, 13; 3:1; 10:12; 12:2; 1 Pet 3:22; Rev 5:1, 7, and in Paul, see Rom 8:34; Eph 1:20; and (implied) 1 Cor 15:25-27.

41. The *ta epi tēs gēs* here corresponds to the *ta epi tēs gēs* of 3:5. The contrast between "above" and "on the earth" is parallel to the lower/higher in the pattern of death and resurrection. Something has to die for there to be new life.

formerly characterized them when they were among the children of disobedience (3:6–7) rather than among the holy ones in the light (1:12). They are to put all these forms of immorality aside (*apothesthe*, 3:8), "since you have taken off the old self with its practices" (*apekdysamenoi ton palaion anthrōpon syn tais praxesin autou*, 3:9). The baptismal action of putting off clothing, entering the water naked, and then being clothed with new clothing is understood again as more than a physical gesture. It represents, as in 2:11, the transformation of the self: it is the "old person" (*palaion anthrōpon*) with all its practices that they have shed.[42]

Paul continues the metaphor: "and [you] have put on the new self [*kai endysamenoi ton neon*], which is being renewed [*ton anakainoumenon*],[43] into recognition [*eis epignōsin*],[44] according to the image of the one who has created it [*kat' eikona tou ktisantos auton*]" (3:10, author's translation).[45] This new person, notably, is one in which religious and ethnic differences are nullified in the unity found in Christ: "Here there is not Greek and Jew, circumcision and uncircumcision, barbarian, Scythian, slave, free; but Christ is all things and in all things" (3:11, adapted).[46] The implication is clear enough: if they have been "clothed" in baptism with the new self that follows the image of Christ its maker, then they exist in a "body" in which circumcision and uncircumcision are no longer religious status markers but the occasion for a diverse and unified church, where not competition but mutual care is the norm.

Just as the existential condition of "having died" called for the moral imperative of putting to death hostile attitudes, and just as the existential

42. For Paul's metaphorical use of clothing elsewhere, see Rom 13:12, 14; 1 Cor 15:53–54; 2 Cor 5:3–4; Gal 3:27; Eph 4:24; 6:11, 14; 1 Thess 5:3.

43. See the use of *anakainōsis* in Rom 12:2 for the transformation of the mind, and in Titus 3:5 for the experience of baptism. Paul also speaks of the "inner self" (*ho esō hēmōn*) as being renewed (*anakainoutai*) day by day (2 Cor 4:16).

44. The NABRE translation has "for knowledge," but I think that misses the distinctive use of *epignōsis* as "recognition" in Colossians (see 1:9, 10; 2:2) and in other Pauline letters (Rom 1:28; 3:20; 10:2; Eph 1:17; 4:13; Phil 1:9; 1 Tim 2:4; 2 Tim 2:25; 3:7; Titus 1:1; Phlm 6).

45. Paul picks up here from Col 1:15; for Christ as the image of God elsewhere in Paul, see Rom 8:29; 1 Cor 15:49; 2 Cor 3:18; 4:4. On the use more broadly, see Eltester, *Eikon im Neuen Testament*; Jervell, *Imago Dei*; Goranson Jacob, *Image of His Son*.

46. This is the only occurrence of the term Scythian in the New Testament. For a discussion of the very lengthy discussion (all the way back to Herodotus) about the meaning, see Yamauchi, "Scythians—Who Were They?" Paul here leaves out "male and female." For the versions of "all in all" (*panta en pasin*), see 1 Cor 12:6; 15:28; Eph 1:23; Phil 4:12.

condition of "putting off" the old self called for a rejection of disruptive moral practices, so, as we have seen, does the existential condition of "rising with Christ" to new life require "seeking the things that are above" and "thinking what is above and not what is on earth." Likewise, "putting on" the new person bears with it the moral imperative of living as "God's chosen ones, holy and beloved" (Col 3:12). What qualities (and practices) of the new person are they to exhibit? They are to put on "heartfelt compassion, kindness, humility, gentleness, and patience, bearing with one another, and forgiving one another if anyone has a grievance against another. Just as Christ has forgiven you, so also should you [forgive each other]" (3:12–13 NABRE, adapted).[47] In a word, the new person "practices" in a manner completely the opposite of the hostile and aggressive and competitive "old person" (cf. 3:12 and 3:5–9).

To conclude his exhortation, Paul extends the baptismal metaphor of unclothing/clothing one step further but also returns to some of the metaphorical language he used in his warning against the agitators. Thus, the Colossians are to express their new identity through mutual love instead of competition: "And above all these, put on love, that is, the bond [*syndesmos*] of perfection [*teleitotētos*]" (3:14, adapted). The term *agapē* ("love") sums up all the qualities of mutual compassion and care that Paul has listed. We remember that Paul's goal is to "present everyone perfect [*teleios*] in Christ" (1:28), and love is the "bond" that holds together the body that is Christ's. The term echoes his startling statement in 2:19 that the agitators do not "[hold] closely to the head, from whom the whole body, supported and held together by its ligaments and bonds [*syndesmon*], achieves the growth that comes from God." Love for each other, Paul declares here, is the most important of such "bonds."

Earlier metaphorical language appears also in Col 3:15: "And let the peace of Christ [*eirēnē tou Christou*] control your hearts [*brabeuetō en tais kardiais hymōn*], the peace into which you were also called in one body." As throughout this exhortation, Paul's verbs and pronouns are plural: these are dispositions that are to be active among all the Colossian believers. Paul here deliberately echoes two earlier statements. The first is in 1:20, where Paul says that Christ made "peace by the blood of his cross."

---

47. The meaning of the Greek words is not difficult, but the syntax of the sentence is tricky: *endysasthe oun hōs eklektoi tou theou hagioi kai ēgapēmenoi splanchna oiktirmou chrēstotēta tapeinophrosynēn prautēta makrothymian anechomenoi allēlōn kai charizomenoi heautois ean tis pros tina echē momphēn kathōs kai ho kyrios echarisato hymin houtōs kai hymeis.* The issue, basically, is how to punctuate, and it is here that the NABRE and I diverge a bit.

The peace of Christ, then, is one that reconciles and forgives (1:22). It is the opposite of the hostility that generates competition for status. The second allusion is Paul's use of *brabeuetō*. The NABRE translates the imperative as "control," and that is possible, but perhaps better would be "act as discerner or judge" within all the hearts in the community, because the verb *brabeuein* has the sense of "act as an umpire," and in 2:16–18 Paul had told the Colossians not to let anyone "judge" (*krinein*) or "disqualify" (*katabrabeuetō*) them on the basis of human regulations and religious status markers. Instead, Paul wants their hearts to be ones that, like Christ on the cross, work for peace and reconciliation.

Conclusion

Paul's language in Colossians is dense, allusive, and demanding. I hope that examining more closely what precisely Paul means by the term *mystērion* and how he uses metaphors has served to exfoliate some of the "hidden treasure" of this letter. As all readers know, Paul turns from his exhortation concerning moral dispositions pertaining to the entire community to the attitudes appropriate for believers in diverse social relations: husbands and wives and children (3:18–21), and at much greater length—in all likelihood, as we have seen, because this letter accompanies the Letter to Philemon[48]—slaves and masters (3:22–4:1). But it is perhaps fitting to close this chapter with Paul's words immediately before those social instructions, words that remind his readers once more of the meaning of the *mystērion* as "Christ within/among you": "And be thankful. Let the word of Christ dwell [*enoikeitō*] in you richly [*plousiōs*], as in all wisdom you teach and admonish one another, singing psalms, hymns, and spiritual songs with gratitude in your hearts to God. And whatever you do, in word or in deed, do everything in the name of the Lord Jesus, giving thanks to God the Father through him" (3:15–17).

48. See vol. 1, chap. 10 ("Paul's Voice—Philemon").

Chapter 16

Doing the Truth in Love

From Eros to Agape

In this chapter I engage Paul's letter to the Ephesians as a way of think-ing about the difficult issues of sexuality, gender, and holiness (or Christian maturity). I have written on these issues a number of times before this. Most of what I have written, however, has been at the nor-mative level, asking what Christians should think about these issues for their own lives, in light of all of Scripture.[1] I do not avoid the normative question in this chapter, but I intend here to focus exclusively on Paul, and to demonstrate the sort of dialectical approach that proves most fruitful, when both history and theology are in play, when Paul and the rest of Scripture are in play, and when the role of the contemporary ex-perience of God is not only acknowledged but made a key factor in the process of thinking.

My effort is based on two convictions. The first is that the either/or approach of many present-day readers is deeply wrong. In this either/ or approach, one option is to take the scriptural texts both literally and normatively, without question: if Paul said it, and Paul's writings are Scripture, and Scripture is the Word of God, the debate is not only over but it cannot even be raised. No questions can be asked, only answers

---

1. The earliest ventures were in Johnson, *Decision Making in the Church*, 95–97, and its enlarged successor, *Scripture and Discernment*, 144–47, which were followed by a series of articles. See, e.g., Johnson, "Abortion, Sexuality, and Catholicism's Pub-lic Presence"; Heim, "Homosexuality, Marriage, and the Church"; Johnson, "Debate and Discernment"; "Disembodied 'Theology of the Body'"; "Biblical Foundations of Matrimony"; "Jesus and the Little Children"; "Scripture and Experience"; "Church and Transgender Identity." See also my review of *Speaking the Christian God* (by Kimel) and *She Who Is* (by Johnson), and my review of Hays's *Moral Vision of the New Testament* in "Why Scripture Isn't Enough," of Scola's *Nuptial Mystery* in "Body Beautiful," and of Farley's *Just Love* in "What's Justice Got to Do with It?"

provided. What applied to the ancient residents of Phrygia applies without remainder to the present-day inhabitants of Pittsburgh. The other option is simply to dismiss Paul's writing (or any other part of Scripture) if it does not agree with the experience of the good people of Paducah. If Paul does not confirm me, he condemns me. Once more, the conversation ceases; we need pay no attention to this ancient nattering Jew. To hell with the Corinthians, hurrah for the Californians! In opposition to the either/or approach, I insist on a dialectical reading, in which both ancient and contemporary voices are taken seriously, precisely because God speaks through both.

The second conviction is that the contemporary focus on sexuality and gender roles has lost sight of what is most important for Paul—and ought to be most important for us—which is not whether we are gay or straight, or whether we are male or female, but whether we are growing toward maturity in Christ. The real issue for Christian readers is holiness in matters of sex and gender, as in all other matters touching on the body and spirit.[2] The question of eros preoccupies us: how and with whom we do it, whether we are accepted or respected for the way God made us sexually. But the question that preoccupies Paul is not eros (the term never occurs) but agape, the distinctive form of mutual self-donation that defines Christian maturity. And it is on this point that Ephesians can instruct us. To get there, though, the steps of the dialectic need to be taken.

The Evidence in Paul on Sex and Gender[3]

As I showed in the first volume of this work,[4] the evidence for Paul's views in the canonical letters corresponds to those held by other Jews (and many Greco-Roman moralists) in the first century. Sexual continence is assumed for those believers who, through call or through circumstance, are single (1 Cor 7:8–40).[5] Sexual excess of any kind, as expressed by

2. See F. Watson, *Agape, Eros, Gender*; Gench, *Encountering God*.

3. For useful discussions on the historical realities, see Osiek and MacDonald, *A Woman's Place*; M. MacDonald, *Power of Children*; Hylen, *Women in the New Testament World*.

4. See vol. 1, chap. 11.

5. Paul's statement in 1 Cor 7:7, "I wish everyone to be as I am, but each has a particular gift from God, one of one kind and one of another," makes clear that his singleness is one of call or choice (see also 1 Cor 9:5–6). Cf. Epictetus's argument that

licentiousness, lust, or suggestive speech, is forbidden to believers (Gal 5:19–21; Col 3:8; Eph 4:19, 22; 5:4; Titus 3:3; 2 Tim 3:3–4). Paul singles out incest (1 Cor 5:5:1–5) and consorting with prostitutes (1 Cor 6:12–20) as forms of *porneia* ("sexual immorality") that are directly harmful to the "body" that is the temple of the living God. As a Jewish moralist, Paul similarly regards male-male and female-female sexual activity as a matter of vice, whether he mentions it passingly in a vice list (1 Cor 6:9; 1 Tim 1:10) or states it explicitly as a distortion of "natural" human relations that results from idolatry (Rom 1:24–29).[6] The evidence suggests that Paul was neither obsessed by the topic of sex[7] nor exceptional among religiously and morally committed persons of the first century.

The evidence of the letters also supports the view that Paul was, for the most part, conventional in his views of gender. He accepted without question the clear distinction between male and female made by Scripture (Gen 1:26), and shared the androcentric bias that made the male, in the order of the first creation, superior to the female in being (1 Cor 11:3, 7–8; 1 Tim 2:13) and ability (2 Cor 11:3; 1 Tim 2:14–15). He subscribed to the conventional complementary view of household roles that placed men at the head of the household, with women, children, and slaves all obedient to the male paterfamilias (Rom 7:1–3; Col 3:18–4:1; Eph 5:21–33; 1 Tim 5:3–16; Titus 2:3–5).[8] Paul's androcentric bias—and concern for good order in the household—probably accounts for the one genuinely sexist remark in his letters (2 Tim 3:6–7).[9]

In other ways, however, Paul was unusual for his recognition of female equality with males in the new creation. He qualifies his comments

---

the true Cynic philosopher must be celibate in order to devote himself totally to the call to be God's scout among humans (*Discourses* 3.2). Unless otherwise indicated, Scripture quotations in this chapter are from the NABRE.

6. As has been observed many times, Paul's screed against the consequences of denying God's presence in the world does not climax in his mention of same-sex relations but in his list of antisocial (not sexual) vices in Rom 1:29–32 and, above all, in the sin of judging others (2:1–11).

7. The contrast with the Hellenistic-Jewish tractate *The Sentences of Pseudo-Phocylides* is both impressive and illuminating.

8. The complementary view of gender roles is classically defined by Aristotle's contemporary Xenophon in his *On Household Management* (*Oeconomicus*).

9. Speaking of false teachers, he says that some of them "slip into homes and make captives of women weighed down by sins, led by various desires, always trying to learn but never able to reach a knowledge of the truth." The sad condition of women deprived of the opportunity to have an education makes this a canny sociological observation, but the designation of them as "little women" (*gynaikaria*) is slighting.

about women deriving from men in 1 Cor 11 by adding, "Woman is not independent of man or man of woman in the Lord. For just as woman came from man, so man is born of woman; but all things are from God" (11:11–12). In his letter to the Galatians, where the ritual of male circumcision is being advocated as a status advancement by agitators, Paul insists that through baptism into Christ, "there is neither Jew nor Greek, there is neither slave nor free person, there is no male and female; for you are all one in Christ Jesus" (Gal 3:28). Women have equal status in the church with men, and a major reason circumcision is to be resisted is that it creates a status marker available only to males.[10] By affirming the positive role "in the Lord" for virgins and widows (1 Cor 7:8–40), Paul implicitly rejected defining women exclusively through their biological roles,[11] and his recognition of the way women were called by God to active roles in the mission field, as well as in household churches, is consistent with the recognition of basic gender equality in the Lord.[12]

Not surprisingly, this very recognition—and the active roles played by such urban and mobile women—created tension within the faith assemblies that held their meetings in patriarchal households, where traditional gender roles would be assumed; thus the conflicted argument concerning the veiling of women prophets in 1 Cor 11:2–16, the forbidding of a teaching role to women in the assembly (1 Cor 14:33–36; 1 Tim 2:11–14), and the nervousness about women "saying what they should not" (NRSV) when they go alone from household to household (1 Tim 5:3–16). Overall, however, Paul has the most "liberated" view of women among ancient male writers.[13]

---

10. It is noteworthy that Paul's other "unification" statements concerning baptism lack the "male/female" element (see 1 Cor 12:13; Col 3:11).

11. The statement in 1 Tim 2:15, "She will be saved through motherhood [*teknogonias*], provided women persevere in faith and love and holiness, with self-control," is notoriously difficult; for discussion, see Johnson, *First and Second Letters to Timothy*.

12. Thus, though needing to be veiled, women do prophesy and pray in the assembly (1 Cor 11:5); Junia is an apostle before Paul (Rom 16:7), while Phoebe is Paul's patron and traveling fundraiser (Rom 16:1). Mary, Tryphaena and Tryphosa, Julia, and Priscilla (Rom 16:3, 6, 12, 15; 1 Cor 16:19) are all named as parts of Paul's missionary team. Women who are prominent in household churches include Chloe (1 Cor 1:11), Euodia and Syntyche (Phil 4:2), Apphia (Phlm 2), and Nympha (Col 4:15).

13. The closest comparison is the Stoic philosopher Musonius Rufus, who argued for the intellectual and moral equality of women and that they should be taught philosophy just as men are, but who also concluded that such an education was to make them better household managers (see *That Women Too Should Study Philosophy*).

Sex and Gender Today

As we approach Paul from the perspective of the contemporary world, it is good to remember two facts. The first is that Paul's views not only remained standard within worldwide Christianity until the nineteenth century but also remain unexceptional for significant portions of Christianity in the twenty-first century.[14] Modernity, in a word, is not only recent; it is also local and partial. The "we" who struggle with Pauline perspectives are located within a time and place that is unique in world history. This observation is not meant to diminish, much less dismiss, the concerns that "we" have, only to recognize that what "we" regard as obviously objectionable in Paul's letters did not and does not seem so for readers in the past two millennia and for many (if not most) readers today.

The second fact is that the social realities connecting to sex and gender in the First World today are connected to remarkable changes in science and technology. Most dramatic is the development of reliable methods of birth control, which has allowed a certain freedom of choice regarding procreation. Simultaneously, the inexpensive availability of "labor-saving" machines liberated women from the labor-intensive cycle of housework that once made the term "homemaker" both onerous and honorable,[15] and challenged the ancient ideal of complementary gender roles that had women bearing children and managing the household while men fought wars and provided financial security.

Technology has given the most ordinary contemporary women what slavery gave the wealthiest women in antiquity—the ability to enter the public realm and to be defined by character and ability rather than biological function. Contemporary women in the public realm are, indeed, continuous with the generations of celibate women (many of them religious) who taught, nursed, and effected social change, precisely because they were not bound by the demands of family.[16] In some academic cir-

14. The present ecclesial divisions between so-called developed and developing nations (or continents) over sexual issues (especially homosexuality and women's ministry) are connected to the diverse social conditions in the respective areas. I am thinking specifically of the tensions between North American and African communities, both Catholic and Protestant.

15. Never more effectively evoked or argued than in the pioneering feminist work by Friedan, *The Feminine Mystique*.

16. A good sense of how deeply entrenched were convictions concerning women's inadequacy, even in the most enlightened Europe of the nineteenth century, is

cles, it has become fashionable to reduce gender itself to a "social construct" (and thus infinitely malleable), but that view remains disputed by other academics who insist on the biological basis for gender (and gender roles). But with respect to women's full equality with men in rights and in capacity, the larger world mostly agrees that where women can go, they should.[17]

The development of biology and psychology, as well as the weight of human experience in many cultures, has also altered contemporary First World views of sexuality. Same-sex erotic attraction and practice, which for the ancients was at best a matter of preference and at worst (as among Jews) a freely chosen vice, has increasingly come to be regarded as a genetically based predisposition that can be resisted but is otherwise as "natural" as heterosexual attraction and practice. Awareness of the centuries of negative labeling and of oppression, often violent oppression, of those who were sexually "different" has also led many present-day believers to see being gay or lesbian as a simple fact of a person's life rather than a definition of their essence or a freely chosen vice.[18] For Paul, in contrast, the notion of a same-sex "orientation" would be entirely foreign. He had in mind the sort of bisexual actions common among many gentile males in his day; not a few Greek and Roman males had wives and children while also having male lovers.[19]

How do the changed conditions and perspectives affect the contemporary reading of Paul? Although biblical literalists—and there are many throughout the world—insist that Paul's first-century androcentric views of male and female ought still to prevail, there is also widespread willingness to take the developments in science and in experience as also revelatory of God's work in the world, and therefore also a willingness to take Paul's time-conditioned words as authoritative but not normative. That is, they are to be taken seriously, but they are not necessarily probative for contemporary outlook and practice.

Such a position is helped by three elements of Paul that already provide an antecedent to change. The first is Paul's insistence in Gal 3:28, in

---

provided by Baird, *Victoria the Queen*. For the active roles of women in the church, see e.g., Weaver, *New Catholic Women*.

17. In some places, this is so much the case that some worry about the social disparagement of men—who continue to perform the most physically onerous and dangerous occupations in society, such as military combat, firefighting, policing, construction, and mining, without commensurate concern for their well-being.

18. See Foucault, *History of Sexuality*, esp. vol. 1; Jordan, *Invention of Sodomy*.

19. Cantarella, *Bisexuality in the Ancient World*.

the face of those arguing for male circumcision as a necessary step to full maturity, that in Christ "male and female" are not categories that affect equality "in Christ." The second is Paul's frank admission in 1 Cor 11:2–16 that the veiling of women while prophesying and praying is a "custom in all the churches" (2:16). But if it is a custom rather than a theological principle (and Paul defeats himself in trying to find such a principle), then it can be changed. And it is significant that Paul does not in the least challenge the fact that women are gifted by God to pray and prophesy in the public assembly.[20] The third is Paul's own recognition of singleness (of both genders) in the service of the Lord (1 Cor 7:8–40) and his recognition of women leaders in his own missionary endeavor. There is a sound basis in Paul's words and practice to support the advancement of women's roles within the Christian community as much as in society at large.[21]

The case of Paul's condemnation of homoeroticism is much more difficult. It must be said, first, that contemporary preoccupation with practices that affect a relatively small percentage of the population appears more and more like a sort of scapegoating that enables both society and the church to avoid dealing with the sexual issues affecting society and the church as a whole: this is an age in which prostitution (and its accompanying human trafficking), pornography, promiscuity, sexual predation (even by ministers) and violence (including rape and assault), and every sort of lurid licentiousness can be found on public display as well as in private practice. Those who identify themselves with what has come to be called the LGBTQ (lesbian, gay, bisexual, transgender, queer) community are right to name such scapegoating for what it is: a deflection from the truly serious diseases infecting the entire body of Christ.[22]

That said, the statements on same-sex practice in Leviticus and Paul

---

20. See, e.g., Wire, *Corinthian Women Prophets*.

21. I hope it is clear that I emphatically do not associate myself with the views on gender current in both Catholic and Protestant circles that use Gen 1–2 and Eph 5 to treat the distinction between male and female in essentialist ways, with correspondingly reactionary social sequelae. The main influence here is Barth, *Church Dogmatics*, vol. III.4, followed (on the Catholic side) by Balthasar, *Theo-Drama*, esp. vols. 2 and 3; John Paul II, *Man and Woman*; and Scola, *Nuptial Mystery*; and (on the Protestant side) by Grenz, "Theological Foundations." For a full examination, see DeFranza, *Sex Difference in Christian Theology*.

22. It is indeed something of an elephant in the room when Christian males gather to condemn same-sex eroticism, when everyone knows, but dare not say, that by far the greater part of the sexual pandemic in First World countries is attributable to self-proclaimed Christian males. Pornography, prostitution, and predatory sexual behavior are not the signature of lesbians. For the difficulties of speaking coherently

represent—if we exclude the ambiguous story of David and Jonathan—
the sum total of scriptural testimony, and it is entirely negative.[23] Unlike
the case of Paul's language with regard to gender, contemporary readers
find no wiggle room in the canonical letters to support any positive valuation of homoeroticism. From the perspective of Paul the Jew, same-sex
practice appeared to be a freely chosen vice, found only among gentiles
and attributed entirely to the effects of idolatry. At the exegetical level,
no relief is to be found by appealing to the subtle nuances of terms; Paul
knew what he saw, and did not like it, and said so. Done and done. For
biblical literalists, this means that there can be no debate, for the explicit propositions in any part of Scripture are, for them, of absolute
and enduring normativity. To accept homosexuality means, in their
eyes, to reject Scripture. The real issue for many, indeed, is not really
the sexual practice but the authority of Scripture. This is the line in the
sand that must be drawn if the forces of secularity are not to take over
Christianity altogether.

Such a position, however, fails to take into account another powerful
authority, this one equally from God—namely, the evidence offered by
the countless persons who have witnessed to the truth that same-sex attraction is not a vice that they have chosen but is a fact of their existence
apart from their willful choice; it is, indeed, the truth of how they have
been created by God.[24] And apart from that narrow sliver of the church
that pretends to live by the principle of *sola scriptura*—a principle that
is both logically incoherent and chronically broken in practice when it

---

about the issue of transgenderism, however, see esp. Brubaker, *Trans*; and for a theological position, see my essay, "The Church and Transgender Identity."

23. As everyone knows, the amount of literature generated by the issue of same-
sex love, above all in relation to Christianity, is virtually endless. The works of John
Boswell about historical attitudes and practices are informative but not always reliable; see *Christianity, Social Tolerance, and Homosexuality* and *Rediscovering Gay History*. For sober arguments on the side of accepting homosexuality within Christianity,
see Helminiak, *What the Bible Really Says about Homosexuality*, and Rogers, *Jesus, the
Bible, and Homosexuality*. For a careful but negative view, see Hays, *Moral Vision of
the New Testament*, and for a harsh negative view, see Gagnon, *Bible and Homosexual
Practice*. For advocates from either side, see Via and Gagnon, *Homosexuality and the
Bible*, and for an account of both sides from one who is a positive advocate, see Siker,
Homosexuality in the Church.

24. Please refer back to vol. 1, chap. 8 ("The Claims of Experience"), for a consideration of the compelling role played by such experience in the shaping of Paul's
own arguments.

suits its advocates[25]—the church universal recognizes the validity and importance of such testimony as providing guidance to the church, even when that experience stands in tension with customary verities concerning Scripture and tradition.

In fact, obedience to the living God in our age, as in every age, demands that faith respond to the truth being revealed through human experience.[26] In other places I have argued that in light of the overwhelming evidence that being gay or lesbian is not a vice that is chosen—as Scripture always assumed—but is a fact of one's creation by God, Christians are obliged, despite our reverence for Scripture, to stand against those texts that declare homosexuality to be only a vice and a sign of sin, and equally to resist those persons who, claiming to be defenders of Scripture, denounce those who are sexually oriented in a manner different than themselves.[27]

At the same time, however, and with equal vigor, I have held that standing against Scripture's explicit prohibitions does not in the least mean dismissing or disregarding Scripture altogether. Instead of attending only to the characterizations and commands found in Scripture concerning same-sex eros, I have called for attention to the narratives, above all in the book of Acts—but also by implication in the letters of Paul[28] — that provide examples of how the experience of the living God demanded from the people of old, as from us, a willingness to discover new meanings in texts through the careful discernment of experience. The primary example, to be sure, is the confession of Jesus as Lord, a confession that is based on the gift of the life-giving Spirit through him, yet stands in contrast to the explicit text of Scripture that declares one crucified as cursed by God (Deut 21:23; see Gal 3:13). A stance of "Scripture alone" disallows the confession of Jesus as the righteous one (Rom 1:17), whose resurrection as well as death was "according to the scripture."

An equally compelling example, found in the narrative of Acts 10–15, is the Spirit-led initiative to include faithful gentiles into full membership in God's people, without requiring of them circumcision or keeping the law of Moses. This decision was made explicitly and entirely on the basis of the narratives concerning the "signs and wonders" that God was doing

---

25. Stanley Hauerwas has been especially effective in showing how the demand of Jesus to turn the other cheek has effectively been suppressed by centuries of war-waging Christians; see *Unleashing the Scripture*.

26. See Johnson, *Faith's Freedom* and *Revelatory Body*.

27. See Johnson, *Scripture and Discernment*, and the essays cited in note 1 above.

28. See chap. 10 in this volume.

among gentile believers (Acts 14:27; 15:3–4) and the outpouring of the Holy Spirit on them, just as it had been on Jewish disciples in the beginning (Acts 10:44–48; see 11:15–18). More to the point I am making here, this decision went against the entire tenor of Scripture, which spoke of converts to Judaism only on the basis of circumcision. Yet, as James of Jerusalem noted, this decision, which apparently overturned all precedent, turned out to be, astonishingly and paradoxically, the fulfillment of Scripture's true intent (Acts 15:15–21).[29]

I have suggested, therefore, that the welcome of gay and lesbian Christians into full membership and participation in the life of the church was analogous to these early and pivotal decisions on the basis of the experience of the living God inscribed in the New Testament itself.[30] Such analogies provide full scriptural warrant for the church's welcome of those who are other than heterosexual.

Reaching that position, to be sure, does not exhaust the topic of our obedience to God in our sexual lives, or the topic of how Scripture might instruct us concerning our sexual lives. While holding to everything I have said to this point, both with respect to what God is disclosing in the lives of humans and with respect to the implications for our reading of Scripture, I propose pursuing further the implications of a thought experiment I suggested a few years ago to the Covenant Network of Presbyterians in a talk titled "Sexuality and the Holiness of the Church."[31]

I begin with Paul's programmatic statement in Gal 3:28 concerning all those who have received the Spirit of adoption as sons and are one in Christ, so that there is neither Jew nor Greek, slave nor free, male and female, and take it one bold but logical step further. We know that in this statement Paul takes all the important status markers of antiquity (ethnicity, social class, and gender) that divide humans in the world, and designates the church as the place where such distinctions are relativized by the transcendent reality of being one in Christ Jesus. Distinctions that once were decisive are now adiaphora—they do not matter. I add, by way of a thought experiment, a fourth distinction, "neither gay nor straight," in order to ask what might happen if we seriously leveled the playing field with regard to sexual orientation. How does sexual activity

29. See the close exegetical analysis in Johnson, *Scripture and Tradition*, 89–108, and *Acts of the Apostles*, 180–202 and 252–81.

30. See esp. Johnson, "Scripture and Experience."

31. The public presentation I made to the Covenant Network of Presbyterians on September 14, 2004, was transcribed and is available at https://covnetpres.org/2004 /11/06/sexuality-and-the-holiness-of-the-church/.

participate in the holiness of the church if we no longer make odious distinctions between humans who are gay or straight? And how does sexual activity harm the holiness of the church if we no longer make being gay or straight distinctions that are implicitly already moral definitions?

What sexual activity that holiness in the church must exclude is clear and has been elaborated in countless sermons. The church cannot say yes to *porneia*.[32] On the side of same-sex activity, this means that holiness must exclude promiscuity, prostitution, pornography, rape, violence, abuse, seduction of the innocent, and predatory activity. But if holiness demands rejection of a gay bathhouse ethos among homosexual Christians, so must it also reject a penthouse ethos among straight Christians: holiness among straights equally excludes heterosexual promiscuity, pornography, prostitution, rape, violence, abuse, seduction of the innocent, and predatory sex. And as I noted earlier, in such evil behaviors, the ledger has been much fuller on the heterosexual side than on the homosexual side.

Of even greater importance is for Christians to ask, as they too seldom do, what sexual holiness might mean positively. Let us grant and even celebrate the role of virginity (as Roman Catholicism has always done) and other forms of committed singleness within the body of Christ (as most other Christians have also long recognized). What can we say about those leading an active sexual life? How does their sexual activity express the signs of holiness that build the body of Christ, rather than corrupt or tear it down? As soon this question is asked, we quickly realize how deficient our positive understanding of sexual holiness is, how much our discourse, even about heterosexual existence, is a matter of avoiding the negative rather than of cultivating the positive. In an effort to fill that void, I propose three qualities that suggest themselves as dimensions of sexual holiness: covenantal loyalty, fruitfulness, and chastity.

Even though heterosexual marriages fail regularly and often messily—even marriages solemnized within the church through the sacrament of matrimony—we nevertheless rightly hold to the ideal of covenantal loyalty between male and female who are married. That the ideal is not always realized does not mean that in the case of heterosexual marriages we opt for promiscuity or open marriages. Cannot the same standard be

32. In the New Testament generally, the Greek term *porneia* refers to sexual immorality of any kind (see Gal 5:19; Col 3:5; Eph 5:3), although specific nuance is sometimes given by context, such as in 1 Cor 5:1 (incest), 1 Cor 6:18 (prostitution), and Matt 5:32 (adultery). See Paul's binary opposition between holiness and sexual immorality in 1 Thess 4:3.

expected in the case of homosexual love? Cannot the church ask that it aim at covenantal loyalty and seek to fulfill that ideal even when circumstances make it difficult? I think, in fact, that this is exactly why gay and lesbian couples desire and seek the approval of society and the church for their union, precisely to strengthen those bonds of loyalty.

Likewise, we look for heterosexual unions to be fruitful or life-giving. Most obviously, this happens through the bearing and faithful rearing of children. We know, however, that many heterosexual couples cannot give birth biologically, and we encourage and support them in adopting children, providing foster care, or generally overcoming a couple's tendency toward narcissism in ways that improve the life of the larger community. There are a variety of ways of being fruitful. The same applies absolutely to homosexual love. If homosexual Christians fixate at the level of celebrating their erotic attraction, then their union fails the ideal of fruitfulness. Just as heterosexual couples who cannot have children through biological birth, homosexual couples—leaving aside the cases of lesbians who can reproduce biologically—can be fruitful through adoption, foster care, and the building of strong households and communities.

The most difficult criterion of sexual holiness is chastity. Chastity is not the same as celibacy or virginity, although it can certainly be found in those states of life. Chastity is, rather, a matter of sexual virtue, including qualities that we seldom talk or think about these days: self-control, reverence, modesty, delicacy, concern for the other, a sense of privacy; in short, a way of being sexual that, while not dismissing all the ways that sex is joyous and fun, recognizes its place within creation as an activity that best thrives when not engaged in crudely, selfishly, or with no more than animal appetite.[33] Chastity can and should be asked of covenanted homosexual love, just as it can and should be asked of heterosexual love— although we are sadly deficient in thinking about what this might mean and how it might manifest itself.

The point of my thought experiment is to assert that for both straight and gay, and, for that matter, those who are transgender and intersex, the call of God transcends all our starting points—all the ways in which we are different, not only sexually but in all other ways as well—and summons us to a shared obedience to the living God. Paul makes this point in 1 Cor 7:19, where he states that neither circumcision (being a

---

33. The term "chastity" derives from the Latin *castitas*, which has the broad sense of moral purity (see Aulus Gellius, *Attic Nights* 15.18.2; Cicero, *Laws* 2.12.29) and can be synonymous with *pudicitia*, or modesty (see Livy, *History of Rome* 1.58).

Jew) nor uncircumcision (being a gentile) matters, but only keeping the commands of God.

He goes on to apply the same principle to being a slave or free, married or unmarried. None of these conditions advances or retards us with respect to the call of God. They are all adiaphora, circumstances that ultimately do not matter. When Paul states as a general principle that people should remain in the condition they were when called by the Lord (1 Cor 7:17, 24), he does not mean that people do not need to change; indeed, his entire argument in the letter is that believers must be transformed according to the mind of Christ (2:16), must move from spiritual infancy to true adulthood (13:11–13). He means that no human condition—and here I would include any sexual orientation—either prevents us from responding to God's call or excuses us from the need for moral change.

A Necessary Excursus

I would hope that what I have said to this point suffices as introduction to the topic I pursue in this chapter—namely, doing the truth in love. The topic is based on the apostle Paul's peculiar statement in Eph 4:15: "Living the truth in love,[34] we should grow in every way into him who is the head, Christ." Paul contrasts such growth to maturity with a childishness that is tossed about by human opinion and error (4:14). The difficult point I want to argue is that the "doing the truth in love" that Paul sees as

---

34. The Greek is *alētheuontes de en agapē auxēsōmen eis auton ta panta hōs estin hē kephalē Christos*. There are a number of translation issues. The verb *alētheuō* can mean simply "speaking the truth" (as in Xenophon, *Memorabilia* 1.1.5), although it can also have the nuance of "proving true" (as in Hippocrates, *Prognosis* 25). The verb form is found elsewhere in the New Testament only in Gal 4:16, where it has the sense of "telling the truth." That may also be the meaning in this passage, and the KJV and its successors, the RSV and the NRSV, have that restrictive verbal sense. The Vulgate renders the Greek as *veritatem autem facientes in caritate* (literally, "but doing the truth in love"), and other translations have that broader connotation; thus the NABRE's "living the truth," Knox's "follow the truth in a spirit of charity," the JB's "live by the truth and in love," Goodspeed's "lovingly hold to the truth," and Moffett's "hold to the truth and by our love grow up wholly unto him." These suggest that the verb connotes not only verbal accuracy but a certain manner of living. As a circumstantial participle, furthermore, the term can suggest cause, "because we speak the truth," or occasion, "as we speak the truth." Then there is the question of where to attach *en agapē*. I follow most translations with "living the truth in love," having "love" modify the telling or doing of truth. But it could go with "let us grow," in this fashion: "By speaking the truth, let us grow in love." Finally, the phrase *ta panta*, which is here translated as "every way," can bear the nuance of "fullness" or "maturity."

the sign of Christian maturity demands of us all a growth past "the truth of eros" by which we are tempted to define ourselves. God's rule calls us to the relational love called "agape," which is not about the desires of our bodies or the realization of our affections, but is, rather, a disposition to will the good for others even if they do not will the good for us.[35]

In response to God's call, it is insufficient for any of us to cling simply to the truth of our starting point (grounded in our personal experience), for the truth to which we are all called is a manner of life shaped by God's revelation of love in Christ Jesus and the gift of the Holy Spirit that empowers us to live according to this larger truth.

I am fully aware of the delicacy required to advance this argument at our precise point in history. Gay and lesbian believers, who have had constantly to cling to the truth of their own experience of sexuality in the face of denial, discrimination, ridicule, and sometimes violent exclusion from society and church, understandably bristle when told that "we are all called" to move to a larger truth. Like others whose most basic right to exist and to participate in society has been denied, gays and lesbians can easily hear such language as another version of "shut up and go away." Similarly, many African Americans resist talk about full integration because they see such discourse as a means of suppressing blackness, and many feminists resist language about gender-blind policy because they see in it an effort to reverse gains that have been made by and for women.

For gays and lesbians, whose very survival has often been at the cost of silence about themselves and of closeting the truth about their sexuality, the language I draw from Ephesians may appear as a form of covert hostility and repression. They can say that they above all must insist on the truth of eros, for that is the necessary starting point of their liberation and authentic humanity, a required truth for themselves and for others to recognize if any conversation among them is to be authentic. They must stand on and defend the truth of their eros, precisely because the massive machinery of repression and denial has not in the least gone away, is still primed to remove the rights won with such great suffering, is still at work to suppress the work for the truth that gays and lesbians themselves have done.

I am especially aware that my argument can cause offense because

---

35. There is no assemblage of the data superior to that of Spicq, *Agape in the New Testament*.

it is made by someone who presumably can afford to ignore the truth of eros in order to move to a higher place because he is among the heterosexual privileged in the church and in society. I have not had to fight, as gays and lesbians have had and still have to fight, for the recognition of my most basic right to be and act sexually in the manner that God has created me. It is because I am acutely aware of the possibility of offense that I have prepared for my argument with such a lengthy preamble, repeating and reinforcing my affirmations on the necessity of responding to the truth concerning eros that God reveals in our mortal bodies.

Out of the same concern to be heard accurately, I offer four further preliminary clarifications.

1. The call of God about which Ephesians speaks is not a call to abandon or deny the truth of eros that has been won with such difficulty, but rather, standing on that truth, a call to grow into a larger vision of truth as agape within the community. Paul does not ask believers to stop being male and female, slave and free, Jew and Greek: differences within the community serve to enhance unity through the diversity of gifts. Thus, homosexual Christians are gifted by heterosexual brothers and sisters, and heterosexual Christians are gifted by gay and lesbian believers.

2. Moving forward is not going backward. To grow into a larger truth about our mutual call from God is not to deny the truth about the condition in which and through which each one of us was called. Growth into the full maturity of Christ cannot be based on a lie about our starting point in Christ.

3. Such growth into maturity is required of all in the body of Christ. It is not required more of gay and lesbian Christians than it is of heterosexual Christians. This point is especially important because of the long history of assigning the need to be "self-sacrificing" to women and slaves rather than males and the free. Indeed, by the logic of agape, it is more incumbent on those ordinarily considered "the strong" to give themselves for those less privileged.

4. Nevertheless, the call of God and the demand of discipleship is required of all in the community, for the rule of God is not simply an approval of ourselves the way we now are; it demands changing into better selves, or rather a better self (that of Christ), not just individually but together as the body of Christ.

Doing the Truth in Love

With these qualifying observations in mind, then, I turn to a reading of Paul's letter to the Ephesians, especially chapters 4–5. I have chosen this letter in particular because in it Paul most explicitly argues that God's plan for humanity lies in the reconciliation of all humans—bringing all things in heaven and on earth into one under Christ's headship (1:10)—and that the place in the world where such reconciliation is to be embodied and enacted is the church (3:10–11).[36] The peace that Christ has accomplished through his death, shattering the enmity between Jew and gentile, and creating in himself one new human in the Spirit so that through him both Jews and gentiles have equal access to God (2:1–18)—this peace is to be realized in the assembly of believers. God's plan to reconcile all creation finds its first realization in the reconciliation achieved in the church, with Jews and gentiles being "members of the same body, and sharers in the promise" (3:6 NRSV).

It is through the church, indeed, that God's wisdom is to be revealed to all the cosmic powers that resist unity: the church is to be the sacrament of the world's possibility (Eph 3:10–11), the sign that what God seeks to have happen everywhere is already happening among those reconciled in Christ and united in God's Spirit. The church's gift is the gift of reconciliation; the church's mandate is to realize such reconciliation. As the gift is mighty, so is the mission daunting, for logically, if the church does not manifest God's reconciling power among humans, then it has no real reason for existing.

Paul's prayer for the Ephesians, then, is that they will activate in their moral lives the gift they have been given: "that Christ may dwell in your hearts through faith; that you, rooted and grounded in love [*agapē*], may have strength to comprehend with all the holy ones what is the breadth and length and height and depth, and to know the love of Christ [*agapēn tou Christou*] that surpasses knowledge, so that you may be filled with all the fullness of God [*hina plērōthēte eis pan to plērōma tou theou*]" (3:17–19). We note that it is the *agapē Christou* that believers are to come to know. The love to which they are called has its origin, form, and goal in the one who has saved them, rather than the love (eros) that arises from their own psychosexual condition.

Paul's exhortation to the Ephesians, as to us, is consequently to "live in a manner worthy of the call you have received," and he spells out the dispositions that comport with that call: "with all humility and gentleness,

36. See pp. 337–56 in this volume.

with patience, bearing with one another through love [*en agapē*], striving to preserve the unity of the spirit through the bond of peace" (4:1–3).[37] We can observe that speaking or doing the truth in love within the community is a speaking and doing that serves the other—that is, an expression of *agapē* rather than eros. It is not, moreover, a matter of "speaking truth to power," of organizing allies, of calling out enemies, or of demanding from others the acknowledgment of our distinctive erotic inclinations. To activate reconciliation, it is not the "truth-telling" that consists in challenge, confrontation, attack, and recrimination that is required, but rather the "truth-doing" that embodies this set of remarkably gentle dispositions. The goal of reconciliation, after all, is not that someone be proven right and someone else be proven wrong, that one wins and another loses, but rather that all be established in right relationship and be at peace.[38]

Paul begins his moral exhortation proper with a reminder of what binds the Ephesians together in the first place, the "unity of the Spirit through the bond of peace," elaborating the elements that constitute them as a single body in Christ:

One body and one Spirit, as you were also called to the one hope of your call; one Lord, one faith, one baptism; one God and Father of all, who is over all and through all and in all. But grace was given to each of us according to the measure of Christ's gift [*kata to metron tēs dōreas tou Christou*].[39] Therefore, it says: "He ascended on high and took prisoners captive;[40] he gave gifts to men." What does "he ascended" mean except that he also descended into the lower regions of the earth? The one who descended is also the one who ascended far above the heavens, that he might fill all the earth.[41] And he gave some as apostles,[42] others as prophets, others as evangelists, others as

37. Cf. the irenic dispositions associated with *agapē* in 1 Cor 13:4–7 and Gal 5:13–14, 22–23.

38. See chap. 8 in this volume.

39. As so often in Paul, the precise character of the genitive construction involving Christ is ambiguous. Here Paul could mean that Christ is the one who measures out the gifts, or that Christ is the measure of the gift (and therefore of its use). In context, I prefer the latter.

40. The first part of this line comes from LXX Ps 68:19, and the phrase "he gave gifts to men" may summarize the point of Ps 68:20–36.

41. Paul plays on the terms "ascend" and "descend" in a manner reminiscent of Phil 2:6–11 and especially Rom 10:5–10. The reader is reminded as well of the cosmic claims for Christ made in Eph 1:3–14.

42. The intensive *autos* ("he himself") makes clear that Christ is the source of the spiritual gifts in the community; cf. 1 Cor 12:3–11.

pastors and teachers,[43] to equip the holy ones for the work of ministry, for building up the body of Christ, until we all attain to the unity of faith and knowledge of the Son of God, to mature manhood [*eis andra teleion*], to the extent of the full stature of Christ [*eis metron hēlikias tou plērōmatos tou Christou*],[44] so that we may no longer be infants, tossed by waves and swept along by every wind of teaching arising from human trickery, from their cunning in the interests of deceitful scheming. Rather, living the truth in love [*alētheuontes de en agapē*], we should grow in every way into him who is the head, Christ, from whom the whole body, joined and held together by every supporting ligament, with the proper functioning of each part, brings about the body's growth and builds itself up in love [*eis oikodomēn heautou en agapē*]. (Eph 4:4–16)[45]

Several aspects of this lengthy passage are especially noteworthy. The first is that Paul includes the leaders of the community as gifted by the Spirit and as dedicated to the work of service for the building of the body. All of the dispositions and practices required of ordinary Christians are demanded of their leaders as well. If meekness and humility are the way to maturity for the rest of us, so are they also for those who hold authority. If "doing the truth in love" according to the measure of Christ is demanded of all members, so is it demanded of the ministers called to build the community in love.

The second significant element in this preliminary recitation of principles is that Paul drops entirely the language concerning Jew and gentile that dominated his earlier argument in Eph 2:1–22. Within the church, Paul does not consider such ethnic starting points as significant for the growth in the Spirit that is demanded of all. It was his entire point in that argument, after all, that Christ's reconciling death was to "create in himself one new person in place of the two, thus establishing peace" (2:15). By analogy, we can say that neither do the starting conditions of being

43. Cf. the list of ministries in 1 Cor 12:27–31.

44. Unusually, the term "manhood" here is gendered (*anēr*) rather than the usual "human person" (*anthrōpos*); once more, the genitive with *plērōmatos* can mean that the "fullness" can either come from Christ or be Christ. In any case, Christ is the "measure" (*hēlikia*).

45. For the contrast between childhood and maturity, see both 1 Cor 3:1–4 and 1 Cor 13:8–13, 19. Note the similarity—and also the difference—between this passage and Col 2:3–15. Despite the similarity in diction and overall tone, the meaning in each passage is distinct.

straight or being gay significantly alter the shared focus of all the gifts of
the Spirit, which are "for building up the body of Christ . . . to the extent
of the full stature of Christ" (4:12–13), and not to enhance the respective
elements of the individuality of members, sexually or otherwise.

The full humanity toward which the community as community strives
is not the sum of its individual members but rather a humanity that has
been revealed through the life, death, and resurrection of Jesus Christ, into
which they, as individual believers from every sort of ethnicity, gender,
social status, and sexuality, have been incorporated through their baptism.
It is not their own native intelligence, will, and energy that enable them to
be transformed into the image of this new humanity, moreover, but rather
the power of the Holy Spirit from God the Father, "who is over all and
through all and in all" (*ho epi pantōn kai dia pantōn kai en pasin,* 4:6).

Paul declares in Eph 4:30 that they have been sealed with the Holy Spirit
for the day of redemption (*to pneuma to hagion tou theou en hō esphrag-
isthēte eis hēmeran apolytrōseōs*). And if the Holy Spirit is the effective cause
of the community's transformation, then Christ himself must be considered
the formal cause. What I mean by this is that the way Jesus lived out his own
humanity forms the pattern of how each member of the community ought
to live, and thereby "build the body" that is Christ's. The church as "sacrament of reconciliation" to the world, then, is one that reveals in its relationships, one member to the other, the pattern of Christ's reconciling love.

As Paul begins to spell out the moral dispositions that should characterize those relationships, then, he constantly reminds the Ephesians—
and us—that it is not self-realization that is to be pursued. What is to
be sought by each one and all together is the realization of Christ's life
among all the members. "Doing the truth in love," he tells them, means
to grow into the full maturity of Christ the head (4:15) as the whole body
builds itself up in love (4:16). Warning them against bad thinking and bad
behavior, he tells them, "That is not how you learned Christ [*hymeis de
ouch houtōs emathete ton Christon*], assuming that you have heard of him
[*ei ge auton ēkousate*] and were taught in him, as truth is in Jesus [*kai en
autō edidachthēte kathōs estin alētheia en tō Iēsou*]" (4:20–21). "As truth
is in Jesus": this remarkable phrase reminds us that whatever we might
think doing the truth in love means, our understanding and practice must
ultimately be measured by the measure who is the human being Jesus.
Given how frequently Paul uses the title "Christ" in this letter, the choice
of the proper name Jesus in this case must be deliberate and meaningful.[46]

46. In Ephesians, Paul uses "Lord Jesus" once, "Jesus Christ" eight times, "Christ

As Paul reminds the Ephesians that they must put aside their old humanity, he states that they must "be renewed in the spirit of [their] minds" (*ananeousthai de tō pneumati tou noos hymōn*, 4:23),[47] putting on "the new self, created in God's way [*ton kata theon ktisthenta*] in righteousness and holiness of truth [*en dikaiosynē kai hosiotēti tēs alētheias*]" (4:24). Precisely this sort of statement shows why "doing or living the truth in love" is perhaps a more adequate translation of *alētheuontes en agapē* than is "speaking the truth in love."

Paul speaks of such transformation of the mind as a growth toward maturity, or adulthood, sought by the community and all its individual members, and he contrasts this, as we have seen, with their "being children" (Eph 4:14). We are reminded of Paul's stating in 1 Cor 13:11, "When I was a child, I used to talk as a child, think as a child, reason as a child; when I became a man, I put aside childish things," and his telling the Corinthians, "Stop being childish in your thinking. In respect to evil be like infants, but in your thinking be mature" (14:20).[48] There is a sense in which children are profoundly and naturally narcissistic; they see themselves as the center of the universe, and adults collude in that fantasy. Children are concerned first and last with the pleasing of the self. Growth toward adulthood, we understand, is a growth toward the awareness of, and concern for, others. The adult is distinguished from the child precisely in the capacity to act for the sake of others even when it does not bring personal pleasure or satisfaction. Such other-directedness is for Paul the essence of agape, or self-donative love; as he states most succinctly in 1 Cor 8:1, "Love [*agapē*] builds up."

As we attend to the specific dispositions and practices advocated by Paul, therefore, we are to hear them as articulations of both truth and love, the specific sort of love displayed by Jesus as he revealed God to us. This is the "truth [that] is in Jesus" (Eph 4:21). Thus, Paul says that we are to be mutually forgiving, "as God has forgiven [us] in Christ" (4:32), and adds, "Be imitators of God, as beloved children,[49] and live in love [*peripateite en agapē*],[50] as Christ loved us [*kathōs ho Christos ēgapēsen*

Jesus" nine times, and "Christ" twenty-seven times. Only here does he use the personal name "Jesus" by itself.

47. The language here is most reminiscent of Rom 12:2; see chap. 3 in this volume.

48. We remember as well that Paul wants the Corinthians to have "the mind of Christ" (*nous Christou*, 1 Cor 2:16), and the Philippians to "reason morally as Christ did" (*touto phroneite en hymin ho kai en Christō Iēsou*, Phil 2:5, author's translation).

49. See Wild, "'Be Imitators of God.'"

50. Literally, "walk in love," another reminder of the embodied character of "doing/living" the truth in love.

hēmas] and handed himself over for us as a sacrificial offering to God for a fragrant aroma" (5:1–2).[51]

What are some of the specific ways in which Paul spells out "doing the truth in love," by which the church grows to the maturity of Christ? Not surprisingly for an exhortation to change, Paul draws a series of five contrasts involving thinking, speaking, and acting with respect to bodily appetites and material possessions. Also not surprising, Paul tends to elaborate the negative characteristics—the things from which we are to turn—more than the positive.

First, with respect to thinking, Paul calls them not only from a child-ishness that is tossed about by error and human opinion (Eph 4:14) but from a way of thinking that was theirs as pagans, with minds empty, with understanding darkened, being estranged from a life in God because of their ignorance and resistance (4:17–18), a way of being that deteriorates through illusion and desire (4:22). In contrast, he speaks simply of learning the truth that is in Jesus (4:21) and having their minds renewed (4:23). The ways of darkening the mind and deceiving the self,[52] Paul seems to suggest, are multiple and complex; the way of thinking truthfully is direct and simple. If they are thoughtful, with a renewed mind, they can avoid acting like fools and can "understand what is the will of the Lord" (5:17). Paul declares, "For you were once darkness, but now you are light in the Lord. Live as children of light, for light produces every kind of goodness and righteousness and truth" (5:8–9).[53]

Second, with respect to the use of possessions, Paul calls them away from the acquisitiveness (*pleonektēs*) that he identifies forthrightly with idolatry (Eph 5:3–5)[54] and that leads them to steal from each other. Instead, he wants them to work with their hands in honest labor, so that they can have something to share with those in need (4:28).

Third, with respect to eating and drinking, Paul says only that they should avoid getting drunk on wine, for that leads to debauchery (Eph 5:18). He recommends instead being filled with the Spirit and "singing and playing to the Lord in your hearts" (5:19).

Fourth, with regard to sexuality, Paul fills up the negative column easily: they are to turn away from lewdness, obscenity, and promiscuity, from silly and suggestive sexual speech, from fornication, from lust, from

51. The note of "handing himself over for us" echoes the language Paul uses in Gal 1:4 and 2:20 and Titus 2:14.

52. The similarity of this trope to Rom 1:18–32 cannot be missed.

53. Notice again the element of "truth" (*alētheia*) in this exhortation.

54. The logic of this identification is traced in Johnson, *Sharing Possessions*.

shameful deeds done in darkness; all these are among the sins that bring down God's wrath on the disobedient, and believers are to have nothing to do with them (Eph 5:3–4). We are not surprised that Paul places nothing in the positive column here, for as I noted earlier in this presentation, Christian discourse has consistently been stronger on the vices than on the virtues of sexual practice. But it is worth noting that neither straight nor gay Christians can have any problem with the negative elements Paul lists, for these all fall within the category of the sort of *porneia* that is incompatible with holiness.

Finally, Paul gives most attention to the manner of speech within the community, and for good reason: modes of speech are indeed most important in the process of tearing down or building up a community. When I get drunk, I do damage to myself, but I do not necessarily harm you. When I am lewd, I offend chastity but do not necessarily weaken the fabric of community love. When I steal, I take something that is yours, but I do not thereby destroy your sense of self or your reputation. But speech, as the Letter of James reminds us, can be a fire lit from hell, consuming the whole cycle of creation, a deadly poison (Jas 3:5–7). Paul begins by stating simply, "Putting away falsehood, speak the truth [*laleite alētheian*], each one to his neighbor, for we are members one of another" (Eph 4:25).[55]

Such truth-speaking is fundamental to all human society, and it is even more essential for the health of the body of Christ that is to live by the truth that is in Jesus. Lying, we remember, is not the same as speaking in error. Lying means that we know what is true and choose not to speak it, or choose to distort it. How grievously the church through the ages and today suffers—how much the body of Christ is weakened—because of such lying. In matters of sexuality, those who have chosen not to speak the truth about themselves because of fear or because of the desire to be approved cloud the capacity of the church to respond to God's self-disclosure in human lives. Even more, those in authority who know the truth about human sexuality yet use speech to deny and distort that truth in order to protect their own position and the church's reputation for consistency damage the capacity of the church to be a sacrament of reconciliation for the world.

Similarly, Paul rejects speech that arises from bitterness, passion, and anger and issues in harsh words, slander, and malice of every kind (Eph 4:31). "No foul speech," he says, "should come out of your mouths" (4:29, adapted). But although Paul rejects speech arising from bitterness, passion, and anger, he does not exclude the emotion of anger as a com-

---

55. The margin of Nestle-Aland correctly spots the verbal similarity to LXX Zech 8:16.

ponent of truthful speech. Indeed, immediately after telling his readers to speak truth to the neighbor because they are members of each other, Paul says, "Be angry but do not sin" (an allusion to Ps 4:4);[56] he continues, "Do not let the sun set on your anger, and do not leave room for the devil" (Eph 4:25–27).[57] It is not, Paul suggests, the clean anger that arises from hurt and gives expression to that emotion in plain speech that offends the community, but the distorted anger that becomes hostility and finds expression in harshness, slander, and malice. Healthy anger, in fact, is a precondition to truthful reconciliation, and the body of Christ needs to enable those who have been badly hurt, even by the church itself, to speak plainly and simply out of that anger, if the body is truly to be healed through reconciliation.

In contrast to such destructive speech, Paul proposes that the community say "only such as is good for needed edification, that it may impart grace to those who hear" (Eph 4:29). Rather than the malicious speech driven by rage, Paul instructs us to "be kind to one another, compassionate, forgiving one another as God has forgiven you in Christ" (4:32). Rather than lewd and suggestive talk, the community should give thanks to God. As they are filled with the Holy Spirit, they should "[address] one another in psalms and hymns and spiritual songs, singing and playing to the Lord in [their] hearts, giving thanks always and for everything in the name of our Lord Jesus Christ to God the Father" (5:20).

Conclusion

This wonderful passage from Ephesians, in which Paul exhorts his ancient readers, and us, to do the truth in love, and thus build the body of Christ to full maturity, reminds us of the dialectical relationship in which we inevitably find ourselves when we seek seriously to interpret Scripture for our lives. Since the obedience of faith must always be directed to the living God whose work in the world is disclosed through God's creation at every moment, above all in the experience of humans—however ambig-

56. The Greek *orgizesthe kai mē hamartanete* is translated literally, "Be angry *and* do not sin."

57. This may sound obscure to contemporary ears, but the sense is plain enough: if humans fall into rage with someone and do not express the truth of that anger and seek reconciliation quickly (before the sun goes down, for example = that same day), then the Tempter has an opportunity to make the anger fester into hostility and true enmity.

uous and in need of the most careful discernment—there are times when such obedience must include a "no" to the explicit word of Scripture.

Such is the case, as I have argued in other places, when Scripture commands sorcerers to be killed, or slaves to be obedient to their masters, or women to be silent in the assembly. Such is also the case, I hold, when Scripture declares homosexuality to be a freely chosen vice that is a sign of sin rather than a sign of God's loving creation in the lives of many humans. But even such a "no" to the normative force of such scriptural texts relies on an overwhelming "yes" to the authority of Scripture in shaping our lives, for we would not know what obedient faith was, would not be able to discern the work of the Holy Spirit in human lives as the work of God, would not even be able to see everyday experience as a disclosure of the living God, were it not for the ways in which Scripture has shaped our imagination and sharpened our vision.

In other cases, as in the text we have read together from Ephesians, Scripture challenges us to grasp a truth that we would never even glimpse from the ordinary run of our daily experience. Such is the way God has disclosed his love for humans through the self-giving love of Jesus. Such is the vision of the church as a community of reconciliation that provides a sign of what God wills all the world to be. Such is the vision of the church as the body of Christ that is built up to full maturity through the loving and forgiving relationships among its members. Only because of the vision provided us by texts such as Ephesians are our minds shaped to the new mind that is according to the truth that is in Christ Jesus.

Only through careful attention to such passages of Scripture do we become aware of the inadequacy of the truth of our experience of sexuality alone—not inadequate as a truth about God's work in the world, which indeed manifests itself in all the diverse forms and expressions of eros—but inadequate with regard to the truth to which God calls us in Christ, the truth of transformation through agape. And when Scripture thus speaks to us, our "yes" to its words are also and at the same time a "yes" to the living God, for we recognize deep in our hearts that we could never have, on our own, come to such a vision, attain to such a truth. In these circumstances, what should we do but give thanks "always and for everything in the name of our Lord Jesus Christ," and "be subordinate to one another out of reverence for Christ" (Eph 5:19–21)?

Chapter 17

Sacrament of the World

The Church in Ephesians

In this chapter I examine the distinctive place of the church in Paul's letter to the Ephesians.[1] Elsewhere I have acknowledged the letter as stylistically and thematically part of the Colossians/Ephesians cluster and have proposed that it was sent as a circular letter (as part of a three- or four-letter packer) to the churches of Phrygia and Asia, carried by Paul's delegate Tychichus.[2] I have also devoted specific attention to the theme of mystery in the letter, its teaching on transformation into the full maturity of Christ, and that part of its household code dealing with slavery.[3] But some peculiar features of Paul's language concerning church demand consideration and lead us eventually to the question of the place and purpose of this powerful Pauline missive.

We can begin with data. Overall, Paul uses the Greek noun *ekklēsia* some sixty-one times. The great majority of instances refer to the local

1. The title of this chapter echoes the usage of *sacramentum mundi* that derived from the work of the Catholic theologian Karl Rahner (as in his six-volume encyclopedia with that very title) and is embedded in the opening of the Second Vatican Council's Dogmatic Constitution on the Church, *Lumen Gentium*, which states, "In her relationship with Christ, the church is a kind of sacrament of intimate union with God, and of the unity of all mankind, that is, she is a sign and an instrument of such union and unity" (1.1). Similar language is found in *The Catechism of the Catholic Church*, which speaks of the church as a "sacrament of the unity of the human race" (see pars. 774–80). These ecclesiastical documents cite Ephesians frequently, and for good reason. The present essay does not seek to support a dogmatic position but seeks to show how Paul's thought about the church takes a distinctive turn in Ephesians, and to suggest the circumstances that may have prompted that turn.

For overall orientation, see Cerfaux, "Revelation of the Mystery of Christ"; Schnackenburg, *Church in the New Testament*.

2. See vol. 1, chap. 10 ("Paul's Voice—Philemon").

3. See, respectively, chaps. 15 and 16 in this volume and chap. 10 in vol. 1.

assemblies of believers, in line with ordinary Greek political and social usage.⁴ Thus, when Paul uses *ekklēsia* five times in Romans, he refers to house-church assemblies (Rom 16:1, 4, 5, 16, 23); the same is the case for twenty of the occurrences in 1 Corinthians (1:2; 4:17; 6:4; 7:17; 10:32; 11:16, 18, 22; 12:28; 14:4, 5, 12, 19, 23, 28, 33, 34, 35; 16:1, 19), the nine instances in 2 Corinthians (1:1; 8:1, 18, 19, 23, 24; 11:8, 18; 12:13), two of the three occurrences in Galatians (1:2, 22), one of the two instances in Philippians (4:15), two of the four uses in Colossians (4:15, 16), the two examples each in 1 and 2 Thessalonians (1 Thess 1:1; 2:14; 2 Thess 1:1, 4), the three in 1 Timothy (3:5, 15; 5:16), and the one instance in Philemon (Phlm 2). In the Pauline correspondence apart from Ephesians, in sum, the only exception to such local usage occurs when Paul speaks of his "persecution of the church" in the singular (1 Cor 15:9; Gal 1:13; Phil 3:6), and when he speaks in Colossians of Christ as the "head of the church" in the singular (Col 1:18, 24)—this last usage explicable on the basis of the literary closeness of Colossians and Ephesians.

In contrast, language concerning *ekklēsia* in Ephesians calls attention to itself in five ways:

- Paul uses *ekklēsia* nine times in this letter, always in the singular, and never with reference to a local assembly. Nor does the singular refer to his practice of persecution as in other letters.
- Six of these nine occurrences appear in Paul's table of household ethics—in his extended comparison between husband and wife on one hand and Christ and the church on the other (Eph 5:23, 24, 25, 27, 29, 32).
- Only here in his correspondence does Paul assign a specific role to the church (as such) in God's plan of salvation for humanity.⁵ In Eph 1:22-23 the climax of Paul's opening thanksgiving for Christ's triumphant resurrection and exaltation is that "[God] put all things beneath his feet and gave him as head over all things to the church [*tē ekklēsia*], which is his body, the fullness of the one who fills all things in every way [*to plērōma tou ta panta en pasin plēroumenou*]."⁶ And in 3:10 Paul speaks of his role in bringing to light God's

4. See the evidence assembled by Karl Ludwig Schmidt, "ἐκκλησία," *TDNT* 3:500–536; Harland, *Associations*; Kloppenborg, "Edwin Hatch, Churches, and Collegia"; and Kloppenborg and Ascough, *Greco-Roman Associations*.

5. This point is anticipated by Dahl, "Cosmic Dimensions"; see also Minear, "Vocation to Invisible Powers."

6. The precise sense of the dative *tē ekklēsia* is unclear, but the most obvious is "in

mystērion, "so that the manifold wisdom of God might now be made known through the church [*hina gnōristhē . . . dia tēs ekklēsias*][7] to the principalities and powers in the heavens" (adapted).[8] The church as church is the instrument of revelation.

- Between these two statements concerning the special role of the church—not the local congregation, note, but the church as cosmic player—Paul elaborates the specific contents of what the church is to reveal in Eph 2:1–22, first with respect to the reconciliation between God and humans (2:1–10) and then with respect to the reconciliation of Jew and gentile in the church (2:11–22).

- Corresponding to Paul's singular, cosmic, conception of *ekklēsia* is his use of language concerning the "principalities and powers" (*archai kai exousiai*) as suprapersonal entities (Eph 1:10; 2:2; 3:10; 6:12), language not lacking in other letters[9] but employed in Ephesians with specific intent—namely, as the context for the role of the cosmic church.

These observations should stir us to a closer examination of the specific conception of the church in Ephesians.

---

the church," so that the church as such is the place where God's victory over all things is to be found. For the notion of *plērōma* here, as also in Col 1:19; 2:9, see Overfield, "Pleroma"; contrary to the position of, e.g., Schlier, *Christus und die Kirche im Epheserbrief*, there is no reason to postulate any influence of Gnosticism.

7. The instrumental *dia* here should be stressed: it is precisely through the *ekklēsia* that God's mystery is revealed to the cosmic powers.

8. Unless otherwise indicated, Scripture quotations in this chapter are from NABRE.

9. Most notably in Col 1:13, 16; 2:10, 15. Colossians, as I have noted several times, was written most probably as part of the same packet of letters as Ephesians. As in other cases, we find the two letters using very similar language but to slightly different ends. Colossians speaks of Christ being creator of the principalities and powers together with all other things (1:16), of believers being rescued from the "power of darkness" (1:13), of Christ being the "head of every principality and power" (2:10), and, through his exaltation, of his stripping the principalities and powers and leading them in triumph (2:15). Colossians also speaks of Christ as "head of the church" (1:18; 2:19), but without the same specific connection to the principalities and powers that we find in Ephesians. For Paul's language about cosmic entities elsewhere, see Rom 8:38; 1 Cor 2:6–8 (possibly); 6:3; 10:19–22; 11:10; 13:1; 15:24–28; 2 Cor 12:7; 2 Thess 2:7–11; 1 Tim 4:1–2; 5:4). I do not think that Paul's language about *ta stoicheia tou kosmou* in Gal 4:3, 9, or Col 2:8, 20, refers to such suprapersonal powers but rather to worldly regulations. For discussion, see Caird, *Principalities and Powers*; Schlier, *Principalities and Powers*; Wink, *Naming the Powers*.

The Church as Place of God's Reconciliation

Paul leads up to his central argument in Eph 2:1–22 in three stages. In his opening prayer of praise, he identifies the *mystērion* of God (1:9) with the plan to recapitulate all things in Christ (*anakephalaiōsasthai ta panta en tō Christō*, 1:10),[10] a recapitulation that includes those who were chosen from the foundation of the world (Jews like himself, 1:4–6) and those who now had received the pledge of the Holy Spirit (the gentiles, 1:13–14).[11] In his prayer of thanksgiving, Paul adds two further elements. He prays that his gentile readers will be given the wisdom to have full insight into "the hope that belongs to his call, what are the riches of glory in his inheritance among the holy ones" (1:18)—in short, that they grasp the gift that has been given to them. Finally, in 1:20–23 Paul connects the exaltation of Christ over every principality and power to his headship over all things *tē ekklēsia* (for or in the church), his body, "the fullness of the one who fills all things in every way."

In his rehearsal of what God has given them in Christ and the new reality in which they find themselves,[12] Paul begins with the cosmic reconciliation between God and humans accomplished by Jesus (Eph 2:1–10).[13] Although the Greek text presents some difficulties regarding the use of pronouns,[14] it is clear from the overall syntax of the sentences that Paul includes both gentiles and Jews in the condition of alienation from God. The gentiles "were dead in [their] transgressions and sins in which [they] once lived following the age of this world"; they were, moreover, under the influence of "the ruler of the power of the air, the

---

10. In rhetoric, the verb *anakephalaioun* meant "to sum up" (as in "bring to a head"); cf. *kephalaion* in Heb 8:1, and see Quintilian, *Institutes of Oratory* 6.1. Paul uses it in Rom 13:9 for love as the "summation" of the law. Because of the distinctive use of *kephalē* language elsewhere in this letter, the term takes on the suggestion of "gathering together" all things under the lordship of Christ (see Eph 1:22; 4:15; 5:23).

11. On the opening blessing, see O'Brien, "Ephesians I"; for the distinctive language of prayer throughout the letter, see Kirby, *Ephesians, Baptism and Pentecost*.

12. See the use of *charis* in Eph 1:2, 6, 7; 2:5, 7, 8; 3:2, 7, 8; 4:7, 29; 6:24, as well as *charitoun* in 1:6 and *charizomai* in 3:1, 14.

13. For discussion of this part of Paul's argument, see Lincoln, "Ephesians 2:8–10."

14. The original hand of Codex Alexandrinus and Codex Bezae have *kai hymeis* ("and you") in 2:3, rather than *kai hemeis* ("and we"), which would make the state of alienation apply only to gentiles. The support of P46, Vaticanus, and the corrected versions of other MSS, as well as the logic of the argument, support the shift to "and we," which includes the Jews in the same condition, "like the rest" (*hōs kai hoi loipoi*). See R. A. Wilson, "'We' and 'You.'"

spirit that is now at work in the disobedient" (2:1–2).[15] In a different sort of diction, Paul describes the state of gentiles in a manner not dissimilar to the description in Rom 1:18–32: the condition of alienation from God is here cast in terms of following cosmic powers rather than idolatry, but in both cases it is faithlessness or disobedience (*apeitheia*) that is decisive (see also Eph 5:6).[16] Also as in Rom 3:17–20, where Paul assigns Jews as well as gentiles under the power of sin, here he says that "we also . . . like all the rest" lived among the gentiles "in the desires of our flesh, following the wishes of the flesh and the impulses, and were by nature children of wrath" (Eph 2:3, adapted). While they may have been alive in their mortal pursuits, dominated by cosmic powers or by deranged desires, they were, both gentile and Jew, "dead" (*nekros*, 2:1, 5) with respect to God.

But just as God's surpassing power had been displayed by raising Christ from the dead and seating him in the heavenly places at his right hand (Eph 1:20), so God's surpassing mercy and love has been shown both to gentiles and Jews alike (2:4) through that same power. He "brought them to life with Christ" (*synezōopoiēsen tō Christō*), raised them up and seated them with Christ in the heavenly places (2:5–6). This reversal of condition, this "salvation" (2:7, 8), has nothing to do with their own efforts and provides them no ground for boasting (2:8). It is entirely a matter of God's gift (2:5, 7, 8), made effective for them through faith (*dia pisteōs*, 2:8). They have been created by God in Christ Jesus for the purpose of living in a new way, "walking" no longer in the darkness of evil but in the good deeds for which God had prepared them (2:10). Eph 2:4–10 provides a set of affirmations concerning salvation that matches, even in diction, those found in Rom 5–6, with the only startling element being the affirmation that believers had been exalted to the heavenly places with Christ. As the rest of Ephesians will make abundantly clear, however, Paul does not mean by this a sort of "realized eschatology" that swallows up the "not yet" with the "already"; Paul's readers still face the challenge of the transformation of their minds and the reform of their morals in accord with the gift they have been given.[17]

The next stage of Paul's argument in Eph 2:11–22 also has a resem-

---

15. The NABRE's translation of *archonta tēs exousias tou aeros* camouflages the appearance of "principality" (*archē*) and "power" (*exousia*).

16. Cf. the incidence of *apeitheia* and *apeithoun* in Rom 2:8; 10:21; 11:30, 31, 32; 15:31.

17. See chap. 16 in this volume.

blance to Rom 9–11 in that it deals with Jew and gentile in God's plan.[18] But there is a decisive difference. In Rom 9–11 the full reconciliation of gentile believers and Israel according to the flesh is future: that "all Israel will be saved" is an eschatological hope; in the present, the dialectic of God's judgment and mercy is still being worked out. In contrast, Ephesians presents the reconciliation of the two peoples as actual and present. And whereas Rom 9–11 displays the dialectic within the grand scheme of history, Ephesians locates the realized reconciliation within the church. Without using the term *ekklēsia* in the passage, Paul's imagery, especially in 2:19–22, makes such a conclusion unmistakable. Once more, then, the cosmic work of God is concentrated in a cosmic conception of church.

With a conviction that has its roots in the stories of the first humans in Genesis (see Gen 2–4), Paul understands that human alienation from God, caused by disobedience, is expressed by enmity between humans, an enmity that leads to literal, and not only moral, death. And for Paul, the perfect expression of such enmity was the long-standing hostile relationship of Jews and gentiles. Separation from God inevitably meant, for Paul, separation between humans. For Jews, to be sure, their own privileged position as God's elect people (see Rom 3:1–4; 9:1–5) inevitably had as its corollary the exclusion of all those who were not Jews. Paul states the Jewish perspective succinctly as he speaks to his gentile readers: "Therefore, remember that at one time [*pote*] you, Gentiles in the flesh, called the uncircumcision by those called the circumcision, which is done in the flesh by human hands, were at that time without Christ [*chōris Christou*, meaning here "apart from a Messiah"], alienated from the community of Israel [*apēllotriōmenoi tēs politeias tou Israēl*] and strangers to the covenants of promise [*xenoi tōn diathēkōn tēs epangelias*], without hope and without God in the world" (Eph 2:11–12; see 1 Thess 4:13). The gentiles' "being without God" in the world meant their "being without the hope" that was based on God's blessing of Israel.[19]

But God's saving act is for all humans, gentiles as well as Jews. And the reconciliation of all humans with God through the death and resurrection of Jesus has the concomitant result of reconciling Jews and gentiles (that is, all humans) to each other: "But now [*nyni*, cf. "then," *pote* in 2:11] in Christ Jesus you who were once far off [*makran*] have become near [*engys*] by

18. For discussion, see Meeks, "In One Body"; Roetzel, "Jewish Christian–Gentile Relations."

19. Cf. the list of Israel's privileges in Rom 3:17–20 and 9:3–5.

the blood of Christ" (Eph 2:13; cf. Rom 3:21–26; 5:1–11).[20] What Jews were always near to, and what gentiles were always remote from—namely, the presence and power of God—is now made available to all through Christ's death ("his blood"). It is important to repeat at this point that Paul envisages the reconciliation of Jew and gentile not as a future historical event but as a present condition. But where is it *now* present in the world, in such fashion that it can shine forth before those cosmic powers whose work it is to foster human alienation (see 2:1)? Within the life of the church.

Although Paul does not use the term *ekklēsia* in the following exposition, he employs two of his favorite metaphors for the church—namely, the body and the temple.[21] All of Eph 2:14–22, indeed, is an elaborate metaphorical structure based on a historical fact about the Jerusalem temple. It is reported several times by Josephus, and has been confirmed by archaeology, that an inscription on the wall dividing the holy place from the court of the gentiles (nations) threatened death to any gentile who transgressed the law by seeking access to what was available only to Jews.[22]

The "wall of division" defining the enmity between ancient Jew and gentile, therefore, quite literally enforced separation and threatened death within the space that was thought to be the place of God's presence. In his development of the temple metaphor, Paul weaves together the work of Christ to destroy that enmity and create reconciliation between all peoples, together with the creation of a new humanity that constitutes a new temple, or dwelling place of the Spirit—and this through Christ's own sacrificial death. Paul declares:

> For he is our peace, he who made both one and broke down the dividing wall of enmity, through his flesh, abolishing the law with its commandments and legal claims, that he might create in himself one new person in place of the two, thus establishing peace, and might reconcile the both with God, in one body, through the cross, putting that enmity to death by it. He came and preached ["proclaimed," *euēngelisato*] peace to you who were far off and peace to those who were near, for through him we both have access in one Spirit to the Father. (Eph 2:14–18)

20. For the distinctive political/diplomatic language in this section especially, see T.-L. Lau, *Politics of Peace*.

21. For the church as *sōma Christou*, see Rom 12:4–5; 1 Cor 6:15; 12:13–15, 27–28; Col 1:18, 24; 2:17; 3:15; for the church as *naos theou*, see 1 Cor 3:16–17; 6:19; 2 Cor 6:16.

22. Josephus, *Jewish War* 5.193–94, 6.124–26; *Jewish Antiquities* 15.417–18; see Bickerman, "Warning Inscriptions."

Paul here combines the metaphorical fields of diplomacy (peace, enmity, reconciliation, proclamation, access [*prosagōgē*]), of forensics (law, commandments, legal claims), and sacrificial cult (blood, death, cross). Christ's death broke down both the wall separating humans from God (2:13) and the wall literally separating humans from each other. The language about law is particularly striking here, since it was precisely the fact of the law (allegiance to it, adherence to its commands) that defined being Jewish and thus metonymically provided the basis for the hostility/enmity (*echthra*) between Jew and gentile.

By his own death, Paul declares, Christ "put to death" (*apokteinas*) the enmity by "destroying" (*katargēsas*) the power of the law to define the difference between peoples. It is impossible not to note the profound consonance between these lines and Paul's argument in Gal 2:19–3:20, in which "the cross" (*stauros*) stands at once as the instrument of salvation and the point of tension with the law (see Gal 2:20; 3:13). Also closely corresponding to Gal 3:28 is Paul's statement here of the goal of creating in Christ one new person (*hina tous duo ktisē en autō eis hena kainon anthrōpon*, Eph 2:15).[23]

This last sentence provides a transition to Paul's final, startling metaphorical turn. The wall of separation that was idolatry and disobedience prevented "access" (*prosagōgē*) of all humans to God, just as the wall of separation that was the law kept gentiles from having the same "access" ritually to God that was available to Jews. The consequence of Christ breaking down those divisions through his death on the cross is that that "both" (*amphoteroi*) Jews and gentiles have equal access, for they are now a single "new human" (Eph 2:15) joined by "a single Spirit" (*en heni pneumati*), and in that one Spirit can together approach the Father (2:18).

From the start of this letter, the gift of God to Jews and gentiles has been expressed in terms of the Holy Spirit (see Eph 1:13, 17). Now Paul's identification of the Spirit as the source of life and unity (cf. Eph 4:3–6) enables him at last to speak of this new, transformed humanity in terms of a living temple that "in the Spirit" grows and reaches maturity as a body does.[24] Paul tells his gentile readers, "So then you are no longer strangers

23. Gal 3:28 reads, "There is neither Jew nor Greek, there is neither slave nor free person, there is not male and female; for you are all one in Christ Jesus [*pantes gar hymeis heis este en Christō Iēsou*]."

24. See Paul's continuing language about the Holy Spirit in Eph 3:5, 16; 4:3,

and sojourners"[25] as they had been when they were without access to the privilege of the Jews. Instead, "you are fellow citizens with the holy ones and members of the household of God [*oikeioi tou theou*], built upon the foundation of the apostles and prophets, with Christ Jesus himself as the cornerstone [*akrogōniaiou*]. Through him the whole structure is held together and grows into a temple sacred in the Lord [*auxei eis vaon hagion en kyriō*]; in him you also are being built both together [*synoiko-domeisthe*] into a dwelling place of God in the Spirit [*eis katoikētērion tou theou en pneumati*]" (2:19–22).

This, then, is Paul's vision of the church in Ephesians. It is a body whose head is Christ. It is simultaneously a temple of the living God through the presence of the Spirit. It is the place in the world where the reconciling effect of Christ's death—breaking the wall of separation between God and humans—is manifest in the reconciliation (peace) among humans. More than that, the church is where a "new humanity" in the Spirit, made up of all humans, both Jews and gentiles, is the dwelling place of God in the world. The *mystērion* hidden from earlier generations but now revealed is that "the gentiles are coheirs [*synklēronoma*], members of the same body [*syssōma*], and copartakers [*symmetocha*] of the promise in Christ Jesus through the gospel" (Eph 3:6, author's translation).[26]

This is the most sweeping and breathtaking statement of human unity and universality enunciated in antiquity, notable above all for its being spoken by one holding the religious and cultural privileges of a Jew, and for its being grounded in the scandal of the violent death of a single human being. It is a highly idealized vision, to be sure. Paul's awareness that the transformation of the members is required—they must "put off" the old humanity with its rivalry and enmity and "put on" the new humanity with its disposition of compassion and kindness—is the subject of Eph 4:1–5:20 (see esp. 4:24).[27] But this process of transformation is the "growing into," or fuller expression of, what has already been given (2:21; 4:15–16).

4, 23, 30; 5:18; 6:17, 18). For context, see Gärtner, *Temple*; McKelvey, "Christ the Cornerstone."

25. In the LXX, the "stranger" (*xenos*) is one who does not belong to a group or tribe (see Ruth 2:10; 2 Sam 15:19; Isa 18:2; Ps 68:8), whereas the "sojourner" (*paroi-kos*) is a foreigner living among others (Gen 15:13; 23:4; Exod 2:22; 12:45; 18:3; Lev 25:23; Num 35:15).

26. See Caragounis, *Ephesian Mysterion*.

27. See chap. 16 in this volume.

The church, then, must truly actualize and exhibit such reconciliation within its life, if it is to be "sacrament of the world"—that is, an effective sign of the world's possibility. Here is the significance of Eph 1:22–23 and 3:10 framing Paul's central exposition concerning God's work in the world. God exalted Christ "and he put all things beneath his feet and gave him as head over all things to the church [*en ekklēsia*, "in the church"], which is his body, the fullness of the one who fills all things in every way" (1:22–23). The church, considered as a cosmic entity, is the embodiment of the reconciling gift of God in Christ. Precisely for that reason, Paul can declare in 3:10 that he has been sent to bring to light the *mystērion* of God previously hidden, "so that the manifold wisdom of God might now be made known through the church [*dia tēs ekklēsias*] to the principalities and powers in the heavens" (adapted).

If the church is the sign of reconciliation in itself (*en ekklēsia*), then it becomes the effective sign (or sacrament) by its living out that reconciliation, so that through the church (*dia tēs ekklēsias*) the mystery of God's plan for humanity can be known. Reconciliation is at once the gift and the mandate of the church. If the church is not such a sign of reconciliation, it could be argued, the Paul of Ephesians would question the reason for its continued existence.

The Church and Christ, Wife and Husband

After his instructions to his readers on the necessity of living according to their calling Christ, which means abandoning all those moral behaviors of the old person and clothing themselves with the dispositions of the new person in the Spirit, a transformation that can be summarized in Eph 5:1 as "Become imitators of God, as beloved children, and live in love, as Christ loved us and handed himself over for us as a sacrificial offering to God for a fragrant aroma" (adapted),[28] Paul addresses the difference these new dispositions ought to make within the basic unit of society, the household (5:21–6:9). As I have noted elsewhere, the basic form of the Hellenistic "table of household codes" was in place for hundreds of years[29] and reflected social arrangements that were virtually universal in the Greco-Roman and Jewish world alike, with authority

28. See Wild, "'Be Imitators of God.'"

29. Xenophon, *Oecumenicus*; see Foucault, *History of Sexuality*; Balch, "Household Codes."

running from top to bottom and submission running from bottom to top in binary pairs: husbands and wives, parents and children, masters and slaves. Despite arguing for the basic equality of slave and free, Greek and Jew, male and female within the *ekklēsia*, Paul, we have seen, does not challenge the fundamental structure of the household or its power dynamics. What Paul does is modify the moral dispositions consonant with a new humanity within the social structures of the old humanity.[30]

In the first volume of this work, I analyzed the passages dealing with masters and slaves in both Colossians and Ephesians, to see how such a "canonical" reading of these letters in conjunction with the Letter to Philemon might affect the way that small letter of commendation might be read.[31] What we discovered was not a rejection of Greco-Roman slavery but the use of language directed at both master and slave that tended to mitigate the harsh realities of that institution. Now I turn my attention to the very extended treatment of marriage in Ephesians, and specifically the relations of husband and wife.[32] As I turn to this passage, I remind myself and my readers of the dangers of anachronistic reading; Paul is working within the realities of first-century, not twenty-first-century, marriage.[33] My reason for considering it here is the way the exhortation concerning marriage intersects Paul's vision of the church in Ephesians.

30. For positive treatments of what is often regarded as a problematic passage, see Gench, *Encountering God*; F. Watson, *Agape, Eros, Gender*; Dawes, *Body in Question*; Sampley, *"And the Two Shall Become One Flesh"*; Miletic, *"One Flesh."*

31. See vol. 1, chap. 10.

32. In Col 3:18–19 Paul disposes of the pairing of husband and wife in only two verses.

33. Twenty-first-century readers (both female and male) tend to suppose that people marry when both parties are adult, that marriage is a consequence of equal partners falling in love, that property considerations are irrelevant, that husbands and wives are of roughly the same age or generation, and that gender roles (and therefore familial responsibilities) are malleable if not interchangeable. None of these assumptions applies to Paul's world. Marriages were often arranged precisely for reasons of property; husbands were most often considerably older than wives, who were sometimes "given in marriage" at a quite young age (sometimes at the onset of puberty); and biological considerations (the need to bear as many children as possible because of infant mortality, on one side, and the need to do "man's work" in field or in battle, on the other side) determined—with the notable exception of those who had slaves to free them from menial obligations—gender roles and expectations. Note how Xenophon assumes that the older husband is to teach his young wife how to run a household and manage slaves; in such circumstances, "submission" of wife to husband is more explicable, however distasteful we might find it in our changed First World environment.

Fully six of the occurrences of *ekklēsia* appear in these twelve verses. The passage is therefore clearly important to understanding Paul's sense of the church in this letter.

Before analyzing the specifics of the passage, it is helpful to remind ourselves of how much the first part of Genesis was on Paul's mind as he wrote his letters. He thinks of the resurrection experience as a "new creation" (Gal 6:15; cf. Gen 16:15) and quotes God's declaration "Let there be light" (Gen 1:3) in 2 Cor 4:6. His statement that in Christ there is neither male nor female (Gal 3:28) may recall Gen 1:26–28. He sees the exalted and heavenly Christ as the "last Adam" in contrast to the "first Adam" (1 Cor 15:45–49), and the human Christ (as "one man") as reversing the sin of the first Adam (as "one man") that placed all humans under the reign of death (Rom 5:12–21).

The account of the creation and sin of Adam and Eve in Gen 2:18–24 and 3:4–7 is also influential. The creation of Eve after (and from) Adam, for example, serves to provide warrant for the subordination of women to men: Paul states succinctly enough in 1 Cor 11:3 that a man is the head of the woman as Christ is the head of a man, and in 11:7 that a man is the image and glory of God, whereas a woman is the glory of man. Why? "For a man did not come from a woman but a woman from man, nor was a man created for woman but woman for man" (11:8–9, author's translation). Now, it is true that Paul mitigates this "natural hierarchy" slightly when he adds, "Woman is not independent of man or man of woman in the Lord, for just as woman came from man, so is man born of woman" (11:11–12, adapted), but there is no question that the second Genesis creation account supports Paul's androcentric views of gender relations.

There are, moreover, practical implications of the hierarchy that Paul assumes. Women should be covered when they pray or prophesy in the assembly (1 Cor 11:3–16). They should not teach in the assembly (1 Cor 14:34; 1 Tim 2:11–15) and certainly should not go about by themselves between households saying what they should not (1 Tim 5:13–16). Women are more easily deceived than men: the serpent deceived Eve (2 Cor 11:2–3) and she sinned before Adam (1 Tim 2:14); women are easily swayed by charlatans who upset households (2 Tim 3:6–7). It is natural that women should also be subordinate to their husbands in the household (Col 3:18–19) and be under the control of their husbands (Titus 2:5). Now, for all contemporary readers, the review of this evidence makes for painful reading. But it is important to recognize, as I have tried to make clear before, that Paul in no way is unusual for holding such views within his culture (both Greco-Roman and Jewish), and that Paul had genuine scriptural support for his views.

There is absolutely no surprise, then, in Paul telling wives to be submissive to their own husbands as to the Lord in Eph 5:22, or to "fear/reverence" their husband in 5:33.[34] What is more distinctive is that he heads up the entire household instruction with "Be subordinate to one another out of reverence for Christ" (5:21). The disposition of submission is not restricted to women; it is to characterize all relations in the community; "reverence/fear" is not the craven terror of repressed persons; it is the expression of attentive respect before the Savior. Paul subtly modulates the severe social structure of antiquity through such intimations of mutuality.[35]

But what draws our attention particularly in Eph 5:21–33 is the disproportionate attention paid to the moral dispositions of the husband within the marriage relationship, and the way in which the husband-wife pairing is made analogous to Christ and the church. We have seen already how complex are the metaphors Paul has used for the unique relationship between Christ and the church—considered here, I remind you, not as the individual community but as a cosmic reality: the church is Christ's body and Christ is the body's head (1:22–23), but the church is also the "dwelling place for God" a living temple that provides access for both Jews and gentiles, as a new humanity, to the presence of God, whose cornerstone is Christ, and that "grows" as a body grows (2:19–22).

Now Paul appropriates an even more ancient metaphor with roots in the prophetic literature, which could speak of the relationship between God and Israel in terms of the marriage relationship, in both positive and negative ways (see Jer 2:1; 3:1–5; Ezek 16:1–63; Hos 1:2–9; 3:1–5).[36] In one other place in his correspondence, Paul draws on this metaphor

---

34. The verb *hypotassō* in the passive can denote a moral disposition as well as it does a subordinate social position; cf., e.g., Rom 3:7, 20; 10:3; 1 Cor 16:16; Titus 3:1. The social position of subordination was in Paul's time a given; the exhortation therefore concerns the disposition of willing submission. Similarly, *phobos* ("fear") frequently enough has the sense of reverence as it does of craven terror (see, e.g., Rom 3:18; 13:7; 2 Cor 5:11; 7:1; and esp. Phil 2:12).

35. Cf. the instructions to slaves and masters in Eph 6:5–9, analyzed in vol. 1, chap. 10.

36. In rabbinic interpretation, the entire Song of Solomon (or Song of Songs) was read as an allegory of the love between Yahweh and Israel, a reading that was taken over by Origen in his *Commentary on the Song of Songs*.

when speaking of himself and the Corinthian church: "Please put up with me, for I am jealous of you with the jealousy of God, since I betrothed you to one husband to present you as a chaste virgin to Christ; but I am afraid that, as the serpent deceived Eve by his cunning, your thoughts may be corrupted from a sincere and pure commitment to Christ" (2 Cor 11:1–3, adapted). Here Paul is the matchmaker, or the father of the bride, who gives the church in marriage to Christ and is afraid that she may be unworthy.

The marriage metaphor need not be connected to Adam and Eve, but it can be, as Paul himself shows by his direct citation of Gen 2:24 in Eph 5:31 (adapted): "For this reason a man shall leave father and mother and be joined to his wife, and the two shall become one flesh." Immediately before this citation, Paul says that "we are members of his body" (5:30). Here is the point of fusion between two metaphorical fields. From one side, the risen Christ is the head of a body with members (the church); from the other side, Christ is the spouse of the church with whom he has become "one flesh" through the Spirit. The merged metaphor communicates at once the intense intimacy and identification of Christ and church, as well as the respective power positions of the two (head to body, husband to wife).

Now, if Paul were simply trying to reinforce those power positions, he would emphasize either the rights of the head/husband over the body/wife (the head can command the body as it will; the husband can order the wife to do what he desires) or the obligations of the body/wife toward the head/husband (the body is but a passive receiver from the head; the wife is but a pliant servant of the husband). But in fact, because it is Jesus Christ (who "loved us and gave himself for us," Eph 5:2, author's translation) who is the model for the head/husband, all the attention falls on the husband's obligations to give of himself for the sake of his wife. Here is the Paul who understands by "the mind of Christ" (1 Cor 2:16; Phil 2:5) the disposition of the stronger to empower the weaker.

When we note what Paul asks of the "husband" in this set of exhortations, we realize that it truly is the church that remains his subject. Indeed, the disposition of the wife within marriage sets the terms of the analogy: "Just as the church is to Christ, so should the wife be submissive to her husband in every respect" (Eph 5:24, author's translation). It is perhaps not too much to suggest that the reconciling love between husband and wife (male and female) within the household is meant by Paul to be a sacrament (effective sign) to the church itself of how it can be an effective sign of reconciliation (of Jew/gentile) to the world. But the husband's obligation to give of himself is even greater than the submission asked of the wife:

- "The husband is head of his wife [cf. 1 Cor 11:3] just as Christ is head of the church [cf. Eph 1:22], he himself is savior of the body" (5:23). The power of Christ/husband is to be used in "saving" the body/wife.
- "Husbands, love your wives, even as Christ loved the church and handed himself over for her" (5:25; see 5:1).
- "To sanctify her, cleansing her by the bath of water with the word" (5:26; see baptism in Eph 4:5). Paul here echoes Ezek 16:4–9.
- "That he might present to himself the church in splendor, without spot or wrinkle or any such thing, that she might be holy and without blemish" (5:27; cf. 2 Cor 11:2–3).
- "So also husbands should love their wives as their own bodies. He who loves his wife loves himself" (5:28; thus the utter intimacy, even identity, in this relationship).
- "For no one hates his own flesh but rather nourishes and cherishes it, even as Christ does the church"—the use of power is the care and growth of the other, rather than the dominance and control of the other—"because we are members of his body" (5:29–30).
- Finally, it is worth noting that the quotation from Gen 2:24 in Eph 5:31 has the man leaving his primary family to join with the flesh of his partner and form with her a new family; they become "one flesh."[37]

Thus, Paul concludes, "Each one of you [husbands] should love his wife as himself" (5:33).

In the (supposedly) egalitarian world of the twenty-first century, Paul's exhortations to the husband, and above all his analogizing the husband as Christ, may appear as making a bad case worse. Does he not thereby provide a supernatural rationale for a structurally unfair family system? Certainly, the passage can be read that way. A more generous (and fairer) reading, however, would credit Paul with placing on the

---

37. Cf. above all 1 Cor 6:12–20, where Paul applies the same text to sex with a prostitute and counters this with "the one clinging to the Lord is one Spirit [with him]" (6:17, author's translation). The man is, according to Genesis/Paul, "joined to his wife" to become one being, rather than the wife "being joined to the husband."

husband the burden of self-giving, of cherishing, of nurturing, of treating his wife as his own body, his own flesh, and would acknowledge that, within the argument as a whole (including the instructions that follow), Paul's goal is to show how such dispositions of self-donation for the sake of the other are the basis of true peace, not only within the household, but also within the church, which he wants to be the sacrament of the world's possibility. It is not by accident that throughout this passage Paul speaks of "the church" as a single entity that is in relation to the risen Christ, not of scattered "churches" in various locales.

It is by no means an intrusion, then, when Paul states in Eph 5:32, while talking about marriage, "This is a great mystery, but I speak with reference to Christ and the church" (*to mystērion touto mega estin; egō de legō eis Christon kai eis tēn ekklēsian*). Yes, that has been his topic all along.

A Nonrealized Eschatology

It would be easy to conclude from Paul's language earlier in the letter about the power of God (Eph 1:19) displayed especially in the exaltation of Christ above all principalities and powers (1:20–21), and the bringing to life and seating of believers in the heavenly places (2:6), that Ephesians has a fully "realized" eschatology: the victory has fully been won,[38] and no further struggle impends. But it is important to remember the extended exhortation to moral transformation in Eph 4–5, which insists on the readers progressively being transformed through their moral dispositions—and empowered by the Holy Spirit (4:23; 5:18)—into full maturity in Christ. The fundamental victory has been won in Christ, but a battle for the good is still being waged by each individual.

And, as we see in Eph 6:10–20, it is also a battle waged by the church as such. The cosmic forces that worked for the destruction and alienation of humans (see 2:2) are still active in the world, and still require resistance.

38. As I have noted before, the language of Colossians and Ephesians, while similar in so many ways, is not identical. The phrase "principalities and powers" is a good example. It appears in Col 1:16–18 and 2:10 to assert the superiority (or headship) of Christ to them all, and in 2:15 to assert that in his death and resurrection, Christ has "stripped" the principalities and powers. By contrast, Eph 1:21 asserts the superiority of Christ to the principalities and powers, but in 3:10, as we have seen, the role of the church is to reveal the mystery of God's recapitulation of all things (and the reconciliation of all humans) to the principalities and powers.

As we have seen, Paul elsewhere does not entirely lack awareness of inimical cosmic forces (e.g., Rom 8:38–39; 16:20; 1 Tim 4:1).[39] The closest parallel to Eph 6:10–20 is found in 2 Cor 10:3–6: "Although we are in the flesh, we do not battle according to the flesh, for the weapons of our battle are not of flesh but are enormously powerful, capable of destroying fortresses." Similarly, he can speak metaphorically of human moral dispositions as pieces of military armor, as in 1 Thess 5:8:[40] "Since we are of the day, let us be sober, putting on the breastplate of faith and love and the helmet that is the hope for salvation." But Eph 6:10–20 is more extensive and elaborate than these examples and possesses an eschatological urgency not found in the Pauline parallels.[41] As Paul turns from the mundane (but far from typical) instructions for the household, his language unfolds in several stages.

He begins with an exhortation that reminds his readers at once of their own weakness and inability to resist the world's evil on their own. They need each other and, above all, the strength of God: "Finally, draw your strength from the Lord and from his mighty power" (Eph 6:10).[42] They are to "put on the armor of God [*endysasthe tēn panoplian tou theou*][43] so that [they] may be able to stand firm against the tactics of the devil [*pros to dynasthai hymas stēnai pros tas methodeias tou diabolou*]" (6:11).[44] We note that the posture of the church is not aggressive; believers are not arming themselves for a "holy war" in which they conquer material or spiritual territory. They arm themselves in order to defend against attack by cosmic enemies; they seek to be able to "stand fast" in

39. My reasons for not regarding the *stoicheia tou kosmou* in Gal 4:3, 9 and Col 2:8, 20 as such entities have been stated elsewhere (see chap. 11, p. 211, note 5, and chap. 10, p. 194, note 14 in this volume).

40. A similar transposed use of military imagery is found in Isa 11:5; 59:16–17; and esp. in Wis 5:17–23.

41. See Wild, "The Warrior and the Prisoner."

42. The Greek is *endynamousthe en kyriō kai en tō kratei tēs ischyos autou.* The verbs are plural: they are all to be empowered in this fashion. For such "empowerment," see Phil 4:13 and 2 Tim 2:1.

43. The ambiguity of the Greek genitive case is here on full display: the armor can be "from God" or "belonging to God," or it can even be, epexegetically, "the armor that is God."

44. The "you" throughout this section is plural. Paul is speaking to all the churches as one church. With all the attention given to the principalities and powers, the cunning ways of the *diabolos* should not be neglected. The term *methodeia* can mean "methods" as well as "devices" or "wiles." Paul gives an example in Eph 4:26–27: the festering anger of humans leads to hostility and hostility to enmity, destroying peace, and "giving a place to the temptor."

their convictions and practices. Nor is their struggle solely in the future. It takes place every day. As Paul says in 5:16, "Redeem the time, because the days are evil" (*exagorazomenoi ton kairon, hoti hai hēmerai ponērai eisin*, author's translation).[45]

The forces against which the church must arm itself are the very cosmic powers that seek to divide humans from each other. Paul sees human freedom as conditioned by the influence of these suprahuman agents: "For our [or "your"][46] struggle [*palē*] is not with flesh and blood but with the principalities [*archas*], with the powers [*exousias*], with the world rulers of this present darkness [cf. Eph 2:1], with the evil spirits in the heavens" (6:12).[47] The cosmic church, made up of reconciled peoples of all nations, in short, must resist, not merely human agents ("flesh and blood"), but the cosmic powers that sponsor human enslavement and alienation. Thus, the church needs a supply of power greater than the resources available to themselves as merely "flesh and blood."

Paul makes this very connection: "Therefore, put on the armor of God, that you may be able to resist [*antistēnai*] on the evil day[48] and, having done everything, to hold your ground [*stenai*]" (Eph 6:13). Paul does not here present the picture of a comfortable, much less a triumphalistic, church. This is a church under threat from evil, a church that must struggle to maintain its countercultural stance of reconciliation.

What, then, does Paul mean by "God's armor"? He lists items of military gear that represent moral dispositions: "So stand fast with your loins girded with truth [*en alētheia*; see Eph 4:15-20], clothed with righteousness as a breastplate [*ton thōraka tēs dikaiosynēs*], and your feet shod in readiness for the gospel of peace [see esp. 2:14, 17; 4:3]. In all circumstances, hold faith as a shield [*ton thyreon tēs pisteōs*], to quench all the flaming arrows of the evil one [*panta ta belē tou ponērou*]. And take the helmet of salvation [see Eph 1:13; 2:5, 8; 5:23] and the sword of the Spirit [*tēn machairan tou pneumatos*; see 1:13, 17; 2:18, 22; 3:5, 16;

---

45. The NABRE has "making the most of the opportunity, because the days are evil."

46. The textual evidence is split, and the difference between the two readings minimal.

47. The Greek, *ta pneumatika tēs ponērias*, can also be translated as "the spirits of evil" (i.e., representing or serving as agents of evil).

48. Paul speaks variously as "the day" (*hē hēmera*) as a future definitive moment (see Rom 2:5; 13:12; 1 Cor 1:3; 3:13; 5:5; 2 Cor 1:14; Phil 1:6, 10; 2:16; 1 Thess 5:2, 4; 2 Thess 1:10; 2:2; 2 Tim 1:12, 18; 3:1; 4:8). Paul speaks of the present in terms of "evil days" (*hai hēmerai ponērai eisin*) in Eph 5:16 and of the "day of redemption" (*hēmeran apolytrōseōs*) in 4:30.

4:3, 4, 23, 30; 5:18], which is the word of God [*rhēma theou*; see 5:26]" (6:14–17). As my suggested cross-references indicate, Paul's readers are to deploy in their defense all the qualities that are theirs through the gift of God. Of particular importance is their call to continue to express the good news that was first carried to them as gentiles—namely, peace to those who are far off and peace to those who are near (2:17). In a world dominated by cosmic powers that seek to divide and alienate through hostility, Paul has shown them how to express what they had been given: "Live in a manner worthy of the call you have received, with all humility and gentleness, with patience, bearing with one another through love, striving to preserve the unity of the Spirit through the bond of peace" (4:1–3, adapted).

Paul asks that his readers connect through prayer with the spiritual power that will enable them to live out this life of witness: "With all prayer and supplication, pray at every opportunity in the Spirit. To that end, be watchful with all perseverance and supplication for all the holy ones" (Eph 6:18). And he asks for prayer for himself as well, that he can continue to "make known with boldness [*parrēsia*] the mystery [*mystērion*] of the gospel" (6:19). The church exists because of God's willing to create a new humanity in the world that can provide an effective sign of what the world itself might become; but so fierce are the forces of the world that oppose unity and love, that only continuous connection with the creator of the church can enable it to sustain its sacramental role.

Coda: The Circumstances of Composition

My analysis of the distinctive portrayal of the church as a singular (organic) entity with a singular role to play in a cosmic drama tends to support my contention that Ephesians was written under Paul's authorization as a circular letter during his lifetime, specifically as part of the epistolary and diplomatic circuit performed by his delegate Tychichus. As Tychichus delivered Onesimus to his owner Philemon with a letter of commendation from Paul, and as he read aloud the letters to the local assemblies at Colossae and Laodicea, he also delivered and read aloud this ecclesial reflection to other communities (including the one at Ephesus) within the circle of Paul's influence. The writing of a single letter to all the churches, as one church, itself has the effect of creating a consciousness of being one united church.

There is another, and quite specifically historical, reason for placing this utopian vision of the cosmic church within the framework of Paul's ministry, for only then could such a vision have any real credibility. After Paul's death (probably between 64 and 68 CE), and particularly after the Jewish war with Rome and the destruction of the Jerusalem temple in 70 CE, relations between Jews and Christians were either hostile or nonexistent. We have seen that some Jewish-Christian literature of (probably) the second or third century was explicitly hostile to Paul.[49] And the writings we have from gentile Christians of the early second century (e.g., Ignatius of Antioch and Polycarp) not only do not evince a vision of Jew-gentile harmony within the church but are hostile to those they consider Judaizers. By the middle of the second century, as Justin's *Dialogue with Trypho* demonstrates, Christianity is conceived of as an entirely gentile religion that in God's plan has superseded Judaism. It is difficult indeed to think of a composition such as Ephesians being composed in such a context.

But it is possible to imagine that Paul, who in Romans thought of the reconciliation of Jew and gentile as God's plan for humanity and wished for "all Israel [to be] saved" (Rom 11:26), could have composed (with his school) this utopian vision of the church as even now being the place of such reconciliation. It is, furthermore, even possible to imagine that Paul could have composed (with his colleagues) precisely this vision as an instrument for accomplishing such unity among discrete assemblies of Christ-believers. The same vision that drove Paul to seek a collection from among gentile churches for the saints in Jerusalem could also have motivated and shaped this distinctive (and immensely generative) conception of a cosmic church through which the powers and principalities could learn of the *mystērion* of reconciliation between Jew and gentile. It is not too much to say that Ephesians both envisaged and helped create out of disparate local *ekklēsiai* a single universal *ekklēsia*.

49. See vol. 1, chap. 1, pp. 23–25.

Chapter 18

Discernment, Edification, and Holiness

1 Thessalonians

The two letters addressed to the *ekklēsia* in the Macedonian city of Thessaloniki provide a privileged perspective on Paul the pastor.[1] Unlike other Pauline letters that respond to issues within multiple assemblies—we think above all of the Corinthian letters, Galatians, and Colossians—these letters are written to a single community. In these letters, furthermore, Paul's own concerns—such as his collection or future travel plans—do not intrude; his focus is entirely on the *ekklēsia* that he addresses.

The two letters, moreover, invite being read in sequence, so that we can observe shifts in Paul's pastoral practice, some of them made necessary by his own words.[2] Because of their singular focus on the stability and security of a single congregation, finally, these short letters give us insight into elements elsewhere in Paul's correspondence that we might otherwise miss. In this chapter and the next, I propose using them in just that fashion.

Before considering Paul's community-building practice, it is helpful to remember what sort of challenge faced him as he sought to establish

1. First Thessalonians is universally recognized as authentically Pauline, in contrast to 2 Thessalonians, whose authenticity is, in the consensus view, debated; more on that in the next chapter. I will not enter into a discussion here of the rhetorical genre of either letter. That 1 Thessalonians is a "paraenetic-pastoral" letter is argued by Malherbe, "Exhortation in 1 Thessalonians." Others have argued that 1 Thessalonians is a letter of consolation; see Chapa, "Letter of Consolation," and A. Smith, *Comfort One Another*. The question of genre is not germane to my own presentation. For the best overall treatment of these letters as instruments of pastoral care, see Malherbe, *Paul and the Thessalonians* and *Letters to the Thessalonians*.

2. I am, to be sure, assuming the authenticity of 2 Thessalonians; for a full and fair discussion of how both letters ought to be read as authentic, see Malherbe, *Letters to the Thessalonians*, 349–75.

and secure in a city shaped by Greco-Roman culture an *ekklēsia Thessalonikeōn en theō patri kai kyriō Iēsou Christo* ("an assembly of Thessalonians in God the Father and the Lord Jesus Christ," 1 Thess 1:1; 2 Thess 1:1, author's translation).[3] Founding an *ekklēsia* in a major city was, in itself, not exceptional. The Roman Empire had scattered through all its major cities voluntary associations of various kinds that provided the experience of face-to-face participation that once was (and in smaller places still was) a feature of the local assembly (*ekklēsia*) of citizens.[4] There were cultic associations, guilds, funeral societies, and, among Jews, synagogues. A distinctive element of such associations, indeed, is the way they are differentiated in one way or another by a common occupation, task, interest, class, ethnicity, or gender. In this respect, the exclusiveness of the Jewish synagogue was no more exceptional than an association made up entirely of Phrygians; the fact that the cult of Bona Dea was female was no more shocking than that the cult of Mithras was male. Likewise, it would have been exceptional for members of the aristocracy to gather with the lower orders, much less with slaves.

Despite such diversity in their respective memberships, the basic structure of such associations tended to be similar: they had administrative boards that handled finances and made required decisions, and they had various (sometimes quite elaborate) ceremonial and practical offices. An association with a "board of elders" (*Gērousia/presbytērion*) and a revolving office of "supervisor" (*episkopos*) and a range of "helpers" (*diakonoi*) would be instantly familiar to members of other groups.[5] Boundaries were maintained by membership lists and (especially in religious cults) lists of rules and sanctions concerning behavior.[6]

On the evidence of 1 Thess 5:12–13, the *ekklēsia* Paul founded (1:5–10) likewise had some sort of recognizable leadership, which Paul wanted to be acknowledged and honored by members: "We ask you, brothers, to respect those who are laboring among you [*kopiōntas en hymin*] and who are over you in the Lord [*kai proistamenous hymōn*] and who admonish you [*kai nouthetountas hymas*], and to show esteem for them with special love on account of their work [*kai hegeisthai autous hyperekperissou en*

3. Unless otherwise indicated, Scripture quotations in this chapter are from the NABRE.

4. See Kloppenborg, "Associations," and Harland, *Associations*.

5. See the massive appendix devoted to association organizational arrangements in Boyles, "Unevolved."

6. For the rules and punishments attached to Greco-Roman temples, for example, see now Suh, "Power and Peril in Corinth."

agapē dia ton ergon autōn]."[7] As we see in other letters, Paul also sought to shape and stabilize a young community under threat (see 1 Thess 2:13–16) through personal visits (2:17–19), the sending of delegates (3:2–6), and, as a last resort, sending letters.[8] In each of the Thessalonian letters, furthermore, Paul seeks to guide the community's thinking and actions during a developing crisis.

But what does Paul propose as guidance for the church in Thessaloniki on an ongoing basis? Do we get clues concerning the elements that Paul sees as critical to the building and maintaining a distinctive identity as an *ekklēsia* dedicated to the "living and true God" (1 Thess 1:9) and the "Lord Jesus Christ" (1:1) in the absence of him or his delegates? Absolutely basic, to be sure, are the experiences and convictions that have drawn them together as an assembly in the first place.[9] They have heard Paul's message as God's word (2:13), and they have experienced as a result the power of the Holy Spirit at work among them (1:5), including through prophetic utterances (5:20). They know that God raised Jesus from the dead and that Jesus will come again (1:9–10). They are strong in faith, hope, and love (1:3), even if their hope needs the sort of reinforcement that Paul provides them (4:13). The question I want to pursue here, though, has to do with the mechanisms, or practices, that Paul wants to be habitual among them as the means of reinforcing community boundaries.[10]

Before considering three of the practices to which Paul exhorts the Thessalonian church, it is important to recognize how difficult it would be to sustain community cohesion and integrity when the community's very existence is dependent on a set of experiences (of the Spirit) that were undoubtedly various in kind and degree, and on a set of convictions (concerning God and Christ) that were inherently difficult to grasp and easy to challenge on the basis of lived experience—such as the death of

---

7. For evidence of local leadership in other letters, see Rom 12:7–8; 1 Cor 6:1–7; 16:15–18; Gal 6:6; Eph 4:11; Phil 1:1; 1 Tim 3:1–13; 5:17–20; 2 Tim 2:2; Titus 1:5–9.

8. The full complement of methods is evident in 1 and 2 Corinthians and Philippians.

9. See vol. 1, chap. 8 ("The Claims of Experience"), as well as chap. 6 ("Paul and Scripture") and chap. 9 ("Convictions, Myths, Symbols, and Metaphors").

10. My discussion is based on the theoretical underpinnings provided by Berger and Luckmann, *Social Construction of Reality*, and Berger, *Sacred Canopy*, and the specific sociological observations made on intentional communities by Kanter, *Commitment and Community*; Zablocki, *Joyful Community*; and B. Wilson, *Social Dimensions of Sectarianism*.

loved ones who seem to be missing out on God's triumph. The Thessalonian assembly was, on the evidence, only newly formed, without the presence of their founder, and experiencing some form of affliction (*thlipsis*, 1 Thess 1:6; 3:3, 7). It was, therefore, triply fragile.

Unlike many Greco-Roman associations, for example, the one Paul founded (and then left) was not based on a shared trade or task, a shared social class, a single gender, or a divinity who enjoyed public exposure through temples and statues—not to mention generous financial patronage. None of these distinguishing, and stabilizing, factors seem to characterize the *ekklēsia* in Thessaloniki. Likewise, in contrast to the Jewish synagogues that flourished across the Mediterranean world, the Thessalonians could look to no familial lineage or ancestral tradition older than that of their Judean colleagues in belief (1 Thess 2:14). As gentiles who have converted to the living God straight from idolatry (1:9), they possess no deep or ready acquaintance with such a well-established code of behavior as that dictated by Torah. Although Paul adopts the diction of the Septuagint throughout 1 Thessalonians, he makes neither citation of nor allusion to the authoritative texts of Judaism.[11] Nevertheless, Paul's language of "calling" (*kalein*) in this letter (2:12; 4:7; 5:24) unmistakably evokes the understanding of this "people called together" (*ekklēsia*) as in some sense continuous with the *qahal Yahweh* that was the people Israel, which the Septuagint translated as *ekklēsia* (see, e.g., Exod 16:3; Num 14:5; Deut 31:30; Ps 22:22).

Finally, despite the allegations that he was personally authoritarian (if not power-crazed),[12] there is no evidence in these letters that Paul had dictated a detailed a Pauline rulebook for leaders or members of the congregation to follow (along the lines of 1QS at Qumran). Nor in either letter does Paul identify individuals and give specific orders concerning them (with the partial exception in 2 Thessalonians that I will note in the following chapter). He does mention the instructions (*parangeliai*) that they had received from him and that he has handed over to them "through the Lord Jesus" (*dia tou kyriou Iēsou*, 1 Thess 4:1–2). These instructions, as we shall see, are such that the Thessalonians are to work out communally as a means of promoting cohesion, through the dispositions appropriate to the character of the *ekklēsia*. In particular, Paul speaks of

11. See vol. 1, chap. 6.

12. For the exaggerated portrayals, see vol. 1, chap. 11 ("Paul, Oppressor or Liberator?"). For a sophisticated contemporary view, see Castelli, *Imitating Paul*. For a careful consideration of the whole issue, see Schütz, *Paul and the Anatomy of Apostolic Authority*.

three elements that, working together, ought to characterize the Thessalonian congregation. They involve disposition and practices that are to be cultivated by the members of the community themselves.

Building the *Ekklēsia* in 1 Thessalonians

The first of these elements is the practice of discernment, or moral judgment. Paul relies on individual members and the group as a whole to make appropriate practical decisions of the sort that would fall into the category of *phronēsis*.[13] Discernment, in turn, should lead to the edification, the building up (*oikodomein*), of the community as such—that is, in its proper identity. Edification can be called the formal criterion of discernment. The third element is holiness (*hagiōsynē*): the *ekklēsia* is to display a fundamental difference from the world while existing within the world, a difference that derives from its belonging to God and the Lord Jesus Christ. Holiness is for Paul the material criterion of discernment. All three of these elements are stated explicitly in 1 Thessalonians. I will look at them in reverse order. After examining them in the context of this letter, I will show how they represent consistent pastoral concerns in other canonical letters of Paul as well.

Holiness

Paul touches on the theme of holiness in his third statement of prayer concerning the community (see 1 Thess 1:2–10; 2:13–16; 3:9–13), when he says, "May the Lord make you increase and abound in love for one another and for all, just as we have for you, so as to strengthen your hearts, to be blameless in holiness [*amemptous en hagiōsynē*] before our God and Father at the coming of the Lord Jesus with all the holy ones ["saints," *hagioi*]" (3:12–13, adapted).

In the symbolic world of Torah, language concerning holiness has to do with *difference*. In the case of Israel, such difference was connected to the holiness of God. Israel was to be different within the world (i.e., different from other peoples in the world) as God was different from the world. The command was a simple one to state: "Be holy as I am holy"

---

13. For *phronēsis* as practical moral reasoning, and the links between Aristotle and Romans in its usage, see chap. 3 in this volume.

(Lev 11:44–45; 19:2). But the elaboration of it required considerable attention. Israel's difference was spelled out first of all by moral behaviors that distinguished it from the surrounding nations (Lev 17:1–19:37). Also essential to holiness, however, were the ritual requirements concerning the necessary "purity" required to be a full member of the people and to approach God in worship (Lev 11:1–15:33). Such ritual "holiness" was requisite for approaching the presence of God: "Sanctify yourselves, then, and be holy; for I, the LORD, your God, am holy" (Lev 20:7). Undoubtedly, Paul shared the same fundamental conviction of the symbolic world of Torah: God is holy and calls humans to be holy so that they can participate in God's presence. Indeed, Paul declares directly in 1 Thess 4:3, "This is the will of God, your holiness" (*touto gar estin thelēma tou theou, ho hagiasmos hymōn*).

Three aspects of Paul's statement in 1 Thess 3:13, however, call for comment in the context of the letter. First, "at the coming of the Lord Jesus Christ" clearly refers back to Paul's statement in 1:10 that they "await [God's] Son from heaven." Holiness therefore represents the telos of preparation for that parousia. Note that the statement of Christ's parousia "with all the holy ones" can refer just as easily to those awaiting him as to those accompanying him: in either case, Paul's making holiness their call and goal signals that they will be in that company.[14]

Second, the term "holiness" takes on specific character in light of the earlier uses of "the Holy Spirit" (*hagion pneuma*) in the letter. In 1:5–6 Paul reminded them that the good news had come to them not in word alone "but also in power and in the Holy Spirit and in much conviction," and that they had received the good news "in great affliction and with joy from the Holy Spirit" (adapted). Paul will subsequently declare that God has called them "not into impurity but into holiness," so that whoever disregards this call disregards "not a human being but God, who gives his Holy Spirit to you" (4:7–8, author's translation). The Holy Spirit whose source is God is both the warrant and the power for Paul's readers to accomplish the goal of holiness.

Third, Paul defines holiness exclusively in moral rather than ritual terms. They are to be "blameless" (*amemptous*) in holiness, just as Paul had acted "blamelessly" (*amemptōs*) when with them (1 Thess 2:10). In the Septuagint and other New Testament texts, the term consistently

14. When Paul demands in 1 Thess 5:27 that this letter be read "to all the brothers" (*pasin tois adelphois*), a textual variant with significant support has "to all the holy ones" (*pasin tois hagiois*).

refers to moral uprightness.[15] In the present case, it explicates Paul's desire, stated in 2:12, that they "conduct [them]selves as worthy of the God [*peripatein hymas axiōs tou theou*] who calls you into his kingdom and glory." Thus, Paul calls for the Thessalonians to abstain from sexual immorality (*porneia*)—for Jews like himself, a vice consistently associated with gentile idolatry (see Wis 14:12–31; Rom 1:18–32)—and to acquire wives "in holiness and honor, not in lustful passions as do the Gentiles who do not know God. . . . For God did not call us to impurity [*akatharsia*] but to holiness" (1 Thess 4:4–5, 7).[16]

In matters of sex and economics (see 1 Thess 4:6), therefore, Paul wants his community's holiness to be visible in the ways they can be distinguished from idolatrous gentiles. He makes the same sort of distinction when it comes to the moral/religious dispositions of faith, hope, and love. Paul begins by praising the community's faith (1:3, 8) and was reassured by Timothy's report concerning the strength of their faith (3:2, 5, 6, 7), even though he would like to come in person to strengthen them further in faith (3:10). Concerning love, Paul again begins with praise for their "labor of love" (1:3) and rejoices over the good report he hears about this disposition (3:6, 12); he tells them in 4:9, "On the subject of mutual charity [*philadelphia*, literally "love for brethren"] you have no need for anyone to write you, for you yourselves have been taught by God to love one another [*eis to agapan allēlous*]."

Hope is another matter. Although Paul begins by praising their "endurance in hope" (1 Thess 1:3), their grief at the loss of loved ones to death reveals a deficiency in this religious/moral disposition: "We do not want you to be unaware, brothers, about those who have fallen asleep, so that you may not grieve like the rest, who have no hope [*kathōs kai hoi loipoi hoi me echontes elpida*]" (4:13). Providing the Thessalonians with an understanding of the Lord's victory that will provide them such hope then takes up his attention, and he leaves behind the explicit language of holiness.[17] He has said enough, however, to show that for this nascent community, holiness, understood as moral and religious dispositions displayed in behavior, is God's will for them. Indeed, he prays at the end of the letter, "May the God of peace himself make you perfectly holy

---

15. See LXX Gen 17:1; Job 1:1, 8; 2:3; 12:4; Wis 10:5; 18:21; see Luke 1:6; Phil 2:15; 3:6.

16. See Yarbrough, *Not Like the Gentiles*.

17. See, among many discussions, R. Longenecker, "Paul's Early Eschatology"; Kaye, "Eschatology and Ethics"; and esp. Meeks, "Social Functions."

[*hagiasai hymas holoteleis*] and may you entirely, spirit, soul, and body, be preserved blameless [*amemptōs*] for the coming of our Lord Jesus Christ" (5:23).

Edification

At the conclusion of his discussion of the way the dead will share in the future coming of Christ, Paul tells the Thessalonians, "Therefore, exhort one another with these words" (*hōste parakaleite allēlous en tois logois toutois*, 1 Thess 4:18, author's translation). Now, the term *parakalein* can certainly mean something like "console" or "comfort,"[18] but in the present instance, I think that the stronger and more common translation of "exhort" is better.[19] What is at stake here is not simply the emotions of believers but their entire view of reality, which has been badly shaken, for some, by the death of loved ones. And in fragile, newly established intentional communities, every defection from the symbolic world threatens the hold of that world by all.

To pick obvious contemporary analogies, the symbolic worlds of higher education and of democracy exist at all because of the willing and even enthusiastic consensus of all who participate in them, and they are weakened to the degree that some members—students or teachers, voters or politicians—defect to another (especially antecedent) ideological framework. Such deviation in thinking or behavior must be met by the "encouragement" or the "reinforcement" of the community's norms by the remaining members. In this case, we see that Paul calls for the exhortation "of each other," using "these words" that he has just written. In short, they are to secure the stability of the community by mutual reassurance in the face of threat: despite appearances (the death of members), God's triumph will include all.

Again, after addressing both the uncertainty of the parousia's timing—with the reminder that they should therefore be on the watch and awake, "not sleeping like the others" (1 Thess 5:1–6)—and the certainty of their "living together with him" (5:10), Paul concludes with this statement: "Therefore encourage one another and build one another up, as indeed you do" (*dio parakaleite allēlous kai oikodomeite eis ton hena, kathōs kai*

---

18. As in 1 Cor 4:13; 2 Cor 1:4, 6; Col 2:2.

19. See in particular the impressive assemblage of evidence pointing to this interpretation of the phrase *logos tēs paraklēseōs* in Heb 13:22 by Holmes, *Sublime Rhetoric*.

poieite, 5:11). The phrase "encourage one another" (NABRE) should once more be translated as "exhort one another." The nuance of summoning to battle in the verb *parakalein* is reinforced by Paul's telling them, immediately prior to this, to put on "the breastplate of faith and love and the helmet that is the hope for salvation" (5:8). These moral and religious dispositions are strengthened like armor when members of the community summon each other to them.

It is the phrase "build one another up" (*kai oikodomeite heis ton hena*) that especially draws our attention. The verb *oikodomein* means literally to build a house or some other material construction, but, as I showed in the first volume, it is employed by Paul in a metaphorical sense of "building up" the character or dispositions of persons; there is some, though not a great deal of, precedent for Paul's metaphorical usage,[20] which seems to derive in part from his conception of the human gathering that was the *ekklēsia* as a building (*oikodomē*) under constant construction, and in part from his own prophetic self-understanding as one who "builds up" and does not "tear down" (see Jer 1:5; 2 Cor 13:10).[21] In the present case, we can ask what it adds to the "exhorting each other (with these words)" of 1 Thess 4:18 and 5:11. First—we cannot know this now but will learn from his usage in other letters—"edification" is more than verbal. It encompasses all of a person's behavior according to the principles and experiences on which the community is grounded. Second, the phrase *heis ton hena,* though odd in construction, does not mean precisely the same as "each other." It has more the sense of "one on one," or "individually."[22] The responsibility to edify the other must be taken up by each member of the assembly and must be directed to each member of the assembly, individually. Paul acknowledges that this sort of mutual "building up" in conviction and practice is already happening: "as indeed you do" (*kathōs kai poieite,* 5:11).

Paul exhorts the members of the assembly to "respect" and "show esteem and special love" for those who preside over the community (*proistamenous*) and whose labor includes "admonishing" (*nouthetountas*) members (1 Thess 5:12). But then he seems to include everyone (*parakaloumen de hymas, adelphoi*) in the task of mutual admonishment and encouragement, elements of which he uses to round out his pastoral letter

20. In the LXX, see only Ruth 4:4; Ps 27:5; and Jer 40:7.

21. See vol. 1, chap. 5 ("What Kind of Jew Is Paul?") and chap. 9 ("Convictions, Myths, Symbols, and Metaphors").

22. See the convincing case made by Malherbe, *Letters to the Thessalonians,* 300–301.

(5:14–22). From the list of positive behaviors that Paul recommends, one stands out for our consideration—namely, discernment or testing.

Discernment

Paul concludes his recommendations concerning mutual upbuilding through positive dispositions in 1 Thess 5:14–18 with a final five commands that are both provocative and puzzling: "Do not quench the Spirit [*to pneuma mē sbennute*]. Do not despise prophetic utterances [*prophēteias mē exoutheneite*]. Test everything [*panta de dokimazete*]; retain what is good [*to kalon katechete*]. Refrain from every kind of evil [*apo pantos eidous ponērou apechesthe*]" (5:19–22). The two prohibitions are especially puzzling. The form (*mē* + present indicative) could be read strongly as "stop extinguishing the Spirit" and "stop despising prophecy," but the Greek allows for the construction to mean simply "do not,"[23] and it is difficult to imagine preemptory commands to desist from specific behaviors in a list of otherwise highly general and positive exhortations. But we are still left to wonder at how Paul conceived of not "extinguishing" the Spirit, unless he meant that the Holy Spirit by which this community came into being and was empowered (1:5, 6; 4:8) should be cultivated and allowed to express itself. Similarly, we wonder how anyone in Thessaloniki might be moved to "despise" or "reject" prophetic speech,[24] when Paul himself had spoken to them about the last times "by the word of the Lord" (4:15). In any case, it is clear that Paul wants to encourage the presence of the Spirit and the practice of prophecy among the Thessalonians.

When Paul concludes by telling the Thessalonians to "test all things,"[25] he directs them to use their own minds to distinguish (or discern) between authentic and inauthentic expressions of the Spirit and prophecy, just as they might "test" the worth of a metal such as gold (see Prov 8:10; Sir 2:5; Wis 3:6). The use of their rational capacities is not opposed to the work of the Spirit but a necessary corollary to it; we remember how Paul, in recounting his first visit among them, distinguished his own manner

---

23. See the discussion in Smyth, *Greek Grammar*, 409–11.

24. For the completely negative meaning of *exouthenein*, see Acts 4:11 (citing Ps 118:22); Rom 14:3, 10; 1 Cor 1:28; 6:4; 16:11; 2 Cor 10:10; Gal 4:14.

25. In my view, the adversative *de* ("but") before "test all things," which is left out of the NABRE translation, should be both included and taken seriously: testing all things applies to all that went before, especially the exercise of the Spirit in prophecy.

of being among them with the manner and methods of false teachers (1 Thess 2:3-6). In the same way, the Thessalonians are expected to exercise discernment between what is true and what is false. The standard Paul proposes is consistent with his way of defining the character of the community in terms of moral uprightness (or "holiness"). The mark of appropriate discernment is "to retain what is good" (*to kalon*) and to "refrain from every form [or "appearance," *eidous*] of evil [*ponērou*]."

It is striking that Paul so entrusts to these recent gentile converts the capacity to assess the rightness and wrongness of behavior (including manifestations of religious inspiration) by such a broad moral standard. Perhaps it is in part because he is confident that God will empower and guide them. So he ends with this confident aspiration: "May the God of peace himself make you perfectly holy, and may you entirely, spirit, soul, and body, be preserved blameless for the coming of our Lord Jesus Christ. The one who calls you is faithful, and he will also accomplish it" (1 Thess 5:23-24).

Community Construction in Other Pauline Letters

Searching for the same elements of holiness, edification, and discernment in such neat and compressed contiguity as in 1 Thessalonians is frustrating, simply because of the diverse character of the Pauline letters. It is striking, for example, that Galatians entirely lacks any language about holiness—not a single cognate of *hagios* appears in the composition, and *oikodomein* appears only with reference to Paul's not building up what he once tore down (Gal 2:18)—yet it is clear that when Paul does use the verb "test" (*dokimazein*), it is with the same pastoral concern for mutual correction, upbuilding, and discernment that we observed in 1 Thessalonians: "Brothers, even if a person is caught in some transgression, you who are spiritual should correct [*katartizete*] that one in a gentle spirit, looking to yourself, so that you also may not be tempted. Bear one another's burdens, and so you will fulfill the law of Christ . . . each one must examine [*dokimatzetō*] his own work, and then he will have reason to boast with regard to himself alone, and not with regard to someone else; for each will bear his own load" (Gal 6:1-5).

Likewise with Philippians. Once more, both the language of holiness[26] and that of edification are absent. Yet Paul is emphatic about the

---

26. As with Galatians, even the liberal use of *pneuma* in Philippians lacks the descriptor *hagion*.

need for them to practice "testing" or "discernment" in their communal life. He wants their love to "increase ever more in knowledge and every form of perception, to discern what is of value (*dokimazein hymas ta diapheronta*) so that you may be pure and blameless in the day of Christ" (1:9–10, adapted). The letter, indeed, is suffused with the term *phronein* (moral reasoning), which is another way of speaking about discernment (see 1:7; 2:2 (2×), 5; 3:15, 19; 4:2, 10).[27] As for the *idea* of edification, Phil 2–3 can scarcely be read without grasping that Paul recommends discernment to lead to "look[ing] . . . to the interests of others" more than one's own interest (2:4 RSV).

Another sort of case is presented by 2 Corinthians. Here we have explicit language concerning holiness (1:1, 12; 6:6; 7:1; 8:4; 9:1, 12; 13:12, 13) together with the understanding of the *ekklēsia* as the temple of God: "For we are the temple of the living God" (*hemeis gar naos theou esmen zōntos*, 6:16). We have the metaphorical sense of "building" with reference to Paul (10:8) and the assembly (5:1; 12:19; 13:10). And the letter is filled with the cognates of "testing" (*dokimazein*; see 8:8, 22; 13:5; see also 2:9; 8:2; 9:13; 10:18; 13:3, 5, 6, 7). Yet all of these are in service of Paul's passionate efforts to repair the tattered relationship between himself and the Corinthians—they think they are "testing" Paul when in fact he is "testing" them by the standard of the character of Christ[28]—and the rich use of the same language Paul used in 1 Thessalonians does not constitute similar advice concerning the ways in which the Corinthians should discern moral and religious issues (or even *ta biōtika*, see 1 Cor 6:3–4).

It is clear, then, that a purely philological analysis is inadequate to our question concerning Paul's desired ways of constructing and maintaining communities. We need, rather, to look for places where, whatever specific language is used, four elements come together. Paul's advises his readers concerning

- the way they are to work together in the construction of the *ekklēsia*—not apart from the role of leaders but as participants in a shared moral effort;
- the ways in which both individuals and the assembly as a whole are called to a process of moral thinking that can broadly be designated as discernment, which can involve both the choice be-

27. See esp. chap. 3 in this volume.
28. See the acute analysis of Stegman, *Character of Jesus*.

tween right and wrong behaviors and the choice between good and better behaviors;

- the ways in which such decision-making has as its goal not the elevation of any individual (by whatever measure) but the strengthening of others or the community at large; and
- the ways in which this process is connected to the distinctive (or "holy") character of the assembly in contrast above all to the gentile world.

A possible case might be made for including 1 Tim 5:3–16 in the list, since Paul appeals (through his delegate) for a thinking through of moral priorities among the Ephesian believers with respect to the support of widows, and very much has in mind the integrity of the assembly already under threat from "Satan" and the negative perception of outsiders. But the sort of language I have garnered from 1 Thessalonians is lacking, and the directions given by Paul concern what the delegate Timothy is to communicate, rather than the practices of the community as such. We are left, then, with three letters that meet our desire to find connections with the pastoral directions of 1 Thessalonians both linguistically and conceptually: 1 Corinthians, Romans, and Ephesians.

1 Corinthians

Paul's first letter to the Corinthians is like 1 Thessalonians in certain ways: it is written to an *ekklēsia* Paul himself founded and is now away from—his communication with the church is carried out through delegates[29] and through the exchange of letters.[30] As in Thessaloniki, Paul assumes the church in Corinth to have leaders, perhaps the householders mentioned in 1 Cor 16:15–18 who could—or should have been able to—settle local disputes over everyday matters (*ta biōtika*) in the manner that was common in associations and synagogues.[31] The real difference in 1 Cor-

29. Paul is in communication with the community through oral reports from the household members attached to Chloe (1 Cor 1:11), and he plans to send to them his delegate Timothy (4:17; 16:10–11).

30. Paul has sent them an earlier letter about relations with outsiders (1 Cor 5:9) and has received a letter from at least some of the congregants with questions they wish he will answer (7:1).

31. In addition to Kloppenborg, "Associations," and Harland, *Associations*, see Mc-

inthians is that the members of the assembly are in such disagreement on a range of issues that they have taken each other to pagan courts to settle cases (6:1–5).[32] Worse, Paul's own authority to instruct the community is under challenge by some within the assembly.[33]

Given such a breakdown in communication among members, it is all the more remarkable that—with the one great exception of 1 Cor 5:1–13, which I will discuss in the next chapter—Paul so consistently invites the active participation of the Corinthians from every side into a process of discernment, seeking to encourage a mode of moral thinking among them that is in accord with the "mind of Christ" (*nous Christou*, 2:16).

First Corinthians is also extraordinarily rich in the vocabulary that I isolated in 1 Thessalonians. The theme of holiness is struck from the very beginning, as Paul declares them to be "sanctified in Christ Jesus, called to be holy" (*hēgiasmenois en Christō Iēsou, klētois hagiois*, 1 Cor 1:2).[34] Holiness, then, is a condition to which they have been gifted in Christ: Paul says in 1:30 that Christ is their sanctification (*hagiasmos*) and that in baptism they "have been sanctified" (*hēgiasthēte*) in the name of the Lord Jesus Christ (6:11). Their sanctification through Christ has been accomplished by the Holy Spirit (*hagion pneuma*), in which they have all been baptized (12:13), which they have all drunk (12:13), and whose presence among them makes of them the temple of God: "Do you not know that you are the temple of God [*naos theou*], and that the Spirit of God dwells within you [*oikei en hymin*]?" (3:16, adapted); their bodies (or the body that they make up together) are "a temple within [or among] you of the Holy Spirit, whom you have from God" (6:19, author's translation).

As the term "called to be holy" (*klētois hagiois*) in 1 Cor 1:2 indicates, however, this status must be actualized in the way they live; they are to exhibit in the life of their assembly a true "difference" from the world around them.[35] As in 1 Thessalonians, the difference is to be expressed in

---

Lean, "Agrippillina Inscription"; R. Campbell, *Elders*; Appelbaum, "Organization"; Burtchaell, *From Synagogue to Church*.

32. A. Mitchell, "1 Cor 6:1–11."

33. See esp. Dahl, "Paul and the Church at Corinth"; Hurd, *Origin of I Corinthians*.

34. The reader is reminded that English translations (as here the NABRE) will choose cognates of "sanctify" or "holy" (as in "saints" or "holy ones") while the Greek terms are always the same, cognates of *hagiazein* ("to make holy, to sanctify").

35. See esp. the distinction drawn between the "holy ones/saints" and "the world" in 6:1–2, and Paul's consistent way in 1 Corinthians of speaking of "the world" (*ho kosmos*) in opposition to the members of the assembly, as something "outside" their holy sphere: "We have not received the Spirit of the World but the Spirit that is of God" (2:12, author's translation; see also 1:20–23; 3:19, 22; 4:19, 13; 5:10; 6:33–34; 11:32).

moral dispositions and behavior, rather than in ritual observance. Thus, Paul speaks of those who will not inherit the kingdom of God through an extensive vice list (6:9–10), declaring, "That is what some of you used to be," before stating how they have been transformed and "made holy" through baptism in the name of the Lord Jesus Christ (6:11).

The difficulty evinced by the enthusiastic and gifted (see 1 Cor 1:5–7) but fractious (see 1:10) Corinthians is just how holiness is to be expressed in the quotidian matters of life together, as well as in the extraordinary expressions of the Spirit in the worship gathering. Because they cannot agree among themselves and communication among them has broken down,[36] Paul seeks to help them "reason together" in a way consonant with the "mind of Christ" (2:16) with which they have been gifted through the Holy Spirit (2:12).

Before turning to specific examples, we should note how rich in "discernment" language 1 Corinthians is. Paul frequently uses cognates of "testing" (*dokimazein*)[37] and "judging/deciding/ discerning" (*krinein*),[38] not as something that he is doing but as something he wants the Corinthians to do. He wants them to learn how to think morally in a manner that accords with the spirit and mind that have been given them in Christ. Even when these specific terms are not used, Paul's argument concerning specific cases clearly wants to engage the Corinthians' minds and gain their assent.

The same can be said concerning edification. Paul uses the terms "edification" (*oikodomē*) and "to edify" (*oikodomein*) and "to be built up upon" (*epoikodomein*) with greater frequency in 1 Corinthians than any other of his letters,[39] but even when these specific terms are absent, the point is made clear that the construction and maintenance of

36. This seems to be the best explanation for members of the community seeking to sue each other concerning *ta biōtika* "before the unrighteous rather than before the saints" (1 Cor 6:1, author's translation). For the social function of such an argot of distinction, see Meeks, *First Urban Christians*.

37. *Dokimazein* in 1 Cor 3:13; 11:28; 16:3; *dokimos* in 11:19; *adokimos* in 9:27.

38. He uses *krinein* in the sense of "discern" in 1 Cor 2:2; 7:37; 10:15; 11:13, 31. The statement in 10:15 illustrates: "I am speaking as to sensible people [*hōs phronimois*]; judge for yourselves what I am saying [*krinate hymeis ho phēmi*]." He uses *krinein* in the sense of judging (sometimes negatively) in 4:5; 5:3, 12–13; 6:1–3, 6; 10:29. But Paul also uses the cognates *anakrinein* (2:14–15; 4:3–4; 9:3; 10:25, 27; 14:24) and *diakrinein* (4:7; 6:5; 11:29, 31; 14:29), both of which have the nuance of "assessing" or "evaluating." He uses *phronein* in 13:11 and *phronimos* in 4:10 and 10:15.

39. For *oikodomē*, see 1 Cor 3:9; 14:3, 5, 12, 26; for *oikodomein*, see 8:1, 10; 10:23; 14:4, 17; for *epoikodomein*, see 3:10, 12, 14.

a community "worthy of its calling" should govern the members' moral reasoning. What makes Paul's confidence in his readers more startling is that living by the mind of Christ is not simply a matter of choosing the good over the bad but of discerning between things that are both good, to see which course of behavior builds the community as such and not simply the individual (see Phil 2:1–4). This is, clearly, not at all an easy sort of thinking to do.

Marriage and Celibacy   Despite lacking much of the distinctive diction concerning discernment, edification, and holiness, Paul's discussion of marriage and singleness in 1 Cor 7:1–40 is an appropriate focus for our analysis, first because it is apparently the first question put to him by the Corinthians' own letter (*peri de hōn egrapsate*, 7:1), and second because it shows how circumstances—including blatant sexual immorality (*porneia*) within the assembly (see 5:1–5; 6:12–20)—have made the topic much more complex, in contrast to his straightforward instructions to the Thessalonians that each should have a wife in holiness and honor (1 Thess 4:4–5).[40]

Most of all, the passage enables Paul to show how he himself practices moral reasoning on a complex issue involving sexual existence, how simple answers to complex somatic realities seldom suffice, and how necessary it is to distinguish those things that "really matter" (*ta diapheronta*) with respect to God's kingdom and those things that are only accidental and not essential (*ta adiapheronta*).

Paul himself is celibate, "anxious about the things of the Lord" rather than about a wife and children (see 1 Cor 7:32–33), and he wishes that everyone were as he was (7:7). He therefore in a real sense agrees with the slogan advanced by his correspondents, "It is a good thing for a man not to touch a woman" (*kalon anthrōpō gynaikos mē haptesthai*, 7:1).[41] The term *kalos* as used throughout this passage (7:1, 8, 26), however, has more the sense of "appropriate" or "noble/honorable" than the strict moral sense of "good" as opposed to "evil" (cf. Rom 14:21; 2 Cor 8:21; Gal 6:9; 1 Tim 1:8, 18; 2:3; 3:1; 2 Tim 2:3; Titus 3:8). Paul's preference for

---

40. For discussion of Paul's discussion in its historical context, see Demming, *Paul on Marriage and Celibacy*; Thaden, *Sex, Christ, and Embodied Cognition*.

41. I agree that this is likely one of the "slogans," to which some in the Corinthian Pauline party have put to their own use, like "all things are lawful for me" (1 Cor 6:12 NRSV) or "food for the stomach and the stomach for food" (6:13), which may indeed have originated with Paul himself.

celibacy, moreover, is very much connected to the present circumstances facing the church.

When he declares that "the world in its present form is passing away" (1 Cor 7:31), he is not simply making a statement concerning the eschaton; he is delivering a fundamental axiom for those who believe in the living God who creates out of nothing at every moment: all things are contingent and therefore transitory. Believers cannot treat the things of the world, and, still less, social arrangements, as permanent, necessary, or ultimate. All things created are "passing away" even as they are brought into being; all are relative rather than absolute. Believers, therefore, are required to be both engaged with and detached from all worldly structures; they must live in the world "as though not" (*hōs mē*, 7:29-31).[42] For those who are married, the affliction (*thlipsis*) generated by the conflicting loyalties to spouse and children on one side (7:32-35) and the demands of the kingdom on the other (7:28) is real, and Paul would like to spare his reader such anxiety (*merimna*, 7:32).

But not everyone has this gift of celibacy: "I wish everyone to be as I am, but each has a particular gift from God [*charisma*], one of one kind and one of another" (1 Cor 7:7).[43] Marriage is therefore to be regarded as equally valid a choice for believers. What is critical here is that it is a choice, one that responds to the human perception of a divine gift. There is no mandatory Christian sexual state demanded of all. Paul notes two conditions that make marriage the more desirable option: when the threat of *porneia* is pressing (7:2; we remember the backdrop of 5:1-6:20), and when sexual desire makes one "aflame with passion," so that one cannot exercise sexual self-control (7:9).

Paul's depiction of marriage in 1 Cor 7:2-6, however, goes far beyond the recommendation of it as a "cure for concupiscence."[44] We note first that, remarkably for the time, Paul speaks of marriage in terms of the agency of both genders: each man should have a wife, and each wife a husband (7:2). The implication is that individual marriages are the choices of partners rather than determinations made by third parties, and that women have as much say as do men in making such choices. Such reciprocity continues in Paul's further instructions. The bodies of husband and wife belong to each other (7:4; cf. 6:19), and sexual con-

42. See the apt characterization of "eschatological detachment" in Bultmann, *Theology of the New Testament*, 1:135.

43. Paul uses the same term here as he does of the "gifts" (*charismata*) of the Holy Spirit in 1 Cor 12:4, 9, 30, 31.

44. The phrase comes from Augustine, *The Good of Marriage* 9.

gress should be willingly granted to the partner (7:3–4). Abstinence from sex should be temporary in order to give attention to prayer (7:5), and after this temporary break, relations should be resumed (7:5). Just as sex with a prostitute has negative spiritual implications (6:16), so does the sexual bonding of husband and wife have positive spiritual implications: they can sanctify each other—even if one partner is an unbeliever—and their children are sanctified (7:14). A spouse may even, although Paul is not certain of this, be "saved" by a marriage partner—that is, brought into the community of the saints through conversion.[45] Marriage is a covenant undertaken between persons, and in 7:10 Paul follows the saying of Jesus (Mark 10:11; Matt 5:32; 19:9; Luke 16:18) forbidding divorce. The only exception is the separation—with freedom—that results from a fundamental spiritual estrangement when one is a Christian and a partner is a pagan, making it impossible for a man and woman to live in peace (7:15).

The premise on which the freedom to discern and decide which gift of God one will live out is Paul's fundamental distinction between the call of God (which is absolute) and diverse states of life (which are always relative). Since all humans are called by God to discipleship, no station in life can either impede or abet the response of obedience to that call: "Circumcision means nothing, and uncircumcision means nothing; what matters is keeping God's commandments" (1 Cor 7:19). Male and female, Jew and gentile, slave and free, married and unmarried are all called to a life of righteousness (7:17–24). In the *ekklēsia*, then, such differences in ethnicity, gender, social status, or sexual commitment are properly regarded as adiaphora—they are not essential to the life of faith.

Given the present circumstances of affliction, Paul himself thinks people should stay in the condition within which they were called (1 Cor 7:24): "Are you bound to a wife? Then do not seek a separation. Are you free of a wife? Then do not look for a wife" (7:27, adapted). But the logic of his premise can as easily give the freedom to change, so long as this change is not identified as essential to the life of faith before God: "If you marry, however, you do not sin, nor does an unmarried woman sin if she marries" (7:28).

As Paul considers the cases of those now single—whether because they are virgins, widows, or (in the obscure situation suggested 1 Cor

45. This is a splendid example of Paul's social understanding of "salvation" as a matter of belonging to a saved, remnant people, which is dominant in his letters; see chap. 2 in this volume.

7:36–38) virgins of marriageable age under the supervision of another—the principles he has already established continue to be applied. He thinks it "better" to be free from familial anxiety in order to devote oneself to the work of the Lord, and his language is provocative: "An unmarried woman or a virgin is anxious about the things of the Lord [*ta tou kyriou*], so that she may be holy in both body and spirit [*hagia kai tō sōmati kai tō pneumati*]" (7:34).[46] But this does not betray the right, even the necessity, of individual believers choosing the path they will follow (7:35–49). In nonessential matters, the only real sin is insisting that something nonessential is in fact essential. Paul's entire discussion in 7:1–40 is to help the Corinthians shift from holding ideological positions ("all must do this" or "only this is holy") to discerning together what things matter and what things don't, what things build the church and what things tear it apart (see esp. 3:16–17).

Eating Food Offered to Idols   If the sexual contact that constitutes *porneia* can infect the body of Christ so that its holiness is diminished—in that it is less "different" from the world of idolatry with which *porneia* was associated—does the same danger lie in contact with idolatry through food?[47] This is the subject that occupies 1 Cor 8–10. It is a lengthy argument, which begins with the case of eating meat purchased at pagan markets (for urban dwellers the only source for meat) that sold as food what was not consumed in idolatrous sacrifices (8:1–13), then moves to provide Paul's own example of relinquishing rights for the sake of others (9:1–26), and then takes up the situation of actually eating at meals dedicated to the gods (10:1–11:1). The first stage represents contact with idolatry only at second- or thirdhand, whereas the last stage represents the possibility of actually participating in what Paul regards as the "table of demons" (10:21). I focus only on the portion of the argument in 8:1–13.

At the surface level, the problem is the legitimacy of contact with food that has been used in idolatrous worship, but at a deeper level, the issue is the tension between the freedom given by knowledge and the constraints imposed by love of neighbor. Paul begins his discussion with a distinction between a knowledge that "puffs up" (*physioi*) (the

46. Note that this condition of total "sanctification" is in contrast to the married person who is anxious about "the things of the world" (*ta tou kosmou*, 7:33–34). Although Paul attached "holiness" to marriage through the "saving" of a spouse and "sanctifying" of children, he seems here to attach a greater degree of holiness—that is, difference from the world—to those who serve the Lord as single persons.

47. For discussion, see Gooch, *Dangerous Food*; Willis, *Idol-Meat in Corinth*.

self, understood) and love that "builds up" (*oikodomei*) (the neighbor, understood]) (1 Cor 8:1). He continues, "If anyone supposes he knows something, he does not yet know as he ought to know. But if one loves God, one is known by him" (8:2–3). And in the last part of his discussion, Paul states, "'Everything is lawful,' but not everything is beneficial [*sympherei*]. 'Everything is lawful,' but not everything builds up [*oikodomei*]. No one should seek his own advantage, but that of his neighbor" (10:23–24; cf. Phil 2:4). Proper discernment within the body of Christ means thinking in terms of what builds the community rather that what puffs up the self. This is how the church is "holy"—that is, different from the world in which self-advantage is always the trump card in every game of human interaction.

The "strong" among the Corinthians are convinced that idols are not real (1 Cor 8:4; 10:19), and therefore that food offered to them is in no way dangerous for believers. Speaking to those confident in their own understanding, Paul states that he concurs in this judgment: "we know that we all have this knowledge" (8:1, author's translation). Idols are not real, because there is but one God who is the source and goal of all that exists (8:4–6). Food, therefore, is among *ta adiaphora*: "Now food will not bring us closer to God. We are no worse off if we do not eat, nor are we better off if we do" (8:8). Therefore, if believers decide to eat such food on the basis of such correct knowledge, they are free to do so.

In the Corinthian *ekklēsia*, however, there are some who do not have the same robust conscience based on the correct facts: "But not all have this knowledge," Paul declares (8:7). There are some within the assembly of believers who have been so steeped in idolatry before their conversion (or conversely, have carried over from a Jewish background that idol-food pollutes) that they cannot shake the conviction that food connected in any way to idolatrous worship must be tainted by idolatry and is therefore dangerous. They have what Paul calls a "weak conscience" (*syneidēsis asthenēs*), because their moral judgment is not secure and confident: in some sense they think idols are real, and the only safe protection from them (the only way to secure the "holiness" of the church) is through complete abstinence from such food. Their conscience tells them that they must abstain.

Since ancient meals—including cultic meals—were communal, observing what and how one's table companions ate was natural. Paul sees that "weak" brothers or sisters might observe the indiscriminate eating of the "strong" as warrant to go against their own conscience and partake of food that they really consider wrong. They therefore "stumble," not because they have eaten one food rather than another, but because they go against the dictate of their own conscience, under the influence of the strong. Using the term ironically, Paul speaks of the fellow believer being "built up" to an action his or her conscience says is wrong: "Make sure that this liberty [*exousia*] of yours in no way becomes a stumbling block [*proskomma*] to the weak. If someone sees you, with your knowledge, reclining at table in the temple of an idol, may not his conscience too, weak as it is, be 'built up' (*oikodomēthēsetai*) to eat the meal sacrificed to idols?" (1 Cor 8:9–10).

Paul regards such carelessness concerning the effect of individual actions on those "who do not all have such knowledge" to cause not simply a minor "offense"—see the strength of *skandalon* ("stumbling block") elsewhere[48]—but the "destruction" or "loss" (*apollytai*)[49] of a brother "for whom Christ died," and is therefore a sin against the living Christ whose body the *ekklēsia* is (1 Cor 8:11–12).[50] This short passage illustrates brilliantly how, for Paul, the "holiness" of the church is not ritual—involving in this case food prohibitions—but a matter of moral dispositions, and that proper moral discernment in practice demands seeking not the rights of the individual but the edification of the community through love.

Glossolalia and Prophecy Paul's discussion in 1 Cor 12–14 calls for a discernment that builds the church in holiness against the backdrop of a gentile religiosity in which forms of ecstatic prophecy (*mania*) were held in the highest esteem,[51] and to which the Christian practice of speaking in tongues bore a phenomenological resemblance and therefore held a definite attraction to those Corinthians who were puffed up "with all discourse and all knowledge" (1:5), to the extent that they considered the ability to speak in tongues as a superior "sign of believers" (see 14:22).

48. See *skandalon* as that which prevents faith in Rom 9:33; 10:19; 14:13; 16:17; 1 Cor 1:23; Gal 5:11; and similarly, *skandalizein* in Rom 14:21 and 2 Cor 11:29.

49. See Paul's use of *apollymi* in 1 Cor 1:18 in contrast to those who are being saved; see also 2 Cor 2:15; 4:3, 9; 2 Thess 2:10.

50. Paul's dense language shows us first how the "story of Jesus" is applied as cause and exemplar (as Christ died for this brother, so should you be willing to give yourself for this brother or sister), and second, how the resurrectd Jesus is identified with the community as such (you are "sinning against Christ" when you sin against a fellow believer).

51. See chap. 6, "Glossolalia and the Embarrassments of Experience," in this volume.

Three important stages precede the passage I consider. First, in 1 Cor 12:1–3 Paul reminds his readers that not all "spiritual phenomena" (*ta pneumatika*) build the community of faith: when they were pagans, they were carried off in ecstasy to idols. Only in the Holy Spirit are they empowered to declare the lordship of Jesus (12:3). His topic, therefore, is not of spiritual things generally but of those "gifts" (*ta charismata*) that come from the Holy Spirit. Second, in 12:4–31 Paul establishes that both the diversity and the unity of such gifts derive from God and are meant to serve the life and growth of the "body of Christ" that is the *ekklēsia*. Third, in 13:1–13 his encomium on *agapē* reminds readers that all gifts—whether tongues or prophecy or knowledge or even faith (13:1–3)—are useless unless in the service of this moral disposition that seeks the benefit of the other more than the self. His contrast between thinking like a child and thinking like an adult (13:11) is not beside the point but very much to the point: if *agapē* "builds up," as he declares in 8:1, then it must possess the quality of "alterity" that is aware of and responsive to others and not simply the self.[52] For Paul, such thinking is that of adulthood, which contrasts with the narcissism of childhood. These three important points prepare for his discussion of two specific gifts in chapter 14, glossolalia and prophecy.

Paul's preference for prophecy is plain, even though he recognizes speaking in tongues as a gift of the Spirit (1 Cor 12:29–30) and acknowledges its value (see 11:3–4; 14:5); indeed, he claims himself to speak in tongues more than any of them (4:18). His reason is plainly stated. As a mode of prayer, glossolalia can glorify God and "edify" (*oikodomein*) the individual who prays (14:4), but because it is unintelligible unless translated, it does not build up the assembly as such. In contrast, Paul regards prophesy as a form of intelligible speech that engages the mind (14:14) and builds up the community (14:4). Tongues is not, as some claimed, "the sign of believers" but can actually be a "sign for disbelievers" since it repels a true understanding of the good news (see 14:21–22). Prophecy, however, calls people to faith and "builds" on the foundation laid by apostolic teaching (see 3:10–15; 12:28).

Paul presents a hypothetical case of outsiders coming to the worship assembly when all were speaking in tongues, and concluding *hōti mainesthe* (1 Cor 14:23)—that is, "these people are raving in the manner of pagan prophets; there is nothing distinctive here." But if they hear believers

---

52. I use the term "alterity" in the manner I here define it, which has some resemblance to, but is not derived from, the philosopher Emmanuel Lévinas (1906–1995) in works such as *Alterity and Transcendence*.

prophesying, then they will be convicted by the good news and declare, "God is truly among you" (*ontōs ho theos en hymin estin*, 14:25). Paul's language here echoes his description of the church as the temple of God indwelt by the Holy Spirit. In different words, he has the pagan observers recognize the "holiness"—that is, the "difference"—of a community built up by prophecy in the assembly.[53]

Paul therefore demands responsibility, maturity, and thought from the Corinthians (1 Cor 14:20). Even in the context of spiritual worship, the whole community must exercise judgment as to what builds it up: "Two or three prophets should speak, and the others discern" (*prophētai de duo ē treis laleitōsan, kai ho alloi diakrinetōsan*, 14:29).[54] The prophets should control their utterances (14:32); glossolalists should be silent if their ecstatic babbling cannot be translated (14:27–28); speech should be orderly and in turn (14:26–31); even though women can speak in tongues and prophesy (11:5), they should not teach in this public assembly (14:34–36); everything should be done "properly and in order" (14:40). But the fundamental principle underlying all behavior and all discernment is what builds up the *ekklēsia* as the dwelling place of God: "Everything should be done for building up" (*panta pros oikodomēn ginesthō*, 14:26).

Romans

In this letter to readers he had not yet met, Paul traces the progression of his gentile readers from their state of alienation from God to their participation in God's righteous people.[55] They began with "undiscerning minds" (*adokimon noun*), which led them into every kind of vice (Rom 1:28), in partial contrast to the Jews who could boast of "being able to discern what is important" (*dokimazein ta diapheronta*, 2:18) but were still under the power of sin (3:9).

---

53. See above all Munoz, "How Not to Go Out of the World."

54. It is possible to read *hoi alloi* as "the other prophets," but I think it makes more sense to have it refer to all those who are listening. I say this despite Paul's question when listing the gifts in 12:30, "do all have the gifts or healing? Do all speak in tongues? Do all discern?" All these questions, introduced by *mē*, expect a negative answer: "No, not everyone heals, or speaks in tongues, or discerns." But these are clearly rhetorical questions intended to make the point that the gifts are distributed as God wills. There is a tension here between this, and Paul's concern that everyone "in [their] thinking be mature" and practice discernment (14:24).

55. See especially Nicolet-Anderson, *Constructing the Self*.

But because God poured the love of God into their hearts through the Holy Spirit (Rom 5:5) through the gift of the death and resurrection of Christ (5:6–21), and because baptism conformed them to the death of Christ and raised them to a new power of life for "righteousness unto holiness" (*dikaiosynē eis hagiasmon,* 6:19), and to bear the fruit of righteousness "for holiness whose goal is eternal life" (*eis hagiasmon to de telos zōēn aiōnion,* 6:22), and because that Holy Spirit "dwells within [them]" (*oikei en hymin,* 8:9), these gentile believers now have the capacity to "walk according to the Spirit" (*peripatein kata pneuma,* 8:4) and to "think morally according to the Spirit" (*phronousin . . . to tou pneumatos,* 8:5; author's translations above). They live according to a new power and a new norm: "If the Spirit of the one who raised Jesus from the dead dwells in you, the one who raised Christ from the dead will give life to your mortal bodies also, through the Spirit who dwells in you [*dia tou enoikountos autou pneumatos en hymin*]" (8:11, adapted).

When Paul turns to the properly hortatory section of his letter in 12:1–2, then, he naturally uses language that evokes the holiness of this new life (their bodies are "living sacrifices" offered to God) and the transformation of the mind according to Christ that enables them to "discern what is the will of God, what is good and pleasing and perfect" (*dokimazein hymas ti to thelēma tou theou, to agathon kai euareston kai teleion,* Rom 12:2). In a passage that strongly echoes 1 Cor 8:1–13, Paul argues in Rom 14:1–15:3 for discernment that leads to edification within a community that has a legitimate plurality of practice concerning *ta adiaphora.*

Here those whom Paul terms "weak in faith" (Rom 14:1) insist on a stricter observance in matters of diet (14:20) as well as in calendar, "judging" some days as more important than others.[56] They judge (in the sense of condemn) those who are strong in faith and treat all food and days alike (14:2), while, in turn, the strong "despise" the weak (14:3). As in 1 Corinthians, Paul agrees intellectually with the strong, declaring, "The kingdom of God is not a matter of food and drink, but of righteousness and peace, and joy in the Holy Spirit" (14:17, adapted; cf. 1 Cor 8:8). The holiness of the church consists not in certain ritual observances but in appropriate moral dispositions toward God and other humans. There

---

56. For the language for discernment/testing in this passage of Romans, see *dokimos* in 14:18 and *dokimazein* in 14:22; *diakrinein* in 14:23 and *krinein* in 14:3, 4, 5, 10, 13 (2×), 22; and *phronein* in 14:6; 15:5. For a helpful analysis of the passage within the overall argument of Romans, see Meeks, "Judgment and the Brother."

can be legitimate diversity of practice in nonessentials, with the essential shared value being the giving of praise to God (14:6). Believers are not answerable to each other as judges of each other, but are answerable to God alone (14:4, 10–12).

Neither condemnation nor contempt is therefore fitting for members of Christ's body (Rom 14:3–4, 10, 13). Freedom of conscience stands as the norm for individual decision-making (14:14, 20). With regard to the neighbor, Paul insists (as in 1 Corinthians) that this freedom must not cause a weaker brother or sister to stumble (14:13): "Do not because of your food destroy him for whom Christ died" (14:15). Positively, individual discernment should always tend to the building up (*oikodomē*) of others (14:19; 15:2).

Paul's theological warrants for these community guidelines tie in with his earlier argument concerning Jews and gentiles in God's plan (Rom 1–11). Believers should accept one another in their diversity of thought and practice because God has accepted all of them, Jew and gentile alike; all humans have been accepted in Christ (14:3). The Messiah died and lived again so that he might be Lord of all, and so that, whether they lived or died, they would belong to him (14:7–8). Christ died for all, and their lives together must follow his story. Christ is therefore the effective cause of their being accepted by God (15:8–9) and the model (15:2–6) of how they are to receive one another in mutual service: "Welcome one another, then, as Christ welcomes you, for the glory of God" (15:7). The renewal of the mind through the Holy Spirit, then, should lead to this disposition and behavior: "Let each of us please our neighbor for the good [*eis to agathon*, see 12:2], for building up [*oikodomēn*]" (15:2).

Ephesians

Among the Pauline canonical letters, Ephesians has a special character. It is not written to a single *ekklēsia* founded by the apostle, like 1 Thessalonians or Philippians, nor to a group of Pauline churches, like Galatians and 1 Corinthians, or even to a local assembly as yet unknown to him, like Romans. Ephesians is, in all likelihood, a circular or encyclical letter written to believers in any number of places who might broadly fall within the circle of the Pauline mission.[57] It is all the more useful to inquire, then, whether the same sensibilities concerning community

57. See vol. 1, chap. 10.

building among believers that appear in other letters might be found in Ephesians as well—albeit perhaps with a distinctive diction.

Our way into the topic is made more difficult by the fact that Ephesians, true to its nature, is notoriously *general* in its teaching and admonition. Here there are no specific cases for Paul to offer guidelines for discernment. Nevertheless, the evidence offered by the composition is intriguing. The theme of holiness is abundantly attested, not only in the designation of the readers as sealed by the Holy Spirit (1:13; see also 4:30) and in the frequent use of "the holy ones/saints" for members of the assembly (1:1, 15, 18; 2:19; 3:5, 8, 18; 5:3; 6:18) but also in the qualification of such holiness in moral terms (reminding us of 1 Thessalonians). Thus, in 1:4 he speaks of God choosing them to be "holy and without blemish" (*hagious kai amōmous*), and similarly in 5:27 he speaks of the church being "holy and without blemish" (*hagia kai amōmos*).

Ephesians' language about holiness merges with that concerning edification, most notably in the description of the cosmic *ekklēsia* as made up of both Jews and gentiles reconciled to God and to each other through Christ: "So then you are no longer strangers and sojourners, but you are fellow citizens with the holy ones [*tois hagiois*] and members of the household of God, built upon [*epoikodomēthentes*] the foundation of the apostles and prophets, with Christ Jesus himself as the capstone. Through him the whole structure is held together and grows into a temple sacred to the Lord [*pasa oikodomē . . . eis naon hagion en kyriō*]; in him you also are being built together into a dwelling place of God in the Spirit [*en hō kai hymeis synoikodomeisthe eis katoikētērion tou theou en pneumati*]" (2:19–22).[58] The language of edification is also turned to the function of ministries within the *ekklēsia*; leaders are to "equip the holy ones for the work of ministry, for building up the body of Christ" (*eis oikodomēn tou sōmatos tou Christou*, Eph 4:12). It recurs when Paul speaks of the goal of such ministries in 4:15–16: "Living the truth in love, we should grow in every way into him who is the head, Christ, from whom the whole body, joined and held together by every supporting ligament, with the proper functioning of each part, brings about the body's growth and builds itself up in love [*eis oikodomēn heautou en agapē*]."[59] Finally, in a manner similar to 1 Cor 14, Paul makes edification

58. In substance, and largely in diction, this description is remarkably close to 1 Cor 3:10–17 and 6:19.

59. As in 2:19–22 and 4:12, Ephesians here distinctively mixes the metaphor of the body and of the building.

the goal of speech within the *ekklēsia*: "No foul language should come out of your mouths, but only such as is good for necessary edification [*alla ei tis agathos pros oikodomēn tēs chreias*]" (4:29, adapted).

Perhaps least obvious is evidence in Ephesians for what I have called discernment, or practical moral reasoning. This is not because language about insight and wisdom generally is lacking (see, e.g., 1:8, 17, 18; 3:4, 9, 17–18), but such language tends to refer to believers' recognition of the mystery proclaimed by Paul. Beginning in 4:14, however, Paul sketches the epistemic transformation of gentile believers in a manner that echoes Rom 1:18–32 and 12:1–2. In 4:14 he declares that they "may no longer be infants, tossed by waves and swept along by every wind of teaching arising from human trickery, from their cunning in the interests of deceitful scheming." In 4:17–19 he characterizes their former lives in this fashion: "You must no longer live as the Gentiles do, in the futility of their minds [*en mataiotēti tou noos autōn*]; darkened in understanding, alienated from the life of God because of their ignorance [*dia tēn agnoian tēn ousan en autois*], because of their hardness of heart, they have become callous and have handed themselves over to licentiousness for the practice of every kind of impurity to excess [*heautous paredōkan tē aselgeia eis ergasian akatharsias pasēs en pleonexia*]." Not only does this passage echo the diction of Rom 1, but it draws the same connection between the corruption of the mind and the degradation of moral practice. In contrast, Paul sketches the entailments for those who have been incorporated into the "dwelling place of God in the Spirit" (2:22) if they have indeed been taught "the truth that is in Jesus" (4:21, author's translation). They are to "put away the old self of [their] former way of life, corrupted through deceitful desires, and be renewed in the spirit of [their] minds [*ananeousthai de tō pneumati tou noos hymon*], and put on the new self, created in God's way in righteousness and holiness of truth [*kata theon ktisthenta en dikaiosynē kai hosiotēti tēs alētheias*]" (4:22–24).

Just as the "old self" was characterized by a *nous* that distorted reality and expressed itself in vice, so is the renewed *nous* of the "new self" created by God to express itself in righteous and holy moral dispositions. The sort of discernment consequent on this new condition is stated clearly in Eph 5:8–10: "For you were once in darkness, but now you are light in the Lord. Live as children of light, for light produces every kind of goodness and righteousness and truth. Try to learn what is pleasing to the Lord [*dokimazontes ti estin euareston tō kyriō*]."[60] He puts it still

---

60. The NABRE translation here, "try to learn," is inadequate. The Greek *doki-*

another way in 5:15–17 (author's translation): "Watch carefully, therefore, how you live, not as foolish persons but as wise [*mē hōs asophoi all' hōs sophoi*]. . . . Do not continue in ignorance, but understand what is the will of the Lord [*syniete ti to thelēma tou kyriou*]." No less than in the letters he wrote to specific communities, then, does Paul in Ephesians advocate the three mechanisms of mutual community strengthening: a commitment to the otherness within the world that is holiness, behavior that builds other members in that shared commitment, and the practical decision-making by each member that conforms to these goals and derives from a renewed mind through the Holy Spirit.

Conclusion

Beginning with 1 Thessalonians, I have shown how in a considerable number of his canonical letters—passingly in Galatians, distinctively in Philippians, idiosyncratically in 2 Corinthians, and explicitly in 1 Corinthians, Romans, and Ephesians—Paul encourages readers to three mechanisms of communal reinforcement: sanctification (being different from the world), edification (building each other up) and discernment (making practical judgments in conformity with them). These mechanisms do not replace the leadership that Paul supposes to be in place (in 1 Thessalonians, 1 Corinthians, Romans, and Ephesians), nor the direct guidance that Paul himself provides through personal visits, the sending of delegates, or the writing of letters. They represent the set of dispositions and practices that are necessary for any other elements of teaching or tradition to work; they are the essential elements of upkeep and maintenance for a nascent intentional community in a pluralistic world with only the least obvious of experiential and convictional premises at its base. They also reveal a side of Paul's pastoral practice that is, perhaps, surprisingly non-autocratic and trusting in the abilities of his readers, not to mention the transforming power of the Holy Spirit.

---

mazontes should be taken as circumstantial, expressing purpose: "so that you can test." The use of *dokimazein* together with *euareston*, furthermore, provides a clear echo of Rom 12:2.

Chapter 19

The Apostle as Crisis Manager

Second Thessalonians

In the previous chapter, I examined the way in which Paul sought to secure his fragile communities through encouraging the mutual practice of discernment and edification. These social dynamics, when active among believers themselves, both built on and strengthened their holiness, which in social terms could be defined as their sense of separateness or difference from the world around them. Beginning with 1 Thessalonians, I showed how Paul asked for the same or similar dispositions and practices among his readers in Galatia, Philippi, Corinth, and Rome, as well as in the circular letter called Ephesians.

Such mutual reinforcement of identity was all the more important, I argued, because Pauline foundations like the one at Thessaloniki were new, had only a small number of members, were under threat from outsiders, and were bereft of their founder.[1] Like all nascent intentional communities, they existed at all because of the collusion of their members; the doubt, disaffection, or apostasy even of a single member posed the sort of threat to their shared "plausibility structure" that would not challenge a long-standing, institutionally structured, and well-populated community.[2] Paul sought to assist them through personal visits, the dispatching of his delegates, and as a last resort, the sending of letters such as 1 Thessalonians. But in addition to these, and to the exhortation and effort of the leaders he had left in place (1 Thess 5:12), Paul desired and needed the members of the *ekklēsia* themselves to discern, edify, and

1. See the quantitative analysis by Stark, *Rise of Christianity*, 129–46.
2. Critical to my reading is the analysis of the social construction of reality in religion, and the effect of threat on an intentional community's "plausibility structure"—that is, the ideological framework constructed and maintained through embodied practices; see Berger, *Sacred Canopy*.

sanctify each other. Their continued existence demanded such mutual reinforcement in disposition and behavior.

But how does Paul respond to crises that are so severe that they do not yield to such dynamics, or when the community's boundaries are threatened to such a degree as to imperil not only the integrity but the existence of the assembly? Paul's second letter to the Thessalonians provides the ideal case study. If, as I hold, this composition is not only authentically Pauline but is written shortly after 1 Thessalonians, and in response to a situation that Paul's first letter to the *ekklēsia* inadvertently helped create,[3] then we are able to trace with some degree of confidence the unfolding of such a crisis and Paul's response to it. We see (1) how Paul's words in 1 Thessalonians could well have been misread; (2) how the changed situation of the Thessalonians abetted such a misreading; (3) how the crisis in the assembly started and how it exhibited itself behaviorally; and (4) how Paul manages the crisis in his second letter to them, through cognitive adjustment and through social engineering. We can then observe how Paul's "crisis management" is not restricted to this letter but can be observed as well in 1 Corinthians, Galatians, 1 Timothy, and Titus.

The Crisis in Thessaloniki

There is much in 2 Thessalonians that is not only obscure but unknowable.[4] As a result, it is a composition subject to more than ordinary scholarly speculation. It is good to remember that in this case, as in all others,

---

3. Although the authenticity of 2 Thessalonians is held by many commentators (see, e.g., Malherbe, *First and Second Thessalonians*) and has everything to recommend it—the discrepancy in eschatological scenarios is explicable, as I will show, on the change in circumstance, the senders and the style are the same in both letters, and the presence of a signature in 3:17 is a problem only to those otherwise committed to inauthenticity—there are still a majority of scholars holding the conventional position. See, e.g., Richard, *First and Second Thessalonians*; Bailey, "Who Wrote II Thessalonians?"; J. Barclay, "Conflict in Thessalonica"; Koester, "Paul's Eschatology"; Laub, "'Paulinische Autorität'"; Lindemann, "Zum Abfassungszweck." An argument for the change in circumstances rather than the passage of time as accounting for the difference in eschatology is made by Moule, "Influence of Circumstances." The most positive use of 2 Thessalonians for understanding Paul theologically is by Munck, *Paul*, 36–68.

4. Uncertainty attends both the exact nature of the circumstances and the obscure references that occur in Paul's "clarification" in 2 Thess 2:3–12.

we are limited by Paul's (and his co-writers') perceptions of the situation. Their uncertainty may indeed match our own. As reported by the letter, however, the basic facts of the crisis seem to be these:

- Probably at a gathering of the assembly—a reasonable assumption, given what happens—some member or members receive and announce a revelation; Paul is uncertain concerning the medium of revelation: Was it by a "spirit" (*pneuma*), "word" (*logos*), or a "letter" (*epistolē*) "as through us" (2:2, author's translation)?[5]
- The burden of the revelation is that the expected "*parousia* of the Lord Jesus Christ" and "our being gathered to him" (2:1) is happening now: "the day of the Lord is here" (2:2, author's translations).[6]
- Some of those hearing this message are immediately (*tacheōs*) "shaken out of [their] minds" (*saleuthēnai hymas apo tou noos*)[7] and "alarmed" (*throeisthai*) (2:2).[8] The two terms in combination suggest both a cognitive and emotional upheaval.
- Paul regards the announcement as deceptive: "Let no one deceive you in any fashion" (*mē tis hymas exapatēsē kata mēdena tropon*, 2:3, author's translations).[9]

---

5. Unless otherwise indicated, Scripture quotations in this chapter are from the NABRE. Paul's ignorance is matched by ours, especially since, phenomenologically, the options within charismatic communities can occur in combination: a "word of prophecy" is "spirit-inspired" and letters can be "spirit-letters," as we know from Rev 1–3 and the Spirit-communications of early Shaker gatherings in America.

6. These are, as we know, the main topics of 4:12–5:10 in Paul's first letter to the community: for *parousia*, see 1 Thess 2:19; 3:13; 4:5; 5:23, and for *hēmera tou kyriou*, see 5:2 and 5:4. The verb *enestēken* (from *enistēmi*) in the prefect tense has the ambiguous sense of "is arriving" and "has come." In either case, as with the verb *engizō* in the announcement by Jesus that "the kingdom of God has come/approached" (Mark 1:15), the note of immediacy and urgency is palpable.

7. The verb *saleuein* literally means physically "to shake" something (see Luke 6:48; Heb 12:26–27), even as violently as in an earthquake (Ps 81:5; see Acts 4:31), but appears in Acts 17:13 in an accusation made (strangely enough) by Thessalonian opponents for Paul's "shaking up and agitating the crowds" in Berea (*saleuontes kai tarassontes tous ochlous*). Here, in combination with *apo tou noos* ("away from mind"), it suggests a severe mental disturbance.

8. The passive of the verb *throeō* is used in the New Testament only three other times, once for the disciples response of terror at the appearance of Jesus after his death (Luke 24:37) and twice for the fear at the events of the future spoken of by Jesus in Mark 13:7 and Matt 24:6.

9. The verb *exapatan* does not suggest an error but a deliberate attempt to deceive

- The behavioral consequence among some in the community is that—presumably on the assumption that ordinary life has ceased or is about to cease with the appearance of God's kingdom—they have become "disorderly" (*ataktoi*, 3:6), which is expressed by their refusal to work (3:11) and instead becoming some form of what we would call "layabouts" or "idlers" (*mēden ergazomenous alla periergazomenous*).[10]

It is fair to ask why this simple sequence of events should be called a "crisis," why it seemed to Paul and his co-writers to represent a more serious one than that they faced in their first letter, and why matters developed in the direction they did. Answering all three questions requires a certain amount of guesswork, but by taking into account the literary evidence together with a certain amount of imagination based on social psychology, a reasonable surmise is possible.

First, it is a crisis because intentional communities newly founded within a pluralistic context all find that the maintenance of community identity and boundaries is difficult. If the Thessalonian assembly were as tiny as we might suppose—possibly consisting in a mere handful of households—then the threat to the plausibility structure of the community is real if only a few of the members are deviant in thought, feeling, or action, especially if the *ekklēsia*'s founder is absent and unable to address such dissidence directly.

Second, the crisis that Paul faces in 2 Thessalonians is considerably greater than the situation he addressed in his first letter to that assembly, because at least some members have moved from "grieving as those do who have no hope" (1 Thess 4:13, author's translation) because of the death of loved ones, to a full-fledged state of mental and emotional confusion, thinking that the "day of the Lord" was upon them; worse, that mental and emotional confusion has led to consequences in action.

(see Josephus, *Jewish Antiquities* 10.111; Epictetus, *Discourses* 2.20.7) either others or oneself; in 2 Cor 11:3 and 1 Tim 2:14, Paul uses it for the deception of Eve (see also Rom 7:11; 16:18; 1 Cor 3:18).

10. The verb combines "about/around" (*peri*) and "to work" (*ergazomai*), thus forming a pun in this verse. It has the sense of (a) being what we would call "busy-busy" or "much ado about nothing" (see Herodotus, *Histories* 4.13), (b) "overdoing" something (Herodotus, *Histories* 3.46), or (c) "meddling in" the affairs of others (Demosthenes, *Oration* 26.15). The NRSV translates "mere busybodies, not doing any work," and the NABRE translates "not keeping busy but minding the business of others," which nicely captures the pun.

Not just cognitive confusion but behavioral deviance results from their panic. The combination of refusing to work (we assume at quotidian tasks) and becoming meddlers in the affairs of others both weakens the bonds of the community and heightens the danger it might face from the outside.[11]

This brings us to the third and most difficult question—namely, how affairs had reached this state. Two causes can be detected. One is the way that Paul inadvertently set up just this sort of overreaction through what he wrote them in his first letter: he meant one thing, but they heard something else. The other is that the assembly's experience of suffering had intensified to the point that the panic that Paul unintentionally set up was triggered.

If we reread 1 Thessalonians in light of the crisis reported in Paul's second letter, a number of things in that first letter can be seen in a new light and help us understand how Paul actually contributed to the crisis.

- Paul speaks of the "affliction" (*thlipsis*) the Thessalonians are now experiencing and that they have experienced from the start (1 Thess 1:6). This is a term that suggests, at the least, pressure or tension and is widely attested in contexts of oppression.[12] Paul is so concerned about the Thessalonians' response that he sent his delegate Timothy precisely to ensure that they were not "moved/shaken" (*sainesthai*) by these afflictions (3:3, 7).
- The affliction is made more concrete by Paul's telling them that they have "suffered the same things" (*ta auta epathete*) from their "fellow tribespeople" (*symphyletōn*) as the churches in Judea did from the Jews (1 Thess 2:14).
- It is not possible directly to connect this suffering at the hands of others with their grieving over "those who have fallen asleep" (1 Thess 4:13), but experiencing the death of loved ones—espe-

11. If *periergozomai* is read in the strong sense as "meddling in the affairs of others," then the idlers can both influence others in the community and bring disrepute to believers in the eyes of outsiders. An approach to the letter compatible with mine is found in three studies by Jewett, "Enthusiastic Radicalism," *Thessalonian Correspondence*, and "Tenement Churches."

12. In the LXX, among many other examples, see Ps 9:9; 19:1; 31:7; 36:39; 54:3; 70:20; especially noteworthy is the expression "day of affliction" (*hēmera tēs thlipseōs*) in Ps 85:7; Obad 12, 14; Nah 1:7; Isa 37:3; and above all Dan 12:1. For Paul's own usage, see Rom 2:9; 5:3; 8:35; 12:12; 1 Cor 7:23; 2 Cor 1:4, 8; 2:4; 8:2; Eph 3:13; Phil 1:17; 4:14; Col 1:24.

cially if it is thought that they would miss out on God's triumph in the parousia—would certainly count as "affliction."

- Paul himself invited such thoughts by the way he spoke of their turning to the living God as "await[ing] his Son from heaven" (1 Thess 1:9) and speaking of the parousia as a reality in which both the dead and those now living would participate (2:19; 3:13; 4:15; 5:23).

- Paul clearly intended his provision of an eschatological scenario in 1 Thess 4:13–18 as a comfort and reassurance to those worried about those who had died. Inadvertently, he encouraged his readers to think of a "being gathered together" with Jesus (2 Thess 2:1) as something that was not only real but would affect those now living: "and thus we will be with the Lord forever" (1 Thess 4:17, author's translation). This stirring of the imagination would only have been reinforced by his solemn summons in 4:18, "Therefore exhort one another with these words" (author's translation).

- Paul's most serious misstep, however, was his introducing the topic of "times and seasons" (*chronoi kai kairoi*) in 1 Thess 5:1. By comparing the day of the Lord to a "thief in the night" (5:2),[13] by saying that it would happen without warning just when people were unprepared, "like labor pains for those who are pregnant" (*hōsper hē ōdin tē en gastri echousē*)[14] from which they will not escape (5:3), Paul actually invites a misunderstanding of his following instructions. By telling them that they should not be in darkness but in the daylight, that they should be "watching" (*grēgorein*, 5:6, 10) and "not sleeping" (5:6, 7, 10), Paul clearly wants them to pay attention to their everyday lives as sober and attentive people, because, despite not knowing when the day will come, "whether watching or sleeping, we shall live with him" (5:10, author's translation). But everything he has said leads people who feel themselves under severe stress and who seek relief to be obsessively "watching" for the thief that comes without warning, to be awake

13. The complexity of the oral tradition in earliest Christianity is illustrated by the fact that the image of the "thief in the night" for the eschaton is attested in a Spirit Letter from the risen Jesus in Rev 3:3, is cited here by Paul in 1 Thess 5:2, and is found in the mouth of Jesus in the eschatological discourse of Matthew (24:42–43) and Luke (12:39).

14. For the literal pains associated with giving birth, see, e.g., Philo, *Life of Moses* 1.280; Isa 51:2; Gal 4:19. As connected to the trials initiating the end time, see Mark 13:8; Matt 24:8.

in order to detect the beginning of the "labor pains" whose arrival is at once certain and unpredictable.

- Finally, among his last instructions to the Thessalonians, he tells them "do not extinguish the Spirit" and "do not despise words of prophecy," and although he follows with "test all things" (1 Thess 5:19–21, author's translations), he has certainly done nothing to discourage the active engagement of the spirit of prophecy by a group under stress.

In short, Paul himself had prepared the tinderbox. The spark that touched this tinderbox and set off the fire of panic and disorder, however, was experiential. The stress under which the Thessalonians live has increased because mere "affliction" has become persecution at the hands of others. At the beginning of the letter, Paul praises their "endurance [*hypomonē*] and faith in all your persecutions [*en pasin tois diōgmois hymōn*] and the afflictions you endure [*kai tais thlipsesin hais anechesthe*]" (2 Thess 1:4). They can be considered worthy of the kingdom of God, "for which you are suffering" (*hyper hēs kai paschete*, 1:5). Notice that the verbs here are in the present: their suffering of persecution is happening now. While persecution is a form of affliction, it is a particularly intense form; it may be the difference between having a loved one die and having them killed, between people slandering us and stoning us.[15]

Corresponding to this intensification of affliction, Paul speaks of a punishment or retribution of those who persecute the community, language that was completely absent from his first letter. "It is surely just on God's part," he says, "to repay with afflictions those who are afflicting you, and to grant rest along with us to you who are undergoing afflictions" (*antapodounai tois thlibousin hymas thlipsin kai hymin tois thliboumenois anesin meth' hēmōn*, 2 Thess 1:6–7). Such retribution, moreover, is to occur at the parousia: "at the revelation of the Lord Jesus from heaven with his mighty angels, in blazing fire, inflicting punishment [*didontes ekdikēsen*] on those who do not acknowledge God and on those who do not obey the gospel of our Lord Jesus" (1:7–8). They will pay the penalty of eternal ruin (*olethron aiōnion*) by being separated from the Lord and his glory (1:9). The mystery of evil that is at work in the world through the influence of Satan, the Lord Jesus will "kill with the breath of his mouth

---

15. Note that neither *diokein* or *diōgmos* appears in 1 Thessalonians. Persecution (which may include prosecution) implies a level of personal animosity and intentionality that is absent from the more general *thlipsis*.

and render powerless by the manifestation of his coming [*tē epiphaneia tēs parousias autou*]" (2:8). The violence of the anticipated retribution corresponds to the violence of the present experience of persecution.

It is difficult to know whether some of the Thessalonians drew the conclusion that "the day is here" because they made the connection between their suffering of persecution and the "labor pains" of which Paul spoke in 1 Thess 5:3, or because of something else about the end time Paul had originally related to them—he says in 2 Thess 2:5, "Do you not recall that while I was still with you I told you these things?"—or on the basis of scriptural antecedents.[16] But draw the connection they did, and in response to a prophetic word or a supposed Pauline letter, the combustible atmosphere of a prayer meeting in the middle of active persecution gave rise to the pronouncement that the day of the Lord was here or near, leading some to abandon their daily lives and occupations to become layabouts who expected the community to continue feeding them even though they contributed nothing to the community (3:10).

Paul's Response to the Crisis

Paul's response to the troubled church takes two basic forms: cognitive correction and social pressure. These alternate with statements of prayer that praise and encourage those members of the assembly who are still thinking straight, are still living in accord with the truth they have been given, and are able to carry out Paul's difficult instructions concerning those whose thinking and behavior are seriously awry (see 2 Thess 1:3-5, 11-12; 2:13-17; 3:3-5, 16).

Cognitive Correction

Although Paul insists that he has told them all these things while he was with them (2 Thess 2:5), and that "they know" (*oidate*, 2:6), much of what Paul tells them to controvert the "lie" concerning the day of the

16. An acquaintance simply with the book of Daniel would have supplied enough images to fuel the imagination: there would be suffering among the faithful before the coming of the son of man (Dan 7:1-9, 23-25), and great distress (12:1, 7), with the faithful being led away by deceit (11:31). One making himself greater than all gods will appear (11:37). The "abomination of desolation" will be set up in the temple (9:26-27; 12:11).

Lord (2:3) remains obscure to present-day readers, both because the events to which he alludes are by no means obvious and because his entire discourse is heavily coded in apocalyptic imagery.[17]

We recognize the familiar Pauline antagonist "Satan," whose power is at work in deceptive signs and wonders and powerful deeds (2 Thess 2:9–10; see Rom 16:20; 1 Cor 5:5; 7:5; 2 Cor 2:11; 11:14; 12:19; 1 Tim 1:20; 5:15), and whose mischief had already impeded Paul in his ministry to them (1 Thess 2:18). And we understand that Paul intends to describe figures and events in "the apostasy" that must occur "first" before the coming of the Lord (*hē apostasia prōton*, 2 Thess 2:3).[18] He provides, in short, a scenario that counters the declaration that the day of the Lord is imminent or had arrived.

But we simply do not, and cannot, know what Paul refers to when he speaks of the "man of lawlessness" and "son of destruction" (2 Thess 2:3, author's translations) who will seat himself in the temple and display himself as God (2:4; see also 2:7–8), still less the "one restraining" (*to katechon*, 2:6, 7) this usurper whose power to deceive is already at work through signs and wonders in order to deceive (2:9) those on whom God has sent a power of deception (2:11).[19]

The point of Paul's complex elaboration of "stages" before the day

17. In addition to the references to the book of Daniel given above, the basic idea of cosmic evils occurring before a messianic rescue can be found in the (difficult to date) Jewish works such as 1 Enoch 91:5–7; 2 Baruch 41:3; 42:4; and 4 Ezra 4:16–5:13. What connection there might be between Paul's language and the "word of the Lord" (see 1 Thess 4:15) found in the Gospels is impossible to determine. There we find the themes of "deception" (Mark 13:6; Matt 24:5), of "labor pains" (Mark 13:8), of "being put on trial" (Mark 13:9; Matt 24:9), of "the Abomination of Desolation standing where he should not" (Mark 13:14; Matt 24:15, author's translation)—Matthew adds "spoken of through Daniel the prophet standing in the holy place"—and of "signs and wonders in order to mislead" (Mark 13:22; Matt 24:24), as well as the exhortation, "Be watchful!" (Mark 13:23), before the description of "'the Son of Man coming in the clouds' with great power and glory" (Mark 13:26); all of this under the general rubric of "tribulation" (*thlipsis*; Mark 13:19, 24; Matt 24:9, 21, 29). Still less certain is the possible date and provenance of the elaborate rendering of "the Great Tribulation" in the book of Revelation (7:14). On the tradition-history problem with the eschatological discourse in this correspondence, see Schippers, "Pre-Synoptic Tradition."

18. The definite article suggests an acquaintance with the term among Paul's readers. The noun *apostasia* (literally, a "standing away from") is used for political division (see Polybius, *History* 5.46.6; Josephus, *The Life* 43) and for religious disaffection (Jer 2:19; Josh 28:22; Acts 21:21).

19. See, e.g., O. Betz, "Der Katechon"; Aus, "God's Plan"; Barnouin, "Les Problemes"; Giblin, "2 Thess 2"; Cullmann, "Der eschatolische Character."

of the Lord is clear enough. Things must happen first that have not yet happened, even though the power that will energize "the apostasy" is already at work. But the things that are yet to happen will be public, if not cosmic: they will involve the temple of God and "all" who lack faith and resist the truth (2 Thess 2:4, 8, 12). The "lawless one" will represent a scale much larger than the troubles of a Macedonian church. In short, the persecution experienced by a tiny community in Thessaloniki is not the start of the cosmic "labor pains" that will bring on the parousia. When these things happen, they will be manifest and unmistakable. They will not require watchmen to "stay awake" and "watch" and work themselves into a panic of expectation. Local suffering does not and cannot equal the cosmic apostasy. In contemporary parlance, Paul's recital of the "big picture" amounts to telling the disrupters in Thessaloniki to "get over themselves."

Social Pressure

Once more, it is not entirely clear what is happening on the ground—or, better, what Paul thinks is happening. He refers to those who are *ataktoi* and not walking according to the traditions he passed on to them (2 Thess 3:6). The term can mean unruly in general (which they would be by not obeying Paul's directions), but their unruliness seems to consist in their failing to do the work expected of them. Paul states that working with his own hands is the example he had set for them: he did not take food from anyone for free but worked day and night so as not to burden anyone (3:8), even though he had the right to be supported (cf. 1 Cor 9:6). In the first letter to them, he had insisted that they live quietly (*hēsychazein*), working with their own hands (1 Thess 4:11), precisely so that they "conduct [themselves] properly toward outsiders and not depend on anyone" (4:12). That the unruliness is expressed by the failure to work is made explicit when Paul reminds them that he had earlier decreed that anyone who would not work should also not eat (2 Thess 3:10) and speaks of those who are not working but are busybodies/meddlers (2:11).

Two difficult interpretive questions arise from this. The first concerns the reason people should stop working. I suggest that it is directly connected, as a social reflex, to the conviction that the day of the Lord is arriving.[20] If the kingdom of God is here, then all quotidian activities seem

20. The distinction suggested by Russell, "Idle in 2 Thess 3.6–12," is, I argue, a false one. The two aspects go hand in hand.

utterly irrelevant. If we are to be swept into another sphere of existence, dusting the front room or paying the mortgage becomes trivial. All our attention must be on the great event, not on keeping this dreary world going. We know from later millenarian movements that the cessation of ordinary activities was a frequent concomitant.[21] The Thessalonians, it appears, may be the first historical evidence for the pattern.[22]

The second question is the connection between working and eating. Paul's command that failure to work means also not eating seems to point to a common meal shared by the community, so that excommunication in the proper sense is intended. This also seems implied by Paul's command that the *ataktoi* should work quietly and "eat their own bread" (*ton heautōn arton esthiōsin*, 2 Thess 3:12, author's translation). If a common meal is envisaged, then the shunning of the unruly members more closely resembles 1 Cor 5:1–5.[23]

Of greatest interest, however, are the behaviors Paul recommends to those members who have not been swayed by panic and its entailments. They are to close the circle to protect themselves against the threat posed by ideological and behavioral deviance. Paul tells them, first, to "shun" (*stellousthai hymas apo*) any brother who does not live according to the tradition (2 Thess 3:6).[24] The deviant are not, indeed, to eat (perhaps from the common stock, 3:10). They are to work quietly and eat their own food (3:12). The phrasing suggests that they are separated from the common meal and they are to support themselves and eat alone.[25] If their

21. From the followers of Moses of Crete in the fifth century, through the adherents of John of Leiden in the sixteenth century and Sabbatai Zevi in the seventeenth century, down to the unfortunate millenarian groups like the Millerites in the nineteenth century, the deluded at Jonestown and Heaven's Gate and the victims among the Branch Davidians in the twentieth century, those expecting the imminent end, or believing it to be already begun, tend to abandon their daily activities, leaving home and families and focusing on the galvanizing event. Helpful observations are found especially in Cohn, *Pursuit of the Millennium*; Festinger, *When Prophecy Fails*; Jenkins, *Mystics and Messiahs*.

22. It also possible that such cessation of work may have been connected to accustomed cultural responses—among new gentile converts—regarding the festivities that accompanied Greco-Roman liturgies and the parousia of rulers to cities; see Strootman, "Hellenistic Royal Court," 289–305; see esp. 298: "The ritual entry of the king into a city was shaped like a divine epiphany, a *Parousia*."

23. See Jewett, "Tenement Churches."

24. In the LXX and in the New Testament, the verb *stellein* appears only in the middle voice, *stellesthai*, meaning "to stay away from or avoid" (see Prov 31:24; Mal 2:5; 2 Cor 8:20).

25. The practice of such excommunication is attested at Qumran; see, e.g., 1QS 7.15–18, and Josephus, *Jewish War* 2.120–34.

disobedience is such that they refuse even the directions in this letter, they are to be "noted" (*semeiousthe*)[26] so that no one mingles with them (*synanamignysthai*) with them (3:14; cf. 1 Cor 5:9). Such marking and exclusion has the purpose of "shaming" (*hina entrapē*) them (3:14), presumably so that they will again conform to the traditions handed down. In the face of behavior that threatens the stability and identity of the community, Paul is perfectly willing to advocate the most basic forms of social coercion: shunning, exclusion, marking, and shame. Such techniques reveal the seriousness of the threat posed. There are times when speech fails and action must be taken. Paul concludes these instructions, to be sure, with an important reminder concerning the disposition accompanying such actions: "Do not regard him as an enemy but admonish him as a brother" (*kai mē hōs echthron hēgeisthe, alla noutheteite hōs adelphon*, 3:15). Even in such circumstances, the member is not banished for damnation but disciplined for amendment.

Social Coercion in Other Canonical Letters

A question raised by 2 Thess 3 is whether Paul's call for shunning and excommunicating the behaviorally deviant who threatened the stability and identity of the *ekklēsia* was a singular and exceptional response to crisis or was one employed in other situations as well. In fact, there is reason to think that Paul regarded such techniques of social pressure as appropriate more often than we might have imagined, especially when we consider—as we have in the previous chapter—how Paul encouraged his readers to take responsibility for maintaining the boundaries of their community through practices of discernment and edification that were motivated by and themselves reinforced the holiness (the "difference") of the church. There exists evidence for one or another of these techniques in the Corinthian correspondence, in Galatians, in 1 Timothy, and in Titus, thus making six letters within the canonical collection in which Paul's crisis management involved not only words but actions.

26. The verb *semeioun* in the middle voice is a New Testament hapax, but from other uses (as in Theophrastus, *Characters* 1.21.7) it seems to mean "take conscious note of for oneself" rather than any form of active "marking" of the other (in contrast to the single LXX instance in Ps 4:6).

First Corinthians

The case of 1 Cor 5:1–13 is all the more surprising because the Corinthian *ekklēsia* was, by every measure, more stable and under less stress than the church in Thessaloniki. According to Acts, Paul had stayed with the community he had founded for over eighteen months (Acts 18:11, 18); it had received the ministrations of Prisca and Aquila (Acts 18:1–4), Timothy and Silas (Acts 18:5), Apollos (and possibly Cephas, 1 Cor 1:10–11; 3:5–23); it had householders and patrons who exercised leadership (1 Cor 16:15–18); and Paul at least expected it to have the equivalent to the synagogue's *gerousia* to settle disputes (1 Cor 6:1–6). Nor was this a community with enlarged or enflamed future eschatological expectations generated by tribulation and persecution; just the opposite: its problem, at least among some of its members, was an exaggerated sense of already ruling within God's kingdom (1 Cor 4:8; 15:12).[27] Small wonder, then, that in such an assembly, so richly endowed with knowledge and speech, as Paul himself acknowledges (1:5), he should so encourage discernment leading to edification among the saints.

The seriousness of the issue that forces Paul to call for the excommunication of one calling himself a brother (1 Cor 5:11) is made evident in 5:1–2: he is committing a form of *porneia* (sexual immorality) not even found among gentiles, and therefore fundamentally breaks the boundary between the "saints" (*hoi hagioi*) and "the world" (*ho kosmos*, 6:1–2).[28] He wants to remain within the believing community while publicly living in a manner that is below even gentile sexual standards. This is not among the adiaphora concerning which Paul invites discernment. This behavior threatens the sanctity of the church as such. Is it to be the temple of God within which the Spirit of the Lord dwells (3:16), and are the bodies of believers together the temple of the Holy Spirit among them (6:19)? If such is the case, then such flagrant *porneia* is nonnegotiable: "If anyone destroys God's temple, God will destroy that person; for the temple of God, which you are, is holy" (3:17). We are reminded that Paul consistently understands holiness to be a matter not of ritual protocol or cultic correctness but of moral righteousness.

27. See, e.g., Doughty, "Presence and Future"; Horsley, "Spiritual Elitism in Corinth"; Pearson, *Pneumatikos-Psychikos Terminology*.

28. We remember Paul's definition of sexual "holiness" in 1 Thess 4:4: "that each of you know how to acquire a wife for himself in holiness and honor, not in lustful passions as do the Gentiles who do not know God." See Yarbrough, *Not Like the Gentiles*.

Paul's response, therefore, is correspondingly swift and decisive. He rebukes the entire membership for its willingness to judge others while being complacent concerning so serious a case of immorality in their midst. They should rather have removed this member from their midst. Paul's own judgment has already been made (1 Cor 5:4); it remains for the *ekklēsia* gathered in the power of the Spirit "to deliver this man to Satan for the destruction of [his?] flesh, so that [his?] spirit may be saved on the day of the Lord."[29] Here is an act of expulsion that is public, formal, and far more instructive to the other members of community than to the one being expelled. Although both he and they are made dramatically aware of what Paul means behaviorally by the holiness of the church, they are put on notice concerning their own subsequent behavior and the boundaries of their ongoing fellowship.

Paul makes clear that when he earlier wrote to them "not to associate with immoral people" (*mē synanamignysthai pornois*, 1 Cor 5:9),[30] he did not mean the "immoral of the world," because to do so would require them to withdraw from society altogether—something he clearly does not advocate. It is not Paul's business to pass judgment on such people, nor is it the community's business (5:12). It is for God to pass judgment on the immoral of the world (5:13). What is their business is maintaining the community as "holy"—that is, as freed from the moral vices associated with the world. They are to practice discernment/judgment on those

29. We are reminded that "Satan" is the dangerous enemy of the believers in 1 Thess 2:18; 3:5; 2 Thess 2:9; now the member is to be "handed over" (the verb *paradidōmi* has the formal sense of "consigned" or "committed"; cf. 1 Cor 11:23) to the power of this enemy. The goal is a form of "destruction" (*olethron*; cf. 1 Thess 5:3; 2 Thess 1:9; 1 Tim 6:9). The critical question is whether "flesh" (*sarx*) in this instance refers to the body of the offender or his moral dispositions (the possessive pronoun "his" supplied by the NABRE is absent from the Greek), and whether the "spirit" (*to pneuma*) is similarly his (again the possessive pronoun is supplied by the NABRE) or should be understood as "the Holy Spirit" dwelling in the community. Is the excommunication here, in other words, intended to have a pedagogical effect on the individual—for example, that he be "shamed" as in 2 Thess 3:14—or is it meant to be a purification of the community so that its possession of the Holy Spirit is "saved/preserved" (*sōthē*) on the day of the Lord? Both the syntax and the logic of the passage point away from a pedagogical purpose for the individual and toward one of purification of the community as such. On this, see esp. Suh, "Τὸ πνεῦμα in 1 Corinthians 5:5."

30. The term *pornos* here could be read in the strict sense as "sexually immoral/prostitute" (see 1 Cor 6:9; Eph 5:5; 1 Tim 1:10), the subsequent list of vices makes clear that it includes any form of immorality. As for the order "not to associate/mingle," the verb *synanamignysthai* is the same as the one used in 2 Thess 3:14.

"bearing the name of brother" (*tis adelphos onomazomenos*) who are sexually immoral, are greedy, practice idolatry, slander, get drunk, or steal from others (5:11). Paul acknowledges in 6:9–11 that before they were baptized, all these things were practiced by them, but now, he says, "you have had yourselves washed, you were sanctified, you were justified in the name of the Lord Jesus Christ and in the Spirit of our God" (6:11).

What such discernment demands in the future is that they are not to "associate" (*synanamignysthai*) with such a member of the assembly or "even to eat with such a person" (*mēde synesthien*, 1 Cor 5:11). Here we see the same practice of shunning and of the refusal of sharing food that we saw in 2 Thess 3:10–12. In the present case, however, the sin of the one calling himself a brother is so egregious that the assembly must carry out the expulsion demanded by Paul, who concludes by quoting Scripture in support: "Purge the evil person from your midst" (*exararte ton ponēron ex hymōn autōn*, 1 Cor 5:13; see Deut 17:7).

Second Corinthians

Among the many obscurities in Paul's second letter to the Corinthians are the events to which he refers in 2:1–11. Paul speaks first of writing a letter to them with "many tears" (2:4) concerning "the one pained by me" (*ho lypoumenos ex emou*, 2:2), writing so that when he, Paul, came, he "might not be pained by those in whom I should have rejoiced" (*hina mē elthōn lypēn schō aph' hōn edei me chairein*, 2:3). To what letter is Paul referring, the letter we know of as 1 Corinthians, or a subsequent one? What is the "pain" (literally, "sorrow," *lypē*) of which he speaks? Who is the individual that Paul pained, and who are "those" that might pain Paul if he visits?

The greater part of the history of interpretation of this obscure passage understood Paul as referring to 1 Corinthians, the one whom Paul caused pain as the incestuous member whom he ordered excommunicated in 1 Cor 5:1–3, and the pain caused by others to be their failure to carry out this act.[31] But the lines immediately following in 2 Cor 2:5–11, while having some points of contact with 1 Cor 5:1–13, also diverge from that earlier situation in significant ways. What is similar? Paul speaks of "one" who has caused "pain" (*lypē*) not just to him but to all of them

31. See the full and helpful discussion of interpretive options in Furnish, *II Corinthians*, 153–68.

(2 Cor 2:5). Paul commands them to act to test their obedience in all things (2:8–9). The majority of the community has indeed carried out a "punishment" (*epitimia*) on this certain one (2:6). Satan is mentioned as a threat to "defraud" Paul and the church (*pleonektēthōmen hypo tou satana*, 2:11).

Even within these broad similarities, however, it is striking that the egregious character of the offense is not mentioned, nor the solemn ceremony of expulsion commanded by Paul, nor the subsequent instructions to shun sinners within the community. Indeed, the dissimilarities are as impressive as the similarities. Here it is entirely a matter of causing pain to Paul and the Corinthians, not a matter of destroying the holiness of the church through *porneia*. Even more significant, the feelings of the one punished by the majority now become a consideration: Paul does not want him "overwhelmed by excessive pain" (2 Cor 2:7). This is a shift from destroying the flesh so that the Spirit might be saved (1 Cor 5:5). As we saw when looking at the passage in 1 Cor 5, the purpose of the excommunication is not the education/improvement of the sinner but the purification of the church. But here the wrongdoer is to be shown love and encouragement. Paul is more than willing to extend forgiveness to him if they forgive the wrongdoer (2 Cor 2:10). These discrepancies lead other interpreters, especially more recent ones, to conclude that "the letter in tears" is a letter other than 1 Corinthians, and that the offender is not the excommunicated incestuous man but one who has offended in a less serious matter.[32]

For my analysis of Paul's pastoral practice, however, resolution of the debate is not critically important. If the event to which he refers is the excommunication in 1 Cor 5, then this passage shows a shift in his posture— not unlike what we saw in 1 and 2 Thessalonians. Circumstances may have changed. The sinful man may have abandoned his sin and sought readmission to the common meals, and Paul now saw his "sorrow" as sufficient. He really does not want Satan to cheat the church out of one who might be saved. If the event to which Paul refers is not that of the incestuous man but that of some unknown offense against Paul and the community, then the passage confirms that Paul was willing to test the obedience of his readers by instructing them to levy a punishment against the miscreant. It shows as well that when true repentance was in evidence and when the community itself wanted to forgive the offender, he was willing to share in their generosity and receive the member back to full communion.

32. See Furnish, *II Corinthians*; Barrett, "HO ADIKESAS (2 Cor 7:12)."

Galatians

In 2 Thessalonians, Paul called for shunning (and possible) excommunication in response to behavior among the *ataktoi* that threatened the stability of that young and fragile community. In 1 Corinthians, he calls for the formal excommunication of one whose *porneia* (public and highly visible) threatened the holiness of the assembly. The agitators within the gentile communities in Galatia present another sort of threat, this time to the character of the *ekklēsia* as inclusive of male and female, Jew and Greek, slave and free: their efforts to propagandize the necessity of circumcision and to coerce gentiles who have received the Spirit through baptism to practice the law of Moses are a covert way of excluding those who do not advance to this further form of "perfection,"[33] by defining the church as "Jewish only." The threat is clear enough. What is less clear is the degree to which Paul responds to the threat with more than impassioned (though highly logical) argument, and the degree to which he calls his gentile foundations to carry out an excommunication of the judaizing troublemakers. In contrast to 2 Thessalonians and 1 Corinthians, Paul does not issue a specific call to action. Reaching the conclusion that he nevertheless expects such action depends on the decipherment of several discrete statements.

The first statements concern Paul's assessment of the agitators' motives and methods. In Gal 6:12–13 Paul declares, "It is those who want to make a good appearance in the flesh who are trying to compel you [*anankouzousin*] to have yourselves circumcised, only that they may not be persecuted for the cross of Christ." In other words, if the Galatians all become Jewish converts, the churches will escape persecution from fellow Jews. Paul continues, "Not even those having themselves circumcised observe the law themselves; they only want you to be circumcised so that they may boast of your flesh." Their coercive pressure, in short, has nothing to do with piety and everything to do with politics.[34] Paul also states with regard to them that "they show interest in you [literally, "are zealous toward you," *zelousin hymas*], but not in a good way [*ou kalos*]; they want to isolate you [*ekkleisai hymas thelousin*],[35] so that you

33. See chaps. 9 and 10 in this volume.

34. I am deliberately playing on the title of Jacob Neusner's classic study of the development of the Pharisaic movement, *From Politics to Piety: The Emergence of Pharisaic Judaism.*

35. Paul uses the verb *ekkleiein* in reference to human boasting "being excluded" in Rom 3:27 (for "shut out," see Herodotus, *Histories* 1.31, 1.141).

may show interest in them [*hina autous zēloute*]" (4:17). The NABRE translation here misses the important nuances in the Greek verb *zēloun*: it can denote "jealousy" (thus: they want you for themselves), but it can also denote "emulation" (thus: they want you to imitate or become like them).[36] In Paul's view, then, the circumcision party is entirely insincere; they are willing to barter the "truth of the good news" concerning a crucified messiah whose death for all humans enables God's power to transform their lives, for the safety of a homogeneous ethnic identity.

Simply on the basis of what we have so far seen, Paul would seem to place such nonobservant Jewish proselytizers under God's "curse," an intimation suggested also by Gal 3:10: "For all those who depend on works of the law are under a curse (*kataran*); for it is written, 'Cursed (*epikataratos*) be everyone who does not persevere in doing all the things written in the book of the law" (see Deut 27:26). Precisely such nonobservance among the agitators is what Paul charges in 6:13. The troublemakers seek to force a law on others that they do not themselves observe.

It is against this backdrop that we must weigh two further passages in the letter. The first occurs in the very beginning, after Paul expresses his astonishment (*thaumazō*) that they have turned so quickly away from the one who had called them by the gift of Christ and "to another gospel [*heteron euangelion*] (not that there is another)" (Gal 1:6–7): "But there are some who are disturbing you [*tarassontas hymas*] and wish to pervert the gospel of Christ [or "concerning Christ"]. But even if we or an angel from heaven should preach to you a gospel other than the one that we preached to you, let that one be accursed [*anathema estō*]! As we have said before, and now I say again, if anyone preaches a gospel other than the one you received, let that one be accursed [*anathema estō*]!" (1:7–9). To grasp the strength of these statements, we need to remember their placement (they set the stage for the entire letter) and the full meaning of the Greek term *anathema*.[37] It is the term used by the Septuagint to translate "put under the ban" (in Hebrew, *cherem*).[38] It is the most severe of penalties, by which a person, group, city, or property is "excommu-

36. See Johnson, "James 3:13–4:10."
37. We have to decide as well whether his statements are performative (i.e., effect what they state), so that he is himself placing them under the ban or excommunicating them.
38. For *anathema*, see Lev 27:28; Deut 7:26; 13:15, 17; 20:17; Josh 6:16–17; 7:1–13; 1 Chron 2:7; Jdt 16:19; Zech 14:11; for *anathematizein* (translating verbal forms of *cherem*), see Num 18:14; 21:2–3; Deut 13:15; 20:17; Josh 6:20.

nicated" in the most severe sense, liable to destruction. We remember Paul's two uses of the term in 1 Corinthians. In 12:3 he declares that no one speaking in the Spirit of God can say "*anathema Iēsous*" just as no one can say "*kyrios Iēsous* except in the Holy Spirit." Clearly, the "placing of Jesus under the ban" here is equivalent to the "curse" (*katara*) borne by Jesus in Gal 3:13 and represents the total repudiation of Jesus as Lord by those who measure by the words of the law alone and not the experience of God through the Holy Spirit. In 1 Cor 16:22 Paul turns the tables: "If anyone does not love [*philei*] the Lord, let him be accursed [*ētō anathema*]. *Marana tha* ["Our Lord, come"]."[39] If we take "let him be anathema" in Gal 1:7–9 as performative, then Paul from the start declares the agitators to be outside the community of faith and "under the ban."

But does he suggest that the gentile believers therefore should "close out" the agitators who are seeking to "exclude" them (Gal 4:17)? Such seems to be the clear inference to be drawn from Paul's allegory concerning Sarah and Hagar in 4:21–31, addressed (rhetorically) to those who "want to be under the law." Paul begins, "Do you not listen to the law?" (*ton nomon ouk akouete?*). There is no need to repeat here the familiar account. But it is worth pondering its conclusion: "Now you, brothers, like Isaac, are children of the promise. But just as then the child of the flesh persecuted the child of the spirit, it is the same now. But what does the Scripture say? 'Drive out the slave woman and her son! For the son of the slave woman shall not share the inheritance with the son' of the freeborn [Gen 21:10]. Therefore, brethren, we are children not of the slave woman but of the freeborn woman" (Gal 4:28–31). It is difficult, indeed, to take the charge "Drive out the slave woman and her son" to mean anything other than the gentile churches' expulsion of those who are trying to impose circumcision and the observance of the Mosaic law. Not for the last time in history, the churches in Galatia experience the paradox that intentional communities that seek (in utopian fashion) to achieve universal acceptance are forced to exclude those persons who persist in the position that only a certain category of person (in this case, law-observant persons) can be fully accepted.

In contrast to the situation in Thessalonica, where excommunication and shunning were demanded by a disorderliness (idleness) arising from confusion, and in contrast to the situation in Corinth, where a public

---

39. The Aramaic can also be read as *maran atha* ("our Lord has come!"). The MSS evidence is understandably mixed and relatively evenly divided. For my point, the difference is insignificant.

form of *porneia* needed to be expelled to save the sanctity (behavioral "otherness") of the community, the crisis in Galatia cut to the very heart of Paul's message concerning the gift of God in the crucified Messiah Jesus: it threatened the "holiness" of the church (although that term is not used) that was exhibited in its egalitarian ethos that broke the barriers between male and female, slave and free, and (not least) Jew and gentile. It threatened the experience and conviction so perfectly expressed in Gal 6:15–16: "For neither does circumcision mean anything, nor does uncircumcision, but only a new creation (*kainē ktisis*). Peace and mercy to all who follow this rule and to the Israel of God."

The Letters to Paul's Delegates

First Timothy, 2 Timothy, and Titus demand separate consideration because in them Paul addresses an ecclesial crisis not directly but indirectly through directions given to his delegates Timothy and Titus: he does not summon the *ekklēsia* as such to action but tells his delegates what they should do, or (in the case of 1 Timothy) takes preemptive action himself.

Of the three letters, 2 Timothy stands out as most distinctive because of its literary form. It is a personal paraenetic letter, with elements of the protreptic. Put more simply, Paul's attention is on Timothy's personal character and professional behavior as his delegate, and the (mostly polemical) statements about troublemakers serve the literary function of presenting a foil to the positive qualities Paul wants his delegate to cultivate.[40] Thus, even though Paul speaks of false teachers who enter into households to captivate women who are "always learning yet never arriving at the recognition of the truth" (2 Tim 3:6, author's translation; see 3:1–9) and predicts the time when people will have itching ears and not be willing to listen to the truth (4:3), he cautions his delegate against entering into verbal battle with such folk (2:16, 22, 23) and instead advocates a mild manner that seeks the conversion of opponents. Yet we see again that they are said to be caught by the snare of the devil: "A slave of the Lord should not quarrel, but should be gentle with everyone, able to teach, tolerant, correcting opponents with kindness. It may be that God will grant them repentance that leads to knowledge of the truth, and that

40. See chap. 22, "Second Timothy and the Polemic against False Teachers," in this volume.

they may return to their senses out of the devil's snare, where they are trapped by him, to do his will" (2:24–26, adapted).

The situation reported in Titus is much more dire, reminding the reader of the crisis Paul faced in the Galatian churches, with this difference, that Paul's responses are couched in the form of advice to his gentile-born delegate, Titus. The description of the Cretan population and of the qualities of leaders that might be expected among converts is not encouraging.[41] The basic rudiments of character and even of conventional household ethics need to be cultivated among a people that—in the perception of Paul—are lacking them. In this near chaotic context, a plausible solution is being offered by some "from the circumcision" who are "upsetting entire households" by advancing the heteronomous ethic of the law, which demands distinctions between what is clean and unclean (Titus 1:10–16, author's translation).

The crisis is the greater because of the newness and fragility of the Christian community. Titus has just been appointing elders and supervisors in every town, who are themselves in all likelihood new converts (Titus 1:5–7). What can be expected even of a supervisor in this context—apart from his moral qualities—is that he is able to hold fast "to the true message as taught so that he will be able both to exhort with sound doctrine and to refute [*elenchein*] opponents" (1:9). As for the message to the Cretan believers, Paul's delegate is to "admonish them sharply [*elenche autous apotomōs*] so that that may be sound in the faith, instead of paying attention to Jewish myths and regulations of people who have repudiated the truth" (1:13–14).

It is at the end of Titus that we find Paul advising the delegate to practice in the face of obduracy the sort of shunning and exclusion that he advocated to the gentile communities in Thessaloniki, Corinth, and Galatia. After telling Titus to "avoid foolish arguments, genealogies, rivalries, and quarrels about the law, for they are useless and futile" (3:9)—advice strikingly similar to that he gave Timothy—he advocates more assertive behavior: "After a first and second warning [*nouthesian*], break off contact [*paraitou*] with a heretic [*hairetikon anthrōpon*], realizing that such a person is perverted and sinful and stands self-condemned" (3:10–11). Avoid arguments, give two warnings, then break off contact. Sometimes, talking just does not work.

First Timothy is similar to Titus in this respect, that some members of the community want to be "teachers of the law" even though they

---

41. See chap. 23, "The Pedagogy of Grace," in this volume.

are ignorant with respect to it, while combining this would-be legalism with an excessive physical asceticism involving both food and sex, and something that resembles a "prosperity gospel"—religion should yield a profit! In contrast both to Titus and 2 Timothy, however, Paul undertakes himself to offer a theological rebuttal on each of these points (see 1 Tim 1:8–11; 4:3–5, 7–8; 6:5–10).

In 1 Timothy 1:18–20, we also see Paul himself performing an apostolic act of excommunication or expulsion in Ephesus, such as he demanded that the Corinthian community perform itself: "I entrust this charge to you, Timothy, my child, in accordance with the prophetic words once spoken about you. Through them may you fight a good fight by having faith and a good conscience. Some, by rejecting conscience, have made a shipwreck of their faith, among them Hymenaeus and Alexander, whom I have handed over to Satan [*hous paredōka tō satana*] to be taught not to blaspheme [*hina paideuthōsin mē blasphēmein*]." The phrase "handing over to Satan" certainly echoes 1 Cor 5:5, but in this case it is not the entire community acting in concert with the Holy Spirit and Paul's spirit, but the apostle acting on his own authority; it is not one individual whose *porneia* is a public threat to the church's sanctity, but two named individuals who have "blasphemed," a term whose precise significance is difficult to pin down;[42] finally, the pedagogical purpose of this exclusion ("so that they might be taught") is absent from the community's act of excommunication in 1 Corinthians.[43] It is impossible to resolve the differences in the two accounts, and there really is no need for resolution. Of greater significance is that 1 Timothy, like several other canonical Pauline letters, deals with crisis through techniques of social pressure, whether to change the behavior of the deviant or to protect the stability and integrity of the community.

42. The verb *blasphēmein* can mean simply to defame or slander someone or something (see Philo, *On the Special Laws* 4.197; Josephus, *The Life* 232; Rom 3:8; 1 Cor 4:13) but is often used with reference to defaming or despising the divine being (see Philo, *On the Special Laws* 1.53; Josephus, *Jewish Antiquities* 4.207; Rom 2:24). Here it could be words or actions detrimental to the mission, as well as to words or actions deprecating God; note that in 1:13 Paul refers to himself in his former life as a "blasphemer."

43. The verb *paideuein* can refer to cultural education in the broadest and most positive sense (see Titus 2:12) or to "discipline/training" in the narrower (and sometimes punitive) sense (see Euripides, *Suppliants* 917; Plato, *Apology* 24E; Xenophon, *Memorabilia* 1.3.5; Aristotle, *Rhetoric* 1389B; 1 Cor 11:32; 2 Cor 6:9). The temptation to harmonize 1 Cor 5:1–13 and 1 Tim 1:19–20 is seductive, as even the careful discussion of Furnish (*II Corinthians*, 163–68) shows.

Conclusion

The Thessalonian correspondence has provided insight into Paul's pastoral practice, beyond the obvious ones of personal visits, sending delegates, and writing letters. In 1 Thessalonians, we saw how he encouraged new gentile converts to cultivate that holiness which defined the church over against the surrounding world, to discern God's will (testing all things, even the movements of the Spirit), and to exhort and build each other up in their distinctive identity. Taking these three elements (discernment, edification, and holiness), we have seen how they were encouraged by Paul in other letters as well (Romans, 1 Corinthians, Ephesians, Philippians).

Taking 2 Thessalonians as a starting point, we have seen how Paul manages those local crises that express themselves in deviant behavior that threatens either the sanctity or the stability of the community. Paul's directive to shun and, if necessary, excommunicate such a person or persons is found not only in 2 Thessalonians but also in 1 Corinthians, 2 Corinthians, Galatians, and (in mediated fashion) 1 Timothy and Titus. Young and fragile Pauline communities sometimes had to take a hard line with respect to their boundaries. The "holiness" of the church was neither a trivial matter nor one to be taken for granted; it was, rather, something to be cultivated and, when necessary, defended.

In the subsequent history of Christianity, the practice of excommunication continued, sometimes with good cause, sometimes with suspect causes. Paul's declaration, *anathema estō*, became a routine feature of church conciliar declarations. Lists of such excommunicatory notices followed the more positive declarations of the councils and were sometimes applied to matters that, from our present-day perspective, seem trivial.[44] A benefit of serious historical analysis of Paul's letters, however, is to remind us (even if we are not church officials) that there is a world of difference between condemnations issued by powerful and imperially supported ecclesiastical institutions and those Paul pronounced when faced with the most serious possible threat to his nascent, fragile, and

---

44. The Council of Nicaea, held in 325 under the direction of the emperor Constantine, had eighty "canons" attached to its profession of faith, but without any anathemas. The Synod of Gangra in 340, in contrast, had twenty canons, all with attached anathemas, and the Council of Ephesus in 430 had nine canons with anathemas. The custom continued in conciliar documents and was only abandoned by Rome in the 1983 Code of Canon Law.

persecuted communities. And for those who tend to skip over the little-read letters of 2 Thessalonians and 2 Timothy, it is helpful to remember that even when separation and "marking" of the disruptive (*ataktoi*) is required, those who follow Paul's example will continue to treat the separated ones not as enemies but as a brothers or sisters (2 Thess 3:15), and with the spirit of gentleness, hoping for the conversion of those who are, for now, caught in the devil's trap (2 Tim 2:25–26).

Chapter 20

Oikonomia Theou

God's Way of Ordering Creation in 1 Timothy

The point of this thought experiment is to assess the theological character of 1 Timothy. The perspective assumed—not argued for—is that of Pauline authorship: at the very least, this means that the letter is to be read as a production of the Pauline mission under the authority of Paul himself within his lifetime.[1] The reader of the present essay should constantly bear in mind that the goal here is not to demonstrate the validity of such a perspective but to use it as a way of viewing this literary composition from what is today considered an unusual angle.

Clarifications and Caveats

Adopting the perspective of Pauline authorship still leaves a number of important questions concerning how 1 Timothy is to be approached. Preliminary discussion of two questions may help prevent later deflections and distractions. The first concerns the corollaries of Pauline authorship: What does it mean for evaluating the data? Certainly, in determining the historical circumstances for the letter's composition it is possible to use the evidence of Acts and the undisputed Pauline letters: the letter can be read in the context of the mid-first-century Pauline mission concerning which we have considerable evidence, rather than in a hypothetical second-century context concerning which we have little evidence. The striking similarities between 1 Timothy and 1 Corinthians, for example, might be read not in terms of one letter imitating the other but in terms of both letters being written to similar situations in similar communities

---

1. See the discussion of Pauline "authorship" in Johnson, *Writings of the New Testament*, 250–59, and vol. 1, chap. 3, pp. 74–92.

during the same period of Paul's ministry. First Timothy 1:3 says Paul has left Timothy in charge for a short period while he travels to Macedonia (see also 3:14; 4:13). We can begin by taking that self-presentation seriously and seeing where it leads. We can appraise information about the community situation, such as the identity and ideology of those whom the author opposes, without reference to other letters. First Timothy can be read in terms of itself rather than with reference to 2 Timothy or Titus, just as Galatians is read in terms of itself rather than with reference to Romans.

First Timothy, in short, is to be treated here like other Pauline letters. It is not assumed to be part of a package composed all at once, and therefore needing to be put at a certain point at the end of Paul's active ministry or after it. Likewise, its literary form is not automatically connected to second-century productions but is compared to other first-century compositions. Its directives are read not as coming from the time of Polycarp and Ignatius but as coming from the generation of Cephas and James. Its thought is not correlated without further ado with Titus and 2 Timothy but is compared to other Pauline letters that might be assumed to have already been written. Thus, if the circumstances presented by 1 Timothy suggest a dating around 55 (the time of Paul's Aegean travels), comparisons are most naturally made with the Thessalonian and Corinthian letters.[2]

A second preliminary question concerns the meaning of theology when used with reference to Paul's letters. The present essay does not assume the existence of a "Pauline theology" as a system of doctrines that exists outside the various compositions bearing his name, or that is identifiable and locatable in specific passages or propositions within those compositions. It does suppose that Paul's language in all his letters not only is religious in its sensibility but also derives from and helps construct a construal of reality that can be properly called "theological." To search for the theology of 1 Timothy, then, is not to seek for those statements that appear to agree or disagree with another set of statements that are identified as "Paul's theology"—a set of statements, furthermore, drawn from a group of compositions that have already been designated as authentically Pauline and against whose steady and secure norm any pretenders must be measured—but is rather to seek for the larger construal of reality as defined by God within which the statements in 1 Timothy gain their specific point and distinctive coherence. Only when the

2. See Robinson, *Redating the New Testament*, 54, 82–85.

individual voice of 1 Timothy is fairly and adequately heard should it be placed into conversation with the voices of the other Pauline letters, in a larger and more complex conversation that might properly be designated as "Pauline theology."

Composition and Setting

The operative assumption here is that 1 Timothy is a real letter written to Paul's delegate, Timothy, during the time of his Aegean ministry. Analysis of the composition's voice can begin with the classic questions of historical criticism. In the case of a letter, we become better readers to the degree that we can grasp something of the form of the composition, the way it constructs its implied author and readers, and the situation it addresses. We work at these questions although we are aware that, even in the case of real letters written to real people, the world thus constructed is not necessarily one its putative participants would have recognized; at best, we gain knowledge of the writer's perception of things.

We begin with the observation that the portrayal of the respective roles of Paul and Timothy make sense within those inscribed for each in the other sources for Paul's mission.[3] Paul is a founder of churches who also travels. He uses associates such as Timothy and Titus as his delegates to local communities in his absence. Their function is to represent Paul to the community, "to remind [them] of [Paul's] ways in Christ, as [Paul] teach[es] them everywhere in every church" (1 Cor 4:17 RSV). In the present case, Timothy is to provide the Ephesian community with "an example in speech and conduct, in love and faith, in purity" (1 Tim 4:12 RSV) and, until Paul's return from his travels, is to oversee the church's worship (4:13) and to communicate Paul's commands (*parangeliai*) on a number of issues (1:3, 5; 4:11; 5:7; 6:13, 17, 18).

The delegate's obligation to be both personal example and surrogate administrator helps account for the peculiar literary form of 1 Timothy. At first glance, the letter appears as a hodgepodge of paraenesis and instruction, without much coherence. The classic explanation considered the personal exhortation as the fictive paraphernalia of pseudepigraphy, and the commands as the first step toward Church Orders.[4] More recent analysis has led to a better classification of 1 Timothy as a *mandata prin-*

3. See M. Mitchell, "New Testament Envoys."
4. See Dibelius and Conzelmann, *Pastoral Epistles*, 5–7.

cipis letter.[5] Such letters were written by rulers to their representatives in particular localities and are attested before the first century CE. One of the fullest extant examples, Tebtunis Papyrus 703, combines a variety of specific directives that the delegate is to have carried out (dealing with agriculture, waterworks, officials' salaries, transport, deserting soldiers) with an exhortation concerning the personal character of the delegate (see lines 257–80). The letter gains its distinctiveness from its mix of private and public elements; it clearly intends a readership wider than the named addressee. When read aloud in the assembly or published by being posted in a public place, such a document accomplished two things: for the delegate, it provided authorization for the practical chores the ruler wanted carried out; for the community, it provided a norm of good behavior in office, against which the delegate could be measured. First Timothy perfectly fits the form and function of such a *mandata principis* letter.

If 1 Timothy is a real letter intended to be read by Paul's delegate and his community, then we should inquire as well into Paul's relationship with this community, such as we can reconstruct it from the remaining evidence, and Paul's perceptions of this community, such as they are constructed by this composition. This is particularly important, since the "theology" of the letter emerges by way of response to the particular features of that situation.

The account in Acts suggests that although Paul was not really the one who started the Christian movement at Ephesus (18:20–21, 24–28), he was an important presence (19:1–7) over a more than two year period (19:10) before becoming persona non grata with the authorities (19:23–41), requiring his poignant farewell to the Ephesian elders to take place in nearby Miletus (20:17–35).[6] That Paul's experiences in Ephesus were not entirely pleasant is shown by his statement, in a letter probably written from that city, that in addition to the great opportunity presented to him there, Ephesus also contained "many opponents" (*antikeimenoi polloi*, 1 Cor 16:9). In the same letter, he mentions "[fighting] with beasts in Ephesus" (1 Cor 15:32)—which may well refer to his struggles with opponents[7]—and in 2 Cor 1:8 he speaks of the "tribulation that befell us in Asia." The letter written to the church at Ephesus in Rev 2:1–7

5. See the discussions in Fiore, *Function of Personal Example*; Wolter, *Die Pastoralbriefe als Paulustradition*, 164–67.
6. For the peculiarities of the Acts narrative in this section, see Johnson, *Acts of the Apostles*, 327–67.
7. See Malherbe, "Beasts at Ephesus."

also suggests that the Pauline character of Christianity in that city was scarcely absolute.

From an analysis of Paul's comments and commandments concerning the community, four salient features emerge. First, this is a church that has been in existence for some time, as indicated by the presence of a leadership structure, an established order of worship and teaching, and a system of caring for widows in the community. One need not suppose much time required for such protocols to emerge, for Paul assumes some form of local leadership even in youthful communities (see 1 Thess 5:12–13), and models were readily available from both *collegia* and synagogues.[8] Second, there are strong indications that some members of the community enjoyed a significant amount of wealth: it is possible for the author to be concerned that women appear at worship in gold or pearls or costly attire (1 Tim 2:9); some female heads of households can assume the financial burden of caring for their relatives who are widows (5:16); some in the community are slave-owners (6:2); and some are sufficiently wealthy to be termed "the rich in the present age" (*tois plousiois en tō nun aiōni,* NABRE) and to be thought of as having "set their hopes on uncertain riches" (6:17 RSV).

Third, 1 Timothy portrays the community as having within it "certain ones" (*tines*; see 1:3, 19; 6:3) who are "teaching otherwise" (*heterodidaskalein,* 1:3). Two of them, Hymenaeus and Alexander, Paul has "handed over to Satan, so that they might be taught not to blaspheme" (1:20). Otherwise, these would-be teachers of the community are not identified. The delineation of Pauline opponents is always problematic, and the heavy use of stereotyped polemic against the opponents in the Pastorals makes the task even more difficult.[9] The charge that rival teachers are "lovers of money," for example, is used so indiscriminately in antiquity that it is impossible to say whether the charge in 6:5 that some consider godliness a source of profit has any referential value.

The depiction of the opponents in 1 Timothy is, however, distinctive. The author uses relatively less vilifying rhetoric and relatively more specific characterization of their teaching. In contrast to 2 Timothy, the opponents are not said to hold a position concerning the resurrection. In contrast to Titus, they are not explicitly identified as belonging to the circumcision party or to be concerned with purity regulations. First

---

8. See now the important monographs by Burtchaell, *From Synagogue to Church,* and R. Campbell, *Elders.*

9. See Karris, "Background and Significance," and chap. 22 in this volume.

Timothy is also distinctive among the Pastorals for actually engaging the issues purportedly advanced by the opponents. We shall find this engagement to be an important dimension of the composition's theology.

For now, we can note that these characters are presumably members of the community, that they want to be teachers of law (*nomodidaskaloi*, 1:7), that they indulge in investigations or disputations (*ekzētēseis*) concerning myths and endless genealogies (1:4), that they forbid marriage and the eating of certain foods (4:2–3), that they (apparently) favor physical asceticism (4:7–8), that (possibly) they think religious profession should lead to profit (6:5), and that what the author calls their "contradictions" (*antitheseis*) they consider to be "knowledge" (*gnōsis*, 6:20). In short, they appear as intellectual elitists who seek to impose standards of behavior on the community on the basis of their expertise. For Paul, they have rejected conscience and shipwrecked faith (1:19).

Finally, the Ephesian church is portrayed as having a leadership crisis. In part, this conclusion can be drawn from the attention given to the moral and managerial qualities desired in those to be chosen as supervisors (*episkopoi*, 1 Tim 3:1–7) and helpers (*diakonoi*, 3:8–13), and in part from reading between the lines of Paul's instructions to his delegate concerning the elders. When we put together the remarks that some think godliness is a source of profit (6:5), that the faults of some people appear only over the course of time (5:24), that Timothy is to avoid haste in appointing leaders and avoid participating in the sins of another (5:22), that charges are being brought against elders (5:19), and that elders who serve well should receive double payment (5:17), we have grounds for concluding that all is not well in the Ephesian *presbyterion*.

First Timothy constructs the profile of a community that is established in its basic structures but is experiencing a leadership crisis involving a lack of management ability and moral weakness; that has a number of members who challenge the Pauline leadership and who claim on the basis of superior knowledge the right to dictate behavioral norms concerning food and marriage; and that has some wealthy members whose display raises serious issues concerning the boundaries between the measure of the world and the measure of faith.

It may be instructive to note how many parallels there are between the situation sketched in 1 Timothy and that found in 1 Corinthians. In each case, Paul uses his delegate Timothy as his representative to remind the community of his teaching and his "ways" (1 Cor 4:17; 16:10–11 // 1 Tim 1:3; 4:11–14). In each case, Paul tries to establish boundaries by "handing over to Satan" those upsetting the community (1 Cor 5:1–5 // 1 Tim 1:20).

Each community contains a certain number of wealthy persons who can disrupt worship by the display of social status (1 Cor 11:17–22 // 1 Tim 2:9–10), and whose ownership of slaves occasions questions concerning the relationship of Christian identity to social class (1 Cor 1:11; 7:21–23 // 1 Tim 6:1–2). In each church, heads of households are recommended as leaders (1 Cor 16:15–18 // 1 Tim 3:4, 12). In each letter, in fact, the image of the "house of God" is applied to the church (*theou oikodomē* in 1 Cor 3:9–11 // *oikō theou* in 1 Tim 3:15). Each letter also presents a remarkably similar set of behavioral issues. Some in the community consider themselves possessed of a superior wisdom or knowledge (*gnōsis*; 1 Cor 1:17; 3:18–19; 8:1 // 1 Tim 1:7; 6:20–21). There are problems with charges being made or lawsuits being instituted (1 Cor 6:1–5 // 1 Tim 5:19–20). There are problems revolving around sexuality: in each case, the statement must be made that women can or should have a husband (1 Cor 7:2 // 1 Tim 5:14) and that marrying is not a sin (1 Cor 7:36 // 1 Tim 4:3); in each church as well, the precise place of widows is uncertain (1 Cor 7:8, 39 // 1 Tim 5:3–16). The place of women in the assembly arises in both churches, revolving in part around what women should wear (1 Cor 11:2–16 // 1 Tim 2:8–10) and in part around whether they should speak or keep silent—in this last case, both letters have Paul respond by an appeal to Torah (1 Cor 14:33–36 // 1 Tim 2:11–15). Both communities have internal disputes over the eating of certain foods (1 Cor 8–10 // 1 Tim 4:3). Finally, in each church, the issue of financial support for ministers is raised (1 Cor 9:1–12 // 1 Tim 5:17–18).

Recognition of this range of parallels serves to give some further plausibility to the assumption that 1 Timothy can be read as a "Pauline" letter of the first generation, and strengthens the proposal that 1 Corinthians is the appropriate "authentic" composition to which 1 Timothy ought to be compared; at the same time, it enables a more precise delineation of the theological voice that speaks in each letter.

The Theological Perspective of 1 Timothy

Paul's response to the crisis posed by a challenge to a weak local leadership is twofold. First, he engages in an explicit rebuttal of the opponents' positions. His strategy here is different from that in 2 Timothy but is functional for a letter in which instructions to his delegate are "overheard" by a larger readership. Second, Paul seeks to strengthen community structures, particularly those dealing with leadership in the community. This twofold strategy, it is argued here, can be subsumed under Paul's overall understanding of *oikonomia theou tē en pistei.*

This key expression occurs at the very beginning of the letter. Paul instructs Timothy to order certain people to stop "teaching otherwise," being preoccupied with myths and genealogies that generate debates "rather than *oikonomian theou tēn en pistei*" (1 Tim 1:4). The placement and the form of the statement would seem to suggest its importance, particularly when Paul proceeds to spell out the telos of the commandment in terms of love, faith, and a good conscience, in opposition to the empty words of those wanting to be teachers of the law (1:5–7). Its precise point, however, seems to have escaped some early scribes, who replaced *oikonomian* with *oikodomēn.*

English translations, in turn, vary tremendously. They include such renderings as "godly edifying which is in faith" (KJV, reading *oiko-domēn*); "the divine order which belongs to faith" (Moffat); "the divine system which operates through faith" (Goodspeed); "the design of God which are [*sic*] revealed in faith" (JB); "God's plan for us, which works through faith" (NEB); "God's work—which is by faith" (NIV). The most recent widely used scholarly translations appear to be wildly undecided. The RSV has "divine training that is in faith," but offers in a note, "or: 'stewardship that is in faith,' or 'order that is in faith.'" The NRSV has "divine training that is known by faith," or "divine plan that is known by faith." The NABRE provides as a first option "plan of God that is to be received by faith," with the backup of "God's trustworthy plan" or "the training in faith that God requires." If 1 Tim 1:4 is critical for understanding the theological perspective of this composition, such a wide range of renderings does not inspire confidence that this perspective has been comprehended.

Part of the problem here is how to translate a cryptic phrase in a way that fits its context. The noun *oikonomia* has as its first meaning "household management" but can be extended from there to notions of "ordering" or "dispensation" in larger spheres, without necessarily losing its basic point of reference in the *oikos.*[10] The genitive *theou* can be read as subjective or objective: Is this God's way of ordering things, or is it the management of a household with reference to God? Finally, what does the prepositional phrase *tē en pistei* modify? Does it specify a mode of the ordering/management, or does it refer to the sphere within

10. For a review of the cognates and their various uses, see Otto Michel, "οἶκος," *TDNT* 5:119–59.

which the ordering is to be placed? All these considerations must be taken into account, making some variety in translations understandable. But a larger problem is the failure to take with sufficient seriousness the metaphorical implications of *oikonomia*, which help give coherence to the rest of the composition.

For the purposes of the present argument, let us translate the phrase as "God's way of ordering reality as it is apprehended by faith." Not terribly elegant, but decisive. The problem with the opponents, Paul says in 1 Tim 1:4, is that they are not paying attention to God's activity, an activity that structures reality, an activity that must be perceived and responded to by faith. With that working translation, we can begin to see how far it can draw us into the theological perspective of 1 Timothy.

Our starting point is a consideration of the metaphorical implications of *oikonomia*. It will be remembered that for the most part—or at least in our surviving literature—the Greco-Roman world did not, as those who are heirs of Rousseau and the age of revolution tend to do, sharply distinguish between humans in their natural state and in their social arrangements. The ordering of society, beginning with the arrangement of its basic unit, the *oikos*, was not perceived as "the social construction of reality" based on equal parts of rational calculation and symbolic need, but as a manifestation of human nature itself. The order of society should be *kata physin*, a reflection of the innate characteristics of humans. The assignment of complementary roles in the household was based on the qualifications assigned by nature.[11] For those who attributed nature itself to a creating God, it would not be much of a step to perceive such arrangements as the *oikonomia theou*.

Just such a perception seems to be at work in 1 Timothy. For this composition, there is no radical discontinuity between the will of God and the structures of society; rather, the structures of *oikos* and *ekklēsia* are not only continuous with each other but part of the dispensation of God in the world. Timothy's work to stabilize and secure such structures is therefore to be in service to the *oikonomia theou* as an expression of *pistis* (1 Tim 1:4).

Because of the tendency to collapse the Pastoral Letters into each other, it is important to be precise on this point. First Timothy's atten-

---

11. See esp. Xenophon, *Oeconomicus* 3.10–15; 7.5–43; 9.15–10.5, and Aristotle, *Politics* 1252b, 1253b, 1254b, 1259b–1260a, 1277b, 1334b–1337a. Even Plato's utopian subversion relies on the same premise: see *Republic* 455C–457E, 459C–461E, 540C; *Leges* 781A–D, 783E–785B, 802E–803C, 804E–807D, 813C–814B, 833D.

tion is not specifically directed to the *oikos* but to the *ekklēsia*, not to the household but to the assembly; it is Titus 2:1–10 that addresses duties within the *oikos*. First Timothy distinguishes the two at the level of social entity. Thus, the supervisor and helper are qualified to manage the assembly *because* they are good managers of their own household (1 Tim 3:1–12). In the discussion of the support of widows in 5:3–16, a sharp distinction is made between the obligations of household and the obligations of the assembly. Children or grandchildren of a widow have a religious duty to support their own family members (5:4); failure to do this is to "disown the faith" and to become worse than an unbeliever (5:8). Note the force of this language: part of apprehending the *oikonomia theou* "in faith" is to perform those obligations incumbent on one as a member of a household. Likewise, a believing woman with relatives who are widows should assist them (5:16). We assume that such a woman is head of a household and able to dispense its resources, much like the younger women Paul mentions in 5:14, whom he wishes will marry, bear children, and "rule their households." In this last case, however, the care for relatives within the *oikos* is explicitly to relieve the *ekklēsia* of a burden it cannot sustain, so that it can take care of "real widows" (5:16).

In one case, Paul acknowledges a clear tension between the social obligations inherent in the *oikos* and the social ethos of the *ekklēsia*. The need to tell slaves of "believing masters" (*pistous despotas*) that they should not "despise" them but should serve them as an act of benefaction clearly arises from the dissonance between the community ethos of egalitarianism ("they are brothers [*adelphoi*]") and the household reality of slavery ("they are masters") (1 Tim 6:2). Paul does not resolve the tension structurally ("Masters, release your slaves who are brothers") but spiritually ("Slaves, act as though you were the masters"), testimony enough to the social conservatism embedded in the perception of society as part of the *oikonomia theou*.

When, therefore, Paul refers to the "assembly of the living God" in 1 Tim 3:15 as the *oikos theou*, we understand that any instructions concerning "how one ought to behave" in this assembly will tend to move in the same conservative direction. If we read the final phrase of 3:15 as a delayed apposition to "how to behave," we see him making the application immediately and directly: a person who knows how to behave properly is a "pillar and foundation for the truth."[12] The essential point, then, is that the assembly of the living God is continuous with those

12. It ruins the metaphor to have the assembly be at once "house" and "pillar/

social arrangements that are assumed to be set by creation, rather than discontinuous with them; both can be apprehended "in faith," and the proper modes of behavior in one are transferable to the other.

The same perspective is operative in 1 Timothy's response to the "so-called *gnōsis*" of the opponents. In 4:3 we see that their "forbidding marriage [and enjoining] abstinence from foods" is attributed to "their consciences being cauterized." To this Paul opposes the perception of those "who have faith and have come to know the truth"—namely, that God created such things to be received with thanksgiving. Note the implications for the broader understanding of *oikonomia theou* in Paul's flat statement: "everything created by God is good and in no way to be rejected when it is received with thanksgiving" (4:4). Once more, the "sanctification" of the created order by "the word of God and prayer" confirms the goodness inherent in creation itself (4:5).

Likewise, Paul's response to those who seek in *eusebeia* a means of profit (1 Tim 6:5) is couched in terms of an attack on *philargyria* ("love of money") as the root of every sort of evil (6:10). The desire for wealth is itself a "wandering from the faith" (6:10). Those who seek to become rich fall into temptation and a trap; their senseless and hurtful passions drive them into ruin and destruction (6:7). It is easy to recognize here the standard topos on *philargyria*.[13] And Paul's alternative, that *eusebeia* should be accompanied by *autarkeia* (6:6), is also standard philosophical fare. If they have food and covering, they should be content (6:8).[14] But when he spells this out in terms of the nakedness of the human condition—"for we brought nothing into the world, because neither can we take anything out of it" (6:7)—the verbal allusion to LXX Job 1:21 is less impressive than the obvious thematic link to the biblical creation story in which humans as created are naked (Gen 3:7, 11) and in which disobedience to God problematizes food and covering (Gen 3:20–24). The rejection of acquisitiveness, in other words, is connected to a claim about the human condition as created by God. Contentment with the meager food and clothing required for survival is to affirm the *oikonomia theou* in faith.

The sense that the *oikonomia theou* includes the way humans are cre-

---

foundation." Proper behavior within the "house of God" enables one to be a pillar of the truth (compare the use of *stylos* in Gal 2:9 and Rev 3:12).

13. See, e.g., Dio Chrysostom, *Orations* 32.9, 11; 35.1; Epictetus, *Discourses* 1.9.19–20, 1.29.45–47, 3.16.3, 111.24.78; Lucian, *The Runaways* 14; *Philosophies for Sale* 24; *The Double Indictment* 31; *Timon* 54; *Hermotimus* 9–10.

14. On *autarkeia*, see Malherbe, *Moral Exhortation*, 112–14, 120, 157; Dibelius and Conzelmann, *Pastoral Epistles*, 85.

ated and the way humans are arranged socially helps account for this composition's view of women. It is entirely consistent with the understanding that social roles should follow on natural or created capacities to state that young women should marry and bear children and rule their own households (1 Tim 5:14). It is consistent with the position that *philargyria* is opposed to faith to urge women not to wear braided hair or gold or pearls or costly attire but "to adorn themselves modestly and sensibly in seemly apparel" and with "good deeds, as befits women who profess *theosebeia*" (2:9–10).[15] It is consistent with a view of gender roles as complementary that women might be allowed to be helpers (*diakonoi*) within the *ekklēsia* if they are "faithful in all things" (3:11 NRSV), but not supervisors (*episkopoi*), whose role is analogous to authority over a household (3:4). Finally, it is consistent with such a creationist perspective that the submissive role of the woman within the *oikos* is carried over into the assembly, with Paul refusing a woman authority over a man, or the role of teaching, but restricting her role to the domestic one of bearing and raising children in the faith. As in the case of *autarkeia*, furthermore, the order in the household and assembly is buttressed by the biblical accounts of the creation and fall (2:11–15; see Gen 1:27; 3:6, 13). In short, the position on the role of women adopted by 1 Timothy is what readers of today would call the "downside" of that positive perception of the order of creation and of society that—on the "upside"—enables in 4:3–5 such a firm rejection of a world-renouncing asceticism. To this point, our examination of the thematic phrase *oikonomia theou* has focused on the ways in which 1 Timothy perceives the order of creation and the order of society as continuous with each other, and in a very deep sense as continuous with the household that is the assembly of the living God as well.

It is important to note also, however, that 1 Timothy places equal or even greater emphasis on the one doing the creating and the ordering—namely, the living God. The phrase "the living God" occurs first in 3:15 to specify the character of the *ekklēsia* and is used once more in 4:10, when in contrast to the value of physical training for the present life, Paul proposes the training in godliness, which "holds promise for the present life and also for the life to come" (4:8), adding as a reliable warrant for this affirmation, "because we have placed our hope in the living God who is the savior of all humans, especially of the faithful" (4:10). The explicit affirmation of *theos* as "the living God" expands the understanding of *oikonomia theou* beyond the order of creation to the order of salvation,

---

15. See the texts displayed in Balch, *Let Wives Be Submissive*, 101.

and leads to the ways in which the gospel not only is continuous with the structures of society but also transcends them.

Paul exhorts the community to pray for all people (1 Tim 2:1), for "this is good and acceptable in the sight of God our savior, who desires all humans to be saved and to come to the knowledge of the truth" (2:3-4). God's desire to save humans—all humans—is the distinctive element in the "glorious good news concerning the blessed God" with which Paul has been entrusted (1:11; 2:7), just as the revelation of Jesus as the "one mediator between God and humans" (2:5) is the distinctive *mystērion tēs eusebeias* that is confessed by the household of God as the "assembly of the living God" (3:15-16). God's *oikonomia* of salvation is grounded in particularity—it is the "human person Jesus Christ" who is the one mediator—yet in scope is universal. It is particular: the human person Jesus "appeared in the flesh" (3:16 RSV); the "sound words of our Lord Jesus Christ" (6:3 NRSV) are remembered and applied to the life of the community, as in the matter of payment for teachers (5:18; see Luke 10:7); his good confession before Pontius Pilate (6:13) is the model for "the good confession before many witnesses" of the delegate, Timothy (6:12); and Jesus's act of giving himself as a ransom for many is his *martyrion* for the appropriate seasons (2:6). It is also universal: the God who "gives life to all things" (6:13) raised Jesus from the dead, so that he was "justified in the Spirit, appeared to angels, was preached among nations, was believed in the world, was taken up in glory" (3:16). We note how the resurrection and the glorification of Jesus are linked to his "being preached among nations."

Jesus's resurrection establishes him as more than a single nation's messiah; he is the revelation of a "hope" (1 Tim 1:1) for all peoples rooted in the power of the living God, that they might share ultimately in God's own life. We remember that Paul's response to physical asceticism was cast in terms of the usefulness of training in godliness, which held a promise for this life and the one to come, "for we have placed our hope in the living God who is the savior of all humans" (4:10). Likewise, the "genuine widow" is one who is aged and left alone, who "has placed her hope in God and has devoted herself to prayers night and day" (5:5). And finally, those who are "rich in this world" are warned "not to hope in deceptive wealth, but in God who richly furnishes us with everything for enjoyment" (6:17). If they expend their wealth in good deeds and generosity, they will "lay up a treasure for themselves as a good foundation for the future, so that they may take hold of that life which is life indeed [*tēs ontōs zōēs*]" (6:19).

The God who "orders reality," in short, is a living God who encounters humans and calls them beyond the frame of creation and the structures of society to a "real life" that can come only from God. This brings us, again, to the opening sequence in 1 Tim 1:3–17. We have seen that Paul contrasts the *oikonomia theou tē en pistei*, whose goal is "love from a pure heart and a good conscience and sincere faith," with the disputes concerning myths and endless genealogies of those who "teach otherwise" (1:4–5). He then connects their foolish speech, which "swerves away" from the qualities of love, conscience, and faith, to a desire to be "teachers of law" (*nomodidaskaloi*) without any awareness of what they are asserting (1:6–7). The next verses (1:8–11) are notoriously difficult to disentangle: on one side, the goodness of the law is asserted when "lawfully used"; on the other side, it is said "not to apply" to the person who is righteous (1:9) according to the good news with which Paul has been entrusted.

The key to understanding the passage is Paul's thanksgiving, which follows it in 1 Tim 1:12–17. Far from being a change of subject, the thanksgiving is Paul's direct witness to the *oikonomia theou* that is to be apprehended by faith. Like those wicked folk listed in 1:9–10, Paul also had been "a blasphemer and persecutor and arrogant man" (1:13). What changed him was an overflowing gift from the Lord (1:13), an empowerment that came "from Christ Jesus our Lord" (1:12) as an act of mercy (1:13). In a word, it was not the law or knowledge of the law that rendered Paul "faithful" (1:12), but the action of the living God through the resurrected Jesus. What happened to him stands as experiential proof for the declaration that "Christ Jesus came into the world to save sinners" (1:15). The *oikonomia theou* that is to be apprehended by faith is, then, not simply the work of God in creation but above all the work of God in the salvation extended to all humans through the death and resurrection of Jesus. This is an *oikonomia* that only God can accomplish. Human wit and work cannot effect it, not by law nor by asceticism, for human effort alone can serve only for this life, whereas God's *oikonomia* extends beyond this life: "I received mercy for this reason, that in me as the foremost, Jesus Christ might display his perfect patience for an example to those who were to believe in him for eternal life" (1:16).

Understanding this, we are also in a position to appreciate why 1 Timothy places such emphasis on "faith" (1:2, 4, 5, 14, 19; 2:7, 15; 3:9, 13; 4:1, 6, 12; 5:8, 12; 6:10, 11, 12, 21) and characterizes the false teachers as having "swerved from" faith (1:19; 6:10, 21); why he places such an emphasis on "conscience" (1:5, 19; 3:9) and characterizes the false teachers as having "their own consciences cauterized" (4:2). Paul calls for a living response to the living God, which is a matter of attitude even before action. Thus, as the gift of the Lord Jesus was abundantly given to Paul "with faith and love" (1:14), so is the goal of the commandment "love from a pure heart, and a good conscience, and sincere faith" (1:5). The living God cannot be comprehended by human reason; God alone "has immortality and dwells in unapproachable light, whom no human has ever seen or can see" (6:16 NRSV). Neither, then, can the response to the living God be constrained by the dictates of law; in response to the faith and love shown humans in the human person of Jesus, only the flexibility of a living faith and the discernment of a good conscience are appropriate.

Conclusion

This sketch of the theological perspective of 1 Timothy has assumed Pauline authorship of the letter but has not really relied on that assumption to establish its reading, except insofar as the self-presentation of the letter and the circumstances it addresses have been taken seriously, and the literary texture of the composition has provided the basis for analysis. The difficult question of how 1 Timothy's theological perspective might be brought into conversation with other Pauline letters must remain unexamined here, but it is clear that if any such conversation is to prove beneficial, it must begin with just such careful inquiry into each composition's voice. Further investigation of the similarities between 1 Timothy and 1 Corinthians might be a profitable starting point. We have seen a remarkable array of parallels in the situations sketched by each letter. Closer analysis will surely also locate points of divergence in each composition's response to its implied situation. But it is at least worth noting how, in 1 Corinthians, Paul calls the church *theou oikodomē* (3:9), speaks of the ministry of himself and Apollos as *oikonomous mystēriōn theou* (4:1)—a role that demands of them above all that they be *pistoi* (4:2)—and refers to his own work of proclaiming the good news as *oikonomian pepisteumai* (9:17).

Response to an Incisive Critique[16]

Professor Mitchell has given a thorough and fair reading to my paper and has raised some important questions. I am pleased to have this chance to

16. This chapter began as a paper for the Society of Biblical Literature session on

respond to them, especially since, written as an effort to stimulate a conversation among other interested scholars in the spirit of an essay rather than a finished publication, my paper has nevertheless—with all its shabbiness—found its way into a public forum. Although Professor Mitchell makes some eight separate points concerning my paper, they can, I believe, be gathered around two fundamental issues. The first concerns the way I conceived and carried out the task of the paper. The second concerns the correctness of my translation of 1 Tim 1:4 and the role I assigned to it.

The Search for a "Theological Voice"

Mitchell thinks, despite the attention I give to the similarities between 1 Timothy and 1 Corinthians, that I do not really come clean on Pauline authorship: Do I think 1 Timothy is by Paul or not? Similarly, she asks why I refer to the "theological voice of 1 Timothy" rather than "Paul's theology in 1 Timothy"—are these the same for me? For that matter, why seek for a single characterization or organizing principle in the first place? And isn't my definition of theology suspiciously like that I ascribe to 1 Timothy—haven't I rigged the game? Finally, I have described 1 Timothy's theological voice in what Mitchell calls "narrative" terms, and she asks why I have shown "no interest in the ontological reality of God as described in the text." I will respond to this cluster of questions with a series of short replies.

A. My definition of theology was as broad and as neutral—and minimal!—as I could make it. And I do not think that "God's way of ordering reality" exhausts the theology of 1 Timothy. Rather, I used that expression in 1 Tim 1:4 as a means of entry into the distinctive theological perspective of the letter. Like all rubrics, its adequacy is tested by how much of what is essential to 1 Timothy it can encompass and how much of what is essential to 1 Timothy it must exclude. By that measure, I think my choice is defensible.

B. The reason why a single rubric or characterization is chosen is that the search is not for everything theological said by a composition but rather its distinctive way of doing theology. I hope that Professor Mitchell would agree that "reconciliation" would serve in the same fashion for 2 Corinthians, and "fellowship" for Philippians; the value is heuristic.

Pauline Theology in 1996. I am including a response to a critique that Prof. Margaret Mitchell wrote in response to this paper; see Luke Timothy Johnson, "Response to Margaret Mitchell," *Horizons in Biblical Theology* 21, no. 2 (1999): 140–44.

C. Such attention to the distinctive setting, language, and themes of *all* the letters ascribed to Paul is, I think, a necessary prerequisite to any attempt to construct a "Pauline theology." All efforts to describe such a Pauline theology have fallen short because of a failure even to acknowledge, far less deal with, the irreducible diversity in the traditional Pauline corpus, or even that smaller collection called "the undisputed letters." Attention to the distinctive voice in a letter is all the more critical in the case of the disputed letters.

D. As with other letters attributed to Paul, it is appropriate to consider the ways in which other such letters resemble or differ from the one under immediate consideration. Thus, it is important to see the ways in which 1 Timothy's use of *oikos* and *oikonomia* resemble the usage in 1 Corinthians. I have suggested there is more resemblance than difference. But it is equally important to avoid employing such usage to interpret them in 1 Timothy. Meaning is contextual, and the rhetorical context of each letter must be taken into account when making such comparisons.

Similarly, I used considerable space to show that 1 Timothy—so often considered a second-century pseudonymous composition—actually faced a rhetorical situation not totally unlike that in the mid-first century, undisputed 1 Corinthians. My point was not thereby to demonstrate Pauline authorship but to show that the premise of Pauline authorship was by no means silly if comparisons are carried out rigorously and fairly.

E. Do I, finally, think that Paul wrote 1 Timothy? Those who have read my *Writings of the New Testament: An Interpretation* know that I take what might be called a radical conservative position on this question. I think the criteria used to challenge the Pauline authorship of various letters are demonstrably either wrongheaded or inapplicable. But I also think that the standard model of Pauline authorship is inadequate, since it does not take into account the complexity of factors involved in the production of all his letters. Since I think that a "Pauline school," while only a hypothesis for the time after Paul's death, is actually demanded for the composition of these diverse letters during his lifetime, then the consideration of letters such as those to Paul's delegates ought, in my view, to be taken up on more neutral grounds, such as I have tried to supply in this essay. My conclusion, after considering all these issues in my forthcoming commentary on 1 and 2 Timothy for the Anchor Bible, is that there are more reasons than not to read 1 Timothy as authored by Paul (in the sense I have defined) during his lifetime.

F. Why did I not show "any metaphysical interest in the ontological reality of God as described in the text"? Mainly because my task was the descriptive one. I do not deny that the text can be engaged metaphysically (as much of patristic interpretation engaged it), but such engagement involves the use of a second-order discourse or, perhaps better, transposition to another set of categories than the ones 1 Timothy is using.

The Translation and Function of 1 Timothy 1:4

Mitchell says, in the kindest way possible, that I goofed in my translation of 1:4. I don't think so, but before I say why, I want to acknowledge that she has raised a very legitimate point, that her interpretation of the evidence is both possible and arguable, and that I failed to support my own (implied) translation in the essay to which she responded. Let me add also that 1:4 is simply difficult, whichever way it is construed. Mitchell says that I have mistaken the syntax of the sentence, that the verb *parechein* should be seen as governing two contrasting accusatives: on one side, speculations, and on the other, *oikonomian theou*. She thinks this is the only possible syntax, since the earlier verb *prosechein* can only take the dative case, whereas *parechein* can only take the accusative. Since I implied that Paul's readers were "attending to" speculations rather than God's way of ordering reality, Mitchell concluded that I had mistakenly taken *prosechein* as the verb governing *oikonomian theou*. She says this is impossible. Furthermore, since, as she claims, *parechein* means "produce/cause," my reading of *oikonomian theou* as "God's way of ordering reality" is all the more unlikely, for how could humans cause or produce this? Finally, Mitchell challenges the rhetorical centrality of 1:4, since she does not see it as establishing a theme developed by the rest of the letter.

I respond with these quick observations:

A. On the translation: a study of the magisterial Greek dictionary of Liddell-Scott-McKenzie shows that both *parechein* and *prosechein*, as their very construction would suggest, have a variety of meanings. It is too narrow to restrict *parechein* to "produce/cause" and then declare my translation suspect, for it can also mean "hand over," "furnish," "provide," "afford," "yield," and, most pertinent, "give oneself up" (with the reflexive pronoun often suppressed). Likewise *prosechein* can mean "hold to" as well as "offer," "turn to or toward," and "attach oneself to." The terms, in other words, can mean different things depending on usage and context—which is precisely at issue here.

B. The two verbs, furthermore, contrary to Mitchell's claim, can each take the accusative or the dative, depending on the usage. Thus, while

Liddell-Scott gives evidence mostly for *parechein* taking the accusative, when it means "give oneself over to," it has been used with the dative. More pertinently, *prosechein* often takes the accusative case, especially when the verb means "to turn towards" something. It is possible, there-fore, for the phrase in the accusative following *mallon hē* to be governed by *prosechein*. It is not obvious or easy, and it would demand of the author the use of two cases for the same verb, but such inconsistencies are not unknown in the Pastorals—or for that matter in Paul's other letters.

C. Since it is impossible, as Mitchell notes, for Paul to be saying that humans can "cause/produce" God's way of ordering reality, he must be saying something else. Some early scribes seem to have shared Mitchell's concern, for they supplied *oikodomēn* as a (humanly achievable and em-inently Pauline) alternative. But since *oikonomian* is almost certainly the correct reading, we must deal with it. My translation provides the sort of adjustment that Mitchell recognizes as possible in her footnote dis-cussing the translation in J. N. D. Kelly's commentary, "apprehension of God's saving plan," to make sense of the verb and contrast with *ekzētēseis*, although she says "there is no justification for this in the wording itself." All translations, though, must make such accommodations if they are to get at the meaning. In this case, Mitchell's dilemma must be resolved on the side of compromising the (most obvious) reading of the syntax. In my forthcoming commentary, I provide this translation: "not to teach dif-ferent doctrine or devote themselves to myths and endless genealogies. These encourage speculations rather than faithful attention to God's way of ordering things." I think the translation gets close to the meaning.

D. Mitchell's objection that 1:4 does not function thematically for the letter simply puzzles me, for the bulk of my essay tried to show the ways in which it did this, both through the condemnation of the speculations of the would-be teachers and through the positive corrections offered in response to them. It was my hope, furthermore, that precisely the combination of these elements throughout the letter would support not only the rhetorical function I assign the verse but also the translation I have given it. I think I have made that case, but it is clear I have not made it for all readers!

I appreciate the positive comments Professor Mitchell made about my paper, and even more her sharp queries. Both exemplify the spirit of col-legiality by prompting this set of what I hope are useful clarifications.

Chapter 21

The Shape of the Struggle

First Timothy 1:1–20

The letters to Paul's delegates seem to require a declaration concerning one's presuppositions concerning the nature of the compositions as a whole before undertaking the examination of any part, because the basic options concerning the historical placement of these letters appear to demand quite different strategies of reading. One must, it seems, choose between regarding these letters as authentically Pauline—produced in the apostle's lifetime under his authorization—or as pseudonymous productions of a later generation.

Among contemporary scholars—and those taught by them—the view that "the Pastoral Letters" are pseudonymous has the status of a virtual dogma. In the face of such overwhelming opinion, few are willing to risk embracing them as authentic Pauline compositions. Such was not always the case. Indeed, for eighteen centuries all readers of these compositions assumed that they were by Paul. Such widespread acceptance is the more notable because of the willingness to challenge the authenticity of other New Testament compositions. The Pauline character of Hebrews was challenged very early, and in the period of the Reformation, the apostolic authorship of James was questioned.[1] Yet, until 1807, when Friedrich Schleiermacher issued the first public challenge to Paul's authorship of 1 Timothy and in the course of the nineteenth century a completely dif-

---

1. Eusebius reports on the doubts concerning the authorship of Hebrews expressed by Origen (*Ecclesiastical History* 6.25.11–24) and others, including the church at Rome (*Ecclesiastical History* 3.3.5). The apostolic authorship of James was challenged by Erasmus in *Annotationes in Epistolam Jacobi* (1516), Thomas de Vio (Cajetan) in *Epistolae Pauli et aliorum Apotolorum ad Graecam Castigate* (1529), and Martin Luther in *Preface to the New Testament* (1522).

ferent consensus was forged,[2] all three letters were read as Pauline in every respect.[3]

Each option has its own angle of vision: if the letters are authentic, we hope to learn something about Paul's thought in response to first-generation ecclesial situations; if they are pseudepigraphical, then we expect to learn something about late first- or early second-century ecclesial conditions and a forger's ideological position with respect to them.[4] Each position has its corollaries: if regarded as authentic, the letters can be read in the same manner as Paul's other missives—that is, as real letters written to actual situations in specific communities, with literary and thematic connections possible with all the other letters; if regarded as inauthentic, they are read not as real but as fictive letters, pieces of a single literary enterprise, and to be interpreted, not in the context of Paul's other letters, but with respect only to each other.[5]

2. J. E. C. Schmidt had three years earlier questioned the possibility of placing 1 Timothy into the ministry of Paul (*Historisch-Kritische Einleitung*), but it was Schleiermacher who explicitly challenged the Pauline authorship of 1 Timothy—partly by contrasting it to the other Pastorals!—in his public letter to Gass, Über den sogenannten Ersten Brief *des Paulus an den Timotheus*. Despite extensive and vigorous rebuttals of Schleiermacher, the adoption of his position by such prominent scholars as J. G. Eichhorn (1812), F. C. Baur (1835), and W. M. L. de Wette (1844) swung scholarly opinion toward his position. By the end of the century, the massive authority of H. J. Holtzmann, *Lehrbuch der historischkritisch Einleitung in das Neue Testament* (1892), established the pseudonymity of all three writings as the only acceptable scholarly position. For this history, see Johnson, *First and Second Letters to Timothy*, 42–54.

3. Martin Luther began a series of lectures on 1 Timothy in 1535, in which he finds nothing that he does not recognize as Pauline. He considers Paul's words on the law in 1:8, for example, "a fine passage about the understanding, or knowledge of the law. Paul explains it more fully in Rom 7." See Hilton C. Oswald, ed., *Luther's Works* 28:229. And in a sermon devoted to 1 Tim 1:5–7, he says, "Now these are deep and genuinely Pauline words, and besides they are very rich, so we must explain them somewhat in order that we might understand it a little and become accustomed to his language" (John W. Doberstein, *Luther's Works* 51:267).

4. Thus, already with Schleiermacher, and then more elaborately in F. C. Baur, the ecclesial situations addressed by the Pastorals were considered to be the second-century controversies stirred by Marcion and the gnostics. More recently, the letters are read as a reaction to women's ministry by an increasingly patriarchal male leadership; see, e.g., D. MacDonald, "Virgins, Widows, and Paul"; Bassler, "Widows' Tale"; S. Davies, *Revolt of the Widows*.

5. Unfortunately, one of the effects of the near-universal acceptance of the pseudonymity hypothesis is that even the few scholars wanting to assert Pauline authorship fall into the trap of reading these letters in isolation from the other Pauline letters.

The passage I consider in this essay sharply exposes the two basic options. In 1 Tim 1:1–20, do we find the first-century Paul instructing his delegate Timothy about real opposition that has arisen in the church at Ephesus in the form of those seeking to be teachers of law? Read this way, the passage enables the interpreter to pose questions about an actual reader and real opponents.[6] The context for answering these questions, in turn, is provided by Paul's ministry as we know it from Acts and his other letters.[7] Read from the perspective of pseudonymity, in contrast, the passage appears to establish a framework of Pauline authority to ground a set of ecclesiastical directives that are thought to be pertinent to Pauline churches in the late first or early second century.[8] The literary presentation is to be understood as a form of code: these are not three letters but a single composition in the form of three discrete letters; the "opposition" (a composite drawn from all three letters) is not set against the Paul and Timothy of the first century, but against unnamed second-century leaders represented by the "Timothy" of the composition who remain loyal to "Paul" in changed circumstances.[9]

When I began to learn biblical criticism as a young monk, I had absolutely no difficulty accepting the dominant hypothesis, in part because I did not have any reason to question the superior judgment of recognized scholars when delivered with such unanimity and authority, in part because I found no theological difficulty associated with pseudonymity; the letters remained part of the canon and therefore part of Scripture, whether they were by Paul or not. I began to break from the scholarly majority only when I began teaching theology students New Testament Introduction at Yale Divinity School in 1976.

I found that, however much energy and intelligence I put into the task, I could not convincingly defend the reasons adduced for the hypothesis, discovering at the same time that most scholars who asserted

6. The "Timothy" to whom the letter is addressed would be constructed from the evidence provided by Acts 16:1; 18:5; 19:22; 1 Thess 3:2; Phil 2:19; 1 Cor 4:17; 16:10–11; Rom 16:21, a real historical figure with a definite character, who, besides serving as Paul's delegate, also was co-sponsor of six of Paul's letters (Philemon, Philippians, 1 Thessalonians, 2 Thessalonians, 2 Corinthians, Colossians). The profile of the opponents, in turn, would be drawn—as in the analysis of other Pauline compositions—from indicators found in 1 Timothy alone, in contrast to the practice of constructing a composite opposition drawn from evidence of all three letters.

7. For just such an effort to reconstruct the social and ecclesial context of 1 Timothy, see Johnson, *First and Second Letters to Timothy*.

8. See, e.g., M. MacDonald, *Pauline Churches*.

9. See, e.g., Redalié, *Paul après Paul*.

the position offered at best only the evidence in favor of the scholarly consensus and none of the evidence that a considerable and substantial body of scholarship had adduced against it.[10] More troubling, I began to see that for many scholars and students alike, there were theological implications deriving from pseudonymity. If not Pauline, then the letters were not considered authoritative and were increasingly moved to the edge or even out of the canon of Scripture.[11]

The main argument against authenticity today is the sheer weight of scholarly consensus. Many commentaries and New Testament introductions don't even bother arguing the case, contenting themselves with a short recitation of selected data that supports the hypothesis of pseudonymity with no consideration of counterevidence; the position is presented not as a hypothesis or theory but as a scholarly dogma.[12] Scholarly monographs simply assume the dominant hypothesis and build on it as though it were solid rock.[13] Yet the criteria for testing the authenticity first developed by Schleiermacher (placement within Paul's ministry, consistency in style and teaching, nature of opposition, degree of institutionalization) have not significantly been developed over the centuries, nor have they gained in plausibility; if anything, the opposite is the case.

10. See, e.g., Kümmel, *Introduction to the New Testament*, 366–87; for a rapid survey of the works that brought significant arguments against pseudonymity, especially in the early years of the nineteenth century, see Johnson, *First and Second Letters to Timothy*, 46–47.

11. As Albert Schweitzer acutely noted in *Paul and His Interpreters*, 27, the rejection of six letters as inauthentic meant that for discussions of Paul and his theology, even those advocating authenticity were forced to use as evidence only those letters agreed by all to be by Paul. A revealing example is found in Furnish, "Pauline Studies," 326. Furnish accurately reports that the Pastorals are not regarded by most as authentic and gives them no more attention. Fair enough. But whereas the volume contains essays on gnostic writings, apocryphal gospels and acts, and all the other New Testament writings (at least in clusters), it has no essays devoted to the disputed Pauline letters. Out of Paul means out of canon, and even out of mind.

12. On scholarly construals achieving the status of dogma, see the remark of Bernhard Weiss concerning the majority position on the Letter of James: "The newer critics also have their unshakeable dogmas and tenacious traditions!" *Der Jakobasbrief*, 50. I provide a list of the overwhelming number of contemporary histories, introductions, and commentaries, in which the majority position is stated with virtually no genuine argument in support, in *First and Second Letters to Timothy*, 50–53.

13. See, e.g., M. MacDonald, *Pauline Churches*; Fiore, *Function of Personal Example*; Wolter, *Der Pastoralbriefe als Paidustradition*; Verner, *Household of God*; Trummer, *Die Paulustradition der Pastoralbriefe*.

The criteria are both formally problematic[14] and materially insufficient.[15] Above all, the hypothesis is shaky because of its dependence (since the time of Eichorn) on the logical fallacy of *petitio principii*.[16] The three letters to Paul's delegates are measured together against an assumed consistent norm found in the seven or ten other letters of Paul. This procedure emphasizes the agreement among the three segregated letters and their contrast to an abstracted characterization of the undisputed letters. But this procedure assumes what must be demonstrated.

While recognizing the distinctive character of these three letters among Paul's letters, I do not regard their collective character as more distinct than that exhibited by any of the other obvious clusters within the Pauline corpus. If we were to segregate and treat separately—emphasizing at every point elements of discontinuity rather than of continuity—it would be child's play to "demonstrate" that any of the groups that any reader of Greek can discern as stylistically and thematically discrete (Galatians/Romans; 1 and 2 Corinthians; 1 and 2 Thessalonians; Colossians/Ephesians) are not "authentic" when measured against a norm consisting of all the remaining letters. Indeed, I am as impressed by the way these letters differ from each other as I am by their clear similarities.[17]

14. The premise that an ancient author should reveal a consistent Greek style—to be determined by word-statistics or use of particles—not only flies in the face of common sense (diction alters according to subject matter) and the actual evidence (Lucian's satires reveal a wide spectrum of styles; Luke-Acts demonstrates distinct styles in different settings; there are real differences within the undisputed letters) but also ignores the fact that in ancient rhetoric the stylistic principle of *prosōpopoiia* (writing in character or according to circumstance) was paramount.

15. It is certainly the case that these letters are difficult to "fit into Paul's ministry"—especially Titus—but the same can be said of the majority of letters ascribed to Paul, and the analysis is not made easier by the insistence that all the letters have to come from the same setting. Using Acts and the entire Pauline corpus, we can with some degree of certainty locate 1 Thessalonians and (if authentic) 2 Thessalonians, 1 and 2 Corinthians, and Romans. Galatians is notoriously difficult to locate either spatially or temporally. And the captivity letters (including Philemon, Philippians, 2 Timothy, Colossians, and Ephesians) are all capable of being placed in diverse times and places. The fact that scholars invent an Ephesian captivity unattested in any source in order to account for the (equally dubious) theory of multiple notes written to the Philippians should indicate that the situation with respect to 1 and 2 Timothy is more severe.

16. The principle that the Pastorals must rise or fall together with regard to authenticity was enunciated by Eichhorn, *Einleitung in das Neue Testament*, esp. part 1 of vol. 3. Eichhorn in fact claims that he had questioned the authenticity of the Pastorals in his lectures before Schleiermacher's book appeared.

17. Not least do they differ with respect to their genre. Contrary to common opinion, 2 Timothy is *not* a form of testamentary literature (which by its very na-

The appeal of the pseudonymity hypothesis is that it enables a plausible explanation for the way in which these letters are Pauline (the forger is imitating Pauline models) and also not authentically Pauline (the imitation is faulty and the situations anachronistic). The weakness of the hypothesis—quite apart from the weakness of the arguments against authenticity in general—is that the distinctiveness of this particular Pauline cluster can be accounted for on grounds other than the passage of time, circumstance, and author. In fact, they can be accounted for in much the same manner as the distinctive Thessalonian or Corinthian correspondence.

In my own work, I have tried to assess the particular character of the three letters to Paul's delegates in terms of four factors: the shape of Paul's ministry, the character of Paul's correspondence (especially the meaning of "authorship" as applied to any of his letters), the role of Paul's delegates, and the literary form of the respective letters.[18] Then I try to consider the specific situation and rhetoric of each letter as I would with any other Pauline epistle, entering into comparison and contrast with other compositions only when the self-presentation of each letter has been given full weight.[19]

The most important adjustment is the critical assessment, not of the "authorship" of the Pastorals, but of what we mean by "authorship" in the case of all the Pauline letters. Several aspects of recent scholarship on Paul converge (or ought to converge) to suggest a more complex model for the composition of Paul's letters, one in which "Paul's school" is present and active in his correspondence during his lifetime.[20] Paul's "author-

---

ture demands pseudonymity) but is the New Testament's most perfect example of a personal paraenetic letter—in form—with elements of protreptic as appropriate to the situation of addressing a delegate. First Timothy and Titus, in turn, are *mandata principis* letters, mixing the *entolai* concerning community life that the delegate is to enforce, and advice directed to the moral character of the delegate; see Johnson, *First and Second Letters to Timothy*, 137–42, 320–24.

18. In addition to my Anchor Bible commentary, see Johnson, *Writings of the New Testament*; *Invitation to the New Testament Epistles III*; *1 Timothy, 2 Timothy, Titus*; and *Letters to Paul's Delegates*.

19. Thus, with respect to argument, 2 Timothy can usefully be put into conversation with Philippians; in each, Paul provides a series of personal examples, including Jesus and himself, to illustrate the point he wants his reader(s) to emulate. With respect to circumstances, similarly, 1 Timothy can most usefully be compared to 1 Corinthians; in each we see the problems caused by an urban setting, wealth, and the ambiguous social roles of women and slaves.

20. The hypothesis concerning a "Pauline school" operating after Paul's death is based entirely on the supposition of pseudepigraphical compositions, with the diversity of the compositions remaining puzzling and their social context entirely specula-

ship" should be seen as a form of "authorizing" compositions that in all likelihood involved the efforts of his fellow workers as well as himself.[21] When all of these factors are taken into account, it is possible to make perfectly good sense of these particular letters as authentically Pauline— that is, as written under Paul's authorization during his ministry.

Having stated the inevitability of dealing with the issue of authenticity in the case of these letters, and having stated my own position on that question, I need to assert as well the importance of bracketing that issue if we are to read these letters freshly and learn anything new from them. Here I return to my earlier point concerning the importance of dealing with each letter individually in terms of its self-presentation. Theories of authorship are of little help when we seek to engage the logic of a specific passage in these or any other letters ascribed to Paul. If we seek historical information, for example, we realize that the two options are less distant than might be supposed. The "historical" Paul, after all, did not report the facts as they were but constructed a rhetorical situation from his own perspective—there is, inevitably, some "fictive" element in all of Paul's letters. Similarly, a pseudepigrapher's fictive literary construction may have had a basis not only in contemporary but also in earlier experience.

Similarly, if we seek understanding of a letter's rhetorical character or religious convictions, theories of authorship seem even less pertinent. They can, in fact, block a close reading of the actual text because we assume we know already what the text is doing. Rather than beginning from the perspective of authorship and date, then, the reading of specific passages should start as much as possible with the self-presentation of the Greek text, and only secondarily reflect on the implications of its

---

tive. In contrast, there are multiple reasons for thinking of a school present with Paul throughout his ministry: the social practices of teaching among philosophers (see Hock, *Social Context of Paul's Ministry*); the complex character of Paul's compositions using community traditions, dictation, and cosponsorship; and the literary residue (in diatribe and midrash) of processes that are fundamentally scholastic in character.

21. An apt analogy is the production of a presidential state of the union address. The president may indicate a set of themes he wants developed, and his staff proceeds to draft them; over the course of time, there is give and take between the executive and his staff, with each proposing wording or examples, and with the president, perhaps even at the last minute, adding his own phrasing. However complex the process, when the president addresses the joint houses of congress, it his speech; he has "authorized" it from beginning to end, even if many minds and hands have contributed to its shaping.

argument for the issue of historical placement. This is the procedure I follow in my reading of 1 Tim 1:1–20.

Preliminary Observations

Some aspects of this introductory passage are clear and require little comment. The personal and filial language Paul addresses to Timothy,[22] the identification of the would-be teachers,[23] and the recollection of both Paul's and Timothy's call to ministry[24] make this passage an appropriate introduction to the specific *mandata* that Paul begins to enumerate in 1 Tim 2:1.[25] Paul and Timothy are together called to a noble battle (*kalēn strateian*, 1:18) for the faith that joins them to each other (*gnēsiō teknō en pistei*, 1:2) in the shared hope (*tēs elpidos hēmōn*, 1:1) who is Christ Jesus. After the greeting, the passage is neatly framed on one side by Paul's exhortation that Timothy should command (*parangeilēs*) certain people not to advance other teaching (1:3) and on the other side by Paul's imposition of the commandment (*parangelian paratithemai*) on Timothy that he engage in battle (1:18). These personal exhortations stand in contrast to the community instructions that Paul begins to elaborate in 2:1–3:13, and they serve to authorize Timothy as Paul's delegate to the Ephesian church.

The image of battle (*strateian*, 1 Tim 1:18) is appropriate, for Paul constructs the rhetorical situation in terms of a stark contrast—indeed a contest—between those certain people (*tines*, 1:3, 7, 19) who "teach other" (*heterodidaskalein*, 1:3),[26] among whom are Hymenaeus and Al-

---

22. Timothy is addressed as "genuine child" (*gnēsiōs teknos*) in 1:2 and in the vocative as "child Timothy" (*teknon Timothee*) in 1:18. Paul speaks to him directly, using the second-person personal pronoun (*se, soi*) in 1:3 and 1:18.

23. The author characterizes the behavior of "some" (*tines*) to avoid in 1:4–7 and 1:19, and provides the names of Hymenaeus and Alexander in 1:20.

24. Paul speaks of being placed in service in 1:12 and of Timothy being commissioned by prophetic utterances in 1:18.

25. For the understanding of 1 Timothy as a *mandata principis* letter, see Johnson, *The First and Second Letters to Timothy*, 137–42.

26. The use of *heterodidaskalein* in 1:3 and 6:3 provided Schleiermacher (*Ersten Brief*, 90–91) with his point of entry for the questioning of the diction throughout 1 Timothy, since he could find no attestation of the term as early as Paul, and it was attested in patristic literature after Paul. Anticipating other selective displays of evidence, he does not mention Paul's fondness generally for *hetero-* constructions (see 1 Cor 14:21; 2 Cor 6:14; 11:4; Gal 1:6).

exander (1:20), and "the healthy teaching according to the good news" (*hygiainousē didaskalia kata to euangelion*, 1:10–11), to which both Paul (1:12) and his delegate Timothy (1:18) have been committed.

The description of the opposition bears marks of the stereotypical slander found in fights among ancient philosophers. Little specific can be learned from the charge that they are devoted to myths and endless genealogies (1 Tim 1:4) that give rise to speculations (1:4), or that they are foolish in speech (1:6), or that they are ignorant, knowing neither the things they are saying nor those on which they insist (1:6–7). Such charges, like those found later in the letter, are standard items in antiquity's catalogs of polemic.[27]

That Paul uses stereotypical slander in the manner of other ancient philosophers is no surprise.[28] There are, however, some aspects of the description of the opposition that suggest a specific profile. Paul does not suggest that these are people outside the community, for example, who are "from the circumcision party" (see Titus 1:10) or who are "sneaking into households" (2 Tim 3:6); rather, they appear to be completely within the range of Paul's and his delegate's authority: Timothy can "command" them (1 Tim 1:3) and Paul can excommunicate them (1:20).[29] Similarly, the charge of ignorance gains some specificity from three further aspects of Paul's depiction. The first is that they have intellectual ambition: they seek or want to be "teachers of law" (*thelontes einai nomodidaskaloi*, 1:7). The second is that they have "missed the mark" (*astochēsantes*) concerning essential things and have "turned aside" (*exetrapēsan*) to foolishness (1:6), have "spurned" (*apōsamenoi*) the essentials and have "suffered shipwreck" (*enauagēsan*, 1:19). The third is that Paul has handed them over to Satan precisely so that they might be "instructed" (*paideuthōsin*, 1:20). The opposition, in short, is long on ambition but short on talent, and because they fail to understand the basic truth, they fall away from it themselves. They miss, Paul says, the *telos tēs parangelias* (1:5), which we might translate as the "point" or the "goal" of the commandment.

This point of the commandment, Paul says, is not the knowledge of extraneous realities ("myths and genealogies") or the imposition of a heteronomous norm ("law") but the cultivation of moral dispositions internal to humans. In 1 Tim 1:5 he speaks of this *telos* as "love from a

27. See Karris, "Background and Significance," and chap. 22 in this volume and (more broadly) Johnson, "New Testament's Anti-Jewish Slander."

28. As in Rom 15:17–19; 2 Cor 10:13–15; Phil 3:19; Gal 6:13; 1 Thess 1:3–6.

29. I am assuming here that the "handing over to Satan" for instructional purposes is more like 1 Cor 5:5 than not.

pure heart and a good conscience, and sincere faith," and in 1:19 speaks of engaging the noble battle with "faith and a good conscience." The occurrence of "faith" (*pistis*) in each statement to characterize the response of Paul and his delegate does not surprise, since, as we have seen, he has called Timothy his genuine child *en pistei* (1:2) and speaks of the mercy shown him by Christ as an example "for those coming to have faith in him" (*tōn mellontōn pisteuein ep' autō*, 1:16).

Indeed, in 1 Tim 1:5 Paul opposes a preoccupation with myths and genealogies that give rise to speculations with the *oikonomia theou en pistei*. Both the text and translation of this sentence are difficult and disputed.[30] I take the phrase *oikonomia theou* as the preferred reading and translate it as "God's way of ordering [or "disposing"] things" (note the echo of *epitagēn theou* in 1:1). The phrase *en pistei*, in turn, can modify either the character of God's dispensation (it is all about faith) or the character of the human response (it is to be received in faith) or even both. But that Paul here sets "faith" (with its internal dispositions) over against the pretenders' understanding of "law" (as a heteronomous norm) is made clear by his conclusion in 1:19 that the spurning of faith and good conscience by some has meant suffering shipwreck *peri tēn pistin*. Two interrelated contrasts, therefore, dominate the passage, that between God's dispensation and human ambition, and that between internal disposition and external norm.

The Exegetical Challenge

The relative clarity of these contrasts throws into greater relief the difficulty presented by the two elements that form the heart of the passage—namely, Paul's "clarifying" statement concerning the law in 1 Tim 1:8–11, and his description of his conversion and call in 1:12–17. Each section poses severe problems. In the first, what does Paul mean by calling the law good, *ean tis autō nomimōs chrētai* (1:8)?[31] For that matter, what does

---

30. See my discussion of the passage in chap. 20, pp. 415–17, and "Response to an Incisive Critique," pp. 423–27, in this volume.

31. *Kalos ho nomos* echoes Rom 7:16, *symphēmi tō nomō hoti kalos*, while the adverb *nomimōs* finds a parallel in 2 Tim 2:5. The verb *chraomai* occurs also in 1 Cor 7:21, 31; 9:12, 15; 2 Cor 1:17; 3:12; 13:10, as well as 1 Tim 5:23, with much the same meaning of "put to use" in each instance; apart from Acts 27:3, 17, the verb is restricted in the New Testament to Paul.

he have in mind by "the law" (*ho nomos*)?[32] What is the precise significance of the wordplay *keitai/antikeitai* in 1:9–10?[33] Why is the vice list of 1:9–10 personal,[34] and why are the characterizations so extreme? Why does the conclusion of the list shift from wicked persons to impersonal vice (*ti heteron*) opposed to the healthy teaching according to the good news (1:10–11)?[35]

In the second section, why does Paul speak of himself not only as a persecutor but also as *blasphēmon* and *hybristēn*,[36] and why does he connect his former *agnoōn* with *apistia* in his explanation for God's mercy toward him (1:13)?[37] Why does he speak of the *charis* that God showed him as an "empowerment" (1:12)[38] and as an outpouring of the "faith and love that are in Christ Jesus" (1:14)?[39] Why does he include

32. Note that the adjective *Ioudaikos* is not used here with reference to "myths and genealogies" in 1:4, in contrast to the *Ioudaikois mythois* in Titus 1:14. That *nomos* here means at least the commandments in Torah is an inference drawn from two things: the ability to discern the frame of the Decalogue beneath 1:9–10, and Paul's usage elsewhere.

33. That the wordplay is deliberate is supported by the play on *nomos/nomimōs* in the same sentence; precisely the fact that the paired terms are rhetorically matched, however, cautions the reader against excessive precision in their translation, particularly when trying to draw conclusions concerning the status of the law for believers generally. Here the application of the terms is made more complex by the disparity of the two phrases in the dative case, *tō dikaiō* (1:9) and *tē hygiainousē didaskalia* (1:10): in my Anchor Bible translation, I have "is not laid down for a righteous person" and "opposed to the healthy teaching."

34. The list of vices in Col 3:8, Eph 5:3–4, Gal 5:19–21, and 1 Tim 6:4 are all impersonal. The list in 1 Cor 6:9–10 is personal, and that in Rom 1:29–31 is mixed, beginning impersonally and shifting to the personal.

35. Contrast the *hoitines* in Rom 1:32 to the *kai ei ti heteron* in 1 Tim 1:10.

36. Although Paul elsewhere singles out his persecution of the church as a salient of his former life, he uses the verb *diōkein* (1 Cor 15:9; Gal 1:13, 23; Phil 3:6) rather than the noun *diōktēs*. Paul nowhere else designates himself as a *blasphēmos*, although he associates the term with opponents (2 Tim 3:2), and the noun *hybristēs* elsewhere occurs in the New Testament only in the vice list of Rom 1:30.

37. Paul uses the noun *apistia* in Romans as "faithlessness," roughly equivalent to "disobedience" (see Rom 3:3; 4:20; 11:20, 23); similarly, the verb *agnoein* also occurs in Romans in connection with (failure to) convert: "not knowing that the mercy [*chrēstos*] of God drives you to repentance" (2:4) and with reference to Paul's fellow Jews, "not knowing the righteousness that comes from God."

38. In 2 Tim 2:1 Paul tells his delegate to "be strengthened by the gift that is in Jesus Christ" (cf. Eph 6:10) and in 4:17 declares that "the Lord stood by me and empowered me." In Phil 4:13 Paul states, "I am able to do all things *en tō endynamounti me*," which may account for the textual variant in 1 Tim 1:12.

39. The secondary attributive construction found in 1 Tim 1:14; 3:13; 2 Tim 1:1; 2:1,

(as a "faithful saying") a statement about Jesus's coming into the world to save sinners,[40] and speak of God's gift to him as an example for those coming to have faith (1:15–16)? And why is this entire section framed as a thanksgiving to Jesus that concludes with a doxology to God (1:17)?

I cannot hope to answer all these questions in a single essay, but I do want to suggest that progress can be made by placing this entire central part of the first chapter within the framework of a dyadic contrast that Paul establishes on either side of it, and then by reading these two sections in light of each other. The approach is as old as Augustine: facing difficult passages, move from the more to the less certain.[41] The premise, however, is that the author is not clumsily laying slabs of tradition side by side, but is actually working out an argument. In this case, the argument proceeds by the juxtaposition of the clarification concerning the law and Paul's account of his conversion.

The explicit link between the two is found in 1 Tim 1:10–12. The vice list concludes with the summary, "anything else that opposes the healthy teaching according to the glorious good news [*euangelion tēs doxēs*] from [or "of"] the blessed God, *with which I have been entrusted* [*ho episteuthēn egō*]" (1:10–11) and the thanksgiving is for the empowerment of Paul by Christ, for, as Paul says, "he has considered me faithful by *putting me into service* [*hoti piston me hēgēsato themenos eis diakonian*]" (1:12).[42] The better knowledge concerning the law—note the "we know" and "since we know" in 1:8–19—is therefore one given by Paul's present perspective concerning "a righteous one" (*dikaios*, 1:9), which he has because of his experience of empowerment and the outpouring of grace from the Lord (1:14).

Recognizing this, we can observe as well three further links between the sections. First, Paul characterizes his former life as one of "ignorance" (*agnoōn*, 1 Tim 1:13), just as the opponents are said to be "without knowledge" (1:7). This further supports the suggestion that Paul's knowledge concerning law is one given by his present experience rather than his former life; he now understands that of which he was formerly igno-

---

10; and 3:15 have the effect of suggesting a quality that belongs to Christ, a personal characteristic that can be communicated to others.

40. The saying echoes Luke 5:32 and 19:10 but finds expression elsewhere in Paul as well: "God shows his love for us in that while we were still sinners Christ died for us" (Rom 5:8).

41. Augustine, *Christian Instruction* 2.9.

42. Note that while Paul from his side had *apistia* (1:13), Christ Jesus "considered [him] faithful [*piston*]" (1:12).

rant. Second, Paul connects this former ignorance to his "faithlessness" (*apistia*), forming a further connection between his earlier life and the present condition of the opponents, who fall away from faith (1:6, 19). Third, Paul's characterization of himself in his earlier life is particularly harsh. To his activity as a persecutor (*diōktēs*), Paul attaches the traits of being a "blasphemer" (*blasphēmos*) and "an insolent person" (*hybristēs*). The harshness of these terms, especially the last,[43] matches the exaggerated terms used in the vice list, and it is striking that at the end of this opening passage, Paul says of his opponents that he has handed them over to Satan so that they might be instructed "not to blaspheme" (*mē blasphēmein*). It is difficult to avoid the impression that Paul is deliberately identifying himself in his former life with those who, in their faithlessness and ignorance, now wish to be teachers of law.

This deliberate linking helps account, in turn, for three further features of the vice list. First, Paul lists "persons with vices" rather than abstract vice designations ("lawless people," *anomoi*, rather than "lawlessness," *anomia*), because the issue raised by the opponents who wish to be teachers of law is how to be a "righteous person" within the community. It is for this reason that Paul puts the argument on the level of persons and their character. Second, Paul's list of unrighteous persons focuses entirely on religious and moral qualities rather than ritual obligations. The suggestion that the Ten Commandments serve as a loose organizing principle for this vice list has merit.[44] Third, throughout the list, Paul chooses words that express extremely negative moral dispositions or characters: they do not simply commit the act of killing, they are "people who kill mothers" (*mētralōais*) and "people who kill fathers" (*patrolōais*); they do not commit adultery, they are "people who fornicate" (*pornois*) and are sexually perverted (*arsenokoitais*); they not only steal, they are "people who sell into slavery" (*andrapodistais*). These dramatic examples match the extravagant characterization of Paul in his former life as a persecutor, blasphemer, and violent man. Paul was, in short, much as the people he lists in his faithlessness, ignorance, violence, and blasphemy.

In light of his own (and, he assumes, Timothy's) experience, Paul can declare of the law "this thing" (*touto*)—namely, that it is not laid down

---

43. Although *hybris* has a wide range of usage, Nicolas R. E. Fisher argues that the element of a shamelessness that willingly dishonors others—gods or humans—dominates (see Fisher, *Hybris*). In the vice list of Rom 1:30, Paul places the *hybristas* between the *theostygeis* (God-haters) and the *hyperēphanous* (arrogant). The combination of *hybristēs* and *hyperēphanos* is found also in Aristotle, *Rhetoric* 1390B, and Diodorus Siculus, *Library of History* 5.55.6.

44. See the analysis in Johnson, *First and Second Letters to Timothy*, 168–72.

(*keitai*) for the righteous person, but rather for those who act in a way contrary (*antikeitai*) to the healthy teaching of the good news from God. What he means, I think, is that the law can identify wicked behavior, but the law cannot generate positive righteous dispositions, and, by implication, if the righteous dispositions are in place, then the law can add nothing to them. The essential moral transformation has already been accomplished not by the keeping of law but by God's gift.

The point of Paul's thanksgiving, in turn, is to assert that, in his case, remarkably, God worked such a moral transformation as an example of what God through Christ offers all sinners. Note that God accomplishes this not through a verbal revelation but through the person of Jesus Christ. Jesus dominates Paul's thanksgiving. Paul states the faithful saying that "Christ Jesus came into the world to save sinners [*hamartōlous sōsai*]" (1 Tim 1:15). Jesus's existence was directed to rescuing humans from their condition of alienation from God and their alienating behavior. He came for the sort of people identified in 1:9–10, and like Paul, who says, "I am the first among them!"

Jesus's salvific will reached Paul, to be sure, through the power of the resurrection. That Jesus now shares God's power is clear from the greeting, where Paul connects his apostolic authority to "God our savior and Christ Jesus our hope" and sends Timothy grace, mercy, and peace "from God Father and Christ Jesus our Lord" (1:1–2), as well as from the use of "our Lord" in 1:14. It is because Christ Jesus shares God's rule over the ages (1:17) that his power can reach across any time or place to transform humans in their dispositions and behavior. So Paul gives thanks to Christ Jesus who "has empowered me" (*endynamōsanti me*, 1:12) in three ways: Jesus "reckoned" (*hēgēsato*) Paul faithful (*piston*) by putting him in his service (1:12); he "poured out abundantly" (*hyperepleonasen*, 1:14) his grace; and he showed Paul mercy (*eleēthēn*, 1:13, 16). Most remarkable, the gift of the Lord to Paul consisted in the very human dispositions found in Jesus himself: "the faith and love that are in Christ Jesus" (*meta pisteōs kai agapēs tēs en Christō Iēsou*, 1:14). Precisely the internal moral dispositions that Paul identifies as "the goal of the commandment" (1:5; see 1:19) are activated within him through Christ's gift.

The mercy that Jesus showed toward Paul was itself a form of proof of what God could do. It was a "demonstration" (*endeixētai*) in the first of sinners of Christ's *hapasan makrothymian* ("all encompassing patience" or "all possible forbearance"),[45] so that Paul stands as an example (*hypotypōsin*) both of the sinner Christ came to save and of the one brought

---

45. For *makrothymia* as God's disposition, see Rom 2:4 and 9:22.

"to believe in him onto eternal life" (1 Tim 1:16). Paul's coming to faith and apostleship was through the *oikonomia theou* (1:4): it was an expression of Christ's faith in him (see *episteuthēn* in 1:11 and *piston me hēgēsato* in 1:12), generated faith and love within him (1:14), and called for a continuing response of faith and thanksgiving (*en pistei*, 1:5). In light of this powerful personal experience of transformation—shared in some degree, Paul intimates, by Timothy (1:18)—a return to a legal norm for behavior would amount to a rejection of the experience itself and becoming shipwrecked with respect to faith (1:19). It would mean, in fact, a rejection of the power of God to save through Christ, a return to the attitude Paul formerly had as persecutor and arrogant man, who was also a blasphemer. Not by accident, then, is the handing over of the pretend teachers to Satan intended to "instruct them not to blaspheme" (*hina paideuthōsin mē blasphēmein*, 1:20).

Further Connections

I have tried to provide a fresh reading of 1 Tim 1:1–20 that takes seriously its rhetorical crafting and its religious argument, which retain their integrity, I submit, whether we consider the letter to have been written by Paul or by a successor. I have tried to identify the heart of the author's argument in a double contrast between, on one hand, the work of God and human ambition and, on the other hand, a manner of life guided by conscience and one guided by law. I have suggested that the very difficult heart of the argument in 1:8–17 becomes clearer when read in light of this double contrast, and when Paul's statements about the law and his own conversion are seen as interconnected.

If this approach makes good sense of the opening of 1 Timothy, four questions arise. First, does this contrast between the experience of the living God and human ambition pervade the rest of 1 Timothy, so that 1:1–20 may be regarded not only as an authorization of Paul's delegate but also as the announcement of the composition's main point? Second, is the focus on character and moral transformation through the gift of Christ, in contrast to human effort, an important or even central preoccupation of the other letters to Paul's delegates? Third, to what degree can we consider this theme, if it is demonstrated to be so pervasively present in the Pastorals, also a preoccupation of Paul's other letters, especially in places where Paul also discusses the law? Fourth and finally, is it possible to ask whether Paul's other major statement with respect to his calling in Gal 1:10–24 has a paradigmatic function within the argument of that letter, as the thanksgiving in 1 Tim 1:12–17 clearly has? In this essay, only the most preliminary and sketchy response can be provided for each of these questions.

1. The contrast between external prescriptions and internal dispositions continues throughout 1 Timothy. In the discussion of bishops (supervisors) and deacons (helpers), the focus is entirely on moral qualities rather than administrative or ritual functions (see 3:2–4, 8–9, 11). Much of the letter is taken up with specific *mandata* concerning worship, leadership, wealth, and community support for widows, but in the sections of the composition that continue the contrast between Paul's delegate Timothy and the opponents, the same distinction observed in 1:1–20 holds.

In the sections of the letter that provide direct advice to Paul's delegate, the positive exhortation of Timothy has as its foil the negative characterization of his opposition, in much the same terms as in 1:1–20. Thus, in 4:2–3 they are said to have their conscience seared, and they seek to forbid the eating of certain foods and the practice of marriage. However strange it might seem for teachers of Jewish law to forbid marriage,[46] the more important point is that they are advocating an external set of observances. Timothy, however, is trained in godliness as he responds to the living God (1 Tim 4:7, 10) and sets an example in his speech and conduct of the internal dispositions of love and faith and purity (4:11–12), in accord with the gift that was given him through prophetic utterance (4:14).

Similarly, at the end of the letter, Timothy's healthy teaching in godliness (1 Tim 6:3) is called a good fight for the faith (6:12)—echoing 1:18—which demands of him such internal dispositions as righteousness, godliness, faith, love, steadfastness, and gentleness (6:11). Against him stand those who focus on controversy and disputes, "from which come envy and strife and reviling speech and evil suspicions" (6:4). Their constant wranglings are the manifestations of "corrupted minds" (6:5) that have been "defrauded from the truth." Insistence on a heteronomous norm, we see once again, not only fails to transform humans through moral

---

46. The combination of elements is found—so far as we know—only among practitioners of Merkabah mysticism; they did not forbid marriage but did combine observance of law, temporary sexual abstinence, and fasting as preparation for the heavenly ascent. See Francis, "Humility and Angelic Worship." The caution, "so far as we know," however, must be taken seriously. Scholars must avoid the conceit that identifies reality with the information that they happen to possess.

virtue; it exacerbates their vice. The conclusion of the composition forms a perfect *inclusio* with 1:1–20: the opposition's profane chatterings and contradictions reflect only their "so-called knowledge" (*tēs pseudōnymou gnōseōs*, 6:20) and show that they have "missed the mark concerning faith" (*peri tēn pistin ēstochēsan*, 6:21; see 1:19, *peri tēn pistin enauagēsan*). In sum, the contrast between internal disposition in response to God and external norm as expression of human ambition carries through 1 Timothy, showing that, as in other Pauline compositions, the opening lines set the agenda for the whole.[47]

2. Can the same be said for 2 Timothy and Titus? Is the contrast between the work of God that effects internal transformation and the futility of the law to effect such change a feature of these letters as well? It is, though much more in Titus than in 2 Timothy. In Titus, the opposition is, as in 1 Timothy, preoccupied with debates and genealogies and "legal battles" (or "battles over the law," *machas nomikas*, 3:9), but are here explicitly identified as being *ek tēs peritomēs* (1:10), involved with "Jewish myths" and "human commandments" (1:14). These commandments, in turn, concern distinctions between what is clean and unclean (1:15). Paul associates the opponents with the *apistois* (1:15) and *apeitheis* (1:16), as people who claim knowledge of God but deny him, namely God, with their deeds (1:16). In contrast, Titus states forcefully that it is the gift (*charis*) of the savior God that has provided them with instruction (*paideuonta*) in how to live with transformed moral character as "a people that [Jesus] has purified as his own people zealous for good deeds" (2:11–14). Again, Paul asserts that it was God's mercy (*eleos*) that saved them, so that "being made righteous by that gift [*charis*] we might become heirs in the hope of eternal life" (3:5–7) rather than "out of works in righteousness that we ourselves performed" (3:5). In Titus, the Jewish character of the oppositions is heightened, and the power of grace to transform humans into moral dispositions desired by God is clearly affirmed.

In 2 Timothy, there is an equally strong emphasis on Timothy's moral character, which has as its foil the negative moral portrayal of the opposition, but the matter is not cast in terms of a contrast between heteronomous norm and divine empowerment. Paul emphatically asserts that Timothy is empowered by grace (2:1) and that he has been given by God "a spirit not of cowardice but of power and love and self-control" (1:7). The composition focuses precisely on these moral dispositions that

47. See Schubert, *Form and Function*, and O'Brien, *Introductory Thanksgivings*.

Timothy is to display as Paul's delegate. But although some things said about the opponents are similar to the charges made in 1 Timothy and Titus—they are filled with every sort of vice (3:1–6), dispute over words (2:14, 23), are corrupted in mind and unproven in faith (3:8), and turn aside to myths (4:4)—nowhere does Paul suggest that they advance a program involving the observance of law; rather, they are accused only of claiming that the resurrection has already occurred (2:18).

The difference in pattern confirms the judgment that 1 Timothy and Titus should be considered as *mandata principis* letters that address genuine pastoral problems facing Paul's delegates arising from claims made about law-observance, and that 2 Timothy is best read as a personal paraenetic/protreptic letter exhorting the delegate to a way of life consonant with his vocation.

3. To ask whether the contrast between internal moral dispositions and external norm is a characteristic of other Pauline letters is to ask a large question, whose tentative and cautious answer here must be a partial yes. In at least four of the compositions that all agree come from Paul (Romans, 2 Corinthians, Philippians, and Galatians), and in two that are disputed (Colossians and Ephesians), the contrast appears with greater or lesser emphasis. Since part of my interest in regenerating conversation about the authenticity of the Pastorals is restoring them to the larger Pauline conversation and setting them individually into more useful comparisons across the Pauline corpus, I will briefly state here how I see this contrast at work in the four undisputed letters I have named.[48]

In Rom 7–8, Paul states the contrast in powerful terms. Even though he acknowledges that the law is good (7:16), holy (7:12), and spiritual (7:14), and that the commandment is holy and righteous and good (7:12), he states that it is powerless to actually change him. But what the law cannot do, the Spirit of life that comes from Christ can do: change humans in their moral dispositions so that they can walk according to the Spirit and not according to the flesh (8:1–11). The imperative that flows from this spirit-empowerment—"grace" (5:2)—is the transformation of the mind so that it can discern "the will of God, the good thing, and the pleasing and perfect thing" (12:1–2); those who have been so empowered

---

48. That Paul exhorts the Corinthians in his first letter to them to live by the Spirit that comes from God and to measure their behavior according to the "mind of Christ" (1 Cor 2:16) and exhibit transformed moral dispositions (6:9–11) is patent, but in that letter the contrast is not drawn between such interior qualities and heteronomous norms.

have "put on the Lord Jesus Christ" and can therefore "walk decently" rather than in vice (13:13–14).

In 2 Cor 3–4, Paul again establishes a strong contrast between "the letter that kills" and "the spirit that gives life" (3:6). In this argument, the stress is placed not so much on the inadequacy of the law—it had its own "glory" (3:7–9)—as on its being eclipsed by the power of life given by the "spirit of the living God" (3:3), with the contrast focused specifically on the external nature of the law ("written on stone tablets") and the internal character of the spirit's imprinting ("written on tablets of fleshly hearts"). Here Paul makes the bold statement that the spirit (who is the Lord) transforms them from glory to glory into the image of the one on whom they gaze (3:17–18). The issue for Paul in this letter is less that the Corinthians will be seduced by an external measure for morality than that they will fail to demonstrate their transformed character in action.[49]

The contrast between law and grace in Phil 3 has still a different emphasis. Here Paul elaborates the "confidence in the flesh" he enjoyed in his former life because of his heritage and observance; he was, he declared, "according to righteousness found in the law, blameless" (3:6). But he regards all of this as nothing compared to "the knowledge of Christ Jesus my Lord" (3:8), for in that relationship he has found "not a righteousness on the basis of law, but through the faith of Christ, the righteousness that comes from God, based on faith" (3:9). Paul cites his own turn from law to faith as the last in a series of examples he presents to the consideration of the Philippians as "looking to other's interests more than one's own" (2:4): the kenotic Christ (2:5–11); the delegate Timothy, whose proven character they know (2:19–24); and the self-giving Epaphroditus (2:25–30). All these display the moral qualities that are found also in Christ and are available to them because of the "fellowship of the Spirit" (2:1–2).

Galatians bears a remarkable resemblance to 1 Timothy with respect to the contrast between those advocating observance of law as a measure of righteousness and Paul's insistence on those who live in the Spirit also walking according to the Spirit (Gal 5:25). As in 1 Timothy, Galatians speaks of actual individuals (*tines*) who are upsetting the communities (1:7) because they "want to be under law" (*hoi hypo nomon thelontes einai*, 4:21) and are "bewitching" gentile believers (3:1) into seeking cir-

---

49. With Stegman, *Character of Jesus*, I read *egrapsa* in 2 Cor 2:9 as epistolary: Paul is writing to test the character of the Corinthians' obedient faith; see esp. 13:5.

cumcision (5:3–12). As in 1 Timothy, Paul suggests that the "child of the slave girl" (meaning those who are "according to the flesh" rather than "according to the spirit") be cast out of the community (4:30). And as in 1 Timothy, Paul establishes a sharp contrast between the "works of the flesh" associated with a life without the power of the Spirit, which cause strife and conflict in the community, and those deep moral dispositions that he calls "the fruit of the Spirit," which include love, joy, peace, patience, gentleness, goodness, faith, meekness, and self-control—exactly the sort of virtue list that characterizes 1 Timothy (Gal 5:19–23). Paul declares, "Against such [dispositions] as these there is no law" (5:23), a statement that strikingly resembles 1 Tim 1:9, "law is not laid down for a righteous person."

4. The character and function of Paul's conversion account in Gal 1:11–16 is remarkably similar to that of his account in 1 Tim 1:12–17. In both, the contrast is drawn between Paul's former life and his call. In both, his persecution of the church is noted. In both, his conversion is cast in terms of a call or appointment to preach the good news. In both, the change is ascribed to grace or gift (*charis*). In 1 Timothy it consists of an empowerment by "Christ Jesus our Lord" with "the faith and love that are in Christ Jesus" (1:12, 14), and in Galatians it is the "revelation of [God's] son in [or "to"] me" (1:16). There are, to be sure, differences as well. In Galatians Paul elaborates that aspect of his former life that was dedicated to the keeping of the law, whereas in 1 Timothy Paul emphasizes his former faithlessness, ignorance, and arrogance as a blasphemer. Galatians focuses on Paul's mission to preach the good news, whereas 1 Timothy focuses on the demonstration of God's forbearance. Gal 1:15 contains an allusion to a prophetic call ("called from the mother's womb") that 1 Timothy lacks (see Isa 49:1 and Jer 1:5). Apart from the specific diction found in each account, however, it must be granted that they are more alike than different.

Even more impressive is the way in which Paul's account of his call/commissioning/conversion in both letters serves an *exemplary* function. I have already indicated how this works in 1 Timothy: Paul is an example not only of how God shows patience with sinners but above all of how God's grace can transform them. Within the context of 1 Timothy 1, Paul's empowerment from God changes him from an arrogant, blaspheming, and persecuting human being filled with faithlessness and ignorance to one put in God's service, gifted by the faith and love that are in Christ Jesus.

In Galatians, the lesson to be drawn is slightly different: Paul's entire opening narrative serves as a model for his Galatian readers who are in danger of being seduced by the proponents of law: Paul was once like them—and he persecuted the church! But once Paul was commissioned by God as an apostle, he did not look back, did not give in, and claimed the authority given him by the experience of Christ in him. The point is that his readers also should not now, having been lavishly gifted by the Holy Spirit (3:1–5), go back precisely to the place Paul formerly occupied, measuring righteousness by the law. As in 1 Timothy, Paul identifies the supposed "advance" represented by the opponents as a "reversal" to a condition that he formerly shared, and from which he was himself an opponent of the living God.

Conclusion

In this essay I have tried to show how 1 Tim 1:1–20 establishes a contrast between the experience of God and human ambition, expressed on one side by internal moral dispositions and on the other side by disputes centering on observance of law. When the clarification concerning the law and the vice list of 1:9–11 is read in connection with Paul's account of his conversion in 1:12–17, the two sides are shown in the person of Paul himself. In his former life he was under the law, yet he was a violent persecutor; now he is an example of God's power to fill a sinner with faith and love. His personal recital therefore bears his argument within itself. I have further tried to show that the conflict between heteronomous norm and transformation of character runs through both the other letters to Paul's delegates and a substantial portion of his undisputed correspondence, most strikingly in Galatians. Finally, I have suggested that the account of Paul's call in Galatians and of his commissioning in 1 Timothy not only have much substantively in common but serve similar exemplary functions. It is my hope that these simple observations will at least serve to show that putting the respective letters to Paul's delegates into sustained conversation with his other writings is neither frivolous nor without point.

Chapter 22

Second Timothy and the Polemic against False Teachers

A Reexamination

I t is not surprising that the passages in the Pastorals that deal with false teachers continue to present problems for interpreters of those letters.[1] In spite of the amount of attention paid to false teachers (some 47 out of 242 verses), little specific information about them can be gained. The few allusions to doctrinal or ascetic positions are vague,[2] and the terms of condemnation, while vigorous, tell us little about the content of their teaching.[3] It is well known that the author of the Pastorals, in contrast to the Paul of 1 or 2 Corinthians, is less concerned with refuting the theological positions of the heretics than with cautioning against their methods and morals and the insidious results of their teaching.[4]

---

1. This is the earliest of the essays included in this book, and it shows how I slowly worked my way from the conventional position to the one reflected in my other essays and in vol. 1.

2. The heretics claim to possess some sort of gnosis (1 Tim 6:20); some among them are teaching that the resurrection has already taken place (2 Tim 2:17–18); they forbid marriage and the eating of certain food (1 Tim 4:3); they claim to be teachers of the law (1 Tim 1:7); the remarks on physical discipline (1 Tim 4:8) also refer to an ascetic bent.

3. It would be difficult to be more general than Titus 1:11: *didaskontes ha mē dei.* Their teaching included myths (1 Tim 4:7), genealogies (1 Tim 1:3), and "speculations" (1 Tim 1:4, 6:4; 2 Tim 2:23; Tit 3:9), which Paul calls "godless chatter" (1 Tim 6:20; 2 Tim 2:14–16), "foolish" (Titus 3:9; 2 Tim 2:23), and "ignorant" (2 Tim 2:23). Their disputes were characterized by bellicosity and harshness (1 Tim 6:4; 2 Tim 2:14, 23; Titus 3:9).

4. The gist of the moral condemnation is conveyed succinctly by Titus 1:16: *theon homologousin eidenai, tois de ergois arnountai.* As 2 Tim 3:6 indicates, the vice list of 3:2–5 applies to the false teachers. It is remarkable primarily for the number of

Attempts to reconstruct the theological positions of these adversaries have not proven very satisfactory. The picture of rigorist, mythically oriented, quasi-gnostic Judaizers results from pushing the few concrete hints to their limit, and sometimes beyond, and still lacks any convincing specificity.[5] More seriously, these attempts at defining the heretics have not advanced our understanding of the letters to a significant degree.

A sounder approach to these polemical passages was initiated by Martin Dibelius[6] and taken up by Hans Conzelmann.[7] They noted that the vocabulary and tone of the polemic is strongly reminiscent of the polemics frequently found in hellenistic writings directed against Sophists. This sort of polemic, which can be found in Aristophanes,[8] had by the Roman period become a stereotyped topos, employed both by rhetoricians and philosophers.[9] Because such topoi are by nature conventional,

"misanthropic" vices it contains. The emphasis is always on belligerence of these false teachers. On the vice list, see McEleney, "Vice-Lists." Although it can generally be stated that the author does not rebut theologically to any great degree, it should be pointed out that in addition to 1 Tim 4:1–5, examined by Karris, "Background and Significance," 549, one should add 1 Tim 1:8–11 and 6:6–8; in each a "misconception" is corrected by the proper understanding. In general, however, the case is accurately stated by Brox, *Die Pastoralbriefe*: "Man kann den Tatbestand so umschreiben, daß die Pastoralbriefe nicht eigentlich die Irrlehre, sondern die Irrlehrer bekämpfen" (39) ("One can say that the pastoral letters do not so much battle false teaching as they do false teachers").

5. Cf. Mangold, *Die Irrlehrer der Pastoralbriefe*; Lütgert, *Die Irrlehrer der Pastoralbriefe*; Dibelius, *Die Briefe des Apostels Paulus*, 166–68; Brox, *Die Pastoralbriefe*, 31–39; Barrett, *Pastoral Epistles*, 12–16; Kelly, *Pastoral Epistles*, 10–12; W. Barclay, *The Letters to Timothy, Titus, and Philemon*, 5–8; Lock, *A Critical and Exegetical Commentary on the Pastoral Epistles*, xvii; Brown, *Pastoral Epistles*, 5; Schierse, *Die Pastoralbriefe*, 31; Spicq, *Saint Paul*, 1:85–119.

6. Dibelius, *Die Briefe des Apostels Paulus* (1913), 149.

7. Dibelius and Conzelmann, *Pastoral Epistles*, 2 and passim. Spicq, *Saint Paul*, 1:85ff., has not only seen the pertinence of this sort of polemic but has collected an enormous number of references to the hellenistic material. Unfortunately, this mass of material is somewhat undigested and does not come into play significantly in his interpretation. Certain aspects of this polemic were also spotted by Colson, "'Myths and Genealogies.'"

8. *The Clouds* (ca. 417 BCE) already attacked Socrates and his students with most of the criticisms later applied to sophists and philosophers: their distinctive appearance; their complicated syllogisms and discussions that obfuscated truth; their arrogance and argumentativeness; their greed; their subversiveness. See *Aristophanes* (Rogers, LCL), 1:275–359.

9. This was not entirely a literary game or matter of academics. Philosophers in particular were distrusted by Roman authorities, and the worthiest of them suffered exile: Musonius Rufus, Dio Chrysostom, Epictetus. Seneca's vicissitudes at court are

it is hazardous to seek within them the individual traits of opponents.[10] More recently, Robert Karris has provided extensive evidence in support of this topos in philosophical writings[11] and has shown that the language of the Pastorals' polemic can best be understood in the light of this literary schema.[12] In spite of the traditional nature of much of this polemic, Karris suggests that a redactional analysis of the Pastorals reveals enough deviations to allow a tentative description of the false teachers.[13]

Although the basic direction established by these authors is correct, and the wealth of materials they adduce from Hellenistic materials is impressive, there remains a certain lack of precision with regard to the *function* of these polemical materials, both within the Hellenistic writings and the Pastorals themselves. This lack of precision regarding function derives from too little attention to the literary form of the writings in which such polemical language appears. After listing the elements of the polemical schema, Karris states, "The schema is intended to cause aversion for the sophists and sympathy for the writer's position in the minds of his readers. . . . Perhaps the most significant function of the schema was to demonstrate who had the right to and actually did impart genuine wisdom and truth."[14] But although it can be argued that the purpose of such polemic was frequently or even generally as Karris suggests, it is important to note that there are instances where the function is quite plainly different.[15] As

---

well known. For the imperial attitude toward philosophers, see Philostratus, *Life of Apollonius of Tyana* 4.35, 5.19, 7.4; and Dio Cassius, *Roman History* 6.175. See also Macmullen, *Enemies of the Roman Order*, 46–94. For a lively portrait of the philosophic ethos during the Roman period, see Dill, *Roman Society*, 289–440.

10. Dibelius and Conzelmann, *Pastoral Epistles*, 2.

11. Karris, "Background and Significance," 551–55. See also his unpublished dissertation, "Parenetic Elements," 3–39.

12. Karris, "Background and Significance," 556–62.

13. Karris, "Background and Significance," 562–63: "The opponents are Jewish Christians who are teachers of the Law." A similar conclusion was reached by Dornier, *Les Épîtres Pastorales*, 14–16.

14. Karris, "Background and Significance," 556.

15. The compositions Karris employs are all directed against Sophists, which is fair enough. But certain methodic qualifications should be noted. First, it is not the case that the polemic was one-sided; just as philosophers attacked sophists, so did sophists (or rhetoricians) attack philosophers. The most outstanding example is Aelius Aristides's (ca. 117–182 CE) *Platonic Discourses*, especially the second, "HUPER TŌN TETTARŌN," in *Aristides*, 1:11, in which the typical elements of polemic appear: philosophers dress ascetically but are interiorly corrupt (307.10); they are pleasure-lovers (307.15), money-lovers (308.5, 10); they are revilers (309.45); they preach virtue but don't practice it (307.6); and their discourses are without profit

I will show in more detail later in this essay, the same polemical language is frequently employed, not to establish the credentials of a writer for his audience, but to provide an antithesis to the description of the ideal teacher—that is, in paraenetic or protreptic discourses.[16] Though the language in these writings is virtually identical to that in the writings cited by Karris, the *function* of the language is altogether different.

When he applies his analysis of the polemical schema to the Pastorals, Karris concludes that "on analogy" with the way the schema was employed in the Hellenistic writings, the author of the Pastorals wished to "dissociate his teaching from that of the heretics . . . to show that he alone has the right to and actually does impart the truth, that he and his disciples alone have the power to teach correctly . . . to cause aversion for his opponents in the minds of his readers and to establish a strong alternative to their view of Pauline tradition."[17] The problem with this conclusion is that it does not correspond to the actual literary shape of the Pastorals. There is no evidence in the Pastorals that the author was attempting to convince readers of his own credentials, or used the polemic as a device to this end. The authority of the author is never in question; it is assumed. The audience, moreover (at least in literary terms), is not the community at large but the author's personal delegates, themselves Christian teachers. The author has no need to convince them of his authority.[18] Further, the entire focus of the letters is on the proper attitudes

---

(309.14–15). Second, the slanders against false philosophers are found in disputes between different *schools* of philosophy. See, e.g., Epictetus, *Discourses* 1.5.9, 2.20, 2.23.21ff., 3.7.21. Third, the language of slander is to be found in discourses advocating the philosophic way of life. We will look at some of these later, but in addition to those, see also Epictetus, *Discourses* 4.8.5ff; Julian the Apostate, *Oration*, "To the Uneducated Cynics," and *Oration* VII, "To the Cynic Heracleios," in *The Works of the Emperor Julian* (Wright, LCL, 1913). Fourth, both sophists and philosophers are attacked with the same sort of slander by *satirists*. We have referred to Aristophanes above. See also the many places in Lucian of Samosata, e.g., *Zeus Rants* 11, 27; *Icaromenippus* 5; *Philosophers for Sale* 20–23; *The Double Indictment* 22, 34; *Dialogues of the Dead* 332, 369; *Timon* 54; *The Fisherman* 31; *The Runaways* 4, 14, 19; *Hermotimus* 18, and many more. (All titles and references to Lucian are as found in LCL.) Fifth, the slander is not always used in an apologetic way—that is, as a negative defense of one's own teaching. The references to Lucian support this distinction. Karris ("Background and Significance," 555) is correct in noting, however, that most frequently it is *teachers* of one sort or another who are the targets for such slander.

16. Later in the essay we will look in some detail at Epictetus, *Discourses* 3.22, Dio Chrysostom's *Oration* 77/78, and Lucian of Samosata's *Demonax* and *Nigrinus*.

17. Karris, "Background and Significance," 563–64.

18. The assertion of Dibelius and Conzelmann (*Pastoral Epistles*, 7) that "the em-

and methods of these delegates *as* teachers. The contrast provided by the false teachers is to them and their teaching, not to the author. The author does not need to clear the way for the acceptance of his own teaching by denigrating the heretics or by confronting them face to face. Both the author and his delegates share the same teaching and recognize the author's authority. The answer to Karris's important question, "Why does the author employ the schema of philosophers against sophists?"[19] is, I suggest, different than the one he offers. The evidence for this must be sought in a careful literary examination of the Pastorals, as well as of the Hellenistic materials pertinent to the investigation.

In this essay I will try to show more precisely the function of the polemical language of the Pastorals, first by a close examination of 2 Timothy's literary form, second by a review of Hellenistic materials with pertinent parallels, and third by a brief look at similar structures in 1 Timothy and Titus. The reason for looking at 2 Timothy apart from the other Pastorals is that the literary pattern I hope to demonstrate is found most clearly there, and that too frequently the Pastorals are considered en bloc, with little attention paid to their distinguishing characteristics.[20]

Second Timothy: A Personal Paraenetic Letter

The tone of the letter is strikingly personal, not only in the reminiscences of Timothy's youth (2 Tim 1:5; 3:15), but in the description of Paul's own

---

phasis upon tradition in the Pastorals means that Paul is being established as the authority for the Church" is based on inferences that depend on the putative purpose for writing. In terms of literary presentation, at least—that is, insofar as the author and his designated readers are concerned—Paul's authority is not in question.

19. Karris, "Background and Significance," 563.

20. While it is true that the Pastorals share many features, it is not good method to ignore the important differences between them. In discussions of the "theology of the Pastorals" or the "life-setting of the Pastorals," evidence is too frequently garnered indiscriminately, without careful enough consideration given to the distinct coloration given to shared elements by the tone or form of each letter. What often results is a construct drawn almost entirely from 1 Timothy and Titus. See, e.g., Marxsen, *Introduction to the New Testament*, 212–15; Kümmel, *Introduction to the New Testament*, 378–87; Spicq, *Saint Paul*, 1:65–83; Dornier, *Les Épîtres Pastorales*, 16–20; Lock, *Pastoral Epistles*, xiii–xxii. Dibelius and Conzelmann, *Pastoral Epistles*, give more attention than most to the distinguishing literary features in the Pastorals (5–7) but conclude, "So the Pastoral Epistles, taken together, are all three expressions of one and the same *concept*" (8; emphasis added).

career (1:12–13, 15–18; 3:10–11; 4:6–18).[21] In this letter, there is no discussion of church order, no *Haustafeln*.[22] The focus of the letter is entirely on Timothy and those who are to share his teaching role. Twice (2:1, 14) these other teachers are mentioned; in both instances the emphasis falls on Timothy's responsibility for rightly instructing them. Otherwise, the letter deals consistently with the attitudes and practices that should characterize Timothy himself. Paul is instructing his disciple in proper Christian pedagogy; the handing on of that pedagogy to others is important, but secondary.

Is this new teaching that Paul is giving Timothy? No. Rather, the letter presents a series of *reminders* to Timothy. Paul is exhorting Timothy to act in a way of which he was already well aware (2 Tim 1:6, 13; 2:8, 14; 3:10, 14–17). The purpose of Paul's reminders is to "rekindle" in Timothy's mind and heart what he had already received, the gift of God, from Paul (1:6, 13). What are the stimulants to this remembering? They include traditional, trustworthy sayings (2:11, 19) and the Scriptures (3:15). But above all, Timothy is to be stirred into new enthusiasm (into active "memory") by the example of Paul's own words (1:13; 2:2; 3:10) and personal example (1:8–2:13; 3:10–11; 4:6–8). This reminding of traditional teaching is paraenetic in nature. Second Timothy is a personal, paraenetic letter.[23] We can look at the literary structure of 2 Timothy more closely and see how the polemical language fits within that structure.

21. Throughout this essay I will use "Paul" when referring to the author of all three Pastorals. It is not appropriate here to rehearse all the old and new arguments concerning authenticity. In my opinion, the question is at present moot, especially with regard to 2 Timothy. See Ellis, *Paul and His Recent Interpreters*, 49–57; Robinson, *Redating the New Testament*, 67–85. The use of "Paul" here expresses fidelity to the presentation of the documents as a real personality writing to other equally real individuals, and not as a cipher for later church discernment.

22. When defining the purpose of the polemic as causing aversion for the opponents so that positive teaching can be given, Karris, "Background and Significance," 563–64, says that this teaching is to be found in the office of the bishop, who hands on Paul's understanding of grace, and in the *Haustafeln*. But in 2 Timothy there are neither bishops nor *Haustafeln*. What, then, is the function of the polemic in this document?

23. This is recognized by Dibelius and Conzelmann, *Pastoral Epistles*, 7, and certain features of paraenesis are noted throughout their commentary (e.g., 107–9), but they do not systematically pursue the implications with regard to the content. Indeed, they are so persuaded of the relationship of the Pastorals to documents like the Didache and the Letter of Polycarp (6–7) that they can state, "The personal sections of *all three epistles* at once fade into the background; their primary purpose, is at any rate, to demonstrate the authorship of Paul" (8; emphasis added). In this

2 Timothy 1:3–2:13

The first section of the letter focuses entirely on Timothy's attitudes. There is throughout this section a subtle interplay of the notions of memory and model. Explicit statements to this effect are supported by wordplay involving "shame" and "suffering." The idea of memory enters at once in the thanksgiving. Paul remembers Timothy constantly in his prayers (2 Tim 1:3), remembers his tears (1:4), and, finally, remembers the sincere faith that was in Timothy as it was in his mother and grandmother (1:5). The last phrase of verse 5, however, may reveal a certain anxiety: *pepeismai de hoti kai en soi*.[24] Paul is evidently concerned that Timothy is weakening in some fashion because of Paul's imprisonment or his own difficulties in the ministry. In verse 6 Paul states the purpose of the letter. It is to remind Timothy (*anamimnēskō*) to stir up again the gift of God that he had received from Paul's hands. The *di' hēn aitian* is particularly interesting. It is Paul's memory of Timothy's heritage of faith, which moves him to stir Timothy's memory of that same reality.[25]

The point of Paul's reminder is to be found in the nature of the gift they share. God had not given them a spirit of cowardice (*deilias*) but one of power and love and self-control (2 Tim 1:7). Therefore (*oun*), Paul is able to tell Timothy, "Do not be ashamed" (*mē epaischynthēs*, 1:8).[26] Of what

---

essay I hope to demonstrate that the personal sections are the main focus of each letter; that this is so at least in the case of 2 Timothy will be established. It is sometimes asserted that the Pastorals, and in particular 2 Timothy, should be viewed as examples of farewell discourses. The major influence here has been Johannes Munck, "Discours d'Adieu," esp. 162–63. Munck himself refers to Stauffer, *New Testament Theology*, 344–47, though Stauffer did not include the Pastorals in his comparative tables. Spicq, *Saint Paul*, 1:45, says, "C'est surtout la seconde lettre qui est un authentique *Testament*," but he does not pursue this in his exegesis. See also Schierse, *Die Pastoralbriefe*, 97; Dibelius and Conzelmann, *Pastoral Epistles*, 107. Incisive remarks on this "Testimonial" form can be found in Neyrey, "Form and Background," 99–103. The second part of this chapter will demonstrate a more convincing literary form from Hellenistic materials.

24. Spicq, *Saint Paul*, 2:706, takes the *pepeismai* at face value as showing Paul's absolute confidence in Timothy: "Le parfait à valeur superlatif." But in the overall context of encouragement, and especially in the light of verse 7, the expression appears to reveal hesitancy.

25. Spicq, *Saint Paul*, 2:707, notes the powerful effect of the fourfold repetition of the idea of memory in these verses. See also Brox, *Die Pastoralbriefe*, 228; Barrett, *Pastoral Epistles*, 93.

26. Clearly a reminiscence of Paul's own self-characterization. Cf. Rom 1:16; 2 Cor 10:8; Phil 1:20. Spicq, *Saint Paul*, 2:711, calls it a form of *litotes*: what is being called for

should he not be ashamed? Either of his own witnessing to the Lord,[27] or of Paul the prisoner of the Lord. Rather, Timothy is to "join in the sufferings for the gospel" (*alla synkakopathēson tō euangeliō*).[28] This verse brings together the notions of suffering and shame. Timothy is not to be ashamed (fearful), because he has been called to be a minister of the gospel as has Paul. Paul now suffers (*paschō*) for the gospel but himself is not ashamed in that suffering (*all' ouk epaischynomai*) because of his great faith (1:12).

Already it is clear that Paul is presenting himself as a model for Timothy to follow. As Paul was called to be a minister of the gospel, so was Timothy; as Paul has had to suffer for the gospel, so must Timothy; and as Paul was not filled with shame because of this suffering, but rather with confidence, so should Timothy. This is the anamnesis to which Paul stirs his delegate: the recollection of his calling and the model he is to follow.

That Paul is a model for Timothy is made explicit in 2 Tim 1:13: *hypotypōsin eche hygiainontōn logōn hōn par' emou ēkousas en pistei kai agapē tē en Christō Iēsou.* Timothy is told to hold to the example provided by Paul's words.[29] His manner of "holding on" is specified as "in the faith and love which are in Christ Jesus."[30] The gift that Timothy and Paul received was characterized by power and love and self-control (1:7); and Paul is able to suffer because of his conviction (*pepeismai*) that the Lord was able (*dynatos*) to guard until that day what was entrusted to him (*parathēkēn mou phylaxai*, 1:12). Because Timothy is enabled by the same Spirit (1:14), he too can "guard what has been entrusted to him" (*tēn kalēn parathēkēn phylaxon*). Paul's model, therefore, is not simply

---

is *parrēsia*. For "shame" in confessing, cf. Mark 8:38; Luke 9:26. For the psychological verisimilitude in regard to Timothy, cf. 1 Cor 16:10.

27. In the context, the genitive appears to be objective. See Kelly, *Pastoral Epistles*, 160; Spicq, *Saint Paul*, 2:711.

28. The expression is used only here and 2:3 in the New Testament; it is not uncharacteristic of Paul to form such *syn-* compounds, of course. Likewise Pauline is the notion of suffering for the gospel. Cf. Phil 1:16; 2 Cor 4:11–12.

29. Cf. Lee, "Words Denoting 'Pattern,'" esp. 168–72, where he shows the relation between *hypotypos* and *hypodeigma*.

30. The placement of the phrase is difficult; see Dibelius and Conzelmann, *Pastoral Epistles*, 105; Barrett, *Pastoral Epistles*, 97. It seems better to attach it to verse 13 than to verse 14. Spicq, *Saint Paul*, 2:721, says that the phrase could be attached to the actual hearing of Paul's words but would better modify *eche*; Timothy is to hold to the model in this fashion. See also Kelly, *Pastoral Epistles*, 166–67. This would fit better with the depiction of Timothy as model in 1 Tim 4:12, where a similar construction is found.

in the words he has spoken but also his manner of life, especially his suffering for the gospel in the faithful conviction that the Lord would enable him to endure.

At first sight, verses 15–18, which describe Paul's prison conditions and his abandonment, appear to be a digression. But the clear inference to be drawn about those who have abandoned Paul (1:15) is that they have done so out of that spirit of cowardice (*deilias*) against which Paul is warning Timothy. Onesiphorus, on the other hand, is praised because he alone was not ashamed of Paul's chains (*ouk epaischynthē*, 1:16). Onesiphorus, therefore, presents another model for the edification of Timothy of confident service in the midst of suffering.[31]

The *su oun teknon mou* of 2:1 must be seen as following directly from these examples.[32] The "therefore" has the force of "seeing that you have these examples of how it can be done." Timothy is to be strong in the grace that, again, is characterized by power (cf. 2 Tim 1:7). Verse 2 advances the thought of 1:13. Timothy is not only to hold to the example of Paul's words and keep them as a deposit; he is also to hand them over to other men (also faithful, *pistois*), who will be able to teach still others. Having so briefly specified Timothy's task of transmitting the tradition, Paul returns to his main paraenetic emphasis: the necessity of suffering for the gospel. The *synkakopathēson* repeats Timothy's essential way of modeling himself on Paul (cf. 1:8). The three examples of the soldier, athlete, and farmer present, respectively, three aspects of the rigors of suffering and its reward. The soldier who keeps himself unentangled with the cares of life suffers thereby but pleases his commander; the athlete who competes by the rules suffers thereby but wins a crown; the farmer who labors hard suffers thereby but shares the firstfruits of the harvest (2:4–6). What unites all three examples is the necessity of suffering if anything good is to come.[33]

---

31. Dibelius and Conzelmann, *Pastoral Epistles*, 106; Kelly, *Pastoral Epistles*, 168. The *oidas* of verse 15 and *su ginōskeis* of verse 18 frame the passage and emphasize a note of urgency. Spicq, *Saint Paul*, 2:731, suggests the *oidas touto* has the strength of exhortation, "Pay attention to this!" See also Schierse, *Die Pastoralbriefe*, 108.

32. Dibelius and Conzelmann, *Pastoral Epistles*, 107, see this verse as beginning a new section of the letter, the "actual paraenesis." It is better to see the first section as continuing through verse 13, for although it is true that Timothy is here commanded, the theme of the model has not yet been fully elaborated, and, as we shall see, the establishment of a model is a distinct aspect of this sort of paraenesis. The concrete directives begin in verse 14.

33. Barrett, *Pastoral Epistles*, 102; Dibelius and Conzelmann, *Pastoral Epistles*, 108.

Verses 8–13 bring together the themes of remembrance, model, and suffering. Timothy is told again to remember (*mnēmoneue*), this time Jesus Christ who was raised from the dead and for the preaching of whom Paul suffers (*kakopathō*, 2 Tim 2:8–9). As in 1:8, Paul's own sufferings for the gospel are to be the model for Timothy's (cf. 2:3). But the remembrance of Jesus is not simply of his glorious resurrection; the remembering here is a taking part in the sort of suffering Jesus himself endured.[34] This is made clear from 2:11: *ei gar synapethanomen, kai syzēsomen*. If both Paul and Timothy suffer together with the Jesus whom they proclaim, they will both share his life. Here Paul presents both the ultimate model of the suffering teacher and the ultimate motivation for following that model. We notice, too, that verse 12 picks up on verse 10. Paul endures all things (*panta hypomenō*) for the sake of the elect. In verse 12 we read, *ei hypomenomen, kai symbasileusomen*. This *logos*, which is itself *pistos*,[35] specifies for the Christian minister the pattern of suffering and reward intimated by the three examples of 2:3–6.

We have seen that the first section of 2 Timothy is carefully constructed. Paul is attempting to stir the teacher Timothy to new enthusiasm. To do this, he presents himself as a model, not only of sound teaching, but, more importantly, of that way of faithful suffering that was demonstrated by Jesus and that leads to the reward of life with Jesus. In this section, there has been no mention of false teachers and only the barest reference to the faithful men to whom Timothy is to entrust the task of teaching others. The entire focus has been on Timothy's need to gain confidence in the face of suffering. Neither has there been attention paid to the way in which Timothy is to teach. It can also he pointed out that the kind of suffering undergone by Paul and enjoined on Timothy is not said to be physical suffering but seems to have a lot to do with being confined and with being abandoned by others. We can bear this in mind as we look further into the letter.

34. The resurrection of Jesus here is equivalent to the fourth example, and the ultimate one, of suffering followed by reward.

35. On *pistos ho logos* (v. 11), see Dibelius and Conzelmann, *Pastoral Epistles*, 28–29; Spicq, *Saint Paul*, 1:277n1; Duncan, "*Pistos ho Logos*." However stereotyped the phrase, we note that it establishes another point of unity between the teaching (1 Tim 1:15; 3:1; 4:9; Titus 1:9; 3:8) and the teachers (1 Tim 1:12; 2 Tim 2:2); both are "faithful." But God alone is truly *pistos* (see 2 Tim 2:13).

2 Timothy 2:14–4:8

The second section of the letter has the same paraenetic intent as the first section, though the literary structure is different. As we shall see, the importance of Paul as the model will reappear in significant places (3:10–11 and 4:6–8), but this example is placed within a different structure than in the first section. Having sketched in 1:3–2:13 the essential outlines of the model Timothy is to follow,[36] the author now explicates and elaborates that model by means of concrete directives. The basic structure of the section is formed by a series of longer and shorter antitheses. Characteristic here is the dominance of the singular imperative (always addressed to Timothy—his attitudes and methods are always in view), alternating with third-person plural descriptions of the false teachers.[37] The commands to Timothy are basically to shun or avoid certain things and to follow or do certain others.[38] It is most important to note that the descriptions of the false teachers—their attitudes and methods—are always contrasted to the attitudes and methods that should characterize Timothy, and in every case the emphasis falls on what Timothy should do, in contrast to what they do.

Two further aspects of these antitheses should be noted. First, since Timothy models himself on the "sound words" (*hygiainontōn logōn*) he has heard from Paul (2 Tim 1:13), his own teaching was to be characterized by the same "healthful" qualities in contrast to the "diseased" teaching of the opponents (2:15–17; 3:2–5); in the same way that Paul's teaching was gentle and patient (3:10), so was Timothy's to be kindly and

36. Lee, "Words Denoting 'Pattern,'" 172, stresses this aspect of the term *hypotōsis*; the model, like a mold, needs filling in with specific directives.

37. The imperatives to Timothy: 2:14, 15, 16, 22 (2×), 23; 3:1, 5, 14; 4:2 (5×); 4:5 (4×); excluding participles, the verbs designating the false teachers: 2:16, 18; 3:2, 6, 8, 9, 13.

38. Negative injunctions to Timothy: *periistaso* (2:16); *pheuge* (2:22); *paraitou* (2:23); *apotrepou* (3:5). Positive injunctions: *hypomimnēske* (2:14); *spoudason* (2:15); *diōke* (2:22); *ginōske* (3:1); *mene* (3:14); *kēryxon, epistēthi, elenxon, epitimēson, parakaleson* (4:2); *nēphe, kakopathēson, poiēson, plērophorēson* (4:5). The false teachers are ones who fall away or turn away (*ēstochēsan, anatrepousin,* 2:18); they "stand against" (*anthistantai,* 3:8). They also "advance" (*prokopsousin,* 2:16; 3:13). It is against this "advance" that Timothy is to remain (*mene,* 3:14) and stand fast (*epistēthi,* 4:2; cf. also *epistōthēs,* 3:14). The visual imagery is arresting. Even though the false teachers are advancing, Paul is sure that they will be found out and will not "advance" (*prokopsousin,* 3:9).

forebearing (2:24; 4:2) in contrast to that of the false teachers, whose methods are characterized by harshness and battles over words (2:14, 23–24; 3:2). Second, it should be observed that Timothy's opponents are not utterly condemned. It is part of Timothy's task to be a teacher of all, even of his opposing teachers (2:24), and the possibility is held that such patient teaching will lead to their repentance. This is stated explicitly in 2:25.

We can see more clearly how this pattern works as we read carefully through the section. The contrast is established immediately in 2 Tim 2:14. Timothy has remembered the model of Paul's teaching and behavior; now he is to remind others how they should teach (*tauta hypomimnēske*). This reminder is intended for him as well; for the focus shifts directly in 2:15 to his own attitude. We note that the negative characteristics to be avoided (following here the punctuation of the UBS text)[39] are balanced by the three positive qualities that Timothy is to pursue, and that these three qualities flow from the model presented earlier. Thus, Timothy is to be *dokimos* (a term associated with endurance of suffering or rejection);[40] to be an "unashamed workman" (*ergatēn anepaischynton*), which clearly recalls 1:8, 12, 16; and one who handles rightly the word of truth (cf. 1:13). The "godless chatter" (*bebēlous kenophōnias*) of the false teachers is to be avoided by Timothy (2:16). The description of this chatter, engaged in by Hymenaeus and Philetus, ends with its result, the upsetting of some peoples' faith (2:18). This picks up from 2:14c: *epi katastrophē tōn akouontōn*. For our purposes, it is important to note that the emphasis here is entirely on Timothy's mode of teaching, and the description of the opponents serves as a contrast to the positive picture of 2:15.

The passage 2 Tim 2:19–21 is a bit confusing.[41] The author's intention in alluding to the Scripture in verse 19 seems to be to support the motif of *avoidance* established in 2:16. Those who call on the name of the Lord are to depart from iniquity. But are they to depart from, separate themselves from, the *iniquitous*? The image of the great house with vessels of varying worth makes the picture more obscure. Verse 21 indicates that a vessel

---

39. Both text and syntax are difficult here. For the textual problem, see Spicq, *Saint Paul*, 1:308; for the sense, Lock, *Pastoral Epistles*, 98; Dornier, *Les Épîtres Pastorales*, 212; Dibelius and Conzelmann, *Pastoral Epistles*, 110. The general meaning is, in any case, clear enough.

40. For *dokimos*, cf. 1 Cor 11:19; 2 Cor 10:18; Jas 1:12; for *hē dokimē*, cf. Rom 5:4; 2 Cor 8:2; 9:13. In reference to Timothy, Phil 2:22.

41. See Barrett, *Pastoral Epistles*, 107–8.

can change from unworthy to worthy by purifying itself. But in that case, the *apo toutōn* must refer to those vessels that are unworthy—namely, the false teachers.[42] This would fulfill the demand of verse 16. Interpreting the passage in this way would make verses 19–21 another antithesis to the false teachers. By avoiding them, Timothy will be purified and be a vessel prepared for every good work.[43]

Verses 22–24 present two contrasts. In each, the negative quality is presented first, followed by the positive attitude of the ideal teacher. Thus in 2:22 Timothy is told to flee from (*pheuge*) youthful (or revolutionary?)[44] passions and to pursue (*diōke de*) justice, faith, and love. It is intriguing that he is to do this with (*meta*) those who call on the Lord from a pure heart. This clearly recalls both verse 19 and verse 21 and seems to strengthen the interpretation of verses 19–21 as advocating Timothy's avoidance of false teachers. The second contrast again first states what Timothy is to avoid (*paraitou*): stupid, senseless controversies because they lead to quarrels (*machas*, 2:23).[45] In contrast, the servant of the Lord is not to be quarrelsome (*ou dei machesthai*) but to demonstrate those qualities of gentleness and forbearance that may lead to the conversion even of the opponents (2:24–26). We see here again that the characteristics of the false teachers function simply as contrast to the image of the ideal Christian teacher.

The alternating pattern continues in 2 Tim 3:1–10. In this passage we find the longest and most detailed description of men who are vice-ridden and among whose number (3:6) are the false teachers opposed to Timothy. The traditional nature of much of this polemic has rightly been pointed out by Karris.[46] It is equally important to note, however, that this polemical language occurs in the same pattern we have been describing. Verse 1 begins: *touto de ginōske*. The adversative *de* should be taken at full force here. These characteristics of the false teachers stand in opposition

42. See Kelly, *Pastoral Epistles*, 188; Lock, *Pastoral Epistles*, 101.

43. For this interpretation, see Spicq, *Saint Paul*, 2:762–63; Dibelius and Conzelmann, *Pastoral Epistles*, 113. It is, of course, of considerable importance that the church is not pictured in sectarian terms; it contains within itself good and evil. See Schierse, *Die Pastoralbriefe*, 119.

44. *Neōterikos* is a biblical hapax. Spicq, *Saint Paul*, 2:764, notes that it is used elsewhere with a nuance of violence, a seeking after novelty that overthrows accepted ways. Reading the verse in this way would shift attention away from Timothy's personal youthfulness to the novelty-seeking of the false teachers.

45. The theme of verse 14, *mē logomachein*, is here picked up again.

46. Karris, "Background and Significance," 560–61; Spicq, *Saint Paul*, 2:771–78, typically has a wealth of illustrative material.

to the ideal sketched in the preceding verses, and their manner is one Timothy should be aware of. The description is broken in 3:5b by the warning to Timothy: *kai toutous apotrepou*. It is Timothy's avoidance of such as these that is of paramount concern. The passage 3:6–9 continues the description of the methods of these false teachers, and the contrasting picture is found immediately in 3:10: *su de parēkolouthēsas mou tē didaskalia*.[47] Timothy has a different model than that provided by the false teachers or their antecedents, Jannes and Jambres. His is the model provided by the teaching, the attitudes, and the suffering demonstrated by Paul.[48] The necessity of suffering for all who wish to lead godly lives is reasserted in 3:12.

To this positive picture is quickly juxtaposed, in 2 Tim 3:13 (though very briefly), the manner of the false teachers: *ponēroi de anthrōpoi kai goētes prokopsousin epi to cheiron planōntes kai planōmenoi*. But, again, the emphasis falls on Timothy's positive attitude in contrast to these: *sy de mene en hois emathes kai epistōthēs* (3:14). After describing the inspired Scripture as that which is able to equip Timothy for every good work (which here clearly means the work of teaching), Paul continues with his most solemn injunction to his delegate, that he should preach the word in every circumstance (4:1–2). Again, when we look at the qualities of such preaching, we see that it is to be done *en pasē makrothymia* (4:2) as was Paul's own (3:10).

The final contrast in 2 Tim 4:3–8 is a poignant one. Verses 3–4 describes, not the methods of the false teachers, but the success they will enjoy. Paul is certain that men will not want to hear sound teaching but will follow after the mythical seductions of teachers who tell them what they want to hear. In contrast to this "turning away" and "wandering off," Timothy is told: *sy de nēphe en pasin, kakopathēson, ergon poiēson euangelistou, tēn diakonian sou plērophorēson* (4:5). Timothy is to remain steady in his ministry of teaching. The resumption of the note of suffering here is most interesting. Is not the real suffering facing Timothy very close to that then being experienced by Paul? Paul was left all alone, abandoned (1:15); everyone had deserted him (4:16); he was suffering and wearing

47. The verb *parakolouthein* further emphasizes the paraenetic nature of the letter. Paul is not giving Timothy new teaching; he is reminding him of what he "has followed." The subsequent elaboration of Paul as model further strengthens this aspect. See Karris, "Background and Significance," 198; Spicq, *Saint Paul*, 2:781.

48. The fact that "the Lord rescued me from all of them" continues the pattern of suffering-reward established earlier and gives hope to Timothy that he too will find release from his suffering.

chains like a criminal (2:9). In spite of this, he carried on, unashamed (1:12), convinced that the word of God was not fettered (2:9) and that his suffering had a positive effect for the elect (2:10). Now we see that Timothy must face abandonment, when men do not wish to listen to his words but follow after false teachers (3:1, 4:3). He will face abandonment just as did the apostle. In the face of this, Timothy is to willingly take part in the suffering, to persevere in his work of preaching and teaching, not filled with cowardice (1:7) or shame (1:8; 3:15) but empowered with that Spirit who is able to sustain him through suffering and rejection (1:8; 2:1) just as it had Paul (1:12).

In this light, the *gar* of 2 Tim 4:6 is striking.[49] Timothy must carry on because Paul himself, who had held the deposit faithfully (1:12), had fought the good fight and kept the faith (4:7), now was at the point of death. What remained to him was the reward for those who suffer with the Lord (4:8; cf. 2:5, 12). The final note of comfort and encouragement to Timothy is that this crown is not for Paul alone but for all who have loved the Lord's appearing (4:8). Timothy, if he endures in the face of suffering and rejection, will receive the same reward that Paul now expects.[50]

This analysis of 2 Timothy leads to the following conclusions. First, the letter is one of personal paraenesis; the entire focus is the ideal of the Christian ministry of preaching and teaching to be carried out by Paul's delegate, Timothy. Second, the first part of the paraenesis centers on the presentation of Paul as the model for Timothy's words and attitudes; the letter functions as a reminder of this model. Third, the second part of the paraenesis uses Paul as a model, but within a framework of concrete commands and warnings that spell out the implications of Paul's exam-

49. As Dibelius and Conzelmann note, "Vv. 6–8 comprise the solemn conclusion of the paraenesis" (*Pastoral Epistles*, 121).

50. Our close analysis of 2 Timothy stops here, but certain aspects of the remaining thirteen verses should be noted: (a) Although the subject is now ever more personal, dealing with Paul's circumstances and needs, the passage is still carried by the typical singular imperative to Timothy: *spoudason* (v. 9); *age* (v. 11); *phere* (v. 13); *phylassou* (v. 15); *aspasai* (v. 19); *spoudason* (v. 21). (b) One of the false teachers is mentioned by name, Alexander the Coppersmith (v. 14), whom we meet with Hymenaeus in 1 Tim 1:20. (c) Typically, the verse about Alexander is structured antithetically: 1. He did me much harm. 2. You stay away from him. 3. He strongly opposed our words. This snippet follows the same pattern as the rest of the letter. (c) Now concerning Paul, we see again the notion of being "strengthened" by the Lord, so that the gospel preaching might be "fulfilled"; earlier we saw these concepts applied to Timothy (2:1, 4:5). Paul continues to the end as model.

ple. Fourth, these commands and warnings follow a pattern of contrasts, in which the emphasis always falls on the picture of Timothy as the ideal. Fifth, the polemical language concerning the false teachers functions within this pattern as the antithesis to that ideal. The false teachers are not spoken of or addressed, except in relation to Timothy. They serve entirely as contrast.

Hellenistic Materials Pertinent to Understanding 2 Timothy

In searching for Hellenistic materials that can shed some light on the function of polemical language in 2 Timothy, we need to consider both the form and the content of such materials. Although it has been recognized that 2 Timothy is a type of paraenesis, little attention has been paid to the literary structure of this paraenesis within the epistolary form.[51] Abraham J. Malherbe, by assembling and analyzing paraenetic materials from a variety of Hellenistic sources, has done much toward providing a more coherent approach to the literary form of paraenetic letters.[52] His application of this approach has been applied to 1 Thessalonians. Here I hope to extend his insights to 2 Timothy, where, if anything, the pattern he discerned in 1 Thessalonians is even more clearly present.

Even though their publication took place after the first century and the attributions of authorship are pseudonymous, the handbooks of rhetorical schools concerning proper letter writing contain a variety of letter forms (together with examples) that shed considerable light on New Testament epistolary style.[53] In the extensive list of letters categorized by Ps.-Libanius, we find a *parainetikē epistolē*.[54] He defines a

---

51. Karris, "Background and Significance," 559–60; Dibelius and Conzelmann, *Pastoral Epistles*, 7. For a broader discussion of New Testament paraenesis, see Dibelius, *James*, 1–11.

52. Malherbe, "Hellenistic Moralists." In addition to surveying the work done on New Testament paraenesis, this article brings together a mass of Hellenistic material pertinent to the subject and interprets 1 Thessalonians as a paraenetic letter.

53. For a discussion of the dating, authorship, and contents of these handbooks, see Koskenniemi, *Studien zur Idee*, 54–63; Thraede, *Grundzüge griechisch-römischer Brieftopik*, 25–27; Malherbe, "Ancient Epistolary Theorists." Malherbe includes texts and translations of the pertinent parts of the handbooks, as well as a wider assortment of theories on letter writing from Greek and Roman authors. The Greek text (with Latin translation) of Ps.-Libanius's and Ps.-Demetrius's handbooks is available in Hercher, *Epistolographi Graeci*.

54. Hercher, *Epistolographi Graeci*, 8.

paraenetic letter as one in which "we exhort [*parainoumen*] someone, advising him [*protrepontes*] to pursue [*hormēsai*] something, or to abstain [*aphechesthai*] from something."[55] He then gives a sample of this sort of letter: "*Zēlōtēs aei, Beltiste, ginou tōn enaretōn andrōn; kreitton gar esti tous agathous zēlounta kalōs akouein hē phaulois hepomenon eponeidiston einai tois pasin*" (Always be an emulator, dear friend, of virtuous men. For it is better to be well spoken of when imitating good men than to be reproached by all for following evil men).[56] It can be seen from this sample that a paraenetic letter was conceived of not simply as a random listing of commands but as a form of exhortation. In the description, we notice that the exhortation is stated antithetically: we exhort someone to follow this and avoid that. In the sample letter, again, we are struck by the role of models.[57] Rather than simply follow instructions, the reader is first of all to be an imitator, an emulator. He is to base his conduct on that of virtuous men. The models themselves are presented antithetically: one can imitate good models or bad. Finally, we note that the motivation for such conduct is the hope for good reputation.

Already, we can see how precisely 2 Timothy follows this form. Paul is presented as a model to Timothy, and Timothy's mode of teaching is presented by means of antithesis to false teachers. He is to pursue certain things and to avoid others.

It is rare that an actual writing so faithfully follows a schoolbook model as Ps.-Isocrates's *Ad Demonicum* does that of Ps.-Libanius's paraenetic letter form.[58] Already in 1913, Dibelius had remarked in passing on the similarity between this document and 2 Timothy but did not pursue the points of resemblance, particularly the formal ones.[59] In this

55. This is very close to the "*symbouletikos*" letter listed by Ps.-Demetrius (Hercher, *Epistolographi Graeci*, 3), in which *protrepomen epi ti ē apotrepomen apo tinos.* On this similarity, see Koskenniemi, *Studien zur*, 56–57.

56. Hercher, *Epistolographi Graeci*, 8.

57. Malherbe, "Hellenistic Moralists," establishes that these formal characteristics are found in the actual letters of Seneca, Pliny, and Cicero, with numerous examples. In addition to the references he gives on the role of model and memory in paraenesis, the following can be added from Ps.-Isocrates's *Ad Nicoclem* 1.13, 26, 31, 35, 37, 38; 2.59, 60, 61. Especially striking is *Ad Nicoclem* 2.57: "*protrepete tous neōterous ep' aretēn mē monon parainountes alla kai peri tas praxeis hypodeiknyontes autois huious einai chrē tous andras tous agathous.*"

58. *Isocrates* (Norlin, LCL), 1:4–35. Malherbe, "Hellenistic Moralists," quotes extensively from the first part of this work in demonstrating the salient features of paraenesis.

59. Dibelius, *Die Briefe des Apostels Paulus*, 138; see also Dibelius and Conzelmann, *Pastoral Epistles*, 7.

work, which could well have been a letter,[60] the author addresses a single person, the young Demonicus, whose father was friend to the author. The point of the missive is made at once: "Since I deem it fitting that those who strive for distinction and are ambitious for education should emulate [*mimētes einai*] the good and not the bad, I have sent you this discourse" (2).

The author distinguishes his work from those protreptic discourses (*protreptikē logoi*), usually written for the young, that encourage them to learn the tricks of sophistry (3). He is writing not a hortatory exercise (*paraklēsin*) but a moral treatise (*parainēsin*)—that is, paraenesis—which will show what things young men should aspire to (*oregesthai*) and avoid (*apechesthai*) on their way to virtue (5).[61]

He begins by proposing models whom Demonicus might imitate. After citing Heracles and Theseus (8), he proposes Demonicus's own father as the best model he could follow: "Nay, if you will but recall [*anamnēstheis*] also your father's principles, you will have from your own house a noble illustration [*kalon hecheis paradeigma*] of what I am telling you" (9). Isocrates begins to sketch this model for Demonicus. He does this by means of three antithetical statements, structured by *ou . . . alla*, in each case with the negative quality offset by and pointing to the positive. Thus, Hipponicus, the father, was not an indolent man given to pleasure but trained his body vigorously; he did not cling to wealth but handled his cares with detachment; he was not small-minded but generous (9–10). Isocrates despairs of presenting the model adequately, and so concludes, "For the present, however, I have produced a sample [*deigma*] of the nature of Hipponicus, after whom you should pattern your life as after an example [*hōsper pros paradeigma*], regarding his conduct as your law, and striving to imitate [*mimētēn*] and emulate [*zēlōtēn*] your father's virtue" (11).

We should note here the combination of memory and model, so frequent in this type of writing, and which we found in 2 Timothy. It is by *remembering*, by calling back into his mind, the virtuous life of his father that Demonicus has a model on which to base his own life. The establishment of this model is the most important consideration for Isocrates, but he considers it necessary to amplify the model by means of moral precepts, for "it is not possible for the mind to be so disposed unless one

60. *'Apestalkē soi tonde ton logon dōrōn*; *Ad Demonicum* 2. References throughout are to paragraph numbers.
61. See also *Ad Nicoclem* 2.2: *oregomenos . . . apechomenos*.

is fraught with many noble maxims; for as it is the nature of the body to be developed by appropriate exercises, it is the nature of the soul to be developed by moral precepts" (12).[62] Again, as in the letter form of Ps.-Libanius, the purpose of the moral instruction is "progress in virtue . . . [and] highest repute in the eyes of all other men" (12).

The moral precepts make up the bulk of the work. They follow in no discernible order. The simple singular imperative dominates throughout, as in 2 Timothy. There is not a rigorously antithetical pattern to the injunctions (such as we saw in the sketch of the model, 9–10), but with some frequency a positive ideal is set off by contrast to its negative (see, e.g., 12, 14, 15, 16, 17, 20, 23, 24, and esp. 38). When he completes the listing of precepts, Isocrates returns to the models. The examples of Heracles and Tantalus (both, appropriately, sons of Zeus and representing examples of virtue and vice) are held up as models of how good is rewarded and evil punished (50). Isocrates concludes, "With these examples before you, you should aspire [*oregesthai*] to nobility of character" (51).

In *Ad Demonicum* we have found paraenesis structured around a model, the remembering of which provides an example of the virtuous life. The model is sketched by means of antithetical statements. The presentation of the model is followed by a list of moral precepts, many of which are stated antithetically. Finally, the models are presented again. There is here not only a faithful rendering of the form of a paraenetic letter but the closest resemblance to the structure of 2 Timothy.

What about the differences? *Ad Demonicum* intends to teach virtue to a young man and presents by means of model and precept the ideal of the virtuous man. Second Timothy, on the other hand, is concerned to inculcate the ideal of the Christian teacher. Although Timothy's personal attitudes and virtue are important, they are so as a quality of his faithful fulfillment of the ministry to which he was called. These differences in content are real and should be recognized. Nevertheless, the form is nearly identical. Perhaps we should ask how *Ad Demonicum* would look if it were a protreptic discourse, if it were encouraging a young man to, say, the calling of a true philosopher?[63] In fact, we have such discourses

---

62. On the role of precepts in paraenesis, see *Ad Nicoclem* 1.41, as well as the numerous examples cited by Malherbe, "Hellenistic Moralists."

63. We have already noted that Ps.-Isocrates distinguished his paraenetic work from the *protreptikoi logoi*. His reason is interesting. He says such discourses ignore the most vital part of philosophy, *to kratiston tēs philosophias*—that is, the inculcation of virtue—and merely encourage skill in oratory (*Ad Demonicum* 3). In the discourses

available to us, and they will show (naturally in differing degrees) a similarity both to *Ad Demonicum* and 2 Timothy.

In examining these writings, we are looking in particular for the presentation of a model to the prospective philosopher, and the presentation of the philosopher as a model for others to follow, as well as the explication of the ideal by means of antithesis. In these antithetic statements we are interested in discovering whether polemical language against false philosophers (whose original context must be sought, as Karris notes, in philosophic/sophist disputes) serves in this new context a paraenetic or protreptic purpose—that is, to offset by means of contrast the positive ideal.

Epictetus

Epictetus was not the sort of philosopher of whom Dio Chrysostom would approve, for his arena was not the marketplace but the lecture hall.[64] Epictetus was not only a philosopher himself; he was also the teacher of young men who wished to be philosophers. Throughout his *Discourses* (or *Diatribes*)[65] we hear him exhorting his students to stop glorying in their abstract discussions and to put virtue to work.[66] In one sense, nearly all his discourses can be called protreptic. This is certainly the case with the famous discourse on the ideal Cynic (3.22). It is addressed to young men (though the interlocutor is typically singular) who wish to take up the cynic's calling. Epictetus uses the occasion to draw a highly idealized picture of the philosopher's calling and way of life.

---

we will be considering, Isocrates's viewpoint will be very much shared. The point of these discourses is not oratorical skill but the virtuous life, lived philosophy. This is clear in Epictetus, *Discourses* 3.23.33–34. After castigating his students for being preoccupied with clever speechifying, he recognizes the value of a protreptic discourse (*ho protreptikos*), placing it with refutation (*ho elenktikos*) and teaching (*ho didaskalikos*) but separating it from orations made for display (*ho epideiktinon*). As far as Epictetus is concerned, the style of the protreptic discourse is found in the ability to convince hearers of their erring ways and move them to conversion (34–37). It is in this broad sense that the term "protreptic" is used here. For the relation of such discourses to philosophic conversion, see Marrou, *History of Education*, 282–83; Nock, *Conversion*, 164–86.

64. Cf. the description of the "so-called philosophers" (*hoi kaloumenoi philosophoi*) to whom Dio contrasts himself in *Oration* 32.8–9.

65. See *Epictetus* (Oldfather, LCL).

66. See 1.4.5; 1.8.4–10; 2.1.31; 2.9, 17–20; 2.10.30; 2.12; 2.16; 2.17.20; 2.18; 3.2.6; 3.3.17ff.; 3.5.17; 3.6.3; 3.13.23; 3.24.38; 4.4; 4.5.36–37; Frag. 10.

Although the term never occurs, the role of models is important throughout the discourse. The great model of the Cynic is, of course, Diogenes, both in his manner of speaking and in his way of life (24, 57, 80, 88, 91–92). Socrates (26) and Heracles (57) are also held up as models for the philosopher. The true Cynic not only patterns himself on the words and deeds of the philosophers of old but himself becomes a model of the philosophic life to others. He demonstrates in his life that a truly virtuous life is possible (87–88).[67]

Also of interest to us is the way the ideal philosopher is contrasted to the false or would-be philosopher by means of antithetical statements. It is here that we find language about false philosophers that would be entirely at home in polemical contexts; here it is used for protreptic purposes. Thus, in paragraph 9 Epictetus says, *kai su bouleusai peri tou pragmatos epimelōs· ouk estin oion dokei soi*, and follows with this thumbnail sketch of the phony philosopher: "I wear a rough cloak even as it is, and I shall have one then; I have a hard bed even now, and so shall I then; I shall take to myself a wallet and staff, and I shall begin to walk around and beg from those I meet, and revile them; and if I see someone who is getting rid of superfluous hair by the aid of pitch-plasters, I will come down hard on him" (10).[68] Epictetus cautions, "If you fancy the affair to be something like this, give it a wide berth, don't come near it, it is nothing for you" (11). Again, after sketching an ideal Cynic, Epictetus declares, "Lo, these are the words that befit a cynic, this is his character, and his plan of life," and follows with the antithesis, "But no, you say, what makes a cynic is a contemptible wallet, a staff and big jaws; to devour everything you give him, or to stow it away, or to revile tactlessly the people he meets, or to show off his fine shoulder."[69] He warns, "Think the matter over more carefully!" (50–53). Again, in 97–100 we find the ideal contrasted to its negative followed by a reiteration of the ideal.

The castigation of false teachers is as harsh as those found in polemical

67. The true Cynic says, *"idou kai touto martys eimi egō kai to sōma to emon"* (3.22.88).

68. For the outer garb of the philosopher as a cloak for vice, see Philostratus, *Life of Apollonius* 2.29; Julian, *Oration* 7.223C and 225A; Dio Chysostom, *Oration* 35.2.3.11; Lucian, *Timon* 54; *The Runaways* 19; *The Fisherman* 42; *The Double Indictment* 6.

69. For *philargyria* as a vice of false philosophers, see Philostratus, *Life of Apollonius* 1.34; Julian, *Oration* 6.181C, 198B; Dio, *Oration* 32.9, 35.1; Epictetus, *Discourses* 1.29.45–47, 1.9.19–20, 2.17.3, 3.24.78, 4.1.139; Lucian, *The Runaways* 14; *Philosophies for Sale* 24; *Timon* 56; *Menippus* 5; *Hermotimus* 9–10; *Dialogues of the Dead* 374; *The Passing of Peregrinus* 15–16; *The Parasite* 52.

contexts. But here the language of slander serves to highlight the ideal of the true philosopher. We can note, finally, that Epictetus views the ideal Cynic as one who will undergo *suffering* for his calling (54), and who has the attitude of a *physician* toward the souls of others (72–73).[70] These themes recur repeatedly in this literature.

Lucian of Samosata

Lucian of Samosata's attitude toward Philosophy was decidedly ambivalent; while being attracted to the ideals of the philosophic way of life, he was repulsed by its practitioners, and he uses every opportunity to lampoon them mercilessly.[71] It is the more surprising, then, to find in his works two discourses that present a favorable, even idealized, portrait of two otherwise unknown philosophers, Demonax and Nigrinus.[72]

He says that he himself was a student of Demonax, who, together with Sostratus, was a man "worthy of fame and remembrance [*logou kai mnēmēs axiōn*]" (*Demonax* 1). The reason he writes about Demonax, "the best of all philosophers I know about," is to provide a model for those who wish to follow the philosophic life: "That he may be retained in memory [*dia mnēmēs*] . . . and that young men who aspire [*hormōntes*] to philosophy may not have to shape themselves by ancient precedents alone [*ta archaia mona tōn paradeigmatōn*] but may have a more recent pattern [*hemeterou biou kanona*] to emulate (*zēloun*)" (2). We see again that the true philosopher provides a model to the prospective philoso-

---

70. Cf. also Epictetus, *Discourses* 3.23.30: "*iatreion estin andres, to tou philosophou scholeion.*"

71. Lucian's sharp tongue lashed out at all philosophers without much discrimination. But he treats sympathetically the philosopher Cyniscus (*The Downward Journey, Zeus Catechized*), delights in the freedom and free speech of Diogenes and Menippus (*Dialogues of the Dead*), and even portrays Pythagoras, so often a figure of fun for him, discoursing reasonably in *The Dream*. He likes the skepticism of the Epicureans before the charlatan Alexander (*Alexander the False Prophet*). In *The Fisherman*, he paints an admiring portrait of philosophy and claims, like Aristides, that he attacks not true philosophy but the imposters who do harm in its name. He even has an honored place for philosophy in his ideal educational program (*Anacharsis*). It is freedom and free speech that Lucian likes most about philosophy, and, given the sorry state of most philosophers, he thinks those ideals should be sought in the life of the "common man" away from the ambit of professional philosophical schools (*Menippus* 21; *Hermotimus* 84).

72. For both *Demonax* and *Nigrinus*, see Harmon, LCL.

pher, a model that is made effective through memory. Lucian continues the model theme in paragraph 3: "He despised all that men count
good, and committing himself unreservedly to liberty and free-speech
[*eleutheria kai parrēsia*] was steadfast in leading a straight [*orthō*], sane
[*hygiei*], irreproachable life [*anepilēptō biō*] and in setting an example
[*paradeigma*] to all who saw and heard him, by his good judgment and
the honesty of his philosophy."

Lucian sketches the ideal picture of Demonax by means of nine antithetical statements, many of them in the *ou . . . alla* form we met in *Ad
Demonicum*. In each case, the positive ideal of Demonax is contrasted
to other practitioners of philosophy. Demonax did not alter his way of
living in order to cause wonderment among people, but led a simple
life and maintained his place in society (thus contrasted to the showy
manner of wandering Cynics).[73] He did not cultivate irony or harshness
of speech, but spoke with Attic charm, so that his hearers were not sent
away gloomy, but full of joy (thus contrasted with Socrates and the harsh
manner of the Cynics).[74] Noteworthy above all was his gentleness, even
when he had to rebuke (*epitiman*) someone. He had the attitude of a doc-
tor, who hated sickness but could feel no anger toward the sick (7). Like
the ideal teacher of 2 Timothy, then, he was himself healthy and tried
to make others healthy. But even though Demonax was much admired,
he too suffered hatred from the masses and had enemies who charged
him with crimes (11). The discourse continues with a lengthy recital of
Demonax's jokes and a pious recountal of his last moments and death
(12–66). At the very end of the discourse (67), Lucian states, "These are
a few of the things, out of many, which I have recalled [*apemnēmoneusa*]
to give my readers a notion of what sort of man he was." His writing has
been an act of reminiscence, of memory.

In *Demonax* we have seen a work that is explicitly protreptic (it
wishes to encourage young men to follow the philosophic way), that
presents the memory of a model for imitation, and that explicates the
model by means of antithetical statements, within the negative part of

73. On the love of glory as a philosophic vice, see Dio, *Oration* 32.10, 11, 19, 20, 24;
33.1, 9–10; Julian, *Oration* 6.190D, 197B, 200C, and *Oration* 7.226A; Lucian, *The Passing of Peregrinus* 1, 4, 20, 38, 42; *The Fisherman* 31, 34, 46; *The Parasite* 52; *Menippus*
5; *The Runaways* 12, 19; *Dialogues of the Dead* 369, 417.

74. The philosopher's speech must be characterized by directness, freedom, and
even severity (Dio, *Oration* 77/78.45, 33.13). Dio says, "A good prince is marked by
compassion, a bad philosopher by lack of severity" (*Oration* 32.18). But this severity
must not be mere abuse (see Dio, *Oration* 4.19, 74; Epictetus, *Discourses* 3.22.10, 90).

which appears language condemnatory of unworthy philosophers. The function here is not to denigrate them in order to establish Demonax's teaching, but to provide a negative shading to the ideal, so that those who wish to be philosophers will know what to avoid as well as what to imitate as they follow that life.

Lucian's *Nigrinus* is a more complex work. It is in the form of a dialogue in which an eager convert to philosophy recounts for a friend the experience that converted him to that life, his association with the philosopher Nigrinus. The major portion of the dialogue consists in a recountal of one of Nigrinus's lectures. Though the work is not explicitly protreptic, it functions as such, for the result of the recountal is the desire of the second young man to seek the philosophical way of life, and they go off together to "seek healing" from the philosopher who had wounded them—that is, spoken in such a way as to stimulate conversion (38). Thus, the literary complexity: Nigrinus spoke in the first instance and converted the first man; the recital of that conversion causes the second to convert; and the implied result of reading this whole dialogue is that the reader, too, will experience such a conversion.

The function of memory in bringing to life the model is particularly well described here. The enthusiastic convert says, "I take pleasure in calling his words to mind [*memnēsthai*] frequently" (6), and he compares himself to lovers away from their beloved, who "by applying their minds to memory of the past [*tē mnēmē tōn parelēlythotōn*] give themselves no time to be annoyed by the present." So he is separated from the master but is comforted by the memory of his words, even calling to mind his face and the sound of his voice (7).

Nigrinus did not teach only by words. In all that he did, he set "no mean examples" (*ou mikra . . . paradeigmata*) for those who wished to imitate him (*tois zēloun ethelousi*) (26).

The ideal represented by Nigrinus is sharpened by attacks on "those self-styled philosophers" (24) who behave contrary to that ideal and their own philosophic precepts. Thus, he condemns those who, even when dressed in their ascetic garb, carouse at parties (the *philēdonē* motif, 25), and those who "put virtue on sale," teaching in lecture halls for hire (the *philargyria* motif, 25). In contrast to them, Nigrinus not only taught contempt for money but demonstrated it in his own life (26). Nigrinus also condemned those who advocated violent physical exercises as a part of philosophic training, considering it better to create toughness in the soul (28), and he himself provided the model of a well-ordered, strenuous, but well-balanced life (27). The antitheses in paragraphs 24–29 run: negative, negative, positive, positive, negative, positive.

In this protreptically oriented dialogue, we find the picture of the ideal philosopher, who is a model for others, and whose words and manner are brought alive by memory. The ideal is expressed in antithetical statements. In the negative statements, we find polemical language typically used against false philosophers. In this literary context, the function of the language is not to establish the teacher's credentials, so that his teaching will be accepted, but to make a negative foil to the ideal, so that hearers will know what to avoid as well as what to follow.

Dio Chrysostom

When we turn to Dio Chrysostom, we find that in four of his orations (12, 32, 33, 35) he approaches a new audience by distinguishing himself from other popular preachers, the sophists in particular, but also other kinds of philosophers.[75] In those discourses, he uses the language of polemic precisely the way Karris has suggested—namely, to clear the way for his own presentation by establishing his superior credentials and authority. But that use of polemic, we have already seen, is not the same as in 2 Timothy.

There remains another discourse of Dio's that deserves closer consideration. Oration 77/78 does not present itself as a protreptic discourse for future philosophers, nor do we find in it the notions of memory and model. What we do find is that Dio presents the picture of the ideal philosopher, and in that picture employs polemical language to establish an antithesis to the ideal. Most interesting here is the way attention is focused on the philosopher's mission of teaching and how that teaching is to be carried out. In this regard, the discourse resembles 2 Timothy.

Oration 77/78 begins as a dialogue on envy (*phthonos*). By paragraph 19, however, the dialogical form is dropped and Dio launches into a sustained discourse; at the same time, the focus of discussion shifts from

75. In addition to the materials on sophists cited by Karris, "Background and Significance," 551–62, one can mention Dio, *Oration* 4.28, 38; 6.21; 8.9; 10.32; 11.14; 33.4–5, 14–15; 35.3–8; 55.7; 66.12; 77/78.27. On false philosophers, in addition to 77/78, which we will look at, see 70.8–10, which is, again, structured antithetically; it should be noted in particular that these passages in Dio contain a remarkably high number of verbal agreements with the Pastorals.

envy as such to the depiction of the noble man who is untouched by envy
(26). Imperceptibly, the image of the noble man becomes the picture of
the ideal philosopher and his mission. This shift in direction seems to
be stimulated by Dio's attention to false or so-called philosophers (*tous
kaloumenous philosophous*) in paragraph 34.

Dio compares these so-called philosophers, who hang about the doors
of the rich and toady to them, to the cowardly (*deilois*) lions who guarded
Circe, lions who were in reality "wretched men, foolish, corrupted by
luxury and idleness" (*dystēnoi anthrōpoi kai anoētai, diephtharmenoi dia
tryphēn kai argian*). In contrast to them, the man of virtue not only refuses to abandon his freedom and liberty of speech (*eleutheria kai parrēsia*) for any payment of riches (*chrēmatōn*) or power (*dynamenos*), but
does not envy those who do so sell themselves; rather, he pities (*eleōn*)
them (37). Having distinguished the true philosopher from the false, Dio
continues with the positive description. The philosopher is one who not
only practices virtue and sobriety himself (*aretēn kai sōphrosynēn*) but
tries to lead all men to do the same (*pantas epi tauta agōn*). What is distinctive about the following passage is the way it resembles 2 Timothy in
its attention to the task of teaching. We notice the antithetical structure
and the sort of language frequently found in polemic: the philosopher
is to teach "partly by persuading and exhorting [*peithōn kai parakalōn*],
partly by abusing and reproaching [*loidoroumenos kai oneidizōn*] in the
hope that he may thereby rescue somebody from folly and low desires
and intemperate and soft living [*aphrosynēs kai phaulōn epithymiōn kai
akrasias kai tryphēs*], taking them aside privately one by one, and also admonishing them in groups. . . . He is sound in words and sound in deeds
[*hygiēs men en logois hygiēs de en ergois*]" (38–39). The resemblance to
2 Tim 2:23–24 is unmistakable. Dio presses home the ideal way of teaching by means of antithesis: "Not arousing strife [*stasin*] or greed [*pleonex-
ian*] or contentions [*eridas*] and jealousies [*phthonous*] and base desires
for gain [*aischra kerdē*] but [*de*] by reminding them [*hypomimnēskōn*] of
sobriety [*sōphrosynēs*] and justice [*dikaiosynēs*] and promoting concord
[*homonoian*]" (39). At times, the philosopher will suffer defeat and be
powerless (40); those who see him training his body will scorn him (*kat-
aphronousi*) and consider him mad (*mainesthai nomizousi*) and dishonor
him (*atimazousin*). But he (*ho de*) does not grow angry (*orgizetai*) and
is kinder (*eunousteros*) to them than a father or brother or friends (42).
He tries, as far as he is able, to help all men (40).

As we have seen repeatedly in these descriptions of the ideal philosophic teacher, the image of the physician is employed. Dio says that

the severity and honesty of the true philosopher is like the severity of the physician, and his only concern is the healing of souls (43–44). He concludes, "Far worse than a corrupt and diseased body is a soul which is corrupt [*psychē diephtharmenē*], not, I swear, because of salves or potions or some consuming poison, but rather because of ignorance [*agnoias*] and depravity [*ponērias*] and insolence [*hybreōs*] and jealousy [*phthonou*] and grief [*lypēs*] and unnumbered desires [*epithymiōn*]. This disease and ailment is more grievous than that of Heracles and requires a far greater and more flaming cautery; and to this healing [*iasin*] and release [*apolysin*], one must summon without demur father or son, kinsman or outsider, citizen or alien" (45).

The points of contact between this oration and 2 Timothy are numerous.[76] The false philosophers are described not in opposition to the speaker but in opposition to the ideal being depicted. The same sort of language as found in polemical documents is here employed. The true teacher does not follow a method that will disturb and upset others, but in a variety of ways *reminds* them (in his words and by the example of his own life) of the way of virtue. He will experience rebuff and mocking, but he tries to help all. He is like a physician, combining severity and gentleness.

From an examination of these materials, we have located precedents for both the form and the content of 2 Timothy. We have seen that 2 Timothy follows with considerable fidelity the form of personal paraenesis described by Ps.-Libanius and illustrated by *Ad Demonicum*. In discourses exhorting others to become philosophers, the ideal teachers of virtue in Hellenism, we found the use of polemical language, ordinarily employed in disputes, to provide a contrast to the ideal model

---

76. *Oration* 77/78.37–45 contains these significant verbal parallels to the passages in the Pastorals that deal with false teachers: *deilos* (cf. 2 Tim 1:7); *anoētoi* (1 Tim 6:9; Titus 3:3); *diephtharmenoi* (1 Tim 6:5; cf. 2 Tim 3:8); *noutheteō* (Titus 3:10); *phthonos* (1 Tim 6:4; Titus 3:3); *diaphylattein* (of the philosopher; cf. *phylassō* in 1 Tim 5:21; 6:20; 2 Tim 1:12, 14; 4:15); *sōphrosynē* (1 Tim 2:9, 15; cf. Titus 2:6); *parakalōn* (1 Tim 1:3; 2:1; 5:1; 6:2; 2 Tim 4:2; Titus 1:9; 2:6, 15); *oneidizōn* (var. reading in 1 Tim 4:10); *phaulōn* (Titus 2:8); *epithymiai* (1 Tim 6:9; 2 Tim 2:22; 3:6; 4:3; Titus 2:12; 3:3); *hygiēs logois* (Titus 2:8; cf. *hygiainousē*, 1 Tim 1:10; 6:3; 2 Tim 1:13; 4:3; Titus 1:9, 13; 2:1–2); *eris* (1 Tim 6:4; Titus 3:9); *aischrou kerdous* (Titus 1:11); *dikaiosynē* (1 Tim 6:11; 2 Tim 2:22; 3:16; 4:8; Titus 3:5); *kathairō* (2 Tim 2:21; cf. *katharos*, 1 Tim 1:5; 3:9; 2 Tim 1:3; 2:22; Titus 1:15); *machomenos* (positively for Dio, negatively for 2 Tim 2:24; cf. also *machas*, 2 Tim 2:23; Titus 3:9); *menō* (of the philosopher; cf. 2 Tim 3:14); *ploutein* (1 Tim 6:9); *nosountas* (cf. *noseō*, 1 Tim 6:4); *agnoias* (cf. *agnoeō*, 1 Tim 1:13); *ponērias* (cf. *ponēros*, 1 Tim 6:4; 2 Tim 3:13); *hypomimnēskō* (2 Tim 2:14).

being sketched. It is among these writings, I suggest, that we find the real parallels to the function of the polemical language in 2 Timothy.

Paraenesis and Polemic in 1 Timothy and Titus

My treatment of these letters must necessarily be schematic and suggestive. We recognize first the obvious and important differences between these letters and 2 Timothy. The tone is less personal, especially in Titus. The concern of the author is not simply the character and methods of his delegates but the task they are to perform within the church. First Timothy 3:14–15 appears to state the theme of that letter: *hina eidēs pōs dei en oikō theou anastrephesthai.* Timothy must not only regulate the affairs of the church; he must also know how to deal with different groups within the church. In Titus, too, the commands concerning church order follow on the opening commission, "This is why I left you in Crete, that you might amend what was defective, and appoint elders in every town as I directed you" (1:5 RSV).

This awareness of the church extends to its relations with outsiders. The "lack of shame" in 2 Timothy changes to "blamelessness" (*anepilēmptos*), a more outward-looking expression, and one that runs through both letters (see 1 Tim 3:2, 7; 4:15; 5:7, 14; 6:1, 11; Titus 1:6, 7; 2:4, 10; 3:8). It affects as well the treatment of the false teachers. First Timothy 1:4 mentions that they are more concerned with their speculations than with the *oikonomian theou,*[77] and Titus 1:11 says, *holous oikous anatrepousin.* Probably as a consequence, the role of the delegates as contrasted to the false teachers is described in more militant terms than in 2 Timothy (see 1 Tim 1:5, 18, and esp. Titus 1:9, 11). But even this militancy is mollified, as in 2 Timothy, by a desire for the heretics' conversion: *di' hēn aitian elenche autous apotomōs, hina hygiainōsin en tē pistei* (Titus 1:13). We cannot, therefore, simply assume that the function of the polemic in these letters is the same as in 2 Timothy. But if we find there is a close similarity and that certain structural/thematic elements are present in both, the case for 2 Timothy is strengthened.

---

77. Whether one reads *oikonomian* here (as the textual evidence demands) or *oikodomē* (as D*, lat, Iren, Ambrst), the "household" associations of the image remain—not only individual believers but the whole "ordering" of God is being upset by the heretics. See Dibelius and Conzelmann, *Pastoral Epistles,* 17; Brox, *Die Pastoralbriefe,* 103; Spicq, *Saint Paul,* 1:323–24; Kelly, *Pastoral Epistles,* 45–46.

First Timothy

It is striking that in the parts of 1 Timothy that deal with the determinations of church order and the evangelist's relations to groups within the community, there is no mention of the false teachers. Nor is there a separate section set aside for an orderly refutation or condemnation of them. Rather, the material dealing with the false teachers occurs in four distinct units: 1:5–20; 3:14–4:16; 6:2–16; and 6:20–21. Let us look at each unit in turn.

The first unit, 1 Tim 1:5–20, has a triadic structure: (1) the first charge to Timothy (vv. 5–11); (2) the example of Paul (vv. 12–17); (3) the commission to Timothy repeated (vv. 18–20).

The first description of false teachers depends on the first command to Timothy: he is to charge certain ones not to teach falsely (1:5). The description of their preoccupations (1:4) is followed immediately by the characterization of the *parangelia*, as love that flows from a pure heart, a good conscience, and a sincere faith (1:5), qualities Timothy himself possesses (1:19) but which the heretics have abandoned: *hōn tines astochēsantes* (1:6), *hēn tines apōsamenoi* (1:19). The heretics are described as those wishing to be teachers of the law (vv. 6–7). This is countered (vv. 8–11) by the proper understanding of the law shared (*oidamen de*) by Paul and Timothy.

The second part of the triadic structure (1:12–17) is particularly interesting. The last thought of verse 11, that Paul had been entrusted with the gospel, is developed into a reflection on Paul's career.[78] That the sinner Paul has been saved stands as proof of the saying that Jesus Christ came into the world to save sinners. Paul presents himself as a model, not in his words and actions, as in 2 Timothy, but of one who had been shown mercy. He is a *hypotypōsin tōn mellontōn pisteuein ep' autō eis zōēn aiōnion* (1:16). The meaning here is obviously different than in 2 Timothy, but here again, in the middle of a section dealing with false teachers, Paul appears as a model.

The third element of this triadic section repeats the charge to Timothy. Paul solemnly commissions Timothy with his charge: *tautēn tēn parangelian paratithemai soi* (1:18). Timothy is to act in accord with the charge itself, with faith and a good conscience (cf. 1:5). Timothy's approach to the false teachers is described as a warfare (*strateian*). The false teachers are briefly described (1:19), and Paul says he handed over two of them to Satan (1:20); Timothy, we suppose, should follow suit.

---

78. We noted a similar shift in 2 Tim 1:9–11.

In the first unit of material dealing with false teachers, Paul is presented as a model for Timothy and all believers, and the descriptions of the false teachers are placed in antithesis to the proper teaching that Timothy, the receiver of Paul's commission, was to carry on.

The second unit dealing with false teachers (1 Tim 3:14–4:16) follows a similar pattern. Paul writes instructions to Timothy so that he will know how to behave until Paul comes (3:14–15). The vagaries of the false teachers are recounted in 4:1–3a. This is countered (as in 1:8–11) by a proper understanding (4:3b–5). Timothy is told that if he puts "these things"—that is, the proper teaching—before the brothers, he will be a *kalēs didaskalias* (4:6). The next verses elaborate this image of the good minister. Timothy is to avoid (*paraitou*) the kinds of myths associated with false teachers. Positively, he is to exercise (*gymnasia*) himself in godliness (4:7). Verse 8a may present the negative alternative of excessive bodily exertion; the value of training in godliness is superior (4:8b).

In 4:11 the command to Timothy is repeated: *parangelle tauta kai didaske*. In verses 12–13 the model motif recurs. Now Timothy is to be the model: *typos ginou tōn pistōn en logō, en anastrophē*. He is to be an example both in words and manner of life. But Timothy's role as a model is subordinate to Paul's. His continues *heōs erchomai* (4:13). The paraenetic commands come quickly in verses 15–16 (RSV): "Practice these duties, devote yourself to them. . . . Take heed to yourself and your teaching, hold to that." The result of Timothy's striving to be the *kalos diakonos* is that his "progress will be manifest to all" (4:15b) and he will save not only himself but those who hear him (4:16b); this is the reason for being a model.

The focus in this unit is unswervingly on Timothy's role as teacher in Paul's absence. We see again the role of the model, the positive and negative commands explicating the model, and the description of the false teachers functioning as foil to this positive presentation.

The third unit dealing with the false teachers (1 Tim 6:2–16) is also the most detailed in slander. Here again the section opens with a command to Timothy: *tauta didaske kai parakalei*—namely, the directives Paul established for various groups in the community. The false teachers are those who refuse to accept the things handed on by Timothy from Paul. Their description continues until 6:5b, where the motivation of the heretics is said to be love of money. As in 1:8–11 and 4:3b–5, their misconception is countered by the proper understanding. The profit gained from the ministry is not riches, as they think, but "godliness in contentment" (6:7–8). This correction is followed by a continuation of the polemic against false teachers (6:9–10). The climax of the section is reached in the command, once more, to Timothy: *sy de, ō anthrōpe theou, tauta pheuge.* Timothy is to avoid both their motivation and methods. Rather (*de*), he is to pursue (*diōke*) justice, faith, love, steadfastness, and gentleness (4:11). The similarity to 2 Tim 2:22 is here particularly strong. As in 2 Tim 4:1–5 also, Paul then continues with a solemn exhortation to Timothy to hold on faithfully in his teaching office. Again, in spite of the extended description of the false teachers in this unit, it seems clear that their characterization has the function of providing a sharp contrast to the path Timothy himself is to follow.

The final unit (1 Tim 6:20–21) is the shortest and ends the letter. It contains the typical antithesis. Timothy is to guard what has been entrusted to him (*parathēkēn phylaxon*, cf. 2 Tim 1:14) and avoid (*ektrepomenos*) the ways of the false teachers, which lead to an abandonment of that deposit.

If one were to eliminate the rest of 1 Timothy and link together the four units dealing with Timothy the ideal teacher as opposed to the false teachers, one would have a fairly coherent personal paraenetic letter, much like 2 Timothy. This suggests, at least, that in spite of the distinguishing characteristics of the letter that we earlier noted, the polemic against the false teachers functions here, as in 2 Timothy, as an antitype to the ideal teacher, who finds his model in Paul and is himself a model in word and in deeds to the faithful.

Titus

The literary pattern in Titus is less clear. The first mention of false teachers comes in contrast not to Titus but to the bishop. The bishop must be a man who is able to teach sound doctrine and refute those who contradict it (1:9). He must do this because there are many who are insubordinate (1:10). The bishop, we are to understand, is responsible for seeing that they are silenced as they should be (1:11).

But in 1:13 the attention shifts to Titus's own role: "Therefore rebuke them sharply" (RSV). The continuing description of the false teachers (1:14–16) is then contrasted to the positive teaching of Titus: *sy de lalei ha prepei tē hygiainousē didaskalia* (2:1), a general enough command, clearly to be contrasted with *didaskontes ha mē dei* in 1:11.

Paul does not appear as a model in this letter. It is Titus who is the model for the faithful: *peri panta, seauton parechomenos typon kalōn ergōn* (2:7). He is to be a model in both words and deeds. This model precludes the accusations of the false teachers.

Again in 2:15, we find the command to Titus to be a teacher: *Tauta lalei kai parakalei kai elenche meta pasēs epitagēs*. Finally, in 3:8 Paul orders Titus to insist on the things he teaches, for they are *useful* to men. In contrast to this, he is to avoid (*periistaso*) the foolish teachings of the opponents because they are not useful (3:9). Titus is to admonish them once or twice but then avoid (*paraitou*) them (3:10).

Titus does give us the picture of Paul's delegate as the ideal teacher who is a model for the community. His way of teaching is contrasted to that of his opponents by means of antithetical statements, within which we find the typical polemical language.

Conclusions

In this essay, I have tried to show that the polemical language against false teachers in 2 Timothy has the function within a paraenetic framework of providing a contrast to the ideal Christian teacher. I have suggested that the Hellenistic materials pertinent to understanding this function are, with regard to form, letters of personal paraenesis and, with regard to content, philosophic protreptic discourses. I have tried to demonstrate, though schematically, that 1 Timothy and Titus, each in its own degree, use the polemical language in a way closely similar to 2 Timothy.

By accepting the position that the polemical language is to a large extent stereotyped and that identifying the opponents is hazardous, I do not suggest that there were no real opponents. The polemic against false teachers in the Hellenistic materials is stereotyped, but there is more than enough evidence that the disputes between philosophic schools and teachers of all sorts were real and bitter. Nor does the position that these polemical passages in the Pastorals serve the paraenetic function I have suggested lead to the inference that the false teachers were just straw men, propped up only to be demolished. The anxious tone of the letters does not permit such a purely literary understanding. But the position I have argued for may help the reader grasp the central interest of the author of the Pastorals and the real point of his teaching. The Pastorals are not thereby diminished but illuminated.

Chapter 23

The Pedagogy of Grace

The Experiential Basis for Character Ethics in Titus

This short study of Paul's letter to Titus rests on three premises. The first is that this most neglected of Pauline letters deserves serious attention as a valuable witness to early Christianity, and deserves even more attention by the church, whose book it properly is in virtue of its canonization, yet which—largely under the influence of academic marginalization—is little read or appreciated.[1]

The second premise is that Titus ought to be read on its own terms as a coherent literary composition, specifically as a real letter from antiquity,[2] before entering into comparisons and contrasts to other Pauline letters, however valuable those might prove.[3] For that matter, Titus ought not too hastily be collapsed into the genre of *mandata principis* correspondence, where it comfortably fits.[4] I hold, in short, that Titus, like other compo-

---

1. Titus is characteristically considered in the distinct context of "the Pastoral Epistles," without significant reference to other canonical literature, a clustering reflected in the commentary tradition; see, e.g., Dibelius and Conzelmann, *Pastoral Epistles*; Knight, *Pastoral Epistles*; Kelly, *Pastoral Epistles*. An exception is the commentary by Quinn, *Letter to Titus*, which regards this letter as having been composed by the evangelist Luke, as the third volume of Luke-Acts. But thematically, the three letters are almost invariably treated together; see, e.g., Verner, *Household of God*; Young, *Theology of the Pastoral Letters*; Towner, *Goal of our Instruction*.

2. The position that the letters to Paul's delegates are inauthentic is often linked to the theory that they are a single pseudonymous composition, with 2 Timothy serving a fictive biographical setting (as a farewell letter) and both 1 Timothy and Titus being proto-examples of Church Orders; see Dibelius and Conzelmann, *Pastoral Epistles*, and, most fully, Redalié, *Paul après Paul*.

3. In the present essay, certain comparisons and contrasts with 1 Timothy are both unavoidable and valuable if the distinctive tone of Titus is to be assessed.

4. Such correspondence between rulers and subordinates in the Hellenistic age— correspondence that contained advice concerning a delegate's personal demeanor

sitions that at first might tempt readers to a hasty reduction to "letters of that sort," yields insight to the degree that its specific and distinctive literary shaping is taken as the most reliable guide to its meaning.

The third premise is most pertinent to our topic: the Letter to Titus is a rhetorical performance. The study of rhetoric both ancient and modern reminds us that rhetoric does not so much report facts as it constructs realities to which it responds.[5] Whether it is the president of the United States making a State of the Union Address, or parents exhorting their children, the set of positive programs and plans suggested always responds to the state of the crisis as constructed by the rhetorician. There may be some factual basis for the construction, but it is to the rhetorical situation rather than the factual situation that the speaker or writer responds. It may be that the country is in great peril from abroad, or that our children are in great peril because of their friends, or that our culture is collapsing from within, but these "realities" are identified and described through the skill of the rhetorician. The situation as the rhetorician sees it, or constructs it, shapes her recommendations or exhortations: we must strengthen our national defense, we must protect our innocent children, we must improve the instruments of cultural transmission.

That third premise, in turn, has three important corollaries. The first corollary is that, in the Letter of Titus just as in Paul's letters to the Galatians and Corinthians, we neither have real knowledge about the facts on the ground concerning the situation in Crete—or Corinth or Galatia—nor do we have any way to go behind the letter's rhetoric to secure such facts. In each case, we are captive to the author's perception of the situation or, to put it even more sharply, to those elements in the situation the author has chosen to highlight as the target for his rhetorical argument. And since good science, or scholarship, consists in pursuing questions for which there are possible answers, so should our attention to Titus focus on the rhetorical situation and rhetorical response shaped by the author.

---

together with instructions (*mandata*) concerning the delegate's commission—is extant in both inscriptions and papyri (such as the Tebtunis Papyri). For the basics, see Welles, *Royal Correspondence.* For the pertinence to 1 Timothy and Titus, see Wolter, *Die Pastoralbriefe als Paulustradition*; Fiore, *Function of Personal Example*; see also M. Mitchell, "New Testament Envoys," although she disagrees with my identification of Paul's letters with this type.

5. See, e.g., Potter, *Representing Reality*; Lucaites, Condit, and Caudill, *Contemporary Rhetorical Theory*; Braun, *Rhetoric and Reality*.

The second corollary follows from the first: such an approach frees us from the exhausting and futile speculations about the historical Titus, his possible connection to Crete, the actual state of affairs on that island, and, above all, whether this letter was written to an actual delegate by the hand of the apostle Paul, or composed by his school at work during his ministry, or (by far the majority view) by his school, or some fragment of it, after the apostle's death.[6] If all rhetoric has a certain element of the fictive to it—insofar as every rhetorician fashions vapors into visions—the issue of pseudonymity, considered so essential when the scholarly task was construed as historical reconstruction rather than rhetorical analysis, loses much of its savor.[7] Whoever wrote Titus, and whenever Titus was written, the only way forward to greater understanding is through engaging the argument crafted by the author.

The third corollary is that to responsibly interpret a composition like the Letter to Titus, we must enter as fully as we can into the rhetorical situation and response as sketched by the author through a risk-filled but thrilling leap of imagination. We must try our best to make sense of the rhetoric, not by the standards by which we think we live, or the principles that we suppose we embrace, but by the terms set by the composition itself. This means we do not ask whether a patriarchal household was a good or bad thing, whether the Roman Empire was a blessing or a curse, or whether Paul's delegate ought to have been a person from an underrepresented population.[8] Instead, we try to enter imaginatively into the world created by the composition, taking seriously what it takes seriously. In a word, since our goal is understanding rather than normative guidance, we need to practice the hermeneutics of generosity rather than the hermeneutics of suspicion.

The Rhetorical Situation

How, then, does Paul portray the situation faced by his delegate Titus? We are offered several kinds of clues. First, Titus is told that he was left[9]

6. For the formation of the majority (indeed, virtually consensus) view and an analysis of its problems, see Johnson, *First and Second Letters to Timothy*, 13–90.

7. In this regard, the approach to Titus is different only in degree from that which ought to characterize the approach to Paul's more familiar letters.

8. See vol. 1, chap. 11 ("Paul, Oppressor or Liberator?").

9. The 28th edition of Nestle-Aland has the aorist of *apoleipō* in preference to the imperfect of the same verb or the aorist of *kataleipō*. Both verbs can mean the literal

on Crete to "set right what is lacking"—an odd sort of construction[10]—
and to appoint elders/supervisors in every city (Titus 1:5). The impression given is not that of a well-established community but one that is
either new or in need of basic structure.[11] Unusual for a *mandata principis*
letter, moreover, the delegate's own need to exemplify virtue is mentioned only briefly in passing: "[show] yourself a model of good deeds
in every respect, with integrity in your teaching, dignity, and sound
speech that cannot be criticized" (2:7–8).[12] It is Paul's delegate's tasks
of teaching and correcting that are stressed. Beyond the appointment
of elders, Titus's role is defined entirely in didactic/rhetorical terms: he
is to "rebuke sharply" (*elenche apotomōs*, 1:13), speak (*lalei*, 2:1), exhort
(*parakalei*, 2:6), "speak, exhort, rebuke" (*lalei, parakalei, elenche*, 2:15),
remind (*hypomimnēske*, 3:1), insist (*diabebaiousthai*, 3:8), warn and avoid
(*nouthesia, paraitou*, 3:10–11). The terms used by Paul do not suggest an
audience that is especially receptive.

Second, the list of qualities asked of new leaders is correspondingly
minimal. The children of elders/supervisors[13] are to be believers (*techna
echōn pista*, Titus 1:6), suggesting that they could well not have been;
once more, the sense is of recent converts, among whom not even all the

---

separation of parties ("we were together but then I had to leave you"; for *apoleipō*, see
Homer, *Odyssey* 9.292; Plato, *Critias* 44D; for *kataleipō*, see Homer, *Odyssey* 15.89);
or a decision concerning placement in position ("I appointed you to remain"; for
apoleipō, see Epictetus, *Discourses* 2.3; P.Oxy. 105.3; for *kataleipō*, see Homer, *Odyssey*
21.33; Herodotus, *Histories* 6.125).

10. Unless otherwise indicated, Scripture quotations in this chapter are from
the NABRE. "Set right what is lacking" is my translation. For the phrase *ta leiponta*
("things lacking"), we would expect "to supply." But the rare verb *epidiorthoun* suggests "correcting" things already in place (see Philo, *Against Flaccus* 124). The ambiguity is caught equally well by the NRSV's "put in order what remained to be done"
and the NABRE's "set right what remains to be done." The impression given is of a
combination of construction and repair.

11. The establishment of local leaders is a consistent Pauline practice (see Rom
12:6–8; 1 Cor 16:15–18; Gal 6:1; Eph 4:11–12; Phil 1:1; Col 1:7; 4:12; 1 Thess 5:12–13;
2 Tim 2:2; see Acts 14:23). But only here and in 2 Tim 2:2 do we find Paul exhorting a
delegate to select such leaders. By contrast, 1 Tim 3:1–13 and 5:17–23 assume leaders
already in place within a well-established community with clear ministries. In Ephesus, Timothy's job is not to establish a structure of leadership but to find persons of
good character to manage a structure already in place.

12. In Greek, *peri panta seauton parechomenos typon kalōn ergōn, en tē didaskalia
aphthorian, semnotēta, logon hygiē akatagnōston*.

13. In contrast to 1 Timothy, the offices of elder (*presbyteros*) and supervisor (*episkopos*) are not clearly distinguished in Titus's brief treatment (Titus 1:5–9).

members of a household could be assumed to be believers. The elder's children, furthermore, are not to have been charged with drunkenness or disorderliness,[14] suggesting that they could well have been (1:6).[15] As for the supervisors (*episkopoi*) to be appointed by Titus, the requirements stress moral qualities rather than administrative abilities. Overall, they are to be "without reproach" (*anenklētos*).[16] Positively, they are to have only one wife (1:6);[17] they are to be hospitable (*philoxenon*), lovers of goodness (*philagathon*), temperate (*sōphrona*), righteous (*dikaion*), holy (*hosion*) and self-controlled (*enkratē*).[18] Their other positive qualities are didactic/rhetorical: they are to teach the sound doctrine and to refute opponents (1:8–9). None of this is surprising: ancient teachers were expected to combine sound teaching with high moral character,[19] and the qualities listed here could find many parallels.[20]

14. The term *katēgoria* can have the sense of "being accused of" or "under the charge of" in the legal sense: see Herodotus, *Histories* 6.50; Thucydides, *History* 1.69. The noun *asōtia* can be used for any form of prodigality or looseness in living (see Plato, *Laws* 560E; Aristotle, *Nicomachean Ethics* 1107B; 2 Macc 6:4; Testament of Judah 16:1). For the connections between a dissolute lifestyle and political unreliability, see the brilliant study by Davidson, *Courtesans and Fishcakes*. Finally, *anypotakta* has the sense of unruly, resistant to control (see Epictetus, *Discourses* 4.1.161; 1 Tim 1:9). That the elders' children should not be "drunk and disorderly" would ordinarily go without saying. Here the author thinks it necessary to say.

15. Note, in contrast, how 1 Tim 3:4 asks only that children be kept in good order, with no reference to their faith or moral proclivities.

16. The same term appears for both elders and supervisors; for *anenklētos*, see Aristotle, *Rhetoric* 1360A. 1 Tim 3:2 has the near synonym *anepilēmptos* (see Philo, *Special Laws* 3.24).

17. For discussion, see Dibelius and Conzelmann, *Pastoral Epistles*, 158–60; Towner, *Letters to Timothy and Titus*, 249–51; Johnson, *First and Second Letters to Timothy*, 213–14.

18. 1 Tim 3:2–7 also lists as positive qualities hospitality (*philoxenon*) and temperance/self-control (*sōphrona*), and adds to these "being decent" (*kosmion*). Distinctive to Titus is being a "lover of goodness" (*philagathon*), "righteous" (*dikaion*), "holy" (*hosion*), and "self-controlled" (*enkratē*). But whereas Titus speaks of the supervisor as "God's household manager" (*theou oikonomon*), 1 Tim 3:4 expands the actual role within the household of the would-be supervisor, making an analogy between his management of his own household and the management of the church. Add to this that 1 Tim 4:6 disqualifies a "recent convert" from the office, and we see once more the picture of a community in Ephesus that is well-established and settled, in contrast to the nascent movement in Crete (where supervisors and elders would necessarily be "recent converts").

19. See the data assembled in Johnson, "New Testament's Anti-Jewish Slander."

20. See, e.g., Onasander's *De imperatoris officio*, discussed in Dibelius and Conzelmann, *Pastoral Epistles*, 158–60.

What may catch us by surprise is the harshness of the terms used for the vices the supervisor is to lack: that he is to be "blameless" (*anenklētos*, or not open to a charge or accusation) as God's household manager is stated twice (Titus 1:6, 7). But the standard is startlingly low: he is not to be arrogant (*authadē*), liable to rage (*orgilon*), a drunkard (*paroinon*), a brawler (*plēktēn*), nor willing to do anything for money (*aischrokerdē*, 1:7).[21] Both the leaders of the community and their children seem to be drawn from materials raw in the extreme. Against such a dismal backdrop, Paul's list of positive character traits shines the brighter. The contrast, though, is between moral dispositions, or habits, between vices and virtues.

Third, the native population of Crete is characterized in entirely negative terms. Quoting a line from "one of their own prophets" that had probably become a popular slogan,[22] Paul declares that "Cretans have always been liars [*pseustai*], vicious beasts [*kaka thēria*], and lazy gluttons [*gasteres argai*]" (Titus 1:12),[23] a line that neatly summarizes the catalog of vices to be rejected by elders and supervisors—all the more so since they presumably are to be selected from the same savage and mendacious population.

Fourth, the description of the opponents—especially those *ek tēs peritomēs* (Titus 1:10) who are advancing *ioudaikoi mythoi* (1:14)[24]— whom Titus and the supervisors are to rebuke, is consistent with the

21. 1 Tim 3:3 shares the elements of "given to drink" (*paroinon*) and "brawler" (*plēktēn*) with this list, adding "not given to battle" (*amachon*) and "no lover of money" (*aphilagyron*). The terms in Titus 1:7, particularly in combination, are negative in the extreme. One who is *authadē* is self-willed and stubborn (Aristotle, *Rhetoric* 1367A; Herodotus, *Histories* 6.92), even "surly" (Theophrastus, *Characters* 15.1); one who is *orgilos* is "prone to rage" or "irascible" as an aspect of character (Aristotle, *Nicomachean Ethics* 1108A); one who is *plēktēs* is pugnacious or bullying (Aristotle, *Eudemian Ethics* 1221B). Similarly, to be "money-grubbing" (*aischrokerdēs*) is worse than simply being a lover of money (see Herodotus, *Histories* 1.187; Testament of Judah 16:1; Philo, *On the Sacrifices of Abel and Cain* 32; and see the description of the opponents in Titus 1:11). In combination with drunkenness and lack of self-control, the list comprises the qualities associated with poor leadership in antiquity; see Johnson, "Taciturnity and True Religion."

22. See Thiselton, "Logical Role."

23. The "empty bellies" can easily stand for the "desire for sordid gain" (*aischrokerdia*); see Kidd, "Titus as Apologia."

24. The term *hoi ek tēs peritomēs* (literally, "the ones out of circumcision") in 1:10 occurs in the New Testament only here and in Gal 2:12; Acts 10:45; 11:2. It clearly means people belonging to a "Jewish party," and in Acts refers to Christ-believers. Whether they are "Jewish Christians" (NABRE) here is less certain.

morally degraded state of the general populace.[25] They are rebellious (*anypotaktoi*), empty talkers (*mataiologoi*), and deceivers (*phrenapatai*, 1:10). They teach what they ought not, through the shameless quest for money (*aiskrou kerdous charin*, 1:11). They have repudiated the truth (1:14); their minds and consciences are tainted (*memiantai*, 1:15). They claim to know God, but by their deeds they deny them.[26] They are "vile" (*bdelyktoi*), disobedient (*apeitheis*), and are unqualified for any good deed (*pros pan ergon agathon adokimoi*, 1:16). In terms of character, they are, if anything, worse than the Cretan population as a whole.

Their betrayal of the truth, moreover, is not only a matter of personal attitude and behavior. They are also false teachers who create social unrest within households. We can infer from Paul's dictum that "to the pure all things are pure but to the defiled and unbelieving everything is impure" (Titus 1:15, author's translation) that the opponents are advancing some version of the Jewish law, with its laws of purity. Law-observance is the very definition of a heteronomous ethic: rightness and wrongness is in such an ethic measured by how actions correspond to an external norm, rather than by the interior disposition of the agent. Paul declares that their own stained and defiled minds and consciences testify to the uselessness of the program they propagate (1:16). Such charlatans could simply be avoided, if they had not infiltrated and influenced this immature church, whose members have been drawn from a misanthropic and devious population. As it is, the opponents are "upsetting entire households" (1:11, author's translation) by teaching for sordid gain what they ought not teach. Some within the community, we can infer, are more than willing to take hold of any set of moral guidelines—the more precise, the better—in a chaotic and culturally debased environment.

Such is the rhetorical situation, or problem, as Paul sketches it. The severity of the crisis faced by Paul's delegate is suggested by Paul's final instruction: "Avoid foolish arguments, genealogies, rivalries, and quarrels about the law, for they are useless and futile. After a first and second warning, break off all contact with a heretic, realizing that such a per-

---

25. We remember, to be sure, the stereotypical character of polemic between members of opposing parties in antiquity, and that Titus is a "rhetorical performance" rather than a disinterested report; it is not surprising to find that the vices of the opponents correspond to the ones that appointed leaders are to avoid; see Johnson, "New Testament's Anti-Jewish Slander."

26. The lack of consonance between profession and performance was the most fundamental of charges laid against would-be philosophers (see, e.g., Lucian of Samosata, *Timon* 54).

son is perverted and sinful and stands self-condemned" (Titus 3:9–11, adapted). We thus understand that "those from the circumcision" are represented by a "party" (*hairetikos*) within the larger community (if not the church), that Titus is in a position to debate with them or rebuke them, and that, ultimately, for the sake of the integrity of the faith, he may have to cut off all contact with them, leaving them to God.

The Rhetorical Response

The basic lines of Paul's response are clear enough. Since the immediate danger of the insidious propagation of a heteronomous ethic is the disruption of households (*oikoi*), attention must be given to the cultivation of proper attitudes and behaviors within the fundamental and essential unit of all societies. Thus, we see that Paul's specific instructions for his delegate in Titus 2:1–10 and 2:15–3:2 concern relations within the household. The church is never even mentioned in this letter.

At a more fundamental level, Paul must provide a convincing alternative to the heteronomous ethic peddled by the opponents. We have already seen how he emphasizes the elements of a character or virtue ethic for elders and supervisors, and we shall see the same stress in his household directives.

These two elements, however, raise questions of their own. First, why are the household directives he enunciates so pedestrian, so basic? Do older men really need instruction in being "temperate, dignified, self-controlled" as well as "sound in faith, love, and endurance" (Titus 2:2)? The last three qualities certainly pertain to fidelity in the faith, but the first three—we might think—should come naturally to civilized folk who are elderly; lack of dignity, lack of self-control, and intemperance are certainly associated more naturally with the wildness of youth than with the weakness of age. But then we remember how elders and supervisors are not to be arrogant or drunkards or brawlers (1:7)! Perhaps the new believers in Crete need rudimentary instruction in basic human virtues; perhaps what does not come naturally or by cultural influence needs to be taught (2:4).

Similarly, in what context is it appropriate for older women to instruct younger women to love their husbands and children (Titus 2:3–5)? Are not such dispositions natural? Experience ancient and modern, alas, teaches that they may not be and that the most basic of maternal (and need we add paternal?) instincts may need to be taught and nurtured.

Likewise, telling slaves not to talk back to their masters and not to pilfer their goods seems a low behavioral bar to meet (2:9–10), unless the very chaotic state of the household encourages such subversive gestures. Finally, we note that Paul includes in his exhortation to civic duty the desire that the Cretans avoid slandering (*blasphēmein*) and violence (*amachoi*, 3:2). Such rudimentary instructions point to a situation in which the basic elements of the household are unstable or, to put it another way, in which the kind of *paideia*, or culture, that Paul might assume among his readers in Ephesus or Rome, he does not assume in Crete.

If we look closer, however, we cannot help but note that Paul's household instructions do not really represent a set of rules—that is, do not replace one heteronomous ethic with another. Just as in his requirements of leaders and complaints about opponents, Paul focuses less on specific rules or procedures than he does on moral dispositions, or virtues. Older men should be temperate (*nēphalios*), dignified (*semnos*), and self-controlled (*sōphrōn*, Titus 2:2). Older women should not be gossipers or drinkers but should be reverent (*hieroprepeis*), teachers of the good (*kalodidaskalous*) so that they are able to share wisdom with younger women (2:3). Younger women are not only to love their husbands and children; they are to be self-controlled (*sōphronas*) and chaste (*agnas*), good managers of the household (*oikourgous agathas*), and submissive to their own husbands (*hypotassomenas tois idiois andrasin*, 2:5).[27] Younger men also are to be self-controlled (*sōphronos*) in every respect (2:6). Slaves should seek to please in all matters and demonstrate complete good faith (*pasan pistis endeiknymenous agathēn*, 2:9–10). And in the civic order, all are to be obedient and open to every good deed (*peitharchein, pros pan ergon agathon hetoimous einai*); they are to be gentle (*epieikeis*), displaying meekness toward all (*prautēta pros pantas anthrōpous*, 3:1–2). In short, Paul wants leaders and members of households to display moral qualities that are the opposite of the malevolent and violent ones of the Cretan population in general.

The second major question raised by this response (basic good behavior, positive moral qualities) is how Paul expects the Cretan believers to be so transformed. This question, in turn, brings us to the otherwise puzzling rhetorical functions of Titus 2:11–14 and 3:3–7. What are they doing rhetorically? A close examination of these passages brings me to the thesis of my essay, which is that Paul seeks to replace a heteronomous

---

27. In this rhetorical situation, submission to "their own husbands," rather than the male teachers who upset entire households makes good sense.

ethic with a character ethic, and that the experience of grace is seen by Paul as itself having the power to educate otherwise savage humans into becoming civilized people.

It is impossible here to do full justice to each of the two extraordinary passages, so I will focus primarily on how they serve Paul's argument. In the first case, Paul states the effect and shape of God's gift. In the second case, Paul asserts the reality of their experience of that gift and, once more, its effect. Efficiency in presentation is perhaps served by reading each passage in full in the NABRE before pointing out its salient features.

The Gift That Teaches

> For the grace of God has appeared, saving all and training us to reject godless ways and worldly desires, and to live temperately, justly, and devoutly in this age, as we await the blessed hope, the appearance of the glory of the great God and of our savior Jesus Christ, who gave himself for us to deliver us from all lawlessness and to cleanse for himself a people as his own, eager to do good. (Titus 2:11–14)

Given the rhetorical situation Paul has sketched, several aspects of this statement leap to our attention. The answer to the question of how such a savage population can be changed into a peaceful people is that the power for such transformation comes as a gift from God: the inferential *gar* here covers not only the immediately preceding sentence but Paul's entire series of instructions concerning good character and right behavior. The Cretan believers can become different *because* of what God has done for them as free gift. The term "gift" is much to be preferred to the term "grace," not simply because "grace" has been so overused and overdissected, but also because it is the gratuitous and experiential character of *charis* that is here important.[28] It is not God's favor from afar but a gift that has appeared in the empirical world. It is a saving gift (*sōtērios*), we observe, that comes from the God who saves and the savior Jesus Christ.[29] It is a gift, moreover, that has been given for or to "all peo-

---

28. See now esp. J. Barclay, *Paul and the Gift*.

29. Titus is rich in salvation language: *sōzein* in 3:5, *sōtērios* in 2:11, and *sōtēr* in 1:3, 4; 2:10, 13; 3:4, 6. See M. Harris, "Titus 2:13"; Marshall, "Salvation in the Pastoral Epistles"; Marshall, "Salvation, Grace and Works." Given the dismal portrayal of

ple" (*pasin anthrōpois*), embracing even (or especially) the unlikely gentile Cretan population. How has it appeared in the world? Through the self-donation of the savior Jesus for all of them in his death (*hos edōken heauton hyper hēmōn*, Titus 2:14). The gift that God gave them was the gift of a man giving himself for the sake of others—a model of humanity totally at odds with their self-serving and misanthropic heritage. Christ is both efficient and formal cause of salvation: he is the giver of the gift and reveals the shape of the gift.[30] Their transformation is not yet complete: they await in hope for the full disclosure of the glory—that is, the presence and power—of God (2:13).

What is most striking about the first line of this passage, however, is Paul's use of the circumstantial participle *paideuousa* followed by a *hina* clause (Titus 2:12). Following the authority of the great Greek grammarian Herbert W. Smyth, I suggest two things concerning syntax and diction. First, syntax: The circumstantial participle in Greek is the most flexible of all instruments, capable of expressing time, occasion, cause, or concession. It can also express purpose, and that is what it does here.[31] God's saving gift has appeared for all humans, Paul says, precisely for the sake of educating them. The *hina* clause expresses the purpose/consequence of such education "so that."

Second, diction: Although *paideuousa* has been translated in a variety of ways,[32] I think that here Paul deliberately seeks the nuance of education in the fullest Greek sense—that is, learning how to be civilized human beings, everything that the Greeks understood by *paideia*, embracing both culture and education.[33] In this case, education through God's empowerment is not a matter of information but one of transformation. The Cretans are to change internally, in their most fundamental orientation to the world and each other. Negatively, by "rejecting" (*arnēsamenoi*)[34] their former vices (Titus 2:12)—godlessness (*asebeia*) and worldly pas-

---

the Cretan population by the author, the language of salvation is particularly apt: they have been transformed from hostile and mutually destructive individuals into a community of virtue.

30. See the language of Christ "giving himself" in Gal 1:4; 2:20 and Eph 5:1. The resemblance in thought to Rom 3:21–5:21 is striking.

31. See specifically Smyth, *Greek Grammar*, 458–59.

32. The Vulgate has *erudiens*, and this broader sense of the term is reflected in the use of "schooling" by Moffatt and Knox, and "teaching" by Hart and the NJB. The narrower sense of "training" is found in KJV, RSV, NRSV, NAB, and Goodspeed.

33. See the classic works by Jaeger, *Paideia*; Marrou, *History of Education*.

34. Cf. the opponents "rejecting" (*arnountai*) God by their practices in Titus 1:16.

sions (*kosmikas epithymias*)—they will be able to live in the present age in a way entirely different from their past: temperately (*sōphronōs*, cf. 1:8; 2:2, 4), justly (*dikaiōs*, cf. 1:8), and devoutly (*eusebōs*). The effect of God's pedagogy—the gift of Christ's self-donation—is the change of persons from vice to virtue, from bad character to good character.

The final clause of this explanatory passage responds directly to the challenge posed by the opponents. Christ died in order to save them from all lawlessness (*anomia*) and to purify for himself (*katharisai heautō*) an elect people (Titus 2:14). The language of "elect people" echoes the language claimed for itself by Israel, for whom the laws of purity are what mark it as separate; Paul, however, sees the change from lawlessness as consisting not in the addition of laws but in the change of heart.

Similarly, the language of purifying here unmistakably recalls Titus 1:15, when Paul states in response to those proposing the law that "to the pure all things are pure" (*panta kathara tois katharois*) but that nothing is pure to those who lack faith and whose minds and consciences are stained. Paul insists that the change in disposition, in character, comes first. And the good deeds follow from such reformed character: this people is "eager to do what is good" or, more literally, "zealous for good deeds" (*zēlōtēn kalōn ergōn*, 2:14). In effect, the members of Cretan households can meet their pedestrian domestic and civic duties because God's gift has educated them in required moral dispositions. But how has this change within them happened?

The Experience of God's Goodness

The second passage follows the instruction to civic orderliness and the display of an irenic disposition "to all people" in Titus 3:1–2, and, like the one cited earlier, begins with the inferential *gar*, suggesting an explanatory function.

> For we ourselves were once foolish, disobedient, deluded, slaves to various desires and pleasures, living in malice and envy, hateful ourselves and hating one another. But when the kindness and generous love of God our savior appeared, not because of any righteous deeds we had done but because of his mercy, he saved us through the bath of rebirth and renewal by the holy Spirit, which he richly poured out on us through Jesus Christ our savior, so that we might be justified by his grace and become heirs in hope of eternal life. (Titus 3:3–7)

This is an altogether remarkable passage. Like 2:11–14, it offers an explanation of why Cretan believers can now live as decent human beings as "an elect people" that is "zealous for good deeds." But it goes much further in connecting the change within and among them to the actual experience of God's power.

We note immediately that the passage moves through three temporal (and existential) stages: they have been moved from their former lives of vice (Titus 3:3), through the experience of God's gift of salvation—specifically connected to baptism and the outpouring of the Holy Spirit (3:4–6)—to a condition of righteousness that enables them now to be heirs of eternal life (3:7). Each stage deserves attention as a narrative elaboration of how the pedagogy of grace stated by 2:11–14 has an experiential basis, showing how kindness and mercy are learned through the experience of God's kindness and mercy, how love for other humans is learned through having experienced God's *philanthrōpia*.

Paul starts by saying that "for we ourselves [or "also"] were once [or "then"]" in a state of alienation from each other and themselves. Rhetorically, the use of the first-person pronoun "we" is powerful, associating the author and his delegate with the implied Cretan readers in their existential condition of need. But something more than rhetorical chumminess is here at work. For just as Paul states in Titus 2:11 that God's gift has appeared to or for all humans (*pasin anthrōpois*), so here he makes clear that all humans—including Titus and himself—are in need of that gift. The list of vices that follows in 3:3 corresponds to the negative portrayal of the Cretan population Paul sketched earlier in the letter: apart from being foolish and deluded slaves to "various desires and pleasures" (cf. "worldly desires" in 2:12), the list is a catalog of misanthropic dispositions: disobedient (*apeitheis*), living in malice and envy (*en kakia kai pthonō diagontes*), hateful themselves (*strygētoi*), and hating each other (*misountes allēlous*). The list not only characterizes humanity in its raw state—and apart from God it remains always raw—but rhetorically prepares for the precise nature of the gift that changes monsters into humans.

Paul's use of "appeared" (*epephanē*) in Titus 3:4 echoes the same verb in 2:11,[35] and the noun "gift/grace" in 2:11 is given specificity by the phrase "the kindness and generous love," perhaps more precisely translated as

---

35. See A. Lau, *Manifest in the Flesh.*

"gentleness" (*chrēstotēs*)[36] and "love for humanity" (*philanthrōpia*).[37] These qualities are the contrary of malice and hatred for others. They are, Paul says, the qualities of "God our savior," and they have "appeared" to and for all humans in the self-giving of Jesus "for us" (*hyper hēmōn*, 2:14). Such a gift was entirely characteristic of the God who saves; it was "according to his mercy" (*kata to autou eleos*), a quality also completely contrary to malice and envy (3:5; see 3:3). And by this gift, Paul declares simply, "he saved us" (3:5).[38] To become merciful, Paul proposes, humans must themselves experience mercy.

But Paul needs to answer two questions that might (at least logically) be posed. The first is whether they might have reached a state of righteousness through some efforts of their own rather than by God's gift. No, it was "not because of any righteous deeds we had done." So the NABRE, but the phrase should be translated, "not in a righteousness [*en dikaiosynē*] based on works [*ex ergōn*] that we ourselves have done [*ha epoiēsamen hemeis*)." So much for the program of the opponents "from the circumcision party."[39] When a change of heart is what is required, the performance of acts is not sufficient, for even admirable acts can be perverted by a twisted heart.

The second, and most pertinent question, is exactly how the merciful act of Jesus's self-donation for them, which displayed God kindness and love for humanity, reached them. Is it merely formal or real, simply an ideological conviction, or an experience of their own lives?[40] Does salvation have an experiential expression? It is essential to Paul's rhetorical argument that the answer be in the affirmative.

Paul states first that they all had experienced "the bath of regeneration" (or: "rebirth," *palingenesia*, Titus 3:5). Although the terminology is distinctive, the reference to the ritual of baptism is unmistakable. Paul and Titus and the Cretan believers alike had undergone a ritual entry into

36. For *chrēstos* and *chrēstotēs* as characteristically Pauline, see Rom 2:4; 3:12; 11:22; 1 Cor 15:33; 2 Cor 6:6; Gal 5:22; Eph 2:7; 4:32; Col 3:12.

37. Although *philanthrōpia* does appear occasionally in Greek literature (see Plato, *Symposium* 189C; *Laws* 713D), the LXX (Wis 1:6; 7:23), and related literature (Josephus, *Jewish Antiquities* 1.24; Philo, *On the Cherubim* 99), its only New Testament appearance is here and in Acts 28:2 (where it is ascribed to barbarians).

38. For God's mercy in Paul, see Rom 9:13, 15, 16, 18; 11:30, 31, 32; 15:9; 1 Cor 7:25; 2 Cor 4:1; Gal 6:16; Phil 2:27; 1 Tim 1:2, 13, 16, 18.

39. It is difficult to avoid the conclusion that the same point is being made here that was argued by Paul in Rom 2–3.

40. Again, this is the question that Paul addresses in Rom 6–8.

the community that "saved" them by giving them a new identity. As elsewhere in the canonical Pauline letters, "salvation" has a present, social dimension. It is not something merely to be hoped for at the end-time appearance of God and Christ (2:13); it is realized now through the ritual inclusion in a people defined by moral convictions and commitments that the one baptized had not previously shared. Taking on, or being gifted with, such a new sort of character is, in social terms, accurately termed a rebirth or regeneration.

Inclusion in a new social group, however, is by no means the heart of the Cretans' experience of transformation from a savage to a civilized people. In immediate conjunction with the community ritual of baptism is the outpouring of the Holy Spirit, which is here associated with newness of life (*anakainōsis*, Titus 3:5). This Spirit of renewal, Paul declares, has been "richly poured out on us" (*execheen eph' hēmas plousiōs*, cf. Rom 5:5). Such an outpouring is "through Jesus Christ our savior" (*dia Iēsou Christou tou sōtēros hēmōn*), and it is the power from God—"Holy Spirit" is the fundamental symbol in the canonical letters for the power that comes from the exalted Lord Jesus—that provides the ability to change internally, to actually have dispositions corresponding to the gift given them, to leave off hating themselves and each other and to live as temperate, righteous, and devout humans in the present age (Titus 2:12).

Paul ends the passage with a purpose clause (Titus 3:7). This rebirth given by God places humans in a new relationship with God and the world. Rather than translate the passive aorist participle *dikaiōthentes* as the NABRE does, "so that we might be justified by his grace," I think we need to render it as "so that, having been made righteous by/through his gift [*tē ekeinou chariti*], we might become heirs according to hope [*kat' elpida*] of eternal life [*klēronomoi zōēs aiōniou*]." The language of inheritance echoes that of "a people of his own" in 2:14. Against the heteronomous program of the circumcision party, Paul claims that real membership in God's people comes through a gift of such overwhelming mercy and graciousness that it changes people from the inside.

The result is that they are "zealous for good deeds" (Titus 2:14 RSV). And Paul reasserts that telos of moral transformation in the passage immediately following. He tells Titus, "I want you to insist of these points, that those who have believed in God [*hoi pepisteukotes theō*] be careful to devote themselves to good works [*kalōn ergōn*]; these are excellent [*kala*] and beneficial to others [*ōphelima tois anthrōpois*]" (3:8). The Cretan believers can change their behavior because of a change in their character; they have changed their character because of the experience of God's gift to them of God's own character through the self-giving of Christ and the rich outpouring of God's Holy Spirit on them.

Conclusion

By treating Paul's letter to Titus as a rhetorically coherent composition, I have been able to offer an answer—I hope a plausible answer—to several puzzles posed by this small writing: Why are the Cretans and opponents portrayed so negatively, the requirements of leaders so minimal, the instructions for the household so basic? And what function is played by the two glorious passages in which everyone recognizes both genuine Pauline diction and theology? I hope I have shown that Paul counters the savage character of the local population with a character ethic rather than an ethic of ritual rules; evil dispositions must be replaced by good ones, savage attitudes by benevolent ones. But I have also tried to show that Paul connects this internal change among his readers to the embodied experience of baptism and an internal empowerment by the Holy Spirit. God's gift (or grace) is the agent of deep human change, not human rule-keeping.

We have seen as well that what is at stake for Paul is not the security of the church—it is never mentioned—but rather civilized existence itself. This is why I made so much of the participle *paideuousa*. According to this rhetorical presentation, the Cretans cannot build on the ancient and noble traditions of Greek *paideia*, in which both positive moral dispositions and social stability could be assumed. Here the population is savage, and the basic unit of every civilization, the household, is both fragile and under attack. In the case of this rhetorically constructed Crete, the pedagogy of grace—what God's gift of mercy and kindness revealed through the self-giving of Jesus and made available to them through the power of the Holy Spirit—must do the heavy lifting of providing the basis of civilization itself.

I ask your indulgence to make one final point. As a rhetorical performance, Titus provides us with a possible scenario in Paul's mission that could have had some basis in fact and therefore has some value as a historical witness. But can we ask also about its possible pertinence as a canonical composition addressed to the church in every age? Canonical writings, after all, wax and wane in their capacity to address the ever-changing circumstances of the church through the ages and throughout all its worldwide instantiations. I suggest that in many places of today's world—at least in what we call the First World, at least in my own coun-try—there are many contexts in which Paul's rhetorical construction seems eerily prescient, where elderly people are addicted to drink and to drugs, where spouses and especially children are not loved—think only of human trafficking—where workers engage in systematic theft, where populations are alienated from the duties of responsible citizenship, and where violence occurs not only in the streets but also in the household. It is not difficult to make the case that much of our world also has lost, or never had, the sort of *paideia* that once could be taken for granted, to be replaced by the shrill ideological conflicts of academia and the media; that the basic unit of civilization, the household, is fragile and sometimes broken; and that those offering easy answers to such barbarism are liars who will say anything for personal gain.

Taking seriously Paul's position that what humanity today needs is a transformation from within that changes malevolent vices into benevo-lent virtues, that such a change in dispositions is the way forward to sta-bilizing culture, and, above all, that such change can and must come from receiving into ourselves the pedagogy of grace taught us by God's love for humanity displayed through the self-giving of Christ and activated within us by the Holy Spirit—taking all this seriously, I say, is highly risky but also highly rewarding. The immediate gain is to once more make Titus a composition of the greatest importance as a source for reflection on our own lives. What a gift!

Conclusion

Having now completed two volumes on the letters of Paul, touching in one way or another on all the canonical letters ascribed to him, and treating each of them individually at least once, I have the sense of being only at the beginning rather than at the end of inquiry into the apostle. So much has been left unattended! So many more struggles with his difficult yet infinitely bracing language might be undertaken! The more that Paul's letters are read as letters, I have found, and the more the temptation to construct a single, overarching "theology" of Paul is resisted, the richer and more protean his compositions appear, and the more capable they are of stimulating questions that cut to the core of Christian identity.

The essays in this volume have by no means lacked theological perspective or point. With Paul, how could it be otherwise? In Romans, for example, I have tried to show that the faith of Jesus is central to Paul's argument concerning God's gift to humans, that salvation has a social and present significance more than an individual and future one, and that Paul sees the life of virtue as empowered and directed by the Spirit that transforms humans according to the mind of Christ. In 1 Corinthians, I showed how Paul's understanding of the resurrection as Christ becoming "life-giving Spirit" has both ontological and social entailments. In 2 Corinthians, I analyzed the complex ways in which "truth and reconciliation" intersect at the levels of both human and divine agency. In Gal 1–4, I pursued the way in which Paul's argument was carried by four interlocking narratives concerning Paul himself, the gentile Galatian assemblies, Israel, and the faithful Jesus, whose obedience was expressed through his giving of himself for others, and then showed how the imperatives of Gal 5–6 flowed from and advanced those narratives.

Taking Philippians as a starting point, I showed how fellowship in suffering was not an incidental but a central element of Paul's perception

498

of discipleship. Taking Colossians as a starting point, I demonstrated how "mystery" and "metaphor" depend on and illumine each other in all the canonical letters. In similar fashion, 1 and 2 Thessalonians led me through a close examination of Paul's pastoral practice in both chronic and critical settings.

Some of these essays have contributed mainly to the understanding of Paul in his historical setting (especially the essays on the "politics of perfection" in Galatia and Colossae [chap. 9], on glossolalia in 1 Corinthians [chap. 6], the development of church order [chap. 13], and the conventions of ancient polemic in 2 Timothy [chap. 2]). In some of these essays I have tried to show that the supposed divide between disputed and undisputed letters is tiny or nonexistent. The essays on 1 Timothy that compare the problems faced by Paul's delegate to the church at Ephesus to those faced by the apostle himself in the church of Corinth (chap. 20), and that show how the argument in 1 Timothy 1:1–20 contrasts a heteronomous to a character ethic in precisely the manner of Galatians (chap. 21), have suggested the sorts of new insights that result from making new connections and comparisons.

Mainly, though, the questions I have asked of the letters have had the issues of present-day Christians in view. I think here especially of the essays on the pedagogy of grace in Titus (chap. 23), eros and agape in Ephesians (chap. 16), truth and reconciliation in 2 Corinthians (chap. 8), and the politics of perfection in Galatians and Colossians (chap. 9). The issues identified and analyzed in these letters remain alive and troublesome for contemporary believers. Most of all, I have tried in the essay on the church as the sacrament of the world in Ephesians (chap. 17) to provide a taste of what it means, substantively, to speak of Paul as the "apostle of the church." Yes, these essays have been thoroughly (and inevitably) immersed in Paul's religious and theological language. But the reader can see that this is possible, indeed enabled, by the absence of some overarching theory concerning Paul's big ideas. All that is necessary is to read each letter for what it says and for how it connects or does not connect to what other (all the other) letters say about the topics on which they speak.

The thirteen letters ascribed to Paul have been, individually and together, the voice of the apostle in the life of the church. They have been such from the earliest days that scattered communities of Christ-believers could be called church. In the early second century, Clement, Ignatius, and Polycarp revered Paul as a martyr and referred to his letters as authoritative. Toward the end of the second century, Irenaeus and Tertullian rescued his letters from the atomistic misreadings of Marcion and the gnostics. From that time forward, Paul's letters—the complete canonical collection—have been read in the assembly, preached by bishops and elders, studied by scholars, cited by councils, and pondered by mystics.

Until the nineteenth century, no Christian writer challenged the authenticity of any letter or the authority of the traditional canonical collection. But since the nineteenth century, there has grown an ever-greater gap between the "assured results of scholarship" and the tradition of the church. For conventional scholarship, the issue has been decided on the grounds of historical analysis. Almost a full half of the canonical collection is, therefore, to be read as "inauthentic" productions of a later generation. My argument is that the consensus is wrong, based on faulty historiographical methods and critically unexamined theological commitments.

We can debate the degree to which the academic consensus, now so massive as to be considered by its adherents self-evidently irrefutable, has affected the life and practice of the church. Certainly, in those denominations whose ministers are trained within institutions totally embracing the canons of modernity, the disputed letters of Paul have less and less a place in proclamation and piety. But the scholarly reconstruction of a "historical Paul" is of no more relevance to the life of the church than is the scholarly reconstruction of the "historical Jesus." The Gospels, not academic theories, present in all their diversity and complexity the portrayals of Jesus that nurture the church. The canonical letters ascribed to Paul shape the character of Christian identity.

It is time, surely, for scholars who call themselves Christian, and who seek to serve the church more than to advance within academic guilds, to once more bring all the letters of Paul back into conversation, both with each other and with the concerns of the believing community. My efforts in these two volumes have had the simple and singular aim of showing that to embrace the entire Pauline collection is intellectually responsible (I would argue, indeed, intellectually demanded) and that such an embrace yields fresh and unexpected insight into the many dimensions of Paul's pastoral practice and theological thinking. If these two volumes have encouraged any other scholars to once more read Paul whole, not with any diminishment but rather with the enhancement of their critical abilities, then I shall conclude that what I have concluded might prove to be another start.

ACKNOWLEDGMENTS

The twenty-three chapters of this book, not including the introduction and conclusion, bring togethers essays old and new. Ten of the twenty-three were written specifically for this volume.

I appreciate *Catholic Biblical Quarterly* for allowing use of "Romans 3:21–26 and the Faith of Jesus: The Soteriological Significance of Christ's Obedience" (chap. 1), *Horizons in Biblical Theology* for "*Oikonomia Theou*: God's Way of Ordering Creation in 1 Timothy" (chap. 20), and *Journal of Religious Studies* for "Second Timothy and the Polemic against False Teachers: A Reexamination" (chap. 22).

I thank SBL Press for permitting inclusion of "The Social Dimensions of *Sōtēria* in Luke-Acts and Paul: Restoration and Belonging" (chap. 2), from *Society of Biblical Literature 1993 Seminar Papers*, edited by Eugene H. Lovering (1993); "The Body in Question: The Social Complexities of Resurrection in 1 Corinthians" (chap. 5), from *Unity and Diversity in the Gospels and Paul*, edited by Kelly R. Iverson and Christopher W. Skinner (2012); and "God Was in Christ: Second Corinthians 5:19 and Mythic Language" (chap. 7), from *Myth and Scripture: Contemporary Perspectives on Religion, Language and Imagination*, edited by Dexter E. Callender (2014).

Brill offered permission to print "Transformation of the Mind and Moral Discernment in Romans: Paul's Spirit-Filled Ethics" (chap. 3), from *Early Christianity and Classical Culture*, edited by John T. Fitzgerald, Thomas H. Olbricht, and L. M. White (2003). The *Stone-Campbell Journal* agreed to the inclusion of "Life-Giving Spirit: The Ontological Implications of Resurrection in 1 Corinthians" (chap. 4), from volume 15, issue 1 (2012). Peeters granted use of "The Shape of the Struggle: First Timothy 1:1–20" (chap. 21), in *1 Timothy Reconsidered*, edited by Karl P. Donfried (2008).

Baylor University Press permitted the inclusion of "The Rise of Church

Order: An Examination of Bultmann's *Theology of the New Testament*" (chap. 13), from *Beyond Bultmann: Reckoning a New Testament Theology*, edited by Bruce W. Longenecker and Mikeal C. Parsons (2014). Cambridge University Press kindly granted permission for use of "Paul's Vision of the Church: The Community of the Risen Lord" (chap. 12), from *Cambridge Companion to Saint Paul*, edited by James D. G. Dunn (2003).

I am grateful as well to Fortress Press for permission to use two essays from my book *Religious Experience in Earliest Christianity: A Missing Dimension in New Testament Studies* (1998)—namely, "Glossolalia and the Embarrassments of Experience: The Corinthians and the Hellenistic World" (chap. 6) and "Ritual Imprinting and the Politics of Perfection: Galatians and Colossians" (chap. 9).

A few of these essays also appeared in *Contested Issues in Christian Origins and the New Testament* (NovTSup [Brill, 2013])—namely, "Romans 3:21–26 and the Faith of Jesus: The Soteriological Significance of Christ's Obedience" (chap. 1); "The Social Dimensions of *Sōtēria* in Luke-Acts and Paul: Restoration and Belonging" (chap. 2); "Transformation of the Mind and Moral Discernment in Romans: Paul's Spirit-Filled Ethics" (chap. 3); "Life-Giving Spirit: The Ontological Implications of Resurrection in 1 Corinthians" (chap. 4); "The Body in Question: The Social Complexities of Resurrection in 1 Corinthians" (chap. 5); "Paul's Vision of the Church: The Community of the Risen Lord" (chap. 12); "*Oikonomia Theou*: God's Way of Ordering Creation in 1 Timothy (chap. 20); "The Shape of the Struggle: First Timothy 1:1–20" (chap. 21); and "Second Timothy and the Polemic against False Teachers: A Reexamination" (chap. 22).

English translations of the New Testament are my own unless noted in the chapters. I sometimes use the Revised Standard Version and sometimes the New Revised Standard Version, and for the chapters written specifically for this volume I primarily use the New American Bible Revised Edition. I am actually always working from the Greek and often alter the published translations, always trying to indicate when I do. Readers of this volume will in every case be able to check on the translation I provide through the constant provision of chapter and verse.

BIBLIOGRAPHY

Adams, Richard Manly. "'The Israel of God': The Narrative Rhetoric of Paul's Letter to the Galatians." PhD diss., Emory University, 2012.

Ahern, Barnabas M. "The Fellowship of His Sufferings (Phil 3,10): A Study of St. Paul's Doctrine on Christian Suffering." *CBQ* 22 (1960): 1–32.

Alderink, Larry J. "The Eleusinian Mysteries in Roman Imperial Times." *ANRW* 2.18.2:1499–1539. Boston: De Gruyter, 2016.

Alexander, Loveday. "Hellenistic Letter Forms and the Structure of Philippians." *JSNT* 12 (1989): 87–101.

Allen, Michael, and Jonathan A. Linebaugh, eds. *Reformation Readings of Paul: Explorations in History and Exegesis.* Downers Grove, IL: IVP Academic, 2015.

Amiot, Francois. *The Key Concepts of St. Paul.* New York: Herder and Herder, 1962.

Andemicael, Awet. "Grace, Equity, Participation: The Economy of God in 2 Corinthians 8:8–15." *Anglican Theological Review* 98 (2016): 621–38.

Andrews, Scott B. "Too Weak Not to Lead: The Form and Function of 2 Cor 11:23b–33." *NTS* 41 (1995): 263–76.

Angus, Samuel. *The Mystery Religions and Christianity: A Study in the Religious Background of Early Christianity.* London: Murray, 1925.

Aristides, Aelius. *Aristides.* Edited by Wilhelm Dindorf. 3 vols. Leipzig: Reimer, 1829.

Aristophanes. *Aristophanes.* Translated by B. B. Rogers. LCL. Cambridge, MA: Harvard University Press, 1924.

Aristotle. *The Nicomachean Ethics.* Translated by H. Rackham. LCL 73. Cambridge, MA: Harvard University Press, 1926.

Ascough, Richard S. "An Analysis of the Baptismal Ritual of the Didache." *Studia Liturgica* 24 (1994): 201–13.

———. "The Completion of a Religious Duty: The Background of 2 Cor 8.1–15." *NTS* 42 (1996): 584–99.

Aune, David E. "Magic in Early Christianity." *ANRW* 23.2:1549–51. Part 2, *Principat*, 23.2. Edited by H. Temporini and W. Haase. New York: De Gruyter, 1989.

———. *Prophecy in Early Christianity and the Ancient Mediterranean World.* Grand Rapids: Eerdmans, 1983.

Aus, Roger D. "God's Plan and God's Power: Isaiah 66 and the Restraining Factors of 2 Thess 2:6–7." *JBL* 96 (1977): 537–53.

Austin, J. L. *How to Do Things with Words: The William James Lectures Delivered at Harvard University in 1955.* Edited by J. O. Urmson. Oxford: Clarendon, 1962.

Bacht, H. "Wahres und Falsches Prophetentum." *Bib* 32 (1951): 237–62.

Bailey, John A. "Who Wrote II Thessalonians?" *NTS* 25 (1979): 131–45.

Baird, Julia. *Victoria the Queen: An Intimate Biography of the Woman Who Ruled an Empire.* New York: Random House, 2016.

Baker, Nena. *The Body Toxic: How the Hazardous Chemistry of Everyday Things Threatens Our Health and Well-Being.* New York: North Point, 2008.

Balch, David L. "Household Codes." Pages 25–50 in *Greco-Roman Literature and the New Testament: Selected Forms and Genres*, edited by David E. Aune. SBLSBS 21. Atlanta: Scholars Press, 1988.

———. *Let Wives Be Submissive: The Domestic Code in 1 Peter.* SBLMS 26. Chico, CA: Scholars Press, 1981.

Balch, David L., Everett Ferguson, and Wayne A. Meeks, eds. *Greeks, Romans and Christians: Essays in Honor of Abraham J. Malherbe.* Minneapolis: Fortress, 1990.

Balthasar, Hans Urs von. *Theo-Drama: Theological Dramatic Theory.* 5 vols. San Francisco: Ignatius, 1988.

Bandstra, A. J. "Did the Colossian Errorists Need a Mediator?" Pages 329–43 in *New Dimensions in New Testament Study*, edited by Richard N. Longenecker and Merrill C. Tenney. Grand Rapids: Zondervan, 1974.

Barclay, John M. G. "Conflict in Thessalonica." *CBQ* 55 (1993): 512–30.

———. *Obeying the Truth: Paul's Ethics in Galatians.* Edinburgh: T&T Clark, 1988.

———. *Paul and the Gift.* Grand Rapids: Eerdmans, 2015.

Barclay, William. *The Letters to Timothy, Titus, and Philemon.* Rev. ed. Philadelphia: Westminster, 1975.

Barnouin, M. "Les Problèmes de Traduction Concernant II Thess. II. 6–7." *NTS* 23 (1977): 482–98.

Barr, James. *The Semantics of Biblical Language.* Oxford: Oxford University Press, 1961.

Barrett, C. K. "The Allegory of Abraham, Sarah, and Hagar in the Argument of Galatians." Pages 154–70 in *Essays on Paul*.

———. *A Commentary on the Epistle to the Romans*. London: Black, 1957.

———. *Essays on Paul*. Philadelphia: Westminster, 1982.

———. *Freedom and Obligation: A Study in the Epistle to the Galatians*. Philadelphia: Westminster, 1985.

———. "HO ADIKESAS (2 Cor 7:12)." Pages 108–17 in *Essays on Paul*.

———. *The Pastoral Epistles in the New English Bible*. Oxford: Clarendon, 1963.

———. "Paul's Opponents in Corinth." Pages 60–86 in *Essays on Paul*.

———. "Sectarian Diversity at Corinth." Pages 287–302 in Burke and Elliott, *Paul and the Corinthians*.

Barth, Karl. *Church Dogmatics*. Vol. III.4, *The Doctrine of Creation*. Edited by G. W. Bromiley and T. F. Torrance. Edinburgh: T&T Clark, 1961.

Barth, Markus. "The Faith of the Messiah." *Heythrop Journal* 10 (1969): 363–70.

———. "The Kerygma of Galatians." *Int* 21 (1967): 131–46.

Basevi, Claudio, and Juan Chapo. "Philippians 2.6–11: The Rhetorical Function of a Pauline Hymn." Pages 338–56 in *Rhetoric and the New Testament: Essays from the 1992 Heidelberg Conference*, edited by Stanley E. Porter and Thomas H. Olbricht. JSNTSup 90. Sheffield: JSOT Press, 2001.

Bassler, Jouette M. "The Widows' Tale: A Fresh Look at 1 Tim 5:3–16." *JBL* 103 (1984): 23–41.

Bates, W. H. "The Integrity of II Corinthians 1." *NTS* 12 (1965): 56–69.

Baumbach, Günther. "Die von Paulus im Philipperbrief bekaempten Irrlehrer." Pages 293–310 in *Gnosis und Neues Testament*, edited by Karl-Wolfgang Tröger. Berlin: Gütersloher Mohn, 1973.

Beale, G. K. "The Old Testament Background of Reconciliation in 2 Corinthians 5–7 and Its Bearing on the Literary Problem of 2 Corinthians 6:14–7:1." *NTS* 35 (1989): 550–81.

Beare, Frank W. "Speaking with Tongues: A Critical Survey of the New Testament Evidence." *JBL* 83 (1964): 229–46.

Beasley-Murray, G. R. *Baptism in the New Testament*. London: Macmillan, 1962.

Beck, Roger. "Mithraism since Franz Cumont." *ANRW* 17.4:2002–15. Part 2, *Principat*, 17.4 Edited by H. Temporini and W. Haase. New York: De Gruyter, 1989.

Beel, A. "Donum Linguarum Juxta Act. Apost. ii.1–13." *Collationes Brugenses* 35 (1935): 417–20.

Beker, Johan Christiaan. *Heirs of Paul: Paul's Legacy in the New Testament and in the Church Today*. Minneapolis: Fortress, 1991.

———. *Paul the Apostle: The Triumph of God in Life and Thought*. Philadelphia: Fortress, 1980.

Bell, Catherine M. *Ritual Theory, Ritual Practice*. New York: Oxford University Press, 1992.

Berger, Peter L. *The Sacred Canopy: Elements in a Sociological Theory of Religion*. New York: Doubleday, 1969.

Berger, Peter L., and Thomas Luckmann. *The Social Construction of Reality: A Treatise in the Sociology of Knowledge*. New York: Doubleday, 1966.

Betz, Hans Dieter. *Galatians: A Commentary on Paul's Letter to the Churches in Galatia*. Hermeneia. Philadelphia: Fortress, 1979.

———. "The Literary Composition and Function of Paul's Letter to the Galatians." *NTS* 21 (1975): 353–79.

———. "2 Cor 6:14–7:1: An Anti-Pauline Fragment?" *JBL* 92 (1973): 88–108.

———. *2 Corinthians 8 and 9: A Commentary on Two Administrative Letters of Paul*. Hermeneia. Philadelphia: Fortress, 1985.

Betz, Otto. "Der Katechon." *NTS* 9 (1963): 276–91.

Bianchi, Ugo. *The Greek Mysteries*. Iconography of Religions 17.3. Leiden: Brill, 1976.

Bickerman, Elias J. "The Warning Inscriptions of Herod's Temple." *Jewish Quarterly Review* 37 (1947): 387–405.

Bieringer, Reimund, ed. *The Corinthian Correspondence*. BETL 125. Leuven: Peeters, 1996.

———. "Reconciliation with God and a Wide-Open Heart for Paul: The Meaning of the Christian Theology and Practice of Reconciliation according to 2 Corinthians 5:11–7:4." *Proceedings of the Irish Biblical Association* 30 (2007): 15–33.

Bieringer, Reimund, Marilou S. Ibita, Dominika A. Kurek-Chomycz, and Thomas A. Vollmer, eds. *Theologizing in the Corinthian Conflict: Studies in the Exegesis and Theology of 2 Corinthians*. Biblical Tools and Studies 16. Leuven: Peeters, 2013.

Black, David A. "The Authorship of Philippians 2:6–11: Some Literary-Critical Observations." *Criswell Theological Review* 2 (1988): 269–89.

———. *Paul, Apostle of Weakness: Astheneia and Its Cognates in the Pauline Literature*. New York: Lang, 1984.

Black, Mark C. "I Cor 11:2–16: A Re-investigation." Pages 1:191–218 in Osburn, *Essays on Women in Earliest Christianity*.

Bligh, John. *Galatians: A Discussion of St. Paul's Epistle*. London: St. Paul, 1969.

Bloomquist, L. Gregory. *The Function of Suffering in Philippians.* JSNTSup 78. Sheffield: Sheffield University Press, 1993.

Boers, Hendrikus. *What Is New Testament Theology? The Rise of Criticism and the Problem of a Theology of the New Testament.* Guides to Biblical Scholarship. Philadelphia: Fortress, 1979.

Bohnenblust, Gottfried. *Beiträge zum Topos Peri Philias.* Berlin: Universitäts-Buchdruckerei von Gustav Shade, 1905.

Bonsirven, Joseph. *Theology of the New Testament.* Westminster, MD: Newman, 1963.

Boring, M. Eugene. "The Language of Universal Salvation in Paul." *JBL* 105 (1986): 269–92.

Bornhäuser, Karl. "Zum Verständnis von Philipper 2,5–11." *NKZ* 44 (1933): 428–34, 453–62.

Bornkamm, Günther. "The Heresy of Colossians." Pages 123–45 in Meeks and Francis, *Conflict at Colossae.*

Boston Women's Health Course Collective. *Our Bodies, Our Selves: A Course by and for Women.* Boston: New England Free Press, 1971.

Boswell, John. *Christianity, Social Tolerance, and Homosexuality: Gay People in Western Europe from the Beginning of the Christian Era to the Fourteenth Century.* Chicago: University of Chicago Press, 1980.

———. *Rediscovering Gay History: Archetypes of Gay Love in Christian History.* Michael Harding Memorial Address 1982. London: Gay Christian Movement, 1982.

Bousset, Wilhelm. *Kyrios Christos: A History of the Belief in Christ from the Beginnings of Christianity to Irenaeus.* Translated by John E. Steely. Nashville: Abingdon, 1970.

Boyarin, Daniel. *A Radical Jew: Paul and the Politics of Identity.* Contraversions: Critical Studies in Jewish Literature, Culture, and Society 1. Oakland: University of California Press, 1997.

Boyle, T. Coraghessan. *The Tortilla Curtain.* New York: Penguin, 1996.

Boyles, John. "Unevolved: A Study in Diverse Christian Social Organization." PhD diss., Emory University, 2016.

Brant, Jo-Ann A. "The Place of *Mimēsis* in Paul's Thought." *SR* 22 (1993): 285–300.

Braun, Willi. *Rhetoric and Reality in Early Christianities.* SCJ 16. Waterloo, ON: Wilfrid Laurier University Press, 2005.

Bremmer, Jan N. *Initiation into the Mysteries of the Ancient World.* Münchner Vorlesungen Zu Antiken Welten 1. Berlin: De Gruyter, 2014.

Brewer, Raymond R. "The Meaning of *Politeuesthe* in Philippians 1:27." *JBL* 73 (1954): 76–83.

Brink, Laurie. "From Wrongdoer to New Creation: Reconciliation in 2 Corinthians." *Int* 71 (2017): 298–309.

Brinsmead, Bernard Hungerford. *Galatians: Dialogical Response to Opponents*. SBLDS 65. Chico, CA: Scholars Press, 1982.

Brown, David. "The Acts of the Apostles, Chapter II: The Day of Pentecost." *Expositor* 1 (1875): 392–408.

Brown, Ernest Faulkner. *The Pastoral Epistles with Introduction and Notes*. Westminster Commentaries. London: Methuen, 1917.

Brown, Raymond E. *The Semitic Background of the Term "Mystery" in the New Testament*. Facet Books, Biblical Series 21. Philadelphia: Fortress, 1968.

Brox, Norbert. "*ANATHEMA IĒSOUS* (1 Kor. 12,3)." *BZ* 12 (1968): 103–11.

———. *Die Pastoralbriefe*. 4th ed. Regensburger Neues Testament 7. Regensburg: Verlag Friedrich Pustet, 1969.

Brubaker, Rogers. *Trans: Gender and Race in an Age of Unsettled Identities*. Princeton: Princeton University Press, 2016.

Bruce, F. F. *The Epistle to the Galatians: A Commentary on the Greek Text*. NIGTC. Grand Rapids: Eerdmans, 1982.

———. "Galatian Problems 2: North or South Galatians?" *Bulletin of the John Rylands Library* 52 (1970): 243–66.

Bruner, Frederick Dale. *A Theology of the Holy Spirit: The Pentecost Experience and the New Testament Witness*. Grand Rapids: Eerdmans, 1970.

Bultmann, Rudolf. *History of the Synoptic Tradition*. Translated by John Marsh. Rev. ed. New York: Harper & Row, 1968.

———. *Theology of the New Testament*. 2 vols. New York: Scribner, 1951.

Bunn, John T. "Glossolalia in Historical Perspective." Pages 36–47 in Mills, *Speaking in Tongues: Let's Talk about It*.

Burke, Trevor J., and J. Keith Elliott. *Paul and the Corinthians: Studies on a Community in Conflict; Essays in Honour of Margaret Thrall*. NovTSup 109. Leiden: Brill, 2003.

Burkert, Walter. *Ancient Mystery Cults*. Cambridge, MA: Harvard University Press, 1987.

———. *Greek Religion*. Translated by John Raffan. Cambridge, MA: Harvard University Press, 1985.

Burtchaell, James T. *From Synagogue to Church: Public Service and Offices in the Earliest Christian Communities*. Cambridge: Cambridge University Press, 1992.

Buttrick, G. A., ed. *The Interpreter's Dictionary of the Bible*. 4 vols. Nashville: Abingdon, 1962.

Caird, George B. *Principalities and Powers: A Study in Pauline Theology.* Oxford: Clarendon, 1956.

Callan, Terrance. "Pauline Midrash: The Exegetical Background of Gal 3:19b." *JBL* 99 (1980): 549–67.

———. "Prophecy and Ecstasy in Greco-Roman Religion and in 1 Corinthians." *NovT* 27 (1985): 125–40.

Campbell, Douglas A. "The Stories of Predecessors and Inheritors in Galatians and Romans." Pages 172–203 in B. Longenecker, *Narrative Dynamics in Paul.*

———. "The Story of Jesus in Romans and Galatians." Pages 97–124 in B. Longenecker, *Narrative Dynamics in Paul.*

Campbell, John Y. "ΚΟΙΝΩΝΙΑ and Its Cognates in the New Testament." Pages 1–28 in *Three New Testament Studies.* Leiden: Brill, 1965.

Campbell, Joseph, ed. *The Mysteries: Papers from the Eranos Yearbooks.* Bollingen Series 30.2. Princeton: Princeton University Press, 1955.

Campbell, R. Alastair. *The Elders: Seniority within Earliest Christianity.* SNTW. Edinburgh: T&T Clark, 1994.

Campenhausen, Hans von. *Ecclesiastical Authority and Spiritual Power in the Church of the First Three Centuries.* Translated by J. A. Baker. Stanford, CA: Stanford University Press, 1969.

Cannon, George E. *The Use of Traditional Material in Colossians.* Macon, GA: Mercer University Press, 1983.

Cantarella, Eva. *Bisexuality in the Ancient World.* New Haven: Yale University Press, 1992.

Capon, Robert Farrar. *The Supper of the Lamb: A Culinary Reflection.* New York: Modern Library, 2002.

Caragounis, Chrys C. *The Ephesian Mysterion: Meaning and Content.* Coniectanea Biblica: New Testament Series 8. Lund: Gleerup, 1977.

Carr, Frederick David. "The Subject of the New Creation: Transformation and Selfhood in Paul's Letters." PhD diss., Emory University, 2019.

Casaubon, Meric. *A Treatise Concerning Enthiusiasme as It Is an Effect of Nature: But Is Mistaken by Many for Either Divine Inspiration or Diabolicall Possession.* 2nd ed. London: Roger Daniel, 1656.

Casel, Odo. *The Mystery of Christian Worship: And Other Writings.* Westminster, MD: Newman, 1962.

Castelli, Elizabeth A. *Imitating Paul: A Discourse of Power.* Louisville: Westminster John Knox, 1991.

The Catechism of the Catholic Church. Vatican City: Libreria Editrice Vaticana, 1994.

Cerfaux, Lucien. *Christ in the Theology of St. Paul*. New York: Herder and Herder, 1951.

———. "Christ Our Justice." Pages 205–29 in *Christ in the Theology of Saint Paul*.

———. *The Church in the Theology of St. Paul*. New York: Herder and Herder, 1959.

———. "Influence des Mystères sur le Judaisme Alexandrin avant Philon." *Le Museon* 37 (1924): 29–88. Repr., pages 65–112 in *Recueil Lucien Cerfaux: Études d'Exégèse et d'Histoire Religieuse*, vol. 1. BETL 6. Gembloux: Duculot, 1954.

———. "L'hymne au Christ-Serviteur de Dieu (Phil II, 6–11 = Is LII, 13–LIII,12)." Pages 425–37 in *Recueil Lucien Cerfaux: Études d'Exégèse et d'Histoire Religieuse*, vol. 2. BETL 71. Leuven: Leuven University Press, 1985.

———. "L'influence des 'Mystères' sur les Épîtres de S. Paul aux Colossiens et aux Ephésiens." Pages 279–85 in *Recueil Lucien Cerfaux: Études d'Exégèse et d'Histoire Religieuse*, vol. 3. BETL 71. Leuven: Leuven University Press, 1985.

———. *Recueil Lucien Cerfaux: Études d'Exégèse et d'Histoire Religieuse*, vol. 3. BETL 71. Leuven: Leuven University Press, 1985.

———. "The Revelation of the Mystery of Christ." Pages 402–38 in *Christ in the Theology of Saint Paul*.

Chapa, Juan. "Is First Thessalonians a Letter of Consolation?" *NTS* 40 (1994): 150–60.

Christie-Murray, David. *Voices from the Gods: Speaking with Tongues*. London: Routledge & Kegan Paul, 1978.

Clark, Kenneth W. "The Meaning of *Energeō* and *Katargeō* in the New Testament." *JBL* 54 (1935): 93–101.

Clinton, Kevin. *Myth and Cult: The Iconography of the Eleusinian Mysteries*. Skrifter utgivna av Svenska institutet i Athen 11, The Martin P. Nilsson Lectures on Greek Religion. Stockholm: Svenska institutet i Athen, 1992.

Cohn, Norman. *The Pursuit of the Millennium: Revolutionary Millenarians and Mystical Anarchists of the Middle Ages*. Rev. ed. New York: Oxford University Press, 1970.

Collins, Adela Yarbro. "The Origins of Christian Baptism." *Studia Liturgica* 19 (1989): 28–46.

Collins, Raymond F., ed. *First Corinthians*. SP 7. Collegeville: Liturgical Press, 1999.

———. "2 Thess 2 Re-read as Pseudepigraphical: A Revised Reaffirmation of the Threat of Faith." Pages 459–69 in R. Collins, *Thessalonian Correspondence*.

————, ed. *The Thessalonian Correspondence*. BETL 87. Leuven: Leuven University Press, 1990

Colson, F. H. "'Myths and Genealogies': A Note on the Polemic of the Pastoral Epistles." *JTS* 19 (1918): 265–71.

Conte, Gian B. *Latin Literature: A History*. Baltimore: Johns Hopkins University Press, 1983.

Conzelmann, Hans. *1 Corinthians: A Commentary on the First Epistle to the Corinthians*. Translated by James W. Leitch. Hermeneia. Philadelphia: Fortress, 1976.

————. *Grundriss der Theologie des Neuen Testaments*. Einführung in die evangelische Theologie 2. Munich: Kaiser, 1967.

Cope, Lamar. "1 Cor 11:2–16: One Step Further." *JBL* 97 (1978): 435–36.

Corrington, Gail Paterson. "The 'Headless Woman': Paul and the Language of the Body in 1 Cor 11:2–16." *PRSt* 18 (1991): 223–31.

Cosmopoulos, Michael B. *Greek Mysteries: The Archaeology of Ancient Greek Secret Cults*. London: Routledge, 2002.

Coulson, Jesse E., and Ray W. Johnson. "Glossolalia and Internal-External Locus of Control." *Journal of Psychology & Theology* 5 (1977): 312–17.

Cousar, Charles B. *Galatians*. Interpretation. Atlanta: John Knox, 1982.

Crace, Jim. *Being Dead*. London: Viking, 1999.

Crehan, Joseph. *Early Christian Baptism and the Creed: A Study in Ante-Nicene Theology*. Bellarmine Series 13. London: Burns, Oates & Washbourne, 1950.

Critchley, Simon, and Robert Bernasconi, eds. *The Cambridge Companion to Levinas*. Cambridge: Cambridge University Press, 2002.

Cullmann, Oscar. *Baptism in the New Testament*. SBT 1. London: SCM, 1950.

————. "Der eschatolische Character des Missionsauftrags und des apostolischen Selbstbewusstseins bei Paulus: Untersuchung zum Begriff des Katechon in 2 Thess 2:6–7." Pages 305–36 in *Vorträge und Aufsätze, 1925–1962*. Tübingen: Mohr Siebeck, 1966.

Cumont, Franz. *The Mysteries of Mithra*. Chicago: Open Court, 1910.

Currie, Stuart D. "'Speaking in Tongues': Early Evidence outside the New Testament Bearing on 'Glōssais Lalein.'" *Int* 19 (1965): 274–94.

Dahl, Nils Alstrup. "Anamnesis: Memory and Commemoration in Early Christianity." Pages 11–29 in *Jesus in the Memory of the Early Church*.

————. "Christ, Creation, and the Church." Pages 120–40 in *Jesus in the Memory of the Early Church*.

————. "Contradictions in Scripture." Pages 159–77 in *Studies in Paul*.

———. "Cosmic Dimensions and Religious Knowledge." Pages 57–75 in *Jesus und Paulus: Festschrift f. Werner Georg Kümmel z. 70. Geburstag*, edited by E. Earle Ellis and Erich Grässer. Göttingen: Vandenhoeck & Ruprecht, 1975.

———. *The Crucified Messiah, and Other Essays*. Minneapolis: Augsburg, 1974.

———. "A Fragment and Its Context: II Cor 6:14–7:1." Pages 62–69 in *Studies in Paul*.

———. *Jesus in the Memory of the Early Church: Essays*. Minneapolis: Augsburg, 1976.

———. "The Messiahship of Jesus in Paul." Pages 37–47 in *Crucified Messiah*.

———. "Paul and the Church at Corinth According to 1 Corinthians 1:10–4:21." Pages 40–61 in *Studies in Paul*.

———. "'A People for His Name' (Acts 15:14)." *NTS* 4 (1958): 319–27.

———. "Rudolf Bultmann's *Theology of the New Testament*." Pages 90–128 in *Crucified Messiah*.

———. "The Story of Abraham in Luke-Acts." Pages 139–58 in *Studies in Luke-Acts: Essays Presented in Honor of Paul Schubert*, edited by Leander E. Keck and James Louis Martyn. Philadelphia: Fortress, 1966.

———. *Studies in Paul: Theology for the Early Christian Mission*. Minneapolis: Augsburg, 1977.

———. "Two Notes on Romans 5." *ST* 5 (1951): 37–48.

Dailey, Thomas. "To Live or Die: Paul's Eschatological Dilemma in Philippians 1:19–26." *Int* 44 (1990): 18–28.

Dalton, William J. "The Integrity of Philippians." *Bib* 60 (1979): 97–102.

Das, A. Andrew. *Paul and the Stories of Israel: Grand Thematic Narratives in Galatians*. Minneapolis: Fortress, 2016.

Davidson, James N. *Courtesans and Fishcakes: The Consuming Passions of Classical Athens*. London: HarperCollins, 1997.

Davies, John G. "Pentecost and Glossolalia." *JTS* 3 (1952): 228–31.

Davies, Stevan L. *The Revolt of the Widows: The Social World of the Apocryphal Acts*. Carbondale: Southern Illinois University Press, 1980.

Davis, Basil S. "Severianus of Gabala and Galatians 6:6–10." *CBQ* 69 (2007): 292–301.

Dawes, Gregory W. *The Body in Question: Metaphor and Meaning in the Interpretation of Ephesians 5:21–33*. Biblical Interpretation Series 30. Leiden: Brill, 1998.

DeFranza, Megan K. *Sex Difference in Christian Theology: Male, Female, and Intersex in the Image of God*. Grand Rapids: Eerdmans, 2015.

Delorme, J. "The Practice of Baptism in Judaism at the Beginning of the

Christian Era." Pages 25–60 in *Baptism in the New Testament: A Symposium*, translated by David Askew. Baltimore: Helicon, 1964.

Deming, Will. *Paul on Marriage and Celibacy: The Hellenistic Background of 1 Cor 7*. SNTSMS 83. Cambridge: Cambridge University Press, 1995.

Derrida, Jacques. *Aporias*. Translated by Thomas Dutoit. Stanford, CA: Stanford University Press, 1993.

———. *Writing and Difference*. Translated by Alan Bass. Chicago: University of Chicago Press, 1978.

DeSilva, David A. "Measuring Penultimate against Ultimate Reality: An Investigation of the Integrity and Argumentation of 2 Corinthians." *JSNT* 52 (1993): 41–70.

———. "No Confidence in the Flesh: The Meaning and Function of Philippians 3:2–21." *TJ* 15 (1994): 27–54.

Dibelius, Martin. *Die Briefe des Apostels Paulus an Timotheus I, II, an Titus*. HNT 13. Tübingen: J. C. B. Mohr, 1913.

———. "The Isis Initiation in Apuleius." Pages 61–121 in *Conflict at Colossae: A Problem in the Interpretation of Early Christianity, Illustrated by Selected Modern Studies*, edited by Wayne A. Meeks and Fred O. Francis. Society of Biblical Literature Sources for Biblical Study 4. Missoula: Scholars Press, 1975.

———. *James: A Commentary on the Epistle of James*. Rev. by Heinrich Greeven. Philadelphia: Fortress, 1976.

Dibelius, Martin, and Hans Conzelmann. *The Pastoral Epistles: A Commentary on the Pastoral Epistles*. Translated by Philip Buttolph and Adela Yarbro. Hermeneia. Philadelphia: Fortress, 1972.

Dill, Samuel. *Roman Society from Nero to Marcus Aurelius*. New York: Macmillan & Co, 1904; repr. Meridian, 1956.

Dindorf, Wilhelm, ed. *Aristides*. 3 vols. G. Reimder, 1829.

Dix, Gregory. *The Shape of the Liturgy*. New York: Seabury, 1982.

Doberstein, John W., ed. *Luther's Works*. Vol. 51, *Sermons 1*. Philadelphia: Fortress, 1959.

Dodds, E. R. *The Greeks and the Irrational*. Berkeley: University of California Press, 1966.

Dornier, Pierre. *Les Épîtres Pastorales*. Sources Biblique. Paris: Gabalda, 1969.

Doughty, Darrell J. "The Presence and Future of Salvation in Corinth." *ZNW* 66 (1975): 61–90.

Downs, David J. *The Offering of the Gentiles: Paul's Collection for Jerusalem in Its Chronological, Cultural, and Cultic Contexts*. Grand Rapids: Eerdmans, 2016.

Droge, Arthur J. "*Mori Lucrum*: Paul and Ancient Theories of Suicide." *NovT* 30 (1988): 263–86.

———. *A Noble Death: Suicide and Martyrdom among Christians and Jews in Antiquity*. San Francisco: HarperSanFrancisco, 1992.

Dugas, Ludovic. *L'amitié Antique d'après les Mœurs Populaires et les Théories des Philosophes*. Paris: Félix Alcan, 1914.

Duncan, J. Garrow. "*Pistos ho Logos*." *ExpTim* 35 (1923): 141.

Dunn, James D. G. *Romans 1–8*. WBC 38A. Grand Rapids: Zondervan, 1988.

———. *Romans 9–16*. WBC 38B. Grand Rapids: Zondervan, 1988.

———. *The Theology of Paul the Apostle*. Grand Rapids: Eerdmans, 1998.

Dupont, Jacques. *Syn Christōi: L'union avec le Christ suivant Saint Paul*. Bruges: Éditions de l'Abbaye de Saint-André, 1952.

Durkheim, Émile. *The Elementary Forms of Religious Life*. Translated by Joseph F. Swain. New York: Free Press, 1915.

Eastman, Susan Grove. *Paul and the Person: Reframing Paul's Anthropology*. Grand Rapids: Eerdmans, 2017.

Eglinger, Ruth. "Der Begriff der Freundschaft in der Philosophie: Eine historische Untersuchung." PhD diss., University of Basel, 1916.

Eichhorn, Johann Gottfried. *Einleitung in das Neue Testament*. Leipzig: Weidmannischen Buchhandlung, 1810.

Eitrem, Samson. "Embateuō: Note sur Col 2:18." *Studia Theologica* 2 (1949): 90–94.

Eliade, Mircea. *Cosmos and History: The Myth of the Eternal Return*. New York: Harper & Row, 1959.

———, ed. *The Encyclopedia of Religion*. New York: Macmillan, 1987.

———. *Le Chamanisme et les Techniques Archaïques de l'Extase*. Paris: Payot, 1951.

———. *Rites and Symbols of Initiation: The Mysteries of Birth and Rebirth*. Translated by Willard R. Trask. New York: Harper & Row, 1958.

———. *The Sacred and the Profane: The Nature of Religion*. Translated by Willard R. Trask. New York: Harcourt, Brace & World, 1957.

Elliott, Mark W. *Galatians in Christian Theology: Justification, the Gospel, and Ethics in Paul's Letter*. Grand Rapids: Baker Academic, 2014.

Ellis, E. Earle. "Paul and His Opponents." Pages 268–98 in *Christianity, Judaism, and Other Greco-Roman Cults: Studies for Morton Smith at Sixty*, edited by Jacob Neusner, vol. 1. Studies in Judaism in Late Antiquity 12. Leiden: Brill, 1975.

———. *Paul and His Recent Interpreters*. Grand Rapids: Eerdmans, 1961.

Eltester, Friedrich W. *Eikon im Neuen Testament*. BZNW 23. Berlin: Töpelmann, 1958.

Epictetus. *Discourses, Books 1–2.* Translated by W. A. Oldfather. 2 vols. LCL. Cambridge, MA: Harvard University Press, 1925.

Esler, Philip F. *The First Christians in Their Social Worlds: Social-Scientific Approaches to New Testament Interpretation.* London: Routledge, 1994.

———. "Glossolalia and the Admission of Gentiles into the Early Christian Community." Pages 37–51 in *The First Christians in Their Social Worlds.*

Evans, Craig A. "The Colossian Mystics." *Bib* 63 (1982): 188–205.

Fascher, Erich. *Prophētēs: Eine sprach- und religionsgeschichtliche Untersuchung.* Giessen: Töpelmann, 1927.

Fee, Gordon D. *The First Epistle to the Corinthians.* NICNT. Grand Rapids: Eerdmans, 1987.

———. "Philippians 2:5–11: Hymn or Exalted Pauline Prose." *BBR* 2 (1992): 29–46.

Feinberg, Paul D. "The Kenosis and Christology: An Exegetical-Theological Analysis of Phil 2:6–11." *TJ* 1 (1980): 21–46.

Festinger, Leon. *When Prophecy Fails: A Social and Psychological Study of a Modern Group That Predicted the End of the World.* New York: Harper, 1956.

Feuillet, André. "L'hymne Christologique de l'Épitre aux Philippiens (II, 6–11)." *RB* 72 (1965): 352–80, 481–507.

Fiore, Benjamin. *The Function of Personal Example in the Socratic and Pastoral Epistles.* Analecta Biblica 105. Rome: Biblical Institute Press, 1986.

Fisher, Nicolas R. E. *Hybris: A Study in the Values of Honour and Shame in Ancient Greece.* Warminster: Aris & Phillips, 1992.

Fitzgerald, John T. *Cracks in an Earthen Vessel: An Examination of the Catalogues of Hardship in the Corinthian Correspondence.* SBLDS 99. Atlanta: Scholars Press, 1988.

———. *Greco-Roman Perspectives on Friendship.* Society of Biblical Literature Resources for Biblical Study 34. Atlanta: Scholars Press, 1997.

———. "Paul and Paradigm Shifts: Reconciliation and Its Linkage Group." Pages 241–62 in *Paul beyond the Judaism/Hellenism Divide,* edited by Troels Engberg-Pedersen. Louisville: Westminster John Knox, 2001.

———. "Paul, the Ancient Epistolary Theorists, and 2 Corinthians 10–13: The Purpose and Literary Genre of a Pauline Letter." Pages 190–200 in *Greeks, Romans, and Christians: Essays in Honor of Abraham J. Malherbe,* edited by David L. Balch, Everett Ferguson, Wayne A. Meeks. Minneapolis: Fortress, 1990.

Fitzgerald, John T., and L. Michael White. *The Tabula of Cebes.* SBLTT 24. Chico, CA: Scholars Press, 1983.

Fitzmyer, Joseph A. *Paul and His Theology: A Brief Sketch.* Englewood Cliffs: Prentice Hall, 1989.

———. *Romans: A New Translation with Introduction and Commentary.* AYB 33. New York: Doubleday, 1992.

———. "'To Know Him and the Power of His Resurrection' (Phil 3:10)." Pages 411–25 in *Mélanges Bibliques en Hommage au R. P. Béda Rigaux*, edited by Albert Descamps and Andre de Halleux. Gembloux: Duculot, 1970.

Flint, Peter W., and James C. VanderKam. *The Dead Sea Scrolls after Fifty Years: A Comprehensive Assessment.* Leiden: Brill, 1998.

Forbes, Christopher. "Early Christian Inspired Speech and Hellenistic Popular Religion." *NovT* 28 (1986): 257–70.

Ford, J. Massingberd. "Toward a Theology of 'Speaking in Tongues.'" *Theological Studies* 32 (1971): 3–29.

Foskett, Mary F. "A Virgin Conceived: Virginity as a Character-Indicator in Luke-Acts and the Protevangelium of James." PhD diss., Emory University, 1995.

Foster, John. *Natural History of Enthusiasm.* 7th ed. London: Holdsworth and Ball, 1834.

Foucault, Michel. *Discipline and Punish: The Birth of the Prison.* New York: Vintage Books, 1979.

———. *The History of Sexuality.* Translated by Robert Hurley. New York: Vintage Books, 1980.

Fowl, Stephen E. *The Story of Christ in the Ethics of Paul: An Analysis of the Function of the Hymnic Material in the Pauline Corpus.* JSNTSup 36. Sheffield: Sheffield Academic, 1990.

Francis, Fred O. "The Background of *Embateuein* (Col 2:18) in Legal Papyri and Oracle Inscriptions." Pages 197–207 in Meeks and Francis, *Conflict at Colossae.*

———. "The Christological Argument of Colossians." Pages 192–208 in Jervell and Meeks, *God's Christ and His People.*

———. "Humility and Angelic Worship in Col. 2:18." Pages 163–95 in Meeks and Francis, *Conflict at Colossae.*

Freedman, David Noel. *The Anchor Bible Dictionary.* 6 vols. New York: Doubleday, 1992.

Freud, Sigmund. "Obsessive Acts and Religious Practices." Pages 9:117–27 in *The Standard Edition of the Complete Psychological Works of Sigmund Freud*, edited by James Strachey. 24 vols. London: Hogarth, 1966–1974.

Friedan, Betty. *The Feminine Mystique.* New York: Norton, 1963.

Froehlich, Karlfried. *Biblical Interpretation from the Church Fathers to the Reformation*. Burlington, VT: Ashgate, 2010.

Fromm, Erich. *Escape from Freedom*. New York: Farrar & Rinehart, 1941.

Furness, J. M. "The Authorship of Philippians ii. 6–11." *ExpTim* 70 (1959): 240–43.

Furnish, Victor Paul. "Pauline Studies." Pages 321–50 in *The New Testament and Its Modern Interpreters*, edited by Eldon Jay Epp and George W. MacRae. Society of Biblical Literature the Bible and Its Modern Interpreters 3. Atlanta: Scholars Press, 1989.

———. *Theology and Ethics in Paul*. Nashville: Abingdon, 1968.

———. *II Corinthians*. AYB 32A. Garden City, NY: Doubleday, 1984.

Gagnon, Robert A. J. *The Bible and Homosexual Practice: Texts and Hermeneutics*. Nashville: Abingdon, 2001.

Gamber, Klaus. "Der Christus-Hymnus im Philipperbrief in liturgiegeschichtlicher Sicht." *Bib* 51 (1970): 369–76.

Garland, David E. "The Composition and Unity of Philippians: Some Neglected Literary Factors." *NovT* 27 (1985): 141–73.

Garrett, Clarke. *Spirit Possession and Popular Religion: From the Camisards to the Shakers*. Baltimore: Johns Hopkins University Press, 1987.

Gärtner, Bertil E. *The Temple and the Community in Qumran and the New Testament: A Comparative Study of the Temple Symbolism of the Qumran Texts and the New Testament*. SNTSMS 1. Cambridge: Cambridge University Press, 1965.

Geertz, Clifford. "Religion as a Cultural System" Pages 88–125 in *The Interpretation of Cultures: Selected Essays*. New York: Basic Books, 1973.

Gench, Frances Taylor. *Encountering God in Tyrannical Texts: Reflections on Paul, Women, and the Authority of Scripture*. Louisville: Westminster John Knox, 2015.

Gennep, Arnold van. *The Rites of Passage*. Translated by Monika B. Vizedom and Gabrielle L. Caffe. Chicago: University of Chicago Press, 1960.

Georgi, Dieter. "Der vorpaulinishe Hymnus Phil ii. 6–11." Pages 263–93 in *Zeit und Geschichte: Dankesgabe an Rudolf Bultmann zum 80. Geburtstag*, edited by Erich Dinkler. Tübingen: Mohr, 1964.

———. *The Opponents of Paul in 2 Corinthians: A Study of Religious Propaganda in Late Antiquity*. Rev. ed. Philadelphia: Fortress, 1985.

———. *Remembering the Poor: The History of Paul's Collection for Jerusalem*. Nashville: Abingdon, 1992.

Gignac, Alan. "Lorsque Paul 'Raconte' Abraham, Agar et L'Autre Femme: Narrativité et Intertextualité en Ga 4,21–5,1." Pages 463–80 in *Analyse Narrative et Bible: Deuxième Colloque International du RRENAB,*

Louvain-la-Neuve, Avril 2004, edited by Camille Focant and André Wénin. BETL 191. Leuven: Leuven University Press, 2005.

Gillespie, Thomas W. *The First Theologians: A Study in Early Christian Prophecy*. Grand Rapids: Eerdmans, 1994.

Gillman, John. "Transformation in 1 Cor 15:50–53." *Ephemerides Theologicae Lovanienses* 58 (1982): 309–33.

Gladd, Benjamin L. *Revealing the Mysterion: The Use of Mystery in Daniel and Second Temple Judaism with Its Bearing on First Corinthians*. BZNW 160. Berlin: De Gruyter, 2009.

Gloer, Hulitt W. "Homologies and Hymns in the New Testament: Form, Content, and Criteria for Identification." *PRSt* 11 (1984): 115–32.

Gnilka, Joachim. "Die Antipaulinische Mission in Philippi." *BZ* 9 (1965): 258–76.

Gonzalez, Heliodora E. "The Theology and Psychology of Glossolalia." PhD diss., Northwestern University, 1978.

Gooch, Peter D. *Dangerous Food: 1 Corinthians 8–10 in Its Context*. SCJ 5. Waterloo, ON: Wilfrid Laurier University Press, 1993.

Goodenough, Erwin R. *By Light, Light: The Mystic Gospel of Hellenistic Judaism*. New Haven: Yale University Press, 1935.

———. *An Introduction to Philo Judæus*. 2nd ed. New York: Barnes & Noble, 1963.

———. *Jewish Symbols in the Greco-Roman Period*. 13 vols. Bollingen Series 37. New York: Pantheon, 1953.

Goodman, Felicitas D. *Speaking in Tongues: A Cross-Cultural Study of Glossolalia*. Chicago: University of Chicago Press, 1972.

Goppelt, Leonhard. *Theology of the New Testament*. 2 vols. Grand Rapids: Eerdmans, 1982.

Goranson Jacob, Haley. *Conformed to the Image of His Son: Reconsidering Paul's Theology of Glory in Romans*. Downers Grove, IL: IVP Academic, 2018.

Gordley, Matthew E. *New Testament Christological Hymns: Exploring Texts, Contexts, and Significance*. Downers Grove, IL: IVP Academic, 2018.

Grayston, Kenneth. "The Opponents in Philippians 3." *ExpTim* 97 (1986): 170–72.

Grenz, Stanley. "Theological Foundations for Male-Female Relationships." *Journal of the Evangelical Theological Society* 41 (1998): 615–30.

Grieb, A. Katherine. *The Story of Romans: A Narrative Defense of God's Righteousness*. Louisville: Westminster John Knox, 2002.

Griffiths, J. Gwyn, ed. *The Isis-Book (Metamorphoses, Book XI)*. Etudes préliminaires aux religions orientales dans l'empire romain 39. Leiden: Brill, 1975.

Grudem, Wayne A. *The Gift of Prophecy in 1 Corinthians*. Washington, DC: University Press of America, 1982.

Gundry, Robert H. "'Ecstatic Utterance' (N. E. B.)?" *JTS* 17 (1966): 299–307.

———. *Sōma in Biblical Theology: With Emphasis on Pauline Anthropology*. SNTSMS 29. Cambridge: Cambridge University Press, 1976.

Gunkel, Hermann. *The Influence of the Holy Spirit: The Popular View of the Apostolic Age and the Teaching of the Apostle Paul; A Biblical-Theologial Study*. Translated by R. A. Harrisville and P. A. Quanbeck II. Philadelphia: Fortress, 1979.

Hall, Robert G. "The Rhetorical Outline for Galatians: A Reconsideration." *JBL* 106 (1987): 277–87.

Hamm, M. Dennis. "Acts 3:1–10: The Healing of the Temple Beggar as Lukan Theology." *Bib* 67 (1986): 305–19.

———. "Luke 19:8 Once Again: Does Zacchaeus Defend or Resolve?" *JBL* 107 (1988): 431–37.

———. "This Sign of Healing, Acts 3:1–10: A Study in Lucan Theology." PhD diss., St. Louis University, 1975.

Hanson, Anthony Tyrrell. "The Conquest of the Powers." Pages 1–12 in *Studies in Paul's Technique and Theology*. Grand Rapids: Eerdmans, 1974.

Harker, Christina. *The Colonizers' Idols: Paul, Galatia, and Empire in New Testament Studies*. WUNT 2.460. Tübingen: Mohr Siebeck, 2018.

Harland, Philip A. *Associations, Synagogues, and Congregations: Claiming a Place in Ancient Mediterranean Society*. Minneapolis: Fortress, 2003.

Harmon, Matthew S. *She Must and Shall Go Free: Paul's Isaianic Gospel in Galatians*. BZNW 168. Berlin: De Gruyter, 2010.

Harpur, Tom W. "The Gift of Tongues and Interpretation." *Canadian Journal of Theology* 12 (1966): 164–71.

Harris, J. Rendel. "Epaphroditus, Scribe and Courier." *Expositor* 8 (1898): 101–10.

Harris, Murray J. "Titus 2:13 and the Deity of Christ." Pages 262–77 in *Pauline Studies: Essays Presented to Professor F. F. Bruce on His 70th Birthday*, edited by Donald A. Hagner and Murray J. Harris. Grand Rapids: Eerdmans, 1980.

Harrisville, Roy A. "Speaking in Tongues: A Lexicographical Study." *CBQ* 38 (1976): 35–48.

Hart, David Bentley. *The New Testament: A Translation*. New Haven: Yale University Press, 2017.

Harvey, A. E. "The Opposition of Paul." Pages 319–32 in *Studia Evangel-*

ica IV (= Texta Untersuchengen 102), edited by F. L. Cross. Berlin: Akademie, 1968.

————. *Renewal through Suffering: A Study of 2 Corinthians.* SNTW. Edinburgh: T&T Clark, 1996.

Harvey, John. "A New Look at the Christ-Hymn in Phil 2.6–11." *ExpTim* 76 (1965): 337–39.

Hauerwas, Stanley. *Unleashing the Scripture: Freeing the Bible from Captivity to America.* Nashville: Abingdon, 1993.

Hawthorne, Gerald F. "The Interpretation and Translation of Philippians 1:28b." *ExpTim* 95 (1983): 80–81.

Hay, David M. *Glory at the Right Hand: Psalm 110 in Early Christianity.* SBLMS 18. Nashville: Abingdon, 1973.

————, ed. *Pauline Theology.* Vol. 2, *1 & 2 Corinthians.* Society of Biblical Literature Symposium Series 22. Atlanta: Society of Biblical Literature, 2002.

Hays, Richard B. "Christology and Ethics in Galatians: The Law of Christ." *CBQ* 49 (1987): 268–90.

————. "Christ Prays the Psalm." Pages 122–36 in *The Future of Christology: Essays in Honor of Leander E. Keck,* edited by Abraham J. Malherbe and Wayne A. Meeks. Minneapolis: Fortress, 1993.

————. *Echoes of Scripture in the Letters of Paul.* New Haven: Yale University Press, 1989.

————. *The Faith of Jesus Christ: The Narrative Substructure of Galatians 3:1–4:11.* SBLDS 56. Chico, CA: Scholars Press, 1983.

————. "*PISTIS* and Paul's Christology: What Is at Stake?" Pages 714–29 in *Pauline Theology,* vol. 4, edited by E. E. Johnson and D. M. Hay. Atlanta: Scholars Press, 1997.

————. "Psalm 143 and the Logic of Romans 3." *JBL* 99 (1980): 107–15.

Hebert, Gabriel. "'Faithfulness' and 'Faith.'" *Theology* 58 (1955): 373–79.

Heil, John. *Philosophy of Mind: A Contemporary Introduction.* 2nd ed. New York: Routledge, 2004.

Heim, David. "Homosexuality, Marriage, and the Church: A Conversation with Luke Johnson, David Matzko, and Max Stackhouse." *Christian Century* 115 (1998): 644–50.

Heitmüller, D. "Zum Problem Paulus und Jesus." *ZNW* 13 (1912): 320–37.

Heliso, Desta. *Pistis and the Righteous One: A Study of Romans 1:17 against the Backdrop of Scripture and Second Temple Jewish Literature.* WUNT 2.235. Tübingen: Mohr Siebeck, 2007.

Helminiak, Daniel A. *What the Bible Really Says about Homosexuality.* San Francisco: Alamo Square, 1994.

Hengel, Martin. *Crucifixion in the Ancient World and the Folly of the Message of the Cross.* London: SCM, 1977.

———. "Hymns and Christology." Pages 78–96 in *Between Jesus and Paul: Studies in the Earliest History of Christianity.* Philadelphia: Fortress, 1983.

Henning, Meghan. *Educating Early Christians through the Rhetoric of Hell: "Weeping and Gnashing of Teeth" in Matthew and the Early Church.* WUNT 2.382. Tübingen: Mohr Siebeck, 2014.

Hercher, Rudolf. *Epistolographi Graeci.* Bibliotheca Scriptorum Graecorum. Paris: Didot, 1873.

Héring, Jean. *La Première Épitre de Saint Paul aux Corinthiens.* Neuchatel: Delachaux & Niestle, 1959.

Hess, Eckhard H. *Imprinting: Early Experience and Developmental Psychobiology of Attachment.* Behavioral Science Series. New York: Van Nostrand Reinhold, 1973.

Heyd, Michael. *"Be Sober and Reasonable": The Critique of Enthusiasm in the Seventeenth and Early Eighteenth Centuries.* Brill's Studies in Intellectual History 63. Leiden: Brill, 1995.

Hickling, Colin J. A. "Baptism in the First-Century Churches: A Case for Caution." Pages 249–67 in *The Bible in Three Dimensions: Essays in Celebration of Forty Years of Biblical Studies at the University of Sheffield,* edited by David J. A. Clines, Stephen E. Fowl, and Stanley E. Porter. Journal for the Study of the Old Testament Supplement Series 87. Sheffield: JSOT Press, 1990.

Himmelfarb, Martha. *Ascent to Heaven in Jewish and Christian Apocalypses.* New York: Oxford University Press, 1993.

Hine, Virginia H. "Pentecostal Glossolalia toward a Functional Interpretation." *JSSR* 8 (1969): 211–26.

Hinson, E. Glenn. "The Significance of Glossolalia in the History of Christianity." Pages 61–80 in Mills, *Speaking in Tongues: Let's Talk about It.*

Hock, Ronald F. *The Social Context of Paul's Ministry: Tentmaking and Apostleship.* Philadelphia: Fortress, 1980.

Hofius, Otfried. *Der Christushymnus Philipper 2, 6–11: Untersuchungen zu Gestalt und Aussage eines urchristlichen Psalms.* WUNT 17. Tübingen: Mohr Siebeck, 1976.

Holladay, Carl R. "I Corinthians 13: Paul as Apostolic Paradigm." Pages 80–98 in Balch, Ferguson, and Meeks, *Greeks, Romans and Christians.*

———. *Fragments from Hellenistic Jewish Authors.* SBLTT 20. Chico, CA: Scholars Press, 1983.

———. "Paul's Opponents in Philippians 3." *Restoration Quarterly* 12 (1969): 77–90.

Holmes, Christopher T. *The Function of Sublime Rhetoric in Hebrews: A Study of Heb 12:18–29.* WUNT 2.465. Tübingen: Mohr Siebeck, 2018.

Hooker, Morna D. "Philippians 2:6–11." Pages 151–64 in *Jesus und Paulus: Festschrift f. Werner Georg Kümmel z. 70. Geburstag*, edited by E. Earle Ellis and Erich Grässer. Göttingen: Vandenhoeck & Ruprecht, 1975.

Horrell, David G. *The Social Ethos of the Corinthian Correspondence: Interests and Ideology from 1 Corinthians to 1 Clement.* SNTW. Edinburgh: T&T Clark, 1996.

Horsley, Richard A. "'How Can Some of You Say That There Is No Resurrection of the Dead?' Spiritual Elitism in Corinth." *NovT* 20 (1978): 203–31.

Howard, George. *Paul: Crisis in Galatia; A Study in Early Christian Theology.* SNTSMS 35. Cambridge: Cambridge University Press, 1989.

———. "Phil 2:6–11 and the Human Christ." *CBQ* 40 (1978): 368–87.

Hultgren, Arland J. "The *Pistis Christou* Formulations in Paul." *NovT* 22 (1980): 248–63.

Hunt, Allen R. *The Inspired Body: Paul, the Corinthians, and Divine Inspiration.* Macon, GA: Mercer University Press, 1996.

Hurd, John C. *The Origin of I Corinthians.* Macon, GA: Mercer University Press, 1983.

Hurst, Lincoln D. "Re-enter the Pre-existent Christ in Philippians 2.5–11?" *NTS* 32 (1986): 449–57.

Hurtado, Larry W. "The Jerusalem Collection and the Book of Galatians." *JSNT* 2 (1979): 46–62.

———. "Jesus as Lordly Example in Philippians 2:5–11." Pages 113–26 in *From Jesus to Paul: Studies in Honour of Francis Wright Beare*, edited by John C. Hurd and Peter Richardson. Canadian Electronic Library. Books Collection. Waterloo, ON: Wilfrid Laurier University Press, 1984.

Hutch, Richard A. "The Personal Ritual of Glossolalia." *JSSR* 19 (1980): 255–66.

Hylen, Susan. *Women in the New Testament World.* Essentials of Biblical Studies. New York: Oxford University Press, 2019.

Ibita, Marilou S. "Mending a Broken Relationship: The Social Relations and the Symbolic Universe of 2 Corinthians 1–7." Pages 43–68 in Bieringer et al., *Theologizing in the Corinthian Conflict.*

Isocrates. *Isocrates.* Translated by George Norlin. LCL. Cambridge, MA: Harvard University Press, 1928.

Jackson, Timothy P. "A House Divided Again: 'Sanctity' vs. 'Dignity' in the Induced Death Debate." Pages 139–63 in *In Defense of Human Dignity: Essays for Our Times*, edited by Robert P. Kraynak and Glenn E. Tinder. Notre Dame, IN: University of Notre Dame Press, 2003.

Jaeger, Werner. *Paideia: The Ideals of Greek Culture*. Translated by Gilbert Highet. 3 vols. New York: Oxford University Press, 1943.

Jaworski, William. *Philosophy of Mind: A Comprehensive Introduction*. Chichester: Wiley-Blackwell, 2011.

Jenkins, Philip. *Mystics and Messiahs: Cults and New Religions in American History*. Oxford: Oxford University Press, 2001.

Jeremias, Joachim. *The Central Message of the New Testament*. New York: Scribner's Sons, 1965.

Jervell, Jacob. *Imago Dei: Gen 1, 26 f. im Spätjudentum, in der Gnosis und in den paulinischen Briefen*. FRLANT 58. Göttingen: Vandenhoeck & Ruprecht, 1960.

———. *Luke and the People of God*. Minneapolis: Augsburg, 1972.

Jervell, Jacob, and Wayne A. Meeks, eds. *God's Christ and His People: Studies in Honor of Nils Alstrup Dahl*. Oslo: Universitetsforlaget, 1977.

Jewett, Robert. "The Agitators and the Galatian Congregation." *NTS* 17 (1971): 198–212.

———. "Conflicting Movements in the Early Church as Reflected in Philippians." *NovT* 12 (1970): 362–90.

———. "Enthusiastic Radicalism and the Thessalonian Correspondence." Pages 181–232 in *The Society of Biblical Literature, 1972 Proceedings*. 2 vols. Missoula: Society of Biblical Literature, 1972.

———. *Paul's Anthropological Terms: A Study of Their Use in Conflict Settings*. Arbeiten zur Geschichte des antiken Judentums und des Urchristentums 10. Leiden: Brill, 1971.

———. "Tenement Churches and Communal Meals in the Early Church: Implications of a Form-Critical Analysis of 2 Thessalonians 3:10." *Biblical Research* 38 (1993): 23–43.

———. *The Thessalonian Correspondence: Pauline Rhetoric and Millenarian Piety*. Foundations and Facets. Philadelphia: Fortress, 1986.

Johanson, Bruce C. "Tongues, a Sign for Unbelievers? A Structural and Exegetical Study of I Corinthians XIV. 20–25 1." *NTS* 25 (1979): 180–203.

John Paul II, Pope. *Man and Woman He Created Them: A Theology of the Body*. Translated by Michael M. Waldstein. Boston: Pauline Books, 2006.

Johnson, Luke Timothy. "Abortion, Sexuality, and Catholicism's Public Presence." Pages 27–38 in *American Catholics, American Culture: Tradition and Resistance*, edited by Margaret O'Brien Steinfels. American Catholics in the Public Square 2. New York: Rowman & Littlefield, 2004.

——. *The Acts of the Apostles*. SP 5. Collegeville: Liturgical Press, 1992.

——. *Among the Gentiles: Greco-Roman Religion and Christianity*. New Haven: Yale University Press, 2009.

——. "The Biblical Foundations of Matrimony." *The Bible Today* 41 (2003): 113–16.

——. "Body Beautiful." *Commonweal* 133, no. 13 (2006): 24–25.

——. "The Body in Pain." Pages 107–29 in *The Revelatory Body: Theology as Inductive Art*. Grand Rapids: Eerdmans, 2015.

——. *Brother of Jesus, Friend of God: Studies in the Letter of James*. Grand Rapids: Eerdmans, 2004.

——. "Caring for the Earth: Why Environmentalism Needs Theology." *Commonweal* 132, no. 13 (2005): 16–20.

——. "The Church and Transgender Identity: Some Cautions, Some Possibilities." *Commonweal* 144, no. 5 (2017): 19–23.

——. "Debate and Discernment: Scripture and the Spirit (Disputed Questions: Homosexuality)." *Commonweal* 121, no. 2 (1994): 11–13.

——. *Decision Making in the Church: A Biblical Model*. Philadelphia: Fortress, 1983.

——. "A Disembodied 'Theology of the Body': John Paul II on Love, Sex, and Pleasure." *Commonweal* 128, no. 2 (2001): 11–17.

——. *Faith's Freedom: A Classic Spirituality for Contemporary Christians*. Minneapolis: Fortress, 1990.

——. *The First and Second Letters to Timothy*. AYB 35A. New York: Doubleday, 2001.

——. *1 Timothy, 2 Timothy, Titus*. John Knox Preaching Guides. Atlanta: John Knox, 1987.

——. *The Gospel of Luke*. SP 3. Collegeville: Liturgical Press, 1990.

——. "Imagining the World Scripture Imagines." *Modern Theology* 14 (1998): 165–80.

——. *Invitation to the New Testament Epistles III: A Commentary on Colossians, Ephesians, 1 Timothy, 2 Timothy, and Titus with Complete Text from the Jerusalem Bible*. New York: Doubleday, 1980.

——. "James' Significance for Early Christianity." Pages 1–23 in *Brother of Jesus, Friend of God*.

——. "James 3:13–4:10 and the *Topos Peri Phthonou*." *NovT* 25 (1983): 327–47.

——. "Jesus and the Little Children." *Priests and People* 17 (2003): 102–5.

———. "*Koinonia*: Diversity and Unity in Early Christianity." *Theology Digest* 46 (1999): 303–13.

———. *The Letter of James: A New Translation with Introduction and Commentary.* AYB 37A. Garden City, NY: Doubleday, 1995.

———. *Letters to Paul's Delegates: 1 Timothy, 2 Timothy, Titus.* New Testament in Context. Valley Forge, PA: Trinity International, 1996.

———. *The Literary Function of Possessions in Luke-Acts.* SBLDS 39. Missoula: Scholars Press, 1977.

———. *Living Jesus: Learning the Heart of the Gospel.* San Francisco: HarperSanFrancisco, 1999.

———. "Making Connections: The Material Expression of Friendship in the New Testament." *Int* 58 (2004): 158–71.

———. "Meals Are Where the Magic Is." Pages 137–79 in *Religious Experience in Earliest Christianity: A Missing Dimension in New Testament Studies.* Minneapolis: Fortress, 1998.

———. "The New Testament's Anti-Jewish Slander and the Conventions of Ancient Polemic." *JBL* 108 (1989): 419–41.

———. "Norms for True and False Prophecy in First Corinthians 12–14." *American Benedictine Review* 22 (1971): 29–45.

———. "Preaching the Resurrection." Pages 37–42 in *The Living Gospel.* New York: Continuum, 2004.

———. *Prophetic Jesus, Prophetic Church: The Challenge of Luke-Acts to Contemporary Christians.* Grand Rapids: Eerdmans, 2011.

———. *Reading Romans: A Literary and Theological Commentary.* Macon, GA: Smyth & Helwys, 2001.

———. *The Real Jesus: The Misguided Quest for the Historical Jesus and the Truth of the Traditional Gospels.* San Francisco: HarperSanFrancisco, 1996.

———. "Response to Margaret Mitchell." *Horizons in Biblical Theology* 21, no. 2 (1999): 140–44.

———. "The Revelatory Body: Notes Toward a Somatic Theology." Pages 69–85 in *The Phenomenology of the Body: The Twentieth Annual Symposium of the Simon Silverman Phenomenology Center.* Pittsburgh: Simon Silverman Phenomenology Center at the University of Duquesne, 2003.

———. *The Revelatory Body: Theology as Inductive Art.* Grand Rapids: Eerdmans, 2015.

———. Review of *Luke and the Pastoral Epistles,* by Stephen G. Wilson. *JBL* 101 (1982): 459–60.

———. Review of *Speaking the Christian God*, by Alvin F. Kimel, and *She Who Is*, by Elizabeth Johnson. *Commonweal* 120, no. 2 (1993): 17–22.

———. Review of Stephen G. Wilson, *Luke and the Pastoral Epistles*. *JBL* 101 (1982): 459–60.

———. *Scripture and Discernment: Decision Making in the Church*. Nashville: Abingdon, 1996.

———. "Scripture and Experience (Homosexuality and the Church: Two Views)." *Commonweal* 134, no. 2 (2007): 14–17.

———. "Scripture for the Life of the Church" Lecture at Boston College School of Theology and Ministry, 18 Oct 2018.

———. *Sharing Possessions: What Faith Demands*. 2nd ed. Grand Rapids: Eerdmans, 2011.

———. "Taciturnity and True Religion (James 1:26–27)." Pages 329–39 in Balch, Ferguson, and Meeks, *Greeks, Romans and Christians*.

———. "The *Topos Peri Phthonou*." Pages 182–201 in *Brother of Jesus, Friend of God*.

———. "What's Justice Got to Do with It?" *Commonweal* 134, no. 2 (2007): 25–27.

———. "Why Scripture Isn't Enough." *Commonweal* 124, no. 11 (1997): 23–25.

———. *The Writings of the New Testament: An Interpretation*. Philadelphia: Fortress, 1986.

———. *The Writings of the New Testament: An Interpretation*. 2nd ed. Minneapolis: Fortress, 1999.

———. *The Writings of the New Testament: An Interpretation*. 3rd ed. Minneapolis: Fortress, 2010.

Jones, Lawrence N. "The Black Pentecostal." Pages 145–58 in *The Charismatic Movement*, edited by Michael P. Hamilton. Grand Rapids: Eerdmans, 1975.

Jordan, Mark D. *The Invention of Sodomy in Christian Theology*. Chicago Series on Sexuality, History, and Society. Chicago: University of Chicago Press, 1997.

Julian, Emperor of Rome. *Works*. Translated by Wilmer C. Wright. LCL. Cambridge, MA: Harvard University Press, 1913.

Kahl, Brigitte. *Galatians Re-imagined: Reading with the Eyes of the Vanquished*. Minneapolis: Fortress, 2010.

Kanter, Rosabeth M. *Commitment and Community: Communes and Utopias in Sociological Perspective*. Cambridge, MA: Harvard University Press, 1972.

Karris, Robert J. "The Background and Significance of the Polemic of the Pastoral Epistles." *JBL* 92 (1973): 549–64.

———. "The Function and Sitz-im-Leben of the Parenetic Elements in the Pastoral Epistles." PhD diss., Harvard University, 1971.

Käsemann, Ernst. *Commentary on Romans*. Grand Rapids: Eerdmans, 1980.

———. "A Critical Analysis of Philippians 2:5–11." *Journal for Theology and the Church* 5 (1968): 45–88.

———. "Ministry and Community in the New Testament." Pages 63–94 in *Essays on New Testament Themes*, translated by W. J. Montague. SBT 41. London: SCM, 1964.

Kaye, B. N. "Eschatology and Ethics in 1 and 2 Thessalonians." *NovT* 17 (1975): 47–57.

Keck, Leander E., and James Louis Martyn, eds. *Studies in Luke-Acts: Essays Presented in Honor of Paul Schubert*. Philadelphia: Fortress, 1966.

Kelly, J. N. D. *A Commentary on the Pastoral Epistles: Timothy I & II, Titus*. Harper New Testament Commentary. New York: Harper & Row, 1963.

Kelsey, Morton T., ed. *Speaking with Tongues: An Experiment in Spiritual Experience*. London: Epworth, 1965.

Kerényi, Karl. *Eleusis: Archetypal Image of Mother and Daughter*. Bollingen Series 65.4. Princeton: Princeton University Press, 1991.

Khobnya, Svetlana. "Reconciliation Must Prevail: A Fresh Look at 2 Corinthians 5:14–6:2." *European Journal of Theology* 25 (2016): 128–36.

Kidd, Reggie M. "Titus as Apologia: Grace for Liars, Beasts, and Bellies." *HBT* 21 (1999): 185–209.

Kilby, Karen. *Balthasar: A (Very) Critical Introduction*. Grand Rapids: Eerdmans, 2012.

Kildahl, John P. "Psychological Observations." Pages 124–42 in *The Charismatic Movement*, edited by Michael P. Hamilton. Grand Rapids: Eerdmans, 1975.

———. *The Psychology of Speaking in Tongues*. New York: Harper & Row, 1972.

Kilpatrick, George D. "*BLEPETE*: Philippians 3:2." Pages 146–48 in *In Memoriam Paul Kahle*, edited by Matthew Black and Georg Fohrer. BZAW 103. Berlin: Töpelmann, 1968.

Kim, Seyoon. "2 Cor. 5:11–21 and the Origin of Paul's Concept of 'Reconciliation.'" *NovT* 39 (1997): 360–84.

Kirby, John C. *Ephesians, Baptism and Pentecost: An Inquiry into the Structure and Purpose of the Epistle to the Ephesians*. London: SPCK, 1968.

Kirk, G. S. *Myth: Its Meaning and Functions in Ancient and Other Cultures*. Sather Classical Lectures 40. Cambridge: Cambridge University Press, 1970.

Kittel, Gerhard, and Gerhard Friedrich, eds. *Theological Dictionary of the New Testament*. 10 vols. Grand Rapids: Eerdmans, 1964.

Klijn, A. F. J. "Paul's Opponents in Philippians III." *NovT* 7 (1965): 278–84.

Kloppenborg, John S. "Associations in the Greco-Roman World." Oxford Bibliographies. https://doi.org/10.1093/OBO/9780195393361-0064.

———. "Edwin Hatch, Churches and Collegia." Pages 212–38 in *Origins and Method: Towards a New Understanding of Judaism and Christianity: Essays in Honour of John C. Hurd*, edited by Bradley H. McLean. JSNTSup 86. Sheffield: JSOT Press, 1993. 212–38

———. "Greco-Roman *Thiasoi*, the *Ekklēsia* at Corinth, and Conflict Management." Pages 187–218 in *Redescribing Paul and the Corinthians*, edited by Ron Cameron and Merrill P. Miller. Early Christianity and Its Literature 5. Atlanta: Society of Biblical Literature, 2011.

Kloppenborg, John S., and Richard S. Ascough. *Greco-Roman Associations, Texts, Translations, and Commentary: Attica, Central Greece, Macedonia, Thrace*. BZNW 181. Berlin: De Gruyter, 2011.

Knight, George W., III. *The Pastoral Epistles: A Commentary on the Greek Text*. NIGTC. Grand Rapids: Eerdmans, 1992.

Knox, Ronald Arbuthnott. *Enthusiasm: A Chapter in the History of Religion, with Special Reference to the XVII and XVIII Centuries*. New York: Oxford University Press, 1950.

Koester, Helmut. "From Paul's Eschatology to the Apocalyptic Schemata of 2 Thessalonians." Pages 441–58 in R. Collins, *Thessalonian Correspondence*.

———. "The Purpose of the Polemic of a Pauline Fragment (Philippians III)." *NTS* 8 (1962): 317–32.

Kolenkow, Anitra Bingham. "Paul and His Opponents in 2 Cor 10–13: *Theioi Andres* and Spiritual Guides." Pages 351–74 in *Religious Propaganda and Missionary Competition in the New Testament World*, edited by Lukas Bormann, Kelly Del Tredici, and Angela Standhartinger. NovTSup 74. Leiden: Brill, 1994.

Konradt, Matthias. "Die Christonomie der Freiheit. Zu Paulus' Entfaltung seines ethischen Ansatzes in Gal 5,13–6,10." *Early Christianity* 1 (2010): 60–81.

Konstan, David, ed. *Friendship in the Classical World*. Cambridge: Cambridge University Press, 1997.

Koopman, Niels. *Ancient Greek Ekphrasis: Between Description and Narration; Five Linguistic and Narratological Case Studies*. Amsterdam Studies in Classical Philology 26. Leiden: Brill, 2018.

Koperski, V. "The Early History of the Dissection of Philippians." *JTS* 44 (1993): 599–603.

Koskenniemi, Heikki. *Studien zur Idee und Phraseologie des Griechischen Briefes bis 400 n. Chr.* Helsinki: Suomalainen Tiedeakatemia, 1956.

Kraftchick, Steven J. "Death in Us, Life in You: The Apostolic Medium." Pages 156–81 in Hay, *Pauline Theology*, vol. 2, *1 & 2 Corinthians*.

———. "A Necessary Detour: Paul's Metaphorical Understanding of the Philippian Hymn." *HBT* 15, no. 1 (1993): 1–37.

Kroeger, Richard, and Catherine Kroeger. "An Inquiry into Evidence of Maenadism in the Corinthian Congregation." Pages 331–462 in *Society of Biblical Literature 1978 Seminar Papers*, vol. 2, edited by Paul J. Achtemeier. SBLSP 14. Missoula: Scholars Press, 1978.

Kümmel, Werner Georg. *Introduction to the New Testament*. Translated by Paul Feine. Rev. ed. Nashville: Abingdon, 1975.

———. *The Theology of the New Testament according to Its Major Witnesses: Jesus-Paul-John*. Nashville: Abingdon, 1973.

Kurz, William S. "Kenotic Imitation of Paul and Christ in Phil 2 and 3." Pages 103–26 in Segovia, *Discipleship in the New Testament*.

———. *Reading Luke-Acts: Dynamics of Biblical Narrative*. Louisville: Westminster John Knox, 1993.

Ladd, George Eldon. *A Theology of the New Testament*. Grand Rapids: Eerdmans, 1974.

La Fontaine, Jean S. *Initiation*. Harmondsworth: Penguin, 1985.

Lambert, Craig. "The Way We Eat Now." *Harvard Magazine* 106, no. 5 (2004): 50–58, 98–99.

Lambrecht, Jan. "Paul's Coherent Admonition in Galatians 6,1–6: Mutual Help and Individual Attentiveness." *Bib* 78 (1997): 33–56.

———. "Strength in Weakness: A Reply to Scott B. Andrews' Exegesis of 2 Cor 11.23b–33." *NTS* 43 (1997): 285–90.

Lampe, G. W. H. *The Seal of the Spirit: A Study in the Doctrine of Baptism and Confirmation in the New Testament and the Fathers*. 2nd ed. London: SPCK, 1967.

Lau, Andrew Y. *Manifest in the Flesh: The Epiphany Christology of the Pastoral Letters*. WUNT 2.86. Tübingen: Mohr Siebeck, 1996.

Lau, Te-Li. *The Politics of Peace: Ephesians, Dio Chrysostom, and the Confucian Four Books*. NovTSup 133. Leiden: Brill, 2010.

Laub, Franz. "Paulinische Autorität in nachapostolischer Zeit (2 Thess)." Pages 403–17 in R. Collins, *Thessalonian Correspondence*.

Laurentin, René. *Catholic Pentecostalism*. New York: Doubleday, 1977.

Lawless, Elaine J. *Handmaidens of the Lord: Pentecostal Women Preachers and Traditional Religion*. Publications of the American Folklore Society 2/9. Philadelphia: University of Pennsylvania Press, 1988.

Lee, E. Kenneth. "Words Denoting 'Pattern' in the New Testament." *NTS* 8 (1962): 166–73.

Lee, Yeong Mee, and Yoon Jong Yoo, eds. *Mapping and Engaging the Bible in Asian Culture: Congress of the Society of Asia for Biblical Studies 2008 Conference*. Korea: Christian Literature Society of Korea, 2009.

Leenhardt, Franz J. *The Epistle to the Romans: A Commentary*. New York: World, 1957.

Leeuw, G. van der. *Religion in Essence and Manifestation: A Study in Phenomenology*. Translated by John E. Turner. New York: Harper & Row, 1933.

Lévinas, Emmanuel. *Alterity and Transcendence*. New York: Columbia University Press, 1999.

Lewis, I. M. *Ecstatic Religion: An Anthropological Study of Spirit Possession and Shamanism*. Baltimore: Penguin, 1971.

Lightfoot, J. B. *St. Paul's Epistle to the Galatians: A Revised Text with Introduction, Notes, and Dissertations*. 3rd ed. London: Macmillan, 1914.

Lincoln, Andrew T. "Ephesians 2:8–10: A Summary of Paul's Gospel?" *CBQ* 45 (1983): 617–30.

Lindars, Barnabas. *New Testament Apologetic: The Doctrinal Significance of Old Testament Quotations*. Philadelphia: Westminster, 1961.

Lindemann, Andreas. "Zum Abfassungszweck des Zweiten Thessalonicherbriefes." *ZNW* 68 (1977): 35–47.

Ljungman, Henrik. *Pistis: A Study of Its Presuppositions and Its Meaning in Pauline Use*. Lund: Gleerup, 1964.

Lock, Walter. *A Critical and Exegetical Commentary on the Pastoral Epistles*. New York: Scribner, 1924.

Lohse, Eduard. *Colossians and Philemon: A Commentary on the Epistles to the Colossians and to Philemon*. Translated by William R. Poehlmann and Robert J. Karris. Hermeneia. Philadelphia: Fortress, 1971.

———. "Pauline Theology in the Letter to the Colossians 1." *NTS* 15 (1969): 211–20.

Loisy, Alfred. *Les Mystères Païens et le Mystère Chrétien*. 2nd ed. Paris: Nourry, 1930.

Longenecker, Bruce W., ed. *Narrative Dynamics in Paul: A Critical Assessment*. Louisville: Westminster John Knox, 2002.

———. "Sharing in Their Spiritual Blessings: The Stories of Israel in Galatians and Romans." Pages 58–84 in B. Longenecker, *Narrative Dynamics in Paul*.

Longenecker, Richard N. "The Nature of Paul's Early Eschatology." *NTS* 31 (1985): 85–95.

Löning, Karl. "Der 'Paulinismus' in der Apostelgeschichte: Ein forschungsgeschichtlicher Überblick." Pages 202–32 in *Paulinismus in der Apostelgeschichte*, edited by Karl Kertelge. QD 89. Freiburg im Breisgau: Herder, 1981.

Loubser, Gysbert M. *Paul Cries Freedom in Galatia! On Ethics in the New Creation*. Theology in Africa 6. Zurich: LIT, 2017.

Lozada, Francisco. *Toward a Latino/a Biblical Interpretation*. SBLSBS 91. Atlanta: SBL Press, 2017.

Lucaites, John Louis, Celeste Michelle Condit, and Sally Caudill. *Contemporary Rhetorical Theory: A Reader*. Revisioning Rhetoric. New York: Guilford, 1999.

Lucian, of Samosata. *Lucian*. Translated by A. M. Harmon. 8 vols. LCL. Cambridge, MA: Harvard University Press, 1921.

Luck, Georg. *Arcana Mundi: Magic and the Occult in the Greek and Roman Worlds*. Baltimore: Johns Hopkins University Press, 1985.

Lull, David John. *The Spirit in Galatia: Paul's Interpretation of PNEUMA as Divine Power*. SBLDS 49. Chico, CA: Scholars Press, 1980.

Lütgert, Wilhelm. *Die Irrlehrer der Pastoralbriefe*. Beiträge zur Förderung christlicher Theologie 13. Gütersloh: Bertelsmann, 1909.

Luther, Martin. *Three Treatises*. Translated by W. A. Lambert. Philadelphia: Fortress, 1957.

Lyotard, Jean-François. *The Postmodern Condition: A Report on Knowledge*. Theory and History of Literature 10. Minneapolis: University of Minnesota Press, 1984.

MacDonald, Dennis R. "Virgins, Widows, and Paul in Second-Century Asia Minor." Pages 165–84 in *Society of Biblical Literature 1979 Seminar Papers*, vol. 1., edited by Paul J. Achtemeier. SBLSP 16. Missoula: Scholars Press, 1979.

MacDonald, Margaret Y. *The Pauline Churches: A Socio-Historical Study of Institutionalization in the Pauline and Deutero-Pauline Writings*. SNTSMS 60. Cambridge: Cambridge University Press, 1988.

———. *The Power of Children: The Construction of Christian Families in the Greco-Roman World*. Waco: Baylor University Press, 2014.

MacDonald, William G. "Glossolalia in the New Testament." *Bulletin of the Evangelical Theological Society* 7 (1964): 59–68.

———. "The Place of Glossolalia in Neo-Pentecostalism." Pages 81–93 in Kelsey, *Speaking with Tongues*.

Mack, Burton L. *A Myth of Innocence: Mark and Christian Origins*. Philadelphia: Fortress, 1988.

———. *Who Wrote the New Testament? The Making of the Christian Myth*. San Francisco: HarperSanFrancisco, 1995.

Macmullen, Ramsay. *Enemies of the Roman Order*. Cambridge, MA: Harvard University Press, 1966.

Malherbe, Abraham J. "Ancient Epistolary Theorists." *Ohio Journal of Religious Studies* 5 (1977): 3–77.

———. "The Beasts at Ephesus." Pages 79–89 in *Paul and the Popular Philosophers*.

———. "Exhortation in 1 Thessalonians." Pages 35–66 in *Paul and the Popular Philosophers*.

———. "'Gentle as a Nurse': The Cynic Background to I Thess II." *NovT* 12 (1970): 203–17.

———. "Hellenistic Moralists and the New Testament." *ANRW* 26.1:675–750. Part 2, *Principat*, 26.1. Edited by H. Temporini and W. Haase. New York: De Gruyter, 1989.

———. *The Letters to the Thessalonians: A New Translation with Introduction and Commentary*. AYB 32B. New York: Doubleday, 2000.

———. "*Mē Genoito* in the Diatribe and Paul." Pages 25–34 in *Paul and the Popular Philosophers*.

———. *Moral Exhortation: A Greco-Roman Sourcebook*. Library of Early Christianity 4. Philadelphia: Westminster, 1986.

———. *Paul and the Popular Philosophers*. Minneapolis: Fortress, 1989.

———. *Paul and the Thessalonians: The Philosophical Tradition of Pastoral Care*. Philadelphia: Fortress, 1987.

———. "A Physical Description of Paul." Pages 165–70 in *Paul and the Popular Philosophers*.

Malony, H. Newton, and A. Adams Lovekin. *Glossolalia: Behavioral Science Perspectives on Speaking in Tongues*. New York: Oxford University Press, 1985.

Maly, Karl. "I Kor 12:1–3: Eine Regel zur Unterscheidung der Geister?" *BZ* 10 (1966): 82–95.

Mangold, Wilhelm. *Die Irrlehrer der Pastoralbriefe: Eine Studie*. Marburg: Elwert'sche Universitäts-Buchhandlung, 1856.

Marcel, Gabriel. *Mystery of Being*. Vol. 1, *Reflection and Mystery*. Translated by C. S. Fraser. Gifford Lectures, 1949 and 1950. Chicago: Regnery, 1950.

———. "Outline of a Phenomenology of Having." Pages 168–89 in *Being and Having*. Translated by Katharine Farrer. London: Dacre, 1949.

Marrou, Henri I. *A History of Education in Antiquity*. Translated by George Lamb. New York: Sheed and Ward, 1956.

Marshall, I. Howard. *Luke: Historian and Theologian*. Grand Rapids: Zondervan, 1970.

———. "Salvation, Grace and Works in the Later Writings in the Pauline Corpus." *NTS* 42 (1996): 339–58.

———. "Salvation in the Pastoral Epistles." Pages 449–69 in *Geschichte-Tradition-Reflexion: Festschrift für Martin Hengel zum 70. Geburtstag*, edited by Hubert Cancik, Hermann Lichtenberger, and Peter Schäfer. Vol. 3. Tübingen: Mohr Siebeck, 1996.

Martin, Dale B. *The Corinthian Body*. New Haven: Yale University Press, 1995.

———. "Tongues of Angels and Other Status Indicators." *JAAR* 59 (1991): 547–89.

Martin, Ralph P. *Reconciliation: A Study of Paul's Theology*. New Foundations Theological Library. Atlanta: John Knox, 1981.

———. "Some Reflections on New Testament Hymns." Pages 37–49 in *Christ the Lord: Studies in Christology Presented to Donald Guthrie*, edited by Harold H. Rowdon. Leicester: Inter-Varsity Press, 1982.

Martyn, J. Louis. "Apocalyptic Antinomies in Paul's Letter to the Galatians." *NTS* 31 (1985): 410–24.

Marxsen, Willi. *Introduction to the New Testament: An Approach to Its Problems*. Philadelphia: Fortress, 1968.

Matera, Frank J. *Galatians*. SP 9. Collegeville: Liturgical Press, 1992.

May, L. Carlyle. "A Survey of Glossolalia and Related Phenomena in Non-Christian Religions." *American Anthropologist* 58, no. 1 (1956): 75–96.

Mayers, Marvin K. "The Behavior of Tongues." Pages 112–27 in Mills, *Speaking in Tongues: Let's Talk about It*.

McDermott, Michael. "The Biblical Doctrine of *KOINŌNIA*." *BZ* 19 (1975): 64–77, 219–33.

McEleney, N. J. "The Vice-Lists of the Pastoral Epistles." *Catholic Biblical Quarterly* 36 (1974): 203–19.

McKelvey, R. J. "Christ the Cornerstone." *NTS* 8 (1962): 352–59.

McLean, Bradley H. "Agrippillina Inscription: Religious Associations and Early Christian Formation." Pages 239–70 in McLean, *Origins and Method*.

———, ed. *Origins and Method: Towards a New Understanding of Judaism and Christianity: Essays in Honour of John C. Hurd*. JSNTSup 86. Sheffield: Sheffield Academic, 1993.

McMichael, W. F. "Be Ye Followers Together of Me: *Symmimētai Mou Gin-esthe*—Phil III.17." *ExpTim* 5 (1893): 287.

Mearns, Chris. "The Identity of Paul's Opponents at Philippi." *NTS* 33 (1987): 194–204.

Meeks, Wayne A. *The First Urban Christians: The Social World of the Apostle Paul*. New Haven: Yale University Press, 1983.

———. "In One Body: The Unity of Humankind in Colossians and Ephesians." Pages 209–21 in Jervell and Meeks, *God's Christ and His People*.

———. "Judgment and the Brother: Romans 14:1–15:13." Pages 153–66 in *In Search of the Early Christians: Selected Essays*, edited by Allen R. Hilton and H. Gregory Snyder. New Haven: Yale University Press, 2002.

———. "Social Functions of Apocalyptic Language in Pauline Christianity." Pages 687–705 in *Apocalypticism in the Mediterranean World and the Near East: Proceedings of the International Colloquium on Apocalypticism, Uppsala, August 12–17, 1979*, edited by David Hellholm. Tübingen: Mohr Siebeck, 1983.

Meeks, Wayne A., and Fred O. Francis, eds. *Conflict at Colossae: A Problem in the Interpretation of Early Christianity, Illustrated by Selected Modern Studies*. SLBSBS 4. Missoula: Scholars Press, 1975.

Merkelbach, Reinhold. *Mithras*. Königstein: Hain, 1984.

Metzger, Bruce M. "A Classified Bibliography of the Graeco-Roman Mystery Religions, 1924–1973, with a Supplement, 1974–1977." *ANRW* 17.3:1259–379. Part 2, *Principat*, 17.3. Edited by H. Temporini and W. Haase. New York: De Gruyter, 1989.

———. "Considerations of Methodology in the Study of the Mystery Religions and Early Christianity." *Harvard Theological Review* 48 (1955): 1–20.

———. *A Textual Commentary on the Greek New Testament*. 3rd ed. London: United Bible Societies, 1975.

Meyer, Marvin W., ed. *The Ancient Mysteries: A Sourcebook*. San Francisco: Harper & Row, 1987.

Michel, Otto. "Zur Exegese von Phil. 2, 5–11." Pages 77–95 in *Theologie als Glaubenswagnis: Festschrift für Karl Heim zum 80. Geburtstag*. Hamburg: Furche-Verlag, 1954.

Miletic, Stephen F. *"One Flesh": Ephesians 5.22–24, 5.31; Marriage and the New Creation*. AnBib 115. Rome: Pontifical Biblical Institute, 1988.

Mills, Watson E. *Speaking in Tongues: A Guide to Research in Glossolalia*. Grand Rapids: Eerdmans, 1986.

———, ed. *Speaking in Tongues: Let's Talk about It*. Waco: Word, 1973.

Milner, Murray, Jr. "Status and Sacredness: Worship and Salvation as Forms of Status Transformation." *JSSR* 33 (1994): 99–109.

Minear, Paul S. "The Vocation to Invisible Powers: Ephesians 3:8–10." Pages 89–106 in *To Die and to Live: Christ's Resurrection and Christian Vocation*, edited by Paul S. Minear. New York: Seabury, 1977.

Mitchell, Alan. "1 Cor 6:1–11: Group Boundaries and the Courts of Corinth." PhD diss., Yale University, 1986.

Mitchell, Margaret M. "New Testament Envoys in the Context of Greco-Roman Diplomatic and Epistolary Conventions: The Example of Timothy and Titus." *JBL* 111 (1992): 641–62.

———. *Paul and the Rhetoric of Reconciliation: An Exegetical Investigation.* Louisville: Westminster John Knox, 1991.

Moessner, David P. *Lord of the Banquet: The Literary and Theological Significance of the Lukan Travel Narrative.* Minneapolis: Fortress, 1989.

———. "Paul in Acts: Preacher of Eschatological Repentance to Israel." *NTS* 34 (1988): 96–104.

Moo, Douglas J. *The Epistle to the Romans.* NICNT. Grand Rapids: Eerdmans, 1996.

Moore, Richard K. "2 Cor 5:21: The Interpretive Key to Paul's Use of *Dikaiosynē Theou*?" Pages 707–15 in Bieringer, *Corinthian Correspondence.*

Motte, A. "Silence et Sécret dans les Mystères d'Eleusis." Pages 317–34 in *Les Rites d'Initiation: Actes du Colloque de Liège et de Louvain-la-Neuve, 20–21 novembre 1984*, edited by Julien Ries. Homo religiosus 13. Louvain-la-Neuve: Centre d'Histoire des Religions, 1986.

Moule, C. F. D. "Further Reflexions on Philippians 2:5–11." Pages 264–76 in *Apostolic History and the Gospel: Biblical and Historical Essays Presented to F. F. Bruce on His 60th Birthday*, edited by W. Ward Gasque and Ralph P. Martin. Grand Rapids: Eerdmans, 1970.

———. "The Influence of Circumstances on the Use of Eschatological Terms." *JTS* 15 (1964): 1–15.

Müller, P. G. "Der 'Paulinismus' in der Apostelgeschichte: Ein forschungsgeschichtlicher Überblick." Pages 157–201 in *Paulus in den neutestamentlichen Spätschriften: Zur Paulusrezeption im Neuen Testament*, edited by Karl Kertelge. QD 89. Freiburg im Breisgau: Herder, 1981.

Munck, Johannes. "Discours d'Adieu dans le Nouveau Testament et dans la Littérature Biblique." Pages 155–70 in *Aux Sources de la Tradition Chrétienne: Mélanges Offerts à M. Maurice Goguel à l'Occasion de Son Soixante-Dixième Anniversaire*. Bibliothèque théologique. Neuchatel: Delachaux & Niestle, 1950.

———. "The Judaizing Gentile Christians." Pages 87–134 in *Paul and the Salvation of Mankind*.

———. *Paul and the Salvation of Mankind*. Translated by Frank Clarke. Richmond, VA: John Knox, 1959.

Munoz, Kevin A. "How Not to Go Out of the World: First Corinthians and the Social Foundation of Early Christian Expansion." PhD diss., Emory University, 2008.

Murphy-O'Connor, Jerome. "Christological Anthropology in Phil., II, 6–11." *RB* 83 (1976): 25–50.

———. "Interpolations in 1 Corinthians." *CBQ* 48 (1986): 81–94.

———. "The Non-Pauline Character of 1 Corinthians 11:2–16?" *JBL* 95 (1976): 615–21.

———. *Paul: A Critical Life*. Oxford: Clarendon, 1996.

———. "The Unwritten Law of Christ (Gal 6:2)." *RB* 119 (2012): 213–31.

Murray, Henry A. *Myth and Mythmaking*. New York: Braziller, 1960.

Nanos, Mark D. *The Galatian Debate: Contemporary Issues in Rhetorical and Historical Interpretation*. Peabody, MA: Hendrickson, 2002.

Nathan, Emmanuel. "Fragmented Theology in 2 Corinthians: The Unsolved Puzzle of 6:14–7:1." Pages 211–28 in Bieringer et al., *Theologizing in the Corinthian Conflict*.

Neusner, Jacob. *From Politics to Piety: The Emergence of Pharisaic Judaism*. Englewood Cliffs, NJ: Prentice Hall, 1972.

Neyrey, Jerome H. "The Form and Background of the Polemic in 2 Peter." PhD diss., Yale University, 1977.

———. *Paul, in Other Words: A Cultural Reading of His Letters*. Louisville: Westminster John Knox, 1990.

Nickle, Keith F. *The Collection: A Study of Paul's Strategy*. SBT 48. London: SCM, 1966.

Nicolet-Anderson, Valérie. *Constructing the Self: Thinking with Paul and Michel Foucault*. WUNT 2.324. Tübingen: Mohr Siebeck, 2012.

Nock, A. D. *Conversion: The Old and New in Religion from Alexander the Great to Augustine of Hippo*. Oxford: Clarendon, 1933.

———. "Hellenistic Mysteries and Christian Sacraments." Pages 791–820 in *Essays on Religion and the Ancient World*. Vol. 2. Oxford: Clarendon, 1972.

———. "Religious Symbols and Symbolism I." Pages 877–94 in *Essays on Religion and the Ancient World*. Vol. 2. Oxford: Clarendon, 1972. Repr. from *Gnomon* 27 (1955): 558–72.

———. "Religious Symbols and Symbolism II." Pages 895–907 in *Essays on*

Religion and the Ancient World. Vol. 2. Oxford: Clarendon, 1972. Repr. from *Gnomon* 29 (1957): 524–33.

——. "Religious Symbols and Symbolism III." Pages 908–18 in *Essays on Religion and the Ancient World.* Vol. 2. Oxford: Clarendon, 1972. Repr. from *Gnomon* 32 (1960): 728–36.

Nussbaum, Martha C. *Anger and Forgiveness: Resentment, Generosity, Justice.* New York: Oxford University Press, 2016.

Nygren, Anders. *Commentary on Romans.* Philadelphia: Fortress, 1949.

Obaje, Yusufu Ameh. *The Miracle of Speaking in Tongues: Which Side Are You?* Ogbomosho, Nigeria: Abebayo Calvary, 1987.

O'Brien, Peter T. "Ephesians I: An Unusual Introduction to a New Testament Letter." *NTS* 25 (1979): 504–16.

——. "The Fellowship Theme in Philippians." *Reformed Theological Review* 37 (1978): 9–18.

——. *Introductory Thanksgivings in the Letters of Paul.* NovTSup 49. Leiden: Brill, 1977.

O'Collins, Gerald G. "Power Made Perfect in Weakness: II Cor 12:9–10." *CBQ* 33 (1971): 528–37.

Oord, Thomas J. *Divine Grace and Emerging Creation: Wesleyan Forays in Science and Theology of Creation.* Eugene: Pickwick, 2009.

Osburn, Carroll D., ed. *Essays on Women in Earliest Christianity.* 2 vols. Joplin, MO: College Press, 1995.

——. "The Interpretation of 1 Cor 14:34–35." Pages 1:219–42 in Osburn, *Essays on Women in Earliest Christianity.*

Osiek, Carolyn, and Margaret Y. MacDonald. *A Woman's Place: House Churches in Earliest Christianity.* Minneapolis: Fortress, 2006.

Oswald, Hilton C., ed. *Luther's Works.* Vol. 28, *Commentary on 1 Corinthians 7, 1 Corinthians 15, Lectures on 1 Timothy.* St. Louis: Concordia, 1973.

O'Toole, Robert F. *The Unity of Luke's Theology: An Analysis of Luke-Acts.* Good News Studies 9. Wilmington, DE: Glazier, 1984.

Overfield, P. D. "Pleroma: A Study in Content and Context." *NTS* 25 (1979): 384–96.

Panikulam, George. *Koinōnia in the New Testament: A Dynamic Expression of Christian Life.* AnBib 85. Rome: Pontifical Biblical Institute, 1979.

Parke, H. W. *Sibyls and Sibylline Prophecy in Classical Antiquity.* London: Routledge, 1988.

Pawlak, Matthew C. "Consistency Isn't Everything: Self-Commendation in 2 Corinthians." *JSNT* 40 (2018): 360–382.

Pearson, Birger A. "Did the Gnostics Curse Jesus?" *JBL* 86 (1967): 301–5.

——. *The Pneumatikos-Psychikos Terminology in 1 Corinthians: A Study in the Theology of the Corinthian Opponents of Paul and Its Relation to Gnosticism*. SBLDS 12. Missoula: Scholars Press, 1971.

Pfitzner, Victor C. *Paul and the Agon Motif: Traditional Athletic Imagery in the Pauline Literature*. NovTSup 16. Leiden: Brill, 1967.

Philo. *Philo*. 12 vols. LCL. Cambridge: Harvard University Press, 1929–1953.

Philostratus. *Life of Apollonius of Tyana*. Translated by F. C. Conybeare. LCL. Cambridge, MA: Harvard University Press, 1927.

Placher, William C. *The Domestication of Transcendence: How Modern Thinking about God Went Wrong*. Louisville: Westminster John Knox, 1996.

Pollard, T. E. "The Integrity of Philippians." *NTS* 13 (1967): 57–66.

Porter, Stanley E. "Reconciliation and 2 Cor 5:18–21." Pages 693–705 in Bieringer, *Corinthian Correspondence*.

Potter, Jonathan. *Representing Reality: Discourse, Rhetoric, and Social Construction*. London: Sage, 1996.

Prokhorov, Alexander V. "Taking the Jews Out of the Equation: Galatians 6.12–17 as a Summons to Cease Evading Persecution." *JSNT* 36 (2013): 172–88.

Proudfoot, C. Merrill. "Imitation or Realistic Participation? A Study of Paul's 'Suffering with Christ.'" *Union Seminary Magazine* 17 (1963): 140–60.

Quinn, Jerome D. *The Letter to Titus: A New Translation with Notes and Commentary and an Introduction to Titus, I and II Timothy, the Pastoral Epistles*. AYB 35. New York: Doubleday, 1990.

Rabens, Volker. "Paul's Rhetoric of Demarcation: Separation from 'Unbelievers' (2 Cor 6:14–7:1) in the Corinthian Conflict." Pages 229–53 in Bieringer et al., *Theologizing in the Corinthian Conflict*.

Rahner, Hugo. "The Christian Mystery and the Pagan Mysteries." Page 337–401 in Joseph Campbell, *Mysteries*.

Rahner, Karl, ed. *Encyclopedia of Theology: The Concise Sacramentum Mundi*. New York: Seabury, 1975.

Rahtjen, B. D. "The Three Letters of Paul to the Philippians." *NTS* 6 (1960): 167–73.

Rawls, John. *A Theory of Justice*. Cambridge, MA: Harvard University Press, 1971.

Redalié, Yann. *Paul après Paul: Le Temps, le Salut, la Morale selon les Épîtres à Timothée et à Tite*. Le Monde de la Bible 31. Geneva: Labor et Fides, 1994.

Reeves, Rodney R. "To Be or Not to Be? That Is Not the Question: Paul's Choice in Philippians 1:22." *PRSt* 19 (1992): 273–89.

Reitzenstein, Richard. *Hellenistic Mystery-Religions: Their Basic Ideas and*

Significance. Translated by John E. Steely. 3rd ed. Pittsburgh: Pickwick, 1978.

Richard, Earl. *First and Second Thessalonians.* SP 11. Collegeville: Liturgical Press, 1995.

Richardson, James T. "Psychological Interpretations of Glossolalia: A Reexamination of Research." *JSSR* 12 (1973): 199–207.

Richardson, William E. "Liturgical Order and Glossolalia in 1 Corinthians 14:26c–33a." *NTS* 32 (1986): 144–53.

Riches, John. *Galatians through the Centuries.* Chichester: Wiley-Blackwell, 2013.

Robbins, Charles J. "Rhetorical Structure of Philippians 2:6–11." *CBQ* 42 (1980): 74–82.

Robbins, Vernon K. *The Tapestry of Early Christian Discourse: Rhetoric, Society and Ideology.* London: Routledge, 1996.

Roberts, Peter. "A Sign: Christian or Pagan?" *The Expository Times* 90, no. 7 (Apr 1979): 199–203.

Robinson, John A. T. *The Body: A Study in Pauline Theology.* Bristol, IN: Wyndham Hall, 1988.

———. *Redating the New Testament.* Philadelphia: Westminster, 1976.

Roetzel, Calvin J. "Jewish Christian–Gentile Christian Relations: A Discussion of Ephesians 2:15a." *ZNW* 74 (1983): 81–89.

Rogers, Jack. *Jesus, the Bible, and Homosexuality: Explode the Myths, Heal the Church.* Louisville: Westminster John Knox, 2009.

Rolland, Philippe. "La Structure Littéraire et l'Unité de l'Épitre aux Philippiens." *RSR* 64 (1990): 213–16.

Roon, A. van. *The Authenticity of Ephesians.* NovTSup 39. Leiden: Brill, 1979.

Rubin, Theodore Isaac. *The Angry Book.* New York: Collier, 1970.

Russell, R. "The Idle in 2 Thess 3.6–12: An Eschatological or a Social Problem?" *NTS* 34 (1988): 105–19.

Safrai, Shemuel, and Menahem Stern. "The Organization of the Jewish Communities in the Diaspora." Pages 464–503 in *The Jewish People in the First Century: Historical Geography, Political History, Social, Cultural and Religious Life and Institutions,* edited by Shemuel Safrai and Menahem Stern. Compendia Rerum Iudaicarum ad Novum Testamentum 1. Philadelphia: Fortress, 1974.

Samarin, William J. "The Linguisticality of Glossolalia." *Hartford Quarterly* 8 (1968): 55–57.

———. *Tongues of Men and Angels: The Religious Language of Pentecostalism.* New York: Macmillan, 1972.

Sampley, John P. *"And the Two Shall Become One Flesh": A Study of Traditions in Ephesians 5:21–32*. SNTSMS 16. Cambridge: Cambridge University Press, 1971.

———. "Paul and His Opponents in 2 Corinthians 10–13 and the Rhetorical Handbooks." Pages 162–77 in *The Social World of Formative Christianity and Judaism: Essays in Tribute to Howard Clarke Kee*, edited by Jacob Neusner, Peder Borgen, Ernest S. Frerichs, and Richard A. Horsley. Philadelphia: Fortress, 1988.

———. *Pauline Partnership in Christ: Christian Commitment and Community in Light of Roman Law*. Philadelphia: Fortress, 1980.

Sanders, E. P. *Judaism: Practice and Belief 63 BCE–66 CE*. London: SCM, 1992.

———. "Literary Dependence in Colossians." *JBL* 85 (1966): 28–45.

———. *Paul and Palestinian Judaism: A Comparison of Patterns of Religion*. Philadelphia: Fortress, 1977.

Schäfer, Peter. "Die Torah der Messianischen Zeit." *ZNW* 65 (1974): 27–42.

Schierse, F. J. *Die Pastoralbriefe*. Düsseldorf: Patmos, 1968.

Schippers, R. "The Pre-Synoptic Tradition in 1 Thessalonians II 13–16." *NovT* 8 (1966): 223–34.

Schleiermacher, Friedrich. *Über den Sogenannten Ersten Brief des Paulus an den Timotheus: Ein kritisches Senschreiben*. Berlin: Realschulbuchhandlung, 1807.

Schlier, Heinrich. *Christus und die Kirche im Epheserbrief*. Beiträge zur historischen Theologie 6. Tübingen: Mohr, 1930.

———. *Der Römerbrief: Kommentar*. Herders Theologischer Kommentar zum Neuen Testament 6. Freiburg im Breisgau: Herder, 1977.

———. *Principalities and Powers in the New Testament*. QD 3. Freiburg im Breisgau: Herder, 1961.

Schmidt, J. E. C. *Historisch-Kritische Einleitung ins Neue Testament*. Giessen: Tasche und Müller, 1804.

Schmithals, Walter. *Paul and the Gnostics*. Translated by John E. Steely. Nashville: Abingdon, 1972.

Schnackenburg, Rudolf. *Baptism in the Thought of St. Paul: A Study in Pauline Theology*. Translated by G. R. Beasley-Murray. New York: Herder and Herder, 1964.

———. *The Church in the New Testament*. New York: Herder and Herder, 1965.

Scholem, Gershom. *Jewish Gnosticism, Merkabah Mysticism and Talmudic Tradition*. New York: Jewish Theological Seminary of America, 1960.

Schrempp, Gregory, and William Hansen, eds. *Myth: A New Symposium*. Bloomington: Indiana University Press, 2002.

Schubert, Paul. *The Form and Function of the Pauline Thanksgiving*. Berlin: Töpelmann, 1939.

Schüssler Fiorenza, Elisabeth. *In Memory of Her: A Feminist Theological Reconstruction of Christian Origins*. New York: Crossroad, 1983.

Schütz, John H. *Paul and the Anatomy of Apostolic Authority*. New Testament Library. SNTSMS 26. Cambridge: Cambridge University Press, 1975.

Schweizer, Eduard. "The Service of Worship: An Exposition of 1 Cor 14." *Int* 13, no. 4 (1959): 400-408.

Schweitzer, Albert. *Paul and His Interpreters: A Critical History*. New York: Schocken Books, 1964.

Scola, Angelo. *The Nuptial Mystery*. Grand Rapids: Eerdmans, 2005.

Scroggs, Robin. "Paul and the Eschatological Woman." *JAAR* 40 (1972): 283-303.

Sebeok, Thomas A. *Myth: A Symposium*. Philadelphia: American Folklore Society, 1955.

Seesemann, Heinrich. *Der Begriff KOINONIA im Neuen Testament*. BZNW14. Giessen: Töpelmann, 1933.

Segovia, Fernando F., ed. *Discipleship in the New Testament*. Philadelphia: Fortress, 1985.

Shepherd, William H. *The Narrative Function of the Holy Spirit as a Character in Luke-Acts*. SBLDS 147. Atlanta: Scholars Press, 1994.

Sherrill, John L. *They Speak with Other Tongues*. New York: McGraw Hill, 1964.

Siker, Jeffrey S. *Homosexuality in the Church: Both Sides of the Debate*. Louisville: Westminster John Knox, 1994.

Sluckin, W. *Imprinting and Early Learning*. Chicago: Aldine, 1965.

Smit, Joop. "The Letter of Paul to the Galatians: A Deliberative Speech." *NTS* 35 (1989): 1-26.

Smith, Abraham. *Comfort One Another: Reconstructing the Rhetoric and Audience of 1 Thessalonians*. Louisville: Westminster John Knox, 1995.

Smith, Jonathan Z. *Drudgery Divine: On the Comparison of Early Christianities and the Religions of Late Antiquity*. Chicago: University of Chicago Press, 1990.

———. *To Take Place: Toward Theory in Ritual*. Chicago Studies in the History of Judaism. Chicago: University of Chicago Press, 1987.

Smith, Morton. "Goodenough's *Jewish Symbols* in Retrospect." *JBL* 86 (1967): 53-68.

Smyth, Herbert W. *Greek Grammar*. Cambridge, MA: Harvard University Press, 1956.

Spicq, Ceslas. *Agape in the New Testament*. St. Louis: Herder, 1963.

—. *Saint Paul: Les Épîtres Pastorales*. 4th ed. Etudes biblique. Paris: Gabalda, 1969.

Stagg, Frank. "The Mind in Christ Jesus: Philippians 1:27–2:18." *Review and Expositor* 77 (1980): 337–47.

Stanley, David M. "Carmenque Christo Quasi Deo Dicere . . ." *CBQ* 20 (1958): 173–91.

Stark, Rodney. *The Rise of Christianity: How the Obscure, Marginal Jesus Movement Became the Dominant Religious Force in the Western World in a Few Centuries*. San Francisco: HarperSanFrancisco, 1997.

Stauffer, Ethelbert. *New Testament Theology*. London: SCM, 1955.

Stegman, Thomas. *The Character of Jesus: The Linchpin of Paul's Argument in 2 Corinthians*. AnBib 158. Rome: Pontifical Biblical Institute, 2005.

Stevenson, Ian. *Unlearned Language: New Studies in Xenoglossy*. Charlottesville: University Press of Virginia, 1984.

—. *Xenoglossy: A Review and Report of a Case*. Charlottesville: University Press of Virginia, 1974.

Stowers, Stanley. "ἐκ πίστεως and διὰ τῆς πίστεως in Romans 3:30." *JBL* 108 (1989): 665–74.

—. *A Rereading of Romans: Justice, Jews, and Gentiles*. New Haven: Yale University Press, 1994.

Strelan, John G. "Burden-Bearing and the Law of Christ: A Re-examination of Galatians 6:2." *JBL* 94 (1975): 266–76.

Strootman, R. "The Hellenistic Royal Court: Court Culture, Ceremonial and Ideology in Greece, Egypt and the Near East, 336–30 BCE." PhD diss., Utrecht University, 2007.

Suh, M. K. W. *Power and Peril: Paul's Use of Temple Discourse in 1 Corinthians*. BZNW 239. Berlin: De Gruyter, 2020.

—. "Τὸ πνεῦμα in 1 Corinthians 5:5: A Reconsideration of Patristic Exegesis." *Vigilae Christiane* 72 (2018): 121–41.

Sumney, Jerry L. *Identifying Paul's Opponents: The Question of Method in 2 Corinthians*. JSNTSup 40. Sheffield: JSOT Press, 1990.

Talbert, Charles H. "The Problem of Pre-existence in Philippians 2:6–11." *JBL* 86 (1967): 141–53.

Tannehill, Robert C. *Dying and Rising with Christ: A Study in Pauline Theology*. BZNW 32. Berlin: Töpelmann, 1967.

—. *The Narrative Unity of Luke-Acts: A Literary Interpretation*. Vol. 1, *The Gospel according to Luke*. Philadelphia: Fortress, 1986.

—. *The Narrative Unity of Luke-Acts: A Literary Interpretation*. Vol 2, *The Acts of the Apostles*. Minneapolis: Fortress, 1990.

Taylor, R. O. P. "The Tongues of Pentecost." *ExpTim* 40 (1929): 300–303.

Thaden, Robert H. von. *Sex, Christ, and Embodied Cognition: Paul's Wisdom for Corinth*. Emory Studies in Early Christianity 16. Dorset, UK: Deo, 2012.

———. "The Wisdom of Fleeing Porneia: Conceptual Blending in 1 Corinthians 6:12–7:7." PhD diss., Emory University, 2007.

Theissen, Gerd. "Social Integration and Sacramental Activity: An Analysis of 1 Cor 11:17–34." Pages 145–74 in *The Social Setting of Pauline Christianity: Essays on Corinth*. Philadelphia: Fortress, 1982.

———. "Soteriologische Symbolik in den paulinischen Schriften." *Kerygma und Dogma* 20 (1974): 282–304.

Thiselton, Anthony C. *The First Epistle to the Corinthians: A Commentary on the Greek Text*. NIGTC. Grand Rapids: Eerdmans, 2000.

———. "The 'Interpretation' of Tongues: A New Suggestion in the Light of Greek Usage in Philo and Josephus." *JTS* 30 (1979): 15–36.

———. "The Logical Role of the Liar Paradox in Titus 1:12, 13." *Biblical Interpretation* 2, no. 2 (1994): 207–23

———. "The Meaning of ΣΑΡΧ in 1 Corinthians 5.5: A Fresh Approach in the Light of Logical and Semantic Factors." *Scottish Journal of Theology* 26 (1973): 204–28.

Thomas, Samuel I. *The "Mysteries" of Qumran: Mystery, Secrecy and Esotericism in the Dead Sea Scrolls*. Early Judaism and Its Literature 25. Atlanta: Society of Biblical Literature, 2009.

Thraede, Klaus. *Grundzüge griechisch-römischer Brieftopik*. Zetemata 48. Munich: Beck, 1970.

Torrance, Thomas F. "One Aspect of the Biblical Conception of Faith." *ExpTim* 68 (1957): 111–14.

Towner, Philip H. *The Goal of Our Instruction: The Structure of Theology and Ethics in the Pastoral Epistles*. JSNTSup 34. Sheffield: JSOT Press, 1989.

———. *The Letters to Timothy and Titus*. NICNT. Grand Rapids: Eerdmans, 2006.

Trummer, Peter. *Die Paulustradition der Pastoralbriefe*. Beiträge zur biblischen Exegese und Theologie 8. Frankfurt: Lang, 1978.

Turner, Victor W. *Process, Performance, and Pilgrimage: A Study in Comparative Symbology*. Ranchi Anthropology Series 1. New Delhi: Concept, 1979.

———. *The Ritual Process: Structure and Anti-Structure*. The Lewis Henry Morgan Lectures. Ithaca, NY: Cornell University Press, 1969.

Tutu, Desmond. *No Future without Forgiveness*. New York: Doubleday, 1999.

Tyson, Joseph B. "Paul's Opponents at Philippi." *PRSt* 3 (1976): 82–95.

————. "Paul's Opponents in Galatia." *NovT* 10 (1968): 241–54.

Van Houtan, Kyle S., and Michael S. Northcott. *Diversity and Dominion: Dialogues in Ecology, Ethics, and Theology.* Eugene: Wipf & Stock, 2010.

Vawter, F. Bruce. "The Colossian Hymn and the Principle of Redaction." *CBQ* 33 (1971): 62–81.

Vegge, Ivar. *2 Corinthians—a Letter about Reconciliation: A Psychagogical, Epistolographical and Rhetorical Analysis.* WUNT 2.239. Tübingen: Mohr Siebeck, 2008.

Verner, David C. *The Household of God: The Social World of the Pastoral Epistles.* SBLDS 71. Chico, CA: Scholars Press, 1983.

Via, Dan O., and Robert A. J. Gagnon. *Homosexuality and the Bible: Two Views.* Minneapolis: Fortress, 2003.

Villepigue, James, and Hugo Rivera. *The Body Sculpting Bible for Women: The Way to Physical Perfection.* Rev. ed. New York: Hatherleigh, 2006.

Vogel, Cornelia J. de. "Reflexions on Philipp. I 23–24." *NovT* 19, no. 4 (1977): 262–74.

Wach, Joachim. *Sociology of Religion.* Chicago: University of Chicago Press, 1944.

Wagner, Günter. *Pauline Baptism and the Pagan Mysteries: The Problem of the Pauline Doctrine of Baptism in Romans VI, 1–11, in the Light of Its Religio-Historical "Parallels."* Translated by J. P. Smith. Edinburgh: Oliver & Boyd, 1967.

Wainwright, Geoffrey. *Christian Initiation.* Ecumenical Studies in History 10. Richmond, VA: John Knox, 1969.

Walker, William O., Jr. "1 Corinthians 11:2–16 and Paul's Views Regarding Women." *JBL* 94 (1975): 94–110.

Wallace, James B. *Snatched into Paradise (2 Cor 12:1–10): Paul's Heavenly Journey in the Context of Early Christian Experience.* BZNW 179. Berlin: De Gruyter, 2011.

Wanamaker, C. A. "Philippians 2.6–11: Son of God or Adamic Christology?" *NTS* 33 (1987): 179–93.

Ward, Roy Bowen. "Musonius and Paul on Marriage." *NTS* 36 (1990): 281–89.

Watson, Duane F. "A Rhetorical Analysis of Philippians and its Implications for the Unity Question." *NovT* 30 (1988): 57–88.

Watson, Francis. *Agape, Eros, Gender: Towards a Pauline Sexual Ethic.* Cambridge: Cambridge University Press, 2000.

————. *Paul, Judaism and the Gentiles: Beyond the New Perspective.* Rev. ed. Grand Rapids: Eerdmans, 2007.

Weaver, Mary J. *New Catholic Women: A Contemporary Challenge to Traditional Religious Authority*. San Francisco: Harper & Row, 1985.

———. "Pneuma in Philo of Alexandria." PhD diss., University of Notre Dame, 1973.

Wedderburn, A. J. M. "2 Corinthians 5:14—a Key to Paul's Soteriology?" Pages 267–86 in Burke and Elliott, *Paul and the Corinthians*.

Weiss, Bernhard. *Der Jakobusbrief und die neuere Kritik*. Leipzig: Deichert, 1904.

Welles, C. Bradford. *Royal Correspondence in the Hellenistic Period: A Study in Greek Epigraphy*. New Haven: Yale University Press, 1934.

Westerholm, Stephen. "'Letter' and 'Spirit': The Foundation of Pauline Ethics." *NTS* 30 (1984): 229–48.

———. "On Fulfilling the Whole Law (Gal 5:14)." *Svensk exegetisk årsbok* 51–52 (1986–1987): 229–37.

———. *Perspectives Old and New on Paul: The "Lutheran" Paul and His Critics*. Grand Rapids: Eerdmans, 2003.

White, L. Michael. "Morality between Two Worlds: A Paradigm of Friendship in Philippians." Pages 201–15 in Balch, Ferguson, and Meeks, *Greeks, Romans and Christians*.

Whiteley, D. E. H. *The Theology of St. Paul*. Philadelphia: Fortress, 1966.

Wikenhauser, Alfred. *Pauline Mysticism: Christ in the Mystical Teaching of Saint Paul*. Freiburg im Breisgau: Herder, 1956.

Wilcox, Max. "'Upon the Tree': Deut 21:22–23 in the New Testament." *JBL* 96 (1977): 85–99.

Wild, Robert A. "'Be Imitators of God': Discipleship in the Letter to the Ephesians." Pages 127–43 in Segovia, *Discipleship in the New Testament*.

———. "The Warrior and the Prisoner: Some Reflections on Ephesians 6:10–20." *CBQ* 46 (1984): 284–98.

Williams, Cyril G. "Ecstaticism in Hebrew Prophecy and Christian Glossolalia." *SR* 3 (1974): 320–38.

———. "Glossolalia in the New Testament." Pages 25–45 in *Tongues of the Spirit*.

———. *Tongues of the Spirit: A Study of Pentecostal Glossolalia and Related Phenomena*. Cardiff: University of Wales Press, 1981.

Williams, Michael A. *Rethinking "Gnosticism": An Argument for Dismantling a Dubious Category*. Princeton: Princeton University Press, 1996.

Williams, Sam K. *Jesus' Death as Saving Event: The Background and Origin of a Concept*. Harvard Dissertations in Religion 2. Missoula: Scholars Press, 1975.

——. "The 'Righteousness of God' in Romans." *JBL* 99 (1980): 241–90.

Willis, Wendell L. *Idol-Meat in Corinth: The Pauline Argument in 1 Corinthians 8 and 10.* SBLDS 68. Chico, CA: Scholars Press, 1985.

Wilson, Bryan R. *The Social Dimensions of Sectarianism: Sects and New Religious Movements in Contemporary Society.* Oxford: Clarendon, 1990.

Wilson, Jim. "The Old Testament Sacrificial Context of 2 Corinthians 8–9." *BBR* 27 (2017): 361–78.

Wilson, R. A. "'We' and 'You' in the Epistle to the Hebrews." Pages 676–80 in *Studia Evangelica II: Papers Presented to the Second International Congress on New Testament Studies Held at Christ Church, Oxford, 1961,* edited by F. L. Cross. TUGAL 87. Berlin: Akademie, 1964.

Wilson, Robert McL. "Gnostics—in Galatia?" Pages 87–134 in *Studia Evangelica IV: Papers Presented to the Second International Congress on New Testament Studies Held at Christ Church, Oxford, 1965,* edited by F. L. Cross. TUGAL 102. Berlin: Akademie, 1968.

Wilson, Robert R. *Prophecy and Society in Ancient Israel.* Philadelphia: Fortress, 1980.

Wilson, Stephen G. *Luke and the Pastoral Epistles.* London: SPCK, 1979.

Wilson, Walter T. *Love without Pretense: Romans 12:9–21 and Hellenistic Jewish Wisdom Literature.* WUNT 2.46. Tübingen: Mohr Siebeck, 1991.

Wimpfheimer, Barry S. *The Talmud: A Biography.* Lives of Great Religious Books. Princeton: Princeton University Press, 2018.

Wink, Walter. "The Hymn of the Cosmic Christ." Pages 235–45 in *The Conversation Continues: Studies in Paul and John in Honor of J. Louis Martyn,* edited by Robert T. Fortna and Beverly R. Gaventa. Nashville: Abingdon, 1990.

——. *Naming the Powers: The Language of Power in the New Testament.* Philadelphia: Fortress, 1984.

Wire, Antoinette C. *The Corinthian Women Prophets: A Reconstruction through Paul's Rhetoric.* Minneapolis: Fortress, 1990.

Witherington, Ben, III. *Conflict and Community in Corinth: A Socio-Rhetorical Commentary on 1 and 2 Corinthians.* Grand Rapids: Eerdmans, 1994.

——. *Friendship and Finances in Philippi: The Letter of Paul to the Philippians.* New Testament in Context. Valley Forge, PA: Trinity International, 1994.

Wolter, Michael. *Die Pastoralbriefe als Paulustradition.* FRLANT 146. Göttingen: Vandenhoeck & Ruprecht, 1988.

Wright, N. T. *The New Testament and the People of God.* Christian Origins and the Question of God 1. Minneapolis: Fortress, 1992.

————. "On Becoming the Righteousness of God: 2 Corinthians 5:21." Pages 200–208 in Hay, *Pauline Theology*, vol. 2, *1 & 2 Corinthians*.

————. *Paul and the Faithfulness of God*. 2 vols. Christian Origins and the Question of God 4. Minneapolis: Fortress, 2013.

————. "Poetry and Theology in Colossians 1.15–20." *NTS* 36 (1990): 444–68.

————. *The Resurrection of the Son of God*. Christian Origins and the Question of God 3. Minneapolis: Fortress, 2003.

Yamauchi, Edwin M. *Pre-Christian Gnosticism: A Survey of the Proposed Evidence*. Grand Rapids: Eerdmans, 1973.

————. "The Scythians—Who Were They? And Why Did Paul Include Them in Colossians 3:11?" *Priscilla Papers* 21, no. 4 (2007): 13–18.

Yarbrough, O. Larry. *Not Like the Gentiles: Marriage Rules in the Letters of Paul*. SBLDS 80. Atlanta: Scholars Press, 1986.

Young, Frances M. *The Theology of the Pastoral Letters*. New Testament Theology. Cambridge: Cambridge University Press, 1994.

Zablocki, Benjamin D. *The Joyful Community: An Account of the Bruderhof, a Communal Movement Now in Its Third Generation*. Baltimore: Penguin, 1971.

INDEX OF AUTHORS

Adams, Richard Manley, 188, 193n15

Aelius Aristides, 224n38, 451n15, 470n71

Ahern, Barnabas M., 272n17

Alderink, Larry J., 171n73, 171n74, 172n77

Alexander, Loveday, 263n3

Allen, Michael, 185n1

Ambrose, 297n14

Amiot, Francois, 40n32

Andemicael, Awet, 139n3

Andrews, E., 109n17

Andrews, Scott B., 150n18

Angus, Samuel, 171n72, 172n75

Apuleius, 113n41, 172–73

Aristophanes, 450–51, 451–52n15

Aristotle, 4, 49, 54–58, 125n91, 126n92, 157n37, 226n39, 263n1, 274n24, 302n23, 303n25, 304n27, 315n8, 361n13, 406n43, 417n11, 440n43, 485n14, 485n16, 486n21

Arnold, C. E., 167n53

Ascough, Richard S., 169n66, 177n123, 181n149, 338n4

Augustine of Hippo, 128, 373n44, 439n41

Aulus Gellius, 324n33

Aune, David E., 109n16, 113n39, 127n103

Aus, Roger D., 393n19

Austin, J. L., 69n2

Bacht, H., 113n34

Bailey, John A., 386n3

Baird, Julia, 317–18n16

Baker, Nena, 88n5

Balch, David L., 346n29, 420n15

Balthasar, Hans Urs von, 245n2, 319n21

Bandstra, A. J., 170n70

Barclay, John M. G., 158n39, 216n12, 386n3, 490n28

Barclay, William, 450n5

Barnouin, M., 393n19

Barr, James, 17

Barrett, C. K., 14n5, 74n21, 140n7, 149n15, 206n45, 210n3, 400n32, 450n5, 455n25, 456n30, 457n33, 460n41

Barth, Karl, 5, 319n21

Barth, Markus, 14, 16n12, 17, 25n33, 170n71

Basevi, Claudio, 275n29

Bassler, Jouette M., 429n4

Bates, W. H., 129n1, 139n4

Bauer, Walter, 256

Baumbach, Günther, 283n43

Baur, F. C., 256, 429n2, 429n4

Beale, G. K., 151n20

Beare, Frank W., 108n10

Beasley-Murray, G. R., 171n72, 180n146, 180n147

Beck, Roger, 171n73

Beel, A., 111n24

Behm, Johannes, 108n9

Beker, Johann Christiaan, 30n12, 31n13, 40n32

Bell, Catherine M., 160n3, 160n4, 160n5

Berger, Peter L., 244, 359n10, 385n2

Bernasconi, Robert, 202n42

Betz, Hans Dieter, 129n1, 139n4, 167n51, 181n150, 193n15

Betz, Otto, 393n19

Bianchi, Ugo, 290n2

Bickerman, Elias J., 343n22

Bieringer, Reimund, 139n6

Black, David A., 268n12, 275n27

Black, Mark C., 123n79, 124n86

Bligh, John, 228n42

Bloomquist, L. Gregory, 272n17

Boers, Hendrikus, 245n1

Bohnenblust, Gottfried, 102n49, 157n34, 263n1

Bonsirven, Joseph, 40n32

Boring, M. Eugene, 31n13, 45n36

Bornhäuser, Karl, 275n30

Bornkamm, Günther, 170n70, 290n2

Boston Women's Health Course Collective, 88n8

Boswell, John, 320n23

Bourguignon, Erika, 166n43

Bousset, Wilhelm, 246

Boyarin, Daniel, 206n46

Boyle, T. Coraghessan, 87n4

Boyles, John, 358n5

Brant, Jo-Ann A., 286n48

Braun, Willi, 482n5

Bremmer, Jan N., 290n2

Brewer, Raymond R., 287n51

Brink, Laurie, 139n3

Brinsmead, Bernard Hungerford, 167n51

Brown, David, 108n11

Brown, Ernest Faulkner, 450n5

Brown, Raymond E., 290n3

Brox, Norbert, 118n62, 449–50n4, 450n5, 455n25, 476n77

Brubaker, Rogers, 319–20n22

Bruce, F. F., 167n46, 227n41

Bruner, Frederick Dale, 107n2, 117n57

Bueschsel, F., 164n35

Bultmann, Rudolf, 17, 21n28, 22n29, 40n32, 41n34, 47n39, 48n2, 86n1, 244–61, 373n42

Bunn, John T., 109n16

Burkert, Walter, 161n6, 162n14, 163n22, 164n27, 171n73, 171n74, 172n78, 173n84, 174n95, 247n10

Burtchaell, James T., 369–70n31, 413n8

Caird, George B., 339n9

Cajetan (Thomas de Vio), 428n1

Callan, Terrance, 117n57, 167n52, 187n5

Calvin, John, 5

Camino, Linda A., 162n15

Campbell, Douglas A., 188n7

Campbell, John Y., 263n2

Campbell, Joseph, 290n2

Campbell, R. Alastair, 369–70n31, 413n8

Campenhausen, Hans von, 257n25

Cannon, George E., 167n47

Cantarella, Eva, 318n19

Capon, Robert Farrar, 101n47

Caragounis, Chrys C., 290n2, 345n26

Carr, Frederick David, 195n23, 271n13, 288n52

Casaubon, Meric, 107n4

Casel, Odo, 171n72

Castelli, Elizabeth A., 142n13, 360n12

Caudill, Sally, 482n5

Celsus, 127

Cerfaux, Lucien, 24n32, 40n32, 169n65, 170n71, 171n72, 174n93, 275n30, 337n1

Chapa, Juan, 275n29, 357n1

Christie-Murray, David, 112n30

Cicero, 112n33, 113n38, 324n33

Clark, Kenneth W., 266n9

Clement of Alexandria, 115n51, 172n77, 297n14

Clinton, Kevin, 290n2

Cohn, Norman, 395n21

Collins, Raymond F., 72n15

Colson, F. H., 450n7

Condit, Celeste Michelle, 482n5

Conte, Gian B., 172n79

Conzelmann, Hans, 41n34, 72n15, 123n81, 164n34, 411n4, 419n14, 450–51, 452n18, 453n20, 454–55n23, 456n30, 457n31, 457n32, 457n33, 458n35, 460n39, 461n43, 463n49, 464n51, 465n59, 476n77, 481n1, 481n2, 485n17, 485n20

Cope, Lamar, 123n81
Corrington, Gail Paterson, 124n87
Cosmopoulos, Michael B., 290n2
Coulson, Jesse E., 122n72
Cousar, Charles B., 227n41
Crace, Jim, 90n16
Crehan, Joseph, 163n23, 180n146
Critchley, Simon, 202n42
Cullmann, Oscar, 165n36, 171n72,
    180n146, 393n19
Cumont, Franz, 172n78
Currie, Stuart D., 110n19

Dahl, Nils Alstrup, 18n19, 25n34, 25n35,
    32n18, 39n31, 104n54, 140n8, 151n20,
    167n52, 170n71, 187n5, 249, 338n5,
    370n33
Dailey, Thomas, 272n19
Dalton, William J., 281–82n41
Das, A. Andrew, 188n7
Davidson, James N., 485n14
Davies, John G., 110n22
Davies, Stevan L., 429n4
Davis, Basil S., 228n42
Dawes, Gregory W., 347n30
DeFranza, Megan K., 319n21
Delorne, J., 162n14, 180n146
Deming, Will, 96n29, 372n40
Demosthenes, 303n25, 388n10
Derrida, Jacques, 7
Descartes, René, 71, 87
DeSilva, David A., 129n1, 139n4, 281n40
Dibelius, Martin, 164n34, 169n65,
    246, 411n4, 419n14, 450–51, 452n18,
    453n20, 454–55n23, 456n30, 457n31,
    457n32, 457n33, 458n35, 460n39,
    461n43, 463n49, 464n51, 465–66,
    476n77, 481n1, 481n2, 485n17, 485n20
Dill, Samuel, 450–51n9
Dio Cassius, 450–51n9
Dio Chrysostom, 93n22, 113n41, 124n86,
    219n22, 223n31, 419n13, 450–51n9,
    452n16, 468, 469n68, 469n69, 471n73,
    471n74, 473–76
Diodorus Siculus, 440n43
Diogenes Laertius, 4, 304n27
Dionysius of Halicarnassus, 304n27

Dix, Gregory, 184n155
Doberstein, John W., 429n3
Dodds, E. R., 113n34
Donaldson, James, 127n100
Donne, John, 90n18
Dornier, Pierre, 451n13, 453n20, 460n39
Doughty, Darrell J., 397n27
Douglas, Mary, 117n58
Downs, David J., 141n12, 157n38
Droge, Arthur J., 272n18
Dugas, Ludovic, 157n34, 263n1
Dunn, James D. G., 40n33, 48n2, 53n11,
    58n18, 58n19, 59n21, 63n27, 86n1
Dupont, Jacques, 273n23
Durkheim, Émile, 160n2

Eastman, Susan Grove, 271n13
Eglinger, Ruth, 263n1
Eichhorn, J. G., 429n2, 432
Eitrem, Samson, 169n65
Eliade, Mircea, 109n15, 160n2, 160n3,
    162n15, 163n22, 164n33, 178n136
Elliott, Mark W., 185n2
Ellis, E. Earle, 283n43, 454n21
Eltester, Friedrich W., 310n45
Epictetus, 180n146, 195n22, 302n24,
    314–15n5, 387–88n9, 419n13, 450–
    51n9, 451–52n15, 452n16, 467–68n63,
    468–70, 483–84n9, 485n14
Epicurus, 4
Epiphanius, 126n96, 126n98
Erasmus of Rotterdam, 428n1
Esler, Philip F., 117n56, 122n76
Euripides, 114n43, 290n2, 304n27,
    406n43
Eusebius, 126n95, 126n97, 126n98,
    127n100, 128n106, 428n1
Evans, Craig A., 170n70

Farley, Margaret, 313n1
Fascher, Erich, 113n34, 114n43
Fee, Gordon D., 72n15, 72n16, 74n21,
    97n34, 123n81, 275n27
Feinberg, Paul D., 275n30
Festinger, Leon, 395n21
Feuillet, André, 275n30
Fiore, Benjamin, 412n5, 431n13,
    481–82n4

Fisher, Nicolas R. E., 440n43

Fitzgerald, John T., 139n4, 139n6, 149n16, 156n56, 200n35, 218n19, 263n1

Fitzmyer, Joseph A., 53n11, 58n18, 58n19, 59n21, 63n27, 265n7

Flint, Peter W., 248n13

Foerster, W., 40n32

Forbes, Christopher, 110n21

Ford, J. Massingberd, 109n12, 110n21

Foskett, Mary F., 125–26

Foster, John, 107n4

Foucault, Michel, 88n9, 96n31, 318n18, 346n29

Fowl, Stephen E., 63n26, 275n29

Francis, Fred O., 169n65, 170n71, 443n46

Freud, Sigmund, 163

Friedan, Betty, 317n15

Froehlich, Karlfried, 185n1

Fromm, Erich, 215n11

Fulgentius, 297n12

Furness, J. M., 275n27

Furnish, Victor Paul, 9n5, 129n1, 131n6, 131n8, 139n4, 216n12, 399n31, 400n32, 406n43, 431n11

Gabler, Johann Philipp, 245n1

Gagnon, Robert A. J., 320n23

Gamber, Klaus, 275n27

Garland, David E., 281–82n41

Garrett, Clarke, 107n2

Gärtner, Bertil E., 344–45n24

Geertz, Clifford, 164n26

Gench, Frances Taylor, 347n30

Gennep, Arnold van, 162n15, 177n123, 177n126, 178–79

Georgi, Dieter, 141n12, 149n15, 275n27

Gignac, Alan, 206n46

Gillespie, Thomas W., 117n57, 118n63

Gillmann, John, 141n11

Gladd, Benjamin L., 290n3

Gloer, Hulitt W., 275n26

Gnilka, Joachim, 283n43

Gonzalez, Heliodora E., 122n74

Gooch, Peter D., 375n47

Goodenough, Erwin R., 174

Goodman, Felicitas D., 109n14, 114n45, 114n47

Goppelt, Leonhard, 41n34

Goranson Jacob, Haley, 310n45

Gordley, Matthew E., 275n26, 299n18

Grayston, Kenneth, 283n43

Greimas, A. J., 35

Grenz, Stanley, 319n21

Grieb, A. Katherine, 188

Griffiths, J. Gwyn, 172n81

Grudem, Wayne A., 117n57

Gundry, Robert H., 86n1, 110n21

Gunkel, Hermann, 120n70

Hall, Robert G., 167n51

Hamm, M. Dennis, 34n22, 34n23, 37–38

Hansen, William, 130n3

Hanson, Anthony Tyrrell, 170n71

Harker, Christina, 185n2

Harland, Philip A., 247n8, 338n4, 358n4, 369n31

Harmon, Matthew S., 210n3, 470n72

Harnack, Adolf von, 253, 258

Harpur, Tom W., 110n21

Harris, J. Rendel, 281n38

Harris, Murray J., 490n29

Harrisville, Roy A., 108n9

Hart, David Bentley, 194n18

Harvey, A. E., 154n28, 187n4

Harvey, John, 275n30

Hauck, F., 263n1

Hauerwas, Stanley, 321n25

Hawthorne, Gerald F., 272n19

Hay, David M., 69n3

Hays, Richard B., 13n2, 31n14, 31n16, 35n25, 61n24, 61n25, 94n25, 170n71, 188, 196n25, 224n34, 313n1, 320n23

Hebert, Gabriel, 17n14, 19n27

Hegel, G. W. F., 4, 5

Heil, John, 88n6

Heim, David, 313n1

Heitmüller, D., 246

Heliso, Desto, 202n40

Helminiak, Daniel A., 320n23

Hengel, Martin, 70n5, 275n26, 276n31

Henning, Meghan, 200n35

Hercher, Rudolf, 464n53, 464n54, 465n56

Héring, Jean, 118n61

Herodotus, 113n35, 113n36, 113n40, 114n43, 290n2, 388n10, 401n35, 483–84n9, 485n14, 486n21

Hess, Eckhard H., 166n44

Heyd, Michael, 107n4

Hickling, Colin J. A., 161n8

Hierocles, 223n31

Hilary of Poitiers, 297n11

Himmelfarb, Martha, 247n11

Hine, Virginia A., 109n14

Hinson, E. Glenn, 107n5

Hippocrates, 126n92, 325n34

Hippolytus, 126n95

Hock, Ronald F., 433–34n20

Hofius, Otfried, 275n30

Holladay, Carl R., 119n65, 174n93, 283n43

Holmes, Christopher T., 364n19

Holtzmann, H. J., 429n2

Homer, 114n43, 483–84n9

Hooker, Morna D., 66n29, 275n29

Horace, 135n9

Horrell, David G., 140n7

Horsley, Richard A., 397n27

Howard, George, 13n2, 24n32, 275n28

Hultgren, Arland J., 13–14, 15n11, 16n12, 18n20, 19n24

Hume, David, 5

Hunt, Allen R., 117n57, 118n63, 119n66

Hurd, John C., 99n38, 117n59, 140n10, 370n33

Hurst, Lincoln D., 275n28

Hurtado, Larry W., 228n42, 275n28

Hutch, Richard A., 114n48

Hylen, Susan, 314n3

Ibita, Marilou S., 154n28

Ignatius of Antioch, 356

Irenaeus of Lyon, 28n2, 127

Jackson, Timothy P., 90n17

Jaeger, Werner, 491n33

Jaworski, William, 88n6

Jenkins, Philip, 395n21

Jeremias, Joachim, 220n26

Jervell, Jacob, 32n18, 310n45

Jewett, Robert, 86n1, 170n70, 187n4, 283n43, 389n11, 395n23

Johanson, Bruce C., 117n59, 119n68

John Chrysostom, 128

John Paul II, 319n21

Johnson, Luke Timothy, 9n6, 10n7, 10n11, 32n17, 32n19, 33n20, 34n21, 34n23, 35n24, 36n26, 38n29, 39n30, 49n4, 53n10, 70n4, 70n6, 70n7, 71n9, 71n12, 89n12, 89n15, 100n45, 102n48, 102n50, 107n1, 111n24, 111n25, 116n53, 116n54, 117n55, 117n57, 119n69, 124n83, 130n4, 157n36, 165n37, 168n54, 170n69, 185n3, 199n33, 201n36, 202n40, 210n4, 218n21, 219n23, 248n14, 256n23, 256n24, 259n26, 259n27, 260n28, 261n29, 264n5, 264n6, 271n15, 287n50, 313n1, 316n11, 321n26, 321n27, 322n29, 322n30, 333n54, 402n36, 409n1, 412n6, 423–24n16, 429n2, 430n7, 431n10, 432–33n17, 433n18, 435n25, 436n27, 440n44, 483n6, 485n17, 485n19, 486n21, 487n25

Johnson, Ray W., 122n72

Jones, Lawrence N., 107n5

Jordan, Mark D., 318n18

Josephus, 169n68, 180n146, 180n147, 343n22, 387–88n9, 393n18, 395n25, 406n42, 494n37

Julian the Apostate, 451–52n15, 469n68, 469n69, 471n73

Justin Martyr, 356

Kahl, Brigitte, 185n2

Kanter, Rosabeth M., 359n10

Karris, Robert J., 413n9, 436n27, 449–50n4, 451–53, 454n22, 461, 462n47, 468, 473n75

Käsemann, Ernst, 14, 24n33, 53n11, 54n15, 58n18, 58n19, 59n20, 59n21, 59n22, 118n60, 275n30

Kaye, B. N., 363n17

Keck, Leander E., 30n9

Keller, Albert, 71n13

Kelly, J. N. D., 427, 456n27, 456n30, 457n31, 461n42, 476n77, 481n1
Kelsey, Morton T., 107n3, 107n5, 109n12, 109n14, 111n23, 114n46, 114n47, 122n74, 122n75
Kerényi, Karl, 164n29, 172n77
Khobnya, Svetlana, 139n3
Kidd, Reggie M., 486n23
Kilby, Karen, 245n2
Kildahl, John P., 109n14, 112n28, 114n47, 122n73, 122n74, 122n75
Kilpatrick, George D., 282n42
Kim, Seyoon, 139n6
Kirby, John C., 340n11
Kirk, G. S., 130n3
Klijn, A. F. J., 283n43
Kloppenborg, John S., 140n7, 338n4, 358n4, 369n31
Knight, George W., III, 481n1
Knox, Ronald A., 107n3, 128n109, 325n34
Koester, Helmut, 281–82n41, 283n43, 386n3
Kolenkow, Anitra Bingham, 149n15
Konradt, Matthias, 224n34
Koopman, Niels, 200n35
Koperski, V., 281n41
Koskenniemi, Heikki, 464n53, 465n55
Kraftchick, Steven J., 150n19, 275–76n30
Kramer, Helmut, 113n34
Kroeger, Catherine, 125n89
Kroeger, Richard, 125n89
Kümmel, Werner Georg, 28n1, 431n10, 453n20
Kurz, William S., 31n15, 65n28, 275n29, 280n37, 281n40

Ladd, George Eldon, 28n1
La Fontaine, Jean S., 163n22, 164n33, 177n124, 177n125, 177n127, 178
Lambert, Craig, 101n46
Lambrecht, Jan, 150n18, 223n29
Lampe, G. W. H., 161n10, 166n45, 180n146
Lau, Andrew Y., 493n35
Lau, T.-L., 343n20

Laub, Franz, 386n3
Laurentin, René, 107n5
Lawless, Elaine J., 107n2
Lee, E. Kenneth, 456n29, 459n36
Lee, Yeong Mee, 185n2
Leenhardt, Franz J., 5, 14
Leeuw, G. van der, 160n1
Lehmann, K., 71n10
Lévinas, Emmanuel, 202n42, 378n52
Lewis, I. M., 122–24, 125, 127–28
Lightfoot, J. B., 167n46
Lincoln, Andrew T., 340n13
Lindars, Barnabas, 187n5
Lindemann, Andreas, 386n3
Linebaugh, Jonathan A., 185n1
Livy, 125n89, 324n33
Ljungman, Henrik, 15n11
Lock, Walter, 450n5, 453n20, 460n39, 461n42
Locke, John, 87n3
Lohse, Eduard, 167n47, 304n29, 307n34
Loisy, Alfred, 171n72
Longenecker, Bruce W., 188n7
Longenecker, Richard N., 363n17
Löning, Karl, 30n10
Loubser, Gysbert M., 210n3
Lovekin, A. Adams, 109n14, 112n28, 112n29
Lozada, Francisco, 185n2
Lucaites, John Louis, 482n5
Lucian of Samosata, 113n42, 126n93, 200n35, 419n13, 451–52n15, 452n16, 469n68, 469n69, 470–73, 487n26
Luck, Georg, 172n76
Luck, U., 53n12
Luckmann, Thomas, 359n10
Lull, David John, 182n152, 191n9
Lütgert, Wilhelm, 450n5
Luther, Martin, 5, 215n11, 428n1, 429n3
Lyotard, Jean-François, 7n2

MacDonald, Dennis R., 429n4
MacDonald, Margaret Y., 314n3, 430n8, 431n13
MacDonald, William G., 107n6, 108n10
Mack, Burton L., 165n37

Macmullen, Ramsay, 450–51n9

Malherbe, Abraham Johannes, 48n1, 88n10, 99n40, 223n33, 357n1, 357n2, 365n22, 386n3, 412n7, 419n14, 464–65, 467n62

Maloney, H. Newton, 109n14, 110n18, 112n28, 112n29, 114n47, 114n49, 114n50, 122n72, 122n74

Maly, Karl, 118n61, 118n62

Mangold, Wilhelm, 450n5

Marcel, Gabriel, 89

Marrou, Henri I., 467–68n63, 491n33

Marshall, I. Howard, 32n18, 490n29

Martin, Dale B., 92n20, 92n21, 97n32, 117n58, 118n64, 124n87, 125–26, 275n26

Martin, Ralph P., 139n6

Martyn, James Louis, 30n9, 224n35

Marx, Karl, 5

Marxsen, Willi, 453n20

Matera, Frank J., 227n41

Maximus of Tyre, 219n22

May, L. Carlyle, 109n15, 110n20, 112n30

Mayers, Marvin K., 122n73

McDermott, Michael, 263n2

McEleney, N. J., 449–50n4

McKelvey, R. J., 344–45n24

McLean, Bradley H., 369–70n31

McMichael, W. F., 286n48

Mearns, Chris, 283n43

Meeks, Wayne A., 162n12, 163n19, 163n21, 163n23, 170n69, 342n18, 363n17, 371n36, 380n56

Merkelbach, Reinhold, 172n78

Metzger, Bruce M., 111n26, 171n72, 171n73, 247n10

Meyer, Marvin W., 171n73

Meyerhoff, Barbara G., 162n15

Michel, Otto, 275–76n30, 416n10

Miletic, Stephen F., 347n30

Mills, Watson E., 108n8, 109n12

Milner, Murray, Jr., 178n134

Minear, Paul S., 338n5

Mitchell, Alan, 370n32

Mitchell, Margaret M., 92n20, 99n38, 118n64, 140n8, 411n3, 423–27, 481–82n4

Moessner, David P., 34n21, 37n27

Moo, Douglas J., 50n6, 53n11, 53n13, 58n18, 58n19, 59n21

Moore, Richard K., 154n29

Motte, A., 171n74

Moule, C. F. D., 275–76n30, 386n3

Müller, P. G., 30n10

Munck, Johannes, 170n70, 187n4, 386n3, 454–55n23

Munoz, Kevin A., 379n53

Murphy-O'Connor, Jerome, 24n32, 123n81, 167n47, 224n34, 275n28

Murray, Henry A., 130n3

Musonius Rufus, 316n13, 450–51n9

Nanos, Mark D., 185n2

Nathan, Emmanuel, 151n20

Neusner, Jacob, 401n34

Neyrey, Jerome H., 92n21, 97n32, 117n58, 192n12, 454–55n23

Nickle, Keith F., 141n12, 228n42

Nicolet-Anderson, Valérie, 96n31, 188, 379n55

Nock, Arthur Darby, 164n29, 171n72, 172n75, 172n76, 172n77, 172n80, 173n89, 174, 467–68n63

Northcott, Michael S., 89n15

Nussbaum, Martha C., 138n2

Nygren, Anders, 14n5

Obaje, Yusufu Ameh, 107n2

O'Brien, Peter T., 153n25, 263n3, 340n11, 444n47

O'Collins, Gerald G., 149n16

Oepke, Albrecht, 162n13, 162n14

Onasander, 485n20

Origen, 127n104, 349n36, 428n1

Osburn, Carroll D., 123n80

Osiek, Carolyn, 314n3

Oswald, Hilton C., 429n3

O'Toole, Robert F., 32n18

Overfield, P. D., 338–39n6

Panikulam, George, 263n2

Parke, H. W., 113n36

Pascal, Blaise, 4

Pausanias, 114n43

Pawlak, Matthew C., 150n17

Pearson, Birger A., 77n27, 118n62, 397n27

Pfitzner, Victor C., 286n46

Philo, 113n37, 174–77, 195n22, 304, 390n14, 406n42, 484n10, 485n16, 486n21, 494n37

Philodemus, 223n31

Philostratus, 224n38, 450–51n9, 469n68, 469n69

Placher, William C., 71n11, 87n2

Plato, 4, 113n36, 113n37, 114n43, 174n95, 290n2, 301n20, 301–2n21, 303n25, 303n26, 406n43, 417n11, 483–84n9, 485n14, 494n37

Pliny, 167n46

Plutarch, 113n37, 113n38, 113n40, 126n93, 157n35, 173n87, 193n14, 223n31, 224n37, 301–2n21

Pollard, T. E., 281–82n41

Polybius, 393n18

Polycarp, 356

Porter, Stanley E., 154n29

Potter, Jonathan, 482n5

Prokhorov, Alexander V., 221n27

Proudfoot, C. Merrill, 272n17

Ps.-Demetrius, 465n55

Ps.-Isocrates, 465–68

Ps.-Libanius, 172n76, 464–66, 475

Puntel, L. B., 71n10

Quinn, Jerome D., 481n1

Quintilian, 340n10

Rabens, Volker, 151n20

Rackham, H., 54n16

Rahner, Hugo, 171n72

Rahner, Karl, 71n10, 71n13, 94n24, 337n1

Rahtjen, B. D., 281–82n41

Rawls, John, 87n3

Redalié, Yann, 430n9, 481n2

Reeves, Rodney R., 272n19

Reitzenstein, Richard, 171n72

Richard, Earl, 386n3

Richardson, James T., 122n72

Richardson, William E., 119n67

Rivera, Hugo, 88n7

Robbins, Charles J., 275–76n30

Robbins, Vernon K., 49n5

Roberts, Alexander, 127n100

Robinson, John A. T., 86n1, 410n2, 454n21

Roetzel, Calvin J., 342n18

Rogers, Jack, 320n23

Rolland, Philippe, 281–82n41

Roon, A. van, 46n37

Rubin, Theodore Isaac, 148n14

Russell, R., 394n20

Samarin, William J., 109n13, 111n23, 112n28, 114n44, 114n46

Sampley, John P., 149n15, 263n3, 294n7, 347n30

Sanders, E. P., 28n4, 40n32, 167n47, 247

Schäfer, Peter, 224n34

Schierse, F. J., 450n5, 454–55n23, 457n31, 461n43

Schippers, R., 393n17

Schlatter, Adolf, 245

Schleiermacher, Friedrich, 428–29, 431–32, 435n26

Schlier, Heinrich, 14n5, 338–39n6, 339n9, 435n26

Schmidt, J. E. C., 429n2

Schmidt, Karl Ludwig, 338n4

Schmithals, Walter, 170n70, 187n4

Schnackenburg, Rudolf, 165n36, 337n1

Scholem, Gershom G., 247n11

Schrempp, Gregory, 130n3

Schubert, Paul, 153n25, 444n47

Schüssler Fiorenza, Elisabeth, 124–25

Schütz, John H., 360n12

Schweitzer, Albert, 431n11

Schweizer, Eduard, 119n67

Scola, Angelo, 313n1, 319n21

Scroggs, Robin, 124n83

Sebeok, Thomas S., 130n3

Seesemann, Heinrich, 263n2

Seneca, 450–51n9

Shepherd, William H., 180n148

Sherrill, John L., 111n23

Siker, Jeffrey S., 320n23

Sluckin, W., 166n44

Smit, Joop, 167n51

Smith, Abraham, 357n1

Smith, Jonathan Z., 29n8, 102n51,
  160n3, 160n4, 163n24, 171n72
Smith, Morton, 174n94
Smyth, Herbert W., 366n23, 491
Sohm, Rudolf, 253–55, 258
Sophocles, 194n19
Spicq, Ceslas, 326n35, 450n5, 450n7,
  453n20, 454–55n23, 455n24, 455n25,
  455n26, 456n27, 456n30, 457n31,
  458n35, 460n39, 461n43, 461n44,
  461n56, 476n77
Splett, J., 94n24
Staehlin, Gustav, 102n49
Stagg, Frank, 275–76n30
Stanley, David M., 275n26
Stark, Rodney, 385n1
Stauffer, Ethelbert, 28n1, 454–55n23
Stegman, Thomas, 129, 139n5, 154n30,
  368n28, 446n49
Stevenson, Ian, 110n20, 112n30
Stowers, Stanley, 54, 57n17, 61n25
Strabo, 167n46
Strelan, John G., 224n34
Strootman, R., 395n22
Suh, M. K. W., 98n37, 358n6, 398n29
Sumney, Jerry L., 149n15

Talbert, Charles H., 24n32, 275n28
Tannehill, Robert C., 32n18, 165n36
Taylor, R. O. P., 111n24
Tertullian, 126–27
Thaden, Robert H. von, 96n29, 372n40
Theissen, Gerd, 31n13, 103n52
Theophrastus, 302n24, 396n26, 486n21
Thiselton, Anthony C., 72n14, 72n15,
  95n26, 97n34, 98n36, 111n27, 486n22
Thomas Aquinas, 5, 68n31, 216n13
Thraede, Klaus, 464n53
Thucydides, 113n35, 290n2, 485n14
Tillich, Paul, 5
Torrance, Thomas F., 17n13
Towner, Philip H., 256n24, 481n1,
  485n17
Trummer, Peter, 431n13
Turner, Edith, 162n15
Turner, Nigel, 13n3
Turner, Victor, 177n123, 178–79

Tutu, Desmond, 138n2
Tyson, Joseph B., 170n70, 187n4,
  283n43

VanderKam, James C., 248n13
Van Houtan, Kyle S., 89n15
Vawter, F. Bruce, 299n18
Vegge, Ivar, 139n5
Verner, David C., 431n13, 481n1
Via, Dan O., 320n23
Vielhauer, Philipp, 30
Villepigue, James, 88n7
Virgil, 113n38, 126n94
Vogel, Cornelia J. de, 272n19

Wach, Joachim, 160n1
Wagner, Günter, 162n14, 164n27,
  171n72, 172n77
Wainwright, Geoffrey, 163n19, 163n20,
  166n45
Walker, William O., Jr., 123n81
Wallace, James Buchanan, 129–30,
  150n18
Wanamaker, C. A., 275n28
Ward, Roy Bowen, 96n30
Watson, Francis, 210n3, 281–82n41,
  314n2, 347n30
Weaver, Mary J., 113n37, 317–18n16
Wedderburn, A. J. M., 154n27
Weiss, Bernhard, 10n8, 431n12
Welles, C. Bradford, 481–82n4
Westerholm, Stephen, 6n1, 216n12,
  217n15
Wette, W. M. L. de, 429n2
White, L. Michael, 200n35, 263n3
Whiteley, D. E. H., 28n1
Wikenhauser, Alfred, 95n27
Wilcox, Max, 167n52, 187n5
Wild, Robert A., 332n49, 346n28,
  353n41
Williams, Cyril G., 108n7, 109n16,
  112n31, 122n72
Williams, Michael A., 247n9
Williams, Sam K., 13n2, 14, 15
Willis, Wendell L., 375n47
Wilson, Bryan R., 359n10
Wilson, Jim, 157n38
Wilson, R. A., 340n14

Wilson, Robert McL., 187n4

Wilson, Robert R., 112n32

Wilson, Stephen G., 30n11

Wilson, Walter T., 50n7, 51n8, 54n14, 57n17

Wimpfheimer, Barry S., 212n7

Wink, Walter, 299n18, 339n9

Wire, Antoinette Clark, 124–25, 319n20

Witherington, Ben, III, 129n2, 263n3

Wolter, Michael, 412n5, 431n13, 481–82n4

Wright, N. T., 10n11, 28–29, 35–36, 47, 71n8, 153n29, 299n18

Xenophon, 193n14, 290n2, 301n21, 302n24, 315n8, 325n34, 346n29, 347n33, 406n43, 417n11

Yamauchi, Edwin M., 247n9, 310n46

Yarbro Collins, Adela, 164n32

Yarbrough, O. Larry, 96n29, 363n16, 397n28

Yoo, Yoon Jong, 185n2

Young, Frances M., 481n1

Zablocki, Benjamin D., 359n10

Zuesse, E. M., 160n4

INDEX OF SUBJECTS

Abraham, 34, 77–78n28; faith of, 13n3, 16, 20–21, 23; and metaphor of the church as family, 237; story of Israel and the promise to, 203–7, 220

Achaia, 158, 159

Acts, 257–58, 321–22; glossolalia, 116–17; salvation language, 27–28, 36–39; social character of salvation, 36–39

Adam: first, 77–79, 91, 94, 348; and Jesus, 25

Ad Demonicum (Ps.-Isocrates), 465–68

adiaphora, 322, 325, 374, 376, 380, 397

agapē, 118–19, 219, 311; "doing the truth in love," 325–35; and glossolalia, 118–19, 378

Alexander the charlatan, 406, 413, 435–36, 463n50, 470n71

anathemas, 402–3, 407

anger, Paul on, 334–35

Antioch of Pisidia, synagogue speech at, 37, 38

apocalyptic worldview as this-worldly restoration (Wright's hypothesis), 28–32, 35–36, 47

Apollo, 125–26

Apollos, 44, 91–92, 140, 141, 147, 237, 397, 423

Apuleius of Madera, 172–73

Aristophanes, 450–51

Aristotle, 4, 54–58; character ethics, 54–58, 61–62; and *koinōnia*, 156–57; *Nicomachean Ethics*, 54–58, 61–62, 64, 67; on prudence (*phronēsis*), 54–58, 65, 67–68

Augustine of Hippo, 128

baptism: Bultmann on, 252; Colossians, 167–71, 181–84, 289, 299–300, 305–12; Corinthian community, 75n23, 94, 103, 105; Galatians' experience of Holy Spirit in, 191–92; and grace for Cretan community, 494–95; of Jesus, 161–62, 165, 180; metaphor of circumcision, 307–8; mystery and metaphor in, 299–300, 305–12; and other Jewish and Christian rituals of initiation, 179–81; proselyte baptism for gentile converts, 179–80; ritual imprinting, 160–84, 301; as single initiation vs. series of rituals, 166–71; symbolism, 162–66. *See also* ritual imprinting

Barnabas, 198–99

Barth, Karl, 5

biblical theology, 17, 245

boasting, 224–25

body: Corinthian correspondence, 75–77, 85, 86–106, 125–26; default modes of thinking about, 87–91; Greco-Roman medical and moral discourse, 125–26; implications of Corinthian meals, 101–5; metaphors for the church, 237–38; Paul on his body, 272–74; *sarx* (flesh), 76, 98n36, 216–17, 398n29; and sexual immorality, 96–101, 106; social body of Corinthian assembly as *sōma Christou*, 91–96; *sōma* and social complexities of resurrection, 75–77, 85, 86–106; spirit and body (*pneuma* and *sōma*), 86–87, 91, 105–6, 125–26

Bona Dea, cult of, 358

Bultmann, Rudolf, 244–61; church and baptism, 252; church and early Catholicism, 253, 257; church and Lord's Supper, 252; church as historical phenomenon, 245–49; development of church order, 253–58; eschatology and church structure, 249–52; on the Hellenistic church and Jewish synagogue, 250–52, 257; historical method, 247–49, 260–61; and New Testament theology, 244–45; on *pistis*, 17, 21n28; on salvation language, 40n32; *Theology of the New Testament*, 244–61

Calvin, John, 5
Capon, Robert Farrar, 101
captivity correspondence, 45–46. *See also* Ephesians; Philippian correspondence
Catechism of the Catholic Church, The, 337n1
Catholicism: Bultmann and, 253, 257; Johnson's, 8n4, 27; Pentecostal, 108n8; and sacrament of the world, 337n1; views on gender and sexuality, 319n21, 323
Celsus, 127
Cephas, 122, 147, 158, 197–99, 266, 410
character ethics: Aristotle, 54–58, 65, 67–68; Corinthians, 64–65; Galatians, 66–67; moral discernment and role of Holy Spirit, 62–64; moral discernment as measure of faith, 58–62; Philippians, 65–66; and prudence (*phronēsis*), 54–58, 65, 67–68; Romans, 48–68; Titus, 481–97
Character of Jesus, The (Stegman), 129
charism, 118, 255, 256
charismatic movement, 108n8
chastity, 324–25, 334
childishness, 119n66, 325–26, 332–33
church (*ekklēsia*), 230–43, 337–56, 357–84; Colossians, 240–41, 338, 339n9; construction of ecclesial community, 357–67, 369–84; Corinthians, 369–79; cultivating mutual edification, 361, 364–66; cultivating practice of mutual discernment, 361, 366–67; cultivation of mutual holiness, 361–64; Ephesians, 240–41, 292–95, 328, 337–56, 381–84, 499; Galatians, 401–4; and Greco-Roman social clubs or societies, 231, 232, 239, 358, 360; and Hellenistic Jewish diaspora synagogues, 231, 239, 250–52, 257, 358, 360; Israel and, 232–35; language of discernment/testing, 361, 366–67, 370, 371, 379–81, 397–99; language of edification, 361, 364–66, 371–72, 382–83; and marriage, 349–52; metaphors, 236–39, 349–52; mission of, 235–36, 292–95, 345–46; and the *mystērion*, 292–95, 345–46; organization in, 239–40; Pastorals, 241–42, 256–57; Paul's crisis management for threats to, 385–408; Paul's focus on stability and integrity, 231–33; as place of God's reconciliation, 236, 328, 331, 334, 336, 339, 340–46, 356; principalities and powers, 293–94, 339, 340, 346, 352n38, 353n44, 354; and the resurrection, 233; role of Holy Spirit, 238; Romans, 379–81; theme of holiness, 361–64, 370–71, 380–81, 382; Thessaloniki community, 357–67, 385–96, 407–8
circumcision: Colossians, 169–71, 177, 181–83, 289, 307–12; Galatians, 169–71, 177, 181–83, 187–88, 192–93, 207, 228–29, 234, 316, 319, 401–4; Luke on gentiles and, 38–39; and men's status in the church, 316; metaphor of baptism, 307–8; Paul's management of threats to the *ekklēsia*, 401–4; Philippians, 283–84; Titus, 405
Clement of Alexandria, 172n77, 247, 256, 499
Code of Canon Law (1983), 407n44
Colossians, 289–312, 499; the church (*ekklēsia*), 240–41, 338, 339n9; circumcision issue, 169–71, 177, 181–83, 289, 307–12; disputed character, 5, 10n11, 170; metaphors of Christian maturity, 301–12; *mystērion* and metaphor, 289–312; mystery of Christ

among the gentiles, 290–300; mystery of "Christ within/among you," 296, 298–300, 305, 307, 309, 312; ritual imprinting and baptism, 167–71, 181–84, 289, 299–300, 305–12

confirmation, rite of, 184

Conzelmann, Hans, 450–51

Corinthian correspondence, 69–85, 86–106, 107–28, 129–37, 138–59, 498; appeal to *koinōnia* (fellowship), 140, 142, 143, 146–47, 151–53, 156–59; baptism, 75n23, 94, 103, 105; the body, 75–77, 85, 86–106, 125–26; the body and sexual immorality, 96–101, 106, 140, 372, 397–99; character ethics, 64–65; church community construction, 369–79; collection of funds from gentiles, 143–44, 145–47, 149, 156, 157–58; Corinthians' allegiance to "super-apostles," 144, 147, 152; on eating food offered to idols, 102–3, 375–77; glossolalia, 107–28, 377–79; glossolalia and prophecy, 107–28, 377–79; immediate literary context of 2 Corinthians, 132–34; language of discernment and testing, 370, 371, 397–99; language of edification, 371–72; marriage and celibacy, 372–75; mythic language, 129–37; parallels to Timothy's community, 409–10, 414–15, 423, 425; Paul's hurt and anger, 144–51, 159, 239–40; *pneuma* and the human spirit/Holy Spirit, 64, 78–81, 86; resurrection, 69–85, 86–106, 136–37, 154–56; rhetorical situation (2 Cor), 140–44; salvation language/social dimension of salvation, 43–44; theme of holiness, 368, 370–71, 397; threats to the church and Paul's crisis management, 97–98, 140, 397–400; truth and reconciliation process, 138–59; women's head coverings/veiling, 123–24, 316, 319; women's speech and roles, 123–26

covenantal nomism, 247

Covenant Network of Presbyterians, 322

Crete, 476, 482–97. *See also* Titus

Cybele, 113–14

Cynics, 314–15n5, 468–70, 471

Dead Sea scrolls, 247

deconstruction, benefits of, 7–11

Delphic oracles, 113, 114, 125–26

Demeter, cult of, 175

Derrida, Jacques, 7

Descartes, René, 71, 87

Dibelius, Martin, 450–51, 465–66

Dio Chrysostom, 473–76

Diogenes Laertius, 4, 469

dogmas, scholarly, 10, 428, 431

Donne, John, 90

Ecstatic Religion (Lewis), 122–23

Eleusinian mysteries, 172, 174n95

Enlightenment, 71, 87n3, 101, 137, 210n4

Enuma Elish, 134

Epaphras, 168, 289, 292, 301, 302

Epaphroditus, 66, 268, 280, 281, 283, 285–86, 446

Ephesians, 328–36, 337–56; the church (*ekklēsia*), 240–41, 292–95, 328, 337–56, 381–84, 499; church as place of God's reconciliation, 328, 331, 334, 336, 339, 340–46, 356; church community construction, 381–84; circumstances of composition, 355–56, 381–82; "doing the truth in love," 325–35; language of discernment, 383–84; language of edification, 382–83; marriage, 346–52; *mystērion* and the church's mission, 292–95, 345–46; nonrealized eschatology and exhortation to moral transformation, 341, 352–56; salvation language/social dimension of salvation, 46; theme of holiness, 382

Ephesus, city of, 141, 142, 412–14; Council of, 407n44; Paul's opponents, 405–6, 412–14, 419, 430, 435–37

Epictetus, 468–70

excommunication, practice of, 394–408; conciliar declarations, 407–8

faith of Jesus Christ (*pistis Christou*), 8–9, 13–26, 201–3, 209–13, 279, 498;

as confession, 18–19; Galatians, 201–3, 209–13; and obedience, 21–26; as response to God, 20–21; Romans, 9, 13–26, 43, 61–62, 202

false teachers, polemic against, 449–80; Dio Chrysostom, 473–76; Epictetus, 468–70; Letter to Titus, 476, 479–80, 486–87; Letters to Timothy, 447–79, 449–53, 459–64; Lucian, 470–73

form criticism, 248, 299n18

Freud, Sigmund, 163

Galatians, 185–208, 209–29, 446–47, 498; baptism, 167–71, 177, 183–84, 191–92; character ethics, 66–67; circumcision issue, 169–71, 177, 181–83, 187–88, 192–93, 207, 228–29, 234, 316, 319, 401–4; deciphering Galatians 6, 220–29; "do not submit to the yoke of slavery," 198n31, 210, 217, 220; epistolary greeting, 189–90; flesh and spirit, 216–19, 227; fourfold narrative on truth of Christian experience, 185–208, 209–10, 222; imperatives on expression of Christian experience, 209–29; list of vices/list of virtues, 218–19; moral heteronomy, 211–15; paradoxical character of Christian freedom, 215–20; Paul's personal narrative, 186–90, 193–99, 208; "politics of perfection," 195, 212, 289, 499; shunning agitators who threatened community stability, 401–4; story of Israel, 203–7, 220; story of Jesus, 200–203; story of the community, 190–93; testing and mutual discernment in communal life, 367; threats to the church, 401–4

Gangra, Synod of, 407n44

gender and sexuality. *See* sexuality

Genesis: creation and sin of Adam and Eve, 348; the first Adam, 77–78, 348; mythic language, 134

glossolalia, 107–28, 377–79; and *agapē*, 118–19, 378; ambiguous character, 120–26; contemporary, 107–8, 109–12, 114, 122; Corinthian community, 107–28, 377–79; and deviance, 126–28; as ecstatic utterance, 108n9, 109n12, 112–15, 115n52, 116, 163; evaluations by other New Testament writers, 116–20; and Greco-Roman mantic prophecy, 109, 112–15, 121, 125, 126–27; as "interpretation of tongues," 110–12, 115; Luke-Acts, 116–17; nature of the phenomenon, 108–15; as ordered babbling, 112–15, 119, 120, 127, 379; pervasiveness, 115–16; and prophecy, 108–9, 112–26, 377–79; psychological aspects, 109–10, 114, 122; *xenoglossia*, 110

Gnosticism, 28, 127, 247, 251–52, 338–39n6, 429n4; Bultmann on, 247, 252, 256; and glossolalia, 127

Goodenough, Erwin, 174

grace, God's, 16–17, 20, 196, 293–94, 447, 481–97

Greco-Roman religion and culture: on boasting, 224; the body in medical and moral discourse, 125–26; cultic meals, 101–2, 376–77; cultic mysteries and ritual initiation, 171–73; Hellenistic materials pertinent to understanding the polemic against false teachers, 464–76; and Jewish diaspora synagogues, 231, 239, 250–52, 257, 358, 360; *koinōnia* and friendship, 156–57, 263–64; mantic prophecy and glossolalia, 109, 112–15, 121, 125, 126–27; *phronēsis*, 274; slavery, 347; structure of local associations and societies, 231, 232, 358, 360; table of household codes, 346–47; virtues, 219

Harnack, Adolf von, 253, 258

heteronomy, moral, 210n4, 211–15

historical-critical method, 10n9

"historical Jesus," 71, 246, 500

History of the Synoptic Tradition (Bultmann), 245, 246

holiness, 361–64; *ekklēsia* and theme of, 361–64, 370–71, 380–81, 382; sexual holiness for modern Christians, 323–25

Holy Spirit: manifestations (gifts) of, 83–84; *pneuma* and the human spirit in 1 Corinthians, 64, 78–81, 86; *pneuma*'s functions, 80–84; role in moral discernment, 62–64; spirit-filled character ethics in Romans, 49–51, 62–64. *See also* glossolalia

household codes, 346–47

Hume, David, 5

Hymenaeus, 406, 413, 435–36, 460, 463n50

idolatry, 20, 52–53, 118, 121, 152, 218n20; and food offerings, 94, 102–3, 375–77; and initiation rituals, 181–82; and vices of sexual immorality, 218n20, 315, 320, 363, 375; and wall of separation from God, 344

Ignatius of Antioch, 247, 255, 256, 257, 356, 410, 499

image of God, 78, 156, 300, 301, 305, 310n45

individualism, 87–88, 90, 101, 103, 106, 210, 216, 240

Irenaeus of Lyons, 28, 127, 499

Isis cult, 169n65, 172–73, 184

James of Jerusalem, 322

Jerusalem temple, 356

Jewish apocalyptic literature, 28, 47

John Chrysostom, 128

John of Leiden, 395n21

John the Baptist, 117, 161–62, 165, 166n43, 180

Josephus, 111, 343

Judaism: cultic meals, 101–2; Philo on mysterious initiation in, 174–77; Second Temple period, 247; story of Israel and reinterpretation of Torah, 203–7

Judaizers, 228n42, 283, 356, 450

Justin Martyr, 356

Karris, Robert, 451–53, 468

koinōnia (fellowship): appeal in 2 Corinthians, 140, 142, 143, 146–47, 151–53, 156–59; Greco-Roman friendship, 156–57, 263–64; imperative to the Galatians, 226, 228; language of friendship (Philippians), 262–64; and sharing meals, 102–3; and suffering, 264

kyrios, 69–70, 79, 81, 202

Lewis, I. M., 122–23, 127–28

love: *agapē*, 118–19, 219, 311, 378; and church community, 363; "doing the truth in love" (Eph 4:15), 325–35; love commandment, 42, 63, 235. *See also* sexuality

Lucian of Samosata, 470–73

Luke, Gospel of: gentiles and circumcision, 38–39; glossolalia, 116–17; salvation language, 27–28, 32–36; social character of salvation, 32–36

Lumen Gentium (Dogmatic Constitution of the Church), 337n1

Luther, Martin, 5, 429n3

Macedonian church, 141, 142–44, 394, 410

Malherbe, Abraham J., 464–65

mandata principis letters, 231, 411–12, 432–33n17, 435, 445, 481–82, 484

mantic prophecy, 109, 112–15, 121, 125, 126–27

Marcion, 127, 429n4, 499–500

marriage: and celibacy, 372–75; and the church, 349–52; contemporary First World views of, 323–24; Corinthians, 372–75; Ephesians, 346–52; gender relations and roles, 348–52; sex in, 96–98, 323–24, 373–74; Timothy, 414, 419, 443

Mary, 35

meals: Greco-Roman cultic, 101–2, 376–77; and idolatry, 94, 102–3, 375–77; Jewish cultic, 101–2; *koinōnia* (fellowship), 102–3; Lord's banquet (Eucharist), 103–5; the *sōma* (body) and implications of, 101–5; Thessaloniki church crisis and shunning members from, 394–96

Merkabah mysticism, 169n65, 443n46

millenarian movements, 395
Millerites, 395n21
mind of Christ, 45–46, 58–68, 85, 95–96, 104–6, 118, 224, 235, 238, 274–86, 332n48, 370
Mithras, cult of, 358
Montanism, 126–27, 256
Moses of Crete, 395n21
Musonius Rufus, 316n13, 450n9
mystery (*mystērion*): ancient cultic mysteries, 171–73, 247; baptism as ritual imprinting, 167–71, 181–84, 289, 299–300, 305–12; Bultmann on, 247; Colossians, 289–312; Eleusinian mysteries, 172, 174n95; Ephesians, 292–95, 345–46; metaphors of Christian maturity, 301–12; *mystērion* (term), 171n72; mysterious initiation in Judaism, 174–77; mystery of Christ among the gentiles, 290–300; mystery of "Christ within/among you," 296, 298–300, 305, 307, 309, 312; Paul's ecclesiology, 292–95, 345–46; Romans, 291–92
mythic language: Corinthians, 129–37; definition of myth, 130; logic of, 134–37; regarding Christ's resurrection experience, 136–37; regarding Jesus's death on the cross, 136–37

necromancy, 166n43
New Testament canon, 9–10, 430–31
New Testament scholarship, 8–11, 244–45
Nicaea, Council of, 407n44
Nock, Arthur Darby, 174
noos (mind), 52–67

obedience and the faith of Jesus Christ (*pistis Christou*), 21–26
oikonomia theou tē en pistei, 416–22, 426, 435, 442
orthodox Christianity, 127–28
Osiris cult, 173

paideia, 489, 491, 496–97
paraenesis, 50–51, 286, 411, 453–64, 454n23

Pastoral Letters: authorship and authenticity, 409, 423–25, 428–35, 454n21, 483; Bultmann on development of church order and, 256–57; the church (*ekklēsia*), 241–42, 256–57; on false teachers, 449–80. *See also* Timothy, letters to; Titus
Pauline school, 7, 425, 433n20
Pauline theology. *See* theology of Paul
Pentecost, 37, 107, 111–12, 116–17, 180
Pentecostal movement, 108n8
petitio principii, logical fallacy of, 13n3, 432
Philippian correspondence, 262–65, 272–88, 498–99; character ethics, 65–66; circumcision issue, 283–84; contrast between law and grace, 446; exhortation to testing and mutual discernment, 367–68; fellowship of suffering, 262–65, 274–88; *koinōnia*, 262–64; mind of Christ, 274–86; *phronēsis* and moral reasoning, 274–75, 287–88; salvation language/social dimension of salvation, 45–46
Philo: on glossolalia, 111; on mystery initiation in Judaism, 174–77
phronēsis: Aristotle on prudence, 54–58, 65, 67–68; Christ's moral reasoning on fellowship of suffering, 274–75, 287–88; and cultivation of discernment, 361; Paul's character ethics, 54–58, 65, 67–68
Phrygia and Phrygian Christians, 167–70, 167n46, 179, 180–84, 301
pistis Christou. See faith of Jesus Christ (*pistis Christou*)
Platonism, 4–5
pneumatikos, 64, 76–77, 81
Polycarp, 356, 410, 454n23, 499
postmodernism, 7
principalities and powers, 293–94, 339, 340, 346, 352n38, 353n44, 354
prophecy: Corinthians, 107–28, 377–79; and glossolalia, 108–9, 112–26, 377–79; Greco-Roman mantic, 109, 112–15, 121, 125, 126–27; women's veiling, 123–24, 316, 319

Ps.-Libanius, 464–65, 475
psychikos, 64, 76–78, 91
Pythian spirit at Philippi, 39, 113n37, 125

Qumran community, 256, 257, 360

reconciliation: alienation between Paul
   and Corinthian community, 140–44;
   church as place of, 328, 331, 334, 336,
   339, 340–46, 356; embodiment of,
   156–58, 159; *koinōnia* (fellowship),
   140, 142, 143, 146–47, 151–53, 156–59;
   roots of, 151–56, 159; significance of,
   for contemporary political situation, 138–39, 158–59; three aspects
   of truth in service of, 144–58; truth
   and reconciliation process (2 Cor),
   138–59; and wall of separation from
   God, 342–45
Reformation, 249, 428–29
restorative justice, 138n1
resurrection: Corinthian correspondence, 69–85, 86–106, 136–37,
   154–56; and God's way of ordering
   creation, 421; moral transformation
   and ontological transformation,
   79–80, 85, 105; mythic language,
   136–37; ontological implications of
   Paul's statements on, 69–85; Paul's
   analogies, 75–80; Paul's ecclesiology,
   233; the resurrection confession,
   69–70, 72; roots of reconciliation and
   paradigm of the cross, 154–56; the
   sōma (body) and social complexities
   of, 75–77, 85, 86–106
ritual imprinting, 160–84, 301;
   cross-cultural anthropological
   studies, 177–79; definition of ritual,
   160–61; initiation into ancient cultic
   mysteries, 171–77; liminality, 179;
   Philo on mysterious initiation in
   Judaism, 174–77. *See also* baptism
Romans, 13–26, 48–68, 498; baptism
   mystery and metaphor, 306; character ethics, 48–68; church community
   construction, 379–81; faith of Jesus
   Christ (*pistis Christou* formulations), 9, 13–26, 43, 61, 202; Jesus as

exemplary moral guide, 61; language
   about Holy Spirit, 49–51; language
   of discernment/testing, 58–64,
   379–81; language of holiness, 380–81;
   moral discernment and role of Holy
   Spirit, 62–64; moral discernment
   as measure of faith, 58–62; on moral
   dispositions, 445–46; *mystērion* in,
   291–92; the noun *noos*, 52–67; origins
   of, 185–86; salvation language/social
   dimension of salvation, 40–43, 46

Sabbatai Zevi, 395n21
salvation. *See* soteriology
sarx (flesh), 76, 98n36, 216–17, 398n29
Schlatter, Adolf, 245
Schleiermacher, Friedrich, 428–31,
   435n26
Schüssler Fiorenza, Elisabeth, 124–25
Schweitzer, Albert, 431n11
Second Temple Judaism, 247
Second Vatican Council, 337n1
sexuality, 313–36; contemporary
   First World views, 317–27, 347n33;
   Corinthian community, 96–101, 106,
   140, 372, 397–99; "doing the truth in
   love" (Eph 4:15), 333–34; and gender,
   314–16; in marriage, 96–98, 323–24,
   372–75; same-sex relations/homosex-
   uality, 315, 318–25, 326–27, 336; sexual
   continence and excess, 314–15; sexual
   holiness for modern Christians,
   323–25; sexual immorality (*porneia*),
   96–101, 106, 140, 218n20, 314–15, 323,
   333–34, 363, 372, 375, 397–99
shamanism, 109, 122
signs and wonders, 51, 116, 148, 155,
   321–22, 393
Sinai, 206–7
Smyth, Herbert W., 491
Snatched into Paradise (2 Cor 2:1–10)
   (Wallace), 129–30
Sohm, Rudolf, 253–55, 258
sola scriptura, 320–21
Sophists, 450–51
sōphrosynē, 54n14, 55, 474
sorcery, 218

sōtēria, 29, 32, 34–47

soteriology, 27–47, 186; apocalyptic worldview as this-worldly restoration, 28–32, 35–36, 47; Bultmann on salvation language, 40n32; and ecclesiology, 229, 232; and faith of Jesus, 26; salvation in Luke-Acts and Paul, 27–47; salvation language in Corinthians, 43–44; salvation language in Romans, 40–43, 46; salvation language in the captivity correspondence, 45–46; salvation language in Thessalonian correspondence, 45; social dimension of salvation, 39–46; *sōtēria*, 29, 32, 34–47; *sōtērion*, 29, 32, 34–35, 39; *sōzein*, 29, 32–37, 490n29; Wright's hypothesis, 28–32, 35–36, 47

sōtērion, 29, 32, 34–35, 39

sōzein, 29, 32–37, 490n29

stoicheia, worldly, 191n8, 193, 211–12, 217, 220, 229, 302, 308

suffering, fellowship of, 262–88; *koinōnia* and language of friendship, 262–64; and the mind of Christ, 274–86; Paul on his body, 272–74; Philippians, 262–65, 272–88; and *phronēsis* (moral reasoning), 274–76, 287–88; power and strength/energy, 265–68, 271–72; as self-emptying and fellowship, 278–80; suffering with/ suffering for, 270–72; weakness, 268–69, 271

"super-apostles," 144, 147, 152

systematic theology, 5, 6, 271n16

ta pneumatika (spiritual powers), 73, 81, 83, 117–18, 120–21, 226, 354n47, 378

Tebtunis Papyri, 412, 481–82n4

Tertullian, 126–27, 499

thanksgiving blessing (2 Cor), 152–53

theology of Paul, 409–11; Johnson's objections to, 3–7, 425, 498; and perspective of 1 Timothy, 409–11, 415–23, 424–26

Theology of the New Testament (Bultmann), 244–61

Thessalonian correspondence, 357–84, 385–408, 499; building the church community, 357–67; church in Thessaloniki, 357–67, 385–96, 407–8; crisis in the church and Paul's response, 386–96, 407–8; cultivating mutual discernment, 361, 366–67; cultivating mutual edification, 361, 364–66; cultivation of mutual holiness, 361–64; Holy Spirit and holiness, 362; salvation language/social dimension of salvation, 45

Thomas Aquinas, 5, 68n31, 216n13

Tillich, Paul, 5

Timothy, letters to, 409–27, 428–48, 449–80, 499; authorship and authenticity, 409, 423–25, 428–35; church at Ephesus, 241–42, 404–6, 412–14; composition and setting, 411–15; God's *oikonomia theou tē en pistei*, 416–22, 426, 435, 442; Hellenistic materials pertinent to understanding, 464–76; list of vices, 438–40; *mandata principis* letters, 411–12, 445; on marriage, 414, 419, 443; parallels to Corinthian church situation, 409–10, 414–15, 423, 425; Paul as model for Timothy to follow, 455–58; Paul's conversion account, 437, 439, 447–48; Paul's opponents, 404–6, 412–14, 419, 430, 435–37; Paul's thanksgiving, 422, 439–41; personal paraenetic letter (2 Tim), 453–64; polemic against false teachers, 449–53, 459–64, 477–79; theological character (1 Tim), 409–27; theological perspective (1 Tim), 415–23, 424–26; threats to the church and Paul's crisis management, 404–6; Timothy as Paul's delegate, 140, 141, 142, 264, 270, 280, 285, 369, 404, 411–15, 430, 435–64; on women as heads of households, 413, 415, 418, 420

Titus, 9, 444, 481–97; authorship, 483; character ethics and pedagogy of grace, 481–97; the church (*ekklēsia*), 241–42, 405; experience of God's goodness, 492–96; God's grace as the gift that teaches, 490–92; household directives, 488–90; polemic against false teachers, 476, 479–80, 486–87; rhetorical performance for Cretan community, 482–90; threats to the church and Paul's crisis management, 405; on vices, 486

tongue-speaking. *See* glossolalia

Torah, Paul's reinterpretation of, 203–7

tradition criticism, 258

truth and reconciliation. *See* reconciliation

Truth and Reconciliation Commission (Canada), 138n1

Truth and Reconciliation Commission (South Africa), 138n1

Turner, Victor, 178–79, 182

Tychichus, 168n54, 168n56, 292, 337, 355

Van Gennep, Arnold, 178–79

vices: idolatry and sexual immorality, 218n20, 315, 320, 363, 375; lists of, 218–19, 438–40, 449–50n4, 486

Wire, Antoinette Clark, 124–25

women: as heads of households, 413, 415, 418, 420; roles of, 123–26, 315–16, 319, 346–52; speech of, 123–26; veiling while prophesying, 123–24, 316, 319

Wright, N. T., 28–29, 35–36, 47

Xenophon, 96n30, 315n8, 347n33

Yale Divinity School, 9, 430

Zacchaeus, 34–35, 37

INDEX OF SCRIPTURE
AND OTHER ANCIENT SOURCES

OLD TESTAMENT

Genesis

1–2	319n21
1:3	348
1:26	315
1:26–28	348
1:27	420
2–4	342
2:4	69n1
2:7	77, 100n43
2:18–24	348
2:24	294n7, 350, 351
3:4–7	348
3:6	420
3:7	419
3:11	419
3:13	420
3:20–24	419
6:1–4	124, 134
12:3	204, 205
15:6	20, 204, 205
15:13	345n25
16:15	348
17:1	363n15
21:10	207, 403
23:4	345n25
31:41	303n25
34:25	169n68

Exodus

2:22	345n25
3:15–16	69n1
12:45	345n25
16:3	360
18:3	345n25
19:10	164n30
20:8–11	211
20:13–15	211
23:19	74n19
34:6	69n1

Leviticus

2:12	74n19
11:1–15:33	362
11:44–45	362
16:19–20	164n30
16:30	164n30
17:1–19:37	362
18:5	205
18:19	217
19:2	362
19:9–10	211
20:7	362
23:10	74n19
25:23	345n25
26:11–12	152n24
27:28	402n38

Numbers

8:21	164n30
14:5	360
15:20–21	74n19
18:12	74n19
18:14	402n38
19:12	164n30
21:2–3	402n38
31:23	164n30
35:15	345n25

Deuteronomy

7:26	402n38
13:15	402n38
13:17	402n38
17:7	399
18:4	74n19
20:17	402n38
21:23	154, 200, 204, 233, 321
23:1–2	232
26:2	74n19
27:26	204, 402
31:30	360
33:21	74n19

Joshua

6:16–17	402n38
6:20	402n38
7:1–13	402n38
9:2	232
28:22	393n18

Ruth

2:10	345n25
4:4	365n20

1 Samuel

10:5–13	112
19:18–24	112

2 Samuel

7:14	152n24
15:19	345n25

2 Kings

5:7	78n29

1 Chronicles

2:7	402n38

Nehemiah

9:6	78n29

Esther

8:17	169n68

Job

1:1	363n15
1:8	363n15
1:21	419
2:3	363n15
12:4	363n15
36:6	78n29

Psalms

4:4	335
4:6	396n26
9:9	389n12
19:1	389n12
21:22	232
22:22	360
24:1	69n1
27:5	365n20
31:7	389n12
36:39	389n12
43:13	226n40
50:1–12	164n31
54:3	389n12
55:8	203n44

68:8	345n25
68:19	329n40
68:20–36	329n40
70:20	78n29, 389n12
79:6	226n40
81:5	387n7
85:7	389n12
95:5	102–3
109:1 (LXX)	69
110:1	69, 309n40
118:22	366n24

Proverbs

1:30	226n40
8:10	366
31:24	395n24

Isaiah

10:22	40
11:5	353n40
18:2	345n25
37:3	389n12
40:5	35
43:6	152n24
49:1	447
49:2	44
49:6	38
51:2	390n14
52:11	152n24
53:1	69n1
54:1	206
57:14	164n31
59:16–17	353n40
66:17	164n31

Jeremiah

1:5	365, 447
2:1	349
2:19	393n18
3:1–5	349
20:7	226n40
40:7	365n20
40:8	164n31

Ezekiel

3:21	223n31
16:1–63	349
16:4–9	351
20:34	152n24
36:25	164n31
37:23	164n31
37:27	152n24

Daniel

2:18	290
2:19	290
2:27	290
2:28	290
2:29	290
2:30	290
2:47	290
4:6	290
7:1–9	392n16
7:23–25	392n16
9:26–27	392n16
11:31	392n16
11:37	392n16
12:1	389n12, 392n16
12:7	392n16
12:11	392n16

Hosea

1:2–9	349
3:1–5	349

Joel

3:1–5	116
3:5	37, 41

Amos

9:6	203n44

Obadiah

12	389n12
14	389n12

Nahum

1:7	389n12

Habakkuk
2:4   26, 202, 205

Zechariah
8:16   334n55
14:11   402n38

Malachi
2:5   395n24

NEW TESTAMENT

Matthew
1:21   33
3:1–16   161n9
3:1–17   162n16, 180n147
3:11   162n17
3:16–17   162n12, 165n40
4:11   164n32
5:32   323n32, 374
6:7   115n52
8:25   33
11:11   161n9
14:2   161n9
14:30   33
15:2   164n30
16:14   161n9
16:18–19   249n16
17:13   161n9
18:20   121
19:9   374
21:25   161n9
24:5   393n17
24:6   387n8
24:8   390n14
24:9   393n17
24:15   393n17
24:21   393n17
24:24   393n17
24:29   393n17
24:42–43   390n13
26:24   309n40
28:19   161n10

Mark
1:1–33   180n147
1:4   164n32

1:4–9   161n9
1:5   162n16
1:8–9   162n17
1:9–11   162n12, 165n40
1:15   387n6
3:4   32
5:23–24   32
6:25   161n9
6:56   32
7:2–5   164n30
8:28   161n9
8:35   32
8:38   455–56n26
10:11   374
10:26   32
10:38–40   165n36
10:52   32
11:30   161n9
12:36   309n40
13:6   393n17
13:7   387n8
13:8   390n14, 393n17
13:9   393n17
13:13   32, 35
13:19   393n17
13:20   35
13:23   393n17
13:24   393n17
13:26   393n17
13:30   32
14:36   220n26
14:62   309n40
15:30–31   32
16:16   161n10
16:17   108n9, 110, 111, 111n26, 115n52

Luke
1:4   116, 163n22
1:6   363n15
1:46–55   35
1:47   30
1:69   34
1:71   34
1:74–75   35
1:75   35
1:77   35

2:11   30, 35
2:30   30, 35
2:32   35
3:2–19   180n147
3:3   164n32
3:6   30, 35
3:7   162n16
3:7–21   161n9
3:16   117
3:21   162n16
3:21–22   162n12, 165n40
4:16–32   33
4:39   33
5:14   33
5:25   33
5:32   439n40
6:9   32, 33
6:20   33
6:48   387n7
7:10   33
7:15   33
7:19–20   161n9
7:22–23   33
7:33   161n9
7:50   33
8:12   33
8:36   33
8:48   33
8:48–50   32, 33
8:48–56   33
9:19   161n9
9:24   28, 32, 35
9:26   455–56n26
9:56   33
10:7   421
12:39   390n13
13:10–17   33, 34, 37
13:23   33, 34
13:24–30   34
14:4   33
15:1–2   33
15:3–32   33
15:11–31   213
15:11–32   33
16:18   374
16:23   35

16:24	108n9	2:12	107n1	9:21	163n23
17:19	33	2:13	107n1, 111n24	10–15	321–22
17:33	35	2:16–18	108	10:36–45	165n39
18:26	32	2:17–18	116	10:37	161n9
18:42	32, 33	2:19	116	10:43	163n23
19:1–10	37	2:21	31, 37, 41	10:44–48	117n56,
19:9	34, 35	2:33	165n39, 166n43		162n12, 322
19:10	33, 34, 439n40	2:33–34	309n40	10:45	117, 486n24
20:8	161n9	2:37	37	10:45–48	165n38
20:42	309n40	2:38	37, 163n23,	10:46	108n9, 114
21:28	35		164n32, 165n38,	10:46–47	163n21
22:69	309n40		180	10:47–48	161n10,
23:35–37	32	2:38–39	117		162n16, 162n18
23:39	33, 35	2:38–41	161n10	11:2	486n24
23:42–43	35	2:39	37	11:14	38
24:37	387n8	2:40	37	11:15–18	322
		2:41	162n16, 162n18	11:16	117, 161n10, 165n38
John		2:42–47	249n17	13:23	30, 37
1:13	164n35	2:44	37	13:24	161n9
1:25–33	161n9	2:47	37	13:26	37, 39
1:26	162n17	3:1–10	37	13:47	38
1:31–34	180n147	3:12–28	161n10	14:9	38
1:32–34	162n12,	3:16	38	14:23	484n11
	165n40	3:19	164n32	14:27	322
1:33	162n17	4:9	38	15	38–39, 249
3:3–8	164n35	4:11	366n24	15:1	39
3:22	180	4:11–12	38	15:3–4	322
3:22–24	180n147	4:12	163n23	15:5	39
3:22–26	161n9	4:30–31	165n39	15:9	164n28, 164n32
4:1–2	161n9, 180n147	4:31	166n43, 387n7	15:11	39
4:2	180	4:32	157	15:14	39
14:25	165n39	4:32–5:11	249	15:15–21	322
20:21–23	165n39	5:31	30, 37, 309n40	15:16	39
		7:25	37	16:1	430n6
Acts		7:55–56	309n40	16:6	167n46
1:3	165n38	8:1–9	249	16:15	161n10, 162n12,
1:5	117, 161n9, 180n147	8:12	162n16		162n16, 162n18,
1:8	165n38	8:16	163n23		163n23
1:21–22	180	8:16–17	165n38	16:17	39
1:22	161n9	8:26–40	162n12	16:26	273n22
2:1–4	163n21, 165n38	8:37	163n23	16:30	39
2:3	108n9	9:3–8	115	16:31	39, 163n23
2:4	108n9, 116	9:5	95n27	16:33	161n10, 162n12,
2:4–11	110, 114, 122	9:14	163n23		162n16, 162n17,
2:6–8	108	9:17	180		162n18
2:8	111	9:17–19	162n12, 165n38	16:34	39
2:11	108n9, 116	9:18	161n10, 180	17:13	387n7

18:1–4	397	1:17	13–14n3, 14–15, 16,	3:17–20	341, 342n19
18:5	397, 430n6		22, 42, 202, 205,	3:18	349n34
18:8	161n10		321	3:20	305n31, 310n44,
18:11	397	1:18	42		349n34
18:18	397	1:18–23	20	3:21	19
18:20–21	412	1:18–32	42, 52, 55, 233,	3:21–26	13–26, 43,
18:24–28	412		333n52, 341, 363,		61, 213, 258,
18:25	161n9, 180n147		383		284–85n45, 343
18:26	163n22	1:18–3:20	14	3:21–5:21	491n30
19:1–5	180	1:20	265, 266	3:22	13n1, 14–15, 25,
19:1–7	162n12, 412	1:21	100n45		26, 234
19:2–3	117	1:23	76n25, 78n30	3:24	25
19:3–4	180n147	1:24	22	3:25	14, 15–16, 24
19:3–5	161n10	1:24–29	315	3:25–26	25
19:5	162n17, 162n18	1:28	305n31, 310n44,	3:26	13n1, 13n3, 14, 16,
19:5–6	165n38		379		19n23
19:6	108n9, 114, 115,	1:28–29	52	3:27	401n35
	117, 163n21, 180	1:29–31	438n34	3:30	26
19:10	412	1:29–32	52, 60, 315n6	4:1	237, 266
19:22	430n6	1:30	438n36, 440n43	4:1–25	16, 234
19:23–41	412	1:32	438n35	4:3	20
19:34	161n9	2–3	494n39	4:5	20
20:17–35	412	2:1–11	315n6	4:11–12	23
21:21	393n18	2:2–3	104n53	4:12	193n14
21:24	193n14	2:4	438n37, 441n45,	4:15	42
22:16	161n10, 163n23,		494n36	4:16	13n3, 16, 20
	164n32	2:5	42, 354n48	4:16b	13n3
27:3	437n31	2:7	76n25	4:16–25	41
27:17	437n31	2:8	23n31, 42, 341n16	4:17	20, 21, 71,
27:20	36	2:9	389n12		77–78n28, 78n29
27:31	36	2:12	52	4:17–25	77–78n28
27:34	36	2:17	18	4:18–20	21n28
28:2	494n37	2:17–20	284	4:19	77–78n28
28:28	30, 39	2:18	379	4:20	23n31, 76n25,
		2:18–20	52		266, 438n37
Romans		2:24	406n42	4:22–24	20
1	383	2:25–29	235	4:24	77–78n28
1–4	23	3:1–4	234, 342	4:25	223n30
1–11	381	3:2	234	5	23, 25
1:4	49, 50, 63, 165n39,	3:3	15n11, 23n31,	5–6	341
	237, 265, 266		438n37	5–8	49
1:5	22, 24, 292	3:5	42	5:1	42, 43
1:7	26, 237	3:7	15n11, 76n25,	5:1–11	343
1:8	13–14n3, 22n29		349n34	5:2	42, 76n25, 445
1:13	228, 232	3:8	104n53, 406n42	5:3	389n12
1:16	40, 42, 232, 265,	3:9	234, 379	5:4	460n40
	266, 455n26	3:12	494n36	5:5	49, 50, 119, 165n38,

	166n43, 237, 380, 495	6:19	99n41, 100n42, 268, 380	8:18	270
5:5–6	268	6:21–22	228	8:18–21	76n25
5:6	268	6:22	380	8:22	19n23
5:6–21	380	7–8	445	8:23	74n19
5:8	439n40	7:1–3	315	8:23–24	43
5:9	19n23	7:4–5	228	8:24	232
5:9–10	42	7:5	99n41, 100n42, 270	8:24–25	21n28
5:11	19n23	7:6	50, 63	8:26	50, 115n52, 268
5:12–21	16, 25, 61, 77, 233, 284–85n45, 348	7:8	216	8:27	50, 53, 62
		7:11	216, 387–88n9	8:29	62, 78n30, 237, 310n45
5:15	25, 223n30	7:12	445	8:34	309n40
5:15–19	25	7:13	194n19	8:35	389n12
5:16	25, 104n53, 223n30	7:14	445	8:38	339n9
		7:15–23	218n18	8:38–39	353
5:17	223n30	7:16	437n31, 445	9–11	40, 42, 203n44, 234–35, 260, 342
5:17–18	42	7:23	52, 99n41, 100n42	9:1	50
5:18	25, 223n30			9:1–3	234
5:18–19	16, 17, 24, 26	7:23–25	52	9:1–5	342
5:18–21	236	7:25	52	9:3–5	342n19
5:19	21, 25–26	8	62	9:4–5	234
5:20	223n30	8:1	19n23	9:6	234
6	23	8:1–3	62	9:6–29	235
6–8	494n40	8:1–11	445	9:10	31
6:1	76n25	8:2	42, 50	9:13	494n38
6:1–11	163n22, 165n36, 166n42, 196, 232, 306	8:2–4	165n39	9:14–23	291
		8:2–11	166n42	9:15	494n38
		8:3	265, 266, 268	9:16	494n38
6:1–23	50	8:4	42, 218n17, 380	9:17	265, 266
6:3	63n26, 161n10	8:4–5	50	9:18	494n38
6:4	42, 63, 218n17, 306	8:5	53, 380	9:22	42, 266, 441n45
6:6	63n26, 196n24, 200n34	8:5–7	22n30	9:23	76n25
		8:5–8	62	9:25	42
6:8	63n26	8:6	53	9:26	42
6:9	63n26	8:7	53, 265	9:27	40
6:11	23, 63n26, 238	8:8	265	9:30–10:3	233–34
6:12	22	8:9	50, 238, 380	9:30–10:4	235
6:12–19	22	8:9–11	165n39	9:33	18n17, 377n48
6:13	23, 24, 99n41, 100n42, 235	8:10	42	10:1	40
		8:11	16, 50, 63, 78n29, 237, 238, 380	10:2	18, 40, 194–95n21, 305n31, 310n44
6:14	23	8:14	50, 62	10:3	20, 349n34
6:16	22, 23	8:15	50, 62, 115n52, 220n26, 237	10:4	42
6:17	22			10:5–10	329n41
6:17–19	23	8:15–17	24, 163n21	10:9	18, 163n23
6:18	22, 235	8:16	50, 63	10:9a	21, 41

10:9b	21, 41	12:1–6	58	14:2	59, 380
10:9–10	41, 42, 43	12:1–15:12	62	14:3	366n24, 380, 381
10:9–13	41	12:2	52, 53, 58, 63,	14:3–4	381
10:10	21, 41		64, 66, 310n43,	14:4	266, 380n56, 381
10:11	18n17		332n47, 380, 381,	14:5	380n56
10:12	41		383–84n60	14:5–6	59
10:13	31, 41, 43	12:2–3	56	14:6	53, 380n56, 381
10:14	18n17	12:3	53, 55, 57, 58,	14:7–8	381
10:15	201n38		59n22, 60	14:7–9	60, 61
10:16	22	12:3–8	115	14:10	366n24,
10:16–17	22	12:3–13:14	51		380n56, 381
10:19	377n48	12:4–5	60, 65, 92, 237,	14:10–12	381
10:21	23n31, 42, 341n16		304n30, 343n21	14:11	18n18
11:1	41, 42	12:5	60n23	14:12	60
11:1–6	235	12:6	57, 59	14:13	377n48, 380n56,
11:2	42	12:6–8	230, 484n11		381
11:5	19n23	12:7–8	257, 359n7	14:14	61, 381
11:8–27	234	12:8	239, 254	14:15	218n17, 236, 381
11:11	41, 223n30, 232	12:10–13	50	14:15a	61
11:11–14	45	12:11	51	14:15b	61
11:12	46, 223n30	12:12	389n12	14:17	51, 235, 380
11:13	52	12:16	53, 65	14:18	60, 380n56
11:13–32	235	12:19	42	14:19	381
11:14	41, 44, 232	13:2	104n53	14:20	380, 381
11:15	46	13:4–5	42	14:21	269, 372, 377n48
11:16	45, 74n19, 237	13:7	349n34	14:22	59, 380n56
11:16–24	237	13:8	42, 63	14:22–23	59
11:20	23n31, 53, 438n37	13:8–10	235	14:23	20, 380n56
11:22	494n36	13:9	217n15, 340n10	15:1	265, 269
11:23	23n31, 201n38,	13:9–10	63	15:1–3	61
	266, 438n37	13:11	42	15:1–7	166n42
11:25	53, 293	13:11–14	44	15:2	381
11:25–26	42, 292	13:12	163n20, 310n42,	15:2–6	381
11:26	28, 46, 356		354n48	15:3	341n16
11:29	232	13:13	60, 65, 194–	15:3–7	61
11:30	19n23, 341n16,		95n21, 218n17	15:4	234
	494n38	13:13–14	446	15:5	53, 380n56
11:30–32	23n31	13:14	60, 63, 65,	15:7	236, 381
11:31	341n16, 494n38		66n30, 236,	15:8	15n11, 301n24
11:32	23n31, 341n16,		310n42	15:8–9	381
	494n38	14	260	15:9	18n18, 494n38
11:33–36	291	14:1	59, 380	15:10–11	42
12–14	49, 62	14:1–2	269	15:13	51, 265, 266
12:1	50, 60	14:1–23	213n9	15:14	237
12:1–2	24, 50, 166n42,	14:1–15:3	380	15:16–19	51
	383, 445	14:1–15:12	51	15:17–19	436n28

15:18	22	1:12	122	2:13–15	223n32
15:19	265, 266	1:12–17	162n17	2:14	64, 77n27, 81, 265
15:24	239	1:13–17	161n10, 306n32	2:14–15	371n38
15:24–32	236	1:15	162n18	2:16	64, 66, 67, 85,
15:25–26	158	1:17	415		95, 104, 105, 118,
15:25–29	143	1:17–2:5	154		166n42, 166n43,
15:27	77n27, 158, 226	1:18	43, 44, 45, 64, 265,		224, 235, 238, 276,
16:1	237, 316n12, 338		266, 377n49		319, 325, 332n48,
16:1–2	239	1:18–30	64		350, 370, 371,
16:1–3	257	1:18–31	95		445n48
16:3	316n12	1:18–2:5	235	2:24	100
16:4	338	1:18–2:16	64	3:1	77n27, 223n32
16:5	74n19, 231, 338	1:20–23	370n35	3:1–2	265
16:6	316n12	1:20–28	76n26	3:1–3	119n66
16:7	316n12	1:21	18n21, 44	3:1–4	81, 92, 330n45
16:12	316n12	1:23	201, 377n48	3:1–12	147
16:15	316n12	1:24	64, 265, 266	3:3	194–95n21
16:16	338	1:25	267, 268	3:3–4	140
16:18	387–88n9	1:26	232, 282n42	3:4–4:6	140
16:19	22n29	1:26–29	95	3:5–23	397
16:20	353, 393	1:27	267, 268	3:6–9	91, 237
16:21	430n6	1:28	71, 77n28, 83,	3:6–17	147
16:23	338		366n24	3:9	238, 371n39, 423
16:25	265, 293	1:30	370	3:9–11	415
16:25–27	292	2:1	232, 291, 298n16	3:9–15	92
16:26	19n23, 22	2:1–5	71, 198n29	3:10	371n39
		2:2	291, 371n38	3:10–15	378
1 Corinthians		2:2–4	64	3:10–17	382n58
1–4	141	2:3	268	3:12	371n39
1:1	147	2:3–5	147	3:13	44, 354n48,
1:2	82, 94, 157, 163n23,	2:4	82, 148, 265, 266		371n37
	238, 338, 370	2:4–5	18n20	3:14	371n39
1:3	354n48	2:5	65, 82, 265, 266	3:15	44
1:4	73	2:6–7	184n154	3:16	81, 82, 152n23,
1:5	118, 155, 377, 397	2:6–8	291, 339n9		370, 397
1:5–6	82	2:8	64	3:16–17	87, 92, 239,
1:5–7	371	2:10	81, 82, 291		343n21, 375
1:6	301n24	2:10–11	64	3:17	82, 397
1:7	118	2:11	80	3:18	387–88n9
1:8	147, 151, 301n24	2:11–12	81	3:18–19	415
1:9	72, 140, 153	2:12	81, 95, 105,	3:18–23	154
1:10	82, 92, 371		370n35, 371	3:19	370n35
1:10–11	397	2:12a	64	3:21	147
1:10–12	122	2:12b	64	3:21–23	147
1:11	237, 316n12,	2:12–13	81	3:22	370n35
	369n29, 415	2:13	82	4:1	291, 298n16, 423

4:1–2	238	5:12–13	371n38	7:2	373, 415
4:2	423	5:13	398, 399	7:2–3	96n30
4:3–4	371n38	6:1	155n31, 371n36	7:2–6	373
4:5	371n38	6:1–2	370n35, 397	7:3	97
4:6	155n31	6:1–3	371n38	7:3–4	374
4:6–13	155	6:1–5	370, 415	7:4	91, 373
4:6–17	147	6:1–6	397	7:5	97, 98, 374, 393
4:7	147, 155, 371n38	6:1–7	359n7	7:7	96, 314n5, 372, 373
4:8	73, 397	6:1–8	257	7:8	372, 415
4:9	308n37	6:1–9	140	7:8–40	314, 316, 319
4:10	267, 371n38	6:2	99n39, 233	7:9	373
4:13	364n18, 370n35,	6:3	99n39, 339n9	7:10	374
	406n42	6:3–4	239, 368	7:10–16	96n30
4:15	164n35, 231	6:4	338, 366n24	7:12	18n22
4:15–16	140	6:5	371n38	7:14	97, 238, 374
4:17	338, 369n29, 411,	6:6	18n22, 371n38	7:15	374
	414, 430n6	6:6–17	81	7:16	44, 97
4:17–21	140	6:7	65	7:17	218n17, 325, 338
4:18	155n31, 231	6:9	99n39, 315, 398n30	7:17–24	374
4:19	155n31, 370n35	6:9–10	371, 438n34	7:19	235, 324–25, 374
4:19–12	154	6:9–11	219, 399, 445n48	7:21	437n31
4:19–20	265, 266	6:10–20	140	7:22	238
4:20	120	6:11	81, 82, 84, 162n11,	7:23	389n12
4:21	80		163n23, 164n32,	7:24	325, 374
5	400		165n39, 370, 371,	7:25	494n38
5–7	96		399	7:26	372
5:1	97, 323n32	6:12	84, 372n41	7:27	374
5:1–2	397	6:12–14	98–99	7:28	373, 374
5:1–3	399	6:12–20	96, 315,	7:29–31	373
5:1–5	44, 232, 242, 315,		351n37, 372	7:31	373, 437n31
	372, 395, 414	6:13	99, 238, 372n41	7:32	373
5:1–12	96, 97, 102	6:14	99, 265, 266,	7:32–33	372
5:1–13	140, 370,		307n35	7:32–34	96
	397–99, 406n43	6:15	87, 99, 343n21	7:32–35	373
5:1–6:20	373	6:15–18	238	7:32–40	96n30
5:2	97, 155n31	6:15–19	165n39	7:33–34	375n46
5:3	80, 98, 371n38	6:15–20	60	7:34	80, 91, 97n33,
5:4	80, 82, 98, 166n43,	6:16	100, 374		375
	265, 266, 398	6:17	100, 238, 351n37	7:35	84
5:5	80, 98, 104, 354n48,	6:18	100, 239, 323n32	7:35–49	375
	393, 400, 406,	6:19	81, 82, 99n39, 100,	7:36	415
	436n29		343n21, 370, 373,	7:36–38	374–75
5:6	97, 99n39		382n58, 397	7:37	371n38
5:9	143, 369n30, 396,	6:20	100	7:39	166n43, 415
	398	6:33–34	370n35	7:40	81, 83, 254
5:10	370n35	7:1	96, 369n30, 372	8–10	375, 415
5:11	97, 397, 399	7:1–40	96, 140, 372,	8:1	94, 105, 232, 238,
5:12	398		375		

	332, 371n39, 376, 378, 415	10:16	103	11:20	103	
8:1–2	117	10:16–17	60	11:21	103	
8:1–3	235	10:16–22	238	11:22	103, 338	
8:1–13	94, 102, 141, 375, 380	10:17	103	11:23	398n29	
		10:18	103, 282n42	11:23–25	104	
8:2–3	376	10:19	376	11:23–29	65	
8:4	376	10:19–22	339n9	11:24	94n25, 104, 105	
8:4–6	376	10:20–21	102	11:26	105	
8:6	69	10:21	375	11:27	104, 105	
8:7	376	10:22	267	11:27–30	238	
8:7–13	236	10:23	84, 117, 371n39	11:28	371n37	
8:8	376, 380	10:23–24	376	11:29	104, 371n38	
8:9–10	377	10:25	371n38	11:30	104	
8:10	371n39	10:27	18n22, 371n38	11:31	371n38	
8:11	61, 94, 105, 236, 269	10:29	371n38	11:32	370n35, 406n43	
		10:31–33	118	11:33	105	
8:11–12	154, 377	10:31–11:1	65	11:34	104	
8:11–13	65	10:32	338	12	92–94, 100, 237	
8:12	95, 101, 105, 118, 269	10:33	44, 68, 84	12–14	73, 108n9, 117n56, 118, 377	
		11	316			
8:14	232	11:1	166n42	12:1	117, 120, 121	
9	146, 157	11:2	124n84	12:1–2	118	
9:1	72, 147, 254	11:2–16	117n58, 123n81, 316, 319, 415	12:1–3	41, 378	
9:1–3	157			12:1–14:40	141	
9:1–12	415	11:3	315, 348, 351	12:2	125	
9:1–26	375	11:3–4	378	12:3	69, 81, 83, 93, 118, 120, 165n39, 233, 265, 378, 403	
9:1–27	102, 144	11:3–5	108			
9:3	371n38	11:3–16	123, 141, 348			
9:5–6	314n5	11:4	123n82	12:3–11	329n42	
9:6	394	11:5	123n82, 316n12, 379	12:4	83, 118, 373n43	
9:7	228	11:5–7	124	12:4–6	83	
9:11	226, 228	11:6	124n85	12:4–7	93, 94	
9:12	437n31	11:7	76n25, 78n30, 348	12:4–11	83	
9:15	437n31	11:7–8	315	12:4–31	378	
9:16	201n38	11:8–9	348	12:6	93, 120, 266, 267, 310n46	
9:17	423	11:10	124, 339n9			
9:19–22	65	11:11–12	316, 348	12:7	83–84, 105, 118	
9:22	44, 269	11:13	123n82, 124, 371n38	12:8	93	
9:24–27	286n46			12:8–9	83	
9:27	91, 371n37	11:14	124	12:8–10	118	
10:1–13	232	11:14–15	124n85	12:9	93, 118, 373n43	
10:1–32	141	11:16	124n84, 338	12:9–10	83	
10:1–11:1	375	11:17	103	12:10	93, 109, 110, 115, 120, 121, 266, 267	
10:2	306n32	11:17–22	415			
10:10–2:16	155	11:17–34	103, 141	12:11	83, 120, 266	
10:14–22	102	11:18	338	12:12	93	
10:15	371n38	11:18–19	103	12:12–13	165n39	
		11:19	371n37, 460n40	12:12–27	304n30	

12:12–31	60, 118	
12:13	81, 83, 94, 120, 161n10, 165n38, 166n43, 238, 306n32, 316n10, 370	
12:13–15	343n21	
12:14–26	92	
12:18	93	
12:22	237, 268	
12:24	93	
12:26	270	
12:27	87, 94, 99n39	
12:27–28	343n21	
12:27–31	330n43	
12:28	118, 120, 239, 254, 257, 266, 338, 378	
12:29	266	
12:29–30	378	
12:30	118, 121, 373n43, 379n54	
12:31	118, 119, 194n19, 194–95n21, 373n43	
13:1	110n19, 111, 119, 120, 339n9	
13:1–3	378	
13:1–7	65	
13:1–13	105, 378	
13:2	291	
13:3	91	
13:4	155n31, 194–95n21	
13:4–7	329n37	
13:5	68	
13:8	119	
13:8–13	330n45	
13:11	119, 120, 332, 371n38, 378	
13:11–13	325	
13:19	330n45	
14	382	
14:1	120, 123n82, 194–95n21	
14:1–5	65	
14:1–34	117n58	
14:2	110n19, 111, 114, 291	

14:2–3	112	
14:3	123n82, 371n39	
14:3–4	119	
14:4	111, 123n82, 338, 371n39, 378	
14:5	119, 123n82, 338, 371n39, 378	
14:6	108n9, 201n38	
14:6–10	119	
14:6–11	108	
14:7–8	120	
14:7–9	111	
14:9	201n38	
14:10–11	110	
14:11	201n38	
14:12	166n43, 194–95n21, 338, 371n39	
14:13	110, 112, 123n82	
14:13–16	119	
14:14	80, 112, 123n82, 201n38	
14:14–15	112, 119	
14:15	123n82	
14:16	115n52	
14:16–17	111	
14:17	112, 371n39	
14:18	108, 111, 121, 122, 378	
14:18–19	119	
14:19	112, 338	
14:20	79, 119n66, 120, 332, 379	
14:20–25	119	
14:21	435n26	
14:21–22	378	
14:22	18n21, 18n22, 117, 377	
14:23	111, 114, 119, 121, 125, 338, 378	
14:24	18n22, 123n82, 371n38, 379n54	
14:25	119, 379	
14:26	237, 371n39, 379	
14:26–31	379	
14:27–28	110, 119, 379	
14:28	110n19, 112, 114, 121, 338	

14:29	371n38, 379	
14:29–32	254	
14:31	121, 123–24n82	
14:31–32	119	
14:32	121, 379	
14:33	338	
14:33–36	242, 316, 415	
14:33b–36	123	
14:33c	124n84	
14:34	125, 338, 348	
14:34–36	379	
14:35	124n85, 338	
14:36	124n84	
14:37	223n32	
14:39	123–24n82, 194–95n21	
14:39–40	126	
14:40	379	
15	72–80, 86	
15:1	72, 291	
15:1–2	73	
15:1–58	141	
15:2	43, 72	
15:3	72	
15:3–4	72	
15:5–6	72	
15:8	72	
15:9	338, 438n36	
15:10	72, 196n26	
15:11	18n20, 72	
15:12	75, 397	
15:12–19	72, 299n18	
15:13	73	
15:13–19	73	
15:14	18n20, 73	
15:15	198n30	
15:16	73	
15:17	73, 79	
15:19	73–74	
15:21–22	74	
15:23	74	
15:24	74, 265, 266	
15:24–28	74, 339n9	
15:25–27	309n40	
15:28	83n33, 93, 310n46	
15:29	75n23, 161n10, 165n36, 306n32	

15:29–34	75	16:15–18	141, 240, 242,	2:8–9	400
15:30–32	75n23		254, 257, 359n7,	2:9	149, 368, 446n49
15:32	412		369, 397, 415,	2:10	400
15:33	79, 494n36		484n11	2:11	98, 393, 400
15:33–34	75n23	16:16	349n34	2:12–13	142
15:34	79	16:18	80, 228	2:13	142
15:35	75, 87	16:19	231, 316n12, 338	2:14	308n37
15:36–38	76	16:22	115n52, 403	2:15	44, 45, 377n49
15:38	76n24			2:17	144, 145, 149
15:39	76	**2 Corinthians**		3	203n44
15:40	76	1–7	139, 155	3–4	446
15:41	76	1–9	140n7	3:1	146
15:42	76, 79n31	1:1	142, 158, 338, 368	3:1–5	147
15:42–44	278n32	1:3–7	152	3:1–6	155
15:43	265, 266, 268	1:4	153n26, 265, 364n18,	3:1–18	142
15:44	77, 87		389n12	3:2–3	148
15:45	74n20, 77, 78,	1:5	270	3:3	446
	86, 91, 93, 94,	1:6	44, 266, 270, 364n18	3:3–18	136
	100n43, 136,	1:7	270	3:6	78n29, 301n20,
	165n39, 233, 238	1:8	194n19, 265, 266,		446
15:45–49	348		389n12, 412	3:7	265
15:46–48	78	1:8–10	142	3:7–9	446
15:49	310n45	1:9	136	3:7–18	232
15:50	79, 265	1:11	151	3:8–10	76n25
15:51	79, 141, 293	1:12	194n17, 368	3:12	437n31
15:52	79	1:14	354n48	3:17	267
15:53	79	1:15–21	142	3:17–18	24, 79, 238, 446
15:53–54	60, 310n42	1:17	145, 437n31	3:18	76n25, 78n30,
15:56	79, 266n8	1:17–20	154		165n39, 310n45
15:58	75	1:19	237	4:1	194n19, 494n38
16:1	228, 338	1:21	301n24	4:1–18	142
16:1–3	141	1:21–22	136	4:2	145, 149
16:1–4	144, 158, 236, 239	1:22	166n45	4:3	377n49
16:1–5	142	1:23	142, 149	4:3–4	234
16:1–18	141	1:23–2:1	143	4:4	18n22, 78n30, 156,
16:3	371n37	1:24	146		310n45
16:4	141	2:1–9	143	4:5–11	156
16:5	141	2:1–11	399	4:6	163n20, 348
16:8	141	2:2	146, 399	4:7	194n19, 266
16:9	141, 266, 412	2:3	399	4:7–12	65
16:10	141, 455–56n26	2:4	146, 149, 389n12,	4:9	377n49
16:10–11	142, 369n29,		399	4:10–12	269
	414, 430n6	2:5	400	4:10–14	16
16:11	366n24	2:5–11	399	4:11–12	456n28
16:12	141	2:6	400	4:12	267n10
16:13	267	2:7	151, 400	4:12–13	154
16:15	74n19	2:8	151	4:13	136

4:14	136	6:16	343n21, 368	10	140n7
4:15	149, 151, 156	7:1	349n34, 368	10–11	149
4:16	310n43	7:2	145, 148	10–12	139
5:1	133, 134, 368	7:2–3	142	10:1–5	149
5:1–2	137	7:5	142, 143	10:1–12:21	148
5:1–21	132–34	7:5–16	142	10:2	146
5:1–6:12	142	7:7	151, 194–95n21	10:3–6	353
5:2	132, 137	7:8–9	143	10:4	266
5:3	60	7:8–10	146	10:5	21
5:3–4	310n42	7:10	44	10:6	21, 149
5:4	132	7:11	151, 194–95n21	10:8	146, 147, 368,
5:5	133, 134, 136	7:12	143, 146, 149, 151		455n26
5:6	132, 133, 137	7:13	142, 151, 228	10:9	146
5:7	132, 133, 218n17	7:14	149	10:10	143, 146, 267n11,
5:9	132	8–9	139, 143, 157,		366n24
5:10	133		228n42, 236	10:11	149
5:11	132, 133, 134, 149,	8:1	338	10:11–14	143
	349n34	8:1–2	142	10:12	147
5:12	132, 133, 146, 147,	8:2	368, 389n12,	10:12–11:6	144
	148, 216		460n40	10:13	146
5:12–21	236	8:3	266	10:13–15	436n28
5:13	132, 133, 134, 146	8:4	368	10:18	368, 460n40
5:14	133, 134, 136, 155	8:4–7	142	11	282
5:15	133, 136	8:6–7	147	11:1–3	148, 350
5:16	19n23, 133	8:8	368	11:2	194–95n21
5:16–21	65	8:9	65, 158, 277	11:2–3	348, 351
5:17	77–78n28, 84, 131,	8:10–12	143	11:3	149, 315,
	133, 136, 233, 267	8:11	147		387–88n9
5:18	131, 133, 134	8:12–14	158	11:3–15	152
5:18–19	250n19	8:13	226	11:4	136, 149, 152,
5:19	129–37, 155,	8:18	338		435n26
	223n30	8:19	338	11:6	146
5:20	132, 133, 134, 155	8:20	146, 395n24	11:8	303, 338
5:21	23, 133, 134, 137,	8:21	372	11:8–10	144
	154, 277	8:22	368	11:9	147
6:1	151	8:23	141, 338	11:9–11	149
6:2	19n23, 44	8:24	338	11:12	216
6:3	44, 146, 148	9:1	368	11:13–15	149
6:4	146	9:2–6	143	11:14	98, 393
6:6	136, 368, 494n36	9:3–4	147, 157	11:16	148
6:7	266	9:3–5	141	11:18	338
6:8	145	9:4	147	11:20	149
6:9	136, 406n43	9:6	228	11:21	131, 149, 268
6:12	148	9:8	266	11:22–23	284
6:14	435n26	9:10	304n27	11:23–32	149
6:14–15	18n22	9:12	368	11:28	231
6:14–7:1	151	9:13	368, 460n40	11:29	269, 377n48

11:29–30	268	1:6–7	402	2:14–19	167n49
12:1–5	150	1:6–9	188, 192	2:15–16	168n61
12:2	170n69	1:7	168n62, 191, 446	2:16	13n1, 13n3, 18, 201,
12:4	110n19	1:7–9	402, 403		216, 218
12:5	268	1:8	167n50	2:16a	19
12:6	148	1:8–9	187, 222	2:18	215, 367
12:7	98, 194n19, 339n9	1:9	167n50, 168n62, 207	2:19	200n34, 201, 215,
12:7–9	150	1:10	207		222
12:9	266, 268, 269, 287	1:10–24	443	2:19–20	219
12:9–10	150	1:11	167n48	2:19–21	196
12:10	266, 268	1:11–16	447	2:19–3:20	344
12:11	148, 150	1:12	167n49	2:20	13n1, 19, 192, 197,
12:12	148, 155, 266	1:13	191, 207, 338,		200, 201, 202, 215,
12:13	338		438n36		215n10, 216, 217,
12:16–18	144	1:13–14	194, 233, 284		224, 238, 333n51,
12:17–18	146	1:14	194, 207, 218n21		344, 491n30
12:18	136	1:15	193, 232, 447	2:20	203
12:19	368, 393	1:15–17	115	2:20a	19
12:19–13:9	149	1:16	195, 200, 216, 233,	2:20b	19
12:20	194–95n21		447	2:21	197, 215
13:1	143	1:16–17	197	2:22	13n1
13:1–11	236	1:17	195, 222	3:1	167n50, 168n62, 187,
13:2	143	1:17–2:10	167n49		198, 200, 200n35,
13:3	266, 268, 368	1:20	198n30		218n20, 446
13:3–4	154	1:20–24	197	3:1–2	191
13:3–10	65	1:22	338	3:1–3	192
13:4	266, 268, 277	1:23	19n23, 197, 438n36	3:1–5	115, 120, 199, 204,
13:5	368, 446n49	2:1	170n69		214, 448
13:6	368	2:1–2	198	3:2	13–14n3, 167n49,
13:7	368	2:1–10	249		168n61, 182, 191,
13:9	151, 266, 268	2:3	167n49, 169n63,		198, 202, 218
13:10	365, 368, 437n31		198	3:3	169n66, 181, 187,
13:12	368	2:4	234		192n13, 216
13:13	136, 368	2:4–5	198	3:4	22, 191, 237, 270
13:14	165n39	2:5	188	3:5	13–14n3, 182, 191,
		2:6	224n36		214, 266, 267,
Galatians		2:7–9	198		304n27, 323n32
1–4	185–208, 220, 498	2:8	168n61, 266	3:5–6	20
1:1	167n50, 195, 202, 237	2:9	418–19n12	3:6	20, 205
1:1–4	222	2:10	143, 158, 199, 227,	3:6–9	204
1:1–5	189–90, 367		236	3:7	13n3, 20
1:2	186, 338	2:11	199	3:8	204
1:3	202	2:11–14	199	3:9	13n3, 204, 205
1:3–4	197	2:12	486n24	3:10	204, 402
1:4	202, 224, 236, 333n51,	2:12–13	199	3:10–13	187
	491n30	2:14	70, 188, 194n18,	3:10–22	167n49
1:6	167n50, 187, 435n26		199, 218n17	3:11	202, 205

3:12	205, 213	4:8–10	193, 206, 210	5:3–12	447
3:13	154, 192, 200, 202, 204, 205, 214, 233, 321, 344, 403	4:9	211n5, 217, 308n38, 339n9, 353n39	5:4	168n61, 182, 207
3:14	182, 202, 205	4:11	167n50, 193	5:5	169n67
3:15–16	205	4:12	215	5:5–6	165n39
3:15–22	203	4:12–20	167n49	5:6	215, 217, 267
3:15–23	204	4:13	198, 216, 231	5:7	167n50, 168n62, 192
3:16	200	4:13–14	197	5:7–12	215
3:16–22	187	4:13–16	191	5:10	168n62, 238
3:17	205	4:13–20	167n48	5:10–11	167n49
3:17–22	205	4:14	198, 216, 232, 366n24	5:11	167n49, 169n63, 200n34, 201, 207, 377n48
3:19	205	4:16	198, 218n21, 325n34	5:12	167n50, 168n62, 187, 207, 286
3:19–22	234	4:17	168n62, 169n67, 194–95n21, 207, 402, 403	5:12–16	221
3:20	205			5:13	66, 98n36, 207, 216, 217, 225, 236, 268
3:21	78n29, 196, 265	4:19	164n35, 193, 198, 203, 236, 390n14		
3:22	202, 205, 206	4:20	193	5:13–14	67, 329n37
3:23–29	205	4:21	168n61, 169n63, 177, 187, 203, 446	5:13–6:5	66
3:23–4:7	206			5:14	169n66, 217, 219, 223, 270
3:26	20, 165n41, 200	4:21–31	187, 203, 232, 403		
3:26–28	202	4:21–5:4	167n49	5:15	67, 217
3:26–29	191	4:22–28	200	5:16	169n66, 217
3:27	61, 94n23, 161n10, 163n19, 182, 202, 306n32, 310n42	4:23	216	5:16–17	98n36
		4:23–24	206	5:16–18	218
		4:23–29	164n35	5:16–21	236
3:27–4:6	165n38	4:24	203, 206	5:16–26	227, 307n36
3:27–4:7	164n35, 182	4:24–31	206	5:17	66, 217
3:28	179, 192, 200, 220, 230, 234, 252, 316, 318–19, 322, 344, 344n23, 348	4:25	234	5:18	66, 167n49
		4:27	206	5:19	98n36, 217, 218, 323n32
		4:28–31	403	5:19–21	66, 182, 219, 315, 438n34
3:29	165n41, 200	4:29	207, 216		
3:30	181	4:30	187, 207, 222, 232, 447	5:19–23	447
4:1–4	228			5:20–21	67
4:1–7	214	4:31	207, 209, 210	5:21	66
4:3	181n150, 191n8, 211n5, 339n9, 353n39	5–6	209–29, 498	5:22	66, 182, 219, 227, 228, 494n36
		5:1	198n31, 210, 216, 225		
4:4	169n66, 200	5:1–6	233, 308n39	5:22–23	66, 219, 329n37
4:4–5	200, 224	5:1–26	220	5:22–24	236
4:5	202	5:2	168n61, 182	5:23	447
4:6	115n52, 163n21, 202, 219, 220n26, 237	5:2–3	167n49	5:24	67, 200n34, 217, 219
4:6–7	165n41, 182, 191	5:2–4	169n63, 214		
4:7	202	5:3–4	192	5:25	66, 166n43, 182,
4:8	181n150, 191				
4:8–9	168n61, 181				

	193n14, 211n5,	1:3–14	329n41	2:8	46, 340n12, 341,
	220, 223n32, 225,	1:4	382		354
	446	1:4–6	340	2:10	341
5:25–6:2	166n42	1:6	340n12	2:11	342
5:26	67, 220–21,	1:7	223n30, 293,	2:11–12	241, 342
	222–23		340n12	2:11–22	339, 341–42
6	220–29	1:8	383	2:13	343, 344
6:1	67, 225, 484n11	1:9	340	2:13–18	241
6:1–2	223	1:9–10	293	2:14	354
6:1–5	222–25, 226	1:9–14	241	2:14–15	241
6:1–10	221, 222	1:10	241, 328, 339, 340	2:14–18	343
6:2	67, 169n66, 202, 236	1:11	266	2:14–22	343
6:3	67	1:13	46, 165n39,	2:15	330, 344
6:3–5	224		166n45, 344, 354,	2:17	354, 355
6:4	67		382	2:18	344, 354
6:5	67	1:13–14	340	2:19	382
6:6	157, 225–29, 240,	1:15	382	2:19–22	241, 342, 345,
	257, 359n7	1:17	305n31, 310n44,		349, 382
6:7	226		344, 354, 383	2:21	345
6:7–8	227	1:18	163n20, 340, 382,	2:21–22	165n39
6:8	216		383	2:22	354, 383
6:9	227, 372	1:19	266, 267, 352	3:1	340n12
6:10	227	1:20	267, 309n40, 341	3:1–12	293–94
6:11	221, 222	1:20–21	352	3:2	241, 340n12
6:12	169n63, 187,	1:20–23	340	3:4	265, 383
	200n34, 221	1:21	266, 352n38	3:5	344n24, 354, 382
6:12–13	167n49, 168n61,	1:22	340n10, 351	3:6	328, 345
	168n62, 169n67,	1:22–23	338, 346, 349	3:7	266, 340n12
	216, 401	1:23	304n30, 310n46	3:8	340n12, 382
6:12–16	221	2:1	223n30, 341, 343,	3:9	163n20, 298n16,
6:13	182n151, 187, 221,		354		383
	224, 402, 436n28	2:1–2	341	3:9–11	241
6:14	197, 200n34, 201	2:1–10	339, 340	3:10	338, 339, 346,
6:15	77–78n28, 84,	2:1–11	241		352n38
	192, 197, 203, 215,	2:1–18	328	3:10–11	328
	222, 234, 267, 348	2:1–22	330, 339, 340	3:13	389n12
6:15–16	404	2:2	339, 352	3:14	340n12
6:16	193n14, 211n5,	2:3	194n17, 340n14,	3:16	266, 267, 344n24,
	220n25, 222, 234,		341		354
	494n38	2:4	341, 494n38	3:17–18	383
6:17	167n49, 167n50,	2:4–10	341	3:17–19	328
	197, 201	2:5	46, 223n30,	3:18	382
			340n12, 341, 354	3:20	265, 266, 267
		2:5–6	341	4–5	328, 352
Ephesians		2:6	352	4:1	235
1:1	382	2:7	340n12, 341,	4:1–3	329, 355
1:2	340n12		494n36	4:1–5:20	345

4:3	241, 344n24, 354, 355	5	319n21	6:10–20	352–53
4:3–6	344	5:1	346, 351, 491n30	6:11	60, 310n42, 353
4:4	60, 344–45n24, 355	5:1–2	333	6:11–16	265
4:4–6	161n7, 165n38	5:2	350	6:12	339, 354
4:4–16	92, 329–30	5:3	323n32, 382	6:13	354
4:5	161n10, 306n32, 351	5:3–4	334, 438n34	6:14	60, 310n42
4:6	331	5:3–5	333	6:14–17	355
4:7	340n12	5:4	315	6:17	30, 46, 344–45n24
4:11	115, 240, 359n7	5:5	398n30	6:18	344–45n24, 355, 382
4:11–12	484n11	5:6	23n31, 341	6:19	355
4:11–16	241	5:8–9	163n20, 333	6:19–20	294, 295
4:12	232, 237, 382	5:8–10	383	6:24	340n12
4:12–13	331	5:12	124n85		
4:13	305n31, 310n44	5:13	163n20	**Philippians**	
4:14	325, 332, 333, 383	5:14	163n20	1:1	240, 252, 257, 264, 280, 359n7, 484n11
4:15	60, 241, 325, 331, 340n10	5:15–17	384	1:4	263–64n4
4:15–16	345, 382	5:16	354, 354n48	1:5	263n3, 263–64n4, 264
4:15–20	354	5:17	333	1:6	263n3, 279, 354n48
4:16	232, 304n27, 304n30, 331	5:18	333, 344–45n24, 352, 355	1:7	65, 263n4, 274–75, 274n25, 368, 389n12
4:17–18	333	5:19	333	1:8	263n4
4:17–19	383	5:19–21	336	1:9	305n31, 310n44
4:19	115n52, 315	5:20	335	1:9–10	368
4:20–21	331	5:21	349	1:10	354n48
4:20–24	166n42	5:21–32	294	1:12	195n22, 264
4:21	332, 333, 383	5:21–33	315, 349	1:15	264
4:22	163n19, 194n17, 315, 333	5:21–6:9	346	1:16	456n28
		5:22	349	1:19	46, 65, 263–64n4, 279, 285
4:22–24	383	5:22–31	241	1:20	274, 455n26
4:23	332, 333, 344–45n24, 352, 355	5:23	30, 46, 338, 340n10, 351, 354	1:20–26	46, 272–74
4:24	61, 84, 310n42, 332, 345	5:24	294, 338, 350	1:27	18n20, 263n3, 274, 278
4:25	334	5:25	294, 338, 351	1:27–28	45
4:25–27	335	5:26	162n11, 164n28, 233, 351, 355	1:29	18, 270
4:26–27	353n44			1:29–30	274
4:28	333	5:26–27	164n32	1:30	263n3
4:29	334, 335, 340n12, 383	5:27	338, 351, 382	2:1	65, 263n3, 263–64n4, 279, 282, 285
		5:28	351		
4:30	166n45, 331, 344–45n24, 354n48, 355, 382	5:29	338		
		5:29–30	351		
		5:30	92, 350		
		5:31	350, 351		
4:31	334	5:32	241, 294, 296, 338, 352		
4:32	332, 335, 494n36	5:33	349, 351		
		6:5–9	349n35		
		6:10	266, 267, 353, 438n38	2:1–2	446

2:1–3:16	286n47	2:26–27	268	4:1	263–64n4, 264
2:1–3:19	287	2:27	494n38	4:2	65, 274n25, 316n12,
2:1–4	236, 276,	2:27–28	281		368
	278–79, 372	2:28	263–64n4	4:2–3	264
2:1–5	165n39, 275, 285	2:28–29	282	4:3	263n3
2:1–11	166n42, 224, 280	2:29	263–64n4, 281	4:10	65, 263–64n4,
2:1–12a	46	2:30	263n3, 281		274n25, 368
2:2	65, 263n3, 263–	3	446	4:10–15	264
	64n4, 274n25, 368	3:1	263–64n4, 281–82	4:10–20	144
2:2–3	264	3:1a	281–82	4:12	310n46
2:3	65	3:1–16	66	4:13	266, 267, 353n42,
2:4	65, 368, 376, 446	3:2	282, 286n48		438n38
2:5	66, 67, 274n25,	3:2–3	283	4:14	263n3, 263–64n4,
	275–77, 278n33,	3:2–14	280		389n12
	279, 286, 287,	3:2–16	273n21, 281–83	4:15	263n3, 263–64n4,
	332n48, 350, 368	3:2–26	282		338
2:5–11	213, 236, 258, 446	3:3	307n33	4:18	281
2:6	263n3, 279n35, 281,	3:5–6	284		
	284	3:6	194–95n21, 233,	**Colossians**	
2:6–8	276, 284–85n45,		282, 338, 363n15,	1:1	168n57
	287		438n36, 446	1:3–8	304–5
2:6–11	24, 65, 275, 279,	3:7	284	1:4	13n3, 168n54
	282, 299n18,	3:7–9	284	1:5	301, 302
	329n41	3:7–11	262–63	1:5–7	168n59
2:7–8	264	3:8	284, 446	1:6	183, 301, 302
2:7b–8	24	3:9	13n1, 196n25, 284,	1:6–7	168n55, 183
2:8	279n34		446	1:7	301, 484n11
2:9–11	277, 287	3:9–10	267	1:9	168n54, 169n66, 305,
2:11	18, 76n25, 274, 285	3:10	263n3, 263–64n4,		310n44
2:12	24, 45, 279,		264, 266, 270,	1:9–10	183
	349n34		277, 287	1:10	183, 301n24, 305,
2:13	267	3:10–11	285		310n44
2:14	264	3:11	285	1:11	266, 267
2:15	363n15	3:14	286	1:12	163n20, 183, 299n17,
2:16	354n48	3:15	65, 274n25, 286,		301, 310
2:17	263n3, 264		368	1:12–13	168n60
2:17–18	263–64n4	3:15–16	66	1:12–14	298
2:18	263n3,	3:16	193n14, 286	1:12–22	298
	263–64n4	3:17	66, 263n3, 282,	1:13	299n17, 300,
2:19	231, 263–64n4,		286, 286n49		301n20, 339n9
	430n6	3:18	286	1:14	299n17
2:19–24	66, 280, 446	3:18–19	283	1:15	78n30, 300, 301,
2:20–21	280	3:19	65, 274n25, 286,		310n45
2:21–22	280		368, 436n28	1:15–17	300
2:22	460n40	3:20	30, 275, 277	1:15–20	168n60, 240
2:25	263n3, 281	3:20–21	264, 278, 288	1:16	308, 339n9
2:25–30	66, 280, 446	3:21	76n25, 263n3,	1:16–18	352n38
2:26	281		265, 266, 274		

1:18	92, 237, 240, 300, 303, 304, 338, 339n9, 343n21	2:9–10	298	3:3–4	309
		2:9–12	240	3:5	309
		2:9–15	240	3:5–9	311
1:19	169n66, 183, 300, 338–39n6	2:10	169n66, 307, 339n9, 352n38	3:5–17	240
				3:6	23n31
1:20	300, 311	2:11	169n64, 183, 240, 283n44, 306, 307, 308n37, 309, 310	3:6–7	310
1:21	168n61, 183, 299n17, 300n19			3:8	310, 315, 438n34
				3:8–12	307n34
1:21–22	299	2:11–12	183	3:9	168n60, 310
1:21–23	168n60	2:11–13	308	3:9–10	84, 163n19
1:22	299n17, 312	2:11–15	168n58, 168n60	3:10	60, 78n30, 305n31, 310
1:22–23	307n36	2:11–3:17	306		
1:23	168n57, 302	2:12	161n10, 266, 298, 306	3:10–17	166n42
1:24	92, 240, 270, 281n39, 303, 338, 343n21, 389n12			3:11	168n61, 169n64, 183, 240, 310, 316n10
		2:12–13	307		
		2:12–15	165n36		
1:24–29	295–97	2:13	168n61, 223n30	3:12	60, 168n60, 311, 494n36
1:25	168n57, 169n66	2:14	308n38		
1:26	19n23, 171n72, 290	2:14–15	308	3:12–13	311
		2:14–3:1	168n60	3:14	169n66, 183, 290, 311
1:26–27	309	2:15	339n9, 352n38		
1:27	76n25, 168n61, 302, 309	2:16	168n62, 169n67, 182, 240, 301, 308	3:15	60, 92, 311, 343n21
1:27–29	168n60	2:16–18	312	3:15–17	312
1:28	169n66, 183, 290, 305, 311	2:17	183, 303, 304, 308, 343n21	3:16	115n52
				3:17	306
1:29	266	2:18	168n62, 169n65, 169n67, 182, 183, 240, 301, 302	3:18–19	347n32, 348
2:1	168n54			3:18–21	312
2:1–3	295, 297			3:18–4:1	315
2:2	169n66, 171n72, 183, 303, 305n31, 310n44, 364n18	2:19	240, 304, 305, 311, 339n9	3:22–4:1	312
				3:28	183
		2:20	168n59, 193n14, 308, 308–9, 339n9, 353n39	4:2	168n60
2:2–3	168n60, 290			4:2–4	168n57
2:3	183, 309			4:3	168n56, 171n72, 290, 295
2:3–15	330n45	2:20–3:4	168n60		
2:4	303	2:20–3:7	165n36	4:7–8	168n54
2:5	13n3, 18, 168n57, 302	2:21	183, 308	4:8–9	168n57
		2:21–22	240	4:9	168n54
2:6	168n60	2:22	168n58, 169n64, 308	4:10	168n56
2:6–7	168n59, 302			4:11	168n61
2:7	305	2:23	169n67, 183, 240, 303, 308	4:12	168n55, 169n66, 183, 305, 484n11
2:8	168n62, 169n67, 193n14, 302, 303, 339n9, 353n39				
		3:1	168n59, 309	4:15	231, 316n12, 338
		3:1–3	306	4:16	168n54, 338
2:9	168n60, 169n66, 300, 302, 306, 338–39n6	3:1–17	183	4:17	169n66, 282n42
		3:2	309	4:18	168n57, 170n69
		3:3	309		

1 Thessalonians

1:1	266, 338, 358, 359
1:2–10	361
1:3	359, 363
1:3–6	436n28
1:5	231, 359, 366
1:5–6	362
1:5–10	358
1:6	360, 366, 389
1:7	18n21
1:8	13n3, 363
1:8–9	20
1:9	233, 359, 360, 390
1:9–10	359
1:10	16, 362
2:3–6	367
2:4–12	232
2:6	265
2:10	18n21, 362
2:12	232, 360, 363
2:13	18n21, 267, 359
2:13–16	359, 361
2:14	270, 338, 360, 389
2:16	45, 234
2:17–18	231
2:17–19	359
2:18	98, 393, 398n29
2:19	387n6, 390
3:2	231, 363, 430n6
3:2–6	359
3:3	360, 389
3:5	363, 398n29
3:6	363
3:7	360, 363, 389
3:9–13	361
3:10	363
3:12	363
3:12–13	361
3:13	362, 387n6, 390
4:1–2	360
4:3	232, 323n32, 362
4:4	397n28
4:4–5	363, 372
4:5	18, 387n6
4:6	363
4:7	360, 363
4:7–8	362
4:8	366
4:9	363
4:11	394
4:12	394
4:12–5:10	387n6
4:13	342, 359, 363, 388, 389
4:13–18	390
4:14	307n35
4:15	366, 390, 393n17
4:17	390
4:18	364, 365, 390
5:1	390
5:1–6	364
5:2	354n48, 387n6, 390, 390n13
5:3	98n36, 310n42, 390, 392, 398n29
5:4	354n48, 387n6
5:6	390
5:7	390
5:8	46, 60, 353, 365
5:8–9	45
5:10	307n35, 364, 390
5:11	232, 238, 365
5:12	239, 257, 285, 365
5:12–13	254, 358, 413, 484n11
5:14	269
5:14–18	366
5:14–22	366
5:19–21	230, 391
5:19–22	366
5:20	359
5:21	254
5:23	364, 387n6, 390
5:23–24	367
5:24	360
5:27	362n14

2 Thessalonians

1:1	338, 358
1:3–5	392
1:4	338, 391
1:5	270, 391
1:6–7	391
1:7	266

1:7–8	391
1:8	21–22
1:9	98n36, 391, 398n29
1:10	18n21, 354n48
1:11	266
1:11–12	392
2:1	387, 390
2:2	131, 354n48, 387
2:3	201n38, 387, 393
2:3–12	386n4
2:4	393, 394
2:5	392
2:6	392, 393
2:7	267n10, 292n6, 393
2:7–8	393
2:7–11	339n9
2:8	392, 394
2:9	98, 266n8, 393, 398n29
2:9–10	393
2:10	45, 377n49
2:11	393, 394
2:12	18n20, 394
2:13	45
2:13–16	234
2:13–17	392
3	396
3:3–5	392
3:6	388, 394, 395
3:8	394
3:10	392, 394, 395
3:10–12	399
3:11	388
3:12	395
3:14	22, 396, 398n29, 398n30
3:14–15	232
3:15	396, 408
3:16	392
3:17	386n3

1 Timothy

1:1	421, 435, 437
1:1–2	441
1:1–20	428–48, 499
1:2	422, 435, 437, 494n38

1:3	410, 411, 413, 414, 435, 436, 449n3, 475n76	1:16	267, 422, 437, 441, 442, 494n38	3:8	422
		1:17	439, 441	3:8–9	443
1:3–17	422	1:18	372, 435, 436, 442, 443, 494n38	3:8–10	242
1:4	242, 414, 416–17, 422, 424–27, 436, 438n32, 442, 449n3			3:8–13	414
		1:18–20	406	3:9	292n6, 422, 475n76
		1:19	413, 414, 422, 435, 436, 437, 440, 441, 442, 444	3:11	242, 420, 443
				3:12	415
1:4–5	422			3:12–13	242
1:4–7	435n23			3:13	422, 438n39
1:5	411, 422, 423, 436–37, 441, 442, 475n76	1:19–20	406n43	3:14	410
		1:20	98, 242, 393, 413, 414, 435n23, 436, 442, 463n50	3:15	194n17, 242, 338, 415, 418, 420
				3:15–16	421
1:5–7	416, 429n3	2:1	435, 475n76	3:16	76n25, 299n18, 421
1:6	436, 440	2:1–3:13	435		
1:6–7	422, 436	2:3	372	4:1	353, 422
1:7	414, 415, 435, 436, 439, 449n2	2:3–4	421	4:1–2	339n9
		2:4	305n31, 310n44	4:1–5	449–50n4
1:8	372, 429n3, 437	2:5	421	4:2	422
1:8–11	406, 422, 437, 449–50n4	2:6	421	4:2–3	414, 443
		2:7	421, 422	4:3	415, 419, 449n2
1:8–17	442	2:8–10	415	4:3–5	406, 420
1:8–19	439	2:9	413, 475n76	4:4	419
1:9	219n24, 422, 438n33, 439, 447, 485n14	2:9–10	415, 420	4:5	419
		2:11–14	316	4:6	422, 485n18
		2:11–15	124n83, 242, 348, 415, 420	4:7	443, 449n3
1:9–10	422, 438, 441			4:7–8	406, 414
1:9–11	448	2:13	315	4:8	420, 449n2
1:10	315, 398n30, 438n33, 475n76	2:14	348, 387–88n9	4:9	458n35
		2:14–15	315	4:10	420, 421, 443, 475n76
1:10–11	436, 438, 439	2:15	316n11, 422, 475n76		
1:10–12	439			4:11	411
1:11	76n25, 198n32, 421	2:21	421	4:11–12	443
1:12	266, 422, 435n24, 436, 438, 438n38, 439, 441, 442, 447, 458n35	3	257	4:11–14	414
		3:1	372, 458n35	4:12	194n17, 411, 422, 456n30
		3:1–7	242, 414		
		3:1–12	418	4:13	410, 411
1:12–17	422, 437, 443, 447, 448	3:1–13	359n7, 484n11	4:14	443
		3:2	485n16	4:15	195n22
1:13	406n42, 422, 438, 439, 441, 475n76, 494n38	3:2–4	443	5	257
		3:2–7	485n18	5:1	475n76
		3:3	486n21	5:3–16	315, 316, 369, 415, 418
1:14	422, 423, 438, 438n39, 439, 441, 442, 447	3:4	242, 415, 420, 485n15, 485n18		
				5:4	339n9, 418
		3:5	338	5:5	421
1:15	422, 441, 458n35	3:6	104n53, 292n6	5:7	411
1:15–16	439				

5:8	418, 422	**2 Timothy**		2:14	445, 449n3, 454,	
5:12	104n53, 422	1:1	438n39		459n37, 459n38,	
5:13–16	348	1:3	455, 475n76		460, 460n45,	
5:14	216, 415, 418, 420	1:3–2:13	455–58, 459		475n76	
5:15	98, 393	1:4	455	2:14c	460	
5:16	338, 413, 418	1:5	453, 455	2:14–16	449n3	
5:17	414	1:6	454, 455	2:14–4:5	242	
5:17–18	415	1:7	266, 444, 455, 456,	2:14–4:8	459–64	
5:17–20	359n7		457, 463, 475n76	2:15	242, 459n37,	
5:17–23	484n11	1:8	266, 455, 457, 458,		459n38, 460	
5:18	421		460, 463	2:15–17	459	
5:19	414	1:8–2:13	454	2:16	404, 459n37,	
5:19–20	415	1:9–11	477n78		459n38, 460–61	
5:21	475n76	1:12	266, 270, 354n48,	2:17–18	449n2	
5:22	414		456, 460, 463,	2:18	445, 459n37,	
5:23	268, 437n31		475n76		459n38, 460	
5:24	414	1:12–13	454	2:19	454, 460, 461	
5:25	265	1:13	198n32, 454, 456,	2:19–21	460–61	
6:1–2	415		457, 459, 460	2:20–23	242	
6:2	265, 413, 418,	1:13–14	165n39	2:21	460–61,	
	475n76	1:14	456, 457n32,		475n76	
6:3	413, 421, 435n26,		475n76	2:22	404, 459n37,	
	443, 475n76	1:15	457, 462		459n38, 461,	
6:4	438n34, 443, 449n3,	1:15–18	454, 457		475n76	
	475n76	1:16	457, 460	2:22–24	461	
6:5	413, 414, 419, 443,	1:18	354n48, 457n31	2:23	404, 445, 449n3,	
	475n76	2:1	266, 353n42,		459n37, 459n38,	
6:5–10	406		438n38, 438n39,		461, 475n76	
6:6	419		444, 454, 457,	2:23–24	460, 474	
6:6–8	449–50n4		463, 463n50	2:24	460, 475n76	
6:7	419	2:1–13	166n42	2:24–26	405, 461	
6:8	419	2:2	359n7, 454, 457,	2:25	305n31, 310n44,	
6:9	98n36, 398n29,		458n35, 484n11		460	
	475n76	2:3	372, 456n28, 458	2:25–26	408	
6:10	419, 422	2:3–6	458	3:1	354n48, 459n37,	
6:11	422, 443, 475n76	2:4–6	457		459n38, 461, 463	
6:12	421, 422, 443	2:5	201n38, 437n31,	3:1–6	445	
6:13	411, 421		463	3:1–9	404	
6:16	423	2:8	454	3:1–10	461–62	
6:17	411, 413, 421	2:8–9	458	3:2	438n36, 459n37,	
6:18	411	2:8–13	458		460	
6:19	421	2:9	463	3:2–5	449n4, 459	
6:20	414, 444, 449n2,	2:10	438–39n39, 458,	3:3–4	315	
	449n3, 475n76		463	3:5	459n37, 459n38	
6:20–21	415	2:11	454, 458	3:5b	462	
6:21	422, 444	2:12	458, 463	3:6	404, 436, 449n4,	
		2:13	458n35			

	459n37, 461,	1:4	490n29		333n51, 491, 492,
	475n76	1:5	484		494, 495
3:6-7	315, 348	1:5-7	405	2:15	475n76, 484
3:6-9	462	1:5-9	242, 359n7,	2:15-3:2	488
3:7	265, 305n31, 310n44		484n13	3:1	349n34, 484
3:8	445, 459n37,	1:6	484-86	3:1-2	489, 492
	459n38, 475n76	1:7	486, 488	3:2	489
3:9	459n37, 459n38	1:8	492	3:3	315, 475n76, 493, 494
3:10	454, 459, 462	1:8-9	485	3:3-7	489, 492
3:10-11	270, 454, 459	1:9	266, 405, 458n35,	3:4	490n29, 493
3:12	462		475n76	3:4-6	493
3:13	459n37, 459n38,	1:10	436, 444, 486-87	3:5	162n11, 164, 310n43,
	462, 475n76	1:10-16	242, 405		444, 475n76,
3:14	459n37, 459n38,	1:11	124n85, 449n3,		490n29, 494, 495
	462, 475n76		475n76, 486n24,	3:5-6	165n38
3:14-17	454		487	3:5-7	306n32, 444
3:15	438-39n39, 453,	1:12	486	3:6	166n43, 490n29
	454, 463	1:13	475n76, 484	3:7	493, 495
3:16	475n76	1:13-14	405	3:8	372, 458n35, 495
4:1-2	462	1:14	438n32, 444,	3:9	405, 444, 449n3,
4:2	459n37, 459n38,		486-87		475n76
	460, 462, 475n76	1:15	444, 475n76, 487,	3:9-11	488
4:3	404, 463, 475n76		492	3:10	475n76
4:3-4	462	1:16	444, 449n4, 487,	3:10-11	405, 484
4:3-8	462		491n34		
4:4	445	2:1	484	**Philemon**	
4:5	459n37, 459n38,	2:1-2	475n76	1-3	240
	462, 463n50,	2:1-10	418, 488	2	231, 316n12, 338
	475n76	2:2	488, 489, 492	2-3	280n37
4:6	463	2:3	489	3	231
4:6-8	454, 459	2:3-5	315, 488	6	267, 310n44
4:6-18	454	2:4	488, 492	7	228
4:7	463	2:5	348, 489	10	164n35
4:8	354n48, 463, 475n76	2:6	475n76, 484, 489	20	228
4:9	463n50	2:7-8	484	21-22	240
4:11	463n50	2:8	475n76	23	168n56
4:13	463n50	2:9-10	489		
4:14	463n50	2:10	490n29	**Hebrews**	
4:15	463n50	2:11	30, 490n29,	1:3	164n28, 309n40
4:16	462		493-94	1:13	309n40
4:17	266, 438n38	2:11-14	444, 489, 490,	3:1	309n40
4:19	463n50		493	5:12	193n14
4:21	463n50	2:12	406n43, 475n76,	6:1-2	180
			491, 493, 495	6:2	163n22
Titus		2:13	490n29, 491, 495	6:4	163n20, 165n38
1:1	305n31, 310n44	2:14	164n28, 164n32,	8:1	340n10
1:3	198n32, 490n29		194-95n21,		

9:14	164n28	**Jude**		2:18	290
10:12	309n40	20–21	165n39	22:22	290
10:22	162n11, 164n28,			27:16	290
	164n32	**Revelation**		27:17	290
10:32	163n20	1–3	387n5	27:21	290
12:2	309n40	1:5	162n11		
12:26–27	387n7	1:9–10	165n39	**2 Maccabees**	
13:12–13	166n42	2:1–7	412–13	2:21	194n18
13:22	364n19	3:3	390n13	6:4	485n14
		3:12	418–19n12	6:23	194n17
James		5:1	309n40	8:1	194n18
1:12	460n40	5:7	309n40	13:21	290
1:21	27	5:9	108n9	14:38	194n18
2:26	91	7:3–8	166n45		
3:5–7	334	7:14	393n17	**4 Maccabees**	
		19:10	165n39	3:18	194n19
1 Peter				4:26	194n18
1:2	16	**DEUTERO-**			
1:3	164n35	**CANONICAL**		**DEAD SEA**	
1:23	164n35	**WORKS**		**SCROLLS**	
2:9	163n20			1QS	360
2:21–25	166n42	**Tobit**		5:24–25	223n31
3:18–20	165n39	12:7	290	7.15–18	395n25
3:18–4:2	165n36	12:11	290		
3:18–4:6	163n22			**ANCIENT JEWISH**	
3:21	161n10, 164n32	**Judith**		**SOURCES**	
3:22	309n40	2:2	290		
4:1–6	166n42	16:19	402n38	**Josephus**	
				Jewish Antiquities	
1 John		**Wisdom of Solomon**		1.24	494n37
1:7	164n28	1:6	494n37	4.207	406n42
2:23	18n18	2:22	290	10.111	387–88n9
3:9	164n35	3:6	366	13.258	169n68
3:18	108n9	5:17–23	353n40	15.417–18	343n22
4:1	121	6:21	290	18.5.2	180n147
4:2	18n18	7:23	494n37	20.38–48	180n146
4:3	18n18	10:5	363n15		
4:13–14	165n39	14:12–31	363	*Jewish War*	
4:15	18n18	14:15	290	2.120–34	395n25
4:17–19	166n42	14:22–31	174	5.193–94	343n22
5:6–8	165n39	14:23	290	6.124–26	343n22
		18:21	363n15	*The Life*	
2 John				43	393n18
7	18n18	**Sirach**		113	169n68
		2:5	366	232	406n42

Philo

Against Flaccus

124	484n10
50	174n96

Allegorical Interpretation

3.71	176n109
3.100	176n108
3.101–3	176n115

Life of Moses

1.175	113n37
1.280	390n14
2.117–35	304n29
2.188–92	113n37
2.291	113n37

On Agriculture

133	175n100
146	175n100
157	176n101
165	175n100

On Dreams

1.128	304n29
1.164	176n118

On Drunkenness

82	176n104

On Flight and Finding

85	176n110

On Rewards and Punishments

36	176n104
121	176n106

On the Change of Names

12	176n104
23–24	176n102

On the Cherubim

42	176n107
48	176n110
49	177n122
69	175n100
99	494n37

On the Contemplative Life

25	177n120
28	177n120

On the Creation of the World

71	176n114

On the Giants

26	176n101
53–54	176n112
54	176n117

On the Life of Abraham

26	176n101
122	176n105, 177n120

On the Life of Moses

1.62	177n121
1.158	176n113
2.40	176n119

On the Migration of Abraham

73	175n100
89–92	174n96
118	175n99

On the Posterity of Cain

132	176n104
173	176n117

On the Sacrifices of Abel and Cain

7	176n103, 195n22
32	486n21
53–54	176n112
61–62	177n121
62	176n111

On the Special Laws

1.53	406n42
1.65	113n37
1.319	175n97
3.24	485n16
3.37–42	175n98
3.184	304n29
4.49	113n37
4.197	406n42

On the Virtues

178	176n116

Questions on Exodus

2.68	304n29
2.117	304n29

Questions on Genesis

3.9	113n37
4.140	113n37
4.196	113n37

That God Is Unchangeable

61	177n120

Who Is the Heir?

121	176n104
264–65	113n37

RABBINIC WORKS

b. Yevamot

46a	180n146

m. Avot

6:2	198n31

m. Shabb

7:2	211n6

m. Yadayim

1:4–4.8	164n30

Pesahim

8.8	180n146
91b–92	180n146

Pirqe Aboth

5:18	223n31

PSEUDEPIGRAPHA

Acts of Paul and Thecla

34	162n17
40	162n17

2 Baruch
41:3   393n17
42:4   393n17

1 Enoch
91:5–7   393n17

4 Ezra
4:16–5:13   393n17

Gospel of the Egyptians
44   127n102
66   127n102

Joseph and Aseneth
14–17   174n93
15:2   124n87

Letter of Aristeas
130   194n17

Pistis Sophia
4.142   127n102

Sibylline Oracles
4.62–78   180n146

Testament of Job
48:1–50:3   110n19

Testament of Judah
16:1   485n14, 486n21
21:8   195n22

Zostrianos
127n102

CLASSICAL AND CHRISTIAN WRITINGS

Aelius Aristides

Orations
28   224n38

33   224n38
34   224n38

Platonic Discourses
1.11   451n15
307.6   451n15
307.10   451n15
307.15   451n15
308.5   451n15
308.10   451n15
309.14–15
         451–52n15
309.45   451n15

Apuleius

Apology
55   172n76

Metamorphoses (Golden Ass)
8.27   113n41
10.38   172n81
11.3–15   172n82
11.23   173n85
11.24   173n86
11.26   172n83
11.27   173n87
11.29   173n88, 173n89,
         173n91
11.30   173n90

Aristotle

Eudemian Ethics
1221B   486n21

Generation of Animals
1.17–21   125n91
1.20   125n91

History of Animals
10.6   126n92

Nicomachean Ethics
1.13.20   55
2.5.6   54
2.6.15   54, 57
2.6.17   57

3.3.10–11   54
5.3.1–12   57
6.5.1   55
6.5.2   54
6.5.4   55
6.5.5   56
6.5.6   55
6.6.2   56
6.8.1   57
6.8.3   56
6.8.4   57
6.8.5   56
6.8.9   56
6.9.4   55
6.10.2   56
6.11.2–3   57
6.11.4   56
6.11.6   56
6.13.4   56
6.13.5   56
6.13.7   56
8–9   226n39
9.9   263n1
10.8.3   55
1107B   485n14
1108A   486n21
1117b.13   54n15
1130b–32b   157n37

On Generation and Corruption
326b   304n27
327a   304n27

Parts of Animals
642a   304n27
655a   302n23

Politics
1252b   417n11
1253b   417n11
1254b   417n11
1259b–1260a   417n11
1277b   417n11
1334b–1337a   417n11

Rhetoric
1360A   485n16

1367A	486n21
1374b	303n25
1389B	406n43
1390B	440n43

Augustine

Baptism

3.18	128n108

Christian Instruction

2.9	439n41

City of God

22.30	216n13

Enchiridion

28.105	216n13

The Good of Marriage

9	373n44

Homilies on First John

6.10	128n108

Aulus Gellius

Attic Nights

15.18.2	324n33

Cicero

De divinatione

18	112n33
32.70	113n38
34	112n33

Laws

2.12–29	324n33

Clement of Alexandria

Stromateis

5.71–72	172n77

Demosthenes

Orations

26.15	388n10
27.29	303n25
41.30	303n25

Dio Cassius

Roman History

6.175	450–51n9

Dio Chrysostom

Orations

4.19	471n74
4.28	473n75
4.38	473n75
4.74	471n74
4.83–96	219n22
6.21	473n75
8.9	473n75
10.23–24	113n41
10.32	473n75
11.14	473n75
12	473
32.8–9	468n64
32.9	419n13, 469n69
32.10	471n73
32.11	419n13, 471n73
32.18	471n74
32.19	471n73
32.20	471n73
32.24	471n73
33	473
33.1	471n73
33.4–5	473n75
33.9–10	471n73
33.13	471n74
33.14–15	473n75
35	473
35.1	419n13, 469n69
35.2.3.11	469n68
35.3–8	473n75
38.9	93n22
38.11	93n22
38.18	93n22
38.20	93n22
38.51	93n22
39.8	93n22
40.5	93n22
40.15	93n22
40.35	93n22
41.10	93n22
55.7	473n75
66.12	473n75

70.8–10	473n75
77–78	452n16, 473–74
77–78.19	473
77–78.26	474
77–78.27	473n75
77–78.34	474
77–78.37	474
77–78.37–45	223n31, 475n76
77–78.38–39	474
77–78.39	474
77–78.40	474
77–78.42	474
77–78.43–44	475
77–78.45	471n74, 475

Diodorus Siculus

Library of History

5.55.6	440n43

Diogenes Laertius

Lives of Eminent Philosophers

5.67	304n27

Dionysius of Halicarnassus

Roman Antiquities

1.42	304n27
10.54	304n27

Epictetus

Discourses

1.4.5	468n66
1.5.9	451–52n15
1.8.4–10	468n66
1.9.19–20	419n13, 469n69
1.9.24	194n17
1.22.13	194n17
1.29.45–47	419n13, 469n69
2.1.31	468n66
2.3	483–84n9
2.9	468n66

2.9.9–21	180n146	111.24–78	419n13	6.52	113n35
2.10.30	468n66	Frag. 10	468n66	6.57	113n35
2.12	468n66			6.66	113n35
2.16	468n66	**Euripides**		6.76	113n35
2.17–20	468n66			7.220	113n35
2.17.3	469n69	*Bacchae*		7.239	113n35
2.17.4	195n22	299	114n43	8.114	113n35
2.17.20	468n66			8.135	113n36, 113n40
2.18	468n66	*Hippolytus*		8.141	113n35
2.18.32	302n24	199	304n27		
2.20	451–52n15			**Hierocles**	
2.20.7	387–88n9	*Suppliants*			
2.23.21ff.	451–52n15	173	290n2	*On Duties*	
3.2	314–15n5	470	290n2	4.25.53	223n31
3.2.6	468n66	917	406n43		
3.3.17ff.	468n66			**Hippocrates**	
3.5.17	468n66	**Eusebius**			
3.6.3	468n66			*Aphorisms*	
3.7.21	451–52n15	*Ecclesiastical History*		5.51	126n92
3.13.23	468n66	3.3.5	428n1		
3.16.3	419n13	5.7.6		*Prognosis*	
3.22	452n16, 468		127n100	25	325n34
3.22.10	471n74	5.15–18	126n95		
3.22.88	469n67	5.16.7–10	126n97	**Hippolytus**	
3.22.90	471n74	5.17.2–4			
3.23.30	470n70		128n106	*Refutation of All Heresies*	
3.23.33–34	467–68n63	5.17.4	126n98	8.12	126n95
3.24.38	468n66	6.25.11–24	428n1	48.4.1	126n96, 126n98
3.24.78	469n69				
4.1–161	485n14	**Herodotus**		**Homer**	
4.1.139	469n69				
4.4	468n66	*Histories*		*Iliad*	
4.5.36–37	468n66	1.31	401n35	6.131	114n43
4.8.5ff.	451–52n15	1.141	401n35		
9	469	1.187	486n21	*Odyssey*	
10	469	2.51	290n2	9.292	483–84n9
11	469	3.46	388n10	15.89	483–84n9
24	469	4.13	388n10	21.33	483–84n9
26	469	6.50	485n14		
50–53	469	6.92	486n21	**Horace**	
54	470	6.125	483–84n9		
57	469			*Odes*	
72–73	470	*Persian Wars*		3.2.13	135n9
80	469	1.51	113n35		
87–88	469	1.61	113n35	**Irenaeus**	
88	469	1.67	113n35		
91–92	469	4.79	114n43	*Against Heresies*	
97–100	469	5.42–43	113n35	*(Adversus haereses)*	
		5.62–63	113n35	1.3	28n2
		5.91	113n35	1.8.2–5	28n2

1.14–16   127n101
1.20.2   28n2
5.6.1   127n100

John Chrysostom

*Homilies on First
Corinthians*
29.32.35   128n107

Julian

Oration
6.181C   469n69
6.190D   471n73
6.197B   471n73
6.200C   471n73
7.26A   471n73
7.223C   469n68
7.225A   469n68
198B   469n69

Letter of Polycarp
6–7   454n23

Livy

Annals of Rome
39.13   125n89
39.15   125n89

History of Rome
1.58   324n33

Lucian of Samosata

*Alexander the False
Prophet*
13   113n42
22   113n42
27–28   113n42
49   113n42
51   113n42
53   113n42

Demonax
1   470
2   470

3   471
7   471
11   471
12–66   471
67   471

Dialogues of the Dead
332   451–52n15
369   451–52n15, 471n73
374   469n69
417   471n73

The Double Indictment
6   469n68
22   451–52n15
31   419n13
34   451–52n15

The Fisherman
31   451–52n15, 471n73
34   471n73
42   469n68
46   471n73

Hermotimus
9–10   419n13, 469n69
18   451–52n15
84   470n71

How to Write History
20   200n35

Icaromenippus
5   451–52n15

Menippus
5   469n69, 471n73
21   470n71

Nigrinus
6   472
7   472
24   472
24–29   473
25   472
26   472
27   473
28   472
38   472

The Parasite
52   469n69, 471n73

The Passing of Peregrinus
1   471n73
4   471n73
15–16   469n69
20   471n73
38   471n73
42   471n73

Pharsalia
5.160–97   126n93

Philosophies for Sale
20–23   451–52n15
24   419n13, 469n69

The Runaways
4   451–52n15
12   471n73
14   419n13, 451–52n15,
                469n69
19   451–52n15, 469n68,
                471n73

Timon
54   419n13, 451–52n15,
            469n68, 487n26
56   469n69

Zeus Rants
11   451–52n15
27   451–52n15

Maximus of Tyre

Discourse
36.2   219n22

Origen

Against Celsus
7.3   127n104
7.9   127n104

Pausanias

Description of Greece
2.7.5   114n43

Philodemus

On Frankness
37   223n31

Philostratus

Life of Apollonius of Tyana
1.34   469n69
2.29   469n68
4.35   450–51n9
5.19   450–51n9
7.4   450–51n9

Loves of the Sophists
582   224n38

Plato

Apology
24E   406n43

Critias
44D   483–84n9

Gorgias
497c   290n2

Ion
534A–D   113n37

Laws (Leges)
560E   485n14
713D   494n37
781A–D   417n11
783E–785B   417n11
802E–803C   417n11
804E–807D   417n11
813C–814B   417n11
833D   417n11
949A   301n20

Menon
76E   290n2

Phaedrus
150B–C   174n95
244A   113n37
244C   114n43

Republic
407B   301–2n21
455C–457E   417n11
459C–461E   417n11
514A–520A   303n26
540C   417n11

Symposium
189C   494n37
209E   174n95

Theaetetus
162C   303n25

Timaeus
71E–72B   113n37
72B   113n36

Pliny the Elder

Natural History
5.95   167n46

Plutarch

The E at Delphi
387B   113n37
391E   113n37

How to Tell a Flatterer from a Friend
30–37   223n31

Isis and Osiris
351D–384C   173n87

Life of Camillus
11   200n35

Moralia
70D–74E   223n31
288E   301–2n21
351D–384C   173n87
404E   126n93
405C   126n93
432D–E   126n93
539B–547F   224n37

The Obsolescence of Oracles
42A   113n40

404E   126n93
405C   126n93
417C   113n38
432A–D   113n37
432D–E   126n93

On Brotherly Love
484B–C   157n35

On Inoffensive Self-Praise
539B–547F   224n37

On the Education of Children
16   193n14

Oracles at Delphi
397C   113n37
399A   113n37

Roman Questions
102   301–2n21

Polybius

History
5.46.6   393n18

P.Oxy (Oxyrhynchus Papyri)
105.3   483–84n9

Ps.-Isocrates

Ad Demonicum
2   466
3   466, 467n63
5   466
8   466
9   466
9–10   466, 467
11   466
12   467
14   467
15   467
16   467
17   467
20   467
23   467

24	467	**Strabo**		3.11.92	113n35
38	467			4.13.118	113n35
50	467	*Geography*		5.15.17	113n35
51	467	12.7.1–5	167n46		

Ad Nicoclem

1.3	465n57	**Tebtunis Papyrus**		**Virgil**	
1.26	465n57	703, lines 257–80	412	*Aeneid*	
1.31	465n57			6.42ff.	113n38
1.35	465n57	**Tertullian**		6.77–101	126n94
1.37	465n57	*Against Marcion*			
1.38	465n57	5.8	127n99	**Xenophon**	
1.41	467n62				
2.2	466n61	**Theophrastus**		*Cyropaedia*	
2.57	465n57			7.5.11	301n21
2.59	465n57	*Characters*		*Hellenica*	
2.60	465n57	1.21	302n24	1.4.27	290n2
2.61	465n57	1.21.7	396n26		
		15.1	486n21	*Memorabilia*	

Quintilian

		Thucydides		1.1.5	325n34
Institutes of Oratory				1.3.5	406n43
6.1	340n10	*History*		2.1.1	193n14
		1.69	485n14	*Oeconomicus*	
Sophocles		6.28	290n2	3.10–15	417n11
				7.5–43	417n11
Oedipus Rex		*Peloponnesian War*		9.15–10.5	417n11
1195	194n19	2.7.55	113n35	19.1	302n24